The People Speak

The People Speak

American Elections in Focus

Washington, D.C.

Congressional Quarterly Inc.

Congressional Quarterly Inc., an editorial research service and publishing company, serves clients in the fields of news, education, business, and government. It combines Congressional Quarterly's specific coverage of Congress, government, and politics with the more general subject range of an affiliated service, Editorial Research Reports.

Congressional Quarterly publishes the *Congressional Quarterly Weekly Report* and a variety of books, including college political science textbooks under the CQ Press imprint and public affairs paperbacks on developing issues and events. CQ also publishes information directories and reference books on the federal government, national elections, and politics, including the *Guide to the Presidency*, the *Guide to Congress*, the *Guide to the U.S. Supreme Court*, the *Guide to U.S. Elections*, *Politics in America*, and *Congress A to Z: CQ's Ready Reference Encyclopedia*. The *CQ Almanac*, a compendium of legislation for one session of Congress, is published each year. *Congress and the Nation*, a record of government for a presidential term, is published every four years.

CQ publishes *The Congressional Monitor*, a daily report on current and future activities of congressional committees, and several newsletters including *Congressional Insight*, a weekly analysis of congressional action, and *Campaign Practices Reports*, a semimonthly update on campaign laws.

An electronic online information system, Washington Alert, provides immediate access to CQ's databases of legislative action, votes, schedules, profiles, and analyses.

Copyright © 1990 Congressional Quarterly Inc.
1414 22nd Street N.W., Washington, D.C. 20037

Printed in the United States of America

Library of Congress Cataloging-in-Publication Data
The People speak.
    p.   cm.
    ISBN 0-87187-513-6
    1. Elections--United States--History. 2. Political parties--United States--History. I. Congressional Quarterly, inc.
JK1967.P39 1989
324.973--dc20   89-37047
                                          CIP

Editor: Ann Davies
Associate editors: John L. Moore, Nancy A. Lammers
Contributors: Bob Benenson, Peter Bragdon, Neil Brown,
   Rhodes Cook, Phil Duncan, Ronald D. Elving, Charles C.
   Euchner, John Anthony Maltese, Alice C. McGillivray,
   Robert Horn Resnick
Production assistants: Jamie R. Holland, Ian Todreas,
   Jennifer Van der Heide
Proofreaders: Denise L. Hubbard, Mara Kapelovitz,
   Jodean Marks, Steve Moyer
Indexer: Patricia R. Ruggiero
Cover Designer: Paula Anderson

Table of Contents

Boxes, Figures, and Tables

Boxes

Figures

Tables

Table of Contents

Part I
Political Parties

The 1988 Delegate Selection

When Sen. John F. Kennedy set his sights on Pennsylvania's eighty-one delegates to the 1960 Democratic convention, there was not much question about how to win their support for the presidential nomination. Rather than setting up an organization in the state, publicly campaigning there, or wooing political activists far and wide, Kennedy and his advisers simply went to the state's powerful Democratic leader, Gov. David L. Lawrence. After intensive personal negotiations, Kennedy won Lawrence's backing, and the legendary political boss delivered sixty-four convention votes to the Massachusetts senator.

Those were the old days of American politics, and they are long gone. While Kennedy sought support among big-city Democratic machines and union locals, the 1988 candidates for the Democratic and Republican presidential nominations haunted the living rooms of a few thousand party activists in Iowa and New Hampshire, the sites of the crucial first contests in the nomination struggle. While Kennedy wooed backers with the customary blandishments of politics—federal patronage and support for other candidates on the party ticket—the 1988 hopefuls lined up allies by voicing interest group concerns and striking up personal relationships with activists in the two early states, where the rewards of victory were modest in terms of delegates but immense in terms of momentum and publicity.

The jump from Los Angeles's Biltmore Hotel, where Kennedy cemented his alliance with Lawrence, to the coffee klatches of Iowa symbolizes the dramatic changes that have reshaped the nation's system for selecting major-party presidential nominees in the past two decades. In short, the nomination system has been opened in a way that Lawrence and others of his time might scarcely have imagined. It has been transformed from a process in which a handful of leaders exercised a dominant voice, if not outright control, over their party's nomination choice to one in which thousands of party workers and millions of primary voters decide the outcome.

This change has not come without costs. Among people who follow the nomination process closely—political scientists, professional politicians, and journalists—there is a growing sense that the system is not up to the task of selecting the two general-election contenders for the most powerful office in the world. Whatever one may think of candidate Gary Hart and his decision to pull out of the Democratic race because of allegations of marital infidelity, there was little doubt that he touched a popular chord when he denounced the current system in his May 8, 1987,

withdrawal speech. "Politics in this country," Hart said, "is on the verge of becoming another form of athletic competition or sporting match."

The presidential nominating system—technically, the complex of party rules, federal laws, media habits, and political realities that determine the selection of delegates to the national party conventions, which formally nominate candidates—seems increasingly to be a troubled political institution. The list of indictments brought by critics against the current system is a lengthy one. The system has been in a state of constant change for the past twenty years, pulled this way and that so often that no two consecutive contests have been fought under the same guidelines. It requires seemingly endless campaigns; when the national party conventions were still a year away, some of the contenders had already been campaigning nearly full time for at least that long. It gives awesome power to voters in a few early states, and to the media, while forcing candidates to go through an arduous process that has little to do with their future ability to govern. It may discourage many qualified potential candidates from seeking the presidency. "This process is absolutely, disgustingly convoluted," Republican political consultant Eddie Mahe has remarked.

The current system did not spring up overnight, nor did anyone set out to create it. It was shaped by a variety of forces, including conflicts within the Democratic party, the long-term decline of the two parties' hold on political power, the growing technological and social power of television, and the aftershocks of the Watergate crisis. Much of the controversy over the evolution of the system has focused on the Democrats. But Republicans have been affected as well; so their 1988 contest will have been fought under essentially the same system as the Democrats'.

After twenty exhausting years of tinkering with their nomination rules, the Democrats seem to have decided, at least for now, that it is better to live with the current system than open up the subject to a new and divisive debate. Republicans have never been eager to make changes in the system. But if the process had misfired in 1988—by producing candidates with little party support, perhaps, or by leading to widespread frustration and chaos—there could have been strong demands for a thorough revamping, possibly through congressional legislation. "Each election, we see more clearly the defects of the present hodgepodge," said Rep. Sander M. Levin, a Michigan Democrat who had proposed major revisions in the presidential primaries. "The unworkability and ineffi-

Speaking of Nomination

Beauty contest. A primary in which voters indicate their preferred presidential candidates but do not select convention delegates. Vermont's March 1, 1988, preference primary, for example, was followed a few weeks later by caucus meetings to choose delegates.

Closed primary. A primary in which participation is limited to voters who are registered as members of either the Democratic or Republican party. Open primaries allow participation by any registered voter.

Front-loading. The tendency of states to schedule their delegate-selection events as early as possible in the election year, in an attempt to maximize their influence in the nomination process.

Superdelegate. A Democratic elected or party official who receives a convention delegate seat by virtue of his or her office rather than by being chosen through the larger delegate-selection process. Unlike other delegates, superdelegates are not required to state their presidential preference before the convention. In 1988 the superdelegates included all members of the Democratic National Committee, the Democratic governors, 80 percent of Democratic members of Congress, and a handful of former high elected officials.

Window. The period of time in the first half of an election year in which the national Democratic party attempts to confine the primaries and caucuses that select convention delegates. The 1988 window ran from March 8 through June 7, although four states (Iowa, New Hampshire, Maine, and Wyoming) were allowed to hold earlier events. Republicans allow much greater latitude in scheduling.

Winner take all. The traditional method of allocating convention delegates, under which the candidate who receives the most votes in a primary wins all the state's delegates. Some state Republican parties continue to use this method. Most Democratic parties use proportional representation, under which candidates receive a share of delegates equal to their percentage of the primary vote. To win any delegates, however, candidates must meet a minimum threshold of support, currently set at 15 percent of the vote.

ciency of the system will catch up with the inertia and desire for respite. I think [legislative changes] will happen after this time around."

Primaries Are Central Feature

Even if the nominating process is, as Levin said, a hodgepodge, political analysts have identified several com-

mon threads that define the current system. The most important characteristic of the system that operated in 1988 was its emphasis on popular participation through mass party primaries. Although Iowa and about eighteen other states select national convention delegates through caucuses or conventions—mass meetings of party members—primaries are by far the more important method.[1] A comparison with the role that primaries played before 1968, the watershed year for the nomination system, highlights how important primaries have become today. (See Presidential Nominating Process, box, p. 6.)

Although the number of primaries has fluctuated over the years, the general trend since 1968 has been upward. (See Table 1.) By the first of January 1988 thirty-eight primaries had been scheduled, which was more than the twenty-five contests held in 1984 and more than the previous record thirty-seven primaries conducted in 1980. In 1968, by contrast, there were only thirteen contested primaries. Moreover, the tendency of the more populous states to hold primaries—nine of the ten biggest states did so in 1988—means that the vast majority of delegates are picked by popular vote. Primaries would select an estimated 75 percent of the chief category of delegates to the 1988 Democratic convention.[2] The comparable figure for 1968 was 38 percent.

The political importance of primaries has also expanded greatly. Primaries were not insignificant under the system used in 1968 and earlier years; politicians tended to look at their results as a useful indicator of popular sentiment. But they were hardly decisive in determining the eventual outcome. In 1968, for example, Minnesota senator Eugene J. McCarthy's strong showing against President Lyndon B. Johnson in the New Hampshire primary helped push the incumbent out of the Democratic race. Yet the eventual winner, Vice President Hubert H. Humphrey, later took the nomination without entering a single primary all year.

Under the current system, by contrast, primary outcomes can take on an exaggerated political effect even when the results turn on a small number of votes. In 1976 Jimmy Carter's 4,663-vote margin over Arizona representative Morris K. Udall in the New Hampshire primary catapulted Carter to the Democratic nomination and the presidency. In 1984 former vice president Walter F. Mondale's entire campaign hinged on a relative handful of primary votes in Georgia. Reeling from a defeat by Hart in the New Hampshire primary, Mondale's candidacy probably would have been finished if he had not prevailed in Georgia, which he carried by only a 3 percent margin. That slim cushion of victory was enough to enable Mondale to survive and eventually win the nomination.

A second characteristic of the current system is that it revolves around individual candidates rather than the established party structure. In the old days, as Kennedy's pursuit of Lawrence shows, campaigning consisted to a large extent of enlisting the support of state and local party organizations around the country. Candidate campaign staffs were small, and endorsements by important figures in the party mattered a great deal.

Today the reverse is true. Candidate committees in effect become their own little "parties," organized in each state outside the regular party structure. Party leaders rarely control their delegations in the way that Lawrence did, and their endorsements seldom produce many primary votes. Indeed, established party leaders were for a time so lightly regarded by the Democrats that they were virtually

Table 1   Votes Cast and Delegates Selected in Presidential Primaries, 1912-1988

Year	Democratic party			Republican party			Total	
	Number of primaries	Votes cast	Delegates selected through primaries (%)	Number of primaries	Votes cast	Delegates selected through primaries (%)	Votes cast	Delegates selected through primaries (%)
1912	12	974,775	32.9	13	2,261,240	41.7	3,236,015	37.3
1916	20	1,187,691	53.5	20	1,923,374	58.9	3,111,065	56.2
1920	16	571,671	44.6	20	3,186,248	57.8	3,757,919	51.2
1924	14	763,858	35.5	17	3,525,185	45.3	4,289,043	40.4
1928	16	1,264,220	42.2	15	4,110,288	44.9	5,374,508	43.5
1932	16	2,952,933	40.0	14	2,346,996	37.7	5,299,929	38.8
1936	14	5,181,808	36.5	12	3,319,810	37.5	8,501,618	37.0
1940	13	4,468,631	35.8	13	3,227,875	38.8	7,696,506	37.3
1944	14	1,867,609	36.7	13	2,271,605	38.7	4,139,214	37.7
1948	14	2,151,865	36.3	12	2,653,255	36.0	4,805,120	36.1
1952	16	4,928,006	38.7	13	7,801,413	39.0	12,729,419	38.8
1956	19	5,832,592	42.7	19	5,828,272	44.8	11,660,864	43.7
1960	16	5,686,664	38.3	15	5,537,967	38.6	11,224,631	38.5
1964	16	6,247,435	45.7	16	5,935,339	45.6	12,182,774	45.6
1968	15	7,535,069	40.2	15	4,473,551	38.1	12,008,620	39.1
1972	21	15,993,965	65.3	20	6,188,281	56.8	22,182,246	61.0
1976	27	16,052,652	76.0	26	10,374,125	71.0	26,426,777	73.5
1980	35	18,747,825	71.8	35	12,690,451	76.0	31,438,276	73.7
1984	30	18,009,217	52.4	25	6,575,651	71.0	24,584,868	59.6
1988	37	22,961,936	66.6	37	12,165,115	76.9	35,481,934	70.2

Sources: Congressional Quarterly's Guide to the Presidency, ed. Michael Nelson (Washington, D.C.: Congressional Quarterly Inc., 1989), 166; *America Votes* 18, ed. Richard M. Scammon and Alice McGillivray (Washington, D.C.: Congressional Quarterly Inc., 1989).

excluded from the 1972, 1976, and 1980 conventions. Democrats have sought to reverse that trend in recent years, by offering automatic convention seats to party and elected officials, and Republicans have continued to encourage participation by party leaders. Nevertheless, candidates in practice have come to treat their parties as little more than conduits for appealing to the public.

The independence of candidates allows them to operate without much interaction with party leaders. For critics of the current system, such as University of California political scientist Nelson W. Polsby, the insularity of candidates has deprived them of the advice of experienced politicians. Such advice might have been able to head off the missteps that have plagued Democratic candidates in recent years, from Sen. George S. McGovern's ill-fated choice of Sen. Thomas F. Eagleton for his running mate in 1972 to Mondale's harmony-shattering effort to dump the sitting chair of the Democratic National Committee in the midst of the 1984 convention. In 1988 Michael Dukakis's campaign was criticized for not paying attention to party regulars. "The candidate's staff becomes an entourage cutting him off from other people. When things go wrong, there is a tendency to circle the wagons and 'burn out,' rather than opening up to other party leaders," Polsby said.

The campaigns of today also differ from those of the past in their length. Under the previous system campaigns tended to be relatively short; it was an unusual campaign that, like Kennedy's in the fall of 1959, formally organized itself more than a year before the election. A little more than eight years later Sen. Robert F. Kennedy announced his campaign after the New Hampshire primary and made a serious run at the nomination until he was shot to death just after winning the California primary.

A late-starting effort like Robert Kennedy's might strike politicians of the 1980s as futile. All four of the nonincumbents to capture the Democratic nomination since 1968 have announced their campaigns more than twenty months before the election and preceded their formal entries with a year or more of advance preparation. Ronald Reagan pursued the Republican nomination, formally and informally, on a more or less full-time basis from the time he left the California governorship in early 1975 until his victory in 1980. The 1988 crop of candidates have followed a similar pattern; even those, like Vice President George Bush, who did not formally declare their candidacies early on, had been hard at work for months laying the groundwork for a run at the nomination.

Even if a candidate had tried to make an eleventh-hour run for the 1988 nomination, he or she would have faced a formidable obstacle in the fourth major element of the nomination system: the restrictive environment in which candidates can raise and spend campaign money. Campaign finance legislation passed by Congress in 1974 has made it impossible for a contemporary candidate to do what many earlier candidates could do with relative ease: raise a lot of money in a hurry. Since there used to be no limitations on amounts that individuals could give to campaigns, candidates frequently could raise all they needed from a few wealthy backers.

Federal campaign finance law has changed all that, however, by limiting individual contributions to no more than $1,000. Candidates must now seek out thousands of small contributors to obtain what a handful of allies once could have provided. The law also shapes campaigns by providing federal matching funds for individual contributions, financed by the $1 presidential campaign "checkoff" on the income-tax form. Candidates must raise $100,000 from at least twenty states, in the form of contributions of

Presidential Nominating Process

Before 1968

Party-Dominated. The nomination decision is largely made by the leaders of the political parties. Candidates win by enlisting support of state and local party machines.

Few Primaries. Most delegates are selected by state party establishments, with little or no public participation. Some primaries are held, but their results do not necessarily determine nominee. Primaries are used to indicate candidate's "electability."

Short Campaigns. Candidates usually begin their public campaign early in the election year.

Easy Money. Candidates frequently raise large amounts of money quickly by tapping a handful of wealthy contributors. There are no federal limits on spending by candidates.

Limited Media Coverage. Campaigns are followed by print journalists and, in later years, by television. But press coverage of campaigns is not intensive and generally does not play a major role in influencing the process.

Late Decisions. Events early in the campaign year, such as the New Hampshire primary, are not decisive. States that choose delegates late in the year, such as California, frequently are important in selecting nominee. Many states enter convention without making final decisions about candidates.

Open Conventions. National party conventions sometimes begin with nomination still undecided. Outcome determined by maneuvering and negotiating among party factions, often stretching over multiple ballots.

Since 1968

Candidate-Dominated. Campaigns are independent of party establishments. Endorsements by party leaders have little effect on nomination choice.

Many Primaries. Most delegates are selected by popular primaries and caucuses. Nominations are determined largely by voters' decisions.

Long Campaigns. Candidates begin laying groundwork for campaigns three or four years before the election. Candidates who are not well organized at least eighteen months before the election may have little chance of winning.

Difficult Fund Raising. Campaign contributions are limited to $1,000 per person, so candidates must work endlessly to raise money from thousands of small contributors. Campaign spending is limited by law, both nationally and for individual states.

Media-Focused. Campaigns are covered intensively by the media, particularly television. Media treatment of candidates plays crucial role in determining the nominee.

"Front-loaded." Early events, such as the Iowa caucuses and the New Hampshire primary, are important. The nomination may be decided even before many major states vote. Early victories attract great media attention, which gives winners free publicity and greater fund-raising ability.

Closed Conventions. Nominee is determined before convention, which does little more than ratify decision made in primaries and caucuses. Convention activities focus on creating favorable media image of candidate for general-election campaign.

$250 or less, to be eligible for federal matching funds. Once that threshold is met, the federal government will match up to $250 of each individual contribution. Candidates will lose their federal matching funds, however, if they fail to win at least 10 percent of the vote in any two consecutive primaries.

In addition, federal law limits the amounts that candidates can spend in seeking the nomination. For 1988, individual candidates were allowed to spend no more than about $23 million nationwide. There were also ceilings on the amounts candidates could spend in individual states, set according to population.

Finally, the media now play a vastly greater role in the nomination process than they did in the past. True, in earlier days the press treated nomination campaigns as major stories, and candidates viewed their relationship with the press as one element in planning and carrying out their campaigns. But the media were not at the center of the system, as they are today. An incident from the 1956 Democratic campaign, recounted by veteran journalist Theodore H. White, illustrates the point.[3] In the Minnesota primary that year Tennessee senator Estes Kefauver achieved an upset victory over Illinois governor Adlai E. Stevenson. Kefauver spent the evening of the primary with White in a hotel room, sharing a bottle of bourbon and scanning the radio for any news of the results.

It is not hard to imagine how different that scene would be today. Any candidate who had pulled off such a dramatic win would undoubtedly divide time between giving interviews with the three television networks, staging an ecstatic press conference, and plotting with advisers on how to take best media advantage of the results. The television networks and major print publications devote intensive resources to covering the nomination races, and candidates return the favor by tailoring every aspect of their campaigns to the goal of creating a positive impression in the media. In a sense the reality of any contemporary campaign is its media image.

A New Breed of Politics Was Born in Iowa

Probably no state exemplifies the transformation of American politics more starkly than Iowa, where grass-roots activism stretches across the landscape like fields of corn.

This transformation is reflected in the Iowa precinct caucuses, those rituals of neighborhood argumentation and political decision making that rivet the nation's attention every four years. These rituals sprang out of the new politics that captured the Democratic party in the late 1960s and early 1970s. Now established as an institutional part of the presidential-nomination process, they help nurture and sustain that new breed of politics.

An understanding of this requires a little history. For decades Iowa Republicans and Democrats began the process of selecting delegates to their national political conventions at precinct caucuses in January. But in the old days the process was firmly in the hands of party regulars, pragmatic pols who selected delegates to county conventions and thus controlled eligibility for national convention delegates.

Sometimes these decisions would be made in the context of broader political deals between important state bosses and particular candidates. But often they would not have anything to do with a delegate's preference for the nomination. These delegates were expected to represent their localities; the job of choosing the party's presidential nominee could be left to later convention delegates.

And rank-and-file voters were not involved. A Democratic county chairman, say, would meet with a few political cronies to choose delegates to the county convention. Sometimes the local bosses did not even meet in caucus, because nobody ever showed up anyway. They would simply run the requisite ad in the local newspaper's legal-notices section, then meet in someone's downtown office or in a bar down the street to select county convention delegates.

Then came Vietnam. Angered and politically energized by the war in 1968, ordinary voters showed up in droves at precinct caucuses across the state. They overwhelmed the political bosses and sent their own antiwar delegates to the county conventions. Their champion was the antiwar insurgent, Sen. Eugene J. McCarthy of Minnesota.

The political pros fought back at the county conventions and reclaimed the levers of power and decision making. But the die was cast. When South Dakota senator George McGovern, another antiwar Democrat, headed up a commission to transform party rules for the 1972 campaign, he ensured that the bosses would never again dominate the process. The regulars were forced into retreat; the activists came into their own.

Thus were born the Iowa caucuses as we know them today. Once in control, the activists quickly saw the party-building potential in the caucuses. With national media attention focused on the caucuses, more and more Democrats would compete in the state. That in turn would bring more activist Democrats to the caucuses and give the party an increasingly potent base for general-election battles with Republicans.

The Iowa precinct caucuses, overwhelmed by insurgency politics nearly two decades ago, now represent insurgency politics institutionalized. For better or worse they are an integral and media-driven part of the process of choosing our presidential candidates.

Wider Participation

The importance of the nominating system lies in the way it shapes the contest for the presidency—the sorts of candidates who are equipped to do well in it and the kinds of campaigns they are compelled to run. Admirers and critics of the contemporary nominating process have been arguing about its political effects ever since it began to emerge after 1968.

The increase in public participation in the nominating process, caused by the spread of primaries and party rules encouraging more people to become involved, is one of the most controversial aspects of the current system. For people like Billie Carr, a veteran liberal Democratic activist from Texas, the opening up of the system to people other than professional politicians is a positive result. "I think a process that includes a lot of people is a good one," she said. "If we hadn't had the reforms, people like me never would have been allowed to participate in the process."

Curtis Gans, director of an organization devoted to increasing public participation in the political process, argued that primaries are the best way to achieve that goal in the nomination campaign.[4] "People may argue over whether the proliferation of primaries most serves the party system," he said. "When you talk about participation, though, there is not much question. If you want to engage people in the process, the primary is the best way."

Critics of the current system point to two important weaknesses in the emphasis on public participation. One is that the electorate as a whole is ill-equipped to evaluate a large number of contenders. Even the most politically aware amateur usually lacks the knowledge to make an intelligent choice from among a field of up to a dozen candidates. As a result the public tends to prefer either tried-and-true candidates with whom it is already familiar or to be swept along in a tide of media-based enthusiasm for some dark-horse hopeful who bursts out of the pack.

These considerations can make for extraordinarily volatile campaigns but not necessarily for a considered judgment of the strengths and weaknesses of the contenders. In 1984 heavy media coverage of Hart, in the wake of his unexpectedly strong showings in Iowa and New Hampshire, allowed him to make a dazzling jump in the polls: from 2 percent in late January to 30 percent in early March. "The less information you have," said Thomas E. Mann, executive director of the American Political Science Association, "the more you are likely to be influenced by new information."

Critics of the system also worry about the other half of the public-participation equation: the reduced role of established party leaders. If the old-style party bosses tended to judge presidential candidates in light of their own self-interests—mainly, by how each would affect party candidates for other offices—at least they often were familiar with the contenders from having observed them in action in previous political activities. The party leaders added an element of "peer review" that is largely missing under the current system. They were not only better acquainted with the candidates but were experienced in judging which of the contenders had the best chance of winning the general election.

Now, say critics of the current system, that broader judgment is often missing—and sometimes supplanted by political forces that tend to be more ideological than before. Particularly in states that use caucuses to select delegates, party leaders have to a considerable extent been supplanted by "special interest" groups working within the parties. The modern caucus system is midway between the primary and the closed system of the past. Caucus meetings are open to all party members. But because attending a caucus requires much more effort than voting in a primary, caucuses tend to be dominated by people who have the extra motivation created by a commitment to a specific cause or organization. Examples of interest groups that are deeply involved in the nomination process are the National Education Association in the Democratic party and anti-abortion groups in the GOP.

For Alvin From, executive director of the moderate-to-conservative Democratic Leadership Council, the trade-off between the party establishment and interest groups has been a poor one indeed: "Under the old system, a limited number of party bosses were able to determine the nominee. But at least most of those bosses did have occasionally to face the electorate. The new bosses are the leaders of the organized interests, who do not have to face the voters. They have much greater influence in the nomination process than they do in the electorate as a whole." [5]

As From's comment suggests, the strength of interest groups in the nomination process can pose serious problems for candidates in the general election. In order to win the nomination, candidates may be forced to espouse positions that are popular with interest groups but unpopular with the mass of voters. Mondale's 1984 general-election campaign, for example, was seriously weakened by the image he had created by his avid courtship of labor, feminist, and minority groups during the nomination race. Some political experts saw a potentially similar problem developing for the Republicans in 1988, as candidates struggled to appeal to the growing Christian Right faction in the party without alienating the broader electorate.

Actually, though, the most powerful "special interest" in either party may not be any economic or ideological group but the voters of Iowa and New Hampshire. The Granite State's first-in-the-nation primary has been an important milestone in the nomination campaign for decades, and Iowa's even earlier caucus meetings have been a crucial arena ever since Carter used a strong 1976 showing there to propel him into the first rank of contenders. But the two states' influence seems to have grown even greater in recent elections, frustrating every effort of national party officials to reduce the disproportionate clout of those tiny electorates. "There seems to be a natural law of the nomination campaign, that everything that happens ends up making Iowa and New Hampshire more important," observed Democratic rules expert Elaine Kamarck, who served as deputy campaign manager for former Arizona governor Bruce Babbitt.

The two states' pivotal role has its defenders. By concentrating the efforts of the campaigns on relatively small groups of people—roughly speaking, about 250,000 primary voters in New Hampshire and 200,000 caucus participants in Iowa—the system encourages direct contact between candidates and voters. In effect, residents of the two states have assumed some of the role of peer review that used to be exercised by party leaders, by studying the candidates intensively and making a "first cut" in the field before the candidates move on to larger arenas. "If you started in a big place, you would never have the kind of one-on-one look that you do in those small states. People get to look at the candidates personally," said Kamarck. "There is no other place in the system where average people can evaluate the candidates. People in Iowa and New Hampshire take all of this very seriously."

Those people also have learned to take advantage of their special situation, critics of the system observe. There is a core of a few hundred party workers in the two states who will exert a crucial effect on the outcomes, and they expect avid pursuit by the candidates in return for their support. New Hampshire residents have long been accustomed to receiving candidates' personal attentions, for example, but now they seem to want more tangible rewards as well. Party and other organizations in the state regularly charge $1,000 and up for candidates to address their members during primary season. In Iowa politicians parlayed the prospect of their support in 1988 into a campaign finance bonanza: Presidential campaign organizations donated nearly $150,000 to candidates for state and local offices in 1986, according to the *Des Moines Register*. "There are maybe five hundred people in Iowa who have learned to manipulate the system. Do we really want these judgments about candidates to be made by a handful of activists?" asked From.

The influence of those small groups of activists is especially troubling, critics argue, when it shifts the nomination decision away from the wishes of party members nationwide. If the electorates of the two states are unrepresentative of the nation as a whole, the process is skewed. Such criticisms are most frequently made against the Iowa Democratic party, which is markedly more liberal than many other state parties.

Equally troubling to some is the way the power of the Iowa and New Hampshire activists affects the behavior of the candidates. Certainly there is nothing inherently objectionable about candidates spending weeks on end in the two states or even, as Bruce Babbitt did, bicycling across Iowa with his family. Nor is there any reason that candidates should not send their wives to meet with party workers, as most have done. But many people question whether these potential presidents are losing their dignity when they do everything short of washing the dishes of important party members in order to curry their favor. Consider, for example, this statement to Iowa Republicans by Sen. Robert Dole of Kansas, the leader of the Senate GOP and one of the most powerful men in government: "I'll make house calls. I'll do windows. I'll do whatever it takes. And if I can't, I'll get Elizabeth [Dole] for you." [6]

Still, the candidates' emphasis on Iowa and New Hampshire is no more exaggerated than the attention lavished on them by the media. News coverage of the two events dwarfs the efforts expended on primaries and caucuses in states with many more convention delegates. Statistical evidence of that tilt comes from Professor William C. Adams of George Washington University, who studied the 1984 campaign as it appeared on the three networks and in the *New York Times*. Adams found that the New Hampshire primary alone received more coverage than the combined total for delegate-selection events in twenty-four states in the South and West. Comparing news coverage with the number of primary participants, Adams found that the typical New Hampshire Democratic voter was the subject of 125 times the media interest devoted to Ohio primary voters.[7]

"Super Tuesday"

The changes wrought by the current system are not confined to the overall outlines of the nomination struggle. Shifts in specific rules and guidelines every four years reshape the political landscape of each campaign, aiding some candidates and harming others in often unpredictable ways. The campaigns for the 1988 Democratic and Republican nominations were no exception.

The major new dynamic of the 1988 campaigns was "Super Tuesday," the March 8 date on which more than twenty states would hold presidential primaries and caucuses. The core of Super Tuesday was the South, where fourteen states held primaries; South Carolina was the only state in the region not to do so. Roughly one-third of all convention delegates would be chosen on that day.

Although party officials in the past two years had decided against any major rules changes, in order to achieve some stability in the system, Super Tuesday developed spontaneously. Governors and legislatures in largely Democratic-dominated states passed laws mandating primaries to replace the caucuses frequently used in the South in past years. As a result state Republican parties found themselves covered by laws that sprang from internal Democratic politics.

The basic rationale for Super Tuesday was to increase the ability of southern moderates and conservatives to influence the Democratic nomination. By clustering their states early in the process, leaders hoped to give a major boost to a candidate with close ties to their region. A big win in the South, they reasoned, would give a moderate candidate the momentum needed to pull past the probably liberal winners of Iowa and New Hampshire.

Many nomination experts, however, wondered if things would turn out that way. Because of the strong advantages possessed by the winners of the earlier events—chiefly, in favorable media coverage—Super Tuesday might end up magnifying, rather than counteracting, the results of Iowa and New Hampshire. Particularly if turnout was low among conservative Democrats, either because they did not vote or because they crossed over and voted in Republican primaries, one of the liberal candidates could well sweep the region and end the day with the nomination within his or her grasp.

"When you win the New Hampshire primary, you get a 15 percent 'blip,' or sudden jump, in support," said Mark Siegel, a Democratic rules expert and member of the party's Compliance Assistance Commission.[8] "This year, within that 15 percent blip, you have twenty states voting." Moreover, Siegel added, the concentration of contests on one day means that the South will have little ability to influence later stages of the campaign. "After March 8 the

South has literally shot its wad," he said.

Still, the biggest effect of the current system on the 1988 nominations may have occurred before the primaries and caucuses began. One of the most striking aspects of the campaign was the degree to which potentially strong candidates had decided not to seek the nomination. In a year in which the Democrats may have had their best chance to capture the White House in more than a decade, a host of possible contenders—including New York governor Mario M. Cuomo, New Jersey senator Bill Bradley, and Arkansas senator Dale Bumpers—had announced that they would not run. The situation was similar in the GOP, where the list of presidential noncontenders included conservative senator William L. Armstrong of Colorado, moderate governor Thomas H. Kean of New Jersey, and White House chief of staff Howard H. Baker, Jr. Although these noncandidates cited personal and other reasons for not running, there was little doubt that the length, complexity, and seeming irrationality of the current system were among the major stumbling blocks.

Changing the System

However serious the loss of such "might-have-been" presidents is to the nation's political strength, it seems unlikely that this or similar concerns about the nominating system will lead to wholesale changes. The desire for stability in the process is so great and the fear that an attempt to thoroughly rewrite the system would stir up damaging political conflicts so pronounced that anything less than a collapse of the system is unlikely to produce a strong movement for change. Chastened by the experience of two decades, in which seemingly harmless changes in the system frequently produced damaging unintended consequences, nomination experts are reluctant to make a plunge to a new system that may be even worse. "Virtually any strategy that requires scrapping the current system and starting anew will probably further undermine rather than enhance quality [of the system]," University of Virginia political scientist James W. Ceaser has written.[9]

A system-shaking event could come in the form of a landslide loss by one of the parties, which might, like the Democratic party in recent elections, be tempted to blame the rules for its political weakness. Alternatively, a candidate who represents only a small fraction of either party might be able to manipulate the system to capture the nomination and thus clearly frustrate the will of the majority. Another possibility is that one or both party contests would remain unresolved by the end of the primary season, leading to an open convention in which the nominee is chosen by floor fights and behind-the-scenes negotiations. Such an event, unprecedented in recent times, could be seen by the public either as a thrilling act of political drama or as a sleazy fiasco culminating a bankrupt process.

There are three arenas for reform if public unhappiness with the system intensifies as a result of the 1988 election. Perhaps the least likely are the national parties themselves. Even if national party officials were willing to attempt to impose changes on the system, as Democrats did in past years, their efforts might well be frustrated by state parties, which have shown increasing resistance to accepting dictates from above. On the other hand, state parties could undertake their own changes, along with the state legislatures, as occurred with Super Tuesday. If a dozen or two states decided to abolish primaries in favor of

What Polls Show—And What They Don't

Public-opinion polls have become a prominent aspect of media coverage of the presidential-nomination campaign in recent years. A year and more before the national conventions, pollsters, the networks, and major newspapers are already busy tracking the minute variations in candidates' fortunes as reflected in the preferences of the public.

But experience suggests that polls are a slim reed on which to base an understanding of a nomination contest. There is ample evidence from past campaigns to show that early polls are not a very good indicator of the eventual outcome. Front-runners in the polls often falter, and candidates who consistently register minimal support in the polls can rise with startling rapidity once their campaigns take a turn for the better—as occurred with Jimmy Carter in 1976 and Gary Hart in 1984.

In fact, many polling experts believe that surveys at this stage of the campaign are far more indicative of the voters' familiarity with the candidates than of their preferences. The "name-recognition" factor is dominant at a time when all but the most politically aware of the voters have given little or no thought to the campaign. When confronted by a pollster, most people are likely to select the candidate they at least have heard of. Nevertheless, polls continue to fascinate campaign observers, who seem to find reassurance in their aura of scientific objectivity. That reliance can put journalists and others in a difficult position, however, when the results of a poll conflict with the basic tenets of political prediction.

That was the case in the 1988 Democratic campaign. When Hart prematurely withdrew from the contest in May 1987, polls regularly showed the Reverend Jesse L. Jackson was favored by more Democrats than any other candidate. Yet most political analysts thought that Jackson, who is black and considerably more liberal than most Democrats, did not have a serious chance of winning the nomination. So organizations that had invested heavily in polls were torn between the impulse to anoint Jackson as front-runner and their knowledge that he almost certainly was not.

Still, consistent poll results can provide some insight into how individual candidates are doing. Many experts have argued that the inability of Democratic senator Joseph R. Biden, Jr., of Delaware and Republican representative Jack F. Kemp of New York—two relatively well known contenders with solid political connections and ample campaign funding—to escape from single digits in the polls indicated some fundamental weakness in their campaigns.

Polls are useful for the candidates themselves, though not in the way they customarily appear in the press. According to Thomas H. Silver, publisher of the *Polling Report*, the detailed information provided by polls can be a political version of market research. "As far as predicting the outcome at this stage in the process, polls have minimal usefulness. But that's not what people in campaigns use them for," he explained. "Campaigns are less concerned with 'trial heats,' which is what usually gets reported in the press, than with what other polling data tell them about designing their media campaigns. They want polls to tell them how to cast their message in a way that doesn't ring any alarm bells with the voters."

caucuses, for example, the system would undergo a major revision. This occurred once before, in the 1920s, when the first wave of enthusiasm for primaries waned. Finally, Congress could approve legislation mandating a new nomination system. "There will be some kind of legislative initiative undertaken after 1988," predicted GOP consultant Mahe. "Congress will not be able to hold off meddling with the process."

Major changes in the current system could follow two different courses. One direction suggested by many would be to convert it into a wholly primary-based process in which the nomination decision was entirely in the hands of the voters. The most dramatic version of that idea is establishment of a national primary to select a nominee. Under such a system candidates would have to file a minimum number of petitions to get on the Democratic or Republican ballots. The candidate with the most votes in each party would be the nominee; a runoff would be held if no one received at least 40 percent of the vote. Conventions would select vice-presidential nominees and approve the party platforms. Other proposals call for a series of mandatory primaries scheduled over several months, organized either by region—the South to vote in March, the West in April, and so on—or, as Representative Levin has proposed, in a series of six primaries composed of randomly selected states.

The idea of a national primary has consistently received strong support in public-opinion polls, but it is anathema to most party professionals and political scientists. Critics of the idea see it undermining what remains of the party system, reducing the nomination contest to a mere popularity contest from which experienced party leaders would be excluded.

Such a system also would greatly expand the influence of the media, critics add, by making any form of campaigning other than press coverage and paid television advertisements impracticable. "Under a national primary, you would get either a Teddy Kennedy or a Lee Iacocca—the best-known candidates would win," said Mahe. "Lesser known candidates, like Pete du Pont or Bruce Babbitt, wouldn't even exist in a national primary."

The opposite approach to nomination reform would be to restore power to established party leaders and strengthen the role of state and local parties in the process. Democrats already have attempted that to a certain extent, through creation of automatic convention seats for party and elected officials. More radical proposals would give the nominating power to a convention entirely composed of party leaders or, as is done in some states for other offices, would allow a convention of officials to nominate a small number of candidates, whose names would then appear on a national primary ballot.

Nomination: Two Centuries of Change

1796-1824   Presidential candidates of the fledgling parties (Democratic-Republican and Federalist) are selected by congressional party caucuses.

1832   Democrats hold their first national convention to select a presidential candidate. Party conventions quickly become the accepted method for picking nominees.

1905   Wisconsin passes a law requiring the selection of national convention delegates by a primary. The number of primaries quickly grows, reaching twenty-six in 1916, but falls in following years.

1920-1968   Full flowering of the "mixed" nomination system. There are some primaries, but most delegates are chosen by autonomous state and local party leaders.

1936   Democrats abolish their longstanding rule requiring candidates to receive a two-thirds majority for the nomination.

1964   The first hints of a movement to "reform" the Democratic party's nominating process. Controversy over the seating of an all-white delegation from Mississippi leads to resolutions barring racial discrimination in delegate selection.

1968   Bitter conflicts within the Democratic party over the Vietnam War and the selection of Vice President Hubert H. Humphrey as presidential nominee produce calls for major changes in the nomination system. Delegates approve establishment of a commission, to be chaired by Sen. George McGovern of South Dakota and Rep. Donald M. Fraser of Minnesota, to revise party rules.

   The commission produces a host of changes in party rules, most notably the requirement that state delegations reflect the racial and sexual makeup of the state (in effect, a quota system for women and minorities). In addition, the panel bars ex officio convention seats for party and elected officials and pushes state parties to use primaries as the preferred method of delegate selection.

1972   Making use of the new rules he helped write, McGovern captures the Democratic nomination. The convention votes to enforce the new rules by expelling Chicago mayor Richard J. Daley, the most powerful Democrat in Illinois. Democrats also appoint another rules commission, headed by Baltimore councilwoman (now senator) Barbara A. Mikulski. The commission ends the quota system used in 1972 but urges continued affirmative action and an equal division of delegations according to sex.

1974   Passage of federal campaign finance legislation, which provides for matching public financing of nomination campaigns and establishes limits on the amounts candidates can spend in pursuit of the nomination.

1975   The Republican National Committee rejects proposals by the Rule 29 Committee, calling for efforts to open up the party and its nomination system to greater public participation. Future GOP rules changes are limited to relatively minor technical improvements.

1976   Democrats appoint a new rules commission, chaired by Michigan Democratic chairman Morley A. Winograd. The panel mandates an equal sexual division of delegations, while also calling for increased efforts to restore participation by party and elected officials.

1980   Democrats pick North Carolina governor James B. Hunt, Jr., to head another rules commission. The Hunt panel recommends that convention seats be reserved for officials, who need not be pledged to any specific candidate. The new official delegates are informally dubbed "superdelegates."

1984   Under pressure from defeated candidates Sen. Gary Hart of Colorado and the Reverend Jesse L. Jackson, the Democratic convention approves a new rules panel, named the "Fairness Commission," to propose major changes in party rules affecting allocation of delegates. The commission, chaired by South Carolina party official Donald L. Fowler, nevertheless recommends against any major rules revisions. The chief thrust of the panel's 1985 report calls for a few more superdelegates.

Delegates from U.S. Territories

They are the wallflowers of presidential politics. Either too far away from the mainland or offering too few delegates to merit candidates' visits, the far-flung territories of the United States held their caucuses in a virtual vacuum, spared the prognostications of national pundits and saturation coverage from the media.

In 1988 Democrats held caucuses in the territories of American Samoa, Guam, and the Virgin Islands. In addition, any American citizen of voting age who lived overseas could have participated in the March 22, 1988, mail-in primary held under the umbrella denomination of "Democrats Abroad."

Breaking from tradition, Democrats in 1988 did not send a separate delegation to the national convention from the Panama Canal Zone. Those Democrats, as well as the rest of the category once known as Latin American Democrats, participated in the Democrats Abroad primary.

Republicans confined their international caucusing to Guam and the Virgin Islands, and the GOP decided at its 1988 convention to initiate delegations for American Samoa for 1992.

The first of these small territories to vote in 1988 was American Samoa, which had four delegate votes at the Democratic convention. Located in the South Pacific about two-thirds of the way from Hawaii to New Zealand, American Samoa held a caucus March 8 to select six delegates (each with one-half vote). Delegates were allocated proportionally to reflect the presidential preferences of caucus participants. American Samoa also had one superdelegate vote, which was divided four ways.

The Democratic delegate-selection plan for the Virgin Islands was similar, but the date was April 2, and there were two district conventions instead of one central caucus meeting.

Both Democrats and Republicans on the Virgin Islands had four delegate votes each at their national conventions. In May Republicans chose their delegates in one round of "club meetings," involving the two thousand or so GOP club members in the Caribbean territory. Two delegates were to be elected from the island of St. Croix, and one each from St. Thomas and St. John.

Each party also awarded four delegate votes to Guam, which is about 3,300 miles west of Hawaii across the international dateline.

Democrats Abroad, entitled to nine delegate votes, held a primary by mail ballot, with ballots due by March 22. It was a direct election primary; voters chose among delegates who were listed on the ballot with their presidential preference. Prospective delegates must have filed petitions signed by fifteen enrolled members of Democrats Abroad by January 15. Ten delegates with one-half vote each were elected in the primary, and four other delegates with one-half vote each were chosen by the governing committee of Democrats Abroad in May to reflect the primary vote. The other two delegate votes were split among eight party officials.

The territories have had a role, albeit a small one, in the nominating process for nearly a century. Alaska first sent delegates to the party conventions in 1892, nearly seventy years before statehood. That year's GOP convention also featured two delegates from the "Indian Territory." They split between Benjamin Harrison and James G. Blaine.

Hawaii entered the nominating sweepstakes in 1900 at both parties' conventions. About the same time the Philippine Islands began sending delegates to the conventions, beginning in 1904 with the GOP. They had a place in the process until gaining independence after World War II.

The territories are not great trend setters. They usually cast their convention votes for the candidate who is clearly going to win the nomination. Participation in their delegate-selection activities vary. In 1984 more than two thousand ballots were cast in the Democrats Abroad primary, while the American Samoa delegation was chosen by seventy Democrats meeting in Pago Pago.

Still, it is hard to imagine either party ever returning to a system ruled by party bosses like Governor Lawrence. "Most of the politicians in both parties think the system needs to be changed," said GOP consultant John Sears. "But they don't want to say so in public, for fear the press will accuse them of trying to move the process back into the back rooms."

"We're never going to be able to close up the system like it used to be," said From of the Democratic Leadership Council. "We can't go back to the 'smoke-filled room.'"

Notes

1. Parties in some states hold both caucuses and primaries; in other states Democrats and Republicans use different methods for selecting delegates.
2. Percentage applies to the 3,517 delegates selected either by primaries or by caucuses. An additional 643 delegate seats would be awarded automatically to party and elected officials.
3. Theodore H. White, *America in Search of Itself* (New York: Harper and Row, 1982), 78.
4. The Committee for the Study of the American Electorate, based in Washington, D.C.
5. The Democratic Leadership Council, based in Washington, D.C., is an organization of elected officials, chiefly from the South and West. Its chairman is Sen. Sam Nunn of Georgia.
6. Quoted in the *Washington Post,* June 16, 1987.
7. From William C. Adams, "As New Hampshire Goes...," in *Media and Momentum: The New Hampshire Primary and Nomination Politics,* ed. Gary R. Orren and Nelson W. Polsby (New York: Chatham House, 1987).
8. The Compliance Assistance Commission reviews the delegate-selection plans submitted by state Democratic parties to make sure they are in accord with national-party rules.
9. From "Improving the Nominating Process," in *Elections, American Style,* ed. A. James Reichley (Washington, D.C.: Brookings Institution, 1987).

1988 Presidential Primaries

In 1988 thirty-six states and the District of Columbia held presidential primaries, although there was no Republican voting in New York and no Democratic voting in South Carolina. Candidates are named in this list only if they received 5 percent or more of the vote. Percentages may not equal 100 because of rounding.

The list gives in parentheses the official state of residence for each candidate registered with the Federal Election Commission.

In some jurisdictions balloting was for delegate slates linked to specific presidential candidates; in others, electors indicated only a personal preference as to their party's nominee.

The major source for this section was *America Votes* 18 (1989), compiled by Richard M. Scammon and Alice V. McGillivray and published by Congressional Quarterly Inc. Other sources were the Federal Election Commission and Congressional Quarterly.

Republican			Democratic		
Candidates	Votes	Percent	Candidates	Votes	Percent

February 16   New Hampshire

Republican			Democratic		
George Bush (Maine)	59,290	37.6	Michael S. Dukakis (Mass.)	44,112	35.7
Robert Dole (Kan.)	44,797	28.4	Richard A. Gephardt (Mo.)	24,513	19.8
Jack F. Kemp (N.Y.)	20,114	12.8	Paul Simon (Ill.)	21,094	17.1
Pierre S. du Pont IV (Del.)	15,885	10.1	Jesse Jackson (Ill.)	9,615	7.8
Pat Robertson (Va.)	14,775	9.4	Albert Gore, Jr. (Tenn.)	8,400	6.8
Alexander M. Haig, Jr. (Pa.)	481	0.3	Bruce Babbitt (Ariz.)	5,644	4.6
Harold E. Stassen (Pa.)	130	—	Gary W. Hart (Colo.)	4,888	4.0
Paul B. Conley (N.Y.)	107	—	William J. du Pont IV (Ill.)	1,349	1.1
Mary Jane Rachner (Minn.)	107	—	David E. Duke (D.C.)	264	0.2
Robert F. Drucker	83	—	Lyndon H. LaRouche (Va.)	188	0.2
William Horrigan (Conn.)	76	—	William A. Marra (N.J.)	142	0.1
Michael S. Levinson (N.Y.)	43	—	Conrad W. Roy	122	0.1
Others [a]	1,756	1.1	Florenzo Di Donato	84	0.1
			Anthony R. Martin-Trigona (Conn.)	61	—
			Steven A. Koczak (D.C.)	47	—
			William King (Fla.)	36	—
			Edward T. O'Donnell	33	—
			Cyril E. Sagan (Pa.)	33	—
			Frank L. Thomas	28	—
			Claude R. Kirk (Fla.)	25	—
			Irwin Zucker	22	—
			Norbert G. Dennerll (Ohio)	18	—
			Osie Thorpe (D.C.)	16	—
			A. A. Van Petten (Calif.)	10	—
			Stanley Lock (Mich.)	9	—
			Others [a]	2,759	2.2

February 23   South Dakota

Republican			Democratic		
Dole slate	51,599	55.2	Gephardt	31,184	43.6
Robertson slate	18,310	19.6	Dukakis	22,349	31.2
Bush slate	17,404	18.6	Gore	5,993	8.4
Kemp slate	4,290	4.6	Simon	3,992	5.6
Unpledged delegates slate	1,226	1.3	Hart	3,875	5.4
du Pont slate	576	0.6	Jackson	3,867	5.4
			Babbitt	346	0.5

March 1   Vermont [b]

Republican			Democratic		
Bush	23,565	49.3	Dukakis	28,353	55.8
Dole	18,655	39.0	Jackson	13,044	25.7
Robertson	2,452	5.1	Gephardt	3,910	7.7
Kemp	1,877	3.9	Simon	2,620	5.2
du Pont	808	1.7	Hart	2,055	4.0
Haig	324	0.7	Others [a]	809	1.6
Others [a]	151	0.3			

Republican			Democratic		
Candidates	Votes	Percent	Candidates	Votes	Percent

March 5   South Carolina

Bush	94,738	48.5			
Dole	40,265	20.6			
Robertson	37,261	19.1			
Kemp	22,431	11.5			
du Pont	316	0.2			
Haig	177	0.1			
Stassen	104	0.1			

March 8   Alabama

Bush	137,807	64.5	Jackson	176,764	43.6
Dole	34,733	16.2	Gore	151,739	37.4
Robertson	29,772	13.9	Dukakis	31,306	7.7
Kemp	10,557	4.9	Gephardt	30,214	7.4
du Pont	392	0.2	Hart	7,530	1.9
Haig	300	0.1	Simon	3,063	0.8
			Babbitt	2,410	0.6
			Unpledged delegates	1,771	0.4
			LaRouche	845	0.2

March 8   Arkansas

Bush	32,114	47.0	Gore	185,758	37.3
Dole	17,667	25.9	Dukakis	94,103	18.9
Robertson	12,918	18.9	Jackson	85,003	17.1
Kemp	3,499	5.1	Gephardt	59,711	12.0
Unpledged delegates	1,402	2.1	Unpledged delegates	35,553	7.1
du Pont	359	0.5	Hart	18,630	3.7
Haig	346	0.5	Simon	9,020	1.8
			Duke	4,805	1.0
			Babbitt	2,614	0.5
			LaRouche	2,347	0.5

March 8   Florida

Bush	559,820	62.1	Dukakis	521,041	40.9
Dole	191,197	21.2	Jackson	254,912	20.0
Robertson	95,826	10.6	Gephardt	182,861	14.4
Kemp	41,795	4.6	Gore	161,165	12.7
du Pont	6,726	0.7	Undecided	79,088	6.2
Haig	5,858	0.7	Hart	·36,315	2.9
			Simon	27,620	2.2
			Babbitt	10,296	0.8

March 8   Georgia

Bush	215,516	53.8	Jackson	247,831	39.8
Dole	94,749	23.6	Gore	201,490	32.6
Robertson	65,163	16.3	Dukakis	97,179	15.6
Kemp	23,409	5.8	Gephardt	41,489	6.7
du Pont	1,309	0.3	Hart	15,852	2.5
Haig	782	0.2	Simon	8,388	1.3
			Unpledged delegates	7,276	1.2
			Babbitt	3,247	0.5

	Republican			Democratic		
Candidates	Votes	Percent	Candidates	Votes	Percent	

March 8   Kentucky

	Republican			Democratic		
Bush	72,020	59.3	Gore	145,988	45.8	
Dole	27,868	23.0	Dukakis	59,433	18.6	
Robertson	13,526	11.1	Jackson	49,667	15.6	
Kemp	4,020	3.3	Gephardt	28,982	9.1	
Unpledged delegates	2,245	1.8	Hart	11,798	3.7	
Stassen	844	0.7	Unpledged delegates	10,465	3.3	
du Pont	457	0.4	Simon	9,393	2.9	
Haig	422	0.3	Babbitt	1,290	0.4	
			LaRouche	681	0.2	
			Martin-Trigona	537	0.2	
			Richard B. Kay (Fla.)	487	0.2	

March 8   Louisiana

	Republican			Democratic		
Bush	83,687	57.8	Jackson	221,532	35.5	
Robertson	26,295	18.2	Gore	174,974	28.0	
Dole	25,626	17.7	Dukakis	95,667	15.3	
Kemp	7,722	5.3	Gephardt	66,434	10.6	
du Pont	853	0.6	Hart	26,442	4.2	
Haig	598	0.4	Duke	23,390	3.7	
			Simon	5,155	0.8	
			Frank Ahern (La.)	3,701	0.6	
			Babbitt	3,076	0.5	
			LaRouche	1,681	0.3	
			Dennerll	1,575	0.3	
			Kay	823	0.1	

March 8   Maryland

	Republican			Democratic		
Bush	107,026	53.3	Dukakis	242,479	45.6	
Dole	64,987	32.8	Jackson	152,642	28.7	
Robertson	12,860	6.5	Gore	46,063	8.7	
Kemp	11,909	5.9	Gephardt	42,059	8.0	
du Pont	2,551	1.8	Simon	16,513	3.1	
Haig	1,421	0.7	Unpledged delegates	14,948	2.8	
			Hart	9,732	1.8	
			Babbitt	4,750	0.9	
			LaRouche	2,149	0.4	

March 8   Massachusetts

	Republican			Democratic		
Bush	141,113	58.6	Dukakis	418,256	58.6	
Dole	63,392	26.3	Jackson	133,141	18.7	
Kemp	16,791	7.0	Gephardt	72,944	10.2	
Robertson	10,891	4.5	Gore	31,631	4.4	
du Pont	3,522	1.5	Simon	26,176	3.6	
No preference	3,416	1.4	No preference	11,866	1.7	
Haig	1,705	0.7	Hart	10,837	1.5	
Others [a]	351	0.1	Babbitt	4,222	0.6	
			DiDonato	1,971	0.3	
			LaRouche	998	0.1	
			Others [a]	1,405	0.2	

Republican			Democratic		
Candidates	Votes	Percent	Candidates	Votes	Percent

March 8   Mississippi

Republican			Democratic		
Bush	104,814	66.1	Jackson	160,651	44.7
Dole	26,855	16.9	Gore	120,364	33.5
Robertson	21,378	13.5	Dukakis	29,941	8.3
Kemp	5,479	3.5	Gephardt	19,693	5.5
			Hart	13,934	3.9
			Unpledged delegates	9,384	2.6
			Simon	2,118	0.6
			Babbitt	2,037	0.6
			LaRouche	1,295	0.4

March 8   Missouri

Republican			Democratic		
Bush	168,812	42.2	Gephardt	305,287	57.8
Dole	164,394	41.1	Jackson	106,386	20.2
Robertson	44,705	11.2	Dukakis	61,303	11.7
Kemp	14,180	3.5	Simon	21,433	4.1
Unpledged delegates	5,563	1.4	Gore	14,549	2.8
du Pont	1,788	0.4	Hart	7,607	1.4
Haig	858	0.2	Unpledged delegates	6,635	1.3
			Duke	1,760	0.3
			Babbitt	1,377	0.3
			LaRouche	664	0.1
			Kay	372	—
			Koczak	241	—
			Dennerll	191	—

March 8   North Carolina

Republican			Democratic		
Bush	124,260	45.4	Gore	235,669	34.7
Dole	107,032	39.1	Jackson	224,177	33.0
Robertson	26,861	9.8	Dukakis	137,993	20.3
Kemp	11,361	4.1	Gephardt	37,553	5.5
No preference	2,797	1.0	Hart	16,381	2.4
du Pont	944	0.3	No preference	16,337	2.4
Haig	546	0.2	Simon	8,032	1.2
			Babbitt	3,816	0.6

March 8   Oklahoma

Republican			Democratic		
Bush	78,224	37.4	Gore	162,584	41.4
Dole	73,016	34.9	Gephardt	82,596	21.0
Robertson	44,067	21.0	Dukakis	66,278	16.9
Kemp	11,439	5.5	Jackson	52,417	13.3
du Pont	938	0.4	Hart	14,336	3.7
Haig	715	0.3	Simon	6,901	1.8
Isabell Masters (Kan.)	539	0.3	Duke	2,388	0.6
			Babbitt	1,601	0.4
			LaRouche	1,078	0.3
			Koczak	1,068	0.3
			Charles R. Doty (Okla.)	1,005	0.3
			Dennerll	475	0.1

March 8   Rhode Island

Republican			Democratic		
Bush	10,401	64.9	Dukakis	34,211	69.7
Dole	3,628	22.6	Jackson	7,445	15.2
Robertson	911	5.7	Gephardt	2,028	4.1
Kemp	792	4.9	Gore	1,939	4.0
Unpledged delegates	174	1.1	Simon	1,395	2.8
du Pont	80	0.5	Unpledged delegates	809	1.7
Haig	49	0.3	Hart	733	1.5
			Babbitt	469	1.0

	Republican			Democratic		
Candidates	Votes	Percent	Candidates	Votes	Percent

March 8   Tennessee

	Republican			Democratic		
Bush	152,515	60.0	Gore	416,861	72.3
Dole	55,027	21.6	Jackson	119,248	20.7
Robertson	32,015	12.6	Dukakis	19,348	3.3
Kemp	10,911	4.3	Gephardt	8,470	1.5
Unpledged delegates	2,340	0.9	Hart	4,706	0.8
Haig	777	0.3	Unpledged delegates	3,032	0.5
du Pont	646	0.3	Simon	2,647	0.5
Others [a]	21	—	Babbitt	1,946	0.3
			Others [a]	56	—

March 8   Texas

	Republican			Democratic		
Bush	648,178	63.9	Dukakis	579,713	32.8
Robertson	155,449	15.3	Jackson	433,335	24.5
Dole	140,795	13.9	Gore	357,764	20.2
Kemp	50,586	5.0	Gephardt	240,158	13.6
Unpledged delegates	12,563	1.2	Hart	82,199	4.7
du Pont	4,245	0.4	Simon	34,499	1.9
Haig	3,140	0.3	Babbitt	11,618	0.7
			LaRouche	9,013	0.5
			Duke	8,808	0.5
			W. A. Williams	6,238	0.4
			Dennerll	3,700	0.2

March 8   Virginia

	Republican			Democratic		
Bush	124,738	53.7	Jackson	164,709	45.1
Dole	60,921	26.0	Gore	81,419	22.3
Robertson	32,173	13.7	Dukakis	80,183	22.0
Kemp	10,809	4.6	Gephardt	15,935	4.4
Unpledged delegates	3,675	1.6	Simon	7,045	1.9
du Pont	1,229	0.5	Hart	6,266	1.7
Haig	597	0.3	Unpledged delegates	6,142	1.7
			Babbitt	2,454	0.7
			LaRouche	746	0.2

March 15   Illinois [d]

	Republican			Democratic		
Bush	469,151	54.6	Simon	635,219	42.3
Dole	309,253	36.0	Jackson	484,233	32.3
Robertson	59,087	6.9	Dukakis	245,289	16.3
Kemp	12,687	1.5	Gore	77,265	5.1
du Pont	4,653	0.5	Gephardt	35,108	2.3
Haig	3,806	0.4	Hart	12,769	0.9
			LaRouche	6,094	0.4
			Babbitt	4,953	0.3

March 29   Connecticut

	Republican			Democratic		
Bush	73,501	70.6	Dukakis	140,291	58.1
Dole	21,005	20.2	Jackson	68,372	28.3
Kemp	3,281	3.1	Gore	18,501	7.7
Unpledged delegates	3,193	3.1	Hart	5,761	2.4
Robertson	3,191	3.1	Simon	3,140	1.3
			Babbitt	2,370	1.0
			Unpledged delegates	1,951	0.8
			Gephardt	1,009	0.4

Republican			Democratic		
Candidates	Votes	Percent	Candidates	Votes	Percent

April 5   Wisconsin

Bush	295,295	82.2	Dukakis	483,172	47.6
Dole	28,460	7.9	Jackson	285,995	28.2
Robertson	24,798	6.9	Gore	176,712	17.4
Kemp	4,915	1.4	Simon	48,419	4.8
Uninstructed delegation	2,372	0.7	Gephardt	7,996	0.8
Haig	1,554	0.4	Hart	7,068	0.7
du Pont	1,504	0.4	Uninstructed delegation	2,554	0.3
Others [a]	396	0.1	Babbitt	2,353	0.2
			Others [a]	513	0.1

April 19   New York

[c]

			Dukakis	801,457	50.9
			Jackson	585,076	37.1
			Gore	157,559	10.0
			Simon	17,011	1.1
			Unpledged delegates	10,258	0.7
			Gephardt	2,672	0.2
			LaRouche	1,153	0.1

April 26   Pennsylvania

Bush	687,323	79.0	Dukakis	1,002,480	66.5
Dole	103,763	11.9	Jackson	411,260	27.3
Robertson	79,463	9.1	Gore	44,542	3.0
			Hart	20,473	1.4
			Simon	9,692	0.6
			Jennifer Alden Wesner (Pa.)	7,546	0.5
			Gephardt	7,254	0.5
			LaRouche	4,443	0.3

May 3   District of Columbia

Bush	5,890	87.6	Jackson	68,840	80.0
Dole	469	7.0	Dukakis	15,415	17.9
Robertson	268	4.0	Simon	769	0.9
Write-ins	93	1.4	Gore	648	0.8
			Gephardt	300	0.3
			Thorpe	80	0.1

May 3   Indiana

Bush	351,829	80.4	Dukakis	449,495	69.6
Dole	42,878	9.8	Jackson	145,021	22.5
Robertson	28,712	6.6	Gore	21,865	3.4
Kemp	14,236	3.6	Gephardt	16,777	2.6
			Simon	12,550	1.9

May 3   Ohio

Bush slate	643,907	81.0	Dukakis slate	869,792	62.9
Dole slate	94,650	11.9	Jackson slate	378,866	27.4
Robertson slate	56,347	7.1	Gore slate	29,931	2.2
			James A. Traficant slate (Ohio)	29,912	2.2
			Hart slate	28,414	2.1
			Douglas Applegate slate (Ohio)	25,068	1.8
			Simon slate	15,524	1.1
			LaRouche slate	6,065	0.4

	Republican			Democratic		
Candidates	Votes	Percent	Candidates		Votes	Percent

May 10 Nebraska [e]

	Republican			Democratic		
Bush	138,784	68.0	Dukakis		106,334	62.9
Dole	45,572	22.3	Jackson		43,380	25.7
Robertson	10,334	5.1	Gephardt		4,948	2.9
Kemp	8,423	4.1	Unpledged delegates		4,763	2.8
Others [a]	936	0.5	Hart		4,220	2.5
			Gore		2,519	1.5
			Simon		2,104	1.2
			LaRouche		416	0.2
			Others [a]		324	0.2

May 10 West Virginia

	Republican			Democratic		
Bush	110,705	77.3	Dukakis		254,289	74.8
Dole	15,600	10.9	Jackson		45,788	13.5
Robertson	10,417	7.3	Gore		11,573	3.4
Kemp	3,820	2.7	Hart		9,284	2.7
Stassen	1,604	1.1	Gephardt		6,130	1.8
Conley	994	0.7	Angus W. McDonald (W.Va.)		3,604	1.1
			Simon		2,280	0.7
			Babbitt		1,978	0.6
			LaRouche		1,482	0.4
			Duke		1,383	0.4
			Dennerll		1,339	0.4
			Traficant		967	0.3

May 17 Oregon

	Republican			Democratic		
Bush	199,938	72.8	Dukakis		221,048	56.8
Dole	49,128	17.9	Jackson		148,207	38.1
Robertson	21,212	7.7	Gephardt		6,772	1.7
Others [a]	4,208	1.5	Gore		5,445	1.4
			Simon		4,757	1.2
			LaRouche		1,562	0.4
			Others [a]		1,141	0.3

May 24 Idaho

	Republican			Democratic		
Bush	55,464	81.2	Dukakis		37,696	73.4
"None of the names shown"	6,935	10.2	Jackson		8,066	15.7
Robertson	5,876	8.6	"None of the names shown"		2,308	4.5
			Gore		1,891	3.7
			Simon		1,409	2.7

June 7 California [f]

	Republican			Democratic		
Bush	1,856,273	82.9	Dukakis		1,910,808	60.9
Dole	289,220	12.9	Jackson		1,102,093	35.1
Robertson	94,779	4.2	Gore		56,645	1.8
Others [a]	115	—	Simon		43,771	1.4
			LaRouche		25,417	0.8

June 7 Montana

	Republican			Democratic		
Bush	63,098	73.0	Dukakis		83,684	68.7
Dole	16,762	19.4	Jackson		26,908	22.1
No preference	6,520	7.5	No preference		4,083	3.4
			Gephardt		3,369	2.8
			Gore		2,261	1.9
			Simon		1,566	1.3

Republican			Democratic		
Candidates	Votes	Percent	Candidates	Votes	Percent

June 7   New Jersey

Bush	241,033	100.0	Dukakis	414,829	63.4
			Jackson	213,705	32.7
			Gore	18,062	2.8
			LaRouche	2,621	0.4
			Marra	2,594	0.4
			Duke	2,491	0.4

June 7   New Mexico

Bush	69,359	78.2	Dukakis	114,968	61.0
Dole	9,305	10.5	Jackson	52,988	28.1
Robertson	5,350	6.0	Hart	6,898	3.7
Unpledged delegates	2,569	2.9	Gore	4,747	2.6
Haig	2,161	2.4	Unpledged delegates	3,275	1.7
			Babbitt	2,913	1.5
			Simon	2,821	1.5

June 14   North Dakota

Bush	37,062	94.0	g		
Rachner	2,372	6.0			

Republican Primary Totals   **Democratic Primary Totals**

Bush	8,254,654	67.9	Dukakis	9,817,185	42.8
Dole	2,333,268	19.2	Jackson	6,685,699	29.1
Robertson	1,097,442	9.0	Gore	3,134,516	13.7
Kemp	331,333	2.7	Gephardt	1,388,356	6.0
du Pont	49,781	0.4	Simon	1,018,136	4.4
Haig	26,617	0.2	Hart	389,003	1.7
Stassen	2,682	—	Babbitt	77,780	0.3
Rachner	2,479	—	LaRouche	70,938	0.3
Conley	1,101	—	Duke	45,289	0.2
Masters	539	—	Traficant	30,879	0.1
Drucker	83	—	Applegate	25,068	0.1
Horrigan	76	—	Dennerll	7,298	—
Levinson	43	—	Wesner	7,546	—
Unpledged delegates	34,950	0.3	Williams	6,238	—
No preference	12,733	0.1	Ahern	3,701	—
"None of the names shown"	6,935	0.1	McDonald	3,604	—
Uninstructed delegation	2,372	—	Marra	2,736	—
Scattered write-in votes	8,027	0.1	Di Nonato	2,055	—
	12,165,115		Kay	1,682	—
			Koczak	1,356	—
			du Pont	1,349	—
			Doty	1,005	—
			Martin-Trigona	598	—
			Roy	122	—
			Thorpe	96	—
			King	36	—
			O'Donnell	33	—
			Sagan	33	—
			Thomas	28	—
			Kirk	25	—
			Zucker	22	—
			Van Petten	10	—
			Lock	9	—
			Unpledged delegates	116,262	0.5
			Undecided	79,088	0.3
			No preference	32,286	0.1
			Uninstructed delegation	2,554	—
			"None of the names shown"	2,308	—
			Scattered write-in votes	7,007	—
				22,961,936	

a. Write-in votes.

b. In Vermont's Liberty Union presidential primary, Willa Kenoyer received 199 votes (68.9 percent), Herb Lewin received 65 votes (22.5 percent), and there were 25 scattered write-in votes (8.7 percent).

c. No primary.

d. In Illinois's Solidarity presidential primary, Lenora B. Fulani received 170 votes (100 percent).

e. In Nebraska's New Alliance presidential primary, Lenora B. Fulani received 10 votes (100 percent).

f. In California's American Independent presidential primary, James C. Griffin received 9,762 votes (64.4 percent), James Gritz received 5,401 votes (35.6 percent), and there were 3 scattered write-in votes (0.0 percent). In the Peace and Freedom presidential primary, Lenora B. Fulani received 2,117 votes (35.7 percent), Shirley Isaacson received 1,222 votes (20.6 percent), Larry Holmes received 1,042 votes (17.6 percent), Herb Lewin received 778 votes (13.1 percent), Willa Kenoyer received 411 votes (6.9 percent), Al Hamburg received 353 votes (6.0 percent), and there were 6 scattered write-in votes (0.1 percent).

g. No candidates' names appeared on the Democratic ballot. Tallied write-in votes were for Dukakis (2,890) and Jackson (515).

The 1988 National Conventions

Both of the major American political parties held their 1988 national nominating conventions in the South. The Democrats met in Atlanta July 18-21 to choose their party's presidential nominee—the first in eight years who would not be facing the popular Ronald Reagan.

With Reagan ineligible to run again after two terms as president, the Republicans met in New Orleans August 15-18 to seek a standard bearer who could keep the presidency in GOP hands, where it had been for most of the previous two decades.

Democrats

After years of internal warfare, the Democrats who nominated Massachusetts governor Michael S. Dukakis for president and Texas senator Lloyd Bentsen for vice president staged a remarkable show of unity. Supercharged by a raucous closing-night celebration, the Democrats left Atlanta brimming with confidence.

Following an acceptance speech that was enthusiastically received by delegates of every ideological stripe, Dukakis had all of his vanquished opponents, including Jesse L. Jackson, join him on the victory platform.

The prospects for party peace were not at all guaranteed as the Democrats gathered for the July 18-21 conclave. A rift had developed after Dukakis selected Bentsen as his running mate, riling Jackson's followers. But on the morning of the convention's opening day, the two candidates announced an agreement that satisfied Jackson's desire for significant input into Dukakis's general-election campaign.

Jackson dominated the early stages of the convention. On July 18 and 19, bright red "Jesse!" signs were more in evidence than Dukakis's blue-hued placards. The night of July 19, Jackson gave a powerful and moving speech, exhorting the poor and disadvantaged to "keep hope alive."

But Jackson, who had threatened floor fights over several liberal platform proposals, agreed to drop or modify most of them. His compromise contributed greatly to the bonhomie of Atlanta, signaling a victory of pragmatism over idealism. For once, the issue-oriented activists who dominated the Democratic nominating process for nearly two decades subordinated their agendas to the goal of party victory.

The Democrats thus avoided the self-inflicted wounds that had marred so many conventions since their 1968 Chicago debacle. In 1984 party conservatives turned away from the liberal ticket of Walter F. Mondale and Geraldine A. Ferraro; black supporters of Jackson, who felt abused by the nominating process, also lacked zeal. But in 1988, Dukakis's détente with Jackson and his outreach to conservatives through Bentsen set the stage for unity.

The result was a tension-free gathering that provided the backdrop for a Hollywood-style finale. Party organizers did all they could to maximize the self-advertising potential of the televised convention. The closing-night climax was a tableau of flags, placards, marching bands, and patriotic music.

The priority given to television production values did mandate certain sacrifices. Atlanta's Omni arena was chosen as the convention site because of its small dimensions: The full seats, crowded aisles and high noise levels created a high-energy environment. But overcrowding resulted in the locking of the arena doors—and the lockout of some delegates—during the July 19 and July 20 sessions.

But any anger over the crowded conditions was washed away by the closing-night fervor, with Democrats buoyed by a wave of optimism that lasted at least until the August Republican convention in New Orleans.

July 18: Opening Day

The Dukakis-Jackson agreement announced early July 18 erased the palpable risk of serious political conflict at the convention. As a result, the atmosphere inside the Omni on opening night was remarkably fraternal.

Dukakis delegates, primed to defend their hard-won victory against the demands of the runner-up, were able to sit back and breathe easy. Jackson supporters—who had been angered to the point of mutiny by what they saw as Dukakis's snub of Jackson—observed the signal of détente sent the morning of July 18 by their candidate. They limited their exhibitions to placard waving and occasional chants of "Jesse! Jesse!"; the chanting rarely went on for more than a few seconds.

But if the "understanding" between the two candidates defused the threat of a disrupted convention, it also removed any sense of drama from the proceedings. Keynote speaker Ann Richards, the Texas state treasurer, did energize the audience of activists with satiric attacks on the Reagan administration and Vice President George Bush. But the delegates' inattention to the other addresses—

including a session-closer by former president Jimmy Carter—gave a vaguely flat feeling to the carefully choreographed first-night "pep rally."

However, the tightly packed Omni proved its merits as a television venue. The 4,210 delegates, packed shoulder to shoulder and crowding the aisles of the cozy arena, assumed the appearance of a far larger mob. The close conditions also amplified the reverberating noise, especially the delegates' roars of approval during Richards's keynote speech.

Meeting of the Minds

The convention approached with some of Jackson's hard-core supporters, such as Rep. Gus Savage of Illinois and Atlanta civil rights activist Hosea Williams, threatening boycotts, protest marches, and walkouts. But a breakthrough came at a three-hour morning meeting July 18 of Dukakis, Jackson, and Bentsen.

At an ensuing news conference held just after 11 a.m., Dukakis praised Jackson for his voter-registration accomplishments and for his efforts to reach out to constituent groups beyond his black base. He then stated, "I want Jesse Jackson to play a major role in this campaign.... He is going to be involved actively, and fully."

Jackson appeared to concur, though he said he would follow through on his plan to have his name placed in nomination the night of July 20 and even joked that he was still hoping for a "Chicago miracle." But he did agree that he and Dukakis had discussed "a relationship of substance ... the commitment to help build a team that will expand our party and carry us to victory in November." In answer to a reporter's question, he said he no longer sought the vice presidency.

Voices in Harmony

The big news of the morning gave a bit of an anticlimactic feel to the floor proceedings, which got under way shortly after 6 p.m. Delegates milled about and conversed as convention business, including the confirmation of House Speaker Jim Wright of Texas as convention chairman, was disposed of in the pre-prime-time hours.

Democratic National Committee Chairman Paul G. Kirk, Jr., persistently underlined the theme of unity, pointing to the fact that the credentials and rules reports—sources of numerous battles and test votes at past conventions—had been previously ratified by the Dukakis and Jackson campaigns. Both were adopted without discussion.

There were a few signs that some Jackson supporters were not ready to forgive those who had slighted their candidate. The first sustained, placard-waving Jackson demonstration came with the introduction of Detroit mayor Coleman A. Young, who had angered Jackson supporters by endorsing Dukakis in 1988 and Mondale in 1984. Some Jackson supporters responded with boos when Atlanta mayor Andrew Young mentioned New York City mayor Edward I. Koch. A supporter of Tennessee senator Albert Gore Jr. in the New York primary, Koch had sharply criticized Jackson.

But the Jackson delegates were otherwise restrained. There was almost no demonstrably negative reaction to the frequent mentions of Bentsen's name.

A few moments appeared to unite the delegates. Both Mondale and his 1984 running mate, former representative Geraldine Ferraro of New York, were warmly received

when their presence in the hall was noted. And while the Democrats eschewed the aggressive flag-waving exercises of their 1984 San Francisco convention, there was a renewed effort to emphasize that Democrats, too, were patriotic. The prime-time proceedings were ushered in by a military brass band playing "God Bless the U.S.A.," the country-pop song so prominent in Ronald Reagan's 1984 reelection campaign. The delegates joined a group of schoolchildren who recited the Pledge of Allegiance, and then performed a full-throated rendition of the national anthem.

Richards Warmly Received

Richards's keynote address, delivered in full Texas twang, centered on a critique of the Republicans' alleged lack of concern for the interests of working Americans. It lacked the philosophical eloquence that made New York governor Mario M. Cuomo's 1984 keynote address famous. But while Richards did not outline a bold new Democratic vision, she won widespread praise for her folksy, personalized delivery and her trademark sense of humor.

Richards immediately drew laughs with jokes about New England-born Bush's adoption of Texas as his home state ("After listening to George Bush all these years, I figured you needed to know what a real Texas accent sounds like") and the capabilities of women ("Ginger Rogers did everything that Fred Astaire did. She just did it backwards and in high heels."). She then fanned the crowd's partisan fire by linking Bush to despised figures of the Reagan administration ("the Reagan-Meese-Deaver-Nofziger-Poindexter-North ... George Bush era").

Richards gave the crowd its biggest thrill of the night with a frontal assault on Bush. She said that for eight years Bush had not "displayed the slightest interest in anything we care about." But now that "he's after a job that he can't get appointed to," she jibed, he had suddenly discovered issues such as child care and education. She topped off her Bush-bashing by drawling, in tones of exaggerated sympathy, "Poor George. He can't help it—he was born with a silver foot in his mouth."

But any excitement that Richards generated was sapped by a series of less-than-enthralling events that followed, which culminated in Carter's address. Although the convention gave Carter an enthusiastic greeting—symbolic of the resurrection of his image within the party—many delegates became distracted during his litany of Democratic party virtues.

July 19: Day Two

Jackson electrified the convention hall, and television viewers beyond, with a high-voltage speech that unfurled his famous call for social justice and offered strong words of praise for Dukakis. Stirring the overflow crowd in the Omni late the night of July 19, Jackson claimed his place in history as the first black candidate to contend seriously for a major-party political nomination. And invoking his rise from poverty as a symbol of hope for poor and working-class Americans, he paid tribute to the civil rights movement that paved his political path.

"I was born in the slum, but the slum was not born in me, and it wasn't born in you, and you can make it," intoned Jackson in a speech that echoed the "I Am Somebody" theme he had used for years to inspire black audiences. He added: "You must not surrender."

Many party professionals had wondered whether Jackson's address might become a vehicle for venting whatever resentment lingered from the rift over the running-mate selection. Even during the July 18 news conference announcing the agreement between Jackson and Dukakis, the black leader had declined to cede the nomination.

But while his July 19 speech stopped short of an outright endorsement of Dukakis, Jackson expressed his solidarity with the Democratic effort to regain the White House. He praised Dukakis for resisting the "temptation to stoop to demagoguery," and said he had demonstrated "a good mind, fast at work, with steel nerves, guiding his campaign out of the crowded field without appeal to the worst in us."

Jackson called on Democrats of all political leanings to find "common ground," saying, "Tonight we choose interdependency in our capacity to act and unite for the greater good." The speech began just before 11 p.m. and lasted nearly an hour.

The Platform Battle

In an afternoon session, the candidates' campaigns had eliminated their last major grounds for argument—the minority planks of the Democratic platform—with a minimum of rancor.

Jackson planks calling for tax increases for corporations and the wealthy, and for a pledge that the United States would make "no first use" of nuclear weapons, were soundly defeated; a plank supporting Palestinian self-determination was withdrawn without a vote.

But without debate the delegates adopted a compromise package of nine other amendments pressed by the Jackson campaign and accepted by Dukakis. These embodied much of the spirit and some of the specifics that Jackson had tried to insert into the platform all along—a denunciation of aid to "irregular" forces in Central America, a national health program, sharply higher spending for education, and a moratorium on missile flight testing.

In the debate on what the Jackson campaign called the "fair tax" plank, Manhattan Borough president David Dinkins said that "the rich and the corporations" received the bulk of the Reagan administration tax cuts, which he blamed for the large federal deficits. He echoed Jackson's line that, in closing the deficit, those tax-cut beneficiaries would now "have to pay for the party."

But Denver mayor Federico Pena called for delegates to reject the plank, warning that its passage would be campaign fodder for Republicans, who persistently portrayed the Democrats as the "tax-and-spend" party. "I don't like throwing softballs to an opponent to knock out of the park," Pena said. The measure was defeated by a delegate vote of 1,091.5 to 2,499. *(See convention ballots, 1988 Democratic, p. 77.)*

There was more emotion over the nuclear-strategy plank, with Jackson supporters waving placards and chanting, "No first use!" Supporters of the plank said it would show Democratic commitment to world peace. But Dukakis supporters, while expressing solidarity with the cause of nuclear disarmament, said the defense strategy that called for use of nuclear weapons in the event of an invasion of Western Europe was a bedrock of the NATO alliance. They also said that, should Dukakis be elected president, the plank could deprive him of a key tool to force the Soviets to the bargaining table.

The minority plank was defeated, 1,220.6 to 2,474.1.

The most divisive issue was that of Palestinian rights. Arab-American activist James Zogby said that while they had agreed not to bring the subject to a vote, supporters of Palestinian self-determination had won a victory by getting the party to debate the issue openly. Plank supporters responded to sharp rebuttals by Sen. Daniel K. Inouye of Hawaii and Rep. Charles E. Schumer of New York—who referred to the Palestine Liberation Organization's terrorism and refusal to recognize Israel's right to exist—with outbursts of booing and catcalls.

Notwithstanding the compromise language inserted into the platform at Jackson's insistence, the overall platform debate represented a victory for the Dukakis forces. From the beginning, they had been bent on keeping the platform a document of general party themes, free of the kinds of commitments to programs and constituency groups that had aided past Republican efforts to label the Democrats the "party of special interests."

Tribute to Liberalism

In the evening session, none of the afternoon's contention was evident. In anticipation of Jackson's speech, the narrow aisles of the arena filled with delegates, guests, reporters, and photographers by the time of the 9 p.m. gaveling. By 10 p.m., the Omni was so packed that convention officials were compelled to close the doors at the suggestion of the fire marshal, shutting out a number of infuriated delegates and media representatives in the process.

If the afternoon session was symbolic of the Democratic party's effort to moderate its national image, the evening session was a tribute to the liberalism that had been the dominant party thread for two decades. The schedule was dominated by leading figures of the party's liberal wing.

A poignant convention moment occurred when law student John F. Kennedy, Jr., son of the slain president, introduced his uncle, Sen. Edward M. Kennedy of Massachusetts, who warmed up the crowd with rousing partisan rhetoric.

The Massachusetts Democrat accused Bush of "burying his head in his hands and hiding from the record of Reagan-Bush mistakes." Kennedy then listed a series of issues—Iran-contra, the Noriega drug connection, domestic budget cuts, civil rights—on which he said the Reagan administration had made wrong choices, following each example with the refrain, "Where was George?" The delegates spontaneously picked up the slogan as a chant.

Texas agriculture commissioner Jim Hightower, a fiery populist and Jackson's most steadfast supporter among white elected officials, also took some sharp jabs at Bush. He referred to the vice president as "a toothache of a man," and satirized him as a country-club snob lacking concern for the common man. "George Bush is a man who was born on third base and thinks that he's hit a triple," Hightower said.

With the session a half-hour behind schedule and pushing close to the end of Eastern prime time television, several speeches praising the platform were shelved. Each of Jackson's five children stepped to the podium, with his eldest son, Jesse Jackson, Jr., making an introduction that showed he had inherited some of his father's oratorical flair.

A campaign-style video on Jackson followed. Then at 10:55 p.m. Jackson entered to a roaring ovation and a sea of red-and-white "Jesse!" placards. As an expression of unity, virtually all of the Dukakis delegates had kept their banners out of sight, and many had given up their passes so Jackson alternates could be on the floor to cheer.

In his speech, Jackson first invoked the heroes of the civil rights movement, including Martin Luther King, Jr., and briefly shared the stage with Rosa Parks, heroine of the 1955 Montgomery, Alabama, bus boycott. He said that his campaign was a historic culmination of earlier black struggles. "As a tribute to the endurance, the patience, the courage of our forefathers and mothers . . . tomorrow night my name will go into nomination for the presidency of the United States of America," Jackson declared.

During his fifty-five-minute address, Jackson called for both liberal and conservative Democrats to find "common ground" of agreement on issues of social welfare, human rights, and world peace.

He called for U.S. allies to pay a greater share of their defense burden so that American resources could be shifted to housing, health care, and other social needs. He called on government to act to protect the family farm and to promote domestic oil production. He made frequent reference to his trademark issue, calling on youths to avoid the temptations of illegal drugs.

Jackson received the most emotional response with a paean to the struggles of the low-income working American. He declaimed the situation of hospital employees who do the dirty work—emptying bedpans, cleaning commodes—"yet when they get sick, they cannot lie in the beds they made up every day."

The speech was climaxed by Jackson's call for Americans to "never surrender" to poverty, drugs, malnutrition, inequality, disease, or physical handicaps. He used his life story as an example, stating that he had risen to his current status despite being born poor and out of wedlock. To those who are told, "You can't make it . . . you're nothing," he declared, "When you see Jesse Jackson, when my name goes in nomination, your name goes in nomination."

He finished on a typically upbeat note: "You must not surrender. . . . We must not surrender. . . . America will get better and better. Keep hope alive."

July 20: Day Three

The night session that ratified Dukakis as the presidential nominee July 20 was a rowdy social reception. Dukakis partygoers, who had weathered more than two days of convention "Jesse-mania" and were busting for their chance to stomp and shout, had little appetite for any agenda item prior to the roll call of the states.

The man who bore the brunt of this restiveness was Arkansas governor Bill Clinton, who placed Dukakis's name in nomination. With his thirty-five-minute nominating speech—more than twice as long as expected—Clinton far exceeded the patience of many Dukakis delegates. When he uttered the words, "And, in closing . . . ," there was a lusty cheer from the crowd.

Clinton's address ended a long night of speechmaking, and the balloting finally began. At 11:27 p.m. the California delegation, which had passed initially, put Dukakis over the top. At the conclusion of the balloting—which Dukakis won with 2,876.25 delegate votes to Jackson's 1,218.5— Jackson conceded by telephone, and the convention ratified the choice of Dukakis by acclamation.

Many Talk, Few Listen

Convention chairman Wright called the session to order at 6 p.m. The first couple of hours featured a series of campaign-style speeches by party disnitaries and 1988 cnadidates. A queue of 1988 Senate candidates who were in high-profile contests stepped to the podium for short statements tht were acknowledged mainly by their cheering home-state delegations. The speakers included incumbents Frank R. Lautenberg of New Jersey and Howard M. Metzenbaum of Ohio, and challengers Richard H. Bryan of Nevada, Richard Licht of Rhode Island, Leo T. McCarthy of California, and Joseph Lieberman of Connecticut.

Later, all the Democratic governors in attendance assembled for a bow; 1984 convention keynoter Cuomo received the loudest cheers by far. The early proceedings also included speakers praising Democratic virtues and criticizing Reagan administration policies on various issues: Sens. Patrick J. Leahy of Vermont and Kent Conrad of North Dakota on agriculture, Mayor Raymond Flynn of Boston and Rep. Charles B. Rangel of New York on illegal drugs, and Rep. Bill Richardson of New Mexico on education. Sen. Christopher J. Dodd of Connecticut, who had nominated Sen. Gary Hart of Colorado at the 1984 convention, spoke on the need for "new ideas" and "new leadership" at the end of the Reagan era.

All the speakers struggled to be heard over the noisy, distracted crowd. Only Coretta Scott King, the widow of Martin Luther, Jr., received a degree of respectful attention. King praised Dukakis for the "consistently high plane" of his campaign activities and said she joined Jackson in calling on the delegates "to keep hope alive."

Though Jackson's reputation for self-promotion had led to a somewhat distant relationship with King over the years, she had high praise for him, stating, "Jesse, Martin would be proud of you, and we're proud of the way you have broadened political participation in America."

End of the Rainbow

As the scheduled 9 p.m. start of the nominating process neared, the Omni again fulfilled the prophecies of those who said it would be too small for the convention. With the seats and aisles filled to capacity, a number of delegates found themselves locked out. Among them were keynote speaker Ann Richards and several members of Congress.

Jackson's name was placed in nomination by a trio intended to symbolize the candidate's concept of the "Rainbow Coalition." International Association of Machinists president William Winpisinger, who is white, made the nominating speech; he was seconded by state senator Olga Mendez of New York, a Puerto Rican, and by black state representative Maxine Waters of California.

Each nominating speech was greeted by cheering and chanting from the enthusiastic Jackson delegates. For Jackson, who had dominated the convention to that point, it was the last hurrah of his 1988 campaign. The rest of the convention would belong to Dukakis.

The Din Wins

Clinton, 41, who was regarded as having long-range designs on the White House, was the personal choice of Dukakis, his friend and fellow governor, to be the nominator. In a speech that will be remembered for its duration rather than its content, he emphasized Dukakis's personal qualities, calling him a man "who plays it straight, and keeps his word, and pays his bills." He escribed Dukakis as "steadfast and consistent" and "tough as nails" when he had to be.

Clinton also praised Dukakis as a political leader, describing him as "a man with vision, a shining vision for this country." He said Dukakis, as governor, had "made the hard decisions, to balance budgets, to create jobs, to fight crime and drug abuse, to increase day care and health care, to do all those things that a leader has to do."

Though Clinton's speech was a strong endorsement on paper, it did not play very well in the hall or on TV. His slightly raspy voice did not carry forcefully over the din on the floor. The delegates let Clinton know several times that they were ready for the roll call, breaking into spontaneous chants of "We Want Mike!" and "Duke! Duke! Duke!" ABC News cut away from the speech for a packaged profile on Dukakis.

The Deed Is Done

The roll call, marked by the usual "Great State of . . ." boosterism, went as predetermined by the primary-and-caucus process. The one surprise came from Minnesota, where three antiabortion delegates registered support for Rep. Richard H. Stallings, D-Idaho, who shared their opposition to abortion.

The only apparent suspense was which state would put Dukakis over the 2,082-vote total he needed to clinch the nomination. But the Dukakis campaign—cognizant of California's importance in November—had even taken care of that detail. They arranged for several delegations to pass on the first call to ensure that California would have the honor. When convention secretary Dorothy Bush made her second call of California, Lt. Gov. McCarthy—a candidate for the Senate—announced that his state's 235 Dukakis delegates had provided "the nominating margin."

The ensuing twelve-minute demonstration, which included traditional patriotic music (but eliminated the customary balloon drop), involved all but a few disaffected Jackson die-hards.

Following the roll call, Speaker Willie Brown, Jr., of the California House, Jackson's national campaign chairman, announced that Jackson had phoned to ask that Dukakis be endorsed by acclamation. A near-unanimous chorus of "ayes" followed.

The celebration was capped by singer Dionne Warwick, who performed her signature song, "That's What Friends Are For," and "America the Beautiful." The delegates then filed out into the warm Atlanta night for what might have been the session's most galvanizing event: a fireworks display that lit up the sky over the Omni and the World Congress Center.

July 21: Closing Day

Led by an assertive, confident Dukakis, and spurred by a carefully orchestrated show of patriotism and party unity, the Democratic delegates unleashed their emotions in an explosive closing-night celebration.

The feeling of promise and solidarity that permeated the final night's proceedings contrasted sharply with the self-doubt and internal divisions that had plagued the Democratic party throughout the Reagan era.

Dukakis did all he could to exploit the opportunity provided by a national convention to project a positive image to the nation. Often described as a dispassionate technocrat, Dukakis appeared accessible and even somewhat uplifted by the adulation of the party faithful.

With Neil Diamond's rock tribute to the nation's immigrant heritage, "Coming to America," thundering over the sound system, Dukakis entered the arena by way of the convention floor and enthusiastically worked the crowd of delegates surging toward him.

Early in his speech, he revived his oft-repeated depiction of the campaign as a "marathon" and asserted, "We're going to win this race."

In general, he delivered a variation on his standard campaign speech, but this time in measured cadences, avoiding his habit of speaking quickly in short bursts. The address was peppered with applause lines, to which the sympathetic audience responded with roars.

It was very difficult to gauge whether the closing-night extravaganza would capture the imagination of TV viewers across the country and dramatically reshape the Democratic party's image; the television networks had complained all week that the general public's lack of interest in the convention had resulted in low ratings.

But one thing was certain: Dukakis's ability to maintain the convention's intensity throughout his address put to rest the satiric profile of him as "Zorba the Accountant." Some other speakers earlier in the evening, notably vice presidential nominee Bentsen and Sen. Bill Bradley of New Jersey, left the audience flat. Dukakis brought them to their feet.

Warm-up Acts

Party officials created a Hollywood-style show for the convention finale. The schedule was crafted with prime-time television foremost in mind, and, in an unusual achievement for the traditionally unruly Democrats, the program went off like clockwork.

The convention was called to order at 5 p.m., so that the podium parade of party officials—this time, House members and local elected officials—could conclude without interfering with the evening's festivities. The carnival atmosphere was enhanced by a brief appearance of a four-hundred-piece combined marching band from several Atlanta-area high schools.

Just after 8 p.m., Wright warmed up the crowd by leading a cheering competition between delegates from different regions of the country. But the audience still had to make it through one last pedagogic speech before shedding its reserve.

Bradley, who played pro basketball before making a national name for himself in the Senate, got a laugh from the audience when he said, "This is the first time I've performed in the Omni in long pants." But his speech on the relationship between presidents and the American people was mainly lost on the milling delegates.

They were quickly reengaged, though, by Illinois representative Dan Rostenkowski's rousing nominating speech for Bentsen. Speaking with the gravelly accents of his Chicago environs, Rostenkowski described Bentsen as "straightforward, smart . . . and tough." He got his strongest response with a passage urging working-class Americans to "come home to your party . . . the party that has contributed so much to our social progress."

Rostenkowski was followed by South Dakota senator Thomas A. Daschle, who praised Bentsen's commitment to rural America. The delegates then gave a long ovation to former Texas representative Barbara C. Jordan, a major figure in the 1974 Judiciary Committee impeachment hearings on President Nixon and the 1976 Democratic convention keynoter.

Jordan, now confined to a wheelchair, praised her longtime ally Bentsen in remarks seemingly aimed at Jackson delegates. Saying that it was a mistake to label him a conservative, Jordan said, "Lloyd Bentsen ... believes in the principles of the Democratic party just like you do."

The compelling need for a defense of Bentsen already had been removed, though. Talk of a challenge to his nomination, so rife early in the week, had been silenced by the Dukakis-Jackson agreement and the ensuing push for unity. Jackson selected Rep. Mickey Leland of Texas to call for Bentsen's nomination by acclamation. The motion was passed overwhelmingly, with just a scattering of "no" votes voiced by delegates carrying signs reading "No Contra Aid."

Fire and Restraint

After an invocation by Greek Orthodox archbishop Iakovos of Boston, Ohio senator John Glenn introduced Bentsen. Glenn, who had been regarded as the front-runner for the vice presidential nomination but was bypassed for his Senate colleague, evidenced no hard feelings, joking, "I just knew I would be making a speech tonight about the vice presidency."

Glenn, whose reputation as a bland speaker had hindered his aspirations for national office, scored one on the skeptics by unleashing an unusually fiery blast at the Reagan administration.

Praising the separation of church and state, and attacking the religious conservative leaders who had allied with Reagan, Glenn said, "The last thing we need is the Gospels of Matthew, Mark, Luke, and John rewritten by Meese, Bakker, Swaggart, and Falwell." Referring to ethical problems in the White House, he said, "They want four more years, but at the rate some of them are going, I think they're going to wind up serving ten to twenty."

Bentsen's address was much more restrained, true to his image as a dignified, formal, and somewhat patrician figure. Shortly into his acceptance speech, Bentsen extended an olive branch to the Jackson supporters who had been deeply offended by Dukakis's vice presidential decision. He told the convention that "equality of opportunity is the ultimate civil right." He then hailed Jackson for "leadership and achievements [that] transcend pride of party and inspire a nation."

The Senate sponsor of the 1988 trade bill, Bentsen received his strongest applause by calling for a plant-closing-notification law. He accused the "Reagan-Bush administration," which opposed the concept, of insisting that "a pink slip in the mail is notice enough."

Bentsen indicted the Reagan presidency as "an eight-year coma in which slogans were confused with solutions and rhetoric passed for reality."

Invoking a familiar Democratic theme, he said that many Americans—Iowa farmers, oil field roughnecks, Ohio factory workers—had missed out on the prosperity of the Reagan years. He accused Reagan of financing prosperity by writing "hot checks for $200 billion a year." Dukakis, Bentsen said, was "talking about putting the American

dream," including home ownership and a college education, "back in the reach of all the American people."

He summed up his speech with the story of his father Lloyd, Sr., now 94, who rose from rugged, pioneer beginnings in the Rio Grande Valley to become a millionaire real estate investor. He said that his father's success in Texas and his own success in Atlanta were symbolic of "the American dream ... of freedom and opportunity."

Though his speech was no rouser, Bentsen, who defeated Bush in a 1970 Senate contest, left the podium to a chant of "Beat Bush Again."

Hollywood Flair

A series of theatrical touches primed the delegates for Dukakis. A specially commissioned musical piece, written by Boston Pops Orchestra director John Williams and conducted by Dukakis's father-in-law, Harry Ellis Dickson, was performed. Dukakis was then introduced by his cousin, Olympia Dukakis, an Oscar-winning actress and New Jersey delegate. In a home movie-style video that meshed with her live speech, she joked about the nominee's legendary stinginess. Pointing to a twenty-five-year-old snowblower that Dukakis used to clear his own sidewalk, she said, "Mike gives the word 'frugal' new dimension."

After making his way to the podium and accepting the delegates' accolades, Dukakis thanked his cousin and recalled her opening command at the Oscar ceremony: "OK, Michael, let's go!"

"She wasn't kidding," Dukakis said, as the delighted delegates picked up the cue and started a night-long chant of "Let's go, Mike!"

Dukakis described himself as a product of the American dream. He paid tribute to his immigrant parents, and tears welled in his eyes when he talked about how proud his late father would have been of his son, and of his adopted country. He cited individuals who represented America's cultural diversity, including Jackson. Seated in the VIP box with former president Carter, Jackson waved and gave Dukakis his trademark "thumbs up" sign.

Dukakis continued to feed the convention's celebratory mood, stating that "the Reagan era is over, and a new era is about to begin." He said it is time "to exchange voodoo economics for can-do economics," adding, "This election isn't about ideology. It's about competence."

Watching His Step

Throughout the speech, Dukakis managed to hit buttons that energized the partisan audience, while avoiding contentious issues, such as tax increases and abortion, that had hurt the Democrats in recent presidential elections. The issues he emphasized were more popular Democratic stands on education, universal health care, and plant-closing notification.

Dukakis stirred the crowd by saying that all Americans were "enriched and ennobled" by the achievements of individuals. He then brought the house down by reciting a tribute to the late Hispanic leader Willie Velasquez in both English and fluent Spanish. Dukakis's speech was interrupted several times by chants form the crowd. When he referred to Bush's failure to intercede to stop the Iran arms sales, the convention delegates reprised their "Where was George? " theme. And in a wave of optimism not seen since the post-Watergate 1976 convention, the delegates chanted, "We're gonna win."

After his speech, Dukakis was joined on the podium by his wife Kitty, the Bentsens, Jackson and his family, Carter and his wife Rosalynn, and eventually by many other party officials. The evening ended with the traditional balloon drop (a concession by some convention officials who had deemed it too old-fashioned) and rafter-ringing renditions of "The Battle Hymn of the Republic" and "America the Beautiful" by singer Jennifer Holliday.

Republicans

Day One belonged to Ronald Reagan, the Republican party's political conqueror, now nearing departure from leadership of his party and nation. He stood before the Republican National Convention, in New Orleans's Louisiana Superdome, in a moment of poignancy and sentiment to bid farewell to his political legions.

Day Two witnessed the passing of the torch—Reagan leaving the city as Vice President George Bush arrived to assume leadership of the GOP. Almost immediately, Bush exercised the prerogative of power, announcing his choice for vice president—Sen. Dan Quayle of Indiana.

Day Three was a time of process and chaos, the nomination rite occurring amid a flurry of questions and concerns about the nominee's young running mate.

Day Four was the dramatic dénouement—the candidate accepting the nomination in words of force and optimism, his junior partner seeking to dispel lingering concerns with his own acceptance address. And for the party's new leader, a political crisis diminished his night of political triumph.

That, in brief, was the Republican National Convention, held in New Orleans August 15-18, 1988. And, as the following diary of the week's events makes clear, it was not exactly the event the GOP or its new leader might have hoped for.

But Bush did not flinch as he sought to present to the nation a unified and upbeat party even as he moved to contain political fallout from revelations about Quayle. As a young man twenty years earlier, it appeared, Quayle had been helped by family connections to get into the Indiana National Guard. He thus avoided the military draft.

Before the event began, top Republicans had announced that one primary aim was to serve up a specific vision of the American future to answer the vagueness of the Democrats and their nominee, Massachusetts governor Michael S. Dukakis, anointed in a similar ritual in Atlanta in July. They also vowed to portray their Democratic rival in what they described as his true liberal colors.

In reality, the assembled Republicans concentrated more on the latter. Speaker after speaker ascended the gigantic podium to decry what they characterized as the Democrats' leftward thinking and to contrast the peace and prosperity of the Reagan years with the economic and foreign policy woes that came before. Little was said about where the Republicans intended to go from here, though Bush did ring a few bells for the future—no new taxes, a big education program, an attack on drugs, help for the disabled, greater government protection of the environment, incentives for the domestic energy industry, and continuation of Reagan's defense and foreign policies.

But all the words of political engagement were diminished by the controversy surrounding the Quayle selection. Already in something of a defensive posture because of questions concerning his image and force of leadership, Bush found himself having to defend his unorthodox choice of a forty-one-year-old senator who clearly lacked the stature of other possible selections.

And Quayle's early performance in meeting the media—the announcement ceremony on August 16, a news conference and national-network interviews the next day—left Bush strategists anxious lest the ticket take on an appearance of weakness even before it managed to propel itself beyond New Orleans. Top Bush hands met late into the night August 17 to thrash out the potential crisis.

Ultimately, the decision was made to tough it out. Bush the morning of August 18 pointedly embraced his running mate in laudatory terms, and the pair completed preparations for the climactic evening of speeches.

August 15: Opening Day

The scene at the Superdome late on the night of August 15 was familiar—Ronald and Nancy Reagan standing atop the Republican convention podium, waving to throngs of adoring delegates as red, white and blue balloons floated from the rafters.

But the situation was very different from the 1980 and 1984 conventions, when the GOP's favorite son accepted his party's accolades en route to two landslide victories and the first eight-year presidency since Dwight D. Eisenhower. This time, the delegates were hailing Reagan's valedictory, a swan song from a politician who had carried GOP conservatives to unprecedented levels of power.

The delegates greeted Reagan as a conquering hero, and they cheered enthusiastically at many of his applause lines. But the mood was tempered by the poignancy of the moment—a realization that Reagan was making his last convention speech as leader of his party and his country, and that the future for Republicans was uncertain.

For his part, Reagan was firm if slightly subdued in a speech that centered on the achievements of his administration and the role of Vice President Bush in those achievements.

The president offered again his optimistic vision of America as a place with no twilight, where it was "sunrise every day," with "fresh new opportunities and dreams to build." He hit a sentimental note early in the speech, thanking the convention for its tribute to Nancy Reagan, who had delivered her own farewell and thank you.

The president took some predictable jabs at his Democratic critics. He accused them of "inflated rhetoric" at their convention in Atlanta, adding, "But, then, inflation is their specialty."

His speech, however, was not so charged as the one he gave to an August 14 GOP pep rally, which contained variations on a theme that the current Democratic leadership was "liberal, liberal, liberal." His convention speech mainly maligned the opposition with statistics contrasting economic hardships under the Carter administration with economic improvements under his leadership.

After portraying seven and a half years of tax cuts, job creation, and reduced inflation and interest rates, he said, "I've noticed they don't call it 'Reaganomics' anymore." And he pointed to his defense and foreign policies as primary factors in international successes, such as the 1987 U.S.-Soviet treaty to eliminate intermediate-range nuclear-force (INF) missiles, the ongoing Soviet withdrawal from Afghanistan and the removal, via a U.S. invasion in October 1983, of Grenada's Communist leadership.

But the most pertinent symbol of Reagan's role in the 1988 campaign was his strong praise of Bush as a key player in his administration. Stating that a regulatory task force headed by Bush had resulted in a reduction in bureaucratic paperwork, Reagan responded to the Democrats' "Where was George?" chant by intoning, "George was there." He also credited Bush with persuading NATO allies to accept American medium-range missiles, a move he said forced the Soviet Union to negotiate the INF treaty.

Reagan's promise of campaign assistance and his call for Bush to "win one for the Gipper" was a lift for Bush supporters, who were disturbed by the Reagans' pallid endorsement of their candidate the previous May. But the adulation afforded the president by the delegates was a reminder of why the party, fearing that the less charismatic Bush could be overshadowed, scheduled Reagan to speak on August 15.

The scheduling allowed the GOP's dominant conservative wing a night to celebrate its successes. Sen. William L. Armstrong of Colorado led the delegates in a tribute to former senator Barry Goldwater of Arizona, whose 1964 landslide defeat by Democratic president Lyndon B. Johnson was regarded by party activists as an act of political martyrdom that set the stage for the triumphs of the 1980s.

Rep. Jack F. Kemp of New York, an unsuccessful primary challenger to Bush and a favorite of party conservatives for the vice presidential nomination, raised his theme that Republicans could appeal to the poor and minorities with a message of self-help and opportunity. He pledged that if the party pursued this tack, a quarter of all blacks, Hispanics, and Asians would be Republicans by 1992.

Sen. John McCain of Arizona had his national profile raised with a prime-time speech centering on his experiences as a Vietnam prisoner of war. Referring to a pet Republican issue—a Dukakis veto, on constitutional grounds, of a bill requiring Massachusetts public-school students to recite the Pledge of Allegiance—McCain told the story of a fellow POW who endured severe beatings from his captors for fashioning a makeshift American flag.

Former transportation secretary Elizabeth H. Dole—who, like her husband, Sen. Robert Dole of Kansas, was still being discussed as a potential vice presidential candidate—used her speech to address the so-called "gender gap." Saying that two-thirds of the jobs created since 1982 went to women, Dole asked women "not just to support us . . . work with us to ensure that this growth continues."

Reagan's speech at the end of the evening session ended a long day that began with a get-acquainted morning meeting gaveled to order at 10 a.m. by Republican National Committee chairman Frank J. Fahrenkopf, Jr.

The advantages of the Superdome as the convention venue were quickly evident. Even though half of it was curtained off, the stadium had room to spare; no delegates would get locked out, as occurred during the Democratic convention in Atlanta's overcrowded Omni Coliseum. The aisles were wide enough for any demonstration the party wanted to stage (including a brassy, Mardi Gras-style parade that warmed up the delegates for the evening session).

However, with delegates spread from end zone to end zone on the floor of the football stadium, the convention lacked the kind of intimacy that contributed to the sense of electricity during key junctures of the Democratic conclave. Many speakers found their words swallowed up by the echoing acoustics of the vast arena.

Russian émigré Yakov Smirnoff, a comedian whose humor about the hardships of Soviet life had made him a favorite of GOP audiences, led the delegates in the Pledge of Allegiance. He was one of several entertainers, including jazz musician and Bush delegate Lionel Hampton, scheduled to perform ceremonial duties during the convention.

Introduced by Maureen Reagan, the president's daughter, a series of Louisianians welcomed the convention to New Orleans. Rep. Jim McCrery, who won a special 1988 election for the District 4 seat vacated by Democratic governor Buddy Roemer, became the first speaker to use a phrase certain to be heard over and over: "liberal Democrats."

The one mildly dissonant note was sounded by Mayor Sidney Barthelemy of the economically troubled host city. A black Democrat, Barthelemy gently prodded his guests to build a "new federal-local partnership" to aid American cities.

The morning session featured two one-time Bush foes—former Delaware governor Pierre S. "Pete" du Pont IV and former secretary of state Alexander M. Haig, Jr.—who had been dispatched early in the GOP nominating process.

Du Pont addressed his remarks as a letter to former presidential candidate Jesse L. Jackson, whose call for poor and working-class Americans to "keep hope alive" electrified the Democratic convention. He said that while Democrats joined union workers on picket lines, slept with the homeless, and said they spoke for senior citizens, the Republicans favored economic policies that would improve these people's conditions. He said Republicans, not Democrats, would guarantee "not only equality of opportunity, but a continued abundance of opportunity."

The morning session ended with a series of showcase speeches by Republican congressional candidates, including Senate incumbent David K. Karnes of Nebraska and challengers Pete Dawkins of New Jersey and Conrad Burns of Montana. The speeches were aimed more at television viewers than the convention audience, and no effort was made to keep the delegates from drifting off to lunch. By the time New Mexico Senate candidate William Valentine made the last statement, only his small home-state delegation and a handful of stragglers were in the hall.

August 16: Day Two

The Republicans had plenty of theater scheduled for August 16, with an agenda that included New Jersey governor Thomas H. Kean's keynote address and speeches by evangelist and former GOP presidential candidate Pat Robertson, former United Nations representative Jeane J. Kirkpatrick, and former president Gerald R. Ford. But Bush himself stole the show with his midafternoon announcement that he had selected dark-horse prospect Sen. Dan Quayle of Indiana as his running mate.

Bush aides had said the candidate would not announce his choice until August 18, to maintain some suspense and keep the television-viewing public focused on the convention. But after being greeted by the departing Reagan at the Belle Chasse Naval Air Station the morning of August 16, Bush told reporters that he had settled on his choice. News soon leaked out of his phone calls to the bypassed prospects—the Doles, Kemp, and senators Alan K. Simpson of Wyoming and Pete V. Domenici of New Mexico.

Riverfront Announcement

Bush made the choice public at a welcoming ceremony on the New Orleans riverfront. He praised Quayle, who was a generation younger than Bush, as "a man of the future." Quayle was clearly overjoyed at his new prominence, grasping Bush by the shoulder, punching the air for emphasis, and shouting, "Let's go get 'em!"

There had been little in the preceding morning session to distract news reporters from their rounds on the vice presidential rumor circuit. Reports of the Credentials, Rules, and Platform committees were approved without debate.

Rep. Newt Gingrich of Georgia, whose complaint led to a House ethics committee probe of Speaker Jim Wright of Texas, said House Democrats embodied an arrogance born of their long years in the majority. Though little change in the partisan makeup of the House was expected in 1988, Gingrich, House Minority Leader Robert H. Michel of Illinois (the convention's permanent chairman), and others called on voters to throw out Democratic incumbents and give the Republicans a House majority. Similar pleas had gone unheeded since the early 1950s.

The morning session concluded with another rollout of congressional candidates, including Sen. Chic Hecht of Nevada and open-seat candidate Rep. Connie Mack of Florida; many delegates again drifted off.

But Virginia Senate candidate Maurice Dawkins, a black lobbyist and former preacher, engaged the dwindling audience with a fiery broadside. Dawkins echoed Goldwater's 1964 admonition that "extremism in defense of liberty is no vice" and got the remaining delegates on their feet, chanting, "We're standing up against drugs." He concluded by leading the convention in a vocal rendition of "God Bless America."

Though the delegates spent much of the evening session discussing what they knew about Quayle—who previously had a low profile outside Indiana—a parade of speakers tried to engage their attention. A series of governors, including Platform Committee chairman Kay A. Orr, governor of Nebraska, praised the GOP platform and compared its specifics with the generalities in the Democratic platform.

The governors signaled the evening's theme, a portrayal of Dukakis and the Democrats as extreme liberals. California Gov. George Deukmejian, noting that Dukakis belonged to the American Civil Liberties Union (ACLU), said ACLU actually meant "Allowing Criminals to Leave Unsupervised" (a reference to a favorite GOP target, the longtime Massachusetts policy of prison furloughs).

Kirkpatrick did not attract the same level of adoration as she did at the 1984 convention in Dallas, where she signaled an intent to switch her party affiliation to Republican. Nor did she coin a memorable slogan, as she did in describing the Mondale-Ferraro ticket that year as the "San Francisco Democrats."

Still, Kirkpatrick's attack on Dukakis's foreign policy stances was warmly received by the Republican delegates. She said the contest between Dukakis and Bush was a choice between a "policy of unilateral concessions and wishful thinking or a policy of clarity and strength." Citing Dukakis's lack of foreign policy experience, Kirkpatrick said that while errors in domestic policy could "cost us jobs and profits . . . serious mistakes in foreign policy [could] cost us jobs, profits—and our freedom."

Kean, whose landslide 1985 reelection as New Jersey governor was attributed to his outreach to minority and blue-collar voters, was expected to emphasize his "politics of inclusion" in the keynote address that followed. But much of his speech was a traditional Republican assault on Democratic liberalism.

Referring to the light shades of red, white, and blue used by the Democrats in Atlanta (lighting conditions at the Omni would have made bright colors look garish on television), Kean said that Americans "have no use for pastel patriotism." Discussing the Democrats' efforts to submerge the differences within their coalition, he cited a quote from a Dukakis supporter who said party constituencies—or special-interest groups, in GOP vernacular—had been told to "just shut up so we can win." Kean then asked, "Should this country tolerate a campaign of deliberate deception?"

Like Massachusetts senator Edward M. Kennedy, who led the "Where was George?" chant in Atlanta, Kean had his own mantra. He gave his version of the Democrats' economic plans, finishing each statement with the question, "What does it add up to?" and leading the delegates with the response: "More taxes!"

In alluding to his trademark subject of outreach, Kean said Republicans would make racism "wither and die," and he added the GOP offered the poor "not the junk food of more big government, but the full meal of good private-sector jobs." He said that "every time we take an unemployed person and give them a job, we take a Democrat and turn him into a Republican." And he compared what he called the Democrats' "politics of delusion and exclusion" with the Republicans' "politics of inclusion."

When he was named keynoter, Kean's reputation as a leading GOP moderate and his pro-choice position on abortion spurred a reaction from a group of conservatives led by New Hampshire senator Gordon J. Humphrey. While there were no signs of opposition to Kean on the convention floor, a group of antiabortion activists seated in the upper reaches of the Superdome held signs and chanted slogans that were lost in the convention din.

Robertson Bloc

But "prolife" activists and religious conservatives, a large bloc within the Republican convention, had their moment with the appearance of Robertson. As a presidential primary candidate, the religious broadcaster and former preacher had fallen well short. But his campaign activists did well in several state caucuses, where they won delegate positions and party influence.

Robertson assailed what he described as the Democratic vision of a polity where "criminals are turned loose . . . disease carriers are protected . . . welfare dependency flourishes . . . [and] the rights of the majority must always take a back seat to the clamorous demands of the special interests." He said Democrats wanted America to be "one big family," with "Jim Wright as the daddy, [Maryland senator] Barbara Mikulski as the momma, and Teddy Kennedy as Big Brother."

Robertson went on to assail the Democrats for eschewing references to God in their platform and said that under the Republicans, "children of this country will once again be allowed to pray to God in the classrooms of America." Picking up on a convention theme, Robertson said Dukakis "will pack the federal courts with ACLU radicals."

Insurgencies by Robertson supporters had led to intraparty divisions in several states. But as delegates waved

"Robertson for Bush" signs, Robertson officially released his delegates and pledged his support for the Republican ticket.

The session ended with Ford's speech, which began after prime TV time in the East. As had the other speakers, Ford hit hard at the Democrats for presenting themselves as the party of the American dream. He referred to differences between Dukakis and his more conservative vice presidential candidate, Sen. Lloyd Bentsen of Texas, and called on Bentsen to "speak up now."

Ford also reviewed Bush's extensive résumé, including his service as emissary to the People's Republic of China and CIA director under Ford. "So where was George?" Ford asked. "For forty-five years, George Bush has been at the center of the action in the service of this great republic." After Ford's rejoinder that "I'll be damned if I will stand and let anyone with a smirk and a sneer discredit the honor, service, accountability, and competence of George Bush," the Republican delegates gave their response to the Democrats' merriment in Atlanta: a chant of "George was there."

August 17: Day Three

As Bush, surrounded by his wife, Barbara, and numerous other family members, watched on television late on the night of August 17, the Republican convention celebrated the culmination of Bush's long pursuit of the party's presidential nomination. At 11:08 p.m. Central Daylight Time, George W. Bush announced the Texas delegation votes that put his father over the top.

But the result had been preordained: Bush, assured of the nomination since his March 8 Super Tuesday sweep and his win in Illinois the next week, was nominated with no dissent. And with the lack of suspense over the proceedings, the national media turned their attention to fleshing out the record of the previously little-known Quayle.

Controversy over Quayle

There was no press "honeymoon" for the prospective vice presidential nominee. A series of tough questions about his background made the day difficult for Quayle—and, by extension, for Bush. Quayle, buoyant and boyishly grinning on August 16, appeared discomfited during his first day under the hot lights of national media scrutiny.

At an afternoon news conference, their first formal appearance as the GOP team, Bush defended his choice of Quayle, who was much younger and had less government experience than many of the bypassed vice presidential prospects. "The accolades from the senators with whom he serves speak eloquently of Dan Quayle's standing to be one heartbeat away from the presidency," Bush said.

However, Quayle's answers to some of the questions he faced were not so deft. His first problem was with a question about a 1980 Florida incident in which Quayle, then a House member, and two colleagues were seen in the company of lobbyist Paula Parkinson, who later posed nude in *Playboy* magazine and said she had had sexual relationships with members of Congress. Quayle's defense at the time, that he had no involvement with Parkinson, never was refuted. But when asked if a version of the events that appeared to back up his story was true, he said, "No." When pressed, he said, "That has been covered, and there's nothing to it."

Quayle, a member of Indiana's Pulliam publishing family and one of the heirs to a family trust, also sought to deflect rumors about his wealth. He denied that his net worth was as high as $200 million.

But by the end of the news conference, it was clear that Quayle would have to deal with a new and potentially explosive issue: whether he had used family influence to gain enlistment in the Indiana National Guard in 1969 to avoid service in the Vietnam War.

Quayle first referred to the question as "a cheap shot." But his answers did not defend his choice of the Guard over the comat services, and he said his thoughts at the time centered on plans for law school, marriage, and family. He raised eyebrows with the off-the-cuff rejoinder, "I did not know in 1969 that I would be in this room today [as a vice presidential candidate], I confess."

His rounds of the TV network convention broadcasts in the evening raised as many questions as they answered. He described himself as willing to defend the country twenty years earlier, stating that if his Guard unit had been called up, as theoretically could have happened, "I would have gone to Vietnam." But he also left himself open to questions about whether his wealthy family had pulled strings to get him into the Guard at a time when he faced prospects of being drafted. He said that he had "let a lot of people know I wanted to get into the National Guard."

The questions about Quayle cast no pall over the exuberant proceedings in the Superdome. He was greeted enthusiastically as he entered to join his wife, Marilyn, and Barbara Bush in the VIP box.

With the media discussing the lack of nonwhite delegates at the convention—about 3 percent were black—the party continued to showcase conservative minority-group figures. One such speaker, Maryland Senate candidate and former State Department official Alan L. Keyes, had publicly objected to a Bush campaign suggestion that he open his speech with the declaration, "I am a black man who happens to be a Republican." His address emphasized his concept of a nation undivided by ethnic or racial differences. "There is a place in every American heart, a place that is neither black nor white, not Asian or Irish or Pole, a place that is just America," Keyes said.

Orange County (California) supervisor Gaddi H. Vasquez, a Hispanic, gave an emphatic explanation of why he was a Republican. "The Democratic candidate may speak Spanish, but he doesn't speak our language," Vasquez said. "His actions and philosophy do not reflect the beliefs or the traditions with which we have been raised."

Sen. Pete Wilson of California, who faced a reelection contest in 1988, repeated the GOP refrain that as governor Dukakis had been soft on crime. Referring to a Massachusetts prison-furlough policy that was rescinded earlier this year, Wilson said Dukakis's challenge to state prisoners was not " 'Make my day,' but 'Have a nice weekend.' " He raised the specter of Willie Horton, a Massachusetts convict who escaped while on furlough, raped a Maryland woman, and stabbed her fiancé.

For Kansas senator Robert Dole, the 1976 Republican vice presidential nominee, his moment before the convention was bittersweet. The delegates hailed his speech, in which he praised Reagan and Bush and criticized Dukakis as a "Massachusetts liberal." But Dole also was making peace with his party and its leader following his second unsuccessful bid for the Republican nomination, a campaign that was marked by several bitter exchanges with

Bush. The Senate minority leader signaled that he wanted to put all that behind him. "I am ready and eager," he said, "to serve as George Bush's 'point man' in a Republican-controlled Senate come January."

A Strong Texas Touch

As it entered its celebratory phase, the convention took on a strong Texas motif. Bush moved to Texas in the late 1940s, and later served in the House from a Houston district. But his Yankee roots and his tendency to spend his free time at a family compound in Maine had forced Bush to defend his claim that he was a Texan. It was no coincidence that when Barbara Bush entered the arena, the orchestra played "Yellow Rose of Texas." Texas senator Phil Gramm, who nominated Bush, was introduced by former Dallas Cowboys quarterback Roger Staubach.

Gramm lambasted "the amnesia Democrats in Atlanta" who "forget that when the Democrats left the White House, inflation and interest rates were at the highest levels in American history." The coauthor of the Gramm-Rudman-Hollings antideficit law assailed Dukakis for raising taxes in his first term as governor, saying, "People called it Taxachusetts."

Gramm later praised Bush's life experiences, including his military heroism as a navy pilot in World War II. He said Bush knew "that peace comes through strength, not wishful thinking." And he described Bush as "the greatest vice president this nation has ever had."

Gramm's speech was followed by an energetic and noisy affirmation of delegate support for Bush. As the convention orchestra blared state anthems and college fight songs, the delegates waved state flags and Bush-Quayle placards, and popped some of the fifty thousand multicolored balloons that showered down from the ceiling.

The nomination was seconded by celebrities such as actress Helen Hayes, Pennsylvania State University football coach Joe Paterno, and Bush's Mexican-American daughter-in-law, Columba Bush. The ensuing roll call turned into a frenzy of state self-promotion that took an hour and a half to complete. *(See convention ballots, 1988 Republican, p. 78.)*

The roll call boosted Bush's image as a family man. The far-flung nature of Bush's large family was evident: Four sons and his one daughter announced the delegate votes from their home states of Colorado, Florida, Maine, Texas, and Virginia.

There was one atypical moment in the roll call. When Massachusetts Senate candidate Joseph Malone announced that he was running against Kennedy, the delegates broke into a spontaneous chant of, "Where was Ted?" Given the buttons and T-shirts being sold around the convention hall referring to Kennedy's 1969 car accident at Chappaquiddick, in which a woman passenger died, the chant seemed also to be a veiled reference to that incident.

August 18: Closing Day

With Bush trailing Dukakis in public-opinion polls, media commentators and Bush supporters alike said he had to make the "speech of his life" on the night of August 18. Bush did not waste the opportunity. Seemingly unfazed by the brush-fire controversy over Quayle's military record—a question that dominated the day's news media coverage—Bush presented an assertive and sometimes commanding persona in an acceptance speech that stirred the Republican delegates.

"I mean to run hard, to fight hard, to stand on the issues—and I mean to win," Bush said early in his speech. And near its conclusion Bush said his experience as vice president had made him the candidate who was prepared to deal with the critical issues that came across the president's desk. "I am that man," Bush said emphatically, as the partisan crowd roared its approval.

If clutch performances under campaign pressure were any indicators of ability to handle the rigors of office, then both Bush and Dukakis proved worthy. Like Dukakis, Bush had long been burdened by his image as an unengaging speaker, one who could not even draw an "Amen" when preaching to the political choir. But their moments at center stage were transcendent events for both candidates.

Dukakis, previously regarded as low-key and boring, spoke with directness, emphasis and emotion in Atlanta and kept the victory-hungry Democrats in a state of high-decibel frenzy. And Bush, often derided for tortured syntax and awkward hand gestures, was clear, concise, and in sync with himself and his conservative audience.

Saving the Day

With his performance, Bush saved for himself a day that had contained the ingredients for a full-scale political disaster. Quayle's muddled answers the previous day to questions about how and why he came to serve in the National Guard during the Vietnam War fueled what was becoming a full-blown controversy. A headline in the New Orleans *Times-Picayune*—"Draft-Dodger Questions Dog Quayle"—was typical of the newspaper coverage of the story. The evening network newscasts led with long inquiries into whether Quayle, a scion of the Pulliam publishing empire, had used family connections to move to the top of the Guard enrollment list in 1969.

The reports quoted retired Indiana National Guard major general Wendell C. Phillippi, the managing editor in 1969 of the Pulliam-owned *Indianapolis News*, who said he contacted Guard officials on Quayle's behalf (as he had for other young men), and recommended him highly. The coverage included discussions about whether the National Guard provided a safe haven at the time for young men looking to shelter themselves from the military draft.

Damage control became the major priority for Bush's new campaign chairman, James A. Baker III. Quayle was to address the Texas and Ohio delegations August 18, but he canceled the campaign appearances, saying he had to rehearse his acceptance speech. That fueled rumors that he was to be dropped from the ticket. Late in the day, Baker, too, canceled several TV interviews. But he emerged early in the evening and trekked between network anchor booths to defend Quayle and roundly reject the rumors that the campaign considered dumping him.

During convention walk-throughs earlier in the day, Bush and Quayle had ignored a barrage of questions about the situation, allowing the convention proceedings to provide their response to the speculation. The answer came quickly. Shortly after a brief address by Barbara Bush—in which she highlighted the presidential nominee's devotion to his large family—Quayle was placed in nomination and anointed with praise by a series of congressional colleagues, including several who had been considered for the vice presidential spot.

Vice Presidents Rarely Win Top Spot

Fully one-third of the forty individuals who have served as president of the United States were first vice presidents, but only five of them got to the Oval Office by being elected to it. The others made it because of the death or resignation of their predecessors.

Of the five vice presidents elevated by election, two—John Adams and Thomas Jefferson—were elected when there was no direct mass participation in the presidential nomination or election process. Martin Van Buren was elected directly to the presidency in 1836, as was George Bush in 1988. Richard M. Nixon lost his bid to move up from the vice presidency in 1960 but was elected eight years later.

Few other vice presidents have come close to attaining the Oval Office. Hubert H. Humphrey was the only other sitting vice president to win a major-party presidential nomination; he lost to Nixon in 1968. Walter F. Mondale won the Democratic presidential nomination in 1984, nearly four years after his term as vice president ended.

Two other vice presidents who never won the White House ran as third party presidential candidates: John C. Breckinridge, Democrat James Buchanan's president (1857-1861), was the nominee of the southern Democrats in 1860, and Henry A. Wallace, Franklin D. Roosevelt's second vice president (1941-1945), was the candidate of the Progressive party in 1948.

The following chart lists the vice presidents who became president as well as those who won a major-party presidential nomination. The names of the presidents under whom they served are noted.

Assumed presidency on death or resignation	Year assumed presidency
John Tyler, Whig (W. H. Harrison)	1841
Millard Fillmore, Whig (Taylor)	1850
Andrew Johnson, R * (Lincoln)	1865
Chester A. Arthur, R (Garfield)	1881
Theodore Roosevelt, R (McKinley)	1901
Calvin Coolidge, R (Harding)	1923
Harry S Truman, D (F. D. Roosevelt)	1945
Lyndon B. Johnson, D (Kennedy)	1963
Gerald R. Ford, R (Nixon)	1974

Elected president directly from vice presidency	Year elected president
John Adams, Federalist (Washington)	1796
Thomas Jefferson, D-R (Adams)	1800
Martin Van Buren, D (Jackson)	1836
George Bush, R (Reagan)	1988

Elected president later	
Richard M. Nixon, R (Eisenhower)	1968

Nominated for president but lost	Year sought presidency
Richard M. Nixon, R (Eisenhower)	1960
Hubert H. Humphrey, D (Johnson)	1968
Walter F. Mondale, D (Carter)	1984

* Although nominated to run with Republican Abraham Lincoln, Andrew Johnson was identified as a Democrat.

Senator Dole, playing the partisan political role he had relished over the years, dared the Democrats to "try to use experience as a measuring stick in this campaign." He compared his version of Dukakis's experience in "raising taxes again and again . . . vetoing the Pledge of Allegiance . . . increasing spending year after year after year," with Quayle's experience "tackling the vital national and international issues that affect the lives of all Americans and the future of our country."

The Indiana senator was nominated by acclamation. A new party rule had eliminated the necessity of a roll call and made it difficult for dissident delegates to call for one if there had been opposition to Bush's choice.

Prior to Quayle's acceptance speech, former Vietnam prisoner of war Everett Alvarez, Jr., led the recitation of the Pledge of Allegiance. A moment of silence for America's war dead followed, as the arena lights dimmed and a bugler played taps.

The Candidates' Vision

Quayle was introduced by Rep. Lynn Martin of Illinois, who described the vigorous campaigner as an "energizer." She said Quayle "doesn't just win elections because he looks good; he wins elections because he makes America look good." Responding to Democratic criticism, Martin countered that Quayle already had more experience in Congress "than John Fitzgerald Kennedy had when he ran for president of the United States."

If Quayle was burdened with concerns over the military service issue, he checked these emotions backstage. The youthful-looking senator tackled his first appearance on the national stage with the cheerleader-like élan for which he was known.

Early on, Quayle confronted the National Guard issue briefly and with a somewhat defiant tone. After expressing pride in his congressional service, he said, "As a young man, I served six years in the National Guard, and like the millions of Americans who have served in the Guard . . . I am proud of it."

Quayle, a native of Huntington, Indiana, described the small-town, Midwestern verities that he said had guided his life: "We believe very strongly in hard work, in getting an education, and in offering an opportunity to families. We love basketball, we love underdogs. But most important, we love our country."

Stating that "the future under George Bush means peace and economic opportunity," Quayle lumped Dukakis in with other Democratic figures who were frequent targets of GOP criticism. "We do not need the future the Democratic party sees, the party of George McGovern, Jimmy Carter, Walter Mondale . . . Ted Kennedy, and his buddy, Michael Dukakis," Quayle said, as the delegates lustily booed each name.

Elucidating his own record, Quayle took credit for authoring the 1982 Job Training Partnership Act and discussed his membership on the Senate Armed Services Committee. He then proclaimed the "profound debt" that his generation—of which he was the first major-party national candidate—owed to Bush's generation "for bringing us to an era of peace and freedom and opportunity."

In his acceptance speech that followed, Bush quickly affirmed his vice presidential choice. "Born in the middle of the century, in the middle of America, and holding the promise of the future, I'm proud to have Dan Quayle at my side," Bush said.

Bush entered the campaign with nearly eight years as vice president, the support of a singularly popular president, and a track record of recent GOP presidential success behind him. But with polls consistently showing him trailing Dukakis, he rallied the delegates by portraying the election as a come-from-behind effort. "There are a lot of great stories in politics about the underdog winning—and this is going to be one of them," he said.

Bush acknowledged the necessity of establishing his own identity. "Ronald Reagan asked for, and received, my candor; he never asked for, but he did receive, my loyalty," Bush said. "But now you must see me for what I am: the Republican candidate for president.... And now I turn to the American people to share my hopes and intentions, and why and where I wish to lead."

Describing his military service and his government jobs as "missions," Bush said that "The most important work of my life is to complete the mission we started in 1980." He described a goal of creating 30 million new jobs in eight years, which he said would be attained if economic growth continued at its current pace.

The vice president contrasted what he said was Dukakis's vision of "a long slow decline for our country" to his own view of America as "a rising nation." Giving credit to the Reagan administration for providing opportunity, economic empowerment for women, controlled inflation, and peace, Bush promised on each, "I'm not going to let them take it away from you."

Bush hit on the conservative hot-button issues—the Pledge of Allegiance, the death penalty, voluntary school prayer, gun ownership, opposition to abortion, prison furloughs—that had been raised by speaker after speaker during the convention.

But Bush prominently listed several social policy areas that had not ranked high in the conservative Republican rhetoric in the 1980s. He called for mainstreaming the disabled, ending ocean garbage-dumping, reducing acid rain, extending racial harmony, and restoring pride and ethics to public service. He seemed to temper the antigovernment sentiment so prominent in Reagan's politics. "I do not hate government," Bush said. "A government that remembers that the people are its masters is a good and needed thing."

Bush, once regarded as an untrustworthy moderate by the party's right wing, also risked the omission of some conservative shibboleths. While pledging "to be a patient friend to anyone ... who will fight for freedom," he made no mention of aid to the Nicaraguan contras. He did not discuss the appointment of conservative judges to the federal judiciary.

But he did delight the delegates with satirical references to critics of Republican policy. Referring to the Democratic campaign's term for regional economic disparities—"the Swiss cheese economy"—Bush said, "That's the way it may look to the three blind mice.... But when they were in charge, it was all holes and no cheese." Restating his promise not to raise taxes, which he said Dukakis would not rule out, Bush said he would tell persistent tax proponents to "Read my lips. 'No new taxes.'"

Bush sought to exhibit his strong family ties and a self-deprecating sense of humor. To be fair to the Democrats, he said, he would "try to hold my charisma in check." Acknowledging his tendency to speak in convoluted phrases, he jokingly dared critics to "Make my twenty-four-hour time period."

Like Reagan, who ended his 1980 acceptance speech with a moment of silent prayer, Bush finished with a flourish. He led the convention in the Pledge of Allegiance, ending a week in which a record may have been set for mentions of the pledge. Enjoying what had been a clear success for him, Bush was joined on the podium by his wife, his many children and grandchildren, Quayle, and other Republican dignitaries. As had been planned as part of Bush's effort to create a separate identity, Reagan waved only from a still photograph flashed on the telescreens.

But the glow would be short-lived, as it always was in politics. The morning after brought with it the reality that in the next eighty-one days Bush had to convince the majority of voters, not just those who attended or watched the convention, that he had truly emerged from Reagan's shadow. And on August 19 the first postconvention campaign stop was in Quayle's hometown of Huntington, a place that held the answers to the questions that came close to ruining Bush's moment of triumph.

The 1988 Convention Texts

In sharp contrast to 1984, when both parties put forth lengthy campaign platforms, the document the Democrats adopted in July 1988 was much shorter than the one the Republicans approved a month later. Instead of trying to placate every interest group, Democratic strategists tried to confine the planks to statements of general party principles. But several speakers at the GOP convention criticized the brief statement, saying it proved that the Democratic party lacked a detailed program to put before the American people. *(See the 1988 National Conventions, pp. 22-34.)*

Following are the texts of both party platforms, and of the acceptance speeches of the nominees for president and vice president.

Dukakis Acceptance

Massachusetts governor Michael S. Dukakis accepted the 1988 Democratic nomination for president at the party's national convention July 21 in Atlanta. Following is the text of his acceptance speech:

A few months ago, when Olympia Dukakis, in front of about a billion and a half television viewers all over the world, raised that Oscar over her head and said, "OK, Michael, let's go," she wasn't kidding.

And Kitty and I are grateful to her for that wonderful introduction and grateful to all of you for making this possible.

This is a wonderful evening for us and we thank you from the bottom of our hearts.

My fellow Democrats, my fellow Americans, sixteen months ago, when I announced my candidacy for the presidency of the United States, I said this campaign would be a marathon.

Tonight, with the wind at our backs, with friends at our sides, and with courage in our hearts, the race to the finish line begins.

And we're going to win this race, we're going to win this race.

We're going to win because we are the party that believes in the American dream.

A dream so powerful that no distance of ground, no expanse of ocean, no barrier of language, no distinction of race or creed or color can weaken its hold on the human heart.

And I know, because, my friends, I'm a product of that dream, and I'm proud of it.

A dream that brought my father to this country seventy-six years ago; that brought Mother and her family here one year later—poor, unable to speak English; but with a burning desire to succeed in their new land of opportunity.

And tonight, in the presence of that marvelous woman who is my mother and who came here seventy-five years ago; with the memory in my heart of the young man who arrived at Ellis Island with only $25 in his pocket, but with a deep and abiding faith in the promise of America—and how I wish he was here tonight. He

would be very proud of his son.

And he'd be very proud of his adopted country, I can assure you.

Tonight, as a son of immigrants with a wonderful wife and now, with Lisa, our lovely daughter-in-law, four terrific children; as a proud public servant who has cherished every minute of the last sixteen months on the campaign trail, I accept your nomination for the presidency of the United States.

My friends, the dream that carried me to this platform is alive tonight in every part of our country—and it's what the Democratic Party is all about.

[San Antonio mayor] Henry Cisneros of Texas, [Rep.] Bob Matsui of California, [Sen.] Barbara Mikulski of Maryland, [Gov.] Mario Cuomo of New York, [Rep.] Claude Pepper of Florida, and Jesse Louis Jackson.

A man who has lifted so many hearts with the dignity and the hope of his message throughout this campaign; a man whose very candidacy has said to every child—aim high; to every citizen—you count; to every voter—you can make a difference; to every American—you are a full shareholder in our dream.

The Reagan Era Is Over

And, my friends, if anyone tells you that the American dream belongs to the privileged few and not to all of us; you tell them that the Reagan era is over. You tell them that the Reagan era is over and that a new era is about to begin.

Because it's time to raise our sights—to look beyond the cramped ideals and the limited ambitions of the past eight years—to recapture the spirit of energy and of confidence and of idealism that John Kennedy and Lyndon Johnson inspired a generation ago.

It's time to meet the challenge of the next American frontier—the challenge of building an economic future for our country that will create good jobs at good wages for every citizen in this land, no matter who they are or where they come from or what the color of their skin.

It's time to rekindle the American spirit of invention and of daring; to exchange voodoo economics for can-do economics; to build the best America by bringing out the best in every American.

It's time to wake up to the new challenges that face the American family.

Time to see that young families in this country are never again forced to choose between the jobs they need and the children they love; time to be sure that parents are never again told that no matter how long they work or how hard their child tries, a college education is a right they can't afford.

It's time to ask why it is that we have run up more debt in this country in the last eight years than we did in the previous two hundred; and to make sure it never happens again.

It's time to understand that the greatest threat to our national security in this hemisphere is not the [Nicaraguan] Sandinistas—

it's the avalanche of drugs that is pouring into this country and poisoning our kids.

Competence and Opportunity

I don't think I have to tell any of you how much we Americans expect of ourselves.

Or how much we have a right to expect from those we elect to public office.

Because this election is not about ideology. It's about competence.

It's not about overthrowing governments in Central America; it's about creating jobs in middle America. That's what this election is all about.

It's not about insider trading on Wall Street; it's about creating opportunity on Main Street.

And it's not about meaningless labels. It's about American values. Old-fashioned values like accountability and responsibility and respect for the truth.

And just as we Democrats believe that there are no limits to what each citizen can do; so we believe that there are no limits to what America can do.

And, yes, I know, this fall, we're going to be hearing a lot of Republican talk about how well some neighborhoods and some regions of this country are doing; about how easy it is for some families to buy a home or to find child care or to pay their doctor's bills or to send their children to college.

But, my friends, maintaining the status quo—running in place standing still—isn't good enough for America. Opportunity for some isn't good enough for America.

My friends, we're going to forge a new era of greatness for America.

We're going to take America's genius out of cold storage and challenge our youngsters; we're going to make our schools and universities and laboratories the finest in the world; and we're going to make teaching a valued and honored profession once again in this country.

We're going to light fires of innovation and enterprise from coast to coast and we're going to give those on welfare the chance to lift themselves out of poverty; to get the child care and the training they need; the chance to step out into the bright sunshine of opportunity and of hope and of dignity.

We're going to invest in our urban neighborhoods; and we're going to work to revitalize small town and rural America. We're going to give our farm families a price they can live on, and farm communities a future they can count on.

We're going to build the kind of America that Lloyd Bentsen has been fighting for for the past forty years; the kind of America where hard work is rewarded; where American goods and American workmanship are the best in the world, the kind of America that provides American workers and their families with at least sixty days' notice when a factory or a plant shuts down.

Now, I know, I have a reputation for being a somewhat frugal man. But let me state for the record that that snow blower is still in good working order, even as it sits in our garage.

In nine years, I've balanced nine more budgets than this administration has and I've just balanced a tenth. And I've worked with the citizens of my state—worked hard to create hundreds of thousands of new jobs—and I mean good jobs, jobs you can raise a family on, jobs you can build a future on, jobs you can count on.

And I'm very proud of our progress, but I'm even prouder of the way we've made that progress—by working together, by excluding no one and including everyone: business and labor, educators and community leaders and just plain citizens—sharing responsibility, exchanging ideas, building confidence about the future.

A Sense of Community

And, my friends, what we have done reflects a simple but very profound idea—an idea as powerful as any in human history.

It is the idea of community. It is the idea of community. The kind of community that binds us here tonight.

It is the idea that we are in this together; that regardless of who we are or where we come from or how much money we have—each of us counts. And that by working together to create opportunity and a good life for all—all of us are enriched—not just in economic terms, but as citizens and as human beings.

The idea of community—an idea that was planted in the New World by the first governor of Massachusetts.

"We must," said John Winthrop, "love one another with a pure heart fervently. We must delight in each other, make each other's condition our own, rejoice together, mourn together, and suffer together.... We must," he said, "be knit together as one."

Now, John Winthrop wasn't talking about material success. He was talking about a country where each of us asks not only what's in it for some of us, but what's good and what's right for all of us.

When a young mother named Dawn Lawson leaves seven years of welfare to become a personnel specialist in a *Fortune* 500 company in Worcester, Mass.—we are all enriched and ennobled.

When a Catholic priest named Bill Kraus helps homeless families in Denver not just by giving them shelter, but by helping them to find the jobs they need to get back on their feet, we are all enriched and ennobled.

When a high school principal named George McKenna and a dedicated staff of teachers and counselors create an environment for learning at the George Washington Preparatory High School in Los Angeles, a high school in Los Angeles that is 90 percent black and 10 percent Hispanic and has 80 percent of its graduates accepted to college, we are all enriched and ennobled.

When a dedicated new management team and fine union in Milwaukee work together to turn Harley-Davidson around and help it come back to life and save twelve hundred good jobs, we are all enriched and ennobled.

And when a man named Willie Velasquez—Y cuando un Willie Velasquez—can register thousands of his fellow citizens as voters—puede inscribir decena de miles de sus conciudadanos para votar—when Willie Velasquez can bring new energy and new ideas and new people—brindando así nuevas energías, nuevas ideas, nuevas personas—into court houses and city halls and state capitals of the southwest—a los gobiernos municipales y estatales del suroeste—my friends, we are all enriched and ennobled—mis amigos, todos nos enriquecemos y enoblecemos.

My friends, as president, I'm going to be setting goals for our country; not goals for our government working alone; I mean goals for our people working together.

I want businesses in this country to be wise enough and innovative enough to retrain their workers, and retool their factories, and to help rebuild their communities. I want students and office workers and retired teachers to share with a neighbor the precious gift of literacy.

I want those of you who are bricklayers and carpenters and developers and housing advocates to work with us to help create decent and affordable housing for every family in America, so that we can once and for all end the shame of homelessness in the United States of America.

I want our young scientists to dedicate their great gifts not to the destruction of life, but to its preservation; I want them to wage war on hunger and pollution and infant mortality; and I want them to work with us to win the war against AIDS, the greatest public health emergency of our lifetime, and a disease that must be conquered.

I want a new attorney general. I want a new attorney general to work with me and with law enforcement officers all over America to reclaim our streets and neighborhoods from those who commit violent crime.

And I want the members of the Congress to work with me—and I'm going to work with them—so that, at long last, we can make good on Harry Truman's commitment to basic health insurance for every family in America.

The Defense of Freedom

My friends, the dream that began in Philadelphia two hundred years ago; the spirit that survived that terrible winter at

Valley Forge and triumphed on the beaches at Normandy; the courage that looked Khrushchev in the eye during the Cuban missile crisis—is as strong and as vibrant today as it has ever been.

We must be—we are—and we will be—militarily strong.

But we must back that military strength with economic strength; we must give the men and women of our armed forces weapons that work; we must have a secretary of defense who will manage—and not be managed by—the Pentagon; and we must have a foreign policy that reflects the decency and the principles and the values of the American people.

President Reagan has set the stage for deep cuts in nuclear arms—and I salute him for that.

He has said that we should judge the Soviet Union not by what it says, but by what it does—and I agree with that.

But we can do a lot more to stop the spread of nuclear and chemical arms in this world. We can do a lot more to bring peace to Central America and the Middle East. And we can and we will do a lot more to end apartheid in South Africa.

John Kennedy once said that America "leads the ... world, not just because we are the richest or the strongest or the most powerful, but because we exert that leadership for the cause of freedom around the globe ... and ... because," in his words, "we are moving on the road to peace."

Yes, we must always be prepared to defend our freedom.

But we must always remember that our greatest strength comes not from what we possess, but from what we believe; not from what we have, but from who we are.

You know, I've been asked many times over the past 16 months if I have one very special goal for these next four years—something that reflects everything I stand for and believe in as an American.

And the answer to that question is yes, I do.

A Government with High Standards

My friends, four years from now, when our citizens walk along Pennsylvania Avenue in Washington, D.C., or when they see a picture of the White House on television, I want them to be proud of their government. I want them to be proud of a government that sets high standards not just for the American people, but high standards for itself.

We're going to have a Justice Department that isn't the laughingstock of the nation. We're going to have a Justice Department that understands what the word "justice" means.

We're going to have nominees to the federal bench who are men and women of integrity and intelligence and who understand the Constitution of the United States. We're going to have an Environmental Protection Agency that is more interested in stopping pollution than in protecting the polluters.

We're going to have a real war, not a phony war, against drugs; and my friends, we won't be doing business with drug-running Panamanian dictators any more.

We're going to have a vice president who won't sit silently by when somebody at the National Security Council comes up with the cockamamie idea that we should trade arms to the ayatollah [Ruhollah Khomeini of Iran] for hostages.

We're going to have a vice president named Lloyd Bentsen who will walk into the Oval Office and say, "Mr. President, this is outrageous and it's got to stop." That's the kind of vice president we're going to have.

And in the Dukakis White House, as in the Dukakis Statehouse, if you accept the privilege of public service, you had better understand the responsibilities of public service. If you violate that trust, you'll be fired. If you violate the law, you'll be prosecuted. And if you sell arms to the ayatollah, don't expect a pardon from the president of the United States.

An Era of Greatness

Monday night, like millions of Americans, I laughed and was moved by the wit and wisdom of Ann Richards. And Tuesday night, along with millions of other Americans, I was inspired, as you were, by the powerful words of Jesse Jackson.

But what stirred me most on Monday was a grandmother talking about her "nearly perfect" granddaughter; and what stirred me most on Tuesday were those handsome and proud and articulate Jackson children—those Jackson children talking about their hopes for the future of their country.

You know, young Jackie Jackson goes to school in my state. And last month, she visited with me in the Statehouse in Boston. She's a remarkable young woman, and I know her parents are very, very proud of her.

My thoughts tonight—and my dreams of America—are about Ann Richards' granddaughter Lily; about young Jackie Jackson; and about the baby that's going to be born to our son John and his wife Lisa in January. As a matter of fact the baby is due on or about January 20.

God willing, our first grandchild will reach the age that Jackie Jackson is now at the beginning of a new century. And we pray that he or she will reach that age with eyes as filled with the sparkle of life and of pride and of optimism as that young woman we watched together two nights ago.

Yes, my friends, it's a time for wonderful new beginnings.

A little baby.

A new administration.

A new era of greatness for America.

And when we leave here tonight, we will leave to build that future together.

To build that future so that when our children and our grandchildren look back in their time on what we did in our time; they will say that we had the wisdom to carry on the dreams of those who came before us; the courage to make our own dreams come true and the foresight to blaze a trail for generations yet to come.

And as I accept your nomination tonight, I can't help recalling that the first marathon was run in ancient Greece, and that on important occasions like this one, the people of Athens would complete their ceremonies by taking a pledge.

That pledge, that covenant, is as eloquent and as timely today as it was two thousand years ago.

"We will never bring disgrace to this, our country—We will never bring disgrace to this, our country, by any act of dishonesty or of cowardice. We will fight for the ideals of this, our country. We will revere and obey the law. We will strive to quicken our sense of civic duty. Thus, in all these ways, we will transmit this country greater, stronger, prouder and more beautiful than it was transmitted to us."

That is my pledge to you, my fellow Democrats.

And that is my pledge to you, my fellow Americans.

Thank you all very, very much.

Bentsen Acceptance

Following is the text of Texas senator Lloyd Bentsen's address, as delivered at the Democratic National Convention July 21, when he accepted the party's 1988 vice presidential nomination.

Thank you very much.

[Sen.] John Glenn [Ohio] is one of the most talented, respected figures in America. And I thank him for a very gracious introduction.

And [Rep.] Danny Rostenkowski [Illinois], [Sen.] Tom Daschle [South Dakota], [former House member] Barbara Jordan [Texas], [Rep.] Mickey Leland [Texas], what great friends you are.

Thank you very much.

And I thank you, my fellow Democrats, for this high honor.

I am proud and pleased to accept your nomination for vice president of the United States of America.

In four months America will elect a new president. And his name will be Michael Dukakis.

His theme will be economic opportunity for all. His values will be honesty, integrity, and fairness. And his party will be a united Democratic Party.

Twenty-eight years ago, our party nominated a president from

Massachusetts and a vice president from Texas. The Texan on that ticket was Lyndon Baines Johnson. Lyndon Johnson knew then what you and I know so well today. The equality of opportunity is the ultimate civil right.

His vision and his victories paved the way for Democratic leaders like Rev. Jesse Jackson whose eloquence, whose leadership and achievements transcend pride of party and inspire a nation.

Tackle the Tough Problems

Tonight the hopes of a nation—the incredible energy and diversity of America—are focused on Atlanta. This convention reflects that energy and diversity.

We are a mirror of America.

We Democrats don't march in lockstep behind some narrow, rigid ideology of indifference. We are not gray grains of oatmeal in a bland porridge of privilege.

Our way, the Democratic way, is to tackle the tough problems. Our way is to search out the honest answers and stand by our principles.

Of course, we have differences of opinion. But on the basic issues of justice and opportunity, we stand united.

Democrats agree that a good job at a fair wage is the passport to opportunity in America.

Democrats agree that America needs a trade policy based on the simple premise of fairness. We demand that nations selling goods freely into our country—that we have full access to their markets.

Democrats agree that the economic, trade, and energy policies of the Reagan-Bush administration have devastated vast areas of America. We see an agricultural economy that has been driven to its knees: We see the energy economy reeling in crisis. We see the loss of more than one million high-paying jobs in manufacturing.

Democrats agree that the American worker who has struggled for twenty years to support his or her family has earned 60 days' notice when that management closes down a plant.

But the Reagan-Bush administration thinks a pink slip in the mail is notice enough. That's their notion of fairness. That's their message to the working men and women of America.

Democrats want a strong national defense, and we will pay the price to defend freedom. But we also demand a careful accounting for our hard-earned dollars. And we will not tolerate the corruption and greed that threatens to undermine our military might.

Democrats agree that decent housing, a clean environment, a good education, and quality health care should be the birthright of every American citizen and not the private domain of a privileged few.

So make no mistake about it. We are united in our commitment to do better for America.

An Eight-Year Coma

My friends, America has just passed through the ultimate epoch of illusion: An eight year coma in which slogans were confused with solutions and rhetoric passed for reality; a time when America tried to borrow its way to prosperity and became the largest debtor nation in the history of mankind; when the Reagan-Bush administration gave lip service to progress while fighting a frantic, losing battle to turn back the clock on civil rights and equal opportunity; a time of tough talk on foreign policy and strange tales of double-dealing Swiss bank accounts, and a botched campaign against a drug-running tin-horn dictator [Panamanian strongman Manuel Antonio Noriega].

The Reagan-Bush administration likes to talk about prosperity. But the farmers in Iowa don't hear them. The oil field workers in Texas and Oklahoma and Louisiana don't hear them. The factory workers in John Glenn's Ohio don't hear them.

My fellow Democrats, it is easy enough to create an illusion of prosperity. All you have to do is write hot checks for $200 billion a year. That's what the Reagan-Bush administration has done. That's how they doubled our national debt in just seven years.

At long last the epoch of illusion is drawing to a close. America is ready for the honest, proven, hands-on, real-world leadership of Michael Dukakis backed by the power of a united, committed Democratic Party.

Land of Opportunity

For two hundred years America has worked better than any society in history. A major reason for our success is that every generation of Americans has accepted responsibility to expand the frontiers of individual opportunity. We have expanded that opportunity through universal education, the Homestead Act, land-grant colleges, women's suffrage, Social Security, the GI bill, civil rights, and health care.

Taken together and placed in the context of the free enterprise system, these progressive actions made America the land of opportunity. They created a magnet that drew millions of people from around the world—people like Michael Dukakis' father from Greece, like my grandfather from Denmark, like your relatives who came here willing to accept enormous risks and dangers in return for the chance for a step up in life.

Recently, it has become more difficult for working Americans to take that step up. Oh, I see the charts and numbers that suggest prosperity. But I also talk with those people and I hear what they say.

I know that if you are a teacher, or a factory worker, or if you are just starting a family, it's almost impossible to buy a house—no matter how hard you work or how carefully you save.

A college education is slipping beyond the reach of millions of hard working Americans. If you have a child that's born today, plan on having $60,000 in the bank when that child reaches the age of eighteen in the hopes of sending that child to a public university. And if the Republicans have their way, you won't have any college loan program to help work it out for you.

Effective Leadership

When Michael Dukakis talks about the economics of opportunity, he is talking about making our country work again. He's talking about putting the American dream back in the reach of all the American people. He is talking sense—and America is listening.

Michael Dukakis understands the reality of America. But even more important, he understands the potential of America. He turned around the economy of Massachusetts, not by writing hot checks, but by careful planning, careful management of the taxpayers' dollar, and a healthy respect for the entrepreneurial system.

When the nation's governors were asked: Who among you is the most effective leader, the answer was Michael Dukakis of Massachusetts. When millions of Democrats went to the polls this year to choose the leader who will blaze America's path during the twenty-first century, they chose Michael Dukakis of Massachusetts.

Michael Dukakis has the uncanny knack of bringing forth the very best in America. He knows that government can't solve all our problems. But he also understands that government has an obligation to lead.

Michael Dukakis and I will lead a government that cares about people, about jobs, about all regions of America, about housing and the homeless, about the defense of freedom, about education and health care, about justice and opportunity for all Americans.

We believe America deserves an administration that will obey the law, tell the truth, and insist all who serve it do the same.

We believe the best way to lead America is by force of character and personal integrity.

The Chance for a Step Up

This convention has been a triumph for Michael Dukakis and the Democratic Party. It has certainly been a proud moment for me and for my family. My wife, B. A., my sons, my daughter and their families are here tonight to share this honor with me. My father is also here. He is ninety-four years old, proud of his country, and proud of his son.

Dad, you have been telling the reporters stories about me lately, so let me tell one about you. My father is a symbol of what people of courage and vision and daring can achieve in America.

He has lived the American dream—the dream we want to come true for our children.

Talk about risk-takers. His family came to this country across the ocean, across the prairie, and homesteaded on the plains of South Dakota when the government would bet you 160 acres that you couldn't make it through the winter.

They built a sod house, and when that first blizzard blew in, they took turns staying awake for thirty-six hours, burning bundles of straw so they wouldn't freeze to death.

But like your ancestors, they made it through the storm. They made it through the winter. They planted and harvested and eventually they prospered.

They made their way in America.

My father made his way to Texas. And I've made my way to Atlanta with Michael Dukakis to stand before my family, before a united Democratic Party, before the American people, to accept your nomination as vice president of the United States of America.

Now, that's the American dream that we have nourished and protected for two hundred years—the dream of freedom and opportunity, the chance for a step up in life.

I want to help Michael Dukakis protect that dream for the next generation. And I want to help Michael Dukakis maintain freedom as the most powerful and persuasive force on earth. And I want to thank all of you for the opportunity to serve America.

Thank you very much.

Democratic Platform

Following is the text of the platform adopted at the Democratic National Convention in Atlanta, Georgia, July 18-21, 1988:

"The Restoration of Competence
and the Revival of Hope"

WE THE PEOPLE OF THE DEMOCRATIC PARTY OF THE UNITED STATES OF AMERICA,

In order to initiate the changes necessary to keep America strong and make America better, in order to restore competence, caring and incorruptibility to the Federal Executive Branch and get it working again fairly for all Americans, and in order to secure for our children a future of liberty and opportunity,

Hereby pledge our Party, our leaders, our elected officials and our every individual effort to fulfilling the following fundamental principles for all members of the American family.

WE BELIEVE that all Americans have a fundamental right to economic justice in a stronger, surer national economy, an economy that must grow steadily without inflation, that can generate a rising standard of living for all and fulfill the desire of all to work in dignity up to their full potential in good health with good jobs at good wages, an economy that is prosperous in every region, from coast to coast, including our rural towns and our older industrial communities, our mining towns, our energy producing areas and the urban areas that have been neglected for the past seven years. We believe that, as a first-rate world power moving into the 21st century, we can have a first-rate full employment economy, with an indexed minimum wage that can help lift and keep families out of poverty, with training and employment programs—including child care and health care—that can help people move from welfare to work, with portable pensions and an adequate Social Security System, safeguarded against emasculation and privatization, that can help assure a comfortable and fulfilling old age, with opportunities for voluntary national public service, above and beyond current services, that can enrich our communities, and with all workers assured the protection of an effective law that guarantees their rights to organize, join the union of their choice, and bargain collectively with their employer, free from anti-union tactics.

WE BELIEVE that the time has come for America to take charge once again of its economic future, to reverse seven years of "voodoo economics," "trickle down" policies, fiscal irresponsibility, and economic violence against poor and working people that have converted this proud country into the world's largest debtor nation, mortgaged our children's future by tripling our national debt, placed home ownership out of reach for most young families, permitted the rise of poverty and homelessness on the streets of America, reduced the buying power of working men and women, and witnessed the decline of our industrial, natural resource and mining base, the unending tragedy of family farm foreclosures, an unhealthy dependence on foreign energy and foreign capital, and the increasing foreign ownership of our land and natural resources.

WE BELIEVE that it is time for America to meet the challenge to change priorities after eight years of devastating Republican policies, to reverse direction and reassert progressive values, to reinvest in its people within a strong commitment to fiscal responsibility. If we are seriously to pursue our commitments to build a secure economic future for all Americans we must provide the resources to care for our newborns, educate our children, house the homeless, heal the sick, wage total war on drugs and protect the environment. Investing in America and reducing the deficit requires that the wealthy and corporations pay their fair share and that we restrain Pentagon spending. We further believe that we must invest in new priorities, in life-long education and training, in targeted economic development, in a healthy small business community and in retooled American industry; that it is time for the broad revitalization of home town America, involving financial institutions in the provision of crucial credit by encouraging special commitments in exchange for bailing out those that are failing, reforming and expanding community reinvestment laws, and reversing the trend of financial concentration and deregulation, all combining to reverse the insecurity that has increasingly troubled our workers and their families in this rapidly changing society that has left some communities and regions behind. There is no good reason why the nation we love, the greatest and richest nation on earth, should rank first among the industrialized nations in output per person but nearly last in infant mortality, first in the percentage of total expenditures devoted to defense but nearly last in the percentage devoted to education and housing.

WE BELIEVE that Government should set the standard in recognizing that worker productivity is enhanced by the principle of pay equity for working women and no substandard wage competition for public contracts; by family leave policies that no longer force employees to choose between their jobs and their children or ailing parents; by safe and healthy work places, now jeopardized by seven callous years of lowered and unenforced occupational safety standards for American workers; and by major increases in assistance making child care more available and affordable to low and middle income families, helping states build a strong child care infrastructure, setting minimum standards for health, safety, and quality, and thereby enabling parents to work and their children to get an early start on their education and personal fulfillment. We believe that the strength of our families is enhanced by programs to prevent abuse and malnutrition among children, crime, dropouts and pregnancy among teenagers and violence in the family; by aggressive child support enforcement; and by emphasizing family preservation and quality foster care. We further believe that our nation faces a crisis of under-investment in our children, particularly in the early years of life. Strong, healthy babies with early opportunities that foster intellectual, emotional and physical growth begin school with an enhanced foundation for learning. There are few better investments for this country than prenatal care, infant nutrition and preschool education, and there are few more successful programs than WIC, Head Start, and prenatal care. We know what works; yet these successful programs have been starved for funds. The Democratic Party pledges to meet this urgent need by providing the funding necessary to reach those unserved children who are—and must be—our national priority.

WE BELIEVE that America needs more trade, fair trade, an administration willing to use all the tools available to better manage our trade in order to export more American goods and fewer

American jobs, an administration willing to recognize in the formulation and enforcement of our trade laws that workers' rights are important human rights abroad as well as at home, and that advance notice of plant closings and major layoffs is not only fundamentally right but also economically sound. We believe that we can and must improve our competitiveness in the world economy, using our best minds to create the most advanced technology in the world through a greater commitment to civilian research and development and to science, engineering and mathematics training, through more public-private and business-labor cooperation and mutual respect, through more intergovernmental partnerships, and through a better balance between fiscal and monetary policy and between military and civilian research and development. We further believe in halting such irresponsible corporate conduct as unproductive takeovers, monopolistic mergers, insider trading, and golden parachutes for executives by reinvigorating our anti-trust and securities laws, reviewing large mergers, and discouraging short-term speculation taking place at the expense of long-term investment.

WE BELIEVE that the education of our citizens, from Head Start to institutions of higher learning, deserves our highest priority; and that history will judge the next administration less by its success in building new weapons of war than by its success in improving young minds. We now spend only two cents of every dollar for education. We pledge to better balance our national priorities by significantly increasing federal funding for education. We believe that this nation needs to invest in its children on the front side of life by expanding the availability of pre-school education for children at risk; to invest in its teachers through training and enrichment programs, including a National Teacher Corps to recruit teachers for tomorrow, especially minorities, with scholarships today; to commit itself for the first time to the principle that no one should be denied the opportunity to attend college for financial reasons; to ensure equal access to education by providing incentives and mechanisms for the equalization of financing among local school districts within each state; to reverse cuts made in compensatory reading, math and enrichment services to low income children; and to expand support for bilingual education, historically Black and Hispanic institutions, the education of those with special needs, the arts and humanities, and an aggressive campaign to end illiteracy.

WE BELIEVE that illegal drugs pose a direct threat to the security of our nation from coast to coast, invading our neighborhoods, classrooms, homes and communities large and small; that every arm and agency of government at every federal, state and local level—including every useful diplomatic, military, educational, medical and law enforcement effort necessary—should at long last be mobilized and coordinated with private efforts under the direction of a National Drug "Czar" to halt both the international supply and the domestic demand for illegal drugs now ravaging our country; and that the legalization of illicit drugs would represent a tragic surrender in a war we intend to win. We believe that this effort should include comprehensive programs to educate our children at the earliest ages on the dangers of alcohol and drug abuse, readily available treatment and counseling for those who seek to address their dependency, the strengthening of vital interdiction agencies such as the U.S. Coast Guard and Customs, a summit of Western Hemispheric nations to coordinate efforts to cut off drugs at the source, and foreign development assistance to reform drug-based economies by promoting crop substitution.

WE BELIEVE that the federal government should provide increased assistance to local criminal justice agencies, enforce a ban on "cop killer" bullets that have no purpose other than the killing and maiming of law enforcement officers, reinforce our commitment to help crime victims, and assume a leadership role in securing the safety of our neighborhoods and homes. We further believe that the repeated toleration in Washington of unethical and unlawful greed among too many of those who have been governing our nation, procuring our weapons and polluting our environment has made far more difficult the daily work of the local policemen, teachers and parents who must convey to our children respect for justice and authority.

WE BELIEVE that we honor our multicultural heritage by assuring equal access to government services, employment, housing, business enterprise and education to every citizen regardless of race, sex, national origin, religion, age, handicapping condition or sexual orientation; that these rights are without exception too precious to be jeopardized by Federal Judges and Justice Department officials chosen during the past seven years—by a political party increasingly monolithic both racially and culturally—more for their unenlightened ideological views than for their respect for the rule of law. We further believe that we must work for the adoption of the Equal Rights Amendment to the Constitution; that the fundamental right of reproductive choice should be guaranteed regardless of ability to pay; that our machinery for civil rights enforcement and legal services to the poor should be rebuilt and vigorously utilized; and that our immigration policy should be reformed to promote fairness, non-discrimination and family reunification and to reflect our constitutional freedoms of speech, association and travel. We further believe that the voting rights of all minorities should be protected, the recent surge in hate violence and negative stereotyping combatted, the discriminatory English-only pressure groups resisted, our treaty commitments with Native Americans enforced by culturally sensitive officials, and the lingering effects of past discrimination eliminated by affirmative action, including goals, timetables, and procurement set-asides.

WE BELIEVE that the housing crisis of the 1980s must be halted—a crisis that has left this country battered by a rising tide of homelessness unprecedented since the Great Depression, by a tightening squeeze on low and moderate income families that is projected to leave seven million people without affordable housing by 1993, and by a bleak outlook for young working families who cannot afford to buy their first home. We believe that steps should be taken to ensure a decent place to live for every American. We believe that homelessness—a national shame—should be ended in America; that the supply of affordable housing should be expanded in order to avoid the projected shortfall; that employer-assisted housing and development by community-based non-profit organizations should be encouraged; that the inventory of public and subsidized housing should be renovated, preserved and increased; that foreclosed government property should be restored to productive use; and that first-time home buyers should be assisted.

WE BELIEVE that we can rebuild America, creating jobs at good wages through a national reinvestment strategy to construct new housing, repair our sewers, rebuild our roads and replace our bridges. We believe that we must pursue needed investment through innovative partnerships and creative financing mechanisms such as a voluntary program to invest a portion of public and private pension funds as a steady source of investment capital by guaranteeing security and a fair rate of return and assuring sound project management.

WE BELIEVE that all Americans should enjoy access to affordable, comprehensive health services for both the physically and mentally ill, from prenatal care for pregnant women at risk to more adequate care for our Vietnam and other veterans, from well-baby care to childhood immunization to Medicare; that a national health program providing federal coordination and leadership is necessary to restrain health care costs while assuring quality care and advanced medical research; that quality, affordable, long-term home and health care should be available to all senior and disabled citizens, allowing them to live with dignity in the most appropriate setting; that an important first step toward comprehensive health services is to ensure that every family should have the security of basic health insurance; and that the HIV/AIDS epidemic is an unprecedented public health emergency requiring increased support for accelerated research on, and expedited FDA approval of, treatments and vaccines, comprehensive education and prevention, compassionate patient care, adoption of the public health community consensus on voluntary and confidential testing and counseling, and protection of the civil rights of those suffering from AIDS or AIDS-Related Complex or testing positive for the HIV antibody.

WE BELIEVE that the last seven years have witnessed an unprecedented assault on our national interest and national security through the poisoning of our air with acid rain, the dumping of toxic wastes into our water, and the destruction of our parks and shores; that pollution must be stopped at the source by shifting to new, environmentally sound manufacturing and farming technologies; that the federal government must promote recycling as the best, least costly way to solve the trash crisis, aggressively enforce toxic waste laws and require polluters to be responsible for future clean-up costs; that this nation must redouble its efforts to provide clean waterways, sound water management and safe drinkable ground water throughout the country; that our national parks, forests, wildlife refuges, and coastal zones must be protected and used only in an environmentally sound manner; that all offshore oil drilling in environmentally sensitive areas should be opposed; and that regular world environmental summits should be convened by the United States to address the depletion of the ozone layer, the "greenhouse effect," the destruction of tropical forests and other global threats and to create a global action plan for environmental restoration.

WE BELIEVE that all Americans, producers and consumers alike, benefit when food and fiber are produced not by a few large corporations and conglomerates but by hundreds of thousands of family farmers obtaining a fair price for their product; that the disastrous farm policies of the last seven years, despite record federal spending, have forced hundreds of thousands of families from their farms while others are struggling to survive; and that a workable agricultural policy should include supply management, reasonable price supports, soil conservation and protection of rural water quality, credit and foreclosure relief, the return of federally held foreclosed lands to minority, beginning and restarting farmers, the development of new uses and markets for American farm products, improved disaster relief, and the revitalization of rural America through new sources of capital for rural business and new federal support for rural health care, housing, education, water supply and infrastructure. We further believe that no person should go to bed hungry and that we must renew the fight against hunger at home and abroad, make food available to those nations who need it and want it, and convene an international conference of food producing nations.

WE BELIEVE that a balanced, coherent energy policy, based on dependable supplies at reasonable prices, is necessary to protect our national security, ensure a clean environment, and promote stable economic growth and prosperity, both nationally and in our energy producing regions; that the inevitable transition from our present, nearly total dependence on increasingly scarce and environmentally damaging non-renewable sources to renewable sources should begin now; that such a policy includes increased cooperation with our hemispheric neighbors, filling the Strategic Petroleum Reserve, promoting the use of natural gas, methanol and ethanol as alternative transportation fuels, encouraging the use of our vast natural gas and coal reserves while aggressively developing clean coal technology to combat acid rain, and providing targeted new incentives for new oil and gas drilling and development, for the development of renewable and alternative sources of energy, and for promotion of energy conservation. We believe that with these changes the country could reduce its reliance on nuclear power while insisting that all plants are safe, environmentally sound, and assured of safe waste disposal.

WE BELIEVE that this country's democratic processes must be revitalized: by securing universal, same day and mail-in voter registration as well as registration on the premises of appropriate government agencies; by preventing the misuse of at-large elections, the abuse of election day challenges and registration roll purges, any undercounting in the national census, and any dilution of the one-person, one-vote principle; by ending discrimination against public employees who are denied the right to full political participation; by supporting statehood for the District of Columbia; by treating the offshore territories under our flag equitably and sensitively under federal policies, assisting their economic and social development and respecting their right to decide their future in their relationship with the United States; by empowering the commonwealth of Puerto Rico with greater autonomy within its relationship with the United States to achieve the economic, social and political goals of its people, and by giving it just and fair participation in federal programs; by assuring and pledging the full

and equal access of women and minorities to elective office and party endorsement; and by minimizing the domination and distortion of our elections by moneyed interests.

WE BELIEVE in a stronger America ready to make the tough choices of leadership in an ever-dangerous world: *militarily* stronger in our overall defense and anti-terrorist capabilities and in the cohesion of our military alliances; *economically* stronger at home and in the global marketplace; *intellectually* stronger in the advances of our schools, science and technology; and *spiritually* stronger in the principles we exemplify to the world.

WE BELIEVE in a clear-headed, tough-minded, decisive American foreign policy that will reflect the changing nature of threats to our security and respond to them in a way that reflects our values and the support of our people, a foreign policy that will respect our Constitution, our Congress and our traditional democratic principles and will in turn be respected for its quiet strength, its bipartisan goals, and its steadfast attention to the concerns and contributions of our allies and international organizations. We believe that we must reassume a role of responsible active international leadership based upon our commitment to democracy, human rights and a more secure world; that this nation, as the world power with the broadest global interests and concerns, has a greater stake than any in building a world at peace and governed by law; that we can neither police the world nor retreat from it; and that to have reliable allies we must be a reliable ally.

WE BELIEVE that our national strength has been sapped by a defense establishment wasting money on duplicative and dubious new weapons instead of investing more in readiness and mobility; that our national strength will be enhanced by more stable defense budgets and by a commitment from our allies to assume a greater share of the costs and responsibilities required to maintain peace and liberty; and that as military spending and priorities change, government should encourage the conversion of affected military facilities and the retraining of workers to facilitate the creation of new forms of communication, space development and new peacetime growth and productivity.

WE BELIEVE in an America that will promote peace and prevent war—not by trading weapons for hostages, not by sending brave Americans to undefined missions in Lebanon and Honduras, not by relaxing our vigilance on the assumption that long-range Soviet interests have permanently changed, not by toasting a tyrant like Marcos as a disciple of democracy, but by maintaining a stable nuclear deterrent sufficient to counter any Soviet threat, by standing up to any American adversary whenever necessary and sitting down with him whenever possible, by making clear our readiness to use force when force is required to protect our essential security commitments, by testing the intentions of the new Soviet leaders about arms control, emigration, human rights and other issues, and by matching them not merely in rhetoric but in reciprocal initiatives and innovation, which takes advantage of what may be the greatest opportunity of our lifetime to establish a new, mutually beneficial relationship with the Soviet Union, in which we engage in joint efforts to combat environmental threats, explore peaceful uses of space and eradicate disease and poverty in the developing world, and in a mutual effort to transform the arms race that neither side can win into a contest for people's minds, a contest we know our side will win.

WE BELIEVE in following up the INF [intermediate-range nuclear-force] Treaty, a commendable first step, with mutual, verifiable and enforceable agreements that will make significant reductions in strategic weapons in a way that diminishes the risk of nuclear attack by either superpower; reduce conventional forces to lower and equivalent levels in Europe, requiring deeper cuts on the Warsaw Pact side; ban chemical and space weapons in their entirety; promptly initiate a mutual moratorium on missile flight testing and halt all nuclear weapons testing while strengthening our efforts to prevent the spread of these weapons to other nations before the nightmare of nuclear terrorism engulfs us all.

WE BELIEVE in an America that recognizes not only the realities of East-West relations, but the challenges and opportunities of the developing world; that will support and strengthen international law and institutions, promote human and political rights and measure them by one yardstick, and work for economic growth and development. We believe that we must provide leadership, compassion and economic assistance to those nations stunted by overwhelming debt, deprivation and austerity, and that we must work to promote active agreements between developing and industrial countries, and the major public and commercial lenders, to provide debt relief and rekindle and sustain economic growth and democracy in Latin America, Asia, and the poorest continent, Africa, which deserves special attention. We further believe that we must enlist the trade surplus nations to join with us in supporting new aid initiatives to fuel growth in developing countries that, though economically depressed, are rich in human and natural potential.

WE BELIEVE this country should work harder to stop the supplies of arms, from both East and West, that fuel conflict in regions such as the Persian Gulf and Angola. Deeply disturbed that the current administration has too long abandoned the peace process in the Middle East and consistently undermined it in Central America, we believe that this country, maintaining the special relationship with Israel founded upon mutually shared values and strategic interests, should provide new leadership to deliver the promise of peace and security through negotiations that has been held out to Israel and its neighbors by the Camp David Accords. We support the sovereignty, independence, and territorial integrity of Lebanon with a central government strong enough to unite its people, maintain order and live in peace in the region. We are committed to Persian Gulf security and freedom of navigation of international waters, and to an end to the Iran-Iraq war by promoting United Nations efforts to achieve a ceasefire and a negotiated settlement, through an arms embargo on the combatants. We further believe that the United States must fully support the Arias Peace Plan, which calls for an end to the fighting, national reconciliation, guarantees of justice, freedom, human rights and democracy, an end to support for irregular forces, and a commitment by the Central American governments to prevent the use of their territory to destabilize others in the region. Instead of the current emphasis on military solutions we will use negotiations and incentives to encourage free and fair elections and security for all nations in the region. We will cease dealing with drug smugglers and seek to reconcile our differences with countries in Central America, enabling the United States and other countries to focus on the pressing social and economic needs of the people of that region. We further believe in pursuing a policy of economic cooperation instead of confrontation with Mexico and our other hemispheric friends; in helping all developing countries build their own peaceful democratic institutions free from foreign troops, subversion and domination and free from domestic dictators and aggressors; in honoring our treaty obligations; and in using all the tools at our disposal, including diplomacy, trade, aid, food, ideas, and ideals, to defend and enlarge the horizons of freedom on this planet.

WE BELIEVE in an America that will promote human rights, human dignity and human opportunity in every country on earth; that will fight discrimination, encourage free speech and association and decry oppression in nations friendly and unfriendly, communist and non-communist; that will encourage our European friends to respect human rights and resolve their long-standing differences over Northern Ireland and Cyprus; that will encourage wherever possible the forces of pluralism and democracy in Eastern Europe and that will support the struggle for human rights in Asia.

WE BELIEVE the apartheid regime in South Africa to be a uniquely repressive regime, ruthlessly deciding every aspect of public and private life by skin color, engaging in unrelenting violence against its citizens at home and promoting naked aggression against its neighbors in Africa. We believe the time has come to end all vestiges of the failed policy of constructive engagement, to declare South Africa a terrorist state, to impose comprehensive sanctions upon its economy, to lead the international community in participation in these actions, and to determine a certain date by which United States corporations must leave South Africa. We further believe that to achieve regional security in Southern Africa, we must press forcefully for Namibia's independence by

calling for the end of South Africa's illegal occupation, a cease fire and elections, must end our counterproductive policy in Angola and must offer support and further assistance to Mozambique and other frontline states.

IN SUM, WE BELIEVE it is time for America to change and move forward again in the interest of all its families—to turn away from an era in which too many of America's children have been homeless or hungry and invest in a new era of hope and progress, an era of secure families in a secure America in a secure world.

WE BELIEVE the American dream of opportunity for every citizen can be a reality for all Americans willing to meet their own responsibilities to help make it come true. We believe that the governments at the national, state and local level, in partnerships between those levels and in partnership with the private sector, exist to help us solve our problems instead of adding to them. We believe in competent, pragmatic governments, accountable to the people, led by men and women dedicated not to self-interest but to service, motivated not by ideology but by American ideals, governing not in a spirit of power and privilege but with a sense of compassion and community. For many years, in state and local capitals across this nation, Democrats have been successfully solving problems and helping people with exactly this kind of innovative government.

THEREFORE, THE DEMOCRATIC PARTY in Convention assembled and united, the Party of hope and change and fairness for all, hereby declares its readiness to end the stalemate in Washington by challenging, encouraging and inviting the American people—challenging them to do their patriotic best to meet their community responsibilities, encouraging them to protect and preserve their families, our most precious assets, and inviting them to join with us in leading the land we love to a brighter and still greater future of opportunity and justice for all.

Bush Acceptance

Following is the text of Vice President George Bush's August 18 speech, in which he formally accepted the 1988 Republican presidential nomination. The text appears as delivered to the Republican National Convention in New Orleans that night.

Thank you ladies and gentlemen, thank you very, very much.

I have many friends to thank tonight. I thank the voters who supported me. I thank the gallant men who entered the contest for this presidency this year, and who've honored me with their support. And, for their kind and stirring words, I thank Governor Tom Kean of New Jersey, Senator, Senator Phil Gramm of Texas, President Gerald Ford—and my friend, and my friend, President Ronald Reagan.

I accept your nomination for president. I mean to run hard, to fight hard, to stand on the issues—and I mean to win.

There are a lot, there are a lot of great stories in politics about the underdog winning—and this is going to be one of them.

And we're going to win with the help of Senator Dan Quayle of Indiana—a young leader who has become a forceful voice in preparing America's workers for the labor force of the future. What a superb job he did here tonight.

Born in the middle of the century, in the middle of America, and holding the promise of the future—I'm proud to have Dan Quayle at my side.

Many of you have asked, many of you have asked, "When will this campaign really begin?" Well, I've come to this hall to tell you, and to tell America: Tonight is the night.

For seven and a half years I've helped the president conduct the most difficult job on Earth. Ronald Reagan asked for, and received, my candor. He never asked for, but he did receive, my loyalty. And those of you who saw the president's speech last week, and listened to the simple truth of his words, will understand my loyalty all these years.

And now, now you must see me for what I am: the Republican candidate for president of the United States. And now I turn to the

American people to share my hopes and intentions, and why and where I wish to lead.

And so tonight is for big things. But I'll try to be fair to the other side. I'll try to hold my charisma in check.

I reject the temptation to engage in personal references. My approach this evening is, as Sergeant Joe Friday used to say, "Just the facts, ma'am."

And after all, after all, the facts are on our side.

Build a Better America

I seek the presidency for a single purpose, a purpose that has motivated millions of Americans across the years and the ocean voyages. I seek the presidency to build a better America. It's that simple—and that big.

I'm a man who sees life in terms of missions—missions defined and missions completed.

And when I was a torpedo bomber pilot they defined the mission for us. And before we took off, we all understood that no matter what, you try to reach the target. And there have been other missions for me—Congress, and China, the CIA. But I'm here tonight, and I am your candidate, because the most important work of my life is to complete the mission we started in 1980. And how, and how do we complete it? We build on it.

The stakes are high this year and the choice is crucial, for the differences between the two candidates are as deep and wide as they have ever been in our long history.

Not only two very different men, but two very different ideas of the future will be voted on this Election Day.

And what it all comes down to is this: My opponent's view of the world sees a long slow decline for our country, an inevitable fall mandated by impersonal historical forces.

But America is not in decline. America is a rising nation.

He sees, he sees America as another pleasant country on the U.N. [United Nations] roll call, somewhere between Albania and Zimbabwe. And I see America as the leader—a unique nation with a special role in the world.

And this has been called the American century, because in it we were the dominant force for good in the world. We saved Europe, cured polio, went to the moon, and lit the world with our culture. And now we are on the verge of a new century, and what country's name will it bear? I say it will be another American century.

Our work is not done, our force is not spent.

"We Can Deliver"

There are those, there are those who say there isn't much of a difference this year. But America, don't let 'em fool ya.

Two parties this year ask for your support. Both will speak of growth and peace. But only one has proved it can deliver. Two parties this year ask for your trust, but only one has earned it.

Eight years ago, eight years ago, I stood here with Ronald Reagan and we promised, together, to break with the past and return America to her greatness. Eight years later, look at what the American people have produced: the highest level of economic growth in our entire history—and the lowest level of world tensions in more than fifty years.

You know, some say this isn't an election about ideology, but it's an election about competence. Well, it's nice of them to want to play on our field. But this election isn't only about competence, for competence is a narrow ideal.

Competence makes the trains run on time but doesn't know where they're going. Competence, competence is the creed of the technocrat who makes sure the gears mesh but doesn't for a second understand the magic of the machine.

The truth is, the truth is, this election is about the beliefs we share, the values we honor and the principles we hold dear.

But, but since someone brought up competence . . .

Consider the size of our triumph: A record number of Americans at work, a record high percentage of our people with jobs, a record high of new businesses, a high rate of new businesses, a record high rate of real personal income.

These are facts.

And one way, and one way we know our opponents know the facts is that to attack our record they have to misrepresent it. They call it a Swiss cheese economy. Well, that's the way it may look to the three blind mice.

But, but when they were in charge it was all holes and no cheese.

Inflation—you know the litany—inflation was 13 percent when we came in. We got it down to four. Interest rates, interest rates were more than 21. We cut them in half. Unemployment, unemployment was up and climbing, and now it's the lowest in fourteen years.

My friends, eight years ago this economy was flat on its back—intensive care. And we came in and gave it emergency treatment: Got the temperature down by lowering regulation, and got the blood pressure down when we lowered taxes. And pretty soon the patient was up, back on his feet, and stronger than ever.

And now who do we hear knocking on the door but the same doctors who made him sick. And they're telling us to put them in charge of the case again? My friends, they're lucky we don't hit 'em with a malpractice suit!

More Jobs: Economic Power

We've created 17 million new jobs [in] the past five years—more than twice as many as Europe and Japan combined. And they're good jobs. The majority of them created in the past six years paid an average—average—of more than $22,000 a year. And someone better take a message to Michael: Tell him, tell him that we have been creating good jobs at good wages. The fact is, they talk and we deliver.

They promise and we perform.

And there are millions of young Americans in their twenties who barely remember, who barely remember the days of gas lines and unemployment lines. And now they're marrying and starting careers. To those young people I say, "You have the opportunity you deserve, and I'm not going to let them take it away from you."

The leaders, the leaders of the expansion have been the women of America who helped create the new jobs, and filled two out of every three of them. And to the women of America I say, "You know better than anyone that equality begins with economic empowerment. You're gaining economic power, and I'm not going to let them take it away from you."

There are millions, there are millions of older Americans who were brutalized by inflation. We arrested it—and we're not going to let it out on furlough.

We're going, and we're going to keep the Social Security trust fund sound, and out of reach of the big spenders. To America's elderly I say. "Once again you have the security that is your right, and I'm not going to let them take it away from you."

I know the liberal Democrats are worried about the economy. They're worried it's going to remain strong. And they're right, it is—with the right leadership it will remain strong.

But let's be frank. Things aren't perfect in this country. There are people who haven't tasted the fruits of the expansion. I've talked to farmers about the bills they can't pay and I've been to the factories that feel the strain of change. And I've seen the urban children who play amidst the shattered glass and the shattered lives. And, you know, there are the homeless. And you know, it doesn't do any good to debate endlessly which policy mistake of the '70s is responsible. They're there, and we have to help them.

But what we must remember if we're to be responsible and compassionate is that economic growth is the key to our endeavors.

I want growth that stays, that broadens, and that touches, finally, all Americans, from the hollows of Kentucky to the sunlit streets of Denver, from the suburbs of Chicago to the broad avenues of New York, and from the oil fields of Oklahoma to the farms of the Great Plains.

And can we do it? Of course we can. We know how. We've done it. If we, if we continue to grow at our current rate, we will be able to produce 30 million jobs in the next eight years.

And we will do it—by maintaining our commitment to free and fair trade, by keeping government spending down, and by keeping taxes down.

Peace through Strength

Our economic life is not the only test of our success. One issue overwhelms all the others, and that is the issue of peace.

Look at the world on this bright August night. The spirit of democracy is sweeping the Pacific rim. China feels the winds of change. New democracies assert themselves in South America. And one by one the unfree places fall, not to the force of arms but to the force of an idea: freedom works.

And we, we have a new relationship with the Soviet Union. The INF [intermediate-range nuclear-force] treaty, the beginning of the Soviet withdrawal from Afghanistan, the beginning of the end of the Soviet proxy war in Angola, and with it the independence of Namibia. Iran and Iraq move toward peace.

It's a watershed. It is no accident.

It happened when we acted on the ancient knowledge that strength and clarity lead to peace—weakness and ambivalence lead to war. You see, you see, weakness tempts aggressors. Strength stops them. I will not allow this country to be made weak again—never.

The tremors in the Soviet world continue. The hard earth there has not yet settled. Perhaps what is happening will change our world forever. And perhaps not. A prudent skepticism is in order. And so is hope.

But either way, we're in an unprecedented position to change the nature of our relationship. Not by preemptive concession, but by keeping our strength. Not by yielding up defense systems with nothing won in return, but by hard, cool engagement in the tug and pull of diplomacy.

My life, my life has been lived in the shadow of war—I almost lost my life in one.

And I hate war. Love peace.

And we have peace.

And I am not going to let anyone take it away from us.

Our economy is stronger but not invulnerable, and the peace is broad but can be broken. And now we must decide. We will surely have change this year, but will it be change that moves us forward? Or change that risks retreat?

In 1940, when I was barely more than a boy, Franklin Roosevelt said we shouldn't change horses in midstream.

My friends, these days the world moves even more quickly, and now, after two great terms, a switch will be made. But when you have to change horses in midstream, doesn't it make sense to switch to one who's going the same way?

Family and Community

An election that is about ideas and values is also about philosophy. And I have one.

At the bright center is the individual. And radiating out from him or her is the family, the essential unit of closeness and of love. For it is the family that communicates to our children—to the twenty-first century—our culture, our religious faith, our traditions and history.

From the individual to the family to the community, and then on out to the town, the church and the school, and, still echoing out, to the county, the state, and the nation—each doing only what it does well, and no more. And I believe that power must always be kept close to the individual, close to the hands that raise the family and run the home.

I am guided by certain traditions. One is that there is a God and he is good, and his love, while free, has a self-imposed cost: We must be good to one another.

I believe in another tradition that is, by now, imbedded in the national soul. It is that learning is good in and of itself. You know, the mothers of the Jewish ghettoes of the east would pour honey on a book so the children would know that learning was sweet. And the parents who settled hungry Kansas would take their children in from the fields when a teacher came. That is our history.

And there is another tradition. And that is the idea of community—a beautiful word with a big meaning. Though liberal Democrats have an odd view of it. They see "community" as a limited cluster of interest groups, locked in odd conformity. And in this view, the country waits passive while Washington sets the rules.

But that's not what community means—not to me.

For we are a nation of communities, of thousands and tens of thousands of ethnic, religious, social, business, labor union, neighborhood, regional and other organizations—all of them varied, voluntary and unique.

This is America: the Knights of Columbus, the Grange, Hadassah, the Disabled American Veterans, the Order of AHEPA [American Hellenic Educational Progressive Association], the Business and Professional Women of America, the union hall, the Bible study group, LULAC [League of United Latin American Citizens], "Holy Name"—a brilliant diversity spread like stars, like a thousand points of light in a broad and peaceful sky.

Does government have a place? Yes. Government is part of the nation of communities—not the whole, just a part.

And I don't hate government. A government that remembers that the people are its master is a good and needed thing.

"Old-Fashioned Common Sense"

I respect old-fashioned common sense, and have no great love, and I have no great love for the imaginings of the social planners. You see, I like what's been tested and found to be true.

For instance.

Should public school teachers be required to lead our children in the pledge of allegiance? My opponent says no—and I say yes.

Should society be allowed to impose the death penalty on those who commit crimes of extraordinary cruelty and violence? My opponent says no—but I say yes.

And should our children, should our children have the right to say a voluntary prayer, or even observe a moment of silence in the schools? My opponent says no—but I say yes.

And should free men and women have the right to own a gun to protect their home? My opponent says no—but I say yes.

And is it right to believe in the sanctity of life and protect the lives of innocent children? My opponent says no—but I say yes.

You see, we must, we must change, we've got to change from abortion to adoption. And let me tell you this: Barbara and I have an adopted granddaughter. And the day of her christening we wept with joy. I thank God that her parents chose life.

I'm the one who believes it is a scandal to give a weekend furlough to a hardened first-degree killer who hasn't even served enough time to be eligible for parole.

I'm the one who says a drug dealer who is responsible for the death of a policeman should be subject to capital punishment.

Policies for the Future

And I'm the one who will not raise taxes. My opponent now says, my opponent now says he'll raise them as a last resort, or a third resort. Well, when a politician talks like that, you know that's one resort he'll be checking into. And, my opponent won't rule out raising taxes. But I will.

And the Congress will push me to raise taxes, and I'll say no, and they'll push, and I'll say no, and they'll push again. And I'll say to them: Read my lips. No new taxes.

Let me tell you more—let me tell you more, let me just tell you more about the mission.

On jobs, my mission is: thirty in eight. Thirty million jobs in the next eight years.

Every one of our children deserves a first-rate school. The liberal Democrats want power in the hands of the federal government. And I want power in the hands of the parents. And, I will—and I will, I will encourage merit schools. I will give more kids a head start. And I'll make it easier to save for college.

I want a drug-free America—and this will not be easy to achieve. But I want to enlist the help of some people who are rarely included. Tonight I challenge the young people of our country to shut down the drug dealers around the world. Unite with us, work with us.

"Zero tolerance" isn't just a policy, it's an attitude. Tell them what you think of people who underwrite the dealers who put poison in our society. And while you're doing that, my administration will be telling the dealers: Whatever we have to do we'll do, but your day is over, you're history.

I am going to do whatever it takes to make sure the disabled are included in the mainstream. For too long they've been left out. But they're not going to be left out anymore.

And I am going to stop ocean dumping. Our beaches should not be garbage dumps and our harbors should not be cesspools.

And I am going to have the FBI trace the medical wastes and we are going to punish the people who dump those infected needles into our oceans, lakes and rivers. And we must clean the air. We must reduce the harm done by acid rain.

And I will put incentives back into the domestic energy industry, for I know from personal experience there is no security for the United States in further dependence on foreign oil.

In foreign affairs I will continue our policy of peace through strength. I will move toward further cuts in strategic and conventional arsenals of both the United States and the Soviet Union and the Eastern Bloc and NATO. I will modernize and preserve our technological edge and that includes strategic defense.

And a priority, a priority: Ban chemical and biological weapons from the face of the Earth. That will be a priority with me.

And I intend to speak for freedom, stand for freedom, be a patient friend to anyone, East or West, who will fight for freedom.

A New Harmony

It seems to me the presidency provides an incomparable opportunity for "gentle persuasion."

And I hope to stand for a new harmony, a greater tolerance. We've come far, but I think we need a new harmony among the races in our country. And we're on a journey into a new century, and we've got to leave that tired old baggage of bigotry behind.

Some people who are enjoying our prosperity have forgotten what it's for. But they diminish our triumph when they act as if wealth is an end in itself.

And there are those who have dropped their standards along the way, as if ethics were too heavy and slowed their rise to the top. There's graft in city hall, and there's greed on Wall Street; there's influence peddling in Washington, and the small corruptions of everyday ambition.

But you see, I believe public service is honorable. And every time I hear that someone has breached the public trust it breaks my heart.

And I wonder sometimes if we have forgotten who we are. But we're the people who sundered a nation rather than allow a sin called slavery—and we're the people who rose from the ghettoes and the deserts.

And we weren't saints, but we lived by standards. We celebrated the individual, but we weren't self-centered. We were practical, but we didn't live only for material things. We believed in getting ahead, but blind ambition wasn't our way.

The fact is prosperity has a purpose. It is to allow us to pursue "the better angels," to give us time to think and grow. Prosperity with a purpose means taking your idealism and making it concrete by certain acts of goodness.

It means helping a child from an unhappy home learn how to read—and I thank my wife Barbara for all her work in helping people to read and all her work for literacy in this country.

It means teaching troubled children through your presence that there is such a thing as reliable love. Some would say it's soft and insufficiently tough to care about these things. But where is it written that we must act as if we do not care, as if we are not moved?

Well, I am moved. I want a kinder and gentler nation.

"Quiet Man"

Two men this year ask for your support. And you must know us.

As for me, I have held high office and done the work of democracy day by day. Yes, my parents were prosperous; and their children sure were lucky. But there were lessons we had to learn about life.

John Kennedy discovered poverty when he campaigned in West Virginia; there were children who had no milk. And young Teddy Roosevelt met the new America when he roamed the immigrant streets of New York. And I learned a few things about life in a place called Texas.

And when I—and when I was, when I was working on this part of the speech, Barbara came in and asked what I was doing. And I looked up, and I said I'm working hard. And she said: "Oh dear, don't worry, relax, sit back, take off your shoes and put up your silver foot."

Now, we moved to West Texas forty years ago—forty years ago this year. The war was over, and we wanted to get out and make it on our own. Those were exciting days. We lived in a little shotgun house, one room for the three of us. Worked in the oil business, and then started my own.

And in time we had six children. Moved from the shotgun to a duplex apartment to a house. And lived the dream—high school football on Friday nights, Little League, neighborhood barbecue.

People don't see their own experience as symbolic of an era—but of course we were.

And so was everyone else who was taking a chance and pushing into unknown territory with kids and a dog and a car.

But the big thing I learned is the satisfaction of creating jobs, which meant creating opportunity, which meant happy families, who in turn could do more to help others and enhance their own lives.

I learned that the good done by a single good job can be felt in ways you can't imagine.

It's been said that I'm not the most compelling speaker, and there are actually those who claim that I don't always communicate in the clearest, most concise way. But I dare them to keep it up—go ahead: Make my twenty-four-hour time period!

Well, I—I may be, may not be the most eloquent, but I learned that, early on, that eloquence won't draw oil from the ground.

And I may sometimes be a little awkward. But there's nothing self-conscious in my love of country.

And I am a quiet man, but—I am a quiet man, but I hear the quiet people others don't. The ones who raise the family, pay the taxes, meet the mortgages.

And I hear them and I am moved, and their concerns are mine.

Man with a Mission

A president must be many things.

He must be a shrewd protector of America's interests; and he must be an idealist who leads those who move for a freer and more democratic planet.

And he must see to it that government intrudes as little as possible in the lives of the people; and yet remember that it is right and proper that a nation's leader take an interest in the nation's character.

And he must be able to define—and lead—a mission.

For seven and a half years, I have worked with a great president—I have seen what crosses that big desk. I have seen the unexpected crisis that arrives in a cable in a young aide's hand.

And I have seen problems that simmer on for decades and suddenly demand resolution. And I have seen modest decisions made with anguish, and crucial decisions made with dispatch.

And so I know that what it all comes down to, this election—what it all comes down to, after all the shouting and the cheers—is the man at the desk. And who should sit at that desk.

My friends, I am that man.

I say it, I say it without boast or bravado.

I've fought for my country, I've served, I've built—and I will go from the hills to the hollows, from the cities to the suburbs to the loneliest town on the quietest street to take our message of hope and growth for every American to every American.

I will keep America moving forward, always forward, for a better America, for an endless enduring dream and a thousand points of light.

This is my mission. And I will complete it.

Thank you.

You know, you know it is customary to end an address with a pledge or a saying that holds a special meaning. And I've chosen one that we all know by heart. One that we all learned in school. And I ask everyone in this great hall to stand and join me in this—we all know it.

I pledge allegiance to the flag of the United States of America and to the republic for which it stands, one nation under God, indivisible, with liberty and justice for all.

Thank you.

Quayle Acceptance

Following is the text of Indiana senator Dan Quayle's address, as delivered at the Republican National Convention August 18, when he accepted the party's 1988 nomination for vice president:

Thank you. Thank you very much.

You're great.

Boy, I can see we're going to have a lot of fun in this campaign. Thank you very much.

Mr. Chairman, Mr. Chairman, fellow Republicans, I accept your nomination for vice president of the United States of America.

Just, just think, eighty-two days from now, George Bush and I are going to win one for you, win one for America's future, and, yes, win one for the Gipper.

My friends, I am standing here tonight because of the decision made by a great man and a great leader, George Bush.

Two days ago, he asked me if I would join him as his running mate. I am deeply grateful for George's confidence in me, and I am humbled by the task ahead.

I would like to add a very personal note. I am also standing here tonight because of the decision my wife, Marilyn, and I made nearly sixteen years ago to be married. Marilyn and our children, Tucker, Benjamin and Corinne, are my strength, my pride, my joy, my love. They are and always will be my total life.

"One Humble Hoosier"

Many this week have asked, who is Dan Quayle?

The people of Indiana know me and now the nation will.

Since 1980, I have been a United States senator from Indiana—and very proud of it. Before that, I was a member of the United States House of Representatives—and proud of it. And, as a young man, I served six years in the National Guard, and, like millions of Americans who have served in the Guard and who serve today—and I am proud of that.

In Indiana, in Indiana they call us Hoosiers, and if you saw the movie *Hoosiers* you have a feeling of what life is like in small towns of our state.

My hometown of Huntington is a little bigger than the town in the movie, and the high school I graduated from is a little bigger than the one that fielded the basketball team in the film.

Still, I identify with that movie, *Hoosiers,* because it reflects the values I grew up with in our small town. We believe very strongly in hard work, in getting an education, in offering an opportunity to our families. Yes, we love basketball, we love underdogs, but most important, we love our country.

So tonight, so tonight, I am one humble Hoosier, whose efforts to devote part of his life to public service have led him here.

I would have been quite happy spending my life in Huntington, in the newspaper business, watching my kids grow, seeing a community with plenty of opportunity to go around. But I looked around me in the midseventies and I saw threats to the future of my family and to the values that could once be taken for granted in our country.

Beyond my town, there were communities torn by crime and drugs, and there were neighborhoods where the very word "opportunity" didn't exist because there were no jobs.

Trying to Change Things

I decided to try to change these things: to make opportunity replace despair, and to make the future just as good as the past for the families of the many Huntingtons of our great land.

That was in 1976, when I was first elected to the House of Representatives. But [with] both houses of Congress and the White House in the hands of liberal Democrats, it was a lot tougher than I ever imagined to turn my determination into reality.

In those Jimmy Carter years, the people running things thought government was the answer, instead of part of the problem. They thought high taxes and big spending would solve anything. I think you know the rest. None of their policies worked and the American people knew it.

In 1980, they voted for a bold new course for the country; a course that brought us more jobs for working Americans, more security for a peace-loving people, more respect from friends and foes around the globe, more opportunity for women and minorities, and a renewed belief that America is a land where you can make your dreams come true.

The Reagan-Bush revolution has already been written on the pages of history. Now, George Bush and Dan Quayle are going to add several bold new chapters to the story of the greatest nation God ever put on this Earth.

"Freedom, Family, and Future"

When I think, when I think of America under the leadership of George Bush, three words come to mind: Freedom. Family. And future.

Freedom first, because without it, nothing else is possible.

When I was a boy, my grandfather used to say to me—and I say it to you here tonight—that America is the greatest nation on Earth because America is free. This is true today and it will always be true.

Next, family. George Bush understands, you understand, I understand, that the family has always been the very heart of civilization. We know the importance of the family to a child growing up. We know the help a family can be to a kid out of school, out of hope, out of luck. And we know the importance of family where one generation helps take care of another, young and old.

And then, there is the future. That word symbolizes hope and opportunity. To make sure hope and opportunity are always there, we need a strong economy so there will be good jobs for all who seek them.

We need an investment in our national defense that brings us long-term security in the world.

We do not need the future the Democratic Party sees, the party of George McGovern, Jimmy Carter, Walter Mondale, just wait, it gets better—Ted Kennedy and now, his buddy, Michael Dukakis. That future has America in retreat. That future has higher taxes and a guaranteed loss of job opportunities. And that future has more government intervention in the lives of all of us.

The future under George Bush means peace and economic opportunity for all.

And, I can tell you, you have George Bush's track record to go on. The tax cuts the Republicans have brought America have resulted in 17 million new jobs being created.

Let me tell you something: George Bush will not raise your taxes, period.

And let me tell you something else: Michael Dukakis will. He has a track record, too, and that is what it tells us: higher taxes.

Job-Training Program

As the new jobs opened up during our current economic expansion, not everyone had the necessary skills for them. Some had lost their jobs and others could not find their first one.

In 1982, the Job Training Partnership Act [JTPA] became law. I was the author of that legislation, and I am proud of it. It established a nationwide training program that has a partnership of government and the private sector. Today, because of the Job

Training Partnership Act, hundreds of thousands of graduates of these programs have jobs with a future.

One of them is Pam Snyder-La Rue of Roy, Utah. A single parent with four children, she was a high school dropout, and on welfare. She joined a JTPA program. First, she earned her high school equivalency credential. Then she earned an accounting certificate. Today, she is a staff accountant at a vocational center. She is off welfare, and proud to be making it on her own. She now has a future.

"Peace, Freedom, and Opportunity"

We could not have a secure economy at home if we [did] not have a peaceful and secure world. As a member of the Senate Armed Services Committee, I know well that it is rebuilding our defense that persuaded the Soviet Union to return to the negotiating table to get us a treaty that, for the first time, actually reduces nuclear arms.

Today, our relationship with the Soviet Union is the best it has been since the end of World War II. George Bush will keep it that way, and I will be right there with him.

Freedom is the most precious commodity our nation has. Let me say again, all else rests on it. We have worked hard for more than two hundred years to preserve freedom. In the Soviet Union, people are trying to get out. In the United States, people are trying to get in. Our freedom is the beacon that draws them.

A great American novelist, the late Thomas Wolfe, once wrote, "This is a fabulous country—the only fabulous country. The one where miracles not only happen, they happen all the time."

Miracles do happen all the time in America because we live in freedom and because the energy and imagination of our people makes their dreams come true every day. I am privileged to be the first person of my generation to be on a national ticket. I don't presume to talk for everyone of my generation, but I know that a great many will agree with me when I express my thanks to the generation of George Bush for bringing us to an era of peace and freedom and opportunity.

My generation has a profound debt to them. We will pay it by making sure that our children and the generations that follow will have the same freedom, the same family values and a future bright with opportunity for all.

Thank you very much. Good night. God bless you. Let's go on to victory.

Republican Platform

Following is the text of the platform adopted at the Republican National Convention in New Orleans, Louisiana, August 15-18, 1988:

Preamble

An election is about the future, about change. But it is also about the values we will carry with us as we journey into tomorrow and about continuity with the best from our past.

On the threshold of a new century, we live in a time of unprecedented technological, social, and cultural development, and a rapidly emerging global economy. This election will bring change. The question is: Will it be change and progress with the Republicans or change and chaos with the Democrats?

Americans want leadership to direct the forces of change, on America's terms, guided by American values. The next stage of the American experiment will be a new dynamic partnership in which people direct government and government empowers people to solve their own problems and to have more choices in their lives.

In 1984, we said, "From freedom comes opportunity; from opportunity comes growth; from growth comes progress."

In 1988, we reaffirm that truth. *Freedom works.* This is not sloganeering, but a verifiable fact. It has been abundantly documented during the Reagan-Bush Administration in terms of

real jobs and real progress for individuals, families and communities urban and rural. Our platform reflects on every page our continuing faith in the creative power of human freedom.

Defending and expanding freedom is our first priority. During the last eight years, the American people joined with the Reagan-Bush Administration in advancing the cause of freedom at home and around the world. Our platform reflects George Bush's belief that military strength, diplomatic resoluteness, and firm leadership are necessary to keep our country and our allies free.

Republicans know the United States is a nation of communities — churches, neighborhoods, social and charitable organizations, professional groups, unions and private and voluntary organizations in city, suburb, and countryside. It is We, the people, building the future in freedom. It is from these innumerable American communities, made up of people with good heads and good hearts, that innovation, creativity, and the works of social justice and mercy naturally flow and flourish. This is why George Bush and all Republicans believe in empowering people and not bureaucracies.

At the very heart of this platform is our belief that the strength of America is its people: free men and women, with faith in God, working for themselves and their families, believing in the inestimable value of every human being from the very young to the very old, building and sustaining communities, quietly performing those "little, nameless, unremembered acts of kindness and love" that make up the best portion of our lives, defending freedom, proud of their diverse heritage. They are still eager to grasp the future, to seize the life's challenges and, through faith and love and work, to transform them into the valuable, the useful, and the beautiful.

This is what the American people do, quietly, patiently, without headlines, as a nation of communities, every day. This is the continuing American revolution of continuity and change.

This is the American people's true miracle of freedom. It is to them that we dedicate this platform.

Jobs, Growth, and Opportunity for All

America again leads the world, confident of our abilities, proud of our products, sure of our future, the pacesetter for all mankind. Moving toward the threshold of the 21st century, the American people are poised to fulfill their dreams to a degree unparalleled in human history.

Our nation of communities is prosperous and free. In the sixth year of unprecedented economic expansion, more people are working than ever before; real family income has risen; inflation is tamed. By almost any measure, Americans are better off than they were eight years ago. The Reagan Revolution has become a Republican renaissance. Our country's back — back in business and back on top again.

Government didn't work this economic wonder. The people did. Republicans got government out of the way, off the backs of households and entrepreneurs, so the people could take charge. Once again our people have the freedom to grow. From that freedom come prosperity and security.

From freedom comes opportunity; from opportunity comes growth; from growth comes progress.

Freedom is not an abstract concept. No, freedom is the inescapable essence of the American spirit, the driving force which makes Americans different from any other people on the face of the globe.

The restoration of our country's tradition of democratic capitalism has ushered in a new age of optimistic expansion. Based on free enterprise, free markets, and limited government, that tradition regards people as a resource, not a problem. And it works.

On every continent, governments are beginning to follow some degree of America's formula to cut tax rates, loosen regulation, free the private sector, and trust the people.

Remember the Carter-Mondale years:

● Taxes skyrocketed every year as the Democrats' inflation pushed everyone into higher brackets.

● Prices spiraled, financially strangling those people least able to keep up. This was heightened by the spending mania of a Democrat-controlled Congress. Savings plunged as prices rose. A dollar saved in 1977 was worth only half by 1981.

● 21.5 percent interest rates — levels not seen before or since — placed the basic needs of life beyond the means of many American families.

● The Democrats threatened workers, investors, and consumers with "industrial policies" that centralized economic planning.

● Joblessness eroded the earnings and dignity of millions under the Democrat Administration.

● The number of poor households grew dramatically during the Democrats' years in power.

● Economic stagnation caused by the Democrats' policies made it harder to find a job, get a promotion, buy a home, raise a family, or plan for old age.

In addition to all of these problems, the Democrats were telling us that there was something wrong with America and something wrong with its people.

Something *was* terribly wrong, but not with the people. A half-century of destructive policies, pitting Americans against one another for the benefit of the Democrats' political machine, had come to a dead end. The Democrats couldn't find a way out, so the voters showed them the door.

Now the ideological heirs of [Jimmy] Carter and [Walter F.] Mondale are trying again to sell the public a false bill of goods. These liberals call America's prosperity an illusion. They fantasize our economy is declining. They claim our future is in the hands of other nations. They aren't operating in the real world.

They can't build the future on fear. Americans know that and are constructing their futures on the solid foundation Republicans have already set in place:

● We are in the midst of the longest peacetime expansion in our country's history. Where once we measured new businesses in the thousands, we now count millions. These small businesses have helped create 17 million well-paying, high-quality new jobs, more than twice the number of jobs that were created during that time in Japan, Canada and Western Europe combined! Small business has accounted for 80 percent of the jobs created during the recovery. Who says America has lost its competitive edge?

● More Americans are working than ever before. Because of Republican pro-growth policies, the unemployment rate has plunged to its lowest level in 14 years.

● Since 1983, 3 million people have risen above the government poverty level. The poverty rate is down for the third consecutive year. The Republican economic program has been the most successful war on poverty.

● Under a Republican Administration, family incomes are growing at the fastest pace recorded in 15 years.

● Under Republican leadership, tax reform removed 6 million low-income people from the income tax rolls and brought financial relief to tens of millions more.

● The typical family is now paying almost $2,000 less per year in income taxes than it would if the Democrats' antiquated income tax system of the 1970s were still in place.

● The Carter "misery index" — the sum of the inflation and unemployment rates — is half of what it was in 1980. Republican economic policies have turned it into a "prosperity index."

● Republicans reduced inflation to one-third of its 1980 level, helping not only average Americans but also low-income Americans and elderly Americans on fixed incomes, who spend most of their income on necessities.

● Interest rates are lower by nearly two-thirds than under the Democrats in 1980.

● Exports are booming. World sales create local jobs!

● Productivity is rising three times as fast under Republican policies as it did during the late 1970s.

● Industrial output increased by one-third during the current expansion.

● Business investment is increasing 20 percent faster, in real terms, than before the Republican economic resurgence.

● The manufacturing sector is now accounting for 23 percent of GNP [gross national product]. U.S. manufacturing jobs have in-creased overall since 1982. The Democrats are wrong about America losing its industrial base, except in Massachusetts, where the Democratic governor of that State has presided over a net decline of 94,000 manufacturing jobs.

This is not a portrait of a people in decline. It is the profile of a can-do country, hopeful and compassionate, on the move. It is America resurgent, renewed, revitalized by an idea: the belief that free men and women, caring for families and supporting voluntary institutions in a nation of communities, constitute the most powerful force for human progress.

In 1980, Ronald Reagan and George Bush called upon us all to recover from a failed political system the power rightly belonging to the people. Now we call upon our fellow citizens, at the bicentennial of our Constitution, in the words of its preamble, to "secure the blessings of liberty to ourselves and our posterity" by opening new vistas of opportunity.

These "blessings of liberty" — the chance to make a decent living, provide for the family, buy a home, give children a superior education, build a secure retirement, help a new generation reach farther and build higher than we were able to — these are the goals that George Bush and the Republican Party seek for every American.

But this prosperity is not an end in itself. It is a beginning. It frees us to grow and be better than we are, to develop things of the spirit and heart. This is the direction in which George Bush will lead our country. It is prosperity with a purpose.

Jobs

The Republican Party puts the creation of jobs and opportunity first. In our 1980 and 1984 platforms, we promised to put Americans back to work by restoring economic growth without inflation. We delivered on our promise:

● Small business entrepreneurs have led the way in creating new job opportunities, particularly for women, minorities, and youths.

● Over 17 million new jobs have been created.

● More than 60% of these new jobs since 1982 are held by women.

● More Americans are working now than at any time in our history.

● The unemployment rate is at its lowest level in 14 years.

● Statistics show that the great majority of the jobs we have created are full-time, quality jobs, paying more than $20,000 per year.

Job growth for minority and ethnic Americans has been even more impressive:

● Minority workers have been finding jobs twice as fast as others.

● Black unemployment has been cut almost in half since 1982. Black Americans gained 2.3 million new jobs in the last few years.

● Black teen unemployment is at its lowest level in 15 years.

● Sales from the top 100 Black firms rose 15 percent between 1982 and 1986. The 7.9 percent growth rate for all Black businesses compares to an overall rate of 5 percent for all business.

● Family incomes of Asian-Americans rank among the highest of all ethnic groups in the United States.

● Hispanic employment increased nearly three times as fast as for all civilian workers. More Hispanics are at work now than at any time since record-keeping began.

We will use new technologies, such as computer data bases and telecommunications, to strengthen and streamline job banks matching people who want work with available jobs.

We advocate incentives for educating, training, and retraining workers for new and better jobs — through programs like the Job Training Partnership Act, which provides for a public/private partnership — as our country surges ahead.

The best jobs program — the one that created 17 million jobs since 1982 — is lower taxes on people. We believe that every person who wants a job should have the opportunity to get a job. We reject the notion that putting more Americans to work causes inflation. The failure of government make-work programs proves that jobs are created by people in a free market.

Opportunity for All

With its message of economic growth and opportunity, the GOP is the natural champion of blacks, minorities, women and ethnic Americans. We urge Republican candidates and officials at all levels to extend to minority Americans everywhere the historic invitation for full participation in our party.

A free economy helps defeat discrimination by fostering opportunity for all. That's why real income for Black families has risen 14 percent since 1982. It's why members of minority groups have been gaining jobs in the Republican recovery twice as fast as everyone else. Upward mobility for all Americans has come back strong.

We are the party of real social progress. Republicans welcome the millions of forward-looking Americans who want an "opportunity society," not a welfare state. We believe our country's greatest resource is its people — all its people. Their ingenuity and imagination are needed to make the most of our common future. So we will remove disincentives that keep the less fortunate out of the productive economy:

● Families struggling near the poverty line are always hurt most by tax increases. Six million poor have been removed from the tax rolls in the 1986 Tax Reform Act — the largest income transfer to lower-income Americans since the early 1970s. We will continue to reduce their burden.

● We advocate a youth training wage to expand opportunities and enable unskilled young people to enter the work force.

● As an alternative to inflationary — and job-destroying — increases in the minimum wage, we will work to boost the incomes of the working poor through the Earned Income Tax Credit, especially for earners who support children. This will mean higher take-home pay for millions of working families.

● We will reform welfare to encourage work as the ticket that guarantees full participation in American life.

● We will undertake a long overdue reform of the unemployment insurance program to reward workers who find new jobs quickly.

● We insist upon the right of Americans to work at home. The Home Work Rule, banning sale of certain items made at home, must go. It idles willing workers, prevents mothers from working and caring for their children in their own homes, limits the country's output, and penalizes innocent persons to please special interests.

● We will fight to end the Social Security earnings limitation for the elderly. It discourages older persons from reentering or remaining in the work force, where their experience and wisdom are increasingly needed. As a first step, we will remove the earnings limitation for those whose income is from child care.

We will continue our efforts, already marked with success, to revitalize our cities. We support, on the federal, State and local levels, enterprise zones to promote investment and job creation in beleaguered neighborhoods.

Entrepreneurship

Our country's 18 million small business entrepreneurs are the superstars of job creation. In the past decade, they created two out of three new jobs. When they are free to invest and innovate, everyone is better off. They are today's pathfinders, the explorers of America's economic future.

Republicans encourage the women and men in small businesses to think big. To help them create jobs, we will cut to 15% the current counter-productive capital gains tax. This will foster investment in new and untried ventures, which often are the cutting edge of constructive change. It will also build the retirement value of workers' pension funds and raise revenues for the federal government.

We will increase, strengthen, and reinvigorate minority business development efforts to afford socially and economically disadvantaged individuals the opportunity for full participation in our free enterprise system.

Workplace benefits should be freely negotiated by employee-employer bargaining. We oppose government requirements that shrink workers' paychecks by diverting money away from wages to pay for federal requirements. These hidden taxes add to labor costs without paying those who labor. That is the liberals' way of replacing collective bargaining with congressional edicts about what's good for employees. It reduces the number of jobs and dishonestly imposes on others the costs of programs the Congress can't afford.

We call for a reasonable state and federal product liability standard that will be fair to small businesses, including professional and amateur sports, and to all who are in liability contests. We propose to return the fault based standard to the civil justice system. Jobs are being lost, useful and sometimes life-saving products are being discontinued, and America's ability to compete is being adversely affected. Reform will lower costs for all and will return fairness to the system for the benefit of everyone. Republicans recognize the basic right of all Americans to seek redress in the courts; however, we strongly oppose frivolous litigation. In addition, we support enactment of fair and balanced reforms of the tort system at the State level.

The remarkable resurgence of small business under the Republican renaissance of the 1980s highlights the key to the future: plant openings, thousands of them in every part of this land, as small businesses lead the way toward yet another decade of compassionate prosperity.

Reducing the Burden of Taxes

The Republican Party restates the unequivocal promise we made in 1984: *We oppose any attempts to increase taxes.* Tax increases harm the economic expansion and reverse the trend to restoring control of the economy to individual Americans.

We reject calls for higher taxes from all quarters — including "bipartisan commissions." The decisions of our government should not be left to a body of unelected officials.

The American people deserve to know, *before the election,* where all candidates stand on the question of tax increases. Republicans unequivocally reiterate the no-tax pledge we have proudly taken. While we wouldn't believe the Democrats even if they took the pledge, they haven't taken it.

The crowning economic achievement of the Republican Party under Ronald Reagan and George Bush has been the dramatic reduction in personal income taxes. The Reagan-Bush Administration has cut the top marginal tax rate from 70 percent to 28 percent. We got government's heavy hand out of the wallets and purses of all our people. That single step has sparked the longest peacetime expansion in our history.

We not only lowered tax rates for all. We tied them to the cost of living so congressional Democrats couldn't secretly boost taxes by pushing people into higher brackets through inflation. We took millions of low-income families off the tax rolls and we doubled the personal exemption for all.

As a result, by 1986 the income tax bill of a typical middle-income family had declined by one-quarter. If the Democrats had defeated our economic recovery program, that family would have paid nearly $6,000 more in taxes between 1982 and 1987. Meanwhile, average Americans and the working poor carry substantially less of the burden. Upper income Americans now pay a larger share of federal taxes than they did in 1980.

Our policies have become the model for much of the world. Through the power of capitalism, governments are rushing to reduce tax rates to save their stagnating economies. This is good for America, for their recovery will make them better trading partners for our own exuberant economy.

Many economists advising the Democrat Party have publicly called for a national sales tax or European-style Value-Added Tax (VAT) which would take billions of dollars out of the hands of American consumers. Such a tax has been imposed on many nations in Europe and has resulted in higher prices, fewer jobs, and higher levels of government spending. We reject the idea of putting a VAT on the backs of the American people.

Republicans know that sustaining the American economic miracle requires a growing pool of private savings. From bank accounts, small stock purchases, and piggy banks, the streams of thrift must flow together and form a mighty tide of capital. That rushing force pushes our society ahead, lifting everyone as it goes. To keep it going:

● We support incentives for private savings, such as our deductibility for IRA contributions.

● We oppose tax withholding on savings.

● To protect savings by ensuring the soundness of our financial system, the federal government must continue to play an active role through its regulatory responsibilities and supervisory duties. We demand stern punishment for those persons, whether in financial institutions or in Congress, whose wheeling and dealing have betrayed the public trust.

● We will reduce to 15 percent the tax rates for long-term capital gains to promote investment in jobs and to raise revenue for the federal government by touching off another surge of economic expansion. In 1978, we cut the capital gains tax from 49.1 percent to 28 percent; in 1981, it was slashed again to 20 percent. The cuts injected a new vitality into the economy, with the result that revenues from this tax rose 184 percent from 1978 to 1985.

● We call for a taxpayers' bill of rights to give everyone simple and inexpensive means to resolve disputes with government. Democrats, using the Massachusetts Revenue Department as a model, intend to squeeze more out of the public by making the IRS [Internal Revenue Service] more intrusive. Republicans will not tolerate tax cheating by anyone, but we know most Americans responsibly pay their fair share. By restoring their confidence in frugal, limited government, we will enhance compliance with tax laws that are simple and fair.

Beating Inflation

Today, the dollar is sound again. The Republican economic program brought inflation under control and lowered interest rates. Ten million more American families have bought homes for the first time. Inflation has been forced down from over 13 percent to 4 percent. Interest rates are only half of what they were at the end of the Carter years.

If the Democrats' inflation rates had continued all these years, a family of four would now be paying an average of $200 a month more for food and over $300 a month more for housing. That's the real cost of the Democrats' bad policies.

The Democrats would drag us back to those dreadful years when inflation was robbing workers of their earnings, consumers of their spending power, and families of their savings. Skyrocketing interest rates were stalling the economy and pushing decent housing out of reach for millions.

We can't let them do it again. To sustain the country's economic expansion, confidence in American monetary policy is vital. The possibility of imprudent action by government breeds fear, and that fear can shake the stock and commodity markets worldwide. To keep markets on an even keel, we urge objective Federal Reserve policies to achieve long-run price stability.

Regulatory Reform

This is a success story for the entire nation. Eight years ago, the country was strangling in red tape. Decades of rules and regulations from official Washington smothered enterprise, hindered job creation, and crippled small businesses. Even worse, the federal bureaucracy was spreading its intrusion into schools, religious institutions, and neighborhoods.

At the outset of his Administration, President Reagan asked Vice President Bush to take charge of an unprecedented exercise in liberty: relieving Americans from oppressive and unnecessary regulations and controls. With George Bush's leadership, Republicans turned the tables on the regulators.

We saved consumers tens of billions of dollars in needless regulatory costs that had been added to the price of virtually every product and service.

● In banking, we ensured that savers would get a fair return on their savings through market interest rates in place of artificially low rates capped by government.

● In energy, transportation, telecommunications, and financial services, we made fundamental changes in the way Americans

could do business. We trusted them. We hacked away at artificial rules that stifled innovation, thwarted competition, and drove up consumer prices. Indeed, telecommunications and computer technology innovations have improved economic performance in nearly every American industry and business.

● In education, housing, and health care, we reduced the chilling effect of regulation upon the private sector and communities. Despite opposition from liberals in the Congress, we have at least slowed the expansion of federal control.

● We turned dozens of narrow programs, full of strings attached, into a few block grants with leeway for State and local administration.

The job isn't over yet. We will resist the calls of Democrats to turn back or eliminate the benefits that reducing regulations have brought to Americans from every walk of life in transportation, finance, energy and many other areas. We want to reduce further the intrusion of government into the lives of our citizens. Consistent with the maintenance of a competitive market place, we are committed to breaking down unnecessary barriers to entry created by regulations, statutes and judicial decisions, to free up capital for productive investment. Let Democrats trust the federal bureaucracy. Republicans trust the creative energy of workers and investors in a free market.

We are committed to further return power from the federal government to state and local governments, which are more responsive to the public and better able to administer critical public services.

Competition in Public Services

Republicans recognize that the American people, in their families, places of work, and voluntary associations, solve problems better and faster than government. That's why the Republican Party trusts people to deal with the needs of individuals and communities, as they have done for centuries.

In recent decades, however, big government elbowed aside the private sector. In the process, it made public services both expensive and inefficient. The federal government should follow the lead of those cities and States which are contracting out for a wide range of activities.

We resolve to defederalize, denationalize, and decentralize government monopolies that poorly serve the public and waste the taxpayer's dollars. To that end, we will foster competition wherever possible.

We advocate privatizing those government assets which would be more productive and better maintained in private ownership. This is especially true of those public properties that have deteriorated under government control, and public housing, where residents should have the option of managing their own project. In other areas as well, citizens and employees should be able to become stockholders and managers of government enterprises that would be more efficiently operated by private enterprise. We will not initiate production of goods and delivery of services by the federal government if they can be procured from the private sector.

Housing

The best housing policy is sound economic policy. Low interest rates, low inflation rates, and the availability of a job with a good paycheck that makes a mortgage affordable are the best housing programs of all.

That has been the key to the rebirth of housing during the Reagan-Bush Administration. If things had continued the way they were in 1980, the average family today would have to pay over $300 more for housing every month. Instead, we curbed inflation, pulled down interest rates, and made housing affordable to more Americans than ever before. We promoted home ownership by stoking the engines of economic growth. The results have been spectacular.

● Mortgage rates have fallen from 17.5 percent to single digits today.

● Home ownership has become affordable for more than 10

million additional families.

- Our regulatory reform campaign, in cooperation with local government and the housing industry, has pointed the way to lower housing through removal of needless rules that inflate prices.

That's only the beginning. We want to foster greater choice in housing for all:

- First and foremost, Republicans stand united in defense of the homeowner's deduction for mortgage interest. That separates us from the Democrats who are already planning to raise taxes by limiting its deductibility.
- We will continue our successful drive for lower interest rates.
- We support the efforts of those in the States who fight to lower property taxes that strike hardest at the poor, the elderly, large families, and family farmers.
- We support programs to allow low-income families to earn possession of their homes through urban and rural homesteading, cooperative ventures in construction and rehabilitation, and other pioneering projects that demonstrate the vitality of the private sector and individual initiative.
- We support the FHA [Federal Housing Administration] mortgage insurance program, the Government National Mortgage Association, the VA [Veterans Administration] guarantee program, and other programs that enhance housing choices for all Americans.
- We pledge to continue to expand opportunities for home ownership and to maintain the strength of savings institutions, including thrifts.
- We call on the Departments of Treasury, Housing and Urban Development, Agriculture, and the Federal Home Loan Bank Board to develop incentives for the private sector to bring housing stock foreclosed on by federal agencies back into service for low and moderate income citizens.
- We call for repeal of rent control laws, which always cause a shortage of decent housing by favoring the affluent with low rents, denying persons with modest incomes access to the housing market.

In public housing, we have turned away from the disasters of the past, when whole neighborhoods became instant slums through federal meddling. We are determined to replace hand-out housing with vouchers that will make low-income families neighbors in communities, not strangers in projects. We have promoted a long-range program of tenant management with encouraging results already. We pledge to continue that drive and to move toward resident ownership of public housing units, which was initiated under Ronald Reagan and George Bush.

To ensure that federal housing funds assist communities, rather than disrupt them, we advocate merging programs into a block grant at the disposal of States and localities for a wide range of needs.

We reaffirm our commitment to open housing as an essential part of the opportunity we seek for all. The Reagan-Bush Administration sponsored a major strengthening of the federal fair housing law. We will enforce it vigorously and will not allow its distortion into quotas controls.

Controlling Federal Spending

The Reagan-Bush policies of economic growth have finally turned around the deficit problem. Through Republican-initiated constraints on spending, the federal budget deficit dropped by over 25 percent last year. With the help of the Gramm-Rudman law and a flexible budget freeze, a balanced budget can be expected by 1993.

But the relentless spending of congressional Democrats can undo our best efforts. No president can cause deficits; Congress votes to spend money. The American people must prevent big-spending congressional Democrats from bringing back big budget deficits; we must return both the Senate and the House of Representatives to Republican control for the first time in 36 years.

In 1981, we inherited a federal spending machine that was out of control. During the Carter-Mondale years, spending grew by 13.6 percent annually. We cut that growth rate in half, but the cancer still expands, as it has in some States such as Massachusetts where the budget has increased more than twice as fast as the

federal budget. We will not be content until government establishes a balanced budget and reduces its demands upon the productivity and earnings of the American people.

We categorically reject the notion that Congress knows how to spend money better than the American people do. Tax hikes are like addictive drugs. Every shot makes Congress want to spend more. Even with the Republican tax cuts of 1981, revenues have increased by about $50 billion every year. But congressional spending has increased even more! For every $1.00 Congress takes in in new taxes, it spends $1.25.

That's why congressional Democrats have sabotaged the Republican program to control the federal budget. They refuse to put any reasonable restraints on appropriations. They smuggle through pork barrel deals in huge "continuing resolutions" larded for the special interests. They oppose the balanced budget amendment and all reforms in the bankrupt process. They mock the restraints legally mandated by our Gramm-Rudman budget plan.

Enough is enough. It's time to push through the Republican agenda for budget reform to teach the Congress the kind of financial responsibility that characterizes the American family:

- We call for structural changes to control government waste, including a two-year budget cycle, a super-majority requirement for raising taxes, a legislatively enacted line-item veto, individual transmission of spending bills, greater rescission authority for the chief executive and other reforms.
- We call for a flexible freeze on current government spending. We insist on the discipline to provide stable funding for important government programs, increasing spending only for true national priorities. We oppose any increase in taxes, so that the economy will continue to expand and revenues from a growing tax base will reduce the deficit.
- We believe the Grace Commission report to eliminate waste, inefficiency, and mismanagement in the federal government must be re-examined; its recommendations should be given a high profile by public policy officials.
- We call for a balanced budget amendment to the Constitution. If congressional Democrats continue to block it, we urge the States to renew their calls for a constitutional convention limited to consideration of such an amendment.
- We will use all constitutional authority to control congressional spending. This will include consideration of the inherent line-item veto power of the president.

Opening Markets Abroad

America's best years lie ahead. Because Republicans have faith in individuals, we welcome the challenge of world competition with confidence in our country's ability to out-produce, out-manage, out-think, and out-sell anyone.

This is the voters' choice in 1988: compete or retreat. The American people and the Republican party are not about to retreat.

To make the 1990s America's decade in international trade, Republicans will advance trade through strength. We will not accept the loss of American jobs to nationalized, subsidized, protected foreign industries and will continue to negotiate assertively the destruction of trade barriers:

- We negotiated a sweeping free trade agreement with Canada, our largest trading partner. Under this agreement, Americans will now be able to trade, invest, and prosper, with no barriers to competition and economic growth.
- We have sought enforcement of U.S. international trade rights more vigorously than any previous administration. The Reagan-Bush Administration was the first to self-initiate formal trade actions against unfair foreign market barriers.
- We launched the "Uruguay Round" of trade talks to promote a more open trading system and address new trade problems that stifle world economic progress.
- We negotiated long and hard to beat back the most protectionist provisions in trade legislation and produced a bill that focuses on opening markets around the world.
- We support multilateral actions to open up foreign markets to U.S. products through the General Agreement on Tariffs and

Trade [GATT]. We will use GATT as well to deal with problems involving agricultural subsidies, trade in services, intellectual property rights, and economic relations with countries that mismanage their economies by suppressing market forces.

We will not tolerate unfair trade and will use free trade as a weapon against it. To ensure that rapid progress is forthcoming from our work through GATT, we stand ready to pursue special arrangements with nations which share our commitment to free trade. We have begun with the U.S.-Israel and U.S.-Canada free trade agreements. These agreements should be used as a model by the entire Western Hemisphere as it moves toward becoming a free trade zone, a powerhouse of productivity that can spur economic growth throughout the continents. We are prepared to negotiate free trade agreements with partners like the Republic of China on Taiwan and the Association of Southeast Asian Nations (ASEAN) countries if they are willing to open their markets to U.S. products.

The emerging global economy has required American workers and consumers to adapt to far-reaching transformations on every continent. These changes will accelerate in the years ahead as nations with free economic systems rush toward a future of incredible promise. International trade among market economies is the driving force behind an unprecedented expansion of opportunity and income.

Unfortunately, international markets are still restricted by antiquated policies: protective tariffs, quotas, and subsidies. These hinder world trade and hurt everyone, producers and consumers alike. It is the politicians and special interests who use protectionism to cover up their failures and enrich themselves at the expense of the country as a whole.

We propose that the General Accounting Office be required to issue regular statistics on the costs of U.S. trade restrictions to American workers, consumers and businesses.

The bosses of the Democratic party have thrown in the towel and abandoned the American worker and producer. They have begun a full-scale retreat into protectionism, an economic narcotic that saps the life out of commerce, closes foreign markets to U.S. producers and growers, and costs American consumers billions of dollars. The Democrats' plans would endanger 200,000 jobs and $8 billion in economic activity in agriculture alone! Over the past year, U.S. exports have expanded by 30 percent. The Democrats would reverse that growth by cowering behind trade barriers.

The bottom line in international trade must be American excellence. Every part of our economy is challenged to renew its commitment to quality. We must redouble our efforts to cut regulation, keep taxes low, and promote capital formation to sustain the advance of science and technology. Changes in both the managing of business and our approach to work, together with a new emphasis on quality and pleasing the customer, are creating a new workplace ethic in our country. We will meet the challenges of international competition by know-how and cooperation, enterprise and daring, and trust in a well trained workforce to achieve more than government can even attempt.

International Economic Policy

Eight years ago, Ronald Reagan and George Bush offered visionary leadership to make a clean break with the failed past of international economics.

Our economic success is now acknowledged worldwide. Countries all over the world, even the Soviet Union, are abandoning worn out industrial policy planning by government in favor of the market-oriented policies underlying what foreign leaders call the "American Miracle."

We encouraged the major economic powers to draw greater guidance for their monetary policies from commodity prices. This was an important step toward ensuring price stability, eliminating volatility of exchange rates, and removing excessive trade imbalances.

We support the Administration's efforts to improve coordination among the industrialized nations regarding their basic economic policies as a means of sustaining non-inflationary growth. It is important that we continue and refine efforts to dampen the volatility of exchange rate fluctuations, which have at times impeded improvements in investment and trade. Further, it is important to guard against the possibility of inflation in all currencies by comparing them with a basket of commodities, including gold.

International price stability will set the stage for developing countries to participate in the transforming process of economic growth. We will not turn our backs on the Third World, where Soviet imperialism preys upon stagnation and poverty. The massive debt of some emerging nations not only cripples their progress but also disrupts world trade and finance.

We will use U.S. economic aid, whether bilateral or through international organizations, to promote free market reforms: lower marginal tax rates, less regulation, reduced trade barriers. We will work with developing nations to make their economies attractive to private investment — both domestic and foreign — the only lasting way to ensure that these nations can secure capital for growth. We support innovations to facilitate repayment of loans, including "debt for equity" swaps. We urge our representatives in all multilateral organizations such as the World Bank to support conditionality with all loans to encourage democracy, private sector development, and individual enterprise. As part of our commitment to the family as the building block of economic progress, we believe decisions on family size should be made freely by each family and remain opposed to U.S. funding for organizations involved in abortion.

To dig their way out of debt, those nations must do more than take out additional loans. They need America's greatest export: capitalism. While sharing the pie of prosperity with others, we will teach its recipe. It is this simple: Where democracy and free markets take root, people live better. Where people live better, they produce and trade more. As capitalism spreads throughout the world, more nations are prospering, international commerce is booming, and U.S. trade is breaking records.

But even more important than economic progress is the advance of freedom. Republicans want not only a better life for the people of developing lands; we want a freer and more peaceful future for them too. Those goals are inextricably linked. It is a case of all or nothing, and we believe that free people can have it all.

From all over the world, capital flows into the United States because of confidence in our future. Direct investment in America creates important economy-wide benefits: jobs, growth, and lower interest rates. We oppose shortsighted attempts to restrict or overly regulate this investment in America that helps our people work, earn, and live better.

Most important, we will lead by example. We will keep the United States a shining model of individual freedom and economic liberty to encourage other peoples of the world to assert their own economic rights and secure opportunity for all.

Strong Families and Strong Communities

Strong families build strong communities. They make us a confident, caring society by fostering the values and character — integrity, responsibility, and altruism — essential for the survival of democracy. America's place in the 21st Century will be determined by the family's place in public policy today.

Republicans believe, as did the framers of the Constitution, that the God-given rights of the family come before those of government. That separates us from liberal Democrats. We seek to strengthen the family. Democrats try to supplant it. In the 1960s and 1970s, the family bore the brunt of liberal attacks on everything the American people cherished. Our whole society paid dearly.

It's time to put things together again. Republicans have started this critical task:

● We brought fairness to the tax code, removed millions of low income families from the rolls, and cut tax rates dramatically.

● We reestablished a pro-family tax system. We doubled the exemption for dependents and protected families from backdoor tax hikes by linking the exemption to inflation.

● We tamed inflation to lower interest rates, protect the savings of the elderly, and make housing more affordable for millions of households.

● We fought to reverse crime rates and launched the nation's first all-out war on drug abuse, though there is still much more to do.

● We appointed judges who respect family rights, family values, and the rights of victims of crime.

● We brought education back to basics, back to parents, and strengthened the principle of local control.

● Through President Reagan's historic executive order on the family, we set standards in law for determining whether policies help or hurt the American family.

Republicans have brought hope to families on the front lines of America's social reconstruction. We pledge to fulfill that hope and to keep the family at its proper place at the center of public policy.

Caring for Children

The family's most important function is to raise the next generation of Americans, handing on to them the Judeo-Christian values of western civilization and our ideals of liberty. More than anything else, the ability of America's families to accomplish those goals will determine the course our country takes in the century ahead.

Our society is in an era of sweeping change. In this era of unprecedented opportunity, more women than ever before have entered the work force. As a result, many households depend upon some form of non-parental care for their youngsters. Relatives, neighbors, churches and synagogues, employers and others in the private sector, are helping to meet the demand for quality care. In the process, we are learning more about the needs of children and about the impact of various forms of care. That knowledge should guide public policy and private options on many issues affecting the way we work and raise our families.

Republicans affirm these commonsense principles of child care:

● The more options families have in child care, the better. Government must not constrain their decisions. Individual choice should determine child care arrangements for the family.

● The best care for most children, especially in the early years, is parental. Government must never hinder it.

● Public policy must acknowledge the full range of family situations. Mothers or fathers who stay at home, who work part-time, or who work full-time, should all receive the same respect and consideration in public policy.

● Child care by close relatives, religious organizations, and other community groups should never be inhibited by government programs or policies.

In sum, this is a perfect example of the difference between the two parties. Republicans want to empower individuals, not bureaucrats. We seek to minimize the financial burdens imposed by government upon families, ensure their options and preserve the role of our traditional voluntary institutions. Democrats propose a new federal program that negates parental choice and disdains religious participation. Republicans would never bar aid to any family for choosing child care that includes a simple prayer.

In returning to our traditional commitment to children, the Republican Party proposes a radically different approach:

● Establish a toddler tax credit for pre-school children as proposed by Vice President Bush, available to all families of modest means, to help them afford and care for their children in a manner best suited to their families' values and traditions.

● Establishment of a plan that does not discriminate against single-earner families with one parent in the home.

● Continue to reverse the Democrats' 30-year erosion of the dependent tax exemption. That exemption has been doubled under Republican leadership. This will empower parents to care for their families in a way that public services can never do.

● Make the dependent care tax credit available to low-income families for young children.

● Eliminate disincentives for grandparents and other seniors to care for children by repealing the earnings limitation for Social Security recipients.

● Encourage States to promote child care programs which allow teen-age mothers to remain in school.

● Promote in-home child care — preferred by almost all parents — by allowing annual, instead of quarterly, payments of income taxes by employees and withholding taxes by employers.

● Encourage employers, including government agencies, to voluntarily address their employees' child care needs and use more flexible work schedules and job sharing to recognize the household demands for their workforce.

● Reform the tort liability system to prevent excessive litigation that discourages child care by groups who stand ready to meet the needs of working parents.

● Reform Federal Home Mortgage Association rules to retain mortgage eligibility for homeowners who offer family child care.

Adoption

Adoption is a special form of caring for children. We recognize the tremendous contributions of adoptive parents and foster parents. The Reagan-Bush Administration has given unprecedented attention to adoption through a presidential task force, whose recommendations point the way toward vastly expanding opportunities for children in need.

Republicans are determined to cut through red tape to facilitate the adoption process for those who can offer strong family life based on traditional values. Trapping minority and special needs children in the foster care system, when there are families ready to adopt these youngsters, is a national disgrace. We urge States to remove obstacles to the permanent placement of foster children and to reform antiquated regulations that make adoption needlessly difficult.

Pornography

America's children deserve a future free from pornography. We applaud Republicans in the 100th Congress who took the lead to ban interstate dial-a-porn. We endorse legislative and regulatory efforts to anchor more securely a standard of decency in telecommunications and to prohibit the sale of sexually explicit materials in outlets operated on federal property. We commend those who refuse to sell pornographic material. We support the rigorous enforcement of "community standards" against pornography.

Health

Americans are accustomed to miracles in health care. The relentless advance of science, boosted by space age technology, has transformed the quality of health care and broadened the exercise of our compassion. By the year 2000, more than 100,000 Americans will be more than 100 years old. Yesterday's science fiction regularly becomes today's medical routine.

The American people almost lost all that in the 1960s and 1970s, when political demagogues offered quack cures for the ills of our health care system. They tried to impose here the nationalized medicine that was disastrous in other countries.

Republicans believe in reduced government control of health care while maintaining an unequivocal commitment to quality health care:

● We fostered competition and consumer choice as the only way to hold down the medical price spiral generated by government's open-ended spending on health programs.

● We gave the hospice movement its important role in federal programs.

● We launched a national campaign to ensure quality treatment and to prevent abuse in nursing homes.

● We led the way to enacting landmark legislation for catastrophic health insurance under Medicare.

● We speeded up the regulatory process for experimental drugs for life-threatening illness and loosened import controls to allow greater choice by patients.

● We promoted home health care through pilot projects in the states. We took extraordinary steps to ensure health care so that chronically ill children under Medicaid would not have to stay in the hospital.

Republicans will continue the recovery of America's health care system from the Democrats' mistakes of the past:

● We will promote continuing innovation to ensure that tomorrow's miracles are affordable and accessible to all. We are encouraged by advances in communications which enable small or isolated facilities to tap the resources of the world's greatest centers of healing. Many breakthroughs in recent years have dramatically reduced the incidence of surgery and replaced lengthy hospital stays with out-patient treatment.

● We will work for continuing progress in providing the most cost-effective, high-quality care.

● We will lead the fight for reform of medical malpractice laws to stop the intolerable escalation of malpractice insurance. It has artificially boosted costs for patients, driven many good doctors out of fields such as obstetrics, and made care unavailable for many patients.

● We are opposed to the establishment of government mandated professional practice fees and services requirements as a condition of professional licensure or license renewal.

● We are committed to avoiding the kind of medical crisis facing Massachusetts — a State the American Medical Association has labelled the "Beirut of medicine" where the delivery of quality health care has deteriorated.

● We will continue to seek opportunities for private and public cooperation in support of hospices.

● We are committed to improving the quality and financing of long term care. We will remove regulatory and tax burdens to encourage private health insurance policies for acute or long term care. We will work for convertibility of savings, IRAs [Individual Retirement Accounts], life insurance, and pensions to pay for long term care.

● We will encourage the trend in the private sector to expand opportunities for home health care to protect the integrity of the family and to provide a less expensive alternative to hospital stays. We want to ensure flexibility for both Medicare and Medicaid in the provision of services to those who need them at home or elsewhere.

● We will foster employee choice in selecting health plans to promote personal responsibility for wellness.

● Recognizing that medical catastrophes can strike regardless of age, we empathize with the plight of the thousands of American families with catastrophically ill children and will work toward making catastrophic health care coverage available to our youngest citizens.

● Recognizing that inequities may exist in the current treatment of health insurance costs for those who are self employed, including farmers, we will study ways to more appropriately balance such costs.

● We will continue to promote alternative forms of group health care that foster competition and lower costs.

● We will make special provision for relief of rural hospitals and health care providers who have been unduly burdened by federal cost control efforts. The availability of health services, especially during a crisis like the current drought, is essential for rural America.

● We will continue generous funding for the National Institutes of Health.

● We will hold down Medicaid costs by promoting State pilot programs to give low-income persons the opportunity to secure health insurance. We demand tough penalties against providers who defraud this and other health programs.

● We will work to assure access to health care for all Americans through public and private initiatives.

● We will promote wellness, especially for the nation's youth. Personal responsibility in behavior and diet will dramatically reduce the incidence of avoidable disease and curb health costs in decades ahead.

● We will call on the Food and Drug Administration to accelerate its certification of technically sound alternatives to animal testing of drugs and cosmetics when considering data regarding product safety and efficacy.

AIDS

Those who suffer from AIDS, their families, and the men and women of medicine who care for the afflicted deserve our compassion and help. The Reagan-Bush Administration launched the nation's fight against AIDS, committing more than $5 billion in the last five years. For 1989, the President's budget recommends a 42 percent increase in current funding.

We will vigorously fight against AIDS, recognizing that the enemy is one of the deadliest diseases to challenge medical research. Continued research on the virus is vital. We will continue as well to provide experimental drugs that may prolong life. We will establish within the Food and Drug Administration a process for expedited review of drugs which may benefit AIDS patients. We will allow supervised usage of experimental treatments.

We must not only marshal our scientific resources against AIDS, but must also protect those who do not have the disease. In this regard, AIDS education plays a critical role. AIDS education should emphasize that abstinence from drug abuse and sexual activity outside of marriage is the safest way to avoid infection with the AIDS virus. It is extremely important that testing and contact tracing measures be carried out and be appropriately confidential, as is the case with the long-standing public health measures to control other communicable diseases that are less dangerous than AIDS.

We will remove barriers to making use of one's own (autologous) blood or blood from a designated donor, and we call for penalties for knowingly donating tainted blood or otherwise deliberately endangering others.

The latency period between infection with the virus and onset of AIDS can be lengthy. People should be encouraged to seek early diagnosis and to remain on the job or in school as long as they are functionally capable.

Healthy Children, Healthy Families

As we strengthen the American family, we improve the health of the nation. From prenatal care to old age, strong family life is the linchpin of wellness and compassion.

This is especially important with regard to babies. We have reduced infant mortality, but it remains a serious problem in areas where alcohol, drugs, and neglect take a fearful toll on newborns. We will target federal health programs to help mothers and infants get a good start in life. We will assist neighborhood institutions, including religious groups, in reaching out to those on the margins of society to save their children, especially from fetal alcohol syndrome, the major cause of birth defects in this country.

Inadequate prenatal care for expectant mothers is the cause of untold numbers of premature and low birth-weight babies. These newborns start life at a severe disadvantage and often require massive health care investments to have a chance for normal childhood. We continue to endorse the provision of adequate prenatal care for all expectant mothers, especially the poor and young.

We hail the way fetal medicine is revolutionizing care of children and dramatically expanding our knowledge of human development. Accordingly, we call for fetal protection, both in the work place and in scientific research.

Most of the health problems of young people today stem from moral confusion and family disruption. Republicans are ready to address the root causes of today's youth crisis:

● We will assert absolutes of right and wrong concerning drug abuse and other forms of self-destructive behavior.

● We will require parental consent for unemancipated minors to receive contraceptives from federally funded family planning clinics.

● We support efforts like the Adolescent Family Life program to teach teens the traditional values of restraint, respect, and the sanctity of marriage.

● We urge all branches of the entertainment industry to exercise greater responsibility in addressing the youth market.

To prepare for tomorrow's expanding opportunities, today's young Americans must be challenged by high values with the support that comes from strong families. That is the surest way to guide them to their own affirmation of life.

Older Americans

Older Americans are both our bridge to all that is precious in our history and the enduring foundation on which we build the future. Young Americans see most clearly when they stand on the shoulders of the past.

After eight years of President Reagan's youthful leadership, older Americans are safer and more secure. In 1980, we promised to put Social Security back on a sound financial footing. We delivered. We established the national commission that developed the plan to restore the system and led the way in enacting its recommendations into law.

Now that Social Security is in healthy shape, congressional Democrats are plotting ways to use its short-term revenue surplus for their own purposes. We make this promise: They shall not do so. We pledge to preserve the integrity of the Social Security trust funds. We encourage public officials at all levels to safeguard the integrity of public and private pension funds against raiding by anyone, in labor, business, or government, such as in Massachusetts where the current Democrat governor has raided $29 million from the State pension reserves to fund his enormous deficit in the State budget.

We will not allow liberal Democrats to imperil the other gains the elderly have made during the Reagan-Bush Administration:

• Inflation, the despoiler of household budgets for the aged, has been reduced to less than one-third of its peak rate under the last Democrat Administration.

• Passage of our anti-crime legislation has helped target resources to fight crime against the elderly, many of whom have been prisoners in their own homes.

• As a result of the Republican economic program, the poverty rate for older Americans has declined by 20 percent during the Republican Administration. When the value of non-cash benefits is counted, the poverty rate is the lowest in history: 3 percent.

• We dramatically cut estate taxes so surviving spouses will not have to sell off the property they worked a lifetime to enjoy just to pay the IRS.

• President Reagan led the Congress in expanding Medicare coverage to include catastrophic health costs.

• Effective spending on Medicare has more than doubled. We have, however, saved money for both taxpayers and beneficiaries through reforms in Medicare procedures.

• Congressional Republicans have supported reauthorization of the broad range of programs under the Older Americans Act.

• The Republican Party reaffirms its long-standing opposition to the earnings test for Social Security recipients. Industrious older persons should not be penalized for continuing to contribute their skills and experience to society.

The 1990s should be the best decade ever for America's older worker. Older Americans will be our natural teachers. In a civilization headed for the stars, they will help us keep our feet on the ground.

The Homeless

Republicans are determined to help the homeless as a matter of ethical commitment, as well as sound public policy. The Reagan-Bush Administration has been at the forefront of the effort:

• In 1987, President Reagan signed a $1 billion aid package to help local governments aid the homeless.

• In 1988, the federal government will spend $400 million on emergency shelters and medical care alone. Today, a total of 45 federally assisted programs are potentially available to the homeless.

• In 1983, we launched an Emergency Food and Shelter Program under the Federal Emergency Management Administration.

• The General Services Administration has donated both buildings and equipment for shelters.

• In 1985, the Department of Housing and Urban Development [HUD] began to lease single family homes at a nominal rent for use as shelters.

• The Department of Agriculture has provided hundreds of millions of dollars worth of surplus food — more than 1.1 billion pounds to soup kitchens and shelters.

• The Alcohol, Drug Abuse and Mental Health Administration gives the States about a half-billion dollars a year to offset the lack of outpatient services.

Homelessness demonstrates the failure of liberalism. It is the result of Democratic policies in the 1960s and 1970s that disrupted mental health care, family stability, low-cost housing, and the authority of towns and cities to deal with people in need. Republicans are ready to deal with the root causes of the problem:

• Our top priority must be homeless families. As part of an overall emphasis on family responsibility, we will strongly enforce child support laws. We call for development of a model divorce reform law that will adequately safeguard the economic and social interests of mothers and children while securing fairness to fathers in decisions concerning child custody and support.

• We will improve safety in federally assisted shelters for the good of all, particularly families.

• We will work with State and local governments to ensure that education is available to homeless children. All appropriate federal education and health programs must make provisions for the special needs of these youngsters.

• We will create, as a national emergency effort, a regulatory reform task force drawn from all levels of government to break through the restrictions that keep 1.7 million housing units unrehabilitated and out of use. We will explore incentives for the private sector to put these housing units back into service.

• As detailed elsewhere in this platform, we will advance tenant management and resident ownership of public housing as a proven means of upgrading the living environment of low-income families.

• We favor expanding Community Development Block Grants for acquiring or rehabilitating buildings for shelters. We urge work requirements, no matter how modest, for shelter residents so they can retain skills and a sense of responsibility for their future.

• Rent controls promise housing below its market cost, but inevitably result in a shortage of decent homes. Our people should not have to underwrite any community which erodes its own housing supply by rent control.

We call upon the courts to cooperate with local officials and police departments in arranging for treatment for persons whose actions disrupt the community or endanger their own or others' safety.

Constitutional Government and Individual Rights

Equal Rights. Since its inception, the Republican Party has stood for the worth of every person. On that ground, we support the pluralism and diversity that have been part of our country's greatness. "Deep in our hearts, we do believe":

• That bigotry has no place in American life. We denounce those persons, organizations, publications and movements which practice or promote racism, anti-Semitism or religious intolerance.

• That the Pledge of Allegiance should be recited daily in schools in all States. Students who learn we are "one nation, under God, with liberty and justice for all" will shun the politics of fear.

• In equal rights for all. The Reagan-Bush Administration has taken to court a record number of civil rights and employment discrimination cases. We will continue our vigorous enforcement of statutes to prevent illegal discrimination on account of sex, race, creed, or national origin.

• In guaranteeing opportunity, not dictating the results of fair competition. We will resist efforts to replace equal rights with discriminatory quota systems and preferential treatment. Quotas are the most insidious form of reverse discrimination against the innocent.

• In defending religious freedom. Mindful of our religious diversity, we firmly support the right of students to engage in voluntary prayer in schools. We call for full enforcement of the Republican legislation that now guarantees equal access to school facilities by student religious groups.

• That the unborn child has a fundamental right to life which cannot be infringed. We therefore reaffirm our support for a human life amendment to the Constitution, and we endorse legislation to make clear that the Fourteenth Amendment's protections apply to unborn children. We oppose the use of public revenues for abortion and will eliminate funding for organizations which advocate or support abortion. We commend the efforts of those individuals and religious and private organizations that are providing positive alternatives to abortion by meeting the physical, emotional, and financial needs of pregnant women and offering adoption services where needed.

• We applaud President Reagan's fine record of judicial appointments, and we reaffirm our support for the appointment of judges at all levels of the judiciary who respect traditional family values and the sanctity of innocent human life.

• That churches, religious schools and any other religious institution should not be taxed. We reject as wrong, bigoted, and a massive violation of the First Amendment the current attempt by the ACLU [American Civil Liberties Union] to tax the Roman Catholic Church or any other religious institutions they target in the future.

Private Property. We believe the right of private property is the cornerstone of liberty. It safeguards for citizens everything of value, including their right to contract to produce and sell goods and services. We want to expand ownership to all Americans, for that is the key for individuals to control their own future.

To advance private stewardship of natural resources, we call for a reduction in the amount of land controlled by government, especially in our western States. Private ownership is best for our economy, best for our environment, and best for our communities. We likewise consider water rights a State issue, not a federal one.

Women's Rights. We renew our historic commitment to equal rights for women. The Republican Party pioneered the right of women to vote and initiated the rights now embodied in the Equal Pay Act, requiring equal pay for equal work. But legal rights mean nothing without opportunity, and that has been the hallmark of Republican policy. In government, the Reagan-Bush team has broken all records for the advancement of women to the most important positions: 28 percent of the top policy-level appointments went to women. But far more important than what we've done in government is what women have accomplished with the economic freedom and incentives our policies have provided them.

We must remove remaining obstacles to women's achieving their full potential and full reward. That does not include the notion of federally mandated comparable worth, which would substitute the decisions of bureaucrats for the judgment of individuals. It does include equal rights for women who work for the Congress. We call upon the Democratic leadership of House and Senate to join Republican Members in applying to Congress the civil rights laws that apply to the rest of the nation. Women should not be second-class citizens anywhere in our country, but least of all beneath the dome of the Capitol.

Recognizing that women represent less than 5 percent of the U.S. Congress, only 12 percent of the nation's statewide offices, plus 15 percent of State legislative positions, the Republican Party strongly supports the achievements of women in seeking an equal role in the governing of our country and is committed to the vigorous recruitment, training, and campaign support of women candidates at all levels.

Americans with Disabilities. One measure of our country's greatness is the way it treats its disabled citizens.

Our citizens are the nation's most precious resource. As Republicans, we are committed to ensuring increased opportunities for every individual to reach his or her maximum potential. This commitment includes providing opportunities for individuals with disabilities. The 1980s have been a revolution, a declaration of independence for persons with disabilities, and Republicans have initiated policies which remove barriers so that such persons are more independent.

The most effective way to increase opportunities for such persons is to remove intentional and unintentional barriers to education, employment, housing, transportation, health care, and other basic services. Republicans have played an important role in removing such barriers:

• Republicans supported the creation of a new program to pro-

vide early intervention services to infants and toddlers with disabilities.

• Republicans initiated a supported employment program that allows individuals with severe disabilities to earn competitive wages in integrated work settings, thus, in many instances, creating first-time taxpayers.

• Republicans initiated changes in the Social Security Act that now permit individuals with disabilities to work without losing health insurance coverage.

• Republicans developed legislation to increase the availability of technology-related assistance for individuals with disabilities, thereby increasing their ability to do things for themselves, others, and their communities.

• Republicans have made a sustained commitment to policies that create opportunities for individuals with disabilities to lead productive and creative lives.

Republicans will continue to support such policies:

• We recognize the great potential of disabled persons and support efforts to remove artificial barriers that inhibit them from reaching their potential, and making their contributions, in education, employment and recreation. This includes the removal, insofar as practicable, of architectural, transportation, communication and attitudinal barriers.

• We support efforts to provide disabled voters full access to the polls and opportunity to participate in all aspects of the political process.

• By promoting vigorous economic growth, we want to provide incentives for the scientific and technological research that may reverse or compensate for many disabilities.

• We pledge to fight discrimination in health care. Following the example of President Reagan, we insist upon full treatment for disabled infants. We find no basis, whether in law or medicine or ethics, for denying care or treatment to any medically dependent or disabled person because of handicap, age, or infirmity.

• We will strongly enforce statutory prohibitions barring discrimination because of handicap in any program receiving federal financial assistance.

• We will protect the rights established under the Education for All Handicapped Children Act, Section 504 of the Rehabilitation Act of 1973, and the Civil Rights of Institutionalized Persons Act. We will balance those rights against the public's right to be protected against diseases and conditions which threaten the health and safety of others.

• We recognize the need to procedural due process rights of persons with disabilities both to prevent their placement into inappropriate programs or settings and to ensure that their rights are represented by guardians or other advocates when necessary.

We endorse policies that give individuals with disabilities the right to participate in decisions related to their education, the right to affect how and where they live and the right to choose or change a job or career.

To further promote the independence and productivity of people with disabilities and their integration into the mainstream of life, the Republican Party supports legislation to remove the bias in the Medicaid program toward serving disabled individuals in isolated institutional settings and ensure that appropriate, community-based services are reimbursable through Medicaid.

Native Americans. We support self-determination for Indian Tribes in managing their own affairs and resources. Recognizing the government-to-government trust responsibility, we will work to end dependency fostered by federal controls. Reservations should be free to become enterprise zones so their people can fully share in America's prosperity. We will work with tribal governments to improve environmental conditions and will ensure equitable participation by Native Americans in federal programs in health, housing, job training and education.

We endorse efforts to preserve the culture of native Hawaiians and to ensure their equitable participation in federal programs that can recognize their unique place in the life of our nation.

The Right of Gun Ownership. Republicans defend the constitutional right to keep and bear arms. When this right is abused by an individual who uses a gun in the commission of a crime, we call for stiff, mandatory penalties.

The Rights of Workers. We affirm the right of all freely to form, join or assist labor organizations to bargain collectively, consistent with state laws. Labor relations must be based on fairness and mutual respect. We renew our long-standing support for the right of states to enact "Right-to-Work" laws. To protect the political rights of every worker, we oppose the use of compulsory dues or fees for partisan purposes. Workers should not have to pay for political activity they oppose, and no worker should be coerced by violence or intimidation by any party to a labor dispute.

The Republican Party supports legislation to amend the Hobbs Act, so that union officials, like all other Americans, are once again subject to the law's prohibition against extortion and violence in labor disputes.

We also support amendments to the National Labor Relations Act to provide greater protection from labor violence for workers who choose to work during strikes.

The Right to Political Participation. Republicans want to broaden involvement in the political process. We oppose government controls that make it harder for average citizens to be politically active. We especially condemn the congressional Democrats' scheme to force taxpayer funding of campaigns.

Because we support citizen participation in politics, we continue to favor whatever legislation may be necessary to permit Americans citizens residing in Guam, the Virgin Islands, American Samoa, the Northern Mariana Islands, and Puerto Rico to vote for president and vice president in national elections and permit their elected federal delegate to have the rights and privileges — except for voting on the floor — of other Members of Congress.

Puerto Rico has been a territory of the United States since 1898. The Republican Party vigorously supports the right of the United States citizens of Puerto Rico to be admitted into the Union as a fully sovereign State after they freely so determine. Therefore, we support the establishment of a presidential task force to prepare the necessary legislation to ensure that the people of Puerto Rico have the opportunity to exercise at the earliest possible date their right to apply for admission into the Union.

We also pledge that a decision of the people of Puerto Rico in favor of statehood will be implemented through an admission bill that would provide for a smooth fiscal transition, recognize the concept of a multicultural society for its citizens, and ensure the right to retain their Spanish language and traditions.

We recognize that the people of Guam have voted for a closer relationship with the United States of America, and we reaffirm our support of their right to improve their political relationship through a commonwealth status.

The Republican Party welcomes, as the newest member of the American family, the people of the Commonwealth of the Northern Marianas Islands, who became U.S. citizens with President Reagan's 1986 presidential proclamation.

Immigration. We welcome those from other lands who bring to America their ideals and industry. At the same time, we insist upon our country's absolute right to control its borders. We call upon our allies to join us in the responsibility shared by all democratic nations for resettlement of refugees, especially those fleeing Communism in Southeast Asia.

Restoring the Constitution. We reassert adherence to the Tenth Amendment, reserving to the States and to the people all powers not expressly delegated to the national government.

Our Constitution provides for a separation of powers among the three branches of government. In that system, judicial power must be exercised with deference towards State and local authority; it must not expand at the expense of our representative institutions. When the courts try to reorder the priorities of the American people, they undermine the stature of the judiciary and erode respect for the rule of law. That is why we commend the Reagan-Bush team for naming to the federal courts distinguished women and men committed to judicial restraint, the rights of law-abiding

citizens, and traditional family values. We pledge to continue their record. Where appropriate, we support congressional use of Article III, section 2 of the Constitution to restrict the jurisdiction of federal courts.

Government Ethics and Congressional Reform. As the United States celebrates the bicentennial of the U.S. Congress, many Americans are becoming painfully aware that they are being disenfranchised and inadequately represented by their elected officials.

Indeed, the process of government has broken down on Capitol Hill. The Founding Fathers of the United States Constitution would be shocked by congressional behavior:

● The Democrat congressional leaders exempt themselves from the laws they impose on the people in areas like health, safety and civil rights.

● Salaries and staff keep growing. Lavish free mailing privileges and other power perks help most incumbents hold onto their offices, election after election.

● Out of 91 appropriations bills in the past seven years, only seven made it to the president's desk on time.

● A catch-all bill to fund the government for 1988 was 2,100 pages long, lumping together 13 money bills that should have been separately subject to presidential review.

● $44 billion is currently being spent for programs not authorized by legislation.

● Special interest spending and pork barrel deals are larded throughout massive bills passed in chaotic late-night sessions.

● Vetoed bills are not dealt with directly by the Congress but are buried in other pending legislation.

● Phony numbers are used to estimate budgets and to cover up the true costs of legislation.

Even worse, outright offenses against ethical standards and public laws are treated lightly. National security leaks go unpunished. In the House of Representatives, the Ethics Committee has become a shield for Democrats who get caught but don't get punished.

After 36 years of one-party rule, the House of Representatives is no longer the people's branch of government. It is the broken branch. It is an arrogant oligarchy that has subverted the Constitution. The Democrat congressional leaders:

● Stole a congressional seat from the people of Indiana by barring a duly elected, and officially certified, Republican Member.

● Flagrantly abuse every standard of accepted procedure by adjourning and, contrary to 200 years of House tradition, immediately reconvening in order to create a "new day" and pass legislation previously defeated.

● Deny the century-old right of the minority party to offer its final alternatives to bills.

● Change House rules to prevent debate and thwart the offering of amendments.

● Rig adoption of substantive legislation on mere procedural votes, so their followers won't be accountable on controversial votes to the people back home.

● Protect their cronies charged with personal misconduct or criminal activities.

● Refuse to allow the House to vote on issues of tremendous concern to the American people and viciously penalize independent Democrats who vote their conscience.

● Rig the subcommittee system to give themselves artificial majorities and additional staff members.

Republicans want to hold accountable to the people, the Congress and every other element of government. We will:

● Extend the independent counsel law to Congress.

● Apply health and safety laws and civil rights statutes to the Congress.

● Give to whistleblowers on Capitol Hill the same legal protection they have in the executive branch, to encourage employees to report illegalities, corruption and sexual harassment.

● Implement the budget reform agenda outlined elsewhere in this platform — a balanced budget amendment, line-item veto, and other steps—to restore accountability, order, and truth in government to the way Congress spends the people's money.

● Support citizen efforts in the Senate to defeat the gerrymanders that steal seats for Democrat congressmen by denying fair representation to the voters.

● Force democracy into the committee system of the House so that committees and staffs reflect the overall composition of the House.

● We favor a constitutional amendment which would place some restriction on the number of consecutive terms a man or woman may serve in the U.S. House of Representatives or the U.S. Senate.

Educating for the Future

Republican leadership has launched a new era in American education. Our vision of excellence has brought education back to parents, back to basics, and back on a track of excellence leading to a brighter and stronger future for America.

Because education is the key to opportunity, we must make America a nation of learners, ready to compete in the rapidly changing world of the future. Our goal is to combine traditional values and enduring truths with the most modern techniques and technology for teaching and learning.

This challenge will be immense. For two decades before 1981, poor public policies had led to an alarming decline in performance in our schools. Unfocused federal spending seemed to worsen the situation, hamstringing education with regulations and wasting resources in faddish programs top-heavy with administrative overhead.

Then President Reagan and Vice President Bush rallied our "nation at risk." The response was in the best traditions of the American people. In every state, indeed, in every community, individuals and organizations have launched a neighborhood movement for education reform. It has brought together Americans of every race and creed in a crusade for our children's future. Since 1980, average salaries for elementary and secondary teachers have increased to over $28,000, an increase of 20 percent after inflation. We can enhance this record of accomplishment by committing ourselves to these principles:

● Parents have the primary right and responsibility for education. Private institutions, communities, States, and the federal government must support and stimulate that parental role. We support the right of parents to educate their children at home.

● Choice and competition in education foster quality and protect consumers' rights.

● Accountability and evaluation of performance at all levels of education is the key to continuing reform in education. We must reward excellence in learning, in teaching and in administration.

● Values are the core of good education. A free society needs a moral foundation for its learning. We oppose any programs in public schools which provide birth control or abortion services or referrals. Our "first line of defense" to protect our youth from contracting AIDS and other sexually communicable diseases, from teen pregnancy, and from illegal drug use must be abstinence education.

● Quality in education should be available to all our children within the communities and neighborhoods. Federal policy should empower low-income families to choose quality and demand accountability in their children's schooling.

● Throughout all levels of education we must initiate action to reduce the deplorable dropout rate which deprives young people of their full potential.

● Federal programs must focus on students at special risk, especially those with physical disabilities or language deficits, to increase their chance at a productive future in the mainstream of American life.

● Because America's future will require increasingly competent leadership in all walks of life, national policy should emphasize the need to provide our most talented students with special programs to challenge their abilities.

Based on these principles, the Republican agenda for better education looks first to home and family, then to communities and States. In States and localities, we support practical, down-to-earth reforms that have made a proven difference in actual operation:

● Choice in education, especially for poor families, fosters the parental involvement that is essential for student success, and States should consider enacting voucher systems or other means of encouraging competition among public schools.

● Performance testing, both for students and teachers, measures progress, assures accountability to parents and the public, and keeps standards high.

● Merit pay, career ladders, or other rewards for superior teachers acknowledge our esteem for them and encourage others to follow their example of dedication to a profession that is critical to our nation's future.

● Making use of volunteerism from the private sector and providing opportunity for accelerated accreditation for those with needed expertise broadens the classroom experience and encourages excellence.

● Expansions of curriculum to include the teaching of the history, culture, geography and, particularly, the languages of key nations of the world is a necessity. To compete successfully throughout the world, we must acquire the ability to speak the languages of our customers.

● Excellence in the teaching of geography is essential to equipping our people with the ability to capture new markets in all parts of the world.

● Discipline is a prerequisite for learning. Our schools must be models of order and decorum, not jungles of drugs and violence.

On the federal level, Republicans have worked to facilitate State and local reform movements:

● We kept the spotlight on the reform movement through White House leadership, and we refocused the Department of Education to recognize and foster excellence.

● We enacted legislation to ensure equal access to schools for student religious groups and led Congressional efforts to restore voluntary school prayer.

● We led a national crusade against illiteracy, following the example of Barbara Bush.

● We put into law protection for pupils in federally funded programs, to shield students and their families from intrusive research and offensive psychological testing.

● We strengthened education programs by proposing to replace federal aid to schools with direct assistance that would give choice to low-income parents.

● We broke new ground in early childhood development programs, such as Even Start, that emphasize the involvement of parents in the learning process and address adult illiteracy and school readiness education holistically.

● We intervened in court cases to defend the right of students to learn in a safe, drug-free environment.

We will continue to advance that agenda and to expand horizons for learning, teaching, and mastering the future:

● We will protect the Pledge of Allegiance in all schools as a reminder of the values which must be at the core of learning for a free society.

● We will use federal programs to foster excellence, rewarding "Merit Schools" which significantly improve education for their students.

● We will urge our local school districts to recognize the value of kindergarten and pre-kindergarten programs.

● We will direct federal matching funds to promote magnet schools that turn students toward the challenges of the future rather than the failures of the past.

● We will support laboratories of educational excellence in every State by refocusing federal funds for educational research.

● We will increase funding for the Head Start program to help children get a fair chance at learning, right from the beginning.

● We will work with local schools and the private sector to develop models for evaluating teachers and other school officials.

● We will continue to support tuition tax credits for parents who choose to educate their children in private educational institutions.

● We would establish a public-private partnership using the Department of Labor's Job Training Partnership Act funds to encourage youth to stay in school and graduate. The Labor Department funds would be made available to local employers and business groups to hire high school students after school and during the summer with the requirement that they keep their grades at a "C" average or above until graduation.

In higher education, Republicans want to promote both opportunity and responsibility:

• We will keep resources focused on low-income students and address the barriers that discourage minority students from entering and succeeding in institutions of higher education.

• We are determined to reverse the intolerable rates of default in the guaranteed student loan program to make more money available to those who really need to borrow it.

• We will keep the spotlight of public attention on the college cost spiral—running far ahead of inflation overall—and challenge administrators to exercise more fiscal responsibility.

• We will create a College Savings Bond program, with tax-exempt interest, to help families save for their children's higher education.

• We will condition federal aid to post-secondary institutions upon their good faith effort to maintain safe and drug-free campuses.

• We will insist freedom of speech is not only a fundamental right, it is one of the first lines of education. This freedom should be afforded to all speakers with a minimum of harassment.

• We will continue education benefits for veterans of military service and advance the principle that those who serve their country in the armed forces have first call on federal education assistance.

• We will continue the Reagan-Bush policy of emphasizing vocational-technical education. A large number of jobs in our society require secondary and post-secondary vocational-technical education. Federal programs and policies must recognize and enhance vocational-technical students.

• We will support educational programs in federal prisons that will allow prisoners the opportunity to become literate and to learn an employable skill. We encourage similar programs at the state level.

To compete globally, our society must prepare our children for the world of work. We cannot allow one of every eight 17-year-olds to remain functionally illiterate. We cannot allow 1 million students to drop out of high school every year, most of them without basic skills; therefore, we must teach them reading, writing and mathematics. We must re-establish their obligation to learn.

Education for the future means more than formal schooling in classrooms. About 75 percent of our current workforce will need some degree of retraining by the year 2000. More than half of all jobs we will create in the 1990s will require some education beyond high school, and much of that will be obtained outside of regular educational institutions. Unprecedented flexibility in working arrangements, career changes, and a stampede of technological advances are ushering us into an era of lifelong learning. Therefore, we support employment training programs at all levels of government such as the Job Training Partnership Act and the recently restructured Worker Adjustment Program for dislocated workers. The placement success of these programs can be directly traced to their public/private sector partnerships and local involvement in their program development and implementation.

In the 1960s and 1970s, we learned what doesn't solve the problems of education: federal financing and regimentation of our schools. In the 1980s, we asserted what works: parental responsibility, community support and local control, good teachers and determined administrators, and a return to the basic values and content of western civilization. That combination gave generations of Americans the world's greatest opportunities for learning. It can guarantee the same for future generations.

Arts and Humanities

Republicans consider the resurgence of the arts and humanities a vital part of getting back to basics in education. Our young people must acquire more than information and skills. They must learn to reason and to appreciate the intellectual achievements that express the enduring values of our civilization. To that end, we will:

• Continue the Republican economic renaissance which has made possible a tremendous outpouring of support for arts and humanities.

• Support full deductibility for donations to tax-exempt cultural institutions in order to encourage the private support of arts and humanities.

• Support the National Endowments for the Arts and Humanities and the Institute of Museum Services in their effort to support America's cultural institutions, artists, and scholars.

• Guard against the misuse of governmental grants by those who attack or derogate any race or creed and oppose the politicization of the National Endowments for the Arts and Humanities.

While recognizing the diversity of our people, we encourage educational institutions to emphasize in the arts and humanities those ideas and cultural accomplishments that address the ethical foundations of our culture.

Science and Technology

Our nation's continuing progress depends on scientific and technological innovation. It is America's economic fountain of youth. Republicans advocate a creative partnership between government and the private sector to ensure the dynamism and creativity of scientific research and technology:

• We recognize that excellence in education, and especially scientific literacy, is a precondition for progress, and that economic growth makes possible the nation's continuing advancement in scientific research.

• We consider a key priority in any increased funding for the National Science Foundation the retooling of science and engineering labs at colleges and universities.

• We endorse major national projects like the superconducting Super Collider.

• We will ensure that tax policy gives optimum incentive for the private sector to fund a high level of advanced research. Toward that end, we will make permanent the current tax credit for research and development and extend it to cooperative research ventures.

• We will strengthen the role of science and engineering in national policy by reinforcing the Office of the President's Science Advisor with the addition of a Science Advisory Council.

• We will encourage exchange of scientific information, especially between business and academic institutions, to speed up the application of research to benefit the public.

• We will improve the acquisition of scientific and technical information from other countries through expedited translation services and more aggressive outreach by federal agencies.

• We will include international technology flows as part of U.S. trade negotiations to ensure that the benefits of foreign advances are available to Americans.

• We will encourage innovation by strengthening protection for intellectual property at home and abroad. We will promote the public benefits that come from commercialization of research conducted under federal sponsorship by allowing private ownership of intellectual property developed in that manner.

• We will oppose regulation which stifles competition and hinders breakthroughs that can transform life for the better in areas like biotechnology.

That is an agenda for more than science and technology. It will broaden economic opportunity, sustain our ability to compete globally, and enhance the quality of life for all.

Space

The Republican Party will re-establish U.S. preeminence in space. It is our nation's frontier, our manifest destiny. President Reagan has set ambitious goals for a space comeback. We are determined to meet them and move on to even greater challenges.

We support further development of the space station, the National Aerospace Plane, Project Pathfinder, a replacement shuttle, and the development of alternate launch vehicles. We endorse Mission to Planet Earth for space science to advance our understanding of environmental and climatic forces.

A resurgent America, renewed economically and in spirit, must get on with its business of greatness. We must commit to manned flight to Mars around the year 2000 and to continued exploration of the Moon.

These goals will be achievable only with full participation by private initiative. We welcome the Reagan-Bush initiative to increase the role of the private sector in transport, particularly in the launch of commercial satellites. The Reagan-Bush Administration's proposed space station will allow the private sector additional opportunities in the area of research and manufacturing.

Our program for freedom in space will allow millions of American investors to put their money on the future. That's one of the ways to lift the conquest of space out of the congressional budget logjam. Republicans believe that America must have a clear vision for the future of the space program, well defined goals, and streamlined implementation, as we reach for the stars.

Strong Communities and Neighborhoods

Crime. Republicans want a free and open society for every American. That means more than economic advancement alone. It requires the safety and security of persons and their property. It demands an end to crime.

Republicans stand with the men and women who put their lives on the line every day, in State and local police forces and in federal law enforcement agencies. We are determined to re-establish safety in the streets of those communities where the poor, the hard-working, and the elderly now live in fear. Despite opposition from liberal Democrats, we've made a start:

• The rate of violent crimes has fallen 20 percent since 1981. Personal thefts fell 21 percent, robberies fell 31 percent, assaults fell 17 percent, and household burglaries fell 30 percent.

• In 1986, crimes against individuals reached their lowest level in 14 years.

• The Reagan-Bush Administration has crusaded for victims' rights in trials and sentencing procedures and has advocated restitution by felons to their victims.

• We have been tough on white-collar crime, too. We have filed more criminal antitrust cases than the previous Administration.

• We pushed an historic reform of toughened sentencing procedures for federal courts to make the punishment fit the crime.

• We appointed to the courts judges who have been sensitive to the rights of victims and law-abiding citizens.

We will forge ahead with the Republican anti-crime agenda:

• We must never allow the presidency and the Department of Justice to fall into the hands of those who coddle hardened criminals. Republicans oppose furloughs for those criminals convicted of first degree murder and others who are serving a life sentence without possibility of parole. We believe that victims' rights should not be accorded less importance than those of convicted felons.

• We will re-establish the federal death penalty.

• We will reform the exclusionary rule, to prevent the release of guilty felons on technicalities.

• We will reform cumbersome habeas corpus procedures, used to delay cases and prevent punishment of the guilty.

• We support State laws implementing preventive detention to allow courts to deny bail to those considered dangerous and likely to commit additional crimes.

The election of 1988 will determine which way our country deals with crime. A Republican President and a Republican Congress can lay the foundation for a safer future.

Drug-Free America. The Republican Party is committed to a drug-free America. Our policy is strict accountability, for users of illegal drugs as well as for those who profit by that usage.

The drug epidemic didn't just happen. It was fueled by the liberal attitudes of the 1960s and 1970s that tolerated drug usage. Drug abuse directly threatens the fabric of our society. It is part of a worldwide narcotics empire whose $300 billion business makes it one of the largest industries on earth.

The Reagan-Bush Administration has set out to destroy it. In the past six years, federal drug arrests have increased by two-thirds. Compared with 1980, two and a half times as many drug offenders were sent to prison in 1987. Federal spending for drug enforcement programs more than tripled in the last seven years. And we have broken new ground by enlisting U.S. intelligence agencies in the fight against drug trafficking.

Drug usage in our armed forces has plummeted as a direct result of an aggressive education and random testing program. In 1983, we instituted random drug testing in the Coast Guard. At that time, 10.3 percent of the tests showed positive drug usage. As a result of this testing program, the positive usage rate fell dramatically to 2.9 percent in 1987. The Reagan-Bush Administration has also undertaken efforts to insure that all those in safety related positions in our transportation system are covered by similar drug testing requirements. We commend this effort.

We are determined to finish the job.

• The Republican Party unequivocally opposes legalizing or decriminalizing any illicit drug.

• We support strong penalties, including the death penalty for major drug traffickers.

• User accountability for drug usage is long overdue. Conviction for any drug crime should make the offender ineligible for discretionary federal assistance, grants, loans and contracts for a period of time.

• To impress young Americans with the seriousness of our fight against drugs, we urge States to suspend eligibility for a driver's license to anyone convicted of a drug offense.

• We urge school districts to get tough on illegal drug use by notifying parents and police whenever it is discovered.

• We will encourage tougher penalties for those who use children in illegal narcotics operations.

• We will require federal contractors and grantees to establish a drug-free workplace with the goal that no American will have to work around drug abuse.

• We will suspend passports from those convicted of major drug offenses.

• To protect residents of public housing, we will evict persons dealing in drugs. We will foster resident review committees to screen out drug abusers and dealers. We will promote tenant management as the surest cure for the drug plague in public projects.

• We will strengthen interdiction of foreign drugs and expand the military's role in stopping traffickers.

• We will work with foreign governments to eradicate drug crops in their countries.

• In a summit of Western Hemisphere nations, we will seek total cooperation from other governments in wiping out the international drug empire.

• In addition to our enforcement activities, we encourage drug education in our schools. These programs should begin as early as the elementary school years, before children are subjected to peer pressure to experiment with drugs, and should continue through high school. Cutting down on the demand for drugs will be of great assistance as we increase our enforcement efforts to reduce drug supply.

• We will encourage seizure and forfeiture programs by the Department of the Treasury and each State to take the profits out of illicit drug sales.

We commend our fellow citizens who are actively joining the war against drugs. Drug dealers are domestic terrorists, and we salute the heroic residents of poor neighborhoods who have boldly shut down crack houses and run traffickers out of their communities.

We recognize the need to improve the availability of drug rehabilitation and treatment.

There's a bright side to the picture. We know the most powerful deterrent to drug abuse: strong, stable family life, along with the absolute approach summed up in "Just Say No." Nancy Reagan has made that phrase the battle-cry of the war against drugs, and it is echoed by more than 10,000 Just Say No clubs. We salute her for pointing the way to our nation's drug-free future.

Opportunity and Assistance. Our country's economic

miracle of the last eight years has been the most successful assault on poverty in our era. Millions of families have worked their way into the mainstream of national life. The poverty rate continues to decline. However, many remain in poverty, and we pledge to help them in their struggle for self-sufficiency and independence.

For most of our country's history, helping those less fortunate was a community responsibility. Strong families pulled together, and strong communities cared for those in need. That is more than a description of the past. It is a prescription for the future, pointing the way toward real reform of today's welfare mess through these Republican principles:

● We support the maintenance of income assistance programs for those who cannot work. In particular, we recognize our responsibility to ensure a decent standard of living for the aged, the disabled, and children dependent upon the community.

● Poverty can be addressed by income assistance or in-kind services. Dependency, on the other hand, requires a comprehensive strategy to change patterns of attitude and behavior. We will work to address both poverty and dependency.

● Work is an essential component of welfare reform, and education is an essential component of employability. Welfare reform must require participation in education and work, and provide day care assistance and continued access to Medicaid during the transition to full independence.

● Fathers of welfare dependent children must be held accountable by mandating paternity determinations and requiring the participation of unemployed fathers in education and work programs.

● State and local administration of education, work, and welfare programs is best for both the taxpayers and those in need.

● State and local pilot programs in welfare are the cutting edge of welfare reform. States should be granted the authority by the federal government to pursue innovative programs which return teen mothers to school and welfare recipients to work. Congressional Democrats are blocking the expansion of this vital process. A Republican Congress will give the States authority to meet local needs.

● Welfare fraud is an offense against both the taxpayers and the poor. Whether perpetrated by participants or providers of services, its eradication is an essential component of a compassionate welfare policy.

We are committed to assisting those in need. We are equally committed to addressing the root causes of poverty. Divorce, desertion, and illegitimacy have been responsible for almost all the increase in child poverty in the last 15 years. Because strong family life is the most remarkable anti-poverty force in history, Republicans will make the reinforcement of family rights and responsibilities an essential component of public policy. Stronger enforcement of child support laws must be an important part of that effort, along with revision of State laws which have left many women and children vulnerable to economic distress.

Children in poverty deserve our strongest support. We are committed to safer neighborhoods and full prosecution for child abuse and exploitation. We will reach out to these children through Head Start and targeted education, basic health and nutrition assistance, local community efforts and individual concern. But something more is required to fulfill the hope for self-sufficiency: a job in an expanding economy. The most compassionate policy for children in need is the chance for families to stand on their own feet in a society filled with opportunity.

Fighting poverty means much more than distributing cash. It includes education and work programs. It means reducing illiteracy, the single greatest indicator of life-long poverty. It involves combating crime so that the homes and earnings of the poor are secure. It includes Republican reforms in public housing, like resident management and ownership. It requires regulatory reforms to open up opportunities for those on the margins of the work force. It means streamlining adoption rules and ensuring poor parents a real say in their children's educations. Above all, it means maintaining a strong, healthy economy that creates jobs.

Urban Revitalization. Urban America is center stage of our country's future. That is why we address its problems and

potential throughout this platform, rather than limiting our concern to a particular section. In doing so, Republicans follow three broad principles:

● Economic growth is the most important urban program. Because we cut taxes, a new prosperity has transformed many towns and cities. Because we forced down inflation, cities pay much lower bond rates. Because we created 17.5 million new jobs through a thriving economy, millions of urban residents have seized the opportunity to escape welfare and unemployment. Because we slashed regulatory burdens, enterprise is transforming areas untouched by government programs of past years.

● Local control is the best form of administration. That's why we merged federal programs into block grants for community development and housing.

● Citizen choice is the key to successful government. Options in education empower parents and attract new residents. Options in public housing transform slums into real communities, bustling with enterprise and hope.

Building on those principles, Republicans will advance our urban agenda which is to:

● Enterprise zones, where tax incentives and regulatory reforms open the way for creating jobs and rebuilding neighborhoods from the ground up which have been blocked by the Democrats in Congress.

● Resident control—both management and ownership—of public housing, with a goal of transferring one-third of the country's public housing space to tenants by 1995.

● Urban homesteading and other programs to ensure affordable housing opportunities in our cities.

● Emergency waiver of Davis-Bacon wage requirements for cities with severe deterioration of the public infrastructure.

● Contract out public services to workers in the private sector.

● Education assistance directed to low-income households instead of aid to institutions that fail to meet their needs.

● Continued reduction in crime rates, especially street crime and the violence that destroys community life.

● Unrelenting war on drugs.

● Greater control by local government in federally assisted programs, especially transportation and housing.

● Steady environmental progress to ensure clean air and clean water to our cities and assist local governments in solving their solid waste disposal problems in order to make our cities safe and healthy places to live.

● Special attention to urban residents in the national census, to ensure that cities are not shortchanged in federal representation or in federal programs based upon population.

Rural Community Development And the Family Farm

Republicans see a robust future for American agriculture. Rural America is our country's heartland and pillar of economic and moral strength. From its small towns and communities comes more than the world's greatest bounty of food. From them also comes a commitment to the land by a proud and independent people.

For much of this century, the first line of defense against world hunger has been the American farmer and rancher. In the future as in the past, the enterprise of rural Americans will be crucial to the progress of our country and of mankind. The entire nation—and indeed, the world—benefits from their unsurpassed productivity.

When farmers and ranchers face adversity, the communities that depend on them do, too. When farmers' income falls, the earnings of others follow. When agriculture suffers, the tax base and public services of whole regions decline.

That is why the current drought is an emergency for our entire country. It will affect every American: the way we live, the food we eat, the land we cherish. We cannot promise to bring rain, but we can bend every arm of government to provide for the expeditious relief of farmers and ranchers in trouble. We pledge to do so. We will focus assistance on those most seriously hurt by the drought.

With strong Republican support in the House and Senate, a major relief bill has been signed by President Reagan.

The Record

Some disasters are man-made. In the late 1970s, American agriculture bore the brunt of bad public policy. Long thereafter, farmers suffered the consequences of those four years of devastating Democrat mismanagement. Inflation drove production costs and farm debt to their highest levels in history. To top it off, the Democrats' embargo of grain and other agricultural products dealt a blow to the nation's heartland from which many farmers never recovered.

NEVER AGAIN!

For eight years, Ronald Reagan and George Bush have provided the leadership to turn that situation around. Despite strong Democrat opposition, Republicans have made a good beginning. Because of Republican policies, America's farm and rural sector is coming alive again:

• Inflation, unemployment, and interest rates are at their lowest levels in years. Our dollar exchange rate is more competitive.

• Land values, the best indicator of farm prospects, have stabilized and are rising in many areas.

• Farm credit institutions, both public and private, are back on their feet.

• Farm debt has been reduced from $193 billion in 1983 to a projected $137 billion in 1988.

• Net farm income increased to its highest level ever in 1987, reaching $46 billion, while net cash income was also a record at $57 billion.

• We have reduced price-depressing surpluses to their lowest levels in many years. Total grain surpluses have been cut in half from their high in 1986.

In summary, increased agricultural exports, higher commodity and livestock prices, increased profits and land values, declining farm debt and surpluses, all these point to a healthier outlook for the rural economy.

The recovery is no accident. Republicans have acted decisively in the interest of rural America. Look at the record:

• In 1981, we immediately halted the Democrats' embargo on grain and other agricultural products and kept our pledge always to be a reliable supplier. We now reaffirm our promise never to use food as a weapon as was done by the last Democrat Administration.

• We have successfully opened more markets for our agricultural commodities and value-added products around the world through competitive pricing, aggressive use of the Export Enhancement Program, the Targeted Export Assistance Program, marketing loans, and generic commodity certificates.

• Through tough trade negotiations, we have opened markets abroad including the Japanese beef and citrus markets. Numerous markets for specialty products have also been opened.

• We ended the notorious "widow's tax" so surviving spouses don't have to sell family farms and ranches to meet inheritance taxes. We also reduced other burdensome inheritance taxes for farm and ranch families.

• In 1985, President Reagan signed one of the most successful farm bills in modern history. The dual goals of protecting farm income while gaining back our lost markets are being achieved.

• We have given farmers the opportunity to profitably retire millions of acres of erodible and generally less productive land through the Conservation Reserve Program, and we enacted legislation to ensure that taxpayers' dollars will not be used to subsidize soil erosion or otherwise damage the environment that makes rural America a place where people want to live.

The Democrats offer nothing for the future of farming. Their plan for mandatory production controls would make productive and efficient American farmers beat a full-scale retreat from the world market:

• It would be a boon to family farms—in Argentina, Brazil, Canada, the European Community, Australia, and other competitor nations.

• It would pull the plug on rural Americans. It would sound a death-knell for rural towns and cities as land is taken from production. According to a United States Department of Agriculture study, it would reduce Gross National Product by $64 billion and wipe out 2.1 million jobs in the private sector.

In short, Democrats want to put farmers on welfare while Republicans want to look after the welfare of all rural Americans.

Our Global Economy

Better than most people, agriculturists know we live in a global economy. America's farmers, ranchers, foresters, and fishermen can compete against anyone in the world if trade rules are fair.

We recognize the historical contribution of agricultural exports to a positive national trade balance and will work on all fronts to improve agricultural trade.

Republicans will aggressively pursue fair and free trade for all U.S. products:

• We will insist that production-, consumption-, and trade-distorting agricultural subsidies of the European Economic Community and others be phased out simultaneously with the phasing out of our farm and export assistance programs.

• We will continue to put free and fair trade for farmers and ranchers on the agenda of every international conference on trade.

• We will use free trade agreements with good trading partners as leverage to open markets elsewhere.

• We will be a reliable supplier of agricultural products to world markets and will not use food as a weapon of foreign policy.

In short, instead of retreat, Republicans promise a full-scale assault on foreign markets.

The Future

Republicans will work to improve agricultural income through market returns at home and abroad, not government controls and subsidies:

• We pledge early action to renew and improve the successful farm programs set to expire in 1990.

• We pledge to continue international food assistance, including programs through the Eisenhower Food for Peace program, to feed the world's hungry and develop markets abroad.

• We will continue to provide leadership in the effort to improve standards of quality for grain and other agricultural products in order to meet international competition.

• We call for greater planting flexibility in federal programs to allow more diversity in farming and more freedom for farmers to grow what they want to grow and to sell their products to whoever will buy them.

• We recognize the need for appropriate multiple-use policy on federal range lands and retention of a fair and equitable grazing fee policy as has been established by the Reagan Administration.

• We support a State's review of the adequacy of crop irrigation capacity under severe water shortage conditions, such as the 1988 drought, to identify areas of potential need and development.

• Water use policy formulation belongs to the States without federal interference; we recognize traditional State supremacy in water law, which is the best bulwark against future water crises.

• We resolve to lower tax rates for long-term capital gains and to work for fairer preproductive expense capitalization laws, including the so-called "heifer tax" as just one example, to promote investment in the production of food and fiber.

• We stand with the nation's foresters and the communities that depend on the forest products industry in supporting an annual timber harvest and multiple-use policy that meets national needs both for a sustained yield of wood products and for sound environmental management.

• We will continue our strong support for agricultural research, including increased emphasis on developing new uses for farm products, such as alternative fuels, food, non-food and industrial products. The agricultural industry is, and always has been, on the leading edge of the technological revolution, and it must continue this tradition in order to be internationally competitive.

• We will encourage public and private research and technical assistance to ensure that the resource base of American agriculture is preserved. Sound stewardship of our land and water resources is important for this and future generations. The soil and water resources of our nation must provide profit for farmers and ranchers and a safe and wholesome food supply. Our Land Grant institutions, working with the private sector, can provide more environmentally safe and biodegradable agrichemicals and improved farming techniques that will help preserve the quality of our underground and surface water supplies.

• We pledge that State farm home exemption and redemption rights shall remain inviolate from federal interference.

Rural Economic Development

Republicans realize that rural communities face challenges that go beyond agricultural concerns. Rural economic development is about more than jobs; it is also about the quality of life. We are ready to address the needs of rural America with creativity and compassion:

• The best jobs program for rural Americans is a good farm program.

• The key to rural development is effective local leadership working in partnership with private businesses and federal, State, and local governments. We will advance, in Congress and at the State level, rural enterprise zones to attract investment and create jobs geared to the opportunities of the century ahead.

• Education is the crucial element to ensuring that rural Americans will be in the mainstream of our national future. We must assure rural youngsters quality education and good schools.

• The roads, bridges, schools, sewer and water systems, and other public works of many rural communities have deteriorated. We will ensure that those communities receive their fair share of aid under federal assistance programs.

• Discrimination against rural hospitals and medical practices in federal reimbursement of health care costs has contributed to reduced medical services in rural America. We pledge to help rural Americans meet their health care needs and will ensure fair treatment for their health care institutions under federal health programs.

• To have full participation in our country's unbounded future, rural people will need access to modern telecommunications and satellite communications systems including commercial decryption devices. Adequate supplies of reasonably priced electric power are also a necessity. We continue to support a strong rural electrification and telephone program. We believe the network of local rural electric and telephone cooperatives that provide these services represents a vital public/private partnership necessary to assure growth and development of the rural economy.

• We will energetically use the Job Training Partnership Act and a newly enacted worker retraining program to ensure that rural workers are fully integrated into the work force of the future.

• We will continue to support programs that enhance housing, business, and industry opportunities for rural Americans; and we will adapt urban homesteading programs to rural communities.

• Sound agricultural policy for rural America demands sound economic policy for all America. We will continue to stabilize fiscal and monetary policies in order to keep inflation in check and interest rates stable. This foundation of economic stability must underly all rural initiatives by all levels of government.

This is our pledge for the continuing renewal of a prosperous rural America.

Energy for the Future

To make real their vision for the future, the American people need adequate, safe, and reliable supplies of energy. Both the security of our nation and the prosperity of our households will depend upon clean and affordable power to light the way ahead and speed a daring society toward its goals. We recognize that energy is a security issue as well as an economic issue. We cannot have a strong nation if we are not energy independent.

We are part way there. In 1981, Republican leadership replaced the Democrats' energy crisis with energy consensus. We rejected scarcity, fostered growth, and set course for an expansive future. We left behind the days of gasoline lines, building temperature controls, the multi-billion dollar boondoggle of Synfuels Corporation, and the cancellation of night baseball games.

The Carter-Mondale years of crippling regulation and exorbitant costs are a thing of the past. We returned the country to policies that encourage rather than discourage domestic production of energy. With a free, more competitive system of producing and marketing energy, American consumers gained a wider range of energy choices at lower prices.

During the Reagan-Bush years, we loosened OPEC's [Organization of Petroleum Exporting Countries] hold on the world's petroleum markets. The United States built up its Strategic Petroleum Reserve and persuaded its allies to increase their emergency petroleum stocks as both a deterrent and a cushion against supply disruptions. When President Reagan and Vice President Bush took office, the Strategic Petroleum Reserve held only 79 million barrels. Now it contains almost 550 million, a three-month cushion in the event of a crisis.

Conservation and energy efficiency, stimulated by the oil shocks of the 1970s, made impressive gains. The nation now consumes less oil, and no more energy in total, than it did in 1977, despite the remarkable growth in our economy under the Reagan-Bush Administration.

Despite these gains, much hard work remains. A strong energy policy is required to assure that the needs of our society are met. Because of low oil prices, domestic oil and gas production has declined significantly. New initiatives will be required to halt the erosion of the domestic oil reserve base, to restore the vitality of the domestic oil and gas industry, to slow the rise in oil imports, and to prevent a return to the vulnerabilities of the 1970s. We must maintain the progress made in conservation and rely more heavily on secure American fuels: domestic oil, natural gas, coal, nuclear energy, alternative sources and renewables.

Oil

The United States is heavily dependent on oil, which represents 40 percent of our total energy consumption. We must have a healthy domestic industry to assure the availability of this fuel to meet our needs. The decline in oil prices has brought exploratory drilling in the country to a virtual standstill, and continuing low prices threaten the hundreds of thousands of small wells that make up the most of U.S. production.

We will set an energy policy for the United States to maintain a viable core industry and to ensure greater energy self sufficiency through private initiatives. We will adopt forceful initiatives to reverse the decline of our domestic oil production. Republicans support:

• Repeal of the counterproductive Windfall Profits Tax.

• Maintenance of our schedule for filling the Strategic Petroleum Reserve to reach 750 million barrels by 1993 and encouragement of our allies to maintain similar reserves.

• Tax incentives to save marginal wells, to encourage exploration for new oil, and to improve the recovery of oil still in place.

• Repeal of the Transfer Rule prohibiting independent producers from using certain tax provisions on acquired properties.

• Elimination of 80 percent of intangible drilling costs as an alternative minimum tax preference item.

• Exploration and development in promising areas, including federal lands and waters, particularly in the Arctic, in a manner that is protective of our environment and is in the best national interest.

Such continued exploration and development of new domestic oil and gas reserves are essential to keep our nation from becoming more dependent on foreign energy sources. Indeed, tax incentives can make our investment in U.S. oil and gas exploration competitive with other countries. They can stimulate drilling, put people back to work, and help maintain our leadership in oilfield technology and services. Incentives and opportunities for increased domestic exploration can also help limit the rise in imports, discourage oil price shocks and enhance energy security.

Natural Gas

Natural gas is a clean, abundant, and reasonably priced fuel secure within the borders of the nation. Increased reliance on natural gas can have significant national security and environmental benefits. While U.S. gas resources are plentiful and recoverable at competitive prices, regulatory burdens and price controls still impede development.

More progress must be made in deregulation of natural gas:

● We support fully decontrolling prices and providing more open access to transportation.

● We also support the flexible use of natural gas to fuel automobiles and boilers.

Over the longer term, natural gas as an alternative fuel could significantly reduce overdependence on imported oil, while also improving air quality. We should support cost effective development and greater use of this fuel.

Coal

The United States enjoys a rich national endowment of enormous supplies of coal which can provide a secure source of energy for hundreds of years.

● We should aggressively pursue the clean coal technology initiative successfully launched by the Reagan-Bush Administration as part of the solution to coal's environmental problem.

● A major effort should be made to encourage coal exports, which could improve the trade balance, put Americans to work, and provide reliable energy supplies to our allies.

Nuclear Power

We must preserve nuclear power as a safe and economic option to meet future electricity needs. It generates 20 percent of our electricity, and we anticipate the continued expansion of renewable energy and environmentally safe nuclear power. We will promote the adoption of standardized, cost-effective, and environmentally safe nuclear plant designs. We should enhance our efforts to manage nuclear waste and will insist on the highest standards of safety.

Technology, Alternatives, Conservation and Regulation

Technology is America's competitive edge, and it should be encouraged in finding new solutions to our energy problems. Energy efficiency improvements such as more efficient cars, better insulated homes, and more efficient industrial processes, have resulted in substantial savings, making the U.S. economy more competitive.

● We support funding for research and development, particularly where current market economics preclude private initiative.

● We will set priorities and, where cost effective, support research and development for alternative fuels such as ethanol, methanol, and compressed natural gas, particularly for use in transportation.

● We will also support research and development for energy efficiency, conservation, renewables, fusion and superconductivity.

● We encourage the improvement of our national electricity transportation network, to achieve the economic and environmental efficiencies and reliability of linking electricity-exporting regions with importers.

Substantial progress has been made in eliminating the intrusive and costly regulatory functions of the Department of Energy and should be continued. Efforts should be made to streamline the department's functions and evaluate its long-term institutional role in setting national energy policy, in discouraging a return to regulation, and in promoting long-term scientific research.

We believe continued economic progress requires an adequate and secure supply of electricity from every possible source in addition to energy conservation. Conservation alone cannot meet the energy needs of a growing economy. Witness the case of Massachusetts, where the State government's energy policy of stopping construction of any significant electric generating plants of all kinds has caused a dangerous shortage.

Preserving and Protecting the Environment

The Republican Party has a long and honored tradition of preserving and protecting our nation's natural resources and environment. We recognize that the preservation, conservation, and protection of our environment contribute to our health and well-being and that, as citizens, we all share in the responsibility to safeguard our God-given resources. A great Republican President, Teddy Roosevelt, once characterized our environmental challenge as "the great central task of leaving this land even a better land for our descendants than it is for us." Satisfying this imperative requires dedication and a commitment both to the protection of our environment and to the development of economic opportunities for all through a growing economy.

Republicans have led the efforts to protect the environment.

● We have dramatically reduced airborne lead contamination. This reduction has been perhaps the most important contribution to the health of Americans living in urban areas.

● By almost any measure, the air is vastly improved from the 1970s. Carbon monoxide, sulphur dioxide, ozone, nitrogen dioxide, and other emissions have declined substantially.

● We brought record numbers of enforcement cases against toxic polluters based on the principle that polluters should pay for the damages they cause.

● We pioneered an international accord for the protection of the stratospheric ozone layer, the first such international agreement.

● Dramatic progress has been made in protecting coastal barrier islands, in reducing coastal erosion, and in protecting estuaries.

● We have led the fight to clean up our Great Lakes and the Chesapeake and Narragansett Bays, some of the most unique and productive ecosystems on earth.

● We encouraged agricultural conservation, enhanced our wetlands, and preserved and restored our national parks, which had suffered tragic neglect in the years preceding the Reagan-Bush Administration.

● Under Republican leadership, the most important soil conservation measure of the last half-century became law as the Conservation Title of the 1985 Farm Bill.

● We established 34 national wildlife refuges in 21 States and territories.

● We reformed U.S. and international aid programs to assist developing nations to assure environmental protection.

Republicans look to the environmental future with confidence in the American people and with a renewed commitment to world leadership in environmental protection. We recognize the necessary role of the federal government only in matters that cannot be managed by regional cooperation or by levels of government closer to the people. Cooperative action by all is needed to advance the nation's agenda for a cleaner, safer environment.

The toughest challenges lie ahead of us. Republicans propose the following program for the environment in the 1990s:

● We will work for further reductions in air and water pollution and effective actions against the threats posed by acid rain. These goals can and must be achieved without harmful economic dislocation.

● We are committed to minimizing the release of toxins into the environment.

● We will continue to lead the effort to develop new clean-coal technologies and to remove the barriers that prevent cleaner, alternative fuels from being used.

● We support a comprehensive plan of action to fight coastal erosion and to protect and restore the nation's beaches, coral reefs, bodies of water, wetlands and estuaries such as the Louisiana coast, Chesapeake Bay, the Great Lakes, San Francisco Bay, Puget Sound, Narragansett Bay, and other environmentally sensitive areas. The restoration of these areas will continue to be a priority.

● A top priority of our country must be the continued improvement of our National Parks and wildlife areas. We must upgrade our recreation, fisheries, and wildlife programs in parks, wildlife refuges, forests, and other public lands. We support efforts, including innovative public-private partnerships, to restore declining waterfowl populations and enhance recreational fisheries.

● We will fight to protect endangered species and to sustain biological diversity worldwide.

● We support federal, State, and local policies, including tax code provisions, which lead to the renewal and revitalization of our environment through restoration and which encourage scenic easements designed to preserve farmland and open spaces.

● We will protect the productive capacity of our lands by minimizing erosion.

● We believe public lands should not be transferred to any special group in a manner inconsistent with current Reagan-Bush Administration policy. To the extent possible, consistent with current policy, we should keep public lands open and accessible.

● We are committed to the historic preservation of our American heritage, including our architectural, archaeological, and maritime resoures.

● We support strong enforcement of our environmental laws and are committed to accelerating the pace of our national effort to clean up hazardous waste sites and to protect our groundwater. We will promote proper use of fertilizers and pesticides to minimize pollution of groundwater.

● Republicans recognize that toxic and hazardous waste production is increasing. Therefore, we will utilize the nation's scientific community to develop solutions to this waste disposal dilemma as an alternative to the continued burying and ocean dumping of these dangerous substances, as they are no more than stop-gap measures with extremely tragic potential.

● We are committed to solving our country's increasing problem of waste disposal. By 1995, half of our existing landfills will be closed, and municipalities will have increased difficulty finding new sites. This is an issue which will require the dedication and resolve of our local communities, the private sector, and all of us as citizens. Resource recovery, recycling, and waste minimalization are critical elements of our solution, and we will work to ensure that innovative approaches to the problem are encouraged.

● We are determined to prevent dumping off our coasts and in international waters. Ocean dumping poses a hazard not only to marine life, but also to those who live along our coasts and to those who use them for recreation. Where federal laws have been violated, we will prosecute polluters to the full extent of the law, including adherence to the 1991 federal ban on ocean dumping of sewage sludge. Where laws need to be strengthened, we will work at the federal, State, and local levels to do so.

● We will support all serious efforts to cope with the special problems of illegal dumping of hospital and medical waste. We pledge close cooperation by the Environmental Protection Agency with States and industry groups to develop new approaches to the most cost-effective means for the safe disposal by responsible medical facilities. Those who continue to dump illegally threaten the very life and health of our communities, and we call for enactment by the States of tough new felony laws that will permit swift prosecution of these criminals.

● We will require that federal departments and agencies meet or exceed the environmental standards set for citizens in the private sector.

Many of the most serious environmental problems that will confront us in the years ahead are global in scope. For example, degradation of the stratospheric ozone layer poses a health hazard not only to Americans, but to all peoples around the globe. The Reagan-Bush Administration successfully pioneered an agreement to attack this problem through worldwide action. In addition, we will continue to lead this effort by promoting private sector initiatives to develop new technologies and adopt processes which protect the ozone layer. A similar ability to develop international agreements to solve complex global problems such as tropical forest destruction, ocean dumping, climate change, and earthquakes will be increasingly vital in the years ahead. All of these efforts will require strong and experienced leadership to lead the other nations of the world in a common effort to combat ecological dangers that threaten all peoples. The Republican Party believes that, toward this end, the National Oceanic and Atmospheric Administration should be joined with the Environmental Protection Agency.

We all have a stake in maintaining the environmental balance and ecological health of our planet and our country. As Republicans, we hold that it is of critical importance to preserve our national heritage. We must assure that programs for economic growth and opportunity sustain the natural abundance of our land and waters and protect the health and well-being of our citizens. As a nation, we should take pride in our accomplishments and look forward to fulfilling our obligation of leaving this land an even better place for our children and future generations.

Transportation for America

Republican leadership has revitalized America's transportation system. Through regulatory reform, we increased efficiency in all major modes of transportation. By making our national transportation system safer, more convenient, and less expensive, we have both strengthened our economy and served the interests of all the American people:

● Aviation deregulation now saves consumers $11 billion annually through improved productivity and lower air fares. Millions more Americans can now afford to fly. Even though more people are flying, the overall safety record for commercial aviation during the past four years has been the best in history.

● The National Airspace System (NAS) Plan is upgrading virtually all the equipment in the air traffic control system to meet safety and capacity needs into the next century.

● Rail freight service has been rescued from the brink of insolvency and revitalized. Railroads have lowered rates for many shippers, helping to keep the transportation cost of coal-generated electric power down and making America's farmers more competitive abroad.

● The creation of regional and short-line railroads has been encouraged by the Reagan-Bush Administration. The development of these small businesses has been a welcome alternative to railroad abandonments, and we will continue to encourage their growth.

● The Reagan-Bush Administration achieved new rail safety legislation which expands federal jurisdiction over drug, alcohol, and safety violations.

● America's trucking industry has also been improved. The number of motor carriers has more than doubled since regulatory barriers to competition were removed. Many of these new carriers are small or minority-owned businesses. Private enterprise has thus been able to restructure routes, reduce empty backhauls, and simplify rates. Reduced regulation saves the American consumer $37 billion annually in lower freight bills, making businesses in every part of America more competitive.

● The successful sale of Conrail through a public offering recouped nearly $2 billion dollars of the taxpayers' investment in bankrupt railroads from the 1970s.

● The Reagan-Bush Administration has undertaken a comprehensive program to upgrade federal interstate highways and bridges.

● Through highway improvements, education, and federal encouragement of tougher State laws against drunk driving, highway safety has vastly improved.

As we look to the future, the Republican Party will continue to press for improved transportation safety, reduced costs, and greater availability and convenience of transportation through more open markets and other mechanisms. The Republican Party believes that:

● Americans demand that those entrusted with their safety while operating commercial motor vehicles, railroads, or aircraft will not use drugs or alcohol. While we will protect individual rights, the Republican Party supports comprehensive efforts to curb drug and alcohol abuse in transportation, including drug and alcohol testing of all those in safety-related positions.

● Our transportation system is based upon a vast public and private investment in infrastructure, which must continue to grow and to be maintained to meet America's needs. We advocate greater local autonomy in decision-making concerning the Highway Trust Fund and the Airport and Airway Trust Fund, and we oppose diversion of their resources to other purposes.

● Research should be developed for new technologies to deal with urban gridlock and congested highways.

● The travel and tourism industry is a positive force in enhancing cultural understanding and sustaining economic prosperity. We recognize its important contributions and should work to encourage its continued growth.

• The federal government and local communities must work together to develop additional airport capacity of all types. At the same time, we support timely completion of the National Airspace System plan and continuing augmentation of air traffic control and aircraft inspection personnel.

• We will further increase American jobs and trade opportunities by assuring that American air carriers are afforded full and fair access to international route authorities.

• We will not abandon the economic flexibility that has so enormously strengthened the health of our railroads and so powerfully benefited the American economy.

• Development of high speed rail systems to meet the needs for intercity travel should be encouraged.

• Year by year since 1981, Amtrak operations have shown improvement. Amtrak's ratio of revenues to costs stood at 48 percent in 1981. Last year, 65 percent of the costs were covered by revenues. Fiscal year 1988 will see the ratio pushing 70 percent. We recognize that intercity rail passenger service plays an important role in our transportation system. At the same time, we support continued reduction in public subsidies.

• A new spirit of competitive enterprise in transportation throughout all levels of government should be encouraged. We will encourage both States and cities to utilize private companies, where effective, to operate commuter bus and transit services at substantial savings over what publicly funded systems cost.

• The engines of innovation powered by regulatory reform have brought forth exciting advances in the technology of trucking, rail, and shipping, particularly as they work together as an integrated system for the movement of goods domestically and abroad. Alternative fuels, that are clean and efficient, will both improve air quality and reduce our dependence on imported oil in meeting transportation needs. These technological approaches are far preferable to outmoded regulation, such as the current design of corporate average fuel economy (CAFE) standards, which create substantial advantages for foreign auto manufacturers and actually promote the export of U.S. jobs.

• We consider a privately owned merchant fleet and domestic shipbuilding capacity necessary to carry our nation's commerce in peace and to support our defense responsibilities. We will support programs to give the American maritime industry greater flexibility and freedom in meeting foreign competition.

• We are committed to continuing the Reagan-Bush Administration efforts to stop foreign protectionism that inhibits U.S. flag vessels from fairly competing abroad.

• Maritime safety, search and rescue, military preparedness, environmental and fisheries enforcement, and drug interdiction have long been the responsibility of the U.S. Coast Guard. The Republican Party supports all of these vital roles, and we will support funding and manpower adequate to enable the Coast Guard to carry out its responsibilities.

America: Leading the World

Under the leadership of President Ronald Reagan and Vice President George Bush, America has led the world through eight years of peace and prosperity.

In the years since 1980, our nation has become in fact what it has always been in principle, "the last best hope of mankind on earth."

Republicans know that free nations are peace loving and do not threaten other democracies. To the extent, therefore, that democracies are established in the world, America will be safer. Consequently, our nation has a compelling interest to encourage and help actively to build the conditions of democracy wherever people strive for freedom.

In 1961, President John Kennedy said, "We shall pay any price, bear any burden, meet any hardship, support any friend, oppose any foe to assure the survival and success of liberty." Seeds sown by the Reagan-Bush Administration to make good on that promise are now bearing fruit.

Today's Republican Party has the only legitimate claim to this legacy, for our opposition to totalitarianism is resolute. For those Democrats who came of age politically under the party of [Harry S.] Truman and Kennedy, the message is clear: The old Democrat world view of realistic anti-communism, with real freedom as its goal, has been abandoned by today's national Democrat Party.

In the tradition of the Republican Party, we have long-term foreign-policy goals and objectives which provide vision and leadership. We also have a *realistic,* long-term strategy to match those goals. The primary objectives of foreign policy must be defending the United States of America and its people; protecting America's vital national interests abroad; and, fostering peace, stability and security throughout the world through democratic self-determination and economic prosperity.

To accomplish these goals, we believe our policies must be built upon three basic pillars: strength, realism, and dialogue.

Republican foreign policy, based on a peace preserved by steadfastly providing for our own security, brought us the INF [Intermediate-Range Nuclear-Force] treaty, which eliminated an entire class of nuclear weapons. America's determination and will, coupled with our European allies' staunch cooperation, brought the Soviets to the bargaining table and won meaningful reductions in nuclear weapons. The INF treaty was not won by unilateral concessions or the unilateral canceling of weapons programs.

Today's Republican foreign policy has been tested and validated. Our formula for success is based on a realistic assessment of the world as it is, not as some would like it to be. The Soviet retreat from Afghanistan is not the result of luck or the need of the Kremlin to save a few rubles. It is a direct result of a Republican policy known as the Reagan Doctrine: our determination to provide meaningful aid to people who would rather die on their feet than live on their knees under the yoke of Soviet-supported oppression. Support for freedom-fighters, coupled with an openness to negotiate, will be the model for our resistance to Marxist expansionism elsewhere.

The world expects the United States to lead. Republicans believe it is in our country's best interest to continue to do so. For this reason, we will engage both our adversaries and friends. We share a common interest in survival and peaceful competition. However, the Reagan-Bush Administration has shown that dialogue and engagement can be successful only if undertaken from a position of strength. We know something the national Democrats seem to have forgotten: If a foreign policy is based upon weakness or unrealistic assumptions about the world, it is doomed to failure. If it is based upon naivete, it will be doomed to disaster.

Under our constitutional system, the execution of foreign policy is the prime responsibility of the executive branch. We therefore denounce the excessive interference in this function by the current Democrat majority in the Congress, as it creates the appearance of weakness and confusion and endangers the successful conduct of American foreign policy.

The world in 1988 shows the success of peace through strength and the Reagan Doctrine advancing America's national interests. Our relations with the Soviets are now based on these determined and realistic policies. Results such as the INF treaty are a concrete example of the soundness of this approach:

• The Afghan people are on the verge of ridding their country of Soviet occupation, and with our continued support they can secure true liberty.

• In Southeast Asia, our policies of isolation toward Vietnam and our support for the Cambodian resistance have contributed to Vietnam's decision to get out of Cambodia.

• In southern Africa, Cuban troops may soon be leaving Angola; Namibia may soon enjoy independence.

• The Iran-Iraq war is closer to a settlement due to the strong leadership of the Reagan-Bush Administration in the United Nations and the American presence in the Persian Gulf.

The party Abraham Lincoln helped to establish—the party of Teddy Roosevelt, Dwight Eisenhower, Ronald Reagan, and George Bush—today offers the United States of America continued leadership, strong and effective. The President of the United States must be a good Commander-in-Chief; the Oval Office is no place for on-the-job training. The Republican Party, tempered by real-world experience, accustomed to making tough choices, is prepared to lead America forward into the 1990s.

The Americas

Our future is intimately tied to the future of the Americas. Family, language, culture, environment and trade link us closely with both Canada and Mexico. Our relations with both of these friends will be based upon continuing cooperation and our mutually shared interests. Our attention to trade and environmental issues will contribute to strong economic growth and prosperity throughout the Americas.

Today, more Latin Americans than ever before live free because of their partnership with the United States to promote self-determination, democracy, and an end to subversion. The Republican party reaffirms its strong support of the Monroe Doctrine as the foundation for our policy throughout the Hemisphere, and pledges to conduct foreign policy in accord with its principles. We therefore seek not only to provide for our own security, but also to create a climate for democracy and self-determination throughout the Americas.

Central America has always been a region of strategic importance for the United States. There, Nicaragua has become a Soviet client state like Cuba. Democratic progress in the region is threatened directly by the Sandinista military machine and armed subversion exported from Nicaragua, Cuba, and the Soviet Union. The Sandinistas are now equipped with Soviet arms which, in quality and quantity, are far in excess of their own defense requirements.

The people of Nicaragua are denied basic human, religious, and political rights by the Sandinista junta. Today, thousands of Nicaraguans are united in a struggle to free their homeland from a totalitarian regime. The Republican Party stands shoulder to shoulder with them with both humanitarian and military aid. Peace without freedom for the Nicaraguan people is not good enough.

If democracy does not prevail, if Nicaragua remains a communist dictatorship dedicated to exporting revolution, the fragile democracies in Central America will be jeopardized. The Republican Party stands with them in their struggle for peace, freedom, and economic growth. We express our emphatic support for the people and government of El Salvador, a target of foreign-directed insurgency. Under Republican leadership, the United States will respond to requests from our Central American neighbors for security assistance to protect their emerging democracies against insurgencies sponsored by the Soviets, Cuba, or others.

Democracy continues to prosper in El Salvador, Guatemala, Honduras, and in Costa Rica, the region's oldest democracy. However, economic growth in these countries has not matched their political progress. The United States must take the lead in strengthening democratic institutions through economic development based on free market principles. We pledge our continued support to the peoples of the Americas who embrace and sustain democratic principles in their self-government.

A Republican Administration will continue to promote policy reforms to free the private sector, such as deregulation of enterprise and privatization of government corporations. We will assist friendly democracies in reviving the institutions of regional economic cooperation and integration, and will allow Nicaragua to participate when it enjoys a free, pluralist society and respects free-market principles.

The growth of democracy and freedom throughout Latin America is one of the most positive foreign policy developments of the 1980s. Republican leadership has created the environment necessary for this growth. Over the past decade, Latin Americans have moved boldly toward democracy, with 26 of 33 nations now democratic or in transition toward democracy. Mexico has a special strategic and economic importance to the United States, and we encourage close cooperation across a wide variety of fronts in order to strengthen further this critical relationship.

We believe the governments of Latin America must band together to defeat the drug trade which now flourishes in the region. We must pledge our full cooperation and support for efforts to induce producers of illicit drug crops to substitute other methods of generating income.

Republicans will continue to oppose any normalization of relations with the government of Cuba as long as Fidel Castro continues to oppress the Cuban people at home and to support international terrorism and drug trafficking abroad. We will vigorously continue our support for establishment of a genuinely representative government directly elected by the Cuban people. We reiterate our support of Radio Marti and urge the creation of TV Marti to better reach the oppressed people of Cuba.

Panama now poses a different challenge to the regional progress made over the past eight years. Our policy must be as firm with respect to military authoritarianism and narco-terrorism as it is with communist tyranny and guerrilla subversion. That policy must include a determined effort to bring to justice any identified narco-terrorist or drug dealer within his or her country of residence or in the courts of the United States of America. Republicans view the Panama Canal as a critical, strategic artery connecting the Atlantic and Pacific. We believe that U.S. access to the Panama Canal must remain free and unencumbered consistent with the foremost principle of the Canal Treaty. We acknowledge, however, the historical partnership and friendship between the American and Panamanian people.

Republicans believe that an active, engaged America, clear of purpose and steady in action, is essential to continued progress in Latin America. Passivity and neglect are a sure prescription for the reversal of freedom and peace in Latin America.

The Soviet Union: New Challenges and Enduring Realities

Steady American leadership is needed now more than ever to deal with the challenges posed by a rapidly changing Soviet Union. Americans cannot afford a future administration which eagerly attempts to embrace perceived, but as yet unproven, changes in Soviet policy. Nor can we indulge naive inexperience or an overly enthusiastic endorsement of current Soviet rhetoric.

The current leaders in the Soviet Union came to power while the United States was undergoing an unsurpassed political, economic, and military resurgence. The Reagan-Bush success story—new jobs and unprecedented economic growth combined with reasserted leadership of the free world—was not lost on the new Soviet regime. It had inherited a bankrupt economy, a society with a Third World standard of living, and military power based upon the sweat of the Soviet workers. Confronted by the failure of their system, the new Soviet leaders have been forced to search for new solutions.

Republicans are proud that it was a Republican President who extended freedom's hand and message to the Soviet Union. It will be a new Republican President who can best build on that progress, ever cautious of communism's long history of expansionism and false promises. We are prepared to embrace real reform, but we will not leave America unprepared should reform prove illusory.

Soviet calls for global peace and harmony ring hollow when compared with ongoing Soviet support for communist guerrillas and governments throughout the Third World. Even in Afghanistan, the Soviet Union is in retreat not as a result of a more benevolent Soviet world view, but because of the courage of determined Mujaheddin freedom fighters fully supported by the United States.

The Soviet military continues to grow. Tanks and aircraft continue to roll off Soviet production lines at a rate two to three times that of the United States.

Soviet military doctrine remains offensive in nature, as illustrated by the intimidating presence of massed Soviet tank divisions in Eastern Europe. This is the reality of Soviet military posture.

With a realistic view of the Soviet Union and the appropriate role of arms reductions in the U.S.-Soviet relationship, the Reagan-Bush Administration concluded the historic INF agreement with the Soviet Union. Ongoing negotiations with the Soviet Union to reduce strategic nuclear weapons by 50 percent are possible because the American people trust Republican leadership. The American people know that, for Republicans, no agreement is better than an agreement detrimental to the security of the free world. To pursue arms control for its own sake or at any cost is naive and dangerous.

Republicans will continue to work with the new Soviet leadership. But the terms of the relationship will be based upon persistent and steady attention to certain fundamental principles:

● Human and religious rights in the Soviet Union.
● Economic reform in the Soviet Union.
● Cessation of Soviet support for communist regimes, radical groups, and terrorists.
● Verified full compliance with all arms control agreements.
● The right of free emigration for all Soviet citizens.
● Reduction in the Soviets' massive offensive strategic and conventional capability. In other words, Soviet military doctrine must match its rhetoric.
● An end to untied credits, particularly general purpose loans which provide the Soviet Union with desperately needed hard currency to bolster its weak economy and facilitate illicit Soviet purchase of U.S. technology.

Republicans proudly reaffirm the Reagan Doctrine: America's commitment to aid freedom-fighters against the communist oppression which destroys freedom and the human spirit. We salute the liberation of Grenada. We affirm our support for the heroic fighters in the Afghan resistance and pledge to see them through to the end of their struggle. We pledge political and material support to democratic liberation movements around the world.

Republicans believe human rights are advanced most where freedom is advanced first. We call on the Soviet government to release political prisoners, allow free emigration for "refuseniks" and others, and introduce full religious tolerance. Soviet Jews, Christians, and other ethnic and religious groups are systematically persecuted, denied the right to emigrate, and prevented from freely practicing their religious beliefs. This situation is intolerable, and Republicans demand an end to all of these discriminatory practices.

We support the desire for freedom and self-determination of all those living in Captive Nations. The Republican Party denounces the oppression of the national free will of Poles, Hungarians, Czechoslovakians, East Germans, Bulgarians, Romanians, and Albanians. We support the desire for freedom of Estonians, Latvians, Lithuanians, Ukrainians, the people of the Caucasus, and other peoples held captive in the Soviet Union. We support the Solidarity free trade union movement in Poland.

We find the violation of human rights on the basis of religion or culture to be morally repugnant to the values we hold. Historical tragedies—like the Holocaust or the terrible persecution suffered by the Armenian people—vividly remind us of the need for vigilance in protecting and promoting human rights. We and others must ensure that such tragedies occur never again.

The Republican Party commends the Reagan-Bush Administration for its far-sighted efforts to modernize our electronic tools of public diplomacy to reach the Captive Nations. The Voice of America, Worldnet, Radio Free Europe and Radio Liberty are on the leading edge of our public diplomacy efforts. These electronic means of communication are force-multipliers of truth. They attack one of the darkest pillars of totalitarianism: the oppression of people through the control of information. We urge the further use of advanced technologies such as Direct Broadcast Satellites and videotape, as well as continuing use of television and radio broadcasting, to articulate the values of individual liberty throughout the world.

Combatting Narcotics: Defending Our Children

By eradication at the source, interdiction in transit, education and deterrence against use, prompt extradition of drug kingpins, or rehabilitation, America must be drug free. No nation can remain free when its children are enslaved by drugs. We consider drugs a major national security threat to the United States.

We urge all nations to unite against this evil. Although we salute our hemispheric neighbors who are fighting the war on drugs, we expect all nations to help stop this deadly commerce. We pledge aggressive interdiction and eradication, with strong penalties against countries which shield or condone the narcotics traffic.

Republicans are proud of the fact that we have dramatically increased the interdiction of dangerous drugs. For example, over the past 6 years, our annual seizure of cocaine has increased by over 1,500 percent. While much has been accomplished in eradicating drugs at the source and in transit, much more remains to be done.

We will use our armed forces in the war on drugs to the maximum extent practical. We must emphasize their special capabilities in surveillance and command and control for interdiction and in special operations for eradication of drugs at the source.

To fight international drug trade, we will stress the swift extradition of traffickers. We support a comprehensive use of America's resources to apprehend and convict drug dealers. To enforce anti-drug policy, we pledge to enhance eradication efforts with increased herbicide use; regulate exports of "precursor chemicals" used in the manufacture of illicit drugs; train and equip cooperating government law-enforcement agencies; emphasize a strategy to "choke off" drug supply routes; and impose the death penalty for drug kingpins and those who kill federal law enforcement agents.

Europe and the Defense of the West

The United States and Europe share a wide array of political, economic, and military relationships, all vitally important to the United States. Together they represent a growing, multifaceted bond between America and the European democracies.

Culturally, as well as militarily, we share common goals with Western Europe. The preservation of liberty is first among these. We will not allow the cultural, economic, or political domination of Western Europe by the Soviet Union. Our own national security requires it, for our democracy cannot flourish in isolation. The United States, led by the Reagan-Bush Administration, and our European allies have successfully reasserted democracy's ideological appeal. This formula is without equal for political and economic progress.

Republicans believe that the continued growth of trade between Europe and the United States is in the best interest of both the American people and their European friends. However, this economic relationship must be based upon the principle of free and fair trade. Protectionism and other barriers to American products will not be tolerated. The American people demand economic fair play in U.S.-European trade.

The recently signed INF treaty has proven that NATO's dual track policy of improving NATO nuclear forces in Europe, while negotiating arms reductions with the Soviet Union, was the only way to make the Soviet leadership accept meaningful nuclear arms reductions. NATO's cohesion as an alliance, when assaulted by Soviet propaganda attacks during the 1980s, proved its resilience. Bolstered by the strong leadership of the United States, Europe stood firm in opposing Soviet demands for a nuclear freeze and unilateral disarmament.

American aid and European industriousness have restored West Europe to a position of global strength. In accord with this, the Republican Party believes that all members of NATO should bear their fair share of the defense burden.

Republicans consider consultation and cooperation with our allies and friends to stop the proliferation of ballistic missile technology is a crucial allied goal. We believe that continued support for the Strategic Defense Initiative will yield the type of defensive insurance policy the American people want for themselves and their allies.

We share a deep concern for peace and justice in Northern Ireland and condemn all violence and terrorism in that strife-torn land. We support the process of peace and reconciliation established by the Anglo-Irish Agreement, and we encourage new investment and economic reconstruction in Northern Ireland on the basis of strict equality of opportunity and non-discrimination in employment.

The Republican Party strongly encourages the peaceful settlement of the long-standing dispute on Cyprus.

The future of U.S. relations with Europe is one of endless opportunity and potential. Increased cooperation and consultation will necessarily lead to greater economic, political and military integration, thus strengthening the natural bonds between the democratic peoples on both sides of the Atlantic. This will require a seasoned American leadership, able to build on the achievements of the Reagan-Bush Administration and prepared to lead the alliance into the 1990s and beyond.

Asia and the Pacific

Democratic capitalism is transforming Asia. Nations of the Pacific Rim have become colleagues in the enterprise of freedom. They have shown a strong capacity for economic growth and capital development.

The Asia-Pacific arena continues to be a vital strategic interest for the U.S. and is an area of increased military, economic, and diplomatic activity for the Soviet Union.

Japan has assumed the role earned by her people as a world economic power. The GOP believes that our relations can only be strengthened by attacking trade barriers, both tariff and nontariff, which not only hurt the U.S. now but also will eventually distort Japan's own economy. We believe that it is time for Japan to assume a greater role in this region and elsewhere. This should include a greater commitment to its own defense, commitment to leading the way in alleviating Third World debt, and fostering economic growth in fragile democracies.

Today, democracy is renewed on Taiwan, the Philippines, and South Korea and is emerging elsewhere in the area. We pledge full cooperation in mutual defense of the Philippines and South Korea and the maintenance of our troops and bases vital for deterring aggression. The United States, with its friends and allies, will strenghten democratic institutions in the Philippines by assisting in its economic development and growth. We reaffirm our commitment to the security of Taiwan and other key friends and allies in the region. We regard any attempt to alter Taiwan's status by force as a threat to the entire region. We adhere to the Taiwan Relations Act, the basis for our continuing cooperation with those who have loyally stood with us, and fought at our side, for half a century.

Today, the communist regime of the People's Republic of China looks to free market practices to salvage its future from stagnant Marxism. We welcome this development. As we draw closer in our relationship, the Republican Party believes that we must continue to encourage the abandonment of political repression in the People's Republic of China and movement toward a free market. We also look toward continued improvement in mutually beneficial trade between our two nations.

We recognize the significant progress made by the Reagan-Bush Administration to assure the end of the Soviet occupation of Afghanistan. We will continue to press for self-determination and the establishment of a genuinely representative government directly elected by the Afghan people. We pledge to continue full military and humanitarian support and supplies for the resistance until complete Soviet withdrawal is realized.

We commend the government of Pakistan for its opposition to the Soviet occupation of Afghanistan and its support of the Afghan people, particularly its refugees. We reaffirm our friendship and will continue the strong security assistance relationship between the United States and Pakistan.

We will press for the withdrawal of Vietnamese occupation of Laos and Cambodia and will continue support for the efforts of the non-Communist resistance.

Republicans insist that Vietnam, Laos, and Cambodia must provide adequate information on American POWs and MIAs. The grief of the POW and MIA families is a constant reminder to all Americans of the patriotic sacrifice made by their missing loved ones. Republicans will not rest until we know the fate of those missing in Indochina. We will continue to press relentlessly for a full accounting of America's POWs and MIAs. We put the government of Vietnam on notice that there will be no improvement in U.S.-Vietnam relations until such a satisfactory full accounting has been provided by the government of Vietnam.

Republicans are committed to providing assistance for refugees fleeing Vietnam, Laos, and Cambodia. Republicans strongly believe that the promise of asylum for these refugees must be met by adequate resources and vigorous administration of refugee programs. We will increase efforts to resettle Vietnamese refugees under the orderly departure program. We are particularly committed to assisting the resettlement of Amerasian children against whom brutal discrimination is practiced.

We recognize the close and special ties we have maintained with Thailand since the days of Abraham Lincoln. Thailand stands tall against the imperialist aggression of Vietnam and the Soviet Union in Southeast Asia.

Republicans strongly support our traditional close bilateral relations with our ally Australia. We also look forward to a rejuvenation of the ANZUS [Australia, New Zealand, and the United States] alliance with its benefits and responsibilities to all partners.

The Middle East

The foundation of our policy in the Middle East has been and must remain the promotion of a stable and lasting peace, recognizing our moral and strategic relationship with Israel. More than any of its predecessors, the Reagan-Bush Administration solidified this partnership. As a result, the relations between the United States and Israel are closer than ever before.

We will continue to maintain Israel's qualitative advantage over any adversary or coalition of adversaries.

We will continue to solidify our strategic relationship with Israel by taking additional concrete steps to further institutionalize our partnership. This will include maintaining adequate levels of security and economic assistance; continuing our meetings on military, political and economic cooperation and coordination; prepositioning military equipment; developing joint contingency plans; and increasing joint naval and air exercises. The growth of the Soviets' military presence in the Eastern Mediterranean and along NATO's southern flank has demonstrated the importance of developing and expanding the U.S.-Israel strategic relationship.

We oppose the creation of an independent Palestinian state; its establishment is inimical to the security interests of Israel, Jordan and the U.S. We will not support the creation of any Palestinian entity that could place Israel's security in jeopardy.

Republicans will build upon the efforts of the Reagan-Bush Administration and work for peace between Israel and her Arab neighbors based upon the following principles:

● A just and lasting peace is essential, urgent, and can be reached only through direct negotiations between Israel and the Arab nations.

● Peace treaties must be reached through direct negotiations and must never be imposed upon unwilling partners.

● The PLO should have no role in the peace process unless it recognizes Israel's right to exist, accepts United Nations Security Council resolutions 242 and 338, renounces terrorism, and removes language from its charter demanding Israel's destruction.

Under Republican leadership, the United States will explore every opportunity to move forward the peace process toward direct negotiations as long as the security of Israel is not compromised. Much work remains to establish a climate in the Middle East where the legitimate rights of all parties, including the Palestinians, can be equitably addressed.

We recognize that Israel votes with the United States at the United Nations more frequently than any other nation. The Reagan-Bush Administration supported legislation mandating that if the U.N. and its agencies were to deny Israel's right to participate, the United States would withhold financial support and withdraw from those bodies until their action was rectified. The Republican Party reaffirms its support for the rescission of U.N. Resolution 3379, which equates Zionism with racism. Failure to repeal that resolution will justify attenuation of our support for the U.N.

We believe that Jerusalem should remain an undivided city, with free and unimpeded access to all holy places by people of all faiths.

Republicans see Egypt as a catalyst in the Arab world for advancing the cause of regional peace and security. For this reason, we believe that the United States has a significant stake in Egypt's continuing economic development and growth. As the only Arab nation to have formally made peace with Israel, it is reaping the benefits. Egypt's support of the Camp David Accords demonstrates that an Arab nation can make peace with Israel, be an ally of the U.S., and remain in good standing in the Arab world. Republicans support the Reagan-Bush Administration's formal designation of Egypt as a major non-NATO ally.

Our continued support of Egypt and other pro-Western Arab states is an essential component of Republican policy. In support of that policy, we deployed a naval task force to join with allies to keep the sea lanes open during the Iran-Iraq war. We also recognize the important role the moderate Arab states play in supporting U.S. security interests.

Republicans will continue to build on the Reagan-Bush achievement of increased security cooperation with the pro-Western Arab states. We recognize that these Arab nations maintain friendly relations with the United States in the face of potential retaliation attempts by radical elements in the Middle East.

Continuing strife in Lebanon is not in the interest of the U.S. Until order is established, Lebanon will be a source of international terrorism and regional instability. To re-establish normalcy in Lebanon, the U.S. must strengthen the hand of the overwhelming majority of Lebanese, who are committed to an independent, peaceful, and democratic Lebanon.

In order to achieve this goal, we will base the policy of the United States on the principles of the unity of Lebanon; the withdrawal of all foreign forces; the territorial integrity of Lebanon; the re-establishment of its government's authority; and the reassertion of Lebanese sovereignty throughout the nation, with recognition that its safekeeping must be the responsibility of the Lebanese government. We will strive to help Lebanon restore its society so that, in the future as in the past, religious groups will live in harmony, international commerce will flourish and international terrorism will not exist.

For nearly four decades, U.S. policy in the Persian Gulf has reflected American strategic, economic, and political interests in the area. Republican policy has three fundamental objectives:

- Maintaining the free flow of oil.
- Preventing the expansion of Soviet influence.
- Supporting the independence and stability of the states in the region.

By pursuing those goals, we have created the political leverage to begin the process of ending the Iran-Iraq war. Our re-flagging of Kuwaitis ships limited the expansion of both Iranian and Soviet influence in the region.

Africa

Republicans have three priorities in our country's relations with Africa. The first is to oppose the forces of Marxist imperialism, which sustain the march of tyranny in Africa. This priority includes giving strong assistance to groups which oppose Soviet and Cuban-sponsored oppression in Africa.

Our second priority is the need to develop and sustain democracies in Africa. Democrats have often taken the view that democracy is unattainable because of Africa's economic condition, yet at the same time they refuse to promote the conditions in which democracies can flourish. Economic freedom and market-based economies are the key to the development of democracy throughout Africa.

Our third area of concern is humanitarian assistance, especially food aid, to African nations. The Reagan-Bush Administration has always provided it.

Republicans salute the Reagan-Bush Administration for responding with characteristic American compassion to famine conditions in Africa by providing record amounts of food, medical supplies, and other life-saving assistance. In spite of our efforts,

the people of Africa continue to suffer. Republicans condemn the cynical Marxist governments, especially in Ethiopia, which use planned starvation as a weapon of war and a tool for forced migration.

The recent African drought and resulting famine were not just natural disasters. They were made worse by poorly conceived development projects which stripped lands of their productive capacity. Republicans recognize that protecting the natural resource base of developing nations is essential to protecting future economic opportunities and assuring stable societies. We are leading the fight worldwide to require sound environmental planning as part of foreign development programs.

We believe that peace in southern Africa can best be achieved by the withdrawal of all foreign forces from Angola, complete independence and self-determination for the people of Namibia, a rapid process of internal reconciliation, and free and fair elections in both places. The Reagan-Bush Administration has worked tirelessly to achieve this outcome; and while obstacles remain, we are closer than ever to a comprehensive settlement of these interrelated conflicts. America's strong support for Angolan freedomfighters has helped make this progress possible. We also oppose the maintenance of communist forces and influence in Mozambique.

Republicans deplore the apartheid system of South Africa and consider it morally repugnant. All who value human liberty understand the evil of apartheid, and we will not rest until apartheid is eliminated from South Africa. That will remain our goal. Republicans call for an effective and coordinated policy that will promote equal rights and a peaceful transition to a truly representative constitutional form of government for all South Africans and the citizens of all nations throughout Africa. We deplore violence employed against innocent blacks and whites from whatever source.

We believe firmly that one element in the evolution of black political progress must be black economic progress; actions designed to pressure the government of South Africa must not have the effect of adversely affecting the rising aspirations and achievements of black South African entrepreneurs and workers and their families. We should also encourage the development of strong democratic black political institutions to aid in the peaceful transition to majority rule. Republicans believe that it is wrong to punish innocent black South Africans for the policies of the apartheid government of South Africa.

Child Survival Program

The health of children in the developing countries of Asia, Africa, the Near East, Latin America and the Caribbean has been a priority of the Reagan-Bush Administration. Republicans have designated the Child Survival Program as one of our highest foreign assistance priorities. With the creation of the Child Survival Fund in early 1985, we have helped to ensure that children in developing countries worldwide get a decent start in life.

Our commitment to the Child Survival Program is more than a compassionate response to this challenge. It is in part an indication of the success of the program. Child Survival funding has been put to good use, and it is making a difference. Experience has shown that a few dollars go a long way in saving a child's life.

Republican efforts have seen results. The pilot studies begun by the Reagan-Bush Administration a few years ago have resulted in child survival programs that today are reaching hundreds of thousands of women and children in the developing world. Policies are in place, health workers are trained, and host governments throughout the world are committed to child survival programs.

Republicans are committed to continuing our contribution to this vital program. As we look forward to the 1990s, many countries will have achieved what only a few years ago seemed like unattainable goals. Those countries need to find ways to sustain those achievements. It will not be easy. For other countries, the road to these goals will be longer as they strive to give every child what should be his or her birthright, a chance to thrive.

We can help them. We can provide leadership and support. We are committed to sustaining this effort to save and improve the lives of the world's children.

We commend the Reagan-Bush Administration for its courageous defense of human life in population programs around the world. We support its refusal to fund international organizations involved in abortion.

Stopping International Terrorism And Dealing with Low-Intensity Conflict

The nature of warfare itself has changed. Terrorism is a unique form of warfare that attacks and threatens security and stability around the world. Ranging from the attempted assassination of the Pope and car-bomb attacks on American USO clubs, to narco-subversion in the nations of the West, terrorism seeks to silence freedom as an inalienable right of Man.

The world of totalitarianism and anti-Western fanatics have joined forces in this campaign of terror. The goals of their undeclared war against the democracies are the withdrawal of our presence internationally and the retraction of our freedoms domestically.

The Republican Party believes that, in order to prevent terrorist attacks, the United States must maintain an unsurpassed intelligence capability. In cases of terrorism where prevention and deterrence are not enough, we believe that the United States must be prepared to use an appropriate mix of diplomatic, political, and military pressure and action to defeat the terrorist attack. The United States must continue to push for a Western commitment to a "no-concessions" policy on terrorism.

The Republican Party understands that many problems facing our country are centered on "Low Intensity Conflicts." These include insurgencies, organized terrorism, paramilitary actions, sabotage, and other forms of violence in the gray area between peace and declared conventional warfare. Unlike the Democrat Party, Republicans understand that the threat against the vital interests of the United States covers a broad spectrum of conflict. We are committed to defending the people of the United States at all levels. To implement that commitment, we will rely on the planning and strategy of the U.S. Special Operations Command and other Department of Defense offices.

We commend the Reagan-Bush Administration for its willingness to provide a measured response to terrorists such as Libya's Colonel Qadhafi. We affirm our determination to continue isolating his outlaw regime. We applaud the Reagan-Bush Administration's dispatch in implementing the Omnibus Diplomatic Security and Anti-Terrorism Act of 1986. We are strongly committed to obtaining the freedom of all Americans held captive by terrorist elements in the Middle East. Where possible, we will hold accountable those responsible for such heinous acts. We also support foreign military assistance that enables friendly nations to provide for their own defense, including defense against terrorism.

We recognize the increasing threat of terrorism to our overall national security. We will pursue a forward-leaning posture toward terrorism, and are prepared to act in concert with other nations or unilaterally, as necessary, to prevent or respond to terrorist attacks. Our policy will emphasize preemptive anti-terrorist measures; allied and international cooperation; negotiation toward an international agreement to facilitate pre-emptive and proactive measures against terrorists and narco-terrorists; and creation of a multi-national strike force, on the authority granted in a multi-national agreement, specializing in counterterrorism, intelligence and narcotics control.

Republicans believe that, when necessary, our own armed forces must have the capability to meet terrorist crises. Our support for defense forces specifically equipped and trained to conduct unconventional warfare has resulted in important improvements in this critical area. Under the Reagan-Bush Administration, major improvements have been made in the special operations force's readiness, manning, and modernization.

The Republican Party is strongly committed to increased support for unconventional forces by streamlining the bureaucracy which supports them, building the weapons and platforms which are a minimal requirement for their success, and funding the research and development needed for their future vigor. We whole-heartedly support greater international cooperation to counter terrorism and to ensure the safety of innocent citizens travelling abroad.

State Department Organization

The United States depends upon effective diplomacy to protect and advance its interests abroad. Modern diplomacy requires an institution capable of integrating the international dimension of our national values and concerns into a coherent foreign policy. That institution must be made fully responsive to the guidance and direction provided by our country's political leadership.

This requires a truly hierarchical decision-making structure in the Department of State to assure that issues not directly decided by the Secretary of State are not out of reach of politically accountable authority.

Republicans commend the efforts initiated by the Reagan Administration, and in particular the Secretary of State, to restructure and streamline management of the department in order to provide for greater flexibility, efficiency and accountability.

We will continue these efforts in the areas of organization, personnel, and responsiveness as part of a long-term program to make the Department of State more immediately responsive to a complex and changing world.

Peace through Strength: A Proven Policy

Peace through strength is now a proven policy. We have modernized our forces, revitalized our military infrastructure, recruited and trained the most capable fighting force in American history. And we have used these tools with care, responsibility, and restraint.

The Reagan-Bush national security program has restored America's credibility in the world. Our security and that of our allies have been dramatically enhanced; the opportunities for the United States to be a positive force for freedom and democracy throughout the world have expanded, and the chances for new breakthroughs for peace have risen dramatically.

Republicans will build upon this record and advance the cause of world freedom and world peace by using our military credibility as a vehicle for security at home and peace abroad.

These new opportunities for peace and world freedom pose new challenges to America.

The INF Treaty, the first treaty to actually reduce the number of nuclear weapons, was made possible by our commitment to peace through strength. It will impose new demands on our armed forces. We will redouble our commitment to correct a dangerous imbalance of conventional forces both through negotiation and through force improvements.

The Carter Administration left our armed forces in a dangerously weakened position. Ten of the Army's 16 divisions were rated as "not combat ready" due to shortages of skilled manpower, spare parts, fuel, ammunition, and training. For the same reasons, more than 40 percent of the U.S. Air Force and Navy combat aircraft were not fully mission-capable.

The vacillating, ineffectual defense policies of the Democratic presidential nominee would similarly weaken our national security. His ideas about strategic weapons are not only out of step with the thinking of the vast majority of Americans, but also in direct conflict with those of his vice presidential running mate and most of the leading Democrats on the Senate and House Armed Services Committees.

Republicans will support U.S. defense capabilities by keeping our economy strong and inflation rates low. Continued economic growth will allow more dollars to be available for defense without consuming a larger portion of the GNP or the federal budget; continued efficiency and economy will assure those dollars are well-spent.

Even as we engage in dialogue with our adversaries to reduce the risks of war, we must continue to rely on nuclear weapons as our chief form of deterrence. This reliance will, however, move toward non-nuclear defensive weapon systems as we deploy the Strategic Defense System. We will greatly enhance security by making the transition from an all-offensive balance of nuclear terror to a deterrent that emphasizes non-nuclear defense against attack.

We must improve conventional deterrence that would prevent our adversaries from being able to advance successfully into allied territory. We stand in unity with our European allies in the conviction that neither a nuclear war nor a conventional war should be fought. Nonetheless, we must stay on the cutting edge of weapon system development and deployment to deter Soviet aggression in Europe and throughout the free world.

Only by maintaining our strength and resolve can we secure peace in the years ahead. Republicans will provide the steady leadership needed to move our nation effectively into the 21st century.

America Defended

We have begun a historic transition from an American threatened by nuclear weapons to an America defended against the possibility of a devastating nuclear attack.

We understand the ominous implications of the proliferation of ballistic missile technology in the Third World. The Reagan-Bush Administration has succeeded in negotiating an agreement among the seven leading industrial countries to stop the spread of this technology. This underscores the need for deployment of the Strategic Defense System commonly known as SDI. SDI represents America's single most important defense program and is the most significant investment we can make in our nation's future security.

SDI is already working for America. It brought the Soviets back to the bargaining table, and it has energized and challenged our research and technology community as never before. It has started to reverse the trend of unmatched heavy Soviet investment. Republicans insist it is unacceptable that today the citizens of Moscow are protected against ballistic missile attack while Americans have no such protections.

The SDI program has been structured to facilitate a smooth transition to a safer world. It emphasizes deployments based upon the following objectives:

• Providing protection against an accidental or unauthorized launch of a nuclear missile or an attack by a rogue nation.

• Changing the emphasis on our deterrent from nuclear offense to non-nuclear defensive weapons and providing the only real safeguard against cheating on offensive arms control agreements.

• Ultimately, providing a comprehensive defense against all ballistic missile attacks.

We are committed to rapid and certain deployment of SDI as technologies permit, and we will determine the exact architecture of the system as technologies are tested and proven.

In response to the dangerous proliferation of ballistic missiles, a joint U.S.-Israeli effort is now underway to produce the free world's first anti-tactical ballistic missile system, "Project Arrow." We will support this use of SDI research funds.

The Democrat nominee for president opposes deployment of any SDI system. He opposes deployment of even a limited ballistic missile defense system to protect Americans against missile attacks that might be launched accidentally or by an outlaw ruler with access to a few nuclear weapons. His position contradicts the sponsorship by certain Democrats in Congress of a system to protect Americans from such missile attacks.

Republicans want to begin with protection and add to deterrence. We applaud the leaders of the scientific community for their confidence in the ability of U.S. technology to enhance deterrence and to provide effective defenses. We urge the universities of our country to continue to cooperate with the government and the private sector in establishing the SDI system.

A Strategy for Deterrence

Republicans will implement a strategic modernization program, emphasizing offensive and defensive strategic forces that are affordable and credible and that provide for a more stable balance. In contrast with the Democrat nominee and his party, we will not jeopardize America's security and undermine the advances we have made for peace and freedom by permitting erosion of our nuclear deterrent.

Over the past 10 years, every administration—Democrat and Republican alike—has understood the importance of maintaining a strategic triad: a mix of ground, air and sea retaliatory forces. Republicans know our country needs a survivable land-based leg of the triad. The current Democrat leadership rejects this integral element of our strategic force posture. This will destroy the triad by neglecting necessary modernization and forgoing the strategic forces essential for preserving deterrence.

The most critical element in enabling the President to preserve peace is to assure his ability to communicate with foreign leaders and our armed forces under the most adverse circumstances. The Democrat nominee has acted to prevent a future President from having this ability by denying the federal government the needed approval to deploy key elements of the Ground Wave Emergency Network (GWEN) in Massachusetts. By doing so, he has demonstrated a shocking disregard for the security of all Americans. This nation cannot afford such irresponsible leadership from one who aspires to be our Commander-in-Chief.

To end our historic reliance on massive nuclear retaliation, we need to develop a comprehensive strategic defense system. This system will deter and protect us against deliberate or accidental ballistic missile attack, from whatever source.

In the conventional area, we need to ensure that our ground, naval, and air forces are outfitted with the finest equipment and weapons that modern technology can provide; we must also assure that they are fully capable of meeting any threats they may face. We put special emphasis on integrating the guard and reserves into effective combat forces. We must sustain and accelerate the progress we have already made to ensure that all of our forces are prepared for special operations warfare. In addition, advances in conventional weapons technology, specifically, "smart," highly accurate weaponry, must be accelerated. These new weapons will deter our adversaries by threatening significant targets with very precise conventional weapons. We must provide sealift and airlift capability needed to project and support U.S. forces anywhere in the world.

We must also deal with the reality of chemical and biological weapons. We must have a deterrent capability; that requires modernization of our own chemical weapons. But we must also strengthen our efforts to achieve a verifiable agreement to eliminate all chemical and biological weapons. Getting a completely verifiable agreement will be difficult, requiring for tough, on-site, on-demand verification. It is, however, essential that we press ahead, particularly given the growing proclivity in some quarters to use chemical and biological weapons.

In recognition of our responsibility to provide optimum protection for the American people from terrorists, accidents and—should deterrence fail—from war, we also believe that a high priority should be given to Civil Defense.

In each aspect of our deterrent forces, Republicans propose to foster and take advantage of our technology and our democratic alliance systems to develop competing strategies for most effectively defending freedom around the world.

An Arms Reduction Strategy

Arms reduction can be an important aspect of our national policy only when agreements enhance the security of the United States and its allies. This is the Reagan-Bush legacy: true arms reductions as a means to improve U.S. security, not just the perception of East-West detente. Clear objectives, steady purpose, and tough negotiating, backed up by the Republican defense program, produced the INF Treaty. This is the first real nuclear arms reduction treaty in history. Until 1981, we had accepted arms "control" as simply a "managed" arms build-up, always waiting for the next agreement to reverse the trend. Republicans insist on mutual arms reductions. We have proven that there are no barriers to mutual reductions except the will and strength to safely achieve them.

We cannot afford to return to failed Democrat approaches to arms control. Democrats treat arms control as an end in itself, over-emphasizing the atmospherics of East-West relations, making unilateral concessions, and reneging on the traditional U.S. commitment to those forces essential to U.S. and allied security. Notwithstanding their stated intentions, the Democrats' approach—particularly a nuclear freeze—would make nuclear war more, not less, likely.

Republicans are committed to completing the work the Reagan-Bush Administration has begun on an unprecedented 50 percent cut in strategic nuclear weapons. We will achieve verifiable and stable reductions by implementing the Republican agenda for a secure America:

• We will consistently undertake necessary improvements in our forces to maintain the effectiveness of our deterrent.

• We will not negotiate in areas which jeopardize our security. In particular, we will not compromise plans for the research, testing, or the rapid and certain deployment of SDI.

• We will insist on effective verification of compliance with any and all treaties and will take proportional, compensatory actions in cases of non-compliance. Specifically, the Soviet ABM [Anti-Ballistic Missile] radar at Krasnoyarsk poses a clear violation of the ABM Treaty and, if not corrected, would constitute a "material breach" of the Treaty.

• We will place special emphasis on negotiating asymmetrical Soviet cutbacks in those areas where a dangerous imbalance exists. For example, during the three-year reign of Mikhail Gorbachev, the Soviet military has added more new conventional weapons than currently exist in the entire armed forces of France and West Germany.

• We will reject naive and dangerous proposals such as those offered by the Democrat nominee to ban the testing of weapons and delivery systems. Those simplistic and destabilizing proposals are designed only for domestic political appeal and would actually jeopardize achievement of stable arms reductions. The accuracies and efficiencies achieved by testing have in fact resulted in 25 percent fewer warheads and 75 percent less megatonnage than 20 years ago. Our more accurate weapons of today enhance stability.

We must always remember—and ever remind our fellow citizens—that, when the future of our country is at stake, no treaty at all is preferable to a bad treaty.

The Space Challenge

The Republican Party is determined to lead our country and the world into the 21st century with a revitalized space program. The American people have never turned back from a frontier.

Our exploration of space has kept this country on the leading edge of science, research, and technology. Our access to space is essential to our national security. In the coming decade, nations around the world will compete for the economic and military advantages afforded by space.

The free and unchallenged use of space offers to the free world, and the Soviet bloc as well, unprecedented strategic, scientific, and economic advantages. The Soviets openly seek these advantages, which must not be denied to the United States and other free nations. Our goal is for the United States to acquire the means to assure that we can enforce a stable and secure space environment for all peoples.

We must establish a permanent manned space station in orbit during the 1990s for a commercial and governmental space presence.

U.S. satellites currently act as the "eyes and ears" for our strategic forces. The survivability of U.S. space assets is vital to American interests.

We believe the U.S. needs an Anti-Satellite (ASAT) capability to protect our space assets from an operational Soviet threat, and we intend to deploy it rapidly. Furthermore, we encourage the responsible Democrat Members of Congress to join us in this effort. Our country's advance in space is essential to achieve the economic transformations which await us in the new century ahead.

Two powerful engines that can re-energize the space program

will be competitive free enterprise and SDI. The United States must regain assured access to space through a balanced mix of space shuttles and unmanned vehicles. We must also expand the role—in investment, operation, and control—of the private sector. Republicans believe that this nation can and must develop a private sector capability to compete effectively in the world market place as a provider of launches and other services.

We applaud those who have pioneered America's rendezvous with the future. We salute those who have lifted the nation's spirit by raising its sights. We remember in special honor those who gave their lives to give our country a leading role in space.

America: A Strong Leader And Reliable Partner

NATO remains the United States' most important political and military alliance. Republican commitment to NATO is unwavering, reflecting shared political and democratic values which link Europe, Canada, and the United States. NATO pools our collective military resources and capabilities, stretching in Europe from Norway in the north to Turkey, our strategic friend and pillar in the south.

Our challenge is to assure that today's positive signals from the Soviets translate into a tangible reduction of their military threat tomorrow. Soviet conventional superiority remains a serious problem for NATO. Soviet-Warsaw Pact military doctrine continues to be predicated upon the Soviet Union's ability to mount a massive conventional offensive against the NATO allies. The NATO allies must strengthen their conventional forces, modernize their remaining nuclear systems, and promote rationalization, standardization and interoperability.

On the critical issues of defense burden sharing, Republicans reflect the belief of the American people that, although we must maintain a strong presence, the alliance has now evolved to a point where our European and Japanese allies, blessed with advanced economies and high standards of living, are capable of shouldering their fair share of our common defense burden.

We are committed to supporting the network of liberty through balanced regional or bilateral alliances with nations sharing our values in all parts of the world, especially our neighbors in Central America. The Republican Party reiterates its support of the people of Central America in their quest for freedom and democracy in their countries.

We are proud of the great economic and democratic progress throughout the world during the Reagan-Bush Administration, and we are committed to strengthening the defensive ties that have thwarted Soviet expansion in the past seven years.

Free Sea Lanes

The United States has always been a maritime nation. We have rebuilt our Navy to permit continued freedom of the seas. Our focus has correctly been on the fighting ships our Navy would use in the event of a conflict. Our successful peace mission in the Persian Gulf is eloquent testimony to the benefits of a blue water Navy.

To protect American interests in remote areas of the world, we require a 600-ship Navy with 15 aircraft carrier battle groups. This number enables us to operate in areas where we lack the infrastructure of bases we enjoy in Western Europe and the western Pacific. A force of this size will enable us to meet both our security interests and commitments into the 21st century. Republicans are also committed to the strategic homeporting of our forces throughout the United States. Notwithstanding the Democrat nominee's claim to support conventional arms improvements, U.S. security interests are jeopardized by his proposal to cancel two aircraft carriers previously authorized and funded by Congress.

Providing new policies for the maritime industry is crucial to this nation's defense capability and its economic strength. These policies must include leadership to help make the industries competitive through reform of government programs, aggressive efforts to remove barriers to the U.S. flag merchant fleet, and a commitment to cooperate with the industries themselves to improve their efficiency, productivity, and competitive positions.

A national commitment to revitalize the commercial ship-building industry is needed in this country. Shipyards and the supplier base for marine equipment necessary to build and maintain a merchant marine must survive and prosper. Our merchant marine must be significantly enlarged and become more competitive in order to vastly increase the amount and proportion of our foreign trade it carries.

Sealift is needed to supply our troops and transport commercial cargo during a prolonged national emergency. As a nation, we must be willing to pay for the strategic sealift capability we require. We can do this by ensuring that the needed ships are built and by helping to sustain the ships and their crews in commercial operation. We must return this nation to its foremost place among the world maritime powers through a comprehensive maritime policy.

Last year Congress slashed the Administration's budget request for the Coast Guard. We urge Congress to adjust the budget process to protect the Coast Guard appropriation, thereby removing the temptation to siphon its funds and personnel into other programs and ensuring improved coordination of government agencies in our nations' war against drugs.

Our Nation's Technology Base

Science and technology are the keys to a better future for all. Many of the miracles we take for granted in everyday life originated in defense and space research. They have not only helped preserve the peace, but also have made America's standard of living the envy of the world.

Because of advances in science and technology, our defense budget today is actually one-third lower, as a fraction of the gross national product, than it was a generation ago.

Today, national security and technological superiority are increasingly linked by the relationship between technology and key strategies of credible and flexible deterrence, defenses against ballistic missiles, and space pre-eminence.

Investment in defense research and development must be maintained at a level commensurate with the Reagan-Bush years. This investment should be focused on efficient and effective areas such as ballistic missile defense, space, command and control, and "smart" munitions.

We support a defense budget with the necessary funds and incentives for industry to invest in new technologies and new plant and equipment. This is needed to preserve and expand our competitive edge, thereby assuring future opportunities for America's next generation in science, engineering, and manufacturing.

Our nation will benefit greatly from patent royalties and technological progress that will be developed through spinoffs, especially in the fields of micro-miniaturization and super-conductivity, which are vital in order for U.S. industry to compete in the world.

We regard the education of American students in the fields of science and technology as vital to our national security.

Our investment in militarily critical knowledge and technology must be safe-guarded against transfer to the Soviet Union and other unfriendly countries.

Defense Acquisition

Americans are prepared to support defense spending adequate to meet the needs of our security. Americans have a right—and the government has a duty—to ensure that their hard-earned tax dollars are well-spent. We Republicans recognize that waste and fraud in the defense acquisition process cheat the American people and weaken our national security. Neither can be tolerated.

Those who loot national security funds must be prosecuted and punished. Mismanagement must also be rooted out. The planning and budgeting process must be improved, and the acquisition process reformed, recognizing that congressionally mandated waste contributes mightily to inefficiencies in the system.

We will sustain consistent necessary appropriations in the defense budget to avoid the destructive impact of wildly fluctuating and unpredictable annual funding.

The Packard Commission recommended a series of important reforms for improved defense management. We are committed to ensuring that these reforms are fully implemented—by Congress, the Defense Department and the defense industry. Most particularly we call for submission of a two-year budget for defense to help us meet these goals. Persons involved in the federal government procurement process must be subject to "revolving door" legislation.

Procurement today is constrained by an adversarial relationship between the Congress and the Defense Department. The result is micro-management by Congress, which has resulted in thousands of regulations that add expensive and time consuming red tape without adding value. Republicans support a firm policy of cooperation, treating Members of Congress as full partners in the acquisition process. This will result in more efficiency and better weapons. An example of what can be accomplished with this partnership is the new base closing legislation.

To make real these reforms, we will once again depend on the professionalism, the diligence, and the patriotism of the men and women who comprise the vast majority of our defense establishment.

Armed Forces Personnel for the Nineties

A free society defends itself freely. That is why Republicans created an all-volunteer force of men and women in the 1970s, and why it has proven to be a tremendous success in the 1980s.

From Grenada to the Persian Gulf, the readiness of those in uniform has made America proud again. Despite a demographic decline in the number of those eligible for service, military recruitment and retention rates are at all time highs. Quality is outstanding, and all sectors of society are participating.

We will continue to make the military family a special priority, recognizing strong home life as an essential component in the morale and performance of the armed forces. Republicans deplore and reject the efforts of those who would support either a numerical cap or a reduction in the number of military dependents able to accompany U.S. servicemen and women overseas. We recognize that a stable and happy family life is the most important prerequisite for retaining these dedicated men and women in the service of our country.

Republicans recognize that a secure national defense depends upon healthy military personnel. We commend the United States Armed Forces for their leadership in proving the utility of testing active duty personnel and applicants for disease and substance abuse.

Republicans will never take the military for granted. We support an all-volunteer force and we will continue to insist on fairness in pay and benefits for military personnel and their families, always striving to keep compensation in line with the civilian economy.

The National Guard and Reserve are essential to the integrated force concept of our armed services. Prior to 1981, the Guard and Reserve were deprived of both modern equipment and integration into the active forces. This policy has been changed to enable the Guard and Reserve to make their full contribution to our security. We recognize the major role played by the men and women of the Guard and Reserves in the total defense policy. These improvements will be sustained.

Veterans

Veterans have paid the price for the freedoms we enjoy. They have earned the benefits they receive, and we will be vigilant in protecting those programs of health care, education and housing.

We believe men and women veterans have earned the right to be heard at the highest levels of government. With the personal support of President Reagan, America's veterans will now have a seat in the president's Cabinet.

The health needs of our aging veterans are of special importance, and Republicans will not retreat from this national commitment. We encourage the new Secretary of the Veterans Department to work with the Federal Council on the Aging, and other agencies and organizations, to assure that the development of new facilities and treatment programs meet the special needs of our elderly veterans. Republicans will provide adequate funding for the policy that, in all areas where there are no VA hospitals or long-term care facilities, veterans needing medical attention for service-connected disabilities should have the option of receiving medical care within their communities with adequate funding.

We must continue to address the unique readjustment problems of Vietnam veterans by continuing the store-front counseling, vocational training and job placement programs. We support veterans preference in federal employment and are vigilant about the serious problems associated with delayed stress reaction in combat veterans, particularly disabled and Vietnam veterans. An intense scientific effort must continue with respect to disabilities that may be related to exposure to ionizing radiation or herbicides.

The Republican Party supports sufficient funding to maintain the integrity of the VA hospital and medical care system and the entitlement and beneficiary system. We also support the efforts of the Department of Labor to properly meet the needs of unemployed veterans, particularly disabled and Vietnam veterans.

Our commitment to America's veterans extends to the men and women of all generations.

Intelligence: An Indispensable Resource at a Critical Time

A crucial part of the Reagan-Bush administration's rebuilding of a strong America has been the restoration of the nation's intelligence capabilities after years of neglect and down-grading by the Carter-Mondale Administration. This renewed emphasis has been essential in conducting diplomacy, supporting our armed forces, confronting terrorism, stopping narcotics traffic, battling Soviet subversion, and influencing events in support of other national policies. Our vital intelligence capability will continue to prevent tragedies and save lives.

In the years ahead, the United States will face a widening range of national security challenges and opportunities. Scores of foreign intelligence services will seek to uncover our secrets and steal our technology. But there will also be opportunities to advance U.S. interests, for freedom and democracy are on the march. Both the threats and the opportunities will place demands on our intelligence capabilities as never before.

The Republican Party endorses covert action as one method of implementing U.S. national security policy. We reject legislative measures that impinge on the President's constitutional prerogatives. Our country must be able to collect from both technical and human sources the vital information which is denied to us by closed societies in troubled regions of the world. Our senior national security officials must be informed about trends in foreign societies, opportunities to advance U.S. interests, and the vulnerabilities of those who seek to harm our interests. This information can then be used, through the proper chain of command, to support our national policies.

To strengthen the decision-making process and further limit access to classified information, we support the concept of a single joint congressional committee for intelligence, made up of appropriate congressional leaders and analogous to the former Joint Atomic Energy Committee.

We will continue to enhance the nation's capability for counter-intelligence. Congressional intrusion into the administration of counter-intelligence must be kept to a minimum.

Leaks of highly sensitive and classified national security information and materials have increased at an alarming rate in recent years. Such leaks often compromise matters critical to our defense and national security; they can result in the tragic loss of life. We advocate a law making it a felony for any present or former officer or employee of the federal government, including Members of Congress, to knowingly disclose classified information or material to a person not authorized to have access to it.

The U.S. must continue to provide political, military, and economic assistance to friends abroad and to those seeking to help us against our adversaries. These activities must always be in support of our national policy, and the U.S. has the right to expect reciprocity wherever possible.

To the extent the Congress requires the President to inform its Members of activities sensitive to national security, the President is entitled to require that Congress will respect that sensitivity.

National Security Strategy for the Future

We have set forth the foreign and defense policies of the Republican Party in the two preceding sections of this Platform. To implement those policies, we propose this integrated national security strategy for the future.

The long-term security of our nation is the most important responsibility of the U.S. government. The domestic well-being of the American people cannot be ensured unless our country is secure from external attack. To guard our borders, preserve our freedom, protect America from ballistic missile attack, foster a climate of international stability and tranquility—so that nations and individuals may develop, interact, and prosper free from the threat of war or intimidation—these are the most important goals of America's foreign and defense policy.

We dare not abandon to others our leadership in pursuit of those goals. International peace and stability require our country's engagement at many levels. While we cannot resolve all issues unilaterally, neither can we abdicate our responsibilities by retrenchment or by relying on the United Nations to secure our interests abroad. Those who advocate America's disengagement from the world forget the dangers that would be unleashed by America's retreat—dangers which inevitably increase the costs and risks of the necessary reassertion of U.S. power.

Republicans learned this lesson well as we implemented the most successful national security policy since World War II. In 1981, we had to deal with the consequences of the Democrats' retreat. We inherited an America in decline, with a crisis of confidence at home and the loss of respect abroad. Re-establishing America's strength, its belief in itself, and its leadership role was the first and most important task facing the Reagan-Bush Administration. We met that task. We repaired our defenses, modernized our strategic nuclear forces, improved our strategy for deterrence with our development of the Strategic Defense Initiative, deployed INF missiles in Europe, and restored pride in our nation's military services.

We also met that task by a policy of engagement. We worked with allies, not against them. We supported friends instead of accommodating foes. We fostered the achievement of genuine self-determination and democracy rather than merely preaching about human rights in the Third World.

The Reagan-Bush approach produced dramatic results. Our policy is proven: To foster peace while resolutely providing for the security of our country and its allies. We have significantly enhanced that security. We have expanded the opportunities for the United States to be a positive force for freedom and democracy throughout the world. The chances for new breakthroughs for peace have risen dramatically.

We secured the first arms reduction agreement, eliminating an entire class of soviet and U.S. nuclear weapons. We laid the basis in START [Strategic Arms Reduction Talks] for unprecedented, radical reductions in strategic nuclear arms.

In regional conflicts, a humiliating Soviet retreat from Afghanistan, made possible by our unyielding support for the Mujahadeen, helped to sober the Soviet rulers about the costs of their adventurism. Our protection of vital U.S. interests in the Persian Gulf against Iranian aggression led to the agreement to start resolving the Persian Gulf War. Our support for freedom fighters in Angola has resulted in the chance of a settlement there and elsewhere in southern Africa. Our isolation of Vietnam has led to the prospect of its withdrawal from Cambodia.

In human rights and the building of democracy, Republican leadership has turned the tide against terror in Central America, aided the restoration of democracy in the Philippines and South Korea, and liberated the island of Grenada from a Cuban-controlled dictatorship

This is a remarkable record of achievement. It shows that our policies of achieving peace through strength have worked. By rebuilding American strength and restoring American self-confidence, Republicans achieved a remarkable series of foreign policy objectives critical to our country's security. The resurgence of American leadership has changed the world and is shaping the future, creating new opportunities not dreamt of eight years ago. This is the true measure of competence.

Although we have established a framework for the future, we cannot rest on our laurels. The young democracies we have helped to flourish may yet be overcome by authoritarian pressures. The Soviet Union can easily revert to past practices. Its current effort for internal restructuring could create a more powerful adversary with unchanged objectives. Arms reductions could again become an excuse for reducing our commitment to defense, thus creating dangerous instabilities. Economic competition could easily slip into protectionism and mercantilism. Both to meet those challenges and to build upon the opportunities created by our success, the U.S. must continue in the strong leadership role it has assumed over the past eight years.

As we face the opportunities and challenges of the future, our policies will be guided by realism, strength, dialogue, and engagement. We must be realistic about the Soviet Union and the world we face. Hostile forces remain in that world. Soviet military capabilities are still dangerous to us. It must be clear to all, except the leadership of the Democrat Party, that we are not beyond the era of threats to the security of the United States.

Our country must have all the military strength that is necessary to deter war and protect our vital interests abroad. Republicans will continue to improve our defense capabilities. We will carefully set priorities within a framework of fiscal conservatism, more stringent measures to increase productivity, and improved management of defense resources. We will continue modernizing our strategic forces, emphasizing a mix of offensive and defensive forces, effective and survivable, employing unique U.S. technological advantages. We will redouble our commitment through force improvement to correct the dangerous imbalance that now exists in conventional forces.

At the same time, we will pursue negotiations designed to eliminate destabilizing asymmetries in strategic and conventional forces. Arms reductions can contribute to our national security only if they are designed to reduce the risk of war and result in greater stability. They must be part of a process of broader dialogue with the Soviet Union, as well as other nations, a process in which we explore possible opportunities to reduce tensions and to create more stable, predictable, and enduring relationships.

As we shape our foreign and defense policies, we must never lose sight of the unique leadership role the United States plays in the world community. No other nation can assume that role. Whether we are dealing with security challenges in the Persian Gulf or terrorism or the scourge of drugs, the willingness of other nations to act resolutely will depend on the readiness of America to lead, to remain vigorously engaged, and to shoulder its unique responsibilities in the world.

The American people and the Republican Party, in the tradition of Ronald Reagan and with the leadership of George Bush, are indeed ready to do so.

1988 Democratic Convention: Key Ballots

| | Presidential Balloting | | | | | Balloting on Platform | | | | | |
| | | | | | | PLANK ON FAIR TAX | | | NO FIRST USE PLANK | | |
Delegates	Total votes [a]	Dukakis	Jackson	Others [b]	Abstained	Y	N	A [c]	Y	N	A [c]
Alabama	65	37	28	0	0	14	35	16	19	38	8
Alaska	17	9	7	1	0	5	7	0	8	8	0
Arizona	43	28	14	0	0	15	21	0	15	25	0
Arkansas	48	31	11	0	1	11	27	0	9	25	0
California	363	235	122	0	0	104	240	0	119.09	192.63	1
Colorado	55	37	18	0	0	20	31	0	20	32	0
Connecticut	63	47	16	0	0	16	42	0	21	39	1
Delaware	19	9	7	2	1	8	11	0	8	11	0
Florida	154	116	35	0	0	33	89	0	33	100	0
Georgia	94	50	42	0	0	30	43	0	36	43	0
Hawaii	28	19	8	0	0	8	19	1	8	19	1
Idaho	24	20	3	0	0	3	18	0	3	18	0
Illinois	200	138	57	0	0	28	75	0	40	62	7
Indiana	89	69.50	18	0	0	18	68	0	19	66	1
Iowa	61	49	12	0	0	11	48	0	21	38	0
Kansas	45	30	15	0	0	12	29.50	0	14.50	28.50	0
Kentucky	65	59	6	0	0	6	43	0	6	46	0
Louisiana	76	41	33	1	0	23	11	1	26	13	0
Maine	29	17	12	0	0	11	15	0	11	14	0
Maryland	84	59	25	0	0	21	58	0	21	58	1
Massachusetts	119	99	19	0	0	20	79	0	23	86	1
Michigan	162	80	80	0	2	78	77	0	78	77	0
Minnesota	91	57	29	3	0	36	45	0	42	46	0
Mississippi	47	19	26	0	0	24	15	1	27	16	0
Missouri	88	50	37	0	0	31	49	0	33	50	0
Montana	28	22	5	0	0	5	21	0	7	19	0
Nebraska	30	22	8	0	0	7	23	0	7	23	0
Nevada	23	16	5	0	0	5	15	0	6	15	0
New Hampshire	22	22	0	0	0	0	22	0	1	21	0
New Jersey	126	107	19	0	0	19	39	68	19	64	43
New Mexico	30	22	8	0	0	7	19	0	7	20	0
New York	292	194	97	0	0	90	181	0	108	173	0
North Carolina	95	58	35	0	0	36	51	0	37	51	0
North Dakota	22	17	3	0	2	46	131	0	5	11	0
Ohio	183	136	46	0	1	46	131	0	48	132	0
Oklahoma	56	52	4	0	0	4	44	0	4	46	0
Oregon	54	35	18	0	0	18	31	0	18	34	0
Pennsylvania	202	179	23	0	0	22	177	0	22	179	1
Rhode Island	28	24	3	0	1	3	15	0	4	16	0
South Carolina	53	22	31	0	0	29	19	0	30	23	0
South Dakota	20	19	1	0	0	2	16	2	2	17	1
Tennessee	84	63	20	0	0	12	54	0	15	57	0
Texas	211	135	71	1	4	72	123	0	72	121	0
Utah	28	25	3	0	0	3	18	0	5	20	0
Vermont	20	9	9	1	0	10	9	0	11	9	0
Virginia	86	42	42	0	2	37	46	0	41	44	0
Washington	77	50	27	0	0	27	46	0	29	42	1
West Virginia	47	47	0	0	0	0	44	0	1	43	0
Wisconsin	91	65	25	0	0	24	59	0	25	59	0
Wyoming	18	14	4	0	0	4	12	0	6	10	0
District of Columbia	25	7	18	0	0	13	6	0	16	8	0
Puerto Rico	57	48.50	8	0	0	3	53	0	8	48	0
Virgin Islands	5	0	5	0	0	5	0	0	5	0	0
American Samoa	6	6	0	0	0	0	6	0	0	6	0
Guam	4	4	0	0	0	0	4	0	0	4	0
Democrats Abroad	9	8.25	0.50	0	0	0.50	8.50	0	1	8	0
Total	4,162	2,876.25	1,218.50	9	14	1,091.50	2,499.00	90	1,220.59	2,474.13	67

a. Totals may not add due to absences.
b. Details on the votes for other candidates: Alaska: Sen. Lloyd Bentsen, D-Texas, 1; Delaware: Sen. Joseph R. Biden, Jr., D-Del., 2; Louisiana: Rep. Richard A. Gephardt, D-Mo., 1; Minnesota: Rep. Richard H. Stallings, D-Idaho, 3; Texas: Gephardt, 1; Vermont: former senator Gary Hart, D-Colo., 1.
c. Abstained.

1988 Republican Convention: Presidential Ballot

Delegation	Total	First presidential ballot, Bush
Alabama	38	38
Alaska	19	19
Arizona	33	33
Arkansas	27	27
California	175	175
Colorado	36	36
Connecticut	35	35
Delaware	17	17
Florida	82	82
Georgia	48	48
Hawaii	20	20
Idaho	22	22
Illinois	92	92
Indiana	51	51
Iowa	37	37
Kansas	34	34
Kentucky	38	38
Louisiana	41	41
Maine	22	22
Maryland	41	41
Massachusetts	52	52
Michigan	77	77
Minnesota	31	31
Mississippi	31	31
Missouri	47	47
Montana	20	20
Nebraska	25	25
Nevada	20	20
New Hampshire	23	23
New Jersey	64	64
New Mexico	26	26
New York	136	136
North Carolina	54	54
North Dakota	16	16
Ohio	88	88
Oklahoma	36	36
Oregon	32	32
Pennsylvania	96	96
Rhode Island	21	21
South Carolina	37	37
South Dakota	18	18
Tennessee	45	45
Texas	111	111
Utah	26	26
Vermont	17	17
Virginia	50	50
Washington	41	41
West Virginia	28	28
Wisconsin	47	47
Wyoming	18	18
District of Columbia	14	14
Puerto Rico	14	14
Virgin Islands	4	4
Guam	4	4
Total	2,277	2,277

Party Affiliations in Congress and the Presidency, 1789-1989

Year	Congress	House Majority party	House Principal minority party	Senate Majority party	Senate Principal minority party	President
1789-1791	1st	Ad-38	Op-26	Ad-17	Op-9	F (Washington)
1791-1793	2d	F-37	DR-33	F-16	DR-13	F (Washington)
1793-1795	3d	DR-57	F-48	F-17	DR-13	F (Washington)
1795-1797	4th	F-54	DR-52	F-19	DR-13	F (Washington)
1797-1799	5th	F-58	DR-48	F-20	DR-12	F (John Adams)
1799-1801	6th	F-64	DR-42	F-19	DR-13	F (John Adams)
1801-1803	7th	DR-69	F-36	DR-18	F-13	DR (Jefferson)
1803-1805	8th	DR-102	F-39	DR-25	F-9	DR (Jefferson)
1805-1807	9th	DR-116	F-25	DR-27	F-7	DR (Jefferson)
1807-1809	10th	DR-118	F-24	DR-28	F-6	DR (Jefferson)
1809-1811	11th	DR-94	F-48	DR-28	F-6	DR (Madison)
1811-1813	12th	DR-108	F-36	DR-30	F-6	DR (Madison)
1813-1815	13th	DR-112	F-68	DR-27	F-9	DR (Madison)
1815-1817	14th	DR-117	F-65	DR-25	F-11	DR (Madison)
1817-1819	15th	DR-141	F-42	DR-34	F-10	DR (Monroe)
1819-1821	16th	DR-156	F-27	DR-35	F-7	DR (Monroe)
1821-1823	17th	DR-158	F-25	DR-44	F-4	DR (Monroe)
1823-1825	18th	DR-187	F-26	DR-44	F-4	DR (Monroe)
1825-1827	19th	Ad-105	J-97	Ad-26	J-20	C (John Q. Adams)
1827-1829	20th	J-119	Ad-94	J-28	Ad-20	C (John Q. Adams)
1829-1831	21st	D-139	NR-74	D-26	NR-22	D (Jackson)
1831-1833	22d	D-141	NR-58	D-25	NR-21	D (Jackson)
1833-1835	23d	D-147	AM-53	D-20	NR-20	D (Jackson)
1835-1837	24th	D-145	W-98	D-27	W-25	D (Jackson)
1837-1839	25th	D-108	W-107	D-30	W-18	D (Van Buren)
1839-1841	26th	D-124	W-118	D-28	W-22	D (Van Buren)
1841-1843	27th	W-133	D-102	W-28	D-22	W (W. Harrison) W (Tyler)
1843-1845	28th	D-142	W-79	W-28	D-25	W (Tyler)
1845-1847	29th	D-143	W-77	D-31	W-25	D (Polk)
1847-1849	30th	W-115	D-108	D-36	W-21	D (Polk)
1849-1851	31st	D-112	W-109	D-35	W-25	W (Taylor) W (Fillmore)
1851-1853	32d	D-140	W-88	D-35	W-24	W (Fillmore)
1853-1855	33d	D-159	W-71	D-38	W-22	D (Pierce)
1855-1857	34th	R-108	D-83	D-40	R-15	D (Pierce)
1857-1859	35th	D-118	R-92	D-36	R-20	D (Buchanan)
1859-1861	36th	R-114	D-92	D-36	R-26	D (Buchanan)
1861-1863	37th	R-105	D-43	R-31	D-8	R (Lincoln)
1863-1865	38th	R-102	D-75	R-36	D-9	R (Lincoln)
1865-1867	39th	U-149	D-42	U-42	D-10	R (Lincoln) R (A. Johnson)
1867-1869	40th	R-143	D-49	R-42	D-11	R (A. Johnson)
1869-1871	41st	R-149	D-63	R-56	D-11	R (Grant)
1871-1873	42d	R-134	D-104	R-52	D-17	R (Grant)
1873-1875	43d	R-194	D-92	R-49	D-19	R (Grant)
1875-1877	44th	D-169	R-109	R-45	D-29	R (Grant)
1877-1879	45th	D-153	R-140	R-39	D-36	R (Hayes)
1879-1881	46th	D-149	R-130	D-42	R-33	R (Hayes)
1881-1883	47th	R-147	D-135	R-37	D-37	R (Garfield) R (Arthur)
1883-1885	48th	D-197	R-118	R-38	D-36	R (Arthur)
1885-1887	49th	D-183	R-140	R-43	D-34	D (Cleveland)
1887-1889	50th	D-169	R-152	R-39	D-37	D (Cleveland)
1889-1891	51st	R-166	D-159	R-39	D-37	R (B. Harrison)
1891-1893	52nd	D-235	R-88	R-47	D-39	R (B. Harrison)
1893-1895	53rd	D-218	R-127	D-44	R-38	D (Cleveland)
1895-1897	54th	R-244	D-105	R-43	D-39	D (Cleveland)

Year	Congress	House		Senate		President
		Majority party	Principal minority party	Majority party	Principal minority party	
1897-1899	55th	R-204	D-113	R-47	D-34	R (McKinley)
1899-1901	56th	R-185	D-163	R-53	D-26	R (McKinley)
1901-1903	57th	R-197	D-151	R-55	D-31	R (McKinley)
						R (T. Roosevelt)
1903-1905	58th	R-208	D-178	R-57	D-33	R (T. Roosevelt)
1905-1907	59th	R-250	D-136	R-57	D-33	R (T. Roosevelt)
1907-1909	60th	R-222	D-164	R-61	D-31	R (T. Roosevelt)
1909-1911	61st	R-219	D-172	R-61	D-32	R (Taft)
1911-1913	62d	D-228	R-161	R-51	D-41	R (Taft)
1913-1915	63d	D-291	R-127	D-51	R-44	D (Wilson)
1915-1917	64th	D-230	R-196	D-56	R-40	D (Wilson)
1917-1919	65th	D-216	R-210	D-53	R-42	D (Wilson)
1919-1921	66th	R-240	D-190	R-49	D-47	D (Wilson)
1921-1923	67th	R-301	D-131	R-59	D-37	R (Harding)
1923-1925	68th	R-225	D-205	R-51	D-43	R (Coolidge)
1925-1927	69th	R-247	D-183	R-56	D-39	R (Coolidge)
1927-1929	70th	R-237	D-195	R-49	D-46	R (Coolidge)
1929-1931	71st	R-267	D-167	R-56	D-39	R (Hoover)
1931-1933	72d	D-220	R-214	R-48	D-47	R (Hoover)
1933-1935	73d	D-310	R-117	D-60	R-35	D (F. Roosevelt)
1935-1937	74th	D-319	R-103	D-69	R-25	D (F. Roosevelt)
1937-1939	75th	D-331	R-89	D-76	R-16	D (F. Roosevelt)
1939-1941	76th	D-261	R-164	D-69	R-23	D (F. Roosevelt)
1941-1943	77th	D-268	R-162	D-66	R-28	D (F. Roosevelt)
1943-1945	78th	D-218	R-208	D-58	R-37	D (F. Roosevelt)
1945-1947	79th	D-242	R-190	D-56	R-38	D (F. Roosevelt)
						D (Truman)
1947-1949	80th	R-245	D-188	R-51	D-45	D (Truman)
1949-1951	81st	D-263	R-171	D-54	R-42	D (Truman)
1951-1953	82d	D-234	R-199	D-49	R-47	D (Truman)
1953-1955	83d	R-221	D-211	R-48	D-47	R (Eisenhower)
1955-1957	84th	D-232	R-203	D-48	R-47	R (Eisenhower)
1957-1959	85th	D-233	R-200	D-49	R-47	R (Eisenhower)
1959-1961	86th	D-283	R-153	D-64	R-34	R (Eisenhower)
1961-1963	87th	D-263	R-174	D-65	R-35	D (Kennedy)
1963-1965	88th	D-258	R-177	D-67	R-33	D (Kennedy)
						D (L. Johnson)
1965-1967	89th	D-295	R-140	D-68	R-32	D (L. Johnson)
1967-1969	90th	D-247	R-187	D-64	R-36	D (L. Johnson)
1969-1971	91st	D-243	R-192	D-57	R-43	R (Nixon)
1971-1973	92d	D-254	R-180	D-54	R-44	R (Nixon)
1973-1975	93d	D-239	R-192	D-56	R-42	R (Nixon)
						R (Ford)
1975-1977	94th	D-291	R-144	D-60	R-37	R (Ford)
1977-1979	95th	D-292	R-143	D-61	R-38	D (Carter)
1979-1981	96th	D-276	R-157	D-58	R-41	D (Carter)
1981-1983	97th	D-243	R-192	R-53	D-46	R (Reagan)
1983-1985	98th	D-269	R-165	R-54	D-46	R (Reagan)
1985-1987	99th	D-252	R-182	R-53	D-47	R (Reagan)
1987-1989	100th	D-258	R-177	D-55	R-45	R (Reagan)
1989-1991	101st	D-260	R-175	D-55	R-45	R (Bush)

Source: American Leaders, 1789-1987 (Washington, D.C.: Congressional Quarterly Inc., 1987).

Note: AD—Administration; AM—Anti-Masonic; C—Coalition; D—Democratic; DR—Democratic-Republican; F—Federalist; J—Jacksonian; NR—National Republican; Op—Opposition; R—Republican; U—Unionist; W—Whig. Figures are for the beginning of the first session of each Congress.

Highlights of National Party Conventions, 1831-1988

1831   First national political convention was held in Baltimore by Anti-Masonic party. Second such convention was held several months later by National Republican party (no relation to modern Republicans).

1832   Democratic party met in Baltimore for its first national political convention and nominated Andrew Jackson. The rule requiring a two-thirds majority for nominations was initiated.

1835   President Jackson called his party's convention more than a year before the election to prevent buildup of opposition to his choice of successor, Martin Van Buren.

1839   Whig party held its first convention and chose the winning slate of William Henry Harrison and John Tyler. Party adopted unit rule for casting state delegations' votes.

1840   To avoid bitter battle over vice-presidential nomination, Democratic party set up a committee to select nominees, subject to approval of convention. In accordance with committee recommendations, Van Buren was nominated for president and no one for vice president.

1844   Democrats nominated James K. Polk—the first "dark horse," or compromise, candidate—after nine ballots. Silas Wright, convention's choice for vice president, declined the nomination. First time a convention nominee refused nomination. Convention subsequently nominated George M. Dallas.

1848   Democratic convention voted to establish continuing committee, known as Democratic National Committee.

1852   Democrats and Whigs both adopted platforms before nominating candidates for president, setting precedent followed almost uniformly ever since.

1854   First Republican state convention held in Jackson, Michigan, to nominate candidate slate. Platform denounced slavery.

1856   First Republican National Convention held in Philadelphia. Kentucky sent the only southern delegation. Nominated John C. Fremont for president.

1860   One of the longest, most turbulent, and most mobile conventions in Democratic history. Democrats met in Charleston, South Carolina, April 23. After ten days and no agreement on a presidential nominee, delegates adjourned and reconvened in Baltimore in mid-July, for what turned out to be another disorderly meeting. Delegates finally nominated Stephen A. Douglas for president.

Benjamin Fitzpatrick, the convention's choice for vice president, became the first candidate to withdraw after convention adjournment and be replaced by a selection of the national committee. Southern delegates who bolted the original convention later joined Baltimore dissidents to nominate Vice President John C. Breckinridge for president on the Southern Democrat ticket.

Republicans nominated Abraham Lincoln for the presidency. First Republican credentials dispute took place over seating delegates from slave states and voting strength of delegates from states where party was comparatively weak. Party rejected unit rule for first time.

Constitutional Union party's platform of national unity nominated John Bell for president.

1864   Civil War led to bitter debate within Democratic party over candidates, including Gen. George B. McClellan, presidential nominee.

In attempt to close ranks during war, Republicans used the name "Union party" at convention. Renominated Lincoln. Platform called for constitutional amendment outlawing slavery.

1868   Susan B. Anthony urged Democratic support for women's suffrage.

For the first time Republicans gave a candidate (Ulysses S. Grant) 100 percent of vote on first ballot. Incumbent Andrew Johnson, who succeeded the assassinated Lincoln, sought nomination unsuccessfully. First Republican convention with full southern representation.

1872   Republicans renominated Grant at Philadelphia. Dissident Liberal Republicans nominated Horace Greeley in Cincinnati. Democrats also nominated Greeley. Victoria Clafin Woodhull, nominated by the Equal Rights party, was first woman presidential candidate. Black leader Frederick Douglass was her running mate.

1876   First time either party nominated incumbent governor for president; both major parties did so that year with Rutherford B. Hayes, R-Ohio, and Samuel J. Tilden, D-N.Y. Republican convention rejected unit rule for second time.

1880   Republicans nominated James A. Garfield for president on thirty-sixth ballot—party's all-time record number of ballots. Unit rule was rejected for third and final time. Republican convention passed loyalty pledge for nominee, binding each delegate to his support.

1884   Democrats turned back Tammany Hall challenge to unit rule.

Republicans nominated James G. Blaine, Maine, for president and John Logan, Illinois, for vice president, reversing twenty-four-year pattern of seeking presidential candidate from the Midwest and vice-presidential candidate from the East. John Roy Lynch, three-term U.S. representative from Mississippi, became first black elected temporary chairman of national nominating convention.

1888   Frederick Douglass was first black to receive a vote in presidential balloting at political convention. He received one vote on fourth ballot at Republican convention. Nineteen names were entered into Republican balloting. Benjamin Harrison won nomination on eighth ballot.

1892   Democrat Grover Cleveland broke convention system tradition by receiving third presidential nomination. People's party (Populists) held first national nominating convention in Omaha, Nebraska, and adopted first platform.

1896   Democrats, divided over silver-gold question, repudiated Cleveland administration and nominated William Jennings Bryan.

Thirty-four Republican delegates against free silver walked out of convention.

1900   Each party had one woman delegate.

1904   Florida Democrats elected national convention delegates in public primary, under first legislation permitting any recognized party to hold general primary elections.

Republicans nominated Theodore Roosevelt, first

time a vice president who had succeeded a deceased president went on to be nominated in his own right.

1908 Democrats, calling for legislation terminating what they called "partnership" between Republicans and corporations, pledged to refuse campaign contributions from corporations.

Call to Republican convention provided for election of delegates by primary method introduced in some states for first time.

1912 Increasing numbers of delegates were selected in primaries held in thirteen states.

First time Republicans renominated entire ticket—William Howard Taft and James S. Sherman. Malapportionment of convention seats as result of Republican decline in South killed Theodore Roosevelt's chances of nomination. Taft renominated, but 349 delegates protested his nomination by refusing to vote. Roosevelt nominated for president on Progressive ticket at separate convention.

1916 Democrats renominated entire ticket—Woodrow Wilson and Thomas R. Marshall—for first time.

Hopes of reuniting Republicans diminished when Roosevelt could not secure their nomination and refused Progressive renomination.

1920 For first time women attended conventions in significant numbers.

1924 Republicans adopted bonus votes for first time—three bonus delegates at large allotted to each state carried by party in preceding presidential election. Republican convention was first to be broadcast on radio.

John W. Davis was nominated by Democrats on record 103rd ballot.

Three Democratic women received one or more votes for presidential nomination.

1928 Democrat Alfred E. Smith, governor of New York, was first Roman Catholic nominated for president by a major party.

1932 Republicans began tradition of appointing party leader from House of Representatives as permanent convention chairman.

Franklin D. Roosevelt appeared before Democratic convention to accept presidential nomination, the first major party candidate to do so.

1936 Democratic party voted to end requirement of two-thirds delegate majority for nomination, a rule adopted at party's first convention and one that sometimes had led to lengthy balloting and selection of dark-horse slates.

Republicans nominated Alfred M. Landon and Frank Knox in vain effort to break new Democratic coalition.

1940 Franklin D. Roosevelt was nominated for unprecedented third term. He then wrote out a refusal of his renomination because of opposition to his vice-presidential choice, Henry A. Wallace. Opposition deferred and Wallace was nominated.

Republicans held first political convention to be televised.

1944 Franklin D. Roosevelt, already having broken tradition by winning third term, was nominated for fourth time. Democrats put system of bonus votes into effect for states that voted Democratic in previous presidential election.

Thomas E. Dewey became first Republican candidate to accept nomination in appearance before the convention.

1948 After Democratic convention adopted strong civil rights plank, entire Mississippi delegation and thirteen of Alabama's twenty-six delegates walked out.

Dissidents from thirteen southern states met several days later and nominated Gov. Strom Thurmond of South Carolina for president on the States' Rights ticket.

Democrats began appointing Speaker of the House as permanent chairman. Practice followed through 1968, with exception of 1960, when Sam Rayburn declined. Since 1948 conventions presidential nominees of both parties have appeared at their conventions. Republicans renominated Thomas E. Dewey, the first time a party renominated a defeated presidential candidate.

1952 Adlai E. Stevenson, who did not seek the nomination, was chosen as Democratic nominee in one of few genuine "drafts" in history of either political party.

Republicans nominated Dwight D. Eisenhower. Women delegates wanted to nominate Sen. Margaret Chase Smith, Maine, for vice president, but Smith requested her name not be put in nomination.

1956 Democratic nominee Adlai E. Stevenson left choice of running mate to convention. Winner of open race was Sen. Estes Kefauver of Tennessee. First time a party loyalty provision was put into effect during delegate selection.

Dwight D. Eisenhower renominated unanimously on first ballot at Republican convention.

1960 Democrats adopted strongest civil rights plank in party history. Presidential nominee Sen. John F. Kennedy of Massachusetts was second Roman Catholic to receive presidential nomination of major party.

Republican nominee Richard Nixon was party's first vice president nominated for president at completion of his term.

1964 Democratic president Lyndon B. Johnson was nominated for second term by acclamation. Fight over credentials of Alabama and Mississippi delegations was overriding issue at the convention.

Sen. Margaret Chase Smith's name was placed in nomination for presidency at Republican convention— first time a woman placed in nomination by a major party. Sen. Barry Goldwater of Arizona won the nomination.

1968 Democratic delegates voted to end unit rule and to eliminate it from all levels of party politics for 1972 convention. Vice President Hubert H. Humphrey nominated for president.

Republicans nominated Richard Nixon, who had made one of the most remarkable political comebacks in American history.

1972 With newly adopted party reform guidelines, the Democratic convention included a record number of women, youth, and minorities. Open debate on many issues occurred, with an unprecedented twenty-three credentials challenges brought to the floor. Sen. George McGovern of South Dakota, who built a following as an antiwar candidate, nominated for president on first ballot. His choice for vice president, Sen. Thomas F. Eagleton of Missouri, became second candidate in American history to withdraw. National committee chose R. Sargent Shriver as replacement.

In harmonious convention Republicans renominated Richard Nixon and Spiro T. Agnew with nearly unanimous votes.

1976 Democrats in unified convention nominated Gov. Jimmy Carter of Georgia. Gathering was notable for lack of bitter floor fights and credentials challenges that had characterized some recent conventions.

Incumbent president Gerald R. Ford received Republican nomination, narrowly surviving a challenge from former governor of California, Ronald Reagan.

1980 Democrats renominated President Jimmy Carter in

convention marked by bitter contests over party platform and rules binding delegates to vote on first ballot for candidates under whose banner they were elected. The struggle pitted Carter forces against supporters of Sen. Edward M. Kennedy, Massachusetts, who were trying to pry nomination away from the president and alter party platform. While the Carter camp prevailed on delegate-binding rule, Kennedy managed to force major concessions in Democratic platform.

In contrast, a harmonious and unified Republican convention nominated Ronald Reagan. Rumors abounded during convention that former president Gerald R. Ford would serve as Reagan's vice-presidential candidate.

After it became obvious that efforts to persuade Ford to join the ticket had failed, Reagan chose George Bush as his running mate.

1984 Democrats nominated Walter F. Mondale, Jimmy Carter's vice president, for presidential slot and in a historic move accepted Rep. Geraldine A. Ferraro of New York as his running mate. Ferraro was first woman placed on national ticket by a major party.

A jubilant Republican party wound up its convention confident that President Ronald Reagan and Vice President George Bush would win in November. With the ticket's renomination certain beforehand, convention was more a celebration than a business meeting of GOP activists.

1988 Democrats rallied behind Gov. Michael Dukakis of Massachusetts and his running mate Sen. Lloyd Bentsen of Texas. The mood was one of unity and compromise, signaling a victory of pragmatism over idealism.

Vice President George Bush arrived at the Republican convention as its all-but-anointed standard bearer. The four days of the convention were filled with unexpected drama as party members awaited news of Bush's running mate. When Sen. Dan Quayle of Indiana was announced, he quickly came under fire about his qualifications and background.

The 1988 Conventions

If there was any doubt that the South was being viewed as a pivotal battleground in the 1988 presidential campaign, it should have been dispelled by the Democrats' choice February 10, 1987, of Atlanta as the host city for the party's national convention. Only three weeks earlier Republicans had chosen New Orleans as their 1988 convention site, making it the first time that either southern city had hosted a convention and the first time since 1860 that even one of the parties had held a convention in the Deep South.

The two parties' interest in the South was understandable. Over the past quarter-century it had helped elect Democrats Lyndon B. Johnson and Jimmy Carter as well as Republicans Richard Nixon and Ronald Reagan. And in 1988 the South would have more electoral votes than any other region. Although the choice of a convention city usually makes little difference in the presidential election, the choice can serve to advertise a party's concern for a particular voting bloc or region.

The Democrats chose Atlanta over four other finalists: Houston, Kansas City, New York City, and Washington, D.C. More than three-fourths of the Site Selection Committee voted for the Georgia city.

The two parties had held their conventions in the same city six times in the past without conflict, but the GOP effectively blocked the Democrats from sharing New Orleans by including a clause in their convention contract with the city that assured them exclusive access to the Superdome up to six weeks before the opening gavel. The two conventions were scheduled to be held less than a month apart in 1988, with the Democrats meeting July 18-21 and the Republicans, August 15-18.

The Democratic National Committee was impressed by the arena and surrounding facilities and strongly considered New Orleans as well. They argued that the GOP was unfair in tying up the Superdome, but the Republican National Committee saw it differently, blaming the Democrats for conducting their site selection process too slowly.

In announcing that the GOP would go to New Orleans, the RNC stressed the superiority of the facilities, which would allow Republicans to produce a media spectacular within the huge Superdome, while the DNC stressed the thematic advantages of picking the Georgia metropolis.

In the past the parties made little effort to hold their national conventions in the South. The Democrats had held two conventions in Dixie, the first in Charleston, S.C., in 1860 and then in Houston, Texas, in 1928. No other conventions were held in the South again until 1968, when the Republicans convened in Miami Beach.

Sites of Major Party Conventions, 1832-1988

The following chart lists the twenty cities selected as the site of a major party convention and the number of conventions they have hosted or were scheduled to host, from the first national gathering for the Democrats (1832) and the Republicans (1856) through the 1988 conventions.

	Total conventions	Democratic conventions		Republican conventions	
		Number	Last hosted	Number	Last hosted
Chicago, Ill.	24	10	1968	14	1960
Baltimore, Md.	10	9	1912	1	1864
Philadelphia, Pa.	7	2	1948	5	1948
St. Louis, Mo.	5	4	1916	1	1896
New York, N.Y.	4	4	1980	0	—
San Francisco, Calif.	4	2	1984	2	1964
Cincinnati, Ohio	3	2	1880	1	1876
Kansas City, Mo.	3	1	1900	2	1976
Miami Beach, Fla.	3	1	1972	2	1972
Cleveland, Ohio	2	0	—	2	1936
Atlanta, Ga.	1	1	1988	0	—
Atlantic City, N.J.	1	1	1964	0	—
Charleston, S.C.	1	1	1860	0	—
Dallas, Texas	1	0	—	1	1984
Denver, Colo.	1	1	1908	0	—
Detroit, Mich.	1	0	—	1	1980
Houston, Texas	1	1	1928	0	—
Los Angeles, Calif.	1	1	1960	0	—
Minneapolis, Minn.	1	0	—	1	1892
New Orleans, La.	1	0	—	1	1988

National Party Chairs

Name	State	Years of service	Name	State	Years of service
Democratic party			**Republican party (continued)**		
B. F. Hallett	Massachusetts	1848-1852	J. Donald Cameron	Pennsylvania	1879-1880
Robert McLane	Maryland	1852-1856	Marshall Jewell	Connecticut	1880-1883
David A. Smalley	Virginia	1856-1860	D. M. Sabin	Minnesota	1883-1884
August Belmont	New York	1860-1872	B. F. Jones	Pennsylvania	1884-1888
Augustus Schell	New York	1872-1876	Matthew S. Quay	Pennsylvania	1888-1891
Abram S. Hewitt	New York	1876-1877	James S. Clarkson	Iowa	1891-1892
William H. Barnum	Connecticut	1877-1889	Thomas H. Carter	Montana	1892-1896
Calvin S. Brice	Ohio	1889-1892	Mark A. Hanna	Ohio	1896-1904
William F. Harrity	Pennsylvania	1892-1896	Henry C. Payne	Wisconsin	1904
James K. Jones	Arkansas	1896-1904	George B. Cortelyou	New York	1904-1907
Thomas Taggart	Indiana	1904-1908	Harry S. New	Indiana	1907-1908
Norman E. Mack	New York	1908-1912	Frank H. Hitchcock	Massachusetts	1908-1909
William F. McCombs	New York	1912-1916	John F. Hill	Maine	1909-1912
Vance C. McCormick	Pennsylvania	1916-1919	Victor Rosewater	Nebraska	1912
Homer S. Cummings	Connecticut	1919-1920	Charles D. Hilles	New York	1912-1916
George White	Ohio	1920-1921	William R. Willcox	New York	1916-1918
Cordell Hull	Tennessee	1921-1924	Will Hays	Indiana	1918-1921
Clem Shaver	West Virginia	1924-1928	John T. Adams	Iowa	1921-1924
John J. Raskob	Maryland	1928-1932	William M. Butler	Massachusetts	1924-1928
James A. Farley	New York	1932-1940	Hubert Work	Colorado	1928-1929
Edward J. Flynn	New York	1940-1943	Claudius H. Huston	Tennessee	1929-1930
Frank C. Walker	Pennsylvania	1943-1944	Simeon D. Fess	Ohio	1930-1932
Robert E. Hannegan	Missouri	1944-1947	Everett Sanders	Indiana	1932-1934
J. Howard McGrath	Rhode Island	1947-1949	Henry P. Fletcher	Pennsylvania	1934-1936
William M. Boyle, Jr.	Missouri	1949-1951	John Hamilton	Kansas	1936-1940
Frank E. McKinney	Indiana	1951-1952	Joseph W. Martin, Jr.	Massachusetts	1940-1942
Stephen A. Mitchell	Illinois	1952-1954	Harrison E. Spangler	Iowa	1942-1944
Paul M. Butler	Indiana	1955-1960	Herbert Brownell, Jr.	New York	1944-1946
Henry M. Jackson	Washington	1960-1961	B. Carroll Reece	Tennessee	1946-1948
John M. Bailey	Connecticut	1961-1968	Hugh D. Scott, Jr.	Pennsylvania	1948-1949
Lawrence F. O'Brien	Massachusetts	1968-1969	Guy George Gabrielson	New Jersey	1949-1952
Fred Harris	Oklahoma	1969-1970	Arthur E. Summerfield	Michigan	1952-1953
Lawrence F. O'Brien	Massachusetts	1970-1972	C. Wesley Roberts	Kansas	1953
Jean Westwood	Utah	1972	Leonard W. Hall	New York	1953-1957
Robert Strauss	Texas	1972-1977	H. Meade Alcorn, Jr.	Connecticut	1957-1959
Kenneth Curtis	Maine	1977-1978	Thruston B. Morton	Kentucky	1959-1961
John White	Texas	1978-1981	William E. Miller	New York	1961-1964
Charles Manatt	California	1981-1985	Dean Burch	Arizona	1964-1965
Paul Kirk	Massachusetts	1985-1989	Ray C. Bliss	Ohio	1965-1969
Ronald H. Brown	Washington, D.C.	1989-	Rogers C. B. Morton	Maryland	1969-1971
			Robert Dole	Kansas	1971-1973
			George Bush	Texas	1973-1974
			Mary Louise Smith	Iowa	1974-1977
Republican party			William Brock	Tennessee	1977-1981
Edwin D. Morgan	New York	1856-1864	Richard Richards	Utah	1981-1983
Henry J. Raymond	New York	1864-1866	Paul Laxalt		
Marcus L. Ward	New Jersey	1866-1868	(general chair)	Nevada	1983-1986
William Claflin	Massachusetts	1868-1872	Frank Fahrenkopf	Nevada	1983-1989
Edwin D. Morgan	New York	1872-1876	Lee Atwater	South Carolina	1989-
Zachariah Chandler	Michigan	1876-1879			

Source: Congressional Quarterly's Guide to the Presidency, ed. Michael Nelson (Washington, D.C.: Congressional Quarterly Inc., 1989), 696.

Democratic Conventions, 1832-1988

Year	City	Dates	Presidential nominee	Vice-presidential nominee	No. of pres. ballots
1832	Baltimore	May 21-23	Andrew Jackson	Martin Van Buren	1
1835	Baltimore	May 20-23	Martin Van Buren	Richard M. Johnson	1
1840	Baltimore	May 5-6	Martin Van Buren	— a	1
1844	Baltimore	May 27-29	James K. Polk	George M. Dallas	9
1848	Baltimore	May 22-25	Lewis Cass	William O. Butler	4
1852	Baltimore	June 1-5	Franklin Pierce	William R. King	49
1856	Cincinnati	June 2-6	James Buchanan	John C. Breckinridge	17
1860	Charleston	April 23-May 3	Deadlocked		57
	Baltimore	June 18-23	Stephen A. Douglas	Benjamin Fitzpatrick Herschel V. Johnson b	2
1864	Chicago	August 29-31	George B. McClellan	George H. Pendleton	1
1868	New York	July 4-9	Horatio Seymour	Francis P. Blair	22
1872	Baltimore	July 9-10	Horace Greeley	Benjamin G. Brown	1
1876	St. Louis	June 27-29	Samuel J. Tilden	Thomas A. Hendricks	2
1880	Cincinnati	June 22-24	Winfield S. Hancock	William H. English	2
1884	Chicago	July 8-11	Grover Cleveland	Thomas A. Hendricks	2
1888	St. Louis	June 5-7	Grover Cleveland	Allen G. Thurman	1
1892	Chicago	June 21-23	Grover Cleveland	Adlai E. Stevenson	1
1896	Chicago	July 7-11	William J. Bryan	Arthur Sewall	5
1900	Kansas City	July 4-6	William J. Bryan	Adlai E. Stevenson	1
1904	St. Louis	July 6-9	Alton S. Parker	Henry G. Davis	1
1908	Denver	July 7-10	William J. Bryan	John W. Kern	1
1912	Baltimore	June 25-July 2	Woodrow Wilson	Thomas R. Marshall	46
1916	St. Louis	June 14-16	Woodrow Wilson	Thomas R. Marshall	1
1920	San Francisco	June 28-July 6	James M. Cox	Franklin D. Roosevelt	44
1924	New York	June 24-July 9	John W. Davis	Charles W. Bryan	103
1928	Houston	June 26-29	Alfred E. Smith	Joseph T. Robinson	1
1932	Chicago	June 27-July 2	Franklin D. Roosevelt	John N. Garner	4
1936	Philadelphia	June 23-27	Franklin D. Roosevelt	John N. Garner	Acclamation
1940	Chicago	July 15-18	Franklin D. Roosevelt	Henry A. Wallace	1
1944	Chicago	July 19-21	Franklin D. Roosevelt	Harry S Truman	1
1948	Philadelphia	July 12-14	Harry S Truman	Alben W. Barkley	1
1952	Chicago	July 21-26	Adlai E. Stevenson	John J. Sparkman	3
1956	Chicago	August 13-17	Adlai E. Stevenson	Estes Kefauver	1
1960	Los Angeles	July 11-15	John F. Kennedy	Lyndon B. Johnson	1
1964	Atlantic City	August 24-27	Lyndon B. Johnson	Hubert H. Humphrey	Acclamation
1968	Chicago	August 26-29	Hubert H. Humphrey	Edmund S. Muskie	1
1972	Miami Beach	July 10-13	George McGovern	Thomas F. Eagleton R. Sargent Shriver c	1
1976	New York	July 12-15	Jimmy Carter	Walter F. Mondale	1
1980	New York	August 11-14	Jimmy Carter	Walter F. Mondale	1
1984	San Francisco	July 16-19	Walter F. Mondale	Geraldine A. Ferraro	1
1988	Atlanta	July 18-21	Michael Dukakis	Lloyd Bentsen	1

a. The 1840 Democratic convention did not nominate a candidate for vice president.

b. The 1860 Democratic convention nominated Benjamin Fitzpatrick, who declined the nomination shortly after the convention adjourned. On June 25 the Democratic National Committee selected Herschel V. Johnson as the party's candidate for vice president.

c. The 1972 Democratic convention nominated Thomas F. Eagleton, who withdrew from the ticket on July 31. On August 8 the Democratic National Committee selected R. Sargent Shriver as the party's candidate for vice president.

Republican Conventions, 1856-1988

Year	City	Dates	Presidential nominee	Vice-presidential nominee	No. of pres. ballots
1856	Philadelphia	June 17-19	John C. Fremont	William L. Dayton	2
1860	Chicago	May 16-18	Abraham Lincoln	Hannibal Hamlin	3
1864	Baltimore	June 7-8	Abraham Lincoln	Andrew Johnson	1
1868	Chicago	May 20-21	Ulysses S. Grant	Schuyler Colfax	1
1872	Philadelphia	June 5-6	Ulysses S. Grant	Henry Wilson	1
1876	Cincinnati	June 14-16	Rutherford B. Hayes	William A. Wheeler	7
1880	Chicago	June 2-8	James A. Garfield	Chester A. Arthur	36
1884	Chicago	June 3-6	James G. Blaine	John A. Logan	4
1888	Chicago	June 19-25	Benjamin Harrison	Levi P. Morton	8
1892	Minneapolis	June 7-10	Benjamin Harrison	Whitelaw Reid	1
1896	St. Louis	June 16-18	William McKinley	Garret A. Hobart	1
1900	Philadelphia	June 19-21	William McKinley	Theodore Roosevelt	1
1904	Chicago	June 21-23	Theodore Roosevelt	Charles W. Fairbanks	1
1908	Chicago	June 16-19	William H. Taft	James S. Sherman	1
1912	Chicago	June 18-22	William H. Taft	James S. Sherman Nicholas Murray Butler *	1
1916	Chicago	June 7-10	Charles E. Hughes	Charles W. Fairbanks	3
1920	Chicago	June 8-12	Warren G. Harding	Calvin Coolidge	10
1924	Cleveland	June 10-12	Calvin Coolidge	Charles G. Dawes	1
1928	Kansas City	June 12-15	Herbert Hoover	Charles Curtis	1
1932	Chicago	June 14-16	Herbert Hoover	Charles Curtis	1
1936	Cleveland	June 9-12	Alfred M. Landon	Frank Knox	1
1940	Philadelphia	June 24-28	Wendell L. Willkie	Charles L. McNary	6
1944	Chicago	June 26-28	Thomas E. Dewey	John W. Bricker	1
1948	Philadelphia	June 21-25	Thomas E. Dewey	Earl Warren	3
1952	Chicago	July 7-11	Dwight D. Eisenhower	Richard M. Nixon	1
1956	San Francisco	August 20-23	Dwight D. Eisenhower	Richard M. Nixon	1
1960	Chicago	July 25-28	Richard Nixon	Henry Cabot Lodge	1
1964	San Francisco	July 13-16	Barry Goldwater	William E. Miller	1
1968	Miami Beach	August 5-8	Richard Nixon	Spiro T. Agnew	1
1972	Miami Beach	August 21-23	Richard Nixon	Spiro T. Agnew	1
1976	Kansas City	August 16-19	Gerald R. Ford	Robert Dole	1
1980	Detroit	July 14-17	Ronald Reagan	George Bush	1
1984	Dallas	August 20-23	Ronald Reagan	George Bush	1
1988	New Orleans	August 15-18	George Bush	Dan Quayle	1

* The 1912 Republican convention nominated James S. Sherman, who died on October 30. The Republican National Committee subsequently selected Nicholas Murray Butler to receive the Republican electoral votes for vice president.

Political Party Nominees 1988 *

The following is a comprehensive listing of major and minor party nominees for president and vice president in 1988. In 1988, as in past years, some minor parties made only token efforts at a presidential campaign. Often third party candidates decline to run after being nominated by the convention, or their names appear on the ballots of only a few states. In some cases the names of minor candidates do not appear on any state ballots and they receive only a scattering of write-in votes, if any.

Democratic party
    President: Michael Stanley Dukakis, Massachusetts
    Vice president: Lloyd Millard Bentsen, Jr., Texas

Republican party
    President: George Herbert Walker Bush, Texas
    Vice president: James Danforth Quayle, Indiana

Libertarian party
    President: Ronald Ernest Paul, Texas
    Vice president: Andre Marrou

New Alliance party
    President: Lenora B. Fulani, New York
    Vice president: Joyce Dattner

Populist party
    President: David E. Duke, Louisiana
    Vice president: Floyd C. Parker

Consumer party
    President: Eugene Joseph McCarthy, Minnesota
    Vice president: Florence Rice

American Independent party
    President: James C. Griffin, California
    Vice president: Charles J. Morsa

National Economic Recovery party
    President: Lyndon H. LaRouche, Jr., Virginia
    Vice president: Debra H. Freeman

Right to Life party
    President: William A. Marra, New Jersey
    Vice president: Joan Andrews

Workers League party
    President: Edward Winn, New York
    Vice president: Barry Porster

Socialist Workers party
    President: James Warren, New Jersey
    Vice president: Kathleen Mickells

Peace and Freedom party
    President: Herbert Lewin
    Vice president: Vikki Murdock

Prohibition party
    President: Earl F. Dodge, Colorado
    Vice president: George D. Ormsby

Workers World party
    President: Larry Holmes, New York
    Vice president: Gloria La Riva, California

Socialist party
    President: Willa Kenoyer, Minnesota
    Vice president: Ron Ehrenreich

American party
    President: Delmar Dennis, Tennessee
    Vice president: Earl Jepson

Grassroots party
    President: Jack E. Herer
    Vice president: (no first name listed) Beal

Independent party
    President: Louie Youngkeit, Utah

Third World Assembly
    President: John G. Martin, District of Columbia
    Vice president: Cleveland Sparrow

Sources: Congressional Quarterly's Guide to the Presidency, ed. Michael Nelson (Washington, D.C.: Congressional Quarterly Inc., 1989), 1451-1452, and Elections Research Center.

* In some cases a party's vice-presidential candidate varied from state to state. Candidates' full names and states were not available from some parties.

Victorious Party in Presidential Races, 1860-1988

State	1860	1864	1868	1872	1876	1880	1884	1888	1892	1896	1900	1904	1908	1912	1916	1920	1924	1928	1932	1936	1940	1944	1948	1952	1956	1960	1964	1968	1972	1976	1980	1984	1988	Dem.	Rep.	Other
Ala.	SD	[b]	R	R	D	D	D	D	D	D	D	D	D	D	D	D	D	D	D	D	D	D	SR	D	D[r]	D[s]	R	AI	R	D	R	R	R	22	7	3
Alaska																										R	D	R	R	R	R	R	R	1	7	0
Ariz.														D	D	R	R	R	D	D	D	D	D	R	R	R	R	R	R	R	R	R	R	7	13	0
Ark.	SD	[b]	R	[d]	D	D	D	D	D	D	D	D	D	D	D	D	D	D	D	D	D	D	D	D	D	D	D	AI	R	D	R	R	R	24	5	2
Calif.	R	R	R	R	R	D[f]	R	R	D[g]	R[l]	R	R	R	PR	D	R	R	R	D	D	D	D	D	R	R	R	D	R	R	R	R	R	R	9	23	1
Colo.					R	R	R	R	PP	D	D	R	D	D	D	R	R	R	D	D	R	R	D	R	R	R	D	R	R	R	R	R	R	9	14	1
Conn.	R	R	R	R	D	R	D	D	D	R	R	R	R	D	R	R	R	R	D	D	D	D	R	R	R	D	D	D	R	R	R	R	R	11	22	0
Del.	SD	D	D	R	D	D	D	R	D	R	R	R	R	D	R	R	R	R	D	D	D	D	D	R	R	D	D	R	R	D	R	R	R	14	18	1
D.C.																										D	D	D	D	D	D	D		7	0	0
Fla.	SD	[b]	R	R	R	D	D	D	D	D	D	D	D	D	D	D	D	R	D	D	D	D	D	R	R	R	D	R	R	D	R	R	R	19	12	2
Ga.	SD	[b]	D	D[e]	D	D	D	D	D	D	D	D	D	D	D	D	D	D	D	D	D	D	D	D	D	D	R	AI	R	D	D	R	R	26	4	2
Hawaii																										D	D	D	R	D	D	R	D	6	2	0
Idaho									PP	D	D	R	R	D	D	R	R	R	D	D	D	D	D	R	R	R	D	R	R	R	R	R	R	10	14	1
Ill.	R	R	R	R	R	R	R	R	D	R	R	R	R	D	R	R	R	R	D	D	D	D	D	R	R	D	D	R	R	R	R	R	R	9	24	0
Ind.	R	R	R	R	D	R	D	R	D	R	R	R	R	D	R	R	R	R	D	D	R	R	R	R	R	R	D	R	R	R	R	R	R	7	26	0
Iowa	R	R	R	R	R	R	R	R	R	R	R	R	R	D	R	R	R	R	D	D	R	R	D	R	R	R	D	R	R	R	R	R	D	6	27	0
Kan.		R	R	R	R	R	R	R	PP	D	R	R	R	D	D	R	R	R	D	D	R	R	R	R	R	R	D	R	R	R	R	R	R	6	25	1
Ky.	CU	D	D	D	D	D	D	D	D	R[m]	D	D	D	D	D	D	R	R	D	D	D	D	D	D	R	R	D	R	R	D	R	R	R	22	10	1
La.	SD	[b]	D	[d]	R	D	D	D	D	D	D	D	D	D	D	D	D	D	D	D	D	D	SR	D	R	D	R	AI	R	D	R	R	R	21	7	3
Maine	R	R	R	R	R	R	R	R	R	R	R	R	R	D	R	R	R	R	R	R	R	R	R	R	R	R	D	D	R	R	R	R	R	3	30	0
Md.	SD	R	D	R	D	D	D	D	D	R	R	D[n]	D[o]	D	D	R	R	R	D	D	D	D	R	R	R	D	D	D	R	D	D	R	R	20	12	1
Mass.	R	R	R	R	R	R	R	R	R	R	R	R	R	D	R	R	R	D	D	D	D	D	D	R	R	D	D	D	D	D	R	R	D	13	20	0
Mich.	R	R	R	R	R	R	R	R	R[h]	R	R	R	R	PR	R	R	R	R	D	D	R	R	D	R	R	D	D	D	R	R	R	R	R	6	26	1
Minn.	R	R	R	R	R	R	R	R	R	R	R	R	R	PR	R	R	R	R	D	D	D	D	D	R	R	D	D	D	R	D	D	D	D	12	20	1
Miss.	SD	[b]	[c]	R	D	D	D	D	D	D	D	D	D	D	D	D	D	D	D	D	D	D	SR	D	D	[t]	R	AI	R	D	R	R	R	21	7	3
Mo.	D	R	R	D	D	D	D	D	D	D	D	R	R	D	D	R	R	R	D	D	D	D	D	R	D	D	D	R	R	D	R	R	R	20	13	0
Mont.									R	D	D	R	R	D	D	R	R	R	D	D	D	D	D	R	R	R	D	R	R	R	R	R	R	10	15	0
Neb.			R	R	R	R	R	R	R	D	R	R	D	D	D	R	R	R	D	D	R	R	R	R	R	R	D	R	R	R	R	R	R	7	24	0
Nev.		R	R	R	R	D	R	R	PP	D	D	R	D	D	D	R	R	R	D	D	D	D	D	R	R	D	D	R	R	R	R	R	R	13	18	1
N.H.	R	R	R	R	R	R	R	R	R	R	R	R	R	D	D	R	R	R	R	D	D	D	R	R	R	R	D	R	R	R	R	R	R	6	27	0
N.J.	R[a]	D	D	R	D	D	D	D	D	R	R	R	R	D	R	R	R	R	D	D	D	D	R	R	R	D	D	R	R	R	R	R	R	14	19	0
N.M.														D	D	R	R	R	D	D	D	D	D	R	R	D	D	R	R	R	R	R	R	9	11	0
N.Y.	R	R	D	R	D	R	D	R	D	R	R	R	R	D	R	R	R	R	D	D	D	D	R	R	R	D	D	D	R	D	R	R	D	13	20	1
N.C.	SD	[b]	R	R	D	D	D	D	D	D	D	D	D	D	D	D	D	R	D	D	D	D	D	D	D	D	R[v]	R	D	R	R	R		23	8	1
N.D.									[i]	R	R	R	R	D	D	R	R	R	D	D	R	R	R	R	R	R	D	R	R	R	R	R	R	5	19	1
Ohio	R	R	R	R	R	R	R	R	R[j]	R	R	R	R	D	D	R	R	R	D	D	D	R	D	R	R	R	D	R	R	D	R	R	R	8	25	0
Okla.													D	D	D	R	D	R	D	D	D	D	D	R	R	R[u]	D	R	R	R	R	R	R	10	11	0
Ore.	R	R	D	R	R	R	R	R	R[k]	R	R	R	R	D	R	R	R	R	D	D	D	D	R	R	R	R	D	R	R	R	R	R	D	8	25	1
Pa.	R	R	R	R	R	R	R	R	R	R	R	R	R	PR	R	R	R	R	R	D	D	D	R	R	R	D	D	D	R	D	R	R	R	7	25	1
R.I.	R	R	R	R	R	R	R	R	R	R	R	R	R	D	R	R	R	D	D	D	D	D	D	R	R	D	D	D	R	D	D	R	D	13	20	0
S.C.	SD	[b]	R	R	R	D	D	D	D	D	D	D	D	D	D	D	D	D	D	D	D	D	SR	D	D	D	R	R	R	D	R	R	R	21	9	2
S.D.									R	D	R	R	R	PR	R	R	R	R	D	D	R	R	R	R	R	R	D	R	R	R	R	R	R	4	20	1
Tenn.	CU	[b]	R	D	D	D	D	D	D	D	D	D	D	D	D	R	D	R	D	D	D	D	D[q]	R	R	R	D	R	R	D	R	R	R	20	11	1
Texas	SD	[b]	[c]	D	D	D	D	D	D	D	D	D	D	D	D	D	D	R	D	D	D	D	D	R	R	D	D	D	R	D	R	R	R	23	7	1
Utah										D	R	R	R	R	D	R	R	R	D	D	D	D	D	R	R	R	D	R	R	R	R	R	R	8	16	0
Vt.	R	R	R	R	R	R	R	R	R	R	R	R	R	R	R	R	R	R	R	R	R	R	R	R	R	R	D	R	R	R	R	R	R	1	32	0
Va.	CU	[b]	[c]	R	D	D	D	D	D	D	D	D	D	D	D	D	D	R	D	D	D	D	D	R	R	R	D	R	R	R[w]	R	R	R	19	11	1
Wash.									R	D	R	R	R	D	D	R	R	R	D	D	D	D	D	R	R	R	D	D	R	R	R	R	D[x]	10	14	1
W.Va.		R	R	R	D	D	D	D	D	R	R	R	R	D	R[p]	R	R	R	D	D	D	D	D	D	R	D	D	D	R	D	D	R	D	18	14	0
Wis.	R	R	R	R	R	R	R	R	D	R	R	R	R	D	R	R	PR	R	D	D	D	R	D	R	R	R	D	R	R	D	R	R	D	9	23	1
Wyo.									R	D	R	R	R	D	D	R	R	R	D	D	D	R	D	R	R	R	D	R	R	R	R	R	R	8	17	0
Winning party	R	R	R	R	R	R	D	R	D	R	R	R	R	D	D	R	R	R	D	D	D	D	D	R	R	D	D	R	R	D	R	R	R	12	21	0

Note: With the exception of the District of Columbia, blanks indicate states not yet admitted to the Union. The District of Columbia received the presidential vote in 1961.

Key: A—American party; AI—American Union party; CU—Constitutional Union party; D—Democratic party; PP—People's party; PR—Progressive (Bull Moose) party; R—Republican party; SD—Southern Democratic party; SR—States' Rights party.

a. Four electors voted Republican; three, Democratic.
b. Confederate States did not vote in 1864.
c. Did not vote in 1868.
d. Votes were not counted.
e. Three votes for Greeley not counted.
f. Five electors voted Democratic; one, Republican.
g. Eight electors voted Democratic; one, Republican.
h. Nine electors voted Republican; five, Democratic.
i. One vote each for Democratic, Republican, and People's party.
j. Twenty-two electors voted Republican, one, Democratic.
k. Three electors voted Republican; one, People's party.
l. Eight electors voted Republican; one, Democratic.
m. Twelve electors voted Republican; one, Democratic.
n. Seven electors voted Democratic; one, Republican.
o. Six electors voted Democratic; two, Republican.
p. Seven electors voted Republican; one, Democratic.
q. Eleven electors voted Democratic; one, States' Rights.
r. One elector voted for Walter Jones.
s. Six of eleven electors voted for Harry F. Byrd.
t. Eight independent electors voted for Byrd.
u. One vote cast for Byrd.
v. Twelve electors voted Republican; one, American Independent.
w. One elector voted Libertarian.
x. One elector voted for Ronald Reagan.

Part II
Presidential Elections

History of Presidential Elections

Presidential elections have been perhaps the most influential events in national politics, giving shape to dominant issues, the makeup of national parties and interest groups, regional economic and political alignments, and the way citizens understand and talk about society.

Campaigns for the White House have shaped U.S. politics in several stages and cycles. As the franchise has expanded and electronic media have exercised greater influence, presidential politics have become more broadbased and concerned about the way government can address the needs and demands of innumerable groups.

Presidential elections throughout U.S. history have been at the center of political controversies involving disputes between the branches of government, federalism, banking, tariffs and other taxes, economic change, corporate power, unions, international affairs, social welfare programs, and consumer issues.

Meanwhile, presidential politics also have moved in cycles of conservatism and liberalism, activism and consolidation, elitism and populism, isolationism and internationalism. Presidential elections have articulated the changing moods of the nation since the very first election.

Original Constitutional Provisions

The method of choosing the president proved to be but one of many vexing problems for the fifty-five men who assembled in Philadelphia in May 1787 to draft the Constitution. The Articles of Confederation, which the Constitution would replace, was riddled with weaknesses. Adopted in 1781, the Articles established an impotent federal government consisting of a weak congress and no single executive (although there was a "Committee of States" with no power worth speaking of that sat when the congress was not in session). By the time the Constitutional Convention convened, the Confederacy was but a "cobweb." [1]

From the start of the convention, it was clear that the federal government would be strengthened and that there would be some sort of executive branch. The convention was split, however, between those who wanted a strong executive (the "presidentialists") and those who were wary of executive authority and wanted to increase the power of the national legislature instead (the "congressionalists"). [2]

There was also the question of whether the "national executive" should consist of several individuals or just one. Congressionalists wanted a plural executive with minimal power. Presidentialists wanted a strong executive with power vested in the hands of one individual. Debate over this point was extremely heated.

As it became clear that the executive power would be singular, the tension between the two camps shifted to the question of presidential selection. Congressionalists, anxious that the executive remain subservient to the legislature, wanted the president to be elected by Congress. Presidentialists, however, did not want Congress to exercise that power.

This issue remained unresolved for most of the summer. By the end of August there was still not a consensus on how to select the president. That issue, along with other "questions not settled," was sent to the Committee on Postponed Matters for resolution. Since the committee was dominated by presidentialists, it pushed for a proposal that would avoid legislative appointment. The result was a compromise that was reported to the convention on September 4, 1787, and that served, with little alteration, as the basis for the actual constitutional provision.

The compromise, as finally approved, provided for indirect election of the president by the so-called electoral college. [3] This system allowed each state to appoint (in the manner directed by its own legislature) the same number of electors as it had senators and representatives in Congress. (Virginia, for example, had two senators and ten representatives in Congress and so could choose twelve electors.) Those electors would then meet in their respective states and vote by ballot for two persons (at least one of whom must be from a state other than that inhabited by the elector). When the ballots of all the electors from all the states were tallied, the candidate with the greatest number of votes would become president (assuming it was a majority), and the second-place candidate would become vice president. In case of a tie or if no candidate received a majority, the decision would be made by the House of Representatives. [4]

The compromise won the support of the convention because it so successfully placated all parties concerned. First of all it provided for the president to be selected by electors. This satisfied the presidentialists who were opposed to appointment by Congress. It also satisfied those who were wary of direct election by the masses. Electors, it was thought, would infuse an element of reason into the selection process, thereby stabilizing the whims of mass opinion.

Second, individual state legislatures were allowed to determine how electors would be chosen in their respective states. The language of the clause left open a wide range of options for that process. As a result the convention did not have to agree upon one method of appointing electors for all the states.

Third, if no candidate received a majority, the election would be decided by the House of Representatives. Since it was widely assumed that no candidate after George Washington would receive a majority of votes from the electors, many thought that selection by the House would become the norm. Thus, congressionalists could argue that they had lost the battle but won the war. From their perspective electors usually would nominate candidates, and the House would select the winner.

Finally, since each elector voted for two persons—one of whom could not be from the elector's state—"favorite son" candidates would tend to cancel one another out. This helped to dispel the fear that large states would consistently elect their own favorite sons. Nevertheless, since the number of electors from each state would equal the state's total number of senators and representatives in Congress, the relative weight of more populous states would not be discounted.

The Framers' View of Parties

Whatever the particular motivations of the Framers, it is clear that they were proponents of moderation. It is also clear that they held a quite different understanding of the presidential selection process than that which is generally accepted today. Most notably the Framers envisaged a nonpartisan process. Political parties (or "factions") were viewed as a political evil. The goal of the selection process was to promote men of civic virtue who would be able to exercise unfettered judgment.

The Framers' view of political parties was a natural outgrowth of the Anglo-American tradition. Opposition parties are now considered an essential part of representative democracy, but the Framers believed they would cause tumult and discord. Political scientist Richard Hofstadter has argued that, in eighteenth-century British political thought, there were three archetypal views of party that could have influenced the Framers.[5]

The first, which he called "the Hamiltonian view" (since it is a position associated with Alexander Hamilton), was based on the antiparty doctrine of Bolingbroke, an English statesman, who wrote two important pamphlets on politics in the 1730s. For Bolingbroke, the best sort of state would be led by a "patriot king," a benign monarch who would subdue factions by good statecraft. To him, parties were by definition antithetical to the common good. Nevertheless, he conceived of instances when a uniting "country party" speaking for the nation as a whole rather than for particular interests could be used to restore stability in a state.

The second view, which Hofstadter termed "Madisonian" after James Madison, was based on the writings of the eighteenth-century Scottish philosopher David Hume. Like Bolingbroke, Hume thought that parties were evil, but unlike Bolingbroke he thought that their existence was inevitable in a free state. Champions of liberty could check

and limit the excesses of parties, but they could not abolish them. Madison expressed this view in *Federalist* No. 10, concluding that the only satisfactory method of "curing the mischiefs of faction" was to control their effects. To remove their cause would be to destroy liberty.

Finally, Hofstadter pointed to the views of British statesman Edmund Burke, who felt that parties were not only inevitable, but—for the most part—good. But Burke's writing, published in 1770, came too late to influence the Framers at the Constitutional Convention. Instead, both the Federalists and Anti-Federalists condemned parties. Each side hoped to eliminate the other, thus forming a united nonpartisan state. From their perspective the common good would triumph over the petty rivalries and selfish interests that political parties would produce.

Thus, the Framers adhered to one or the other of Hofstadter's first two archetypes. It was the resulting doctrine of nonpartisanship that allowed for the original vice-presidential selection process. Since the Framers did not contemplate partisan contests among candidates, they did not foresee a problem with having the second-place candidate become vice president.

Voting Requirements

Aside from the Framers' views of political parties, the electorate in the eighteenth century was quite different from the electorate today. The Constitution left it to the states to determine voting requirements. In all states only men could vote. Furthermore, in many states property ownership was a prerequisite for the right to vote. Indeed, property qualifications had existed in all the colonies and endured in many of the states, although the exact qualifications differed among states. Colonial restrictions tended to be harsher than those adopted by the states and were often based on a measure of real estate. Some colonies, such as Massachusetts, had religious qualifications for voting.[6]

Virginia, the home of some of the most important members of the Constitutional Convention and four of the first five presidents, is a good example. Property possession had been a prerequisite for the vote there since 1677. From 1705 until 1736 the laws were liberal: any male tenant who held land for life (his own or that of another person such as his wife or child) was considered a "freeholder" and could vote. In other words, as a qualification to vote, leasing property for the duration of one's own lifetime or for that of a family member was the equivalent of owning property. From 1736 onward the definition of *freeholder* was more restrictive. A man living in the country had to hold twenty-five acres of cultivated land with a house or one hundred acres (changed to fifty in 1762) of uncleared land with no settlement, in order to vote. A man living in town had to hold a house with a lot.[7] By the standards of the time those requirements were not excessive.[8]

The American Revolution brought no suffrage reform to Virginia, although it did to other states. The Virginia constitution of 1776 stated that voting requirements "shall remain as exercised at present."[9] Thus, even those who paid taxes or fought in the militia could not vote unless they held the requisite amount of land. By 1800 Virginia was one of five states that retained real estate property qualifications. (At the other extreme four states had established universal manhood suffrage by 1800.) While various other states allowed personal property or the payment of taxes to substitute for holding real estate, Virginia held on to its old property qualifications until 1830. By that time it was the only state to retain freehold suffrage throughout. Even the reform of 1830 brought little change. Householders were added to the franchise—a very modest step toward universal manhood suffrage.[10]

Property requirements of one sort or another were not abandoned by all the states until 1856. It is not entirely clear how much of the electorate was excluded by property requirements; historians differ on this point, sometimes quite markedly.[11] One should keep in mind, however, that the effect of property qualifications, while certainly restrictive, can be overstated. Because the United States was predominantly a middle-class society with fairly widespread ownership of property, such qualifications were not as significant a limit as they may first appear.

Conceptions of political parties and suffrage different from those we are accustomed to today were part of the milieu in which the original constitutional provision for presidential selection was created. Elements of that provision soon proved to be flawed and were superseded by the Twelfth Amendment, which provided for presidential and vice-presidential votes to be tallied on separate ballots. Nevertheless, the provision met the needs of the moment: it was an acceptable compromise of the diverse positions both within the Constitutional Convention and among the states that would ratify it.

The Electoral College

The Founders intended the selection of the president to be the work of the "electoral college," a group comprised of the nation's most learned and public-spirited citizens. The electors were to be selected by the states as they saw fit; the electors then would meet in their separate states sometime after their selection to pick the next president. As it operates today, electors meet in state capitals on the first Monday after the second Wednesday of December and prepare a statement of their vote to send to Washington, where Congress counts the votes January 6. Since 1836 all the states except Maine have allocated delegates to candidates on a "winner-take-all" basis. (Maine allocates delegates by special presidential-elector districts.) States receive one elector for each representative and senator in Congress. If no candidate wins an electoral majority, the House of Representatives decides the election, with each state casting one vote.

The winner-take-all system is a moderating influence on U.S. politics. Political strategies depend on attracting as many diverse groups as possible under the same political banner in order to win the whole state rather than only a part of the state. Systems of proportional representation (in which parties or candidates receive representation according to their percentage of the popular vote) tend to complicate bargaining and to fragment coalitions by giving representation to minority parties.

Concern has been expressed about a possible deadlock in the electoral college if the election involves more than two candidates. If no candidate wins a majority of all electoral votes, the election is to be decided by the House. If a third-party candidate wins one or two states in a close race, he or she could play an important "broker" role either in the electoral college or in the House. The legitimacy of a race decided by backroom deals, for example, would be in serious question.

When the Electoral College Is Deadlocked

When no presidential candidate receives a majority of the electoral vote, the Constitution directs that the election be decided by the House of Representatives. Originally, the House also selected the vice president in such a situation (as it did in 1800) since there was then no separate ballot for presidential and vice-presidential candidates. Under that system the second-place candidate became vice president. That changed in 1804 with the ratification of the Twelfth Amendment, which directed that electors vote for president and vice president on separate ballots. Since then the House has been directed to select the president and the Senate the vice president when the election is deadlocked.

The Framers of the Constitution originally thought that most presidential elections would be deadlocked. George Mason, for one, predicted that nineteen out of twenty elections would be decided by the House.[1] In fact, only two presidential elections—those of 1800 and 1824—have been so decided.

Procedure. If an election is thrown to the House, the newly elected representatives select the president from among the three candidates with the most electoral votes. The fact that the new House, rather than the "lame-duck" House, selects the president is provided for by statute. The Twentieth Amendment to the Constitution (ratified in 1933) specifies that the new Congress convene on January 3 and the inauguration take place January 20. Before that amendment both the new Congress and the new presidential term began on March 4; thus, the old lame-duck Congress was forced to select the president.

The changes brought about by the Twentieth Amendment meant that Congress would have considerably less time to choose a president if the electoral college were deadlocked. Originally, the Twelfth Amendment gave the House until March 4 to select the president. If the House did not make a decision by that date, the amendment called for the vice president-elect (chosen, if necessary, by the Senate) to "act as president as in the case of the death or other constitutional disability of the president."[2] Under the current system the House has only about two weeks to make a choice before the inaugural date of January 20. If the House is deadlocked and cannot make a choice by that date, the Twentieth Amendment directs that the vice president-elect "shall act as president *until a president shall have qualified.*"[3]

The language surrounding that provision can be read in different ways. For instance, legal scholars Laurence H. Tribe and Thomas M. Rollins of Harvard have argued that the House, if deadlocked, "could go on voting, with interruptions for other business and indeed with an infusion of members in midterm, for four full years." They pointed out that this would transform our government into a "quasi-parliamentary system," since the acting president would be "subject to termination at any time until the House deadlock is finally broken."[4] Political scientist Allan P. Sindler has argued, however, that the deadline of March 4 that was imposed by the Twelfth Amendment was not superseded by the Twentieth Amendment. As such, he argues that the House can replace the acting president only *until* that time. If the House acts before March 4, the acting president becomes vice president.[5]

When selecting the president, each state delegation in

the House has one vote, and no vote is cast if the delegation is evenly divided. Members of the delegation vote by secret ballot, and an absolute majority of the delegations (twenty-six of the fifty states) is necessary for election.[6]

If no vice-presidential candidate receives a majority of votes in the electoral college, the selection is made by the Senate between the two candidates with the most electoral votes. Unlike the House procedure, the Senate procedure allows each senator one vote. Again, an absolute majority—fifty-one votes—is needed for the election. Since the Senate chooses among only the top two candidates and is not beset with the potential problems of split delegations, the vice-presidential selection process is somewhat less complicated than the presidential selection process. By statute the new Senate (as convened on January 3) makes the decision.

The selection process is further complicated if neither a president nor a vice president can be decided upon by the date set for inauguration. In such an event the Twentieth Amendment empowers Congress to decide "who shall then act as President, or the manner in which one who is to act shall be selected, and such person shall act accordingly until a President or Vice President shall have qualified."[7]

The Presidential Succession Act of 1947 now covers such a circumstance. The act calls for the Speaker of the House and the president pro tempore of the Senate, in that order, to serve as acting president until a candidate qualifies. To so serve, they must resign their seat in the legislature.[8] If they refuse, the line of succession reverts to members of the cabinet of the incumbent (previous) administration in the order in which the cabinet offices were established (beginning with secretary of state). Although there were two earlier presidential succession acts (in 1792 and 1886), the 1947 act—in conformity with the Twentieth Amendment—was the first to deal with vacancies caused by the failure of candidates to qualify.[9]

Neither the constitutional provisions nor the succession act specifies what criteria legislators should use in choosing among the designated candidates. As many commentators have pointed out, this raises several problems. Should legislators vote for the candidate with the most electoral votes or the most popular votes? If they base their decision on the popular vote, should they look at the popular vote in their district or their state or in the nation as a whole? Or should they simply vote for the candidate of their party or of their conscience? Could they bargain away their votes to the "highest bidder," so to speak?[10] Although there is little to guide legislators in making such decisions, there no doubt would be considerable pressure to act in a fashion that would foster an orderly and legitimate transfer of power.

Precedents: 1800 and 1824. Presidential elections have been thrown to the House of Representatives only twice in our history: in 1800 and 1824. In the first case the deadlock was brought on by the old method of electors voting for the president and vice president on the same ballot. Each elector had two votes, and when all the votes were tallied, the second-place candidate became vice president. The Federalist ticket consisted of John Adams for president and Charles Cotesworth Pinckney for vice president; the Republican ticket consisted of Thomas Jefferson and Aaron Burr. When the electors voted in December 1800, the two Republican candidates tied for first place.

This example illustrates some of the pitfalls of the legislative selection process. Under the provisions then in

The People's Choice?

Most presidential winners have sought to portray their victory as a mandate from the American people. But even landslide victors in the nationwide popular vote have been the choice of barely one-third of the entire voting-age population.

The chart below compares the percentage of the popular vote that presidential winners since 1932 have received with the percentage of the entire voting-age population that their vote total represents. The latter percentage is based on voting-age population estimates updated each election year by the Census Bureau.

Year	Winner (Party)	Percentage of total popular vote	Percentage of voting-age population
1932	Roosevelt (D)	57.4	30.1
1936	Roosevelt (D)	60.8	34.6
1940	Roosevelt (D)	54.7	32.2
1944	Roosevelt (D)	53.4	29.9
1948	Truman (D)	49.6	25.3
1952	Eisenhower (R)	55.1	34.0
1956	Eisenhower (R)	57.4	34.1
1960	Kennedy (D)	49.7	31.2
1964	Johnson (D)	61.1	37.8
1968	Nixon (R)	43.4	26.4
1972	Nixon (R)	60.7	33.5
1976	Carter (D)	50.1	26.8
1980	Reagan (R)	50.7	26.7
1984	Reagan (R)	58.8	31.2
1988	Bush (R)	53.4	26.8

effect, the old lame-duck House (which had a Federalist majority) selected the president. Many Federalists considered Aaron Burr less repugnant than Thomas Jefferson and therefore plotted to elect him president (even though it was clear that Jefferson was the presidential candidate and Burr was the vice-presidential candidate).

Although Alexander Hamilton strongly discouraged the idea, the majority of Federalists in the House backed Burr. If the Constitution had allowed the decision to be made by the vote of individual members (rather than by the bloc votes of state delegations), Burr would have won. As it stood, the situation remained deadlocked. Balloting began on February 11, 1801, but no candidate received a majority. It soon became apparent that the House deadlock would not be broken quickly. One observer recalled: "Many [congressmen] sent home for night caps and pillows, and wrapped in shawls and great-coats, lay about the floor of the committee rooms or sat sleeping in their seats. At one, two, and half-past two, the tellers roused the members from their slumbers, and took the same ballot as before."[11]

Seven days and thirty-six ballots later, the tide turned. The day before, Federalist representative James Bayard of

Delaware told a party caucus that balloting had gone on long enough. To delay the process any longer would run risk to the Constitution. After receiving word from Maryland Republican boss Samuel Smith that Jefferson would preserve the Hamiltonian financial system, respect the integrity of the navy, and refrain from dismissing Federalists in subordinate government jobs simply on the grounds of politics, Bayard was convinced that the Federalists must relent. Thus, on the thirty-sixth ballot Bayard and the Burr supporters from Maryland, South Carolina, and Vermont cast blank ballots, giving the presidency to Jefferson and the vice presidency to Burr.[12]

The election of 1824 is the only one thrown to the House since the adoption of the Twelfth Amendment. The fact that no candidate received a majority of the electoral vote count that year was largely a result of the crowded field of candidates. By 1824 the Federalist party was dead. It appeared that whoever was nominated by the Republicans' "King Caucus" would surely be elected president. The congressional caucus, however, was subject to increasing criticism. The caucus system was a holdover from an age that distrusted mass democratic sentiments, and that age was coming to an end.

As it turned out, attendance at the caucus was meager. The caucus nominated William H. Crawford (who had served as secretary of the Treasury under President James Monroe), but others balked at the choice, for two reasons. First, Crawford had suffered a paralytic stroke the year before that left him greatly impaired. Second, populist sentiment was rising, and Crawford's selection by a small group of legislators smacked of political manipulation. State legislatures promptly nominated John Quincy Adams, John C. Calhoun, Henry Clay, and Andrew Jackson for president.

Attempts were made to limit the field of candidates, but they were to little avail. Crawford's men dropped his running mate, Albert Gallatin, in the hopes that they could persuade Clay to take his place. Their plan was that Clay supporters, recognizing that Crawford might not live out his term, would push Crawford to victory. Clay, preferring to gamble on the possibility of winning on his own merits, refused.[13] Among the candidates only Calhoun withdrew from the presidential race.

When the votes of the electoral college were in, no candidate had a majority. Jackson stood in front with ninety-nine electoral votes, followed by Adams with eighty-four, Crawford with forty-one, and Clay with thirty-seven. In accord with the Twelfth Amendment, the names of Jackson, Adams, and Crawford were placed before the House. It was immediately evident that the support of Clay would tip the balance between the two front-runners.

Clay was not fond of either candidate, but he clearly felt that Adams was the lesser of two evils. In early January, Clay and Adams conferred, and Clay let it be known that he would support Adams in the House election. Soon thereafter a letter in a Philadelphia newspaper alleged that Adams had offered Clay the post of secretary of state in return for his support. Jackson was furious, and his rage was all the worse when Adams won the House election with a bare minimum of thirteen out of twenty-four state delegations and proceeded to name Clay secretary of state. Thus, Jackson, who had more popular and electoral votes than any of the other candidates in the general election, did not become president.

The Senate has chosen a vice president only once, in 1837. Martin Van Buren was elected president that year

with 170 of 294 electoral votes. His running mate, Richard M. Johnson of Kentucky, however, received only 147 electoral votes (one less than a majority). A group of twenty-three Virginia electors who supported Van Buren boycotted Johnson because of his long-term romantic entanglement with a black woman.[14] The remainder of the electoral votes were split among three other candidates. Francis Granger of New York received 77 electoral votes, John Tyler of Virginia received 47, and William Smith of Alabama received 23.

The names of the top two candidates were sent to the Senate. In making the selection, the Senate adopted a resolution that called for the senators to vote by voice vote in alphabetical order.[15] The Senate confirmed Johnson's election by a vote of thirty-three to sixteen.

Threats. Although no presidential election has been thrown to the House since 1824, several have come close. The elections of Abraham Lincoln in 1860 and John F. Kennedy in 1960, for instance, would have gone to the House given a shift of only thirty thousand popular votes.[16] A relatively small shift of votes could also have sent the elections of 1836, 1856, 1892, 1948, 1968, and 1976 to the House. *(See "Chronology of Elections," p. 99.)*

Often threats are precipitated by the presence of a third party candidate in the race. In 1948 a group of disgruntled southern Democrats formed the States' Rights (or Dixiecrat) party in opposition to a strong civil rights plank adopted at the Democratic National Convention. The Dixiecrats' candidate, Gov. J. Strom Thurmond of South Carolina, captured thirty-nine electoral votes.

In 1968 Alabama governor George C. Wallace ran as a strong third party candidate, receiving forty-six electoral votes. There was widespread fear that year that Wallace would deadlock the election and throw it to the House. Well aware of his strategic position, Wallace elicited written affidavits from his electors promising that they would vote as he instructed them. Wallace took a hard stance on the terms that he required for delivering those votes to another candidate. Among other things he called for the repeal of all civil rights legislation, the repeal of the federal antipoverty program, and the criminal indictment of anyone advocating Viet Cong victory in the Vietnam War.[17]

Although the independent candidacy of John Anderson failed to win any electoral votes in 1980, and Ronald Reagan won the race by a wide margin, there was fear early on in the campaign that Anderson's presence would deadlock that election. At the 1980 Republican National Convention, former president Gerald R. Ford predicted precisely such an outcome.[18] Similar fears were expressed about the third party candidacies of Theodore Roosevelt in 1912 and Robert La Follette in 1924.

To an extent, such fears are fanned by party regulars in an attempt to discount the influence of a third party candidate. A vote for such a candidate is worse than just a wasted vote, they argue; it is one that could lead to a "constitutional crisis." It is not just the presence of third party candidates that threatens to deadlock presidential elections, however. Neck-in-neck races between Kennedy and Nixon in 1960 and between Carter and Ford in 1976 came close to such a deadlock.

Ironically, the Constitution's Framers took great pride in the same system of House election that we now view with great fear. Whether that fear is justified or not is a matter of debate. Nonetheless, it is a fear that periodically haunts our political landscape.

Proposed Reforms
in the Electoral College

Numerous reforms have been proposed to alter both the fundamental concept of the electoral college and some of its obsolete and odd aspects. One reform would eliminate faithless electors by automatically casting a state's electoral votes for the candidate receiving the most popular votes. A second reform would allocate electoral votes by congressional district rather than by state and would give the state's two electors who represent its senators to the top presidential candidate as a bonus. A third proposal would provide for proportional allocation of a state's electoral votes—which could lead to more deadlocks and congressional selection of presidents because there would be more opportunity for third and fourth parties to garner electors. A fourth proposal would do away with the electoral college altogether through direct election of the president, with a runoff if no candidate achieved a majority. Another reform would give the popular-vote victor "bonus" electors for each state. A final proposal would alter the way Congress voted in the event of an electoral college deadlock by allowing House members to vote individually rather than having one vote for each state.

Congress has never passed a constitutional reform of presidential elections for submission to the states, although the Senate passed a direct election proposal in the 1970s. Any of these changes would require a constitutional amendment, and amending the Constitution is a long and arduous process. Under the most prominent method, Congress submits the proposed amendment to the states for ratification, and two-thirds of all state legislatures must approve the amendment for it to become law. In the absence of a major crisis, an overhaul of the electoral college is unlikely.

Chronology of Presidential Elections

The presidential selection process has changed significantly since George Washington was elected to his first term in 1789. In part, this is because the constitutional provisions for presidential selection are so vague.

There are no provisions for organizing political parties, for nominating candidates, or for campaigning for office. Indeed, the Framers assumed (incorrectly) that the selection process would be a reasoned one that would transcend petty partisanship. Furthermore, the original provision for balloting by the electoral college was flawed and had to be superseded by the Twelfth Amendment in 1804.

As a result of the Constitution's ambiguities, the method of choosing presidential and vice-presidential candidates has gone through several distinct phases. Political scientist Richard P. McCormick has identified four such phases.[1]

The first phase was a period marked by uncertain and hazardous rules that lasted until the Twelfth Amendment was ratified in 1804. The second phase, continuing through 1820, was dominated by the Democratic-Republicans and is associated with the nomination of candidates by congressional caucus. The third phase was precipitated by the demise of "'King Caucus" in 1824 and was characterized by factional politics and a period of time when the rules for selecting candidates were in flux. The fourth phase—ongoing today—evolved between 1832 and 1844 and is characterized by a two-party system that nominates candidates by national conventions.

Election of 1789

The Constitution was ratified in July 1788—nearly nine months after the close of the Constitutional Convention in Philadelphia. The continental Congress then decided that the seat of government would be New York City. There, on September 13, 1788, Congress passed a resolution that the states should appoint electors on the first Wednesday in January, that those electors would assemble and vote in their respective states on the first Wednesday in February, and that the new government would convene on the first Wednesday in March.

The method of choosing electors was left up to the individual state legislatures. The fact that all electors had to be chosen on the same day proved to be troublesome for the states since some did not have time to call elections.

In 1789 there was no formal nomination of candidates. It had been obvious since the close of the Constitutional Convention that George Washington would be president, even though he was not anxious to serve. The only real question was who would be vice president. Federalist leaders ultimately decided to support John Adams.

Under the existing constitutional provision, each elector cast two votes. The two votes had to be for different persons—one of whom could not be from the same state as the elector. The individual receiving the votes of a majority of the electors was named president, and the person receiv-

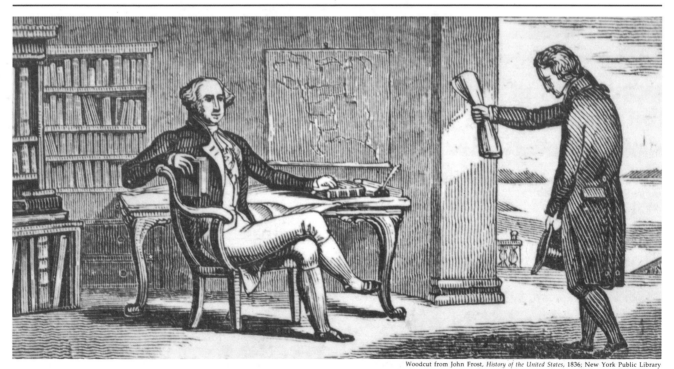

Woodcut from John Frost, *History of the United States,* 1836; New York Public Library

After riding his horse for a full week, Charles Thomson, secretary of the Continental Congress, arrived at Mt. Vernon on April 14, 1789, with the official news of George Washington's election as the first president of the United States.

ing the second highest total was named vice president. Since no distinction was made between balloting for president and vice president, it was possible for both candidates to receive an equal number of votes, thus throwing the election to the House of Representatives. It also was possible that the candidate for vice president—through fluke or machination—actually could end up with the most votes and therefore become president.

Federalist leader Alexander Hamilton recognized the danger all too clearly. Hamilton's concern was further fueled by his personal animosity toward Adams. He therefore plotted to siphon away votes from Adams. In a letter to James Wilson of Pennsylvania, Hamilton wrote: "Everybody is aware of that defect in the constitution which renders it possible that the man intended for vice president may in fact turn up president." To prevent that, Hamilton recommended that several votes that would otherwise have gone to Adams be thrown away on other candidates: "I have proposed to friends in Connecticut to throw away 2 [votes], to others in New Jersey to throw away an equal number and I submit to you whether it would not be well to lose three or four in Pennsylvania...."[2]

Hamilton's efforts were successful. Washington was unanimously elected president with sixty-nine electoral votes. Adams, however, won the vice presidency with only thirty-four electoral votes. Only two states—New Hampshire and his own Massachusetts—voted solidly for Adams. In other states, Federalist leaders withheld support from Adams and sometimes worked against him. Adams did not receive *any* votes from Delaware, Georgia, Maryland, or South Carolina, and he received only one vote from New Jersey. The remaining votes were spread among ten other candidates, including John Jay, John Hancock, Robert Harrison, John Rutledge, and George Clinton.

Although the new government was supposed to begin on March 4, 1789, not enough members of Congress had arrived in New York City by that date to have a quorum. The Senate finally convened on April 6 to count the electoral votes. A messenger was dispatched by horse to deliver news of the election's outcome to president-elect Washington, who was in Mount Vernon. He received the news on April 14. Washington then set out for New York, where he was sworn in on April 30.

The election of 1789 demonstrated the potential for partisanship and intrigue in presidential contests. It also pointed out the weaknesses of the existing election calendar (which had made it difficult for New York to participate in the election) and reminded participants of the danger of the constitutional "defect" in the selection process that made it possible for the person intended to be vice president to become president.

Washington's Reelection: 1792

The election of 1792 was different from its predecessor in at least two ways. First, the election calendar was changed and made more flexible by an act of Congress. That law remained in effect until 1845. It allowed states to choose electors within a thirty-four-day span before the first Wednesday in December when the electors met to vote. The second difference was that an overtly partisan contest broke out between the Federalists and the Democratic-Republicans over the vice presidency when the Democratic-Republicans decided to contest the reelection of

Thomas Pinckney, the Federalist vice-presidential candidate, lost in the 1796 election, although his running mate, presidential candidate John Adams, won. Democratic-Republican Thomas Jefferson won the vice presidency. The Twelfth Amendment (1804) precluded future split-ticket administrations.

Library of Congress

Adams. No attempt was made to displace President Washington.

Thomas Jefferson, the leader of the Democratic-Republicans, chose not to run for vice president, in part because he came from the same state as President Washington. (Since electors could vote for only one candidate from their own state, Jefferson was tacitly precluded from receiving the large electoral vote of Virginia. Besides, a "balanced ticket" required a regional diversity.) Instead, Democratic-Republican leaders from New York, Pennsylvania, Virginia, and South Carolina chose New York governor George Clinton as their candidate at a meeting in Philadelphia in October 1792. The endorsement of Clinton was a milestone in the evolution of the presidential nominating process and a step away from the Framers' original understanding of the selection process.

Both Washington and Adams were reelected, although Clinton scored well in the electoral college. Adams received 77 electoral votes to Clinton's 50 (with 4 votes going to Jefferson and 1 to Aaron Burr), and Washington was reelected president by a unanimous electoral vote of 132.

The First Contest: 1796

George Washington chose not to run for president again in 1796, although there was no prohibition against his doing so. With Washington out of the race, the United States witnessed its first partisan contest for president.

On the Democratic-Republican side, there was no opposition to Jefferson as the presidential candidate, and he was considered the party's standard-bearer by a consensus of party leaders. A caucus of Democratic-Republican senators was unable, however, to agree on a running mate, producing a tie vote for Sen. Aaron Burr of New York and Sen. Pierce Butler of South Carolina that ended with a walk-out by Butler's supporters. As a result, there was no formal Democratic-Republican candidate to run with Jefferson.

The Federalists, by contrast, held what historian Roy F. Nichols described as a "quasi caucus" of the party's members of Congress in Philadelphia in May 1796.[3] The gathering chose Vice President Adams and Minister to Great Britain Thomas Pinckney of South Carolina as the

LOOK ON THIS PICTURE, AND ON THIS.

This 1807 anti-Jefferson cartoon compares Washington and Jefferson in contrasting images of good and evil.

Federalist candidates. The choice of Adams was all but obligatory given that he was Washington's vice president. Nonetheless, Adams was unpopular in the South, and he continued to be disliked by Hamilton. As a result, Hamilton tried to use the "defect" in the Constitution to make Pinckney rather than Adams president. He urged northern electors to give equal support to Adams and Pinckney in the hopes that the South would not vote for Adams and that Pinckney would therefore win the most votes.

Had northern electors followed Hamilton's advice, Pinckney might have won the presidency. Instead, eighteen votes were thrown to other Federalists. As a result, Adams won the presidency with seventy-one electoral votes, but Pinckney—with fifty-nine votes—was not even able to win the vice presidency. Instead, Jefferson (from the opposing Democratic-Republican ticket) came in second with sixty-eight votes and thus was named Adams's vice president. Although the results again played up the defects in the constitutional procedure for electing presidents, Federalists and Democratic-Republicans did not seem unduly concerned that the president and vice president were of opposing parties. Both sides felt that they had prevented the opposition from gaining total victory.

Jefferson's 1800 Victory

The election of 1800 was the first in which both parties used congressional caucuses to nominate candidates for their tickets. Such caucuses were an important innovation in the development of the presidential selection process. They were illustrative of partisan alignments in Congress and demonstrated the emergence of organized political parties.

Federalist members of Congress met in the Senate chamber in Philadelphia on May 3, 1800, to choose their candidates. As in previous presidential election years, Federalists were divided in their support of Adams. Nonetheless, Federalists felt that they had to nominate Adams since he was the incumbent president. Because of their ambivalence toward Adams, they nominated both Adams and Maj. Gen. Charles Cotesworth Pinckney of South Carolina without giving preference to one or the other for president. Pinckney was the elder brother of the Federalist vice-presidential candidate in 1796.

The choice of Pinckney was made at Hamilton's insistence. Once again Hamilton was plotting to use the constitutional defect against Adams. In 1796, South Carolina had voted for an all-southern ticket—Jefferson and Thomas Pinckney—even though the two were of opposing parties. Hamilton hoped that South Carolina would vote the same way in 1800 and that all other Federalist electors could be persuaded to vote for Adams and Charles Pinckney. That would give Pinckney more votes than Adams, thus making him president.

Although the deliberations of the Federalist caucus were secret, the existence of the meeting was not. It was described by the local Democratic-Republican paper, the Philadelphia *Aurora*, as a "Jacobinical conclave." Further denunciations by the paper's editor, Benjamin F. Bache, earned him a personal rebuke from the U.S. Senate.

The Democratic-Republicans once again chose Jefferson as the presidential candidate by consensus. On May 11, a caucus of Democratic-Republican members of Congress met at Marache's boarding house in Philadelphia to choose a running mate. Their unanimous choice was Aaron Burr. Although there was no such thing as a formal party platform in 1800, Jefferson wrote fairly detailed statements of principle in letters to various correspondents. Partisan newspapers also helped to spread the Democratic-Republican position. Among other things, the Democratic-Republicans believed in states' rights, a small national government, and a relatively weak executive. They opposed standing armies in peacetime, a large naval force, and alliances with other countries. And they denounced the Alien and Sedition Acts, which had been passed by the Federalists in 1798 for the ostensible purpose of protecting the nation from subversives given the threat of war with France.

When the electors voted in December, the constitutional defect did not work as Hamilton had hoped. Instead of resulting in a Pinckney victory, the defect produced an unexpected tie vote between the two Democratic-Republican candidates, Jefferson and Burr—each of whom had seventy-three electoral votes. Adams came in third with sixty-five, and Pinckney followed with sixty-four. In accord with the constitutional provision, the election was thrown to the Federalist-controlled House of Representatives. *(See "Jefferson's 1800 Victory," p. 101.)*

Some Federalists felt that Burr was the lesser of the two evils and plotted to elect him president instead of Jefferson—even though Jefferson was clearly the presidential candidate. Hamilton helped to squelch the idea. After thirty-six ballots, Jefferson received a majority in the House of Representatives. The crisis—which could have fatally wounded the nation by calling into question the legitimacy of the new president—was over. Jefferson was elected president and Burr vice president.

The near disaster brought about by the constitutional defect led to the passage of the Twelfth Amendment to the Constitution in September 1804. It called for electors to vote for president and vice president on separate ballots, thereby clarifying who was the presidential candidate and eliminating the possibility of a tie between the principal candidate and the running mate.

The election of 1800 is also important because it was the first to witness active campaigning designed to rally voter support for particular political parties. Despite attempts by the Federalists to muzzle the opposition press with the passage of the Sedition Act of 1798, partisan newspapers on both sides actively defamed the opposition. In fact, the Sedition Act ultimately worked against the Federalists since it helped to turn the Democratic-Republicans into champions of a free press.

Finally, increased partisan activity spurred voter participation. Since electors still were chosen indirectly in twelve of the sixteen states, voters often expressed themselves through state legislative elections as a means of influencing future presidential elections.[4] The seeds were being sowed for a new phase in the development of the presidential election process.

Jefferson's Reelection: 1804

The 1804 election was the first one held after the Twelfth Amendment to the Constitution went into effect, requiring electors to cast separate votes for president and vice president. With ratification of the amendment, parties in 1804 and thereafter specifically designated their presidential and vice-presidential candidates.

The Democratic-Republicans retained the caucus system of nomination in 1804, as they did for the next two decades, and for the first time they publicly reported their

deliberations. The party caucus met on February 25, 1804, and attracted 108 of the party's senators and representatives. President Jefferson was renominated by acclamation, but Vice President Burr, who had fallen out with his party, was not considered for a second term. On the first nominating roll call publicly reported in U.S. political history, New York governor George Clinton was chosen by the caucus to run for vice president. He received sixty-seven votes and easily defeated Sen. John Breckinridge of Kentucky, who collected twenty votes. To "avoid unpleasant discussions" no names were placed in nomination, and the vote was taken by written ballot.

Before adjourning, the caucus appointed a thirteen-member committee to conduct the campaign and promote the success of Democratic-Republican candidates. A forerunner of party national committees, the new campaign group included members of both the House and Senate, but with no two persons from the same state. Since the Twelfth Amendment had not yet been passed when the caucus met, the committee was designed to "manage" the vote of Democratic-Republican electors to make sure that the events of 1800 were not repeated. In fact, that precaution was not necessary since the Twelfth Amendment was ratified in September—well before the electors voted.

By 1804, the Federalist party had deteriorated badly. The new era of dominance by the Virginia-led Democratic-Republicans had begun. The Federalists did not even hold a congressional caucus to select their nominees. Instead, Federalist leaders in 1804 informally chose Charles Cotesworth Pinckney for president and Rufus King of New York for vice president. The exact details of how Federalists formulated this ticket are not clear. There is no record in 1804 of any formal meeting to nominate Federalist candidates.

The Federalists mounted a disorganized and dispirited national campaign. Despite concerted efforts to win at least the votes of New England, the Federalists failed miserably. Pinckney received only 14 electoral votes—those of Connecticut and Delaware, plus 2 from Maryland. Jefferson, the Democratic-Republican candidate, was the overwhelming victor with 162 electoral votes.

Madison's 1808 Victory

President Jefferson refused to seek a third term of office, and the authority of the Democratic-Republican congressional caucus to choose a candidate to succeed Jefferson was put to a test. The caucus met on January 23, 1808. For the first time a formal call was issued. Sen. Stephen R. Bradley of Vermont, chairman of the 1804 caucus, issued the call to all 146 Democratic-Republicans in Congress and several Federalists sympathetic to the Democratic-Republican cause. Several party leaders questioned Bradley's authority to call the caucus, but various reports indicate that eighty-nine to ninety-four members of Congress attended.

As in 1804 the balloting was done without the formal placing of names in nomination. For president, Jefferson's handpicked successor, Secretary of State James Madison, was the easy winner with eighty-three votes. Despite earlier support for James Monroe among Democratic-Republicans in Virginia, and Vice President Clinton's own desire to be president, each received only three votes at the caucus. For vice president, the caucus overwhelmingly renominated

Clinton. He received seventy-nine votes, while runner-up John Langdon of New Hampshire collected five.

The Democratic-Republican caucus also repeated its practice of appointing a committee to conduct the campaign. Membership was expanded to fifteen House and Senate members, and it was formally called the "committee of correspondence and arrangement." The committee was authorized to fill any vacancies on the national ticket, should any occur. Before the caucus adjourned, it passed a resolution defending the caucus system as "the most practicable mode of consulting and respecting the interest and wishes of all." Later caucuses adopted similar resolutions throughout the history of the system.

Still, there were divisions among Democratic-Republicans. Forty percent of the Democratic-Republican members of Congress refused to attend the nominating caucus. Monroe refused to withdraw from the presidential race even after being defeated at the caucus. Even Clinton, although he was nominated for vice president, was angry at not being nominated for president. Clinton publicly denounced the caucus, as did Monroe's supporters. Pro-Clinton newspapers in New York launched harsh attacks on Madison and even suggested a Clinton-Monroe ticket. Some Clinton supporters went so far as to hope that Federalists would nominate Clinton for president later in the year. Such a thought was unpalatable to the Federalists, who ultimately nominated Charles Cotesworth Pinckney.

The Federalists chose their ticket at a secret meeting of party leaders in New York City in August 1808. The meeting was initially called by the Federalist members of the Massachusetts legislature. Twenty-five to thirty party leaders from seven states, all north of the Potomac River except South Carolina, attended the national meeting. Despite the suggestion from Massachusetts representatives that Clinton be nominated, the gathering decided to run the same ticket they had chosen in 1804—Pinckney and King.

Federalists did not actively publicize their ticket. The party itself was divided and devoid of leadership. Many Virginia Federalists formally endorsed Monroe, even though he was a Democratic-Republican. Others preferred to align themselves with Clinton. In the end, Madison achieved a wide margin of victory with 122 electoral votes. For the sake of future party unity, Democratic-Republicans retained Clinton as their vice-presidential nominee even though he had tried to subvert Madison's candidacy. Clinton received 113 electoral votes for vice president, thus winning that office; he received six electoral votes from New York for president. Pinckney came in second for president with 47 electoral votes. Monroe received no electoral votes.

Madison's Reelection: 1812

The Democratic-Republican party held its quadrennial nominating caucus on May 18, 1812. Only 83 of the 178 Democratic-Republicans in Congress participated. New England and New York delegations in particular were poorly represented. Many of the New Yorkers supported the candidacy of their state's lieutenant governor, De Witt Clinton (George Clinton's nephew), who also was maneuvering for the Federalist nomination. New England was noticeably upset with Madison's foreign policy, which was leading to war with England. Others did not attend the caucus because they opposed the system in principle.

Madison was renominated by a near-unanimous vote of the caucus, receiving eighty-two votes. John Langdon of New Hampshire was chosen for vice president by a wide margin, collecting sixty-four votes to sixteen for Gov. Elbridge Gerry of Massachusetts. But Langdon declined the nomination, citing his age (seventy) as the reason. As a result, the Democratic-Republicans held a second caucus on June 8 to select another vice-presidential candidate. Gerry was the clear winner with seventy-four votes. He responded with a formal letter of acceptance. Ten members of Congress who had not been present at the first caucus also took the opportunity to endorse the presidential candidacy of Madison.

Democratic-Republicans from New York were unwilling to accept the choice of Madison. They therefore held their own caucus, consisting of nearly all of the ninety-five Democratic-Republicans in the New York state legislature. They unanimously nominated Clinton, who issued a written "Address" that was a precursor to party platforms. Later, Clinton also was nominated by the Federalists. As they had four years earlier, Federalists convened a three-day secret meeting in New York City. The September meeting was more than twice the size of the 1808 gathering, with seventy representatives from eleven states attending. Delegates were sent to the conference by Federalist general committees, with all but nine of the delegates coming from the New England and Middle Atlantic states.

Debate centered on whether to run a separate Federalist ticket or to endorse the candidacy of Clinton. After much debate, they decided to endorse Clinton. They nominated Jared Ingersoll of Pennsylvania as vice president. Originally, the caucus's decision was meant to be kept a secret, but leaks eventually were reported by Democratic-Republican newspapers.

The United States had declared war on England in June, making the presidential election of 1812 the first wartime election. Federalists aligned themselves with the cause of peace and unimpeded commerce. In some northern states, the Federalists even adopted the Peace party label. Still, Clinton lost with 89 electoral votes to Madison's 128. That vote reflected the growing split between southern agricultural states, which supported Madison, and northern commercial states, which supported Clinton. Indeed, the common bond that held the Clinton coalition together was a hatred of Virginia—the kingmaker of the Democratic-Republican party.

Monroe's 1816 Victory

The Federalist party was nearly extinct by 1816. Rufus King had tried to win the governorship of New York and thus revive the party, but he was defeated in April 1816. Afterwards, he said it was a "fruitless struggle" to maintain the party. Despite efforts by Federalists in Philadelphia to convene another secret meeting to nominate candidates for president and vice president, the party did not hold any type of meeting for such purposes. With the Federalists not running candidates, nomination by the Democratic-Republican caucus was tantamount to election.

Despite his opposition to Madison in 1808, Monroe had been accepted back into the Democratic-Republican fold in the years that followed. In 1811, Madison named him secretary of state. By 1816, he was Madison's heir apparent, but many states were increasingly jealous of the Virginia dynasty that had held a grip on the presidency since 1804. Democratic-Republicans in such states opposed Monroe (himself a Virginian) and favored Secretary of War William H. Crawford of Georgia.

A Democratic-Republican caucus met in the House chamber on March 12, 1816, but only 58 members of Congress—mostly Crawford supporters—attended. With the expectation of better attendance, a second caucus was held on March 16. It drew 119 of the 141 Democratic-Republicans in Congress. There, Monroe narrowly defeated Crawford by a vote of 65-54. Forty of Crawford's votes came from five states: Georgia, Kentucky, New Jersey, New York, and North Carolina. The vice-presidential nomination went to New York governor Daniel D. Tompkins, who easily outdistanced Pennsylvania governor Simon Snyder, 85-30.

The nominations of Monroe and Tompkins revived a Virginia-New York alliance that extended back to the late eighteenth century. With the lone exception of 1812, every Democratic-Republican ticket from 1800 to 1824 was composed of a presidential candidate from Virginia and a vice-presidential candidate from New York.

With the Federalist party in disarray, the Democratic-Republican ticket won easily. Monroe received 183 electoral votes. Three states—Connecticut, Delaware, and Massachusetts—chose Federalist electors, who cast their 34 electoral votes for Rufus King.

Although the collapse of the Federalists ensured Democratic-Republican rule, it also increased intraparty friction and spurred further attacks on the caucus system. Twenty-two Democratic-Republican members of Congress were absent from the second party caucus, and at least fifteen were known to be opposed to the system. Historian Edward Stanwood wrote that there were mass meetings around the country to protest the caucus system.[5] Opponents asserted that the writers of the Constitution did not envision the caucus, that presidential nominating should not be a function of Congress, and that the caucus system encouraged candidates to curry the favor of Congress.

Monroe's Reelection: 1820

The 1820 election came during the "Era of Good Feelings," a phrase coined by a Boston publication, the *Columbian Centinel*, to describe a brief period of virtual one-party rule in the United States. Yet, that phrase glosses over serious sectional divisions that were growing during Monroe's presidency. Indeed, sectional strife was on the brink of explosion during Monroe's first term over the admission of Missouri as a new state. Tensions had grown in recent years between northern and southern states. In the Senate a tenuous balance existed between the two regions, with eleven free states and eleven slave states. The admission of Missouri threatened that balance. The two sides finally agreed to a compromise in which both Missouri and Maine would apply for statehood at the same time. Maine would apply as a free state and Missouri as a slave state. Monroe remained neutral in the debate leading up to the compromise. Despite a financial panic in 1819, he retained overwhelming popular support, bolstered by peace and a wave of nationalistic feeling that overshadowed any partisan divisions.

Although several rival Democratic-Republican candidates aspired to win the presidency when Monroe retired in 1824, none wanted to challenge his reelection in 1820. A nominating caucus was called for early March, but fewer than forty members of Congress showed up. The caucus voted unanimously to make no nominations and passed a resolution explaining that it was inexpedient to do so. Although Monroe and Tompkins were not formally renominated, electoral slates were filed on their behalf.

Because the Federalist party was dead, Monroe ran virtually unopposed. Even John Adams, the last Federalist president, voted for Monroe as an elector from Massachusetts. Only one elector, a Democratic-Republican from New Hampshire, cast a vote against Monroe, supporting instead the young John Quincy Adams, son of the former president.

Last of the Old Order: 1824

With virtual one-party rule in 1820, nomination by the Democratic-Republicans' King Caucus had all but ensured election. There was still only one party in 1824, but within that party an abundance of candidates were vying for the presidency: Secretary of State John Quincy Adams of Massachusetts, Sen. Andrew Jackson of Tennessee, Secretary of War John C. Calhoun of South Carolina, House Speaker Henry Clay of Kentucky, and Secretary of the Treasury William H. Crawford. The number of candidates, coupled with the growing democratization of the U.S. political system, led to the demise of King Caucus in 1824. As McCormick has written, the events of 1824 led to the rise of an interim period of factionalism that characterized the next phase in the evolution of the presidential selection process.

Early on, Crawford was the leading candidate. He had strong southern support and appeared likely to win the support of New York Democratic-Republicans. Since it was assumed that he would win a caucus if one were held, Crawford's opponents joined the growing list of caucus opponents. But Crawford's apparent invincibility suddenly ended in September 1823 when he suffered a paralytic stroke. Nearly blind and unable even to sign his name, he was incapacitated and kept in seclusion for months.

In early February 1824, 11 Democratic-Republican members of Congress issued a call for a caucus to be held in the middle of the month. Their call was countered by 24 other members of Congress from fifteen states who deemed it "inexpedient under existing circumstances" to hold a caucus. They claimed that 181 members of Congress were resolved not to attend if a caucus were held.

The caucus did convene in mid-February, but only 66 members of Congress were present. Three-quarters of those attending came from just four states—Georgia, New York, North Carolina, and Virginia. Despite his illness, Crawford won the caucus nomination with sixty-four votes. Albert Gallatin of Pennsylvania was selected for vice president with fifty-seven votes. The caucus adopted a resolution defending its actions as "the best means of collecting and concentrating the feelings and wishes of the people of the Union upon this important subject." The caucus also appointed a committee to write an address to the people. As written, the text of the address viewed with alarm the "dismemberment" of the Democratic-Republican party.

In fact, the action of the caucus actually led to the further dismemberment of the party. Since so few members of Congress—almost all of them Crawford supporters—attended the caucus, opponents could argue that the choice was not representative even of the Democratic-Republican voice in Congress, much less "the people of the Union." As a result, Crawford was roundly criticized as being an illegitimate candidate. His opponents derided King Caucus, and Crawford's physical condition made it even easier for them to reject his nomination. As it stood, other candidates simply refused to follow the caucus's decision. Never again were candidates chosen by the caucus system.

With the caucus devoid of power and the party lacking unity or leadership, there was no chance of rallying behind a single ticket. In addition, many political issues proved to be divisive. Western expansion and protective tariffs, for example, benefited some parts of the country but hurt others. Thus, the various candidates came to represent sectional interests.

The candidates themselves recognized that such a crowded field was dangerous. The election would be thrown to the House of Representatives if no candidate received a majority.

The candidates therefore made efforts to join forces. Adams tried to lure Jackson as his running mate. Adams was a short, stocky, aloof, well-educated New Englander who came from a family of Federalists, while Jackson was a tall, thin, hot-tempered war hero with little education who came to epitomize a new brand of populist democracy. In trying to lure Jackson onto their team, Adams supporters envisaged a ticket of "the writer and the fighter," but Jackson would have nothing of it.

In the meantime, Crawford dropped Gallatin as his vice-presidential running mate. His supporters then tried to get Clay to drop his own quest for the presidency and join the Crawford team. They hinted that Crawford's physical condition was such that he would probably not finish out a term of office if elected (in fact, he lived ten more years). But Clay was not swayed. Instead, Calhoun dropped his race for the presidency and joined efforts with Crawford.

Still, four candidates remained in the field and each collected electoral votes. None, however, received a majority. Jackson received the most with ninety-nine, followed by Adams with eighty-four, Crawford with forty-one, and Clay with thirty-seven. Thus, the election was thrown to the House of Representatives.

In accordance with the Twelfth Amendment, the names of the top three candidates—Jackson, Adams, and Crawford—were placed before the House. Clay, who had come in fourth place and was Speaker of the House, would play a major role in tipping the balance in favor of one of the candidates. In contrast to Jackson, Adams actively lobbied for support, and Washington rocked with rumors of corruption. Clay informed Adams in January that he would support Adams in the House election—a major blow to Jackson. Shortly thereafter, a letter in a Philadelphia newspaper alleged that Adams had offered Clay the post of secretary of state in return for his support. Adams went on to win the House election narrowly. Each state delegation had one vote, and Adams won the vote of thirteen out of twenty-four states. Jackson came in second with seven, and Crawford third with the remaining four. Thus, the candidate who won the most electoral votes and the most popular votes did not win the presidency.

Jackson was furious at what he considered unfair bargaining between Adams and Clay. He felt that the will of the people had been thwarted, and he seethed when President Adams proceeded to name Clay secretary of state as rumor had indicated he would. The events of 1824 kindled the flame of popular democracy. The stage was set for a rematch between Adams and Jackson in 1828.

The Age of Jackson

Andrew Jackson was in many ways the perfect man to usher in an age of popular politics, although his rhetoric was more populist than his true style of governing. The textbook version of U.S. history depicts Jackson as a coarse man of the frontier, a war hero, a battler of banks and moneyed interests, and a leader of the unschooled and exploited men who built a mass party on patronage and charismatic leadership. Jackson was the first politician to break the Virginia dynasty that had governed the country since the Revolution. After his bitter defeat in the 1824 election, Jackson fought back and grabbed the reins of government in a turbulent election in 1828. These two elections signaled the passing of elite politics and the rise of popular politics. In 1828 Jackson roused the people to turn Adams and his aristocratic clique out of office.

But the Jacksonian folklore has serious flaws. Jackson traveled in elite business circles, for example, and one of his greatest contributions as president was the creation of a more rationally organized bureaucracy.[6] Still, the textbook depiction suffices to show some trends in U.S. politics, including the development of a stable mass party system, sectionalism, urbanization, and shifts in the debate about U.S. expansionism.

As President Adams struggled with the factions and turf battles in Washington, an opposition force gathered strength. The opposition was able to deal the president a number of humiliating defeats. Adams's desire for a national program of roads and canals, education, and research in the arts and sciences antagonized even the most nationalistic groups in the country. U.S. participation in a conference of countries from the Western Hemisphere and the imposition of a tariff (a tax on imported goods designed either to raise revenues and to protect domestic industries from foreign competition) were also divisive issues. But even though Adams was under constant personal attack, the opposition was divided on the same issues. The opposition was united, however, behind Old Hickory.[7]

Jackson, the Battle of New Orleans hero in the War of 1812, had a strong appeal to the common man even though he traveled in the circles of southern gentlemen. People who met with Jackson talked of his unerring "intuition." Jackson's decision to push for reforms of the punishment of debtors was an important gesture to small businessmen and workers who were held to a kind of indentured servitude. Martin Van Buren said the people "were his blood relations—the only blood relations he had." [8]

Jackson's 1828 Victory

Jackson and his running mate, John C. Calhoun, easily beat Adams in their 1828 rematch; Jackson won 178 electoral votes, and Adams won 83. (Calhoun also had been vice president under John Quincy Adams.) Of the popular vote, Jackson received 643,000 votes (56.0 percent) to Adams's 501,000 (43.6 percent). Sectional splits showed in the vote distribution. Adams held all but 1 of New England's electoral votes, all of Delaware's and New Jersey's, 16 of New York's 36 votes, and 6 of Maryland's 11 votes. Jackson took all the rest—the South and the West. The election was decided by the thousands of votes from newly enfranchised voters in the burgeoning regions of the country. The U.S. electorate was expanding not only in the West but also in the original states. Voter participation grew from 3.8 percent to 16.7 percent of the total popula-

GENERAL JACKSON SLAYING THE MANY HEADED MONSTER.

Library of Congress

This 1836 cartoon depicts Jackson attacking the Bank of the United States with his veto stick. Vice President Van Buren, center, helps kill the monster, whose heads represent Nicholas Biddle, president of the bank, and directors of the state branches.

tion between 1824 and 1856.[9]

Jackson has only begun to exert his electoral influence with his revenge victory over Adams. The expanded pool of politically involved citizens that brought Jackson victory also brought him demands for patronage jobs with the federal government. Van Buren, a master machine politician from New York State, tutored the beleaguered new president on dealing with the office seekers. Jackson replaced fewer than one-fifth of the government's employees, which he defended as a perfectly reasonable "rotation in office" that would keep the ranks of the bureaucracy fresh. But the effect of his system was greater. Appointees of previous administrations were able to retain their jobs only when they expressed loyalty to Jackson and his party. Far more important than any government turnover, Jackson's spoils system inaugurated an age in which mass party loyalty was a paramount concern in politics.

The central element of the Jacksonian program was expansion. Much as twentieth-century politicians would talk about economic growth as the key to opportunity, Jackson maintained that movement West "enlarg[ed] the area of freedom."[10] The administration fought to decentralize the management of expansion. Jackson railed against the "corrupt bargain" between the government and banks, joint-stock companies, and monopolies, which, he said, were squeezing out the average person seeking opportunity. Jackson opposed the Bank of the United States and promoted state banks because of his desire to free finance capital from central control.

The increased importance of loyalty, to the president and to the party, became clear with Jackson's dispute with Vice President Calhoun and the subsequent purging of the cabinet. A growing feud between Jackson and Calhoun

came to a head when a personal letter by Calhoun became public. The letter criticized Jackson's conduct of the Seminole Indian campaign and the 1818 invasion of Florida. In a letter to Calhoun during the crisis, Jackson wrote: "Et tu, Brute." A purge of Calhoun men in the cabinet followed the incident. Secretary of State Van Buren enabled the president to make the purge when he and Secretary of War John Eaton, both Jackson allies, resigned their posts; the president then called on the whole cabinet to quit.

Jackson's political strength was further underscored with the introduction of a quintessentially party-oriented institution: the national party convention. Jacksonians from New Hampshire proposed the Democratic convention of 1832, and the president and his advisers jumped at the opportunity. The only previous national convention had been held by the Anti-Masonic party in 1831. Conventions had been the principal means of selecting candidates for local offices since the early part of the century. Especially compared with the caucus system that preceded it, the convention system was a democratic leap forward.

The convention system enabled the parties to gather partisans from all geographic areas, and it welded them together as a cohesive unit that ultimately was accountable to the electorate, if only in a plebiscitary way. Voters had the opportunity to give approval or disapproval to a party program with one vote. Historian Eugene H. Roseboom has written: "It was representative in character; it divorced nominations from congressional control and added to the independence of the executive; it permitted an authoritative formulation of a party program; and it concentrated the party's strength behind a single ticket, the product of compromise of personal rivalries and group or sectional interests."[11]

Jackson's presidency was activist from the beginning. The president in his first term carried on a long-running battle with Nicholas Biddle, the head of the Bank of the United States, and with Congress over the status of the bank. Alexander Hamilton created the bank to manage the nation's monetary policy and investment but Jackson opposed it as a tool of the eastern financial establishment. Jackson failed to close the bank but neutered it when he placed its deposits in a number of regional institutions.

The Jackson administration also negotiated treaties with France, the Ottoman Empire, Russia, and Mexico. Jackson established a distinctive system of federalism when he vetoed a number of public improvements bills as unconstitutional infringements of local affairs. Jackson also called for a tariff that would yield revenues for dispersal to the states for their own public projects—an early form of "revenue sharing." Jackson signed the Indian Removal Act of 1830, which provided for settlement of the territory west of the Mississippi River. Late in his first term, Jackson's strong stand defeated the South Carolina legislature's claim to "nullify," or declare "null and void," federal tariff legislation that the state disliked.

Jackson's 1832 Victory

There was never any doubt that Jackson would be renominated in 1832; in fact, several state legislatures endorsed him before the convention. The purpose of the convention was to rally behind the president and select a new vice-presidential candidate. Van Buren got the nomination, despite lingering resistance from Calhoun supporters and various "favorite sons" (prominent state and local figures).

Jackson's opposition was fragmented as usual. The Whigs—the opposition party that developed from grassroots protests in the North and West against Jackson's tariff and development policies—met in convention in Baltimore in December 1831 and unanimously nominated Henry Clay of Kentucky. Eighteen states used a variety of selection procedures to determine who would be their convention delegates. The party's platform sharply criticized the administration's patronage practices, relations with Great Britain, criticism of Supreme Court decisions, and ill-tempered congressional relations.

The incumbent easily dispatched the opposition in 1832. "The news from the voting states blows over us like a great cold storm," wrote Rufus Choate, a prominent lawyer, to a friend.[12] Despite last-minute maneuvering to unite the opposition to Jackson and a well-financed campaign by the National Bank, the president won 219 electoral votes to Clay's 49, Independent John Floyd's 11, and Anti-Mason William Wirt's 7. Jackson won all but seven states. Clay won Kentucky, Massachusetts, Rhode Island, Connecticut, and Delaware, plus five electors from Maryland. Jackson won 702,000 popular votes to Clay's 484,000 and Wirt's 101,000.[13]

Before Jackson finally left the political stage in 1837, he had changed the face of U.S. politics. Even if his pretensions to being an everyman were overstated, he did open up the system to mass participation and force politicians to listen to popular demands. He developed the notion of a strong party organization. He fought, and eventually defeated, the National Bank by withdrawing its funds and placing them in state banks. He strongly opposed two forces that could have torn the nation apart—the nullification principle of state sovereignty and the Supreme Court's

bid for broader discretion over political issues—by simply proclaiming the law to be "unauthorized by the Constitution" and "therefore null and void."

Van Buren's 1836 Win

Many historians consider the election of 1836 to be the most important event in the development of the party system. Van Buren, a Democratic follower of Jackson and a theorist on the role of political parties in a democratic system, easily won the election over an uncoordinated Whig party. The defeat eventually convinced Whig leaders of the need for a permanent organization for political competition. The emergence of two permanent parties extinguished the American suspicion of the morality of a party system based upon unabashed competition for the levers of power.

Van Buren, who had allied with Jackson during the cabinet controversies and promoted his philosophy of parties and patronage, received the Democratic nomination in 1836 at a convention packed with Jackson administration appointees. The vice-presidential nomination of Richard M. Johnson of Kentucky, whose past relationship with a mulatto woman caused controversy in the South, damaged the ticket in the South, but the Democrats won anyway.

The Whigs' campaign strategy was to run several favorite sons to prevent any candidate from getting a majority of the electoral votes, thereby throwing the election into the House of Representatives. As one Whig put the matter: "The disease [Democratic rule] is to be treated as a local disorder—apply local remedies."[14] The Whig expectation was that Gen. William Henry Harrison of Ohio or Hugh Lawson White of Tennessee would be selected by the House after the electoral college vote proved inconclusive.

Van Buren, however, had Jackson's machine and his personal backing and was able to overcome the Whigs' local strategy. In the last race for the White House before presidential elections became dominated by two national parties, Van Buren took 170 electoral votes—22 more than he needed for election. Of the Whig candidates, Harrison received 73 electoral votes; White, 26; and Daniel Webster of Massachusetts, 14. Willie Mangum, an Independent Democrat from North Carolina, received 11 electoral votes from the South Carolina legislature, which was hostile to White because of his role in nullification politics. Van Buren won 764,000 popular votes (50.8 percent); Harrison, 551,000 (36.6 percent); White, 146,000 (9.7 percent); and Webster, 41,000 (2.7 percent). For the only time in history, the Senate selected the vice president, Richard M. Johnson, who fell one vote shy of election by the electoral college and defeated Francis Granger by a 33-16 Senate vote.

Van Buren was besieged practically from the minute he took the oath of office in March 1837. The economy crashed after years of feverish business growth, overspeculation in land and business, huge private debt accumulation, and unregulated financial and trade practices. Van Buren's approach to the economic crisis was either stubborn refusal to fix a mess that he had not created or action that was guaranteed to antagonize key interest groups.

When Van Buren moved to create an independent treasury to give the federal government insulation from state financial institutions, he was opposed by conservative Democrats who were supporters of the state financial institutions that Jackson had promoted in his legendary National Bank battles. When Van Buren was not hit from the right, he was hit from the left. The nascent labor movement called for protection of jobs and wages and made protests against monopoly and privilege.

The Idea of a Party System

Whatever problems Van Buren had in governing, he can receive credit at least for helping to establish the principle of party government in the United States. That principle—much derided in the early days of the nation's history—has come to enjoy unquestioned allegiance in the United States.

Van Buren's arguments on behalf of a party system—contained in his 1867 book, *An Inquiry into the Origin and Course of Political Parties in the United States*—are similar to the economic principle of Adam Smith that the pursuit of selfish ends redounds to the good of the entire community. American leaders from George Washington through John Quincy Adams had stated that self-interested factions endangered the functioning and virtue of the Republic. These leaders also warned against the dangers of democracy, which they often called "mob rule." The worst of all possible scenarios pictured permanent parties with strong ideological stances appealing to the mass public for support. Most of the Framers feared that democratic institutions would undermine the ability of national leaders to guide public virtue.[15]

The basic tension that Van Buren had to resolve was the system's need for stability and responsible leadership and the party system's imperative to gain office. How could a party's selfish desire to run the government and award patronage and contracts to political allies benefit the whole system?

Van Buren argued that the absence of parties—collections of people from disparate backgrounds—resulted in a system of personal politics that fueled demagogy, perpetual campaigns, and a lack of accountability. Personal presidential politics were more polarizing than the politics of consensus or of coalition building. Presidents should be able to do their job without constant carping from outsiders who fancy themselves to be prospective presidents. Mass parties with certain partisan principles would enable presidents to get the backing they needed to do their work.

The existence of two parties would enable the nation to move beyond its many cleavages—toward the general interest and away from simple clashes of particular interests. Competition among parties, like competition among economic enterprises, would bring about a situation in which disparate demands are promoted by a party. The key is to achieve a balance of competing forces. Political scientist James W. Ceaser has written:

> Established parties ... may stand 'over' the raw electoral cleavages, possessing some leeway or discretion about which potential issues and electoral divisions will be emphasized and which will be suppressed or kept at the fringes. This discretion is exercised according to the interests of the organizations and the judgement of their leaders. But it is important to keep in mind that the degree of this discretion is limited.... Their discretion is always threatened or held in check by the possibility that they might be displaced by a new party having as its goal the advancement of a certain policy.... When a sufficiently powerful and enduring issue exists, an impartial reading of American party history suggests that the party system in the end will have to respond to it, regardless of how the established parties initially react.[16]

The Age of Jackson brought a fundamental shift from republican to democratic values as the nation's territory and activities expanded. Republicanism was the product of a variety of strains of thought—from the Romans Cicero and Tacitus and the Greek Polybius to the Frenchman Montesquieu—that stressed the need for a balancing of interests to produce public virtue. Republicans worried about excess in any single form of governance. Of particular concern was "mob rule"—the excess of democracy. *Democracy* was a term of derision. The Constitution contained many buffers against this and other forms of excess.

Republicanism declined in many stages. A greater stress on the individual's role in society, embodied in the work of Adam Smith and David Hume, reduced the sphere open to public pursuits.

The pace of economic change undermined established patterns. As the nation demanded large-scale projects, and as rival factions looked to the mobilization of larger and larger parts of the electorate to augment their strength, democratic rhetoric gained respectability. Mass party participation became a vehicle for pursuing civic virtue and balance. The notion of a constant opposition party gained strength. If the democratic process had enough "checks," political thinkers now reasoned, the harmful "mob" aspects of democracy could be tempered. The development of the Jacksonian party as a way of arbitrating interests was the final stage in republican decline and democratic ascendance.

Political scientist Russell Hanson has noted that the new democratic ethos sprang from one of the same goals as the old republican ethos: development of a public spirit by rising above particular restraints. "Support for popular sovereignty became the lowest common denominator for a Democratic Party composed of interests seeking liberation from a variety of sectionally specific restraints on the 'will of the people.' "[17]

A two-party system persisted as the nation drifted toward civil war, but it was not a simple two-party system. The Democrats and Whigs competed for the presidency and other political offices until 1856, when the Republican party fielded its first national ticket and made the Whigs obsolete. But the parties were so unstable that their many elements were constantly forming and breaking up coalitions—and threatening to bolt from the system itself. A series of third parties entered the national electoral arena for short periods, applying or relieving pressures on the two major parties.[18]

Only by examining the parties and their various factions and struggles can one understand the presidential contests in the years before the Civil War, and the way that the Civil War revealed the basic fault lines of U.S. politics.

The Whigs' 1840 Victory

The Whigs developed to fill the role of their British namesake, which had been to mount a republican opposition to the royal ruling power. The rise of Andrew Jackson and his supposedly imperial presidency threatened the "balance" of the United States, and the Whigs rose to restore that balance. The Whigs saw Jackson's Democrats as a faction of the most dangerous variety—a majority faction that had the ability to trample liberties in its mad scramble for spoils.

The key to Whiggery was the notion of balanced development. The Whigs opposed the war with Mexico and other expansionist programs because they feared the perils of overextending the nation's abilities and getting entangled with foreign powers. The Whigs favored internal improvements, but only as a way of maintaining balance and staving off the corruption of the Jackson era. The protective tariff was central to the Whigs' program of internal development and protection from outsiders. Political scientist Russell Hanson has described the Whig philosophy:

> Even in America, which was uniquely blessed by an abundance of natural resources and a citizenry of hardy stock, there was need for informed guidance and direction of progress. For the Whigs, government was the primary agent of this progress. Government represented a strong and positive force to be used in calling forth a richer society from the unsettled possibilities of America. In the economic realm this meant that government was responsible for providing the essential conditions for a sound economy, namely, a reliable currency, ample credit, and the impetus for internal improvements. And in the social realm, the government was responsible for promoting virtue in its citizenry through education and exhortation.[19]

The Whig desire for balance and compromise was intended to give the party a national rather than a sectional identity. A series of Senate battles with President Jackson, especially the tariff battles of 1833, which resulted in an unsatisfying compromise, gave impetus to grass-roots organizations in the North and West and to southern Democratic opponents. The tendency of the Whigs to nominate widely popular military heroes helped create at least the illusion of a party of national dimensions. The Whigs developed first in the South where voters were dissatisfied with Jackson's selection of Van Buren as his running mate. Loose coalitions elected candidates in the 1834 and 1835 state and congressional elections in the South. Westerners also organized to oppose the Democratic party that was headed by a New Yorker.

The first serious Whig presidential contest was a loss, but an encouraging one. In 1836, the Whig ticket headed by Harrison showed surprising appeal in the loss to the Democrat Van Buren. The Whig strategy was to run a number of favorite sons and produce inconclusive results in the electoral college, sending the contest to the House of Representatives for resolution. The Whigs won Jackson's home state of Tennessee and the neighboring Georgia, as well as three border slave states, and were strong competitors elsewhere. Harrison carried the old Northwest (now the Midwest) and came close in northern states like Pennsylvania.

Because of the rise of the antislavery "conscience Whigs," the Whigs eventually moved to a completely different base of support—the North rather than the South and West—but their early organizing at least broke the Democratic stranglehold on the latter two regions. The Whigs nominated Harrison in 1840 after a nomination struggle with Clay. A Clay supporter, John Tyler of Virginia, was the vice-presidential nominee. This time, the popular if politically inexperienced hero of the War of 1812 won his ticket to the White House. Harrison defeated the incumbent Van Buren in an electoral vote landslide, receiving 234 of the 294 electoral votes—all the states except Alabama, Arkansas, Illinois, Missouri, New Hampshire, South Carolina, and Virginia. Harrison won 1.3 million popular votes (52.9 percent) to Van Buren's 1.1 million (46.8 percent).

According to Richard P. McCormick:

> The campaign of 1840 brought the American party system at last to fruition. In every region of the country, and indeed in every state, politics was conducted within the framework of a two party system, and in all but a handful of states the parties were so closely balanced as to be competitive. In broad terms, it was the contest for the presidency that shaped this party system and defined its essential purpose.[20]

Harrison's campaign was as vague as his government experience was unimpressive. The image of Harrison as a sort of frontier everyman—which received its popular expression when a Baltimore newspaper mocked him as a sedentary man who would sit in a log cabin and drink cider rather than perform great deeds of leadership—was the theme of numerous parades and mass meetings. On issues from banking and currency to slavery, Harrison spoke in generalities. He did not have an opportunity to do much as president besides discipline the aggressive Clay. Clay assumed that he and the rest of the congressional leadership would play the leading role in the government, and Harrison wrote a quick note rebuking him. But one month after his inauguration, the sixty-eight-year-old Harrison, physically weakened by the pressures of office, developed pneumonia and died. On April 6, 1841, the burdens of the presidency fell upon Vice President John Tyler.

The rift between the White House and Congress widened under Tyler. Clay acted as if he were prime minister during a special session of Congress, pushing through a legislative program that included a recharter of the long-controversial National Bank, higher import taxes, and distribution of proceeds from land sales to the states. Tyler, a lifetime states' rights advocate, vetoed two bills for a national bank, and the Whigs in Congress and his own cabinet entered a bitter feud with the president. In 1842 Clay left the Senate to promote his presidential aspirations, and everyone in the cabinet except Secretary of State Daniel Webster quit. Tyler was all alone, but he did manage to defeat the Whig program in his four years as president.

Polk's Dark-Horse Victory in 1844

The Democrats were transformed into a well-organized mass by Andrew Jackson and Martin Van Buren between 1828 and 1836. But, like the Whigs, the Democratic party became vulnerable because of the irreconcilable difference among many of its parts.

From the beginning, the Democratic party had contained contradictory elements. According to Sundquist: "The party had been formed originally as an alliance between Southern planters and New Yorkers and had always spanned both regions. Northern men of abolitionist sympathies were accustomed to sitting with slaveholders in presidential cabinets and collaborating with them in the halls of Congress."[21] Northerners went so far as to organize antiabolitionist rallies in their cities and towns, and newspapers and churches also defended slavery.

The deepest Democratic divisions—which eventually would lead to the failure not only of the party but also of the nation—were the regional differences based on slavery. Although slavery and the regional split it engendered were a constant and growing theme in U.S. politics, other, more complex divisions also affected the operation of the Democratic party. When the party was able to reconcile or even delay action on the divisive issues, it won. When the divisions burst into the open, the party was in trouble.

James K. Polk of Tennessee, the first "dark-horse" candidate in history, defeated the Whig Henry Clay in 1844 by supporting an expansionist program and winning the support of the solid South. One of the key issues in the campaign was whether Texas should be admitted to the Union and, if so, whether it should be slave or free. President Van Buren in 1840 opposed annexation—opposition that might have cost him the presidency—and the Democrats and Whigs hedged on the issue for the next eight years. In 1844, Polk endorsed the annexation of Texas as a slave state; that was enough for him to lock up the South.

During the 1844 nominating convention, the Democrats finessed the sectional dangers of the Texas issue by combining it with a call for occupying Oregon and for eventually bringing that state into the Union. The Democrats also appealed to Pennsylvania and the rest of the Northeast by supporting a high tariff. Both parties spoke out against the growing foreign elements in the cities, but the Whigs were more effective because of the Democrats' swelling immigrant ranks.

Polk defeated Clay, winning 1.34 million votes (49.5 percent) to Clay's 1.30 million (48.1 percent) and 170 electoral votes to Clay's 105. Clay received his strongest support from five northeastern states and five border slave states. Of the expansionist Northwest, only Ohio fell in the Clay column.

The Liberty party's abolitionist campaign may have been the deciding factor in the 1844 race. Although it received only 2.3 percent of the popular vote and no electoral votes, the Liberty party was strong enough in New York to prevent the Whigs from winning that state's crucial thirty-six electoral votes. Those votes went to the Democrat Polk rather than to the Whig Clay.

The depth of the Democrats' divisions were agonizingly evident even when the party won elections and started to pass out spoils and make policy. Like Harrison, the Whig who had won the presidency four years before, President Polk faced the antagonisms of party factions when he began making appointments after his 1844 win. Westerners were angry when they were shut out of the cabinet and Polk vetoed a rivers and harbors bill. Supporters of both Van Buren and John Calhoun were angry that their faction did not win more prominent positions. Northeasterners were upset at tariff cuts. The New York split between the reformist "Barnburners" and the party-regular "Hunkers"—who disagreed on every issue, including banks, currency, internal improvements, and political reforms—also disrupted the administration.

Creating still more dissension was the war with Mexico (1846-1848), fought because of the dispute over the Texas border and the possible annexation of California. Patronage was intensely controversial, and Northerners resented the country's fighting Mexico over a slave state. Among the war's more prominent opponents was Henry David Thoreau.

Whig Success under Taylor in 1848

In 1848 the Whigs recaptured the White House behind another military hero, Gen. Zachary Taylor, who was vague on most political issues. Taylor defeated the irrepressible Clay and Gen. Winfield Scott for the nomination on the fourth convention ballot. Clay mounted an impressive public campaign that drew large crowds, but the Whigs had lost too many times with Clay. The Whig ticket was headed by the Louisiana slave-owning Taylor, and his running mate was New Yorker Millard Fillmore.

The Whigs were so determined to avoid sectional and other issue splits that they not only nominated the popular Taylor but also eschewed writing a platform. Despite such extreme measures to maintain unity, the convention was disturbed by squabbles between pro- and antislavery forces on the question of the Wilmot Proviso, which would ban slavery in any territory obtained from Mexico.

Sen. Lewis Cass of Michigan defeated Sen. James Buchanan of Pennsylvania and Supreme Court Justice Levi Woodbury for the Democratic nomination, and Gen. William Butler was picked as his running mate. But the convention experienced splits between the New York factions of the Barnburners, who were part of the antislavery movement, and the Hunkers, who had ties to Southerners. The Barnburners defected from the party to become part of the Free Soil party.

The Democrats behind Cass praised the administration of the beleaguered Polk, defended the war with Mexico, congratulated the French Republic that emerged from the wave of revolution in Europe, and did everything it could to avoid the nasty slavery issue. The nomination of Cass—a "doughface," or Northerner with Southern principles—was expected to appeal to both sides of the simmering issue.

Taylor defeated Cass, winning 1.4 million popular votes (47.3 percent) to Cass's 1.2 million (42.5 percent). New York Democrat Martin Van Buren, the former president, running on the Free Soil ticket, won 291,500 votes (10 percent) but no electoral votes. Taylor received 163 electoral votes to Cass's 127, with a strong showing in the North. Taylor won Connecticut, Massachusetts, New Jersey, New York, Pennsylvania, Rhode Island, and Vermont in the North; Delaware, Kentucky, Maryland, North Carolina, and Tennessee in the border states; and Florida, Georgia, and Louisiana in the Deep South. This combination was enough to beat Cass's coalition of seven slave states, six northwestern states, and two New England states.

On July 10, 1850, Fillmore succeeded to the presidency when President Taylor suddenly died. After consuming too many refreshments at a Fourth of July celebration, Taylor developed cramps, then a fatal illness, probably typhoid fever. Fillmore, however, was unable to secure the party nomination in 1852 despite an early lead in convention polling. General Scott won the nomination, and the Whigs entered into permanent decline.

Slavery Divides the Whigs

Try as they might with the selection of military heroes as candidates and vague issue statements, the Whigs could not cover over the nation's disagreements forever. When divisive issues burst into the open, the party was in trouble. The tariff issue and their mildly probusiness stance gave the Whigs strength in the North. But the Whigs, like the Democrats, needed to attract support also in the South; so they tried to keep the slavery question out of their rhetoric. The Whigs could count on being competitive in the border slave states, but not in the rest of Dixie. In 1844, Clay had won only the northern rim of slave states (Delaware, Kentucky, Maryland, North Carolina, and Tennessee).

As political scientist James L. Sundquist has noted, both the Whig and Democratic parties in the pre-Civil War era attempted to ignore the slavery issue, but the Whigs had less room to maneuver. The Democrats' agrarian and populist position gave them the solid South as a foundation, and they could make a variety of antiabolitionist appeals to the rest of the electorate. Democrats could argue that their support for slavery in the South was compatible with many "moderate" positions. The appeal of Stephen Douglas and Buchanan rested on such a coalition-building strategy. The Whigs, however, included vociferous opponents of slavery that could not be reconciled easily with "moderate" positions. Abolitionism had upper-class and religious roots that were difficult to use as a foundation. The support the Whigs were able to retain in the South was based on their positions on local issues. In sum, the Whigs did not have the same potential to build a national party organization as the Democrats.

Both parties contained slavery sympathizers and opponents; neither was willing to make a principled stand against the institution, particularly where it already existed. The parties were more competitive over issues such as westward expansion, banking questions, public improvements, the tariff, and foreign relations. It was up to third parties such as the Liberty and Free Soil parties to press the slavery issue. Sectional cleavages were so strong that Congress in 1836 passed a "gag rule" that forbade the reading of antislavery statements in Congress. Such attempts to silence abolitionist fervor were in vain, however, as politics were entering an age of mass communication and organization. The slavery issue would become irrepressible.

The beginning of the abolitionist movement, which may be dated to the founding of William Lloyd Garrison's newspaper, *The Liberator*, in 1831, posed problems for the Whigs that eventually proved fatal. The antislavery belt developed in the Whigs' strongest territory—New England—and westward into what today would be called the Midwest. Abolitionism was largely an upper- or middle-class and religious cause. But it also was a partisan issue: the Whigs, the party out of power for years, needed an issue with which to confront the Democrats. Slavery was a useful issue, even if the Whigs' antislavery stance in the North contradicted their accommodating stance in the South.

The slavery issue split the Whigs badly with the controversy over the admission of Texas to the Union in 1845. A splinter group of young party members calling themselves the "Conscience Whigs" argued for a straightforward statement of principle against slavery. An opposition group called the "Cotton Whigs" wanted to defuse the slavery issue by ignoring moral arguments and simply calling for a halt to annexation. The party split became complete with Clay's Compromise of 1850, which admitted California as a free state, ended slave trade in the District of Columbia, and admitted Texas but reduced its size by splitting off the New Mexico territory. After agitation from Conscience Whigs and General Scott's nomination in 1852, the party was irreparably rent by the slavery issue.

The Whigs attempted to make concessions to the South, but many of their efforts only antagonized Northern supporters. The 1852 Whig convention platform contained several statements supporting states' rights and the principles behind Clay's compromise.[22] Northern Whigs made these concessions to win Southern support for their presidential favorite, General Scott. When no Whigs voted for the Kansas-Nebraska Act in 1854, which permitted state determination of the slavery question, the Whigs' remaining ties to Dixie were severed.

The Whigs' strength in the Northwest was almost nonexistent. Only Ohio, in 1844, went for the Whigs even once over the course of the 1844, 1848, and 1852 presidential elections. Previously strong ties between the "lake region" and the South deteriorated as immigrants and others moved from the Northeast to the Northwest and, after the completion of railroad links, the two regions developed strong economic ties.

The Whigs' last gasp came in 1852, when Scott was demolished by Democrat Franklin Pierce. Pierce won all the states except two in New England (Massachussetts and Vermont) and two border states (Kentucky and Tennessee). Pierce won twenty-seven states and 254 electoral votes to Scott's four states and 42 electoral votes.

Whig divisions were most evident in 1856 as the Whigs split their votes among the Democrat Buchanan, the former Whig Fillmore, and the Republican John C. Fremont. Not all Whigs were ready yet to join the nascent Republican party, because of the extremism of some of the party's abolitionists. The majority of Whigs folded into the Republicans in 1860 when Abraham Lincoln avoided a white "backlash" by insisting that he supported slavery where it existed and opposed its spread only because of how it would affect the economic fortunes of poor Northern whites.

Slavery Divides the Democrats

The Democrats suffered a North-South cleavage that Lincoln exploited in the 1860 election against Stephen Douglas. Southern Democrats were intent on protecting slavery, and they felt that control of Congress was necessary to their strategy. Extension of slavery to the new states joining the Union was necessary to maintain congressional strength.

Northern Democrats were willing to allow Dixie to maintain its peculiar institution but were scared about their own electoral prospects if slavery should expand. Northern Democrats at first rallied to Douglas's doctrine of "popular sovereignty" (under which the people of new states could decide whether to adopt slavery), but they got nervous when Lincoln hammered away at his argument that any unchecked slavery threatened the freedom of whites as well as blacks. Lincoln argued that Democrats such as Douglas wanted to make slavery a nationwide, rather than a selective state-by-state, institution.

Lincoln planted seeds of doubt about partial solutions to the slavery question by asserting that slavery could extend to whites if it were nationalized: "If free negroes should be made *things,* how long, think you, before they will begin to make *things* out of poor white men?"[23] Lincoln also maintained that the extension of slavery into new territories would close off the territories for whites seeking upward mobility: "The whole nation is interested that the best use be made of these Territories. We want them for homes of free white people. This they cannot be, to any considerable extent, if slavery shall be planted within them."[24]

The growing movement against the extension of slavery was based on a concern for the upward mobility of labor. Rather than stressing the common interests of blacks and poor, Northern, white laborers, the antiextension movement followed Lincoln's lead in playing up the competition between the two groups. Horace Greeley's vision of the frontier as "the great regulator of the relations of Labor and Capital, the safety valve of our industrial and social engine"[25] left little room for the extension of slavery into the new territories. The extension of slavery was the issue that most divided the Democratic party.

Democrat Pierce's Victory in 1852

Clay's congressional compromise on slavery in the territories, known as the Compromise of 1850, turned out to be the major reason for the Democrats' 1852 victory. President Taylor stalled action for months and even suggested that California and New Mexico might become independent nations. But his successor, Fillmore, threw his support behind the compromise. The Whigs were divided on the proposal. The compromise addressed the slavery question in all of the new U.S. territories by making concessions to both sides of the struggle. For the North, California would be admitted as a free state, and the slave trade (but not slavery itself) would be abolished in the District of Columbia. For the South, fugitive slave laws would be strengthened, and the New Mexico territory would be divided into two states where popular sovereignty would decide the slave issue.

The compromise was designed to settle the issue of slavery in new territories once and for all. But the slavery issue could not be contained by region; it had an increasingly important "spillover" effect. Because of concerns for the congressional balance of power and the difficulties of enforcing slavery provisions such as the fugitive-slave law in states that opposed slavery, it was impossible to isolate the slavery question into particular regions as Clay intended.

General Scott won the Whig nomination in 1852 after platform concessions to the party's Southern delegation. Scott's appeal was always limited to the North, while Fillmore appealed to the South and Daniel Webster appealed to New England. Scott won on the fifty-third ballot.

Franklin Pierce of New Hampshire, a dark horse who gained fame with his Mexican War record, won the Democratic nomination in 1852. The vice-presidential candidate was Sen. William Rufus de Vane King of Alabama. The party held together a coalition of groups with contradictory positions on the slavery issue and regional affairs. The convention, meeting in Baltimore, pledged to "abide by, and adhere to" Clay's compromise and to do what it could to smother the slavery issue.

Attempts to inject issues of economics and foreign affairs into the election failed, and the campaign degenerated into squabbles over personalities. Pierce easily won with 1.6 million popular votes (50.4 percent) to Scott's 1.4 million (43.9 percent). Pierce had twenty-seven states and 254 electoral votes to Scott's four states and 42 electoral votes.

The Democrats' Bruising 1856 Victory

By 1856, the North-South split had eliminated the Whigs as a national party and fatally damaged the Democrats' chances for winning a national election for decades.

Congress opened the slavery issue by passing the Kansas-Nebraska Act of 1854. The act declared "null and void" the Missouri Compromise, which prohibited slavery in new territories north of the 36°30′ parallel except in Missouri.

The 1854 legislation created two territories (Kansas and Nebraska) from the original Nebraska territory and left the slavery issue to be determined by popular sovereignty there and in the Utah and New Mexico territories.

The Kansas-Nebraska Act was a vehicle to spur the development of the West. Such development was part of a longstanding American approach to creating opportunity and freedom via growth. Sen. Stephen A. Douglas of Illinois—the promoter of the law and the main advocate of popular sovereignty—held that the law was necessary if the country was to be bound together by rail and telegraph lines and was to drive Great Britain off the continent. The latter goal was intertwined with a widely held suspicion that Britain was exploiting the slavery issue to distract American politics and stunt American growth.

Whatever the economic motives for unification, the Kansas-Nebraska Act was bitterly divisive. Northern state legislatures passed resolutions denouncing the law. The development of sectional parties continued.

A flood of new settlers into Kansas, and the terror-filled balloting over whether Kansas was to be a free or a slave state, further inflamed passions. Neighboring Missourians took part in the controversy, arguing that their status as slave owners would be undermined if Kansas voted to be free. Especially with the Supreme Court's infamous 1857 *Dred Scott* decision, which defined slaves as property, and the Lincoln-Douglas debates in Illinois in 1858, the slavery question was becoming decisive in American politics.

The Democrats won the White House in 1856 when the party endorsed the Kansas-Nebraska Act and nominated the pro-Southern James Buchanan as its presidential candidate. John Breckinridge of Kentucky, who later served in the Confederate Army, was Buchanan's running mate. The Democrats, who were becoming almost exclusively a Southern party, benefited from close wins in Buchanan's home state of Pennsylvania and in New Jersey, and in western states such as Illinois, Indiana, and California. But the only strong region for the Democrats was the South. Buchanan won all the slave states except Maryland. Overall, Buchanan won 1.8 million popular votes (45.3 percent) to Fremont's 1.3 million (33.1 percent). The electoral college gave Buchanan a 174-114 victory.

The nativist American party—or the "Know-Nothings," as they were called—nominated former Whig president Millard Fillmore, but the party was never able to move beyond an urban strength based on parochial resistance to immigration and Catholicism. Fillmore won only the state of Maryland; overall, he got 873,000 popular votes (21.5 percent) and 8 electoral votes.

After an 1854 meeting in Ripon, Wisconsin, where a new national party was first proposed, the Republican party developed quickly. The Republicans had a strong grass-roots organization in the Northwest after the Kansas-Nebraska Act and attracted Whigs, Know-Nothings, and Northern Democrats who were troubled by the possible extension of slavery. Uncertainty about how the extension of slavery would affect laborers who sought opportunity in the territories also helped unite the new coalition.

The first GOP presidential convention met in Philadelphia in 1856 with delegates from all of the free states, four border states, three territories, and the District of Columbia. The party's opposition to slavery was far from unanimous, but its willingness to address rather than suppress the issue enabled it to redefine the political dialogue. Besides strong antislavery statements, the party platform contained proposals for several internal improvements

Stephen Douglas, at 5'4", was the 1864 Democratic candidate for president.

advantageous to the North. The party did not offer anything to the solidly Democratic South. To win a national election, it would have to sweep the North. Col. John Charles Fremont was named the Republicans' first presidential candidate. Former Whig senator William Dayton of New Jersey received the vice-presidential nomination.

In 1860, the Democratic split was complete when the party's Southern elements supported Vice President Breckinridge and Northerners backed Stephen Douglas. The Buchanan administration earlier had waged war on Douglas by ousting Douglas allies from the federal bureaucracy for opposing the administration's pro-Southern stance on the Kansas issue.

When the time came for the 1860 presidential campaign, the Democrats were hopelessly split over slavery. The biggest sticking point was the *Dred Scott* decison, which held that Congress had no power to prohibit the slave trade in a territory. The decision was just what Southerners favoring popular sovereignty wanted, but it also created uncertainty about any legislature's authority over slavery. If the federal legislature could not regulate slavery, could state legislatures? The Republicans were able to use the decision as a rallying point for popular control of government; the Democrats were in the uncustomary position of defending the Supreme Court, which since Thomas Jefferson they had pictured as elitist. Douglas, the eventual Democratic nominee and architect of the platform, insisted on state resolution of the issue. Jefferson Davis of Mississippi, the eventual president of the Confederate States of America, fought in Congress for the right of Congress to promote and protect slavery in new territories.

Eventually, the Davis Democrats held their own convention and nominated Vice President Breckinridge for the presidency. Although these "Dixiecrats"—a term used to distinguish Southern from Northern Democrats—insisted that they were the backbone of the party and had been strong enough to elect Buchanan four years before, the party divided would not be able to win a national election.

Democratic party splits enabled Lincoln to win the 1860 election, resulting in the secession of seven Southern states from the Union even before his inauguration. (The remaining four states forming the Confederacy seceded after the fall of Fort Sumter, April 13, 1861.)

The Fateful Election of 1860

The regional splits that had been tearing the nation apart for decades reached their peak in 1860. None of the four major candidates who sought the presidency could compete seriously throughout the nation. The winner would probably be a candidate from the North, the region with the most electoral votes. The two Northern candidates were former U.S. representative Abraham Lincoln of Illinois and Stephen Douglas, a Democrat, who defeated Lincoln for the Illinois Senate seat in 1858. Moderate Constitutional Union nominee John Bell of Tennessee and Democrat John Breckinridge of Kentucky were the candidates competing in the South.

The Republican party developed out of disgruntled elements of the Whigs, the Know-Nothings, abolitionists, members of the Liberty and Free-Soil parties, anti-imperialists, high-tariff supporters, temperance activists, and states' rights advocates. The Republicans succeeded in 1860 because they were able to pull together a variety of potentially warring factions. Above all else, the Republicans stood against the extension of slavery into new territories. By accepting slavery where it already existed but warning against the nationalization of the system, the Republicans divided the Democrats and picked up support from a diverse array of otherwise contentious factions—abolitionists, moderate abolitionists, and whites who feared for their position in the economy.

The *Dred Scott* decision enabled the Republicans to rail publicly against the high court in the tradition of Jefferson and Jackson. While opposing the Democratic doctrine of popular sovereignty, the Republicans picked up some states' rights sympathizers.

Lincoln won the nomination at a frenzied convention in Chicago. After the convention blocked several radical candidates, Lincoln emerged as the consensus compromise choice. Lincoln was known widely throughout Illinois, which improved his chances at the Chicago convention.

Among the Democrats, Douglas was Lincoln's principal rival. Douglas managed several moderate platform victories at the Democratic convention in Charleston, S.C., defeating resolutions that called for acceptance of the *Dred Scott* decision and protection of slavery in the territories. But Douglas's success prompted delegates from ten Southern states to bolt the convention. After disputes over quorum rules and fifty-seven ballots, the Democrats were unable to muster the necessary two-thirds majority for Douglas. The convention adjourned, reassembled at Baltimore, and faced disputes about the seating of delegates that caused further defections from the South. With Southern radicals effectively eliminated from the convention, Douglas swept to a unanimous nomination victory.

The Democratic defectors named Vice President Breckinridge to run for president in the South. The Constitutional Union party, which developed as a futile attempt to repair the nation's geographic divisions, nominated Bell to oppose Breckinridge. These two candidates were doomed from the start, however, since the South's electoral-vote total was significantly below that of just a few major Northern states.

The Republicans assembled the wide-ranging coalition that eluded the Whigs in their last years of existence. Lincoln could count on strength in the areas that Fremont had won in 1856—New England and the upper Northwest, as well as New York and Ohio. The GOP offered an internal-improvements program to attract settlers in the frontier. Lincoln's local ties would help him in Illinois and Indiana, and his Whig background was a plus in the Ohio valley. The coal and iron regions of Pennsylvania and Ohio were attracted to the party's high-tariff policy. Urban immigrants, particularly Germans, were attracted by the GOP support of homestead (that is, frontier settlement) legislation and the Lincoln campaign's "Vote Yourself a Farm" appeal.[26] The vice-presidential selection of Hannibal Hamlin of Maine, a former Democrat, broadened the coalition beyond partisan lines. Lincoln's oft-stated desire to protect slavery where it then existed was an appeal to border states.

Lincoln easily won with a total of 180 electoral votes to Breckinridge's 72, Bell's 39, and Douglas's 12. Lincoln's closest competitor in the popular vote was Douglas. Lincoln had 1.9 million popular votes (40.0 percent); Douglas had 1.4 million (29.5 percent) spread out geographically. The two other principal candidates received much less support, which was concentrated in the South: Breckinridge won 848,000 popular votes (18.1 percent); Bell, 591,000 (12.6 percent).

Republican presidential candidate Abraham Lincoln stood tall at 6'4".

President of the Confederacy

In 1861, two weeks before Abraham Lincoln was inaugurated in Washington, D.C., as the sixteenth president of the United States, another president was inaugurated in Montgomery, Alabama. On February 18, 1861, Jefferson Davis became the first and only president of the Confederate States of America.

Davis was born in Christian (now Todd) County, Kentucky, on June 3, 1808. He was the youngest of the ten children of Samuel and Jane Davis, who moved their family to a small Mississippi plantation when Jefferson was a boy. He attended private schools and Transylvania University in Lexington, Kentucky, before his oldest brother, Joseph, secured his appointment to West Point in 1824.

After graduating from the academy, Davis was stationed in Wisconsin under Col. Zachary Taylor. There he saw action in the Black Hawk War during the early 1830s and fell in love with Taylor's daughter, Sarah Knox. In 1835 he left the army, married Sarah, and settled on a one-thousand-acre plantation in Mississippi, which was given to him by his brother Joseph. Tragically, Sarah died from malaria three months after the wedding, and for several years Davis devoted himself to developing his land and wealth.

In 1845 Davis married Varina Howell, a member of the Mississippi aristocracy, and was elected to the U.S. House of Representatives. He served in Washington less

**Jefferson
Davis**

than a year before the Mexican War began, and he gave up his seat to accept a commission as a colonel. He became a national hero when his company made a stand at the Battle of Buena Vista that was said to have saved Gen. Zachary Taylor's army from defeat.

In 1847 he left the army and was elected to the Senate. He served there until 1851, when he ran unsuccessfully for governor of Mississippi. He returned to Washington in 1853 after being appointed secretary of war by President Franklin Pierce. Davis was credited with strengthening the armed forces during his time in office. He also was influential in bringing about the Gadsden Purchase from Mexico in 1853, which added areas of present-day Arizona and New Mexico to the United States.

In 1857 Davis was reelected to the Senate. Although he became a leading spokesman for the South, he did not advocate secession until 1860 when it had become inevitable. Davis hoped to be appointed commanding general of the South's army, but instead he was chosen as president by a convention of the seceding states.

Davis believed his first priority as president was to preserve Southern independence. He tried to secure French and British assistance for the Confederacy, but he was largely unsuccessful. Like Lincoln he helped develop military strategy and on occasion interfered with the plans of his generals. In managing the war effort, Davis was hampered by his paradoxical position. The South could fight most effectively as a unified nation run by the central government in Richmond, but the Southern states had seceded in part to preserve their rights as independent states. Davis took actions, including the suspension of *habeas corpus* and the establishment of conscription, that were regarded as despotic by many Southerners.

When the Union's victory appeared imminent in early 1865, Davis fled south from Richmond and was captured by federal troops. He was indicted for treason and imprisoned for two years, but he never stood trial. He lived in Canada and Europe for several years before retiring to Mississippi. There he wrote his *Rise and Fall of the Confederate States*, which was published in 1881. He died in New Orleans on December 6, 1889.

Southerners had vowed to secede from the Union if Lincoln won the election. In the period before Lincoln's inauguration, congressional committees sought to put together a compromise that would save the nation from civil war, but they always failed because of Lincoln's refusal to abandon his policy of containment of slavery. Lincoln rejected proposals for popular sovereignty or a slave-free geographic division of Western states. Lincoln would not comment on proposals for constitutional amendments or popular referenda on the issue.

After Lincoln was elected, South Carolina, Louisiana, Mississippi, Alabama, Georgia, Texas, and Florida seceded from the Union and on February 7, 1861, adopted a con-

stitution forming the Confederate States of America. After a protracted standoff between Union soldiers who held Fort Sumter and the Confederate soldiers who controlled South Carolina, the Confederates fired on the fort. Virginia, Arkansas, North Carolina, and Tennessee then joined the Confederacy, and the Civil War was under way.

The Civil War Election

The Union's military difficulties in 1861 and 1862 created resentment and impatience with President Lincoln, and splits that developed in the Republican party seemed to imperil his chances for renomination and reelection.

From the very beginning of his administration Lincoln suffered because of the difficulty he had finding a general who could successfully prosecute the war. Repeated military setbacks and stalemates—such as the battles of Fredericksburg and Chancellorsville, Confederate general Robert E. Lee's escape after the battle of Antietam (Sharpsburg), and heavy casualties in the drive to Richmond—hurt the Republicans. Publicized conflicts with generals such as George McClellan caused further damage. In addition to the military problems, the president's announcement of the emancipation of slaves in rebellious states in September 1862 (the Emancipation Proclamation) created legal and political controversy.

The Republicans experienced widespread losses in congressional and state elections in the 1862 midterm elections. Among the more bitter defeats for Lincoln was John Stuart's victory in the president's old congressional district in Illinois. By the time of the election, Stuart, a former law partner of the president, was an ardent political foe.

The military frustrations gave rise to deep divisions within Lincoln's own cabinet. Treasury Secretary Salmon P. Chase led a radical faction of the administration, and the Philadelphia banker Jay Gould briefly led a movement for Chase's nomination for president in 1864. Chase withdrew only after the Lincoln forces dealt him a severe blow at the party caucus in his home state of Ohio. Other radicals met in Cleveland in May 1864 and named John Fremont to run against Lincoln in the fall. Fremont withdrew only after a series of Union military victories strengthened Lincoln's political standing.

The president manipulated the GOP convention in Baltimore brilliantly, ensuring not only his own renomination but also the selection of pro-Union governor Andrew Johnson of Tennessee as the vice-presidential candidate. Lincoln professed indifference about a possible running mate. "Wish not to interfere about V.P. Cannot interfere about platform," he said in a letter. "Convention must judge for itself." [27] Nonetheless, he maneuvered to build support for Johnson. Johnson's selection was in accord with the desire of the party, which called itself the Union party as a way to attract Democrats and to develop nationwide unity. Yet Lincoln's reelection drive was so uncertain that he obliged his cabinet in August 1864 to sign a statement pledging an orderly transition of power if he lost. The statement read: "This morning, as for some days past, it seems exceedingly probable that this Administration will not be reelected. Then it will be my duty to so cooperate with the President-elect, as to save the Union between the election and the inauguration; as he will have secured his election on such ground that he cannot possibly save it afterwards." [28]

The man for whom Lincoln anticipated arranging a wartime transition was General McClellan, the Democratic nominee whom Lincoln had fired as general in January 1863. McClellan had won the Democratic nomination with the strong backing of "peace Democrats" such as Clement L. Vallandigham of Ohio, who was arrested by Union general Ambrose E. Burnside after making a series of antiwar speeches. (Vallandigham later took up exile in Canada.) McClellan's running mate was Rep. George Pendleton of Ohio, who would later sponsor landmark civil-service reform legislation.

McClellan was a vocal critic of the administration. The general did not win a single major battle despite constant infusions of extra troops, but he blamed Lincoln for the losses. McClellan was popular with the soldiers, and his campaign was built around a call for a cease-fire and a convention to restore the Union. McClellan and other peace Democrats also criticized the administration's violation of civil liberties and other unconstitutional actions.

Lincoln's fortunes improved in the two months before the election. When Gen. William Tecumseh Sherman took Atlanta after a scorched-earth march through the South, the Confederacy was left badly divided geographically. The military victory cut off Gulf states from the Confederate capital of Richmond. Gen. Philip Sheridan had important successes in the Shenandoah Valley, and Gen. Ulysses Grant did well in Virginia.

Not only did the Democrats face a GOP reconstituted for the war election as the Union party and united by recent military victories, but McClellan also had a difficult time developing consistent campaign themes. He was at various times conciliatory toward the Confederacy and solicitous of the soldiers who fought for the Union. The balancing problem was underscored by the inclusion of both war and peace songs in the *McClellan Campaign Songster*, a piece of campaign literature. [29] McClellan also had a difficult time selling his message to Northern industrialists who profited from munitions procurement.

Not until the arrival of election results from three state elections on October 11 were Lincoln and the Unionists confident that they would win the national election in November. Republican victories in Indiana, Ohio, and Pennsylvania were the first concrete indications that Lincoln's fortunes had turned around.

Lincoln overwhelmed McClellan by winning all of the loyal states except Delaware, Kentucky, and New Jersey for a 212-21 electoral-vote victory. Lincoln garnered 2.2 million popular votes (55.0 percent) to McClellan's 1.8 million (45.0 percent). The electoral votes of Louisiana and Tennessee, the first Confederate states to return to the Union, were not accepted by Congress.

Postwar Radicalism

The Civil War's end left the nation almost as divided as it had been in the antebellum years. Concerns about punishment of the rebel states, the status of the freedmen, and economic development replaced slavery as the principal sources of disagreement

The nation undoubtedly would have experienced bitter splits no matter who served as chief executive, but the assassination of President Lincoln on April 14, 1865, shortly after the Confederate surrender, created a crisis of leadership. Lincoln's vice president, Andrew Johnson, ascended to the presidency and immediately came into conflict with the radical Northern Republicans who controlled Congress. Johnson, a Democrat from Tennessee, was stubborn, which only aggravated the troubles that were inevitable anyway because of his party and regional background.

Johnson intended to continue Lincoln's plans for a reconstruction of North and South "with malice toward none," but the Congress was intent on establishing political institutions that would respect the rights of former slaves and promote economic growth. [30] A states' rights politician, Johnson attempted to put together a coalition of moderates from all parts of the country that would bring about a quick reconciliation. He chafed at the notion of the South as a conquered territory. Johnson and Congress fought over bills that would extend the life of the Freedmen's Bureau and guarantee the franchise and equal protection to blacks. Johnson vetoed both bills. Johnson also opposed the Fourteenth Amendment, which guaranteed equal protection, as well as the stipulation that Confederate states approve the amendment as a condition of their readmission to the Union.

When the Radicals took over Congress in the 1866 midterm elections, the war with Johnson began in earnest. In March 1867 Congress established limited military rule in recalcitrant Southern states and passed the Tenure of Office Act limiting the president's right to dismiss his appointees. Johnson contemptuously disregarded the tenure act and fired Edwin Stanton, his secretary of war. For this action Johnson was impeached by the House and tried by the Senate. When the Senate voted in May 1868, he avoided conviction by a single vote (35-19).

The Grant Years, 1869-1877

Ulysses S. Grant was more than a concerned citizen during the dispute between Johnson and Congress. Despite its portrayal in many history books as a clear instance of congressional abuse of power, the affair was more complicated. All of the players in the drama negotiated their way with care, and almost none of them escaped without major scars. Grant was a central figure, and his style of maneuvering was dictated by his ambition to succeed Johnson as president.

Radical Republicans in Congress achieved a lasting victory when they secured passage of the Civil Rights Act of 1866 over President Johnson's veto, but they were increasingly disturbed by reports that the statute was not being enforced. A congressional investigation of violence against blacks in Memphis concluded that the Freedmen's Bureau could not enforce civil rights without help. Radicals began to look to Secretary of War Stanton to enforce the law that the president clearly disliked and repeatedly subverted.

Stanton indicated that he would carry out the law in the Confederacy as Congress intended, and Johnson began to think about replacing him. Congress passed the Tenure of Office Act over Johnson's veto in May 1867, reasoning that its constitutional "advise and consent" powers over appointments extended to removal as well. Johnson decided to test the law's constitutionality. Johnson's concern—and indeed the concern of all involved—was who could be given the post with minimal threat to his own position.

Johnson first considered General Sherman but decided to appoint Grant on a temporary basis. Originally a Democrat and supporter of moderate Southern policies, Grant worried about appearing too close to the unpopular president. After vaguely assuring Johnson that he would accept a temporary appointment, Grant hedged. He increasingly expressed support for the notion that appointees should interpret and obey laws according to congressional intent. Eventually, Grant told the president in a letter that he could not accept the appointment.

After the drama of impeachment, Grant was in a good position to seek the White House. He had avoided allying himself with controversy both during Johnson's search for a replacement for Stanton and in the ensuing impeachment battle. Everyone but Grant and Chief Justice Salmon

Chase was tainted by the affair. Grant even managed to maintain his public posture of disinterested duty. Thus during one of the nation's ugliest political episodes, Grant looked clean. He was ready for a presidential campaign.

As Johnson endured his Senate impeachment trial in March, Grant won his first electoral victory. A New Hampshire congressional campaign, which normally would favor the Democrat, became an early Grant referendum when Republican candidate Donald Sickles told voters that a vote for a Republican was a vote for Grant; Sickles won. Just before the GOP convention in May, a Soldiers and Sailors Convention "nominated" Grant. Grant avoided an excessively military image when he vowed to reduce the size of the standing army. Grant was on his way.

Grant won the nomination without opposition. The real battle at the 1868 Republican convention was for the vice-presidential nomination. Schuyler Colfax of Indiana, the Speaker of the House, won on the sixth ballot.

The Democrats had a difficult time finding a nominee. Johnson sought the Democratic nomination, but his appeal was to the South; and, because many Southern states were still outside the Union, Northern politicians were selecting the nominee. Chase, highly regarded for his fairness during Johnson's Senate trial, was a possibility, but his strong stand for black suffrage was a barrier. Thomas Hendricks of Indiana was strong in the East, and George Pendleton of Ohio was strong in the West. Gen. Winfield Hancock of Pennsylvania presented the opportunity of running one military hero against another.

After twenty-three bitter ballots in a sweltering New York City, Horatio Seymour, the party chair and popular war governor of New York, accepted the Democratic nomination against his will. Gen. Francis P. Blair, Jr., of Missouri was the vice-presidential nominee. The party platform called for a rapid reentry of Confederate states to the Union, state authority over suffrage questions, and the "Ohio Idea," which set an inflationary money supply and helped the indebted South.

Both sides were well financed in the election, but the Republicans had the edge. The GOP's positions on the tariff, railroad grants, and the currency attracted millions of dollars. Newspapers and magazines tended to be pro-Republican.

Grant ran his campaign from his home in Galena, Illinois. He was vague about issues ranging from the currency to voting rights. Appearances in Colorado with fellow generals Sherman and Sheridan were taken to be endorsements. Everything seemed to go Grant's way. Even the traditional campaign gossip about the sexual activities of candidates did not hurt him. Charges that Grant was excessively problack—"I am Captain Grant of the Black Marines, The stupidest man that was ever seen" were the lyrics of one ditty[31]—helped him with the recently enfranchised citizens. Without the black vote, Grant probably would have lost the popular vote and maybe the electoral vote.

Results from October state elections that favored the Republicans created a brief movement for Seymour and Blair to quit the contest so that the Democrats could name a new ticket. Seymour instead took the October results as an incentive to get to the campaign stump. Seymour was a good speaker, but nothing he could do could help the Democrats.

Grant defeated Seymour 3.0 million (52.7 percent) to 2.7 million votes (47.3 percent). The electoral vote tally was 214 for Grant and 80 for Seymour. Grant won all but eight of the thirty-four states taking part in the election. He benefited from Radical Republican reconstructionist sentiment in the North and newly enfranchised blacks in the South.

With Grant's ascension to the presidency in 1869, the Republican party entered a new era—what the German sociologist Max Weber would call a shift from "charismatic" to "rational" institutional authority. The party shifted its devotion from a great moral cause to its own survival as an organization. The party began as a coalition of activists fervently opposed to the expansion of slavery (many opposed to slavery itself) and to the rebellion of Southern states from the Union. The Republicans' 1868 victory under Grant was the first not dominated wholly by crisis conditions.

The Republicans had a strong base of support: eastern bankers, manufacturers, railroads, and land speculators. With the old Confederacy under the control of military governments and with blacks given the franchise, the Republicans had strength in the South. The West was restive, however, because of depressed farm prices, high taxes, and debt. The industrial-agrarian split between North and South before the Civil War would be resumed as an East-West split in the years after the war.

Republican leadership was turning over to new hands. Age was claiming a number of the early Republican leaders, such as Thaddeus Stevens, William Seward, Benjamin Wade, Charles Sumner, James Grimes, Stanton, and Chase. New party leaders included Senators Roscoe Conkling of New York, Oliver Morton of Indiana, Simon Cameron of Pennsylvania, and Zachariah Chandler of Michigan, and Representatives Benjamin Butler of Massachusetts, John Logan of Illinois, James Garfield of Ohio, and James G. Blaine of Maine.

The Grant administration was undistinguished. The new president's inaugural address—spoken without the traditional company of the outgoing president, since Grant neglected to respond to Johnson's polite letters—was decent but uninspiring. Grant vowed that "all laws will be faithfully executed, whether they meet my approval or not," that debtors would not be tolerated, and that blacks should get the vote throughout the country, and Indians should be offered "civilization and ultimate citizenship."[32] With a few important exceptions, cabinet positions went to old Grant cronies.

The nation experienced a financial panic when financiers Jay Gould and Jim Fisk attempted to corner the world's gold market. Their scheme led to "Black Friday," September 24, 1869. Gould and Fisk met with President Grant and urged him not to sell government gold—therefore keeping the price of gold high. At the last minute, however, Grant decided to reject their advice and dumped $4 million worth of gold on the market. That dumping caused a severe drop in gold prices, breaking up the Gould-Fisk conspiracy but also causing tremendous losses for thousands of speculators. It was the worst disaster on Wall Street up to that time. Although it did not cause a depression, the South and West were hard hit by the financial retrenchment program that followed. Tariff rates remained high on most manufactured goods, despite tentative efforts to reform the system. The spoils system was in full swing during the Grant years. Grant himself was not involved in the scramble for booty, but his family and aides were often shameless in their greed. When Grant learned that liberal Republicans were planning an independent presidential campaign against him in 1872, he took the edge off the

Currier & Ives; Library of Congress

The 1872 Republican campaign called voters' attention to the humble backgrounds of presidential candidate Ulysses S. Grant and his running mate, Henry Wilson.

spoils issue by creating the Civil Service Reform Commission, but his neglect of the commission made it ineffective.

Before the 1872 election, the *New York Sun* exposed the Crédit Mobilier scandal. The newspaper reported that the firm's board of directors had many of the same members as the Union Pacific Railroad Company, which hired it to build a transcontinental route, and that Crédit Mobilier had paid its board exorbitant profits. To avoid a public investigation, Crédit Mobilier offered stock to Vice President Colfax and Representative Garfield (later president). Colfax lost his place on the Republican ticket for his role in the scandal; Sen. Henry Wilson of New Hampshire took his position as the vice-presidential candidate in 1872.

Liberal Republicans, discontent with protective tariffs, spoils, and uneven administration of the Southern states, bolted the party in 1872. The group was interested in policies such as civil service and free trade that would promote individual virtue in a laissez-faire economic system. The reformers thought they had a chance to win. The German-born senator Carl Schurz of Missouri wrote to a friend that "the administration with its train of offices and officemongers [is] the great incubus pressing upon the party. . . . The superstition that Grant is the necessary man is rapidly giving way. The spell is broken, and we have only to push through the breach."[33]

Candidates for the nomination from this group of Republicans included former ambassador to Great Britain

Charles Francis Adams, son of President John Quincy Adams and grandson of President John Adams; Supreme Court Justice David Davis; Salmon Chase; Sen. Lyman Trumbull of Illinois; and Horace Greeley, editor of the *New York Tribune*. Greeley won the nomination on the sixth ballot. The Democrats were so weak that they did not field a candidate of their own. They endorsed the Greeley ticket.

Since his early days as a newspaper reporter, when he described President Van Buren as an effeminate failure, Greeley had won fame as a pungent social critic. He was a crusading, abolitionist editor and a dedicated reformer, but his rumpled appearance and unpolished speaking style made him appear "unpresidential." Greeley was unable to parlay an amalgam of promises to various interest groups— blacks, soldiers, immigrants, and laborers—into a victory over Grant. Groups that Greeley actively courted found him wanting for a variety of reasons, and even though Greeley advocated the tariff favored by the North, he could not cut into Grant's northeastern strength. A Republican cartoon showed Greeley's difficult task: Sitting on the fence are a laborer, skeptical because of Greeley's stand against strikes, and a black, concerned because of Greeley's advocacy of amnesty for Confederates. Sitting on the sidelines is a German upset because of Greeley's prohibitionist stance. He says: "Oh! Yaw! You would take my Lager away, den you must get widout me along!" [34]

Even though he went on the stump and delivered a series of impressive speeches, Greeley never had a chance. Republican gubernatorial victories in North Carolina in August and in Pennsylvania, Ohio, and Indiana in October were clear harbingers that the GOP would do well in November. Grant took the entire North and the newly admitted South with 3.6 million popular votes (55.6 percent). Greeley won three border states, as well as Tennessee, Texas, and Georgia, with 2.8 million popular votes (43.9 percent). Less than a month after the election, Greeley died. Of the electoral votes, which were cast after Greeley's death, Grant received 286; the Democrats' 63 electoral votes were scattered among various candidates, and 17 Democratic electoral votes were not cast.

The Compromise of 1876

The pattern of Republican, Northern, and business domination of presidential politics was institutionalized in the 1876 election. Republican Rutherford B. Hayes, the three-time governor of Ohio, lost the popular vote and had a questionable hold on the electoral-college vote, but he managed to beat Democrat Samuel J. Tilden for the presidency when the election was settled by a special commission created by Congress. (Hayes won 4.0 million votes to Tilden's 4.3 million, or 48-51 percent of the vote.) Perhaps the most controversial election outcome in history, some feared it would set off a second civil war.

The problem arose when the vote tallies in Florida, South Carolina, and Louisiana were called into question. Violence attended the voting in all three states, but President Grant did not send in federal troops to ensure fair balloting. On those states hung the electoral outcome. There was good reason to be suspicious of any vote count in those and other Southern states. While the Republicans controlled the balloting places and mounted vigorous drives to get blacks to the polls, the Democrats used physical intimidation and bribery to keep blacks away. The bitterness between Northern interests and Southern whites

was apparent in the violence that often took place at polls.

State election board recounts and investigations did not settle the question, and Congress took it up. An electoral commission made up of five senators (three majority party Republicans, two minority Democrats), five representatives (three majority party Democrats, two minority Republicans), and five Supreme Court justices (two from each party, one independent) assembled to hear complaints about the disputed states. At the last minute the independent justice could not serve; his place was taken by a Republican who was accepted by Democrats because they considered him to be the most independent of possibilities. Weeks of bargaining followed, during which the Republican vote totals of the disputed states were confirmed, and the Southern Democrats extracted promises of financial aid and political independence from the federal government.

When the validity of the Florida vote count for Hayes was challenged, the commission responded that it did not have the capacity to judge the actual conduct of the balloting, only the validity of the certificates presented to Congress. That decision gave the state to Hayes. Challenges to the vote counts of Louisiana, South Carolina, and Oregon were dismissed in a similar way, so Hayes was awarded the presidency.

The compromise not only settled the partisan dispute between Hayes and Tilden; it also established a rigid alignment of political interests that would dominate U.S. politics for the next half-century. Although Democrats won occasional victories, the Republican, eastern, conservative, business-oriented establishment held sway over the system until Franklin Roosevelt's election in 1932. The institutional form of the regional splits created by the compromise remained much longer.

Historian C. Vann Woodward has argued that secret wheeling and dealing among congressional and party leaders institutionally divided the political system by party, region, economic interest, and governmental branches. Northern Republican industrial interests were given control of the presidential election process, and Southern Democratic agricultural interests were given autonomy over their regional politics that led to domination of Congress.[35] This alignment was not completely dislodged until the passage of important civil rights legislation in the 1960s. In return for throwing the election to the Republican Hayes, Northern politicians agreed to pull federal troops out of the South and to allow Southern whites to take over the system. Within months, Southern states were erecting a powerful edifice of racial discrimination that would last until the 1960s. Former South Carolina governor Daniel H. Chamberlain later summed up the deal:

> What is the president's Southern policy? [I]t consists in the abandonment of Southern Republicans and especially the colored race, to the control and rule not only of the Democratic Party, but of that class of the South which regarded slavery as a Divine Institution, which waged four years of destructive war for its perpetuation, which steadily opposed citizenship and suffrage for the negro— in a word, a class whose traditions, principles, and history are opposed to every step and feature of what Republicans call our national progress since 1860.[36]

The Age of Republicanism

From 1860 until 1908, the Republicans won nine elections; the Democrats won only two. Only Grover Cleveland could put together a Democratic win, and he was as conservative on most issues as the Republicans of the period. Presidential election winners after the Great Compromise were Hayes (1876), James Garfield (1880), Cleveland (1884), Benjamin Harrison (1888), Cleveland (1892), William McKinley (1896 and 1900), Theodore Roosevelt (1904), and William Howard Taft (1908).

The political aspirants of the day were required to adhere to the religion of high tariffs, laissez-faire economics, and tight money. Tight money policies—the restricted issuance of currency, which favored bankers and other established interests but hurt debtors and those seeking more rapid expansion of some kinds of investment and spending—provided rare openings for resistance to Republican hegemony. Resistance also developed when the scramble for tariff protections created obvious inequities among businesses and hardships for the consumer. Populist uprisings such as Democrat William Jennings Bryan's 1896 campaign faltered, however, because of strong mobilization by the Republicans and divisions within the Democratic ranks. Bryan failed to bring a likely Democratic constituency—the worker—into the fold. Eastern businessmen were able to portray their interest in industrial growth as a common concern with labor and Bryan's western agrarian alliance as a danger to that growth.

While the GOP dominated presidential politics, the parties were well-balanced in Congress and in state governments until the class and sectional cleavages of the 1890s. The Senate was split in 1881, 37-37, and two years later the Republicans had a 38-36 edge. Democrats made gains in Northern congressional races, and Republicans were making smaller gains in the South. The House tended to provide a majority for the presidential party in power.

Garfield Carries the GOP Banner

Hayes honored his pledge to serve only one term, setting off a scramble for the parties' nominations in 1880. When the momentum for a third term for Grant faltered, the Republican contest became a battle between Grant, House Speaker James Blaine, and General John Sherman. Grant was able to muster a first-ballot plurality but could not attract new supporters as the balloting proceeded. A stalemate between Blaine and Sherman ensued.

Rep. James Garfield of Ohio, a former preacher who was impressive in his oratory and organization for Sherman, was the compromise choice for the nomination. He selected as his running mate Chester A. Arthur, the collector of the Port of New York, an important patronage job.

The Democrats named Gen. Winfield Hancock and former Rep. William English to head their ticket. The Democrats' platform advocated the gold standard, a tariff to raise revenue, civil service reform, restrictions on Chinese immigration, and a belated criticism of the 1876 deal that gave the presidency to Hayes. Except for the tariff and 1876 questions, the Democrats' platform was close to the Republicans' statement of principles.

The regional breakdown of support, with most of the North and West falling in Garfield's camp and the South lining up behind Hancock, gave the presidency to Garfield. The popular vote was close—4.45 million (48.27 percent) to 4.44 million (48.25 percent)—but Garfield won a 214-155 electoral-vote victory.

The festering issue of patronage and civil service came

to a head shortly after Garfield's inauguration. On July 2, 1881, Charles Guiteau, a man history textbooks have described as a "disappointed office-seeker," shot Garfield in a railroad depot while Garfield was traveling to Williams College to deliver a commencement address. Garfield died in September, and Arthur became president. The outstanding feature of Arthur's presidency was the easy passage of the Pendleton Act. The legislation set up a commission to regulate the provision of federal jobs and the behavior of civil servants. The number of federal workers removed from the patronage system was at first small, but successive presidents widened the coverage of nonpartisan workers so that today less than 1 percent of all federal workers are appointed by the White House.[37]

The tariff question also emerged as crucial. The Tariff Act of 1883 "gave little or no relief to the consumer and took care of every important industrial interest." [38] The Democrats opposed the bill and later worked for gradual lowering of rates, but failed. The tariff would be a major issue in later elections.

The next three elections, 1884, 1888, and 1892, revolved around Democrat Grover Cleveland of New York, a city politician who worked his way up to the governorship. Cleveland defeated Blaine for the presidency in 1884, lost to Harrison in 1888, then came back to defeat Harrison in 1892. Even after his two staggered terms, Cleveland remained involved in Democratic presidential politics. He emerged as the chief foe of Bryan in 1896 and was even considered for the presidency in 1900.

Democrat Cleveland Wins

Arthur wanted the Republican nomination in 1884, and his record as stand-in for the assassinated Garfield arguably should have earned him the nomination. Not only was he an important player in the civil service reform and the tariff issue, but he began the modernization of the navy and vetoed the Chinese Exclusion Act of 1883. He was a model of fiscal probity with his veto of the $19 million river and harbor bill.

James G. Blaine of Maine—secretary of state in Arthur's own administration—stood in Arthur's way. After months of public appeals by old-line Republicans interested in stronger leadership and more generous patronage from their own party, Blaine quit his administration position and opposed Arthur for the nomination.

Blaine was the most charismatic figure of the period. A former teacher, editor, state legislator, and member of Congress, Blaine's fiery oratory captured the imagination of the political establishment. He had made a national name for himself when he opposed an 1876 congressional resolution expressing forgiveness to Civil War rebels including the Confederate president, Jefferson Davis. Col. Robert G. Ingersoll, a rising political figure in the Republican party, said of Blaine: "Like an armed warrior, like a plumed knight, James G. Blaine marched down the halls of the American Congress and threw his shining lance full and fair against the brazen forehead of every traitor to his country." [39]

The Republican convention in Chicago praised Arthur's administration and fudged the tariff issue. The tariff that passed in 1883 was the product of swarms of lobbyists for private interests. The GOP platform promised better protection for raw wool interests, angered by their treat-

The fiery oratory of 1884 Republican candidate James G. Blaine captured the imagination of the political establishment, but it was not enough to win him the election over Democrat Grover Cleveland.

ment in 1883, and a generally protective stance for domestic industry. The platform also called for an international currency conference, railway regulation, a national agency for labor affairs, and further improvements in the navy.

At a frenzied convention, Blaine took the lead over Arthur on the first ballot. Old-line party leaders quickly united behind Blaine, while Arthur was unable to consolidate the support of reform Republicans still skeptical of his leadership abilities from his days as a patronage politician and collector of the Port of New York. Blaine won the nomination on the fourth ballot. Gen. John Logan of Illinois received the vice-presidential nomination.

The Democrats nominated Grover Cleveland after skirmishes with Sen. Thomas Bayard of Delaware and Sen. Thomas Hendricks of Indiana. Hendricks, whose liberal expansionist currency stance would balance the more conservative stance of Cleveland, was named the vice-presidential candidate. The Democratic platform vaguely promised reform of the tariff laws to make them more fair and, even more vaguely, promised a more honest and efficient administration.

Cleveland was a former teacher, lawyer, assistant district attorney, and reform mayor of Buffalo who had won the governorship of New York only two years before. Members of both parties consistently underestimated Cleveland's intellect and resolve. As governor, he made enemies through vetoes of low public-transit fares and aid to sectarian schools. He also defied Tammany Hall, the Democratic party organization that dominated New York politics, especially in New York City.

Cleveland's nomination signaled a triumph for the "educational politics" characteristic of urban progressivism. In a move away from the highly partisan and vitriolic campaigns of the post-Civil War era, Cleveland and other disciples of former New York governor Samuel Tilden promoted their program through a "literary bureau" that distributed pamphlets describing the party's policy positions. Campaign themes were developed at the national level and disseminated via the mails and meetings with the many professional and community organizations. The educational style was adopted by Republican Harrison in 1888.[40]

Blaine's campaign was one of the dirtiest in U.S. history. Blaine first attempted to spark sectional antagonisms with his "bloody shirt" warnings that the South was trying to reassert its rebel ways through Cleveland. Blaine also tried to rouse business fears with claims that Cleveland would institute free trade policies damaging to domestic industries. That appeal failed because the Democratic platform's plank on the tariff laws specifically supported protection of those interests. Finally, Blaine tried to make a scandal of Cleveland's fathering of a child out of wedlock years before. Among the charges against Cleveland was that he kidnapped and immured both the mother and child to cover up the story.

The campaign eventually turned on Cleveland's victory in New York, which resulted from a number of blunders by Blaine. One blunder had occurred years before, when Blaine mocked New York party boss Roscoe Conkling: "The contempt of that large-minded gentleman is so wilted, his haughty disdain, his grandiloquent swell, his majestic, supereminent, overpowering, turkey-gobbler strut, has been so crushing to myself that I know it was an act of the greatest temerity to venture upon a controversy with him." [41] Conkling was so peeved by the turkey image that he spent his whole career battling Blaine, including the presidential campaign of 1884. Blaine's own running mate, Logan, sympathized with Conkling in the dispute.

The other Blaine faux pas occurred a week before the election when a Protestant minister praised Blaine and proclaimed, "We are Republicans, and do not propose to leave our party and identify ourselves with the party whose antecedents have been rum, Romanism, and rebellion." Blaine did not separate himself from the remark, which angered New York Democrats and cost him votes. Later the same day, Blaine attended a formal dinner with a number of wealthy persons that became known as "the millionaires dinner"; the event belied Blaine's claims to speak for ordinary people.

Blaine, of Irish background, appealed to Irish immigrants in New York for their votes. But Cleveland countered Blaine's Irish tactic with the last-minute endorsement of the powerful Tammany leader Edward Kelly. Cleveland made two campaign speeches and attended a public rally in Buffalo. On the Saturday before the election, he attended a parade in New York City that attracted forty thousand people chanting: "Blaine, Blaine, James G. Blaine, the Monumental Liar from the State of Maine!" With the help of an economic downturn and the "Mugwumps"—independents and liberal Republicans offended by Blaine—Cleveland won the presidency.

The race however, was close. Cleveland received 4.9 million votes (48.5 percent) to Blaine's 4.8 million (48.3 percent). He won the solid South, Indiana, Connecticut, New Jersey, and, most important, New York (although by only 1,047 out of 1.13 million votes cast). Still, the election controversy did not end with the balloting. The *New York*

Tribune reported that Blaine won the race, fueling fears about an election deadlock similar to the Hayes-Tilden contest of 1876. But Cleveland received 219 electoral votes to Blaine's 182, making the Democrat the clear winner.

Cleveland's first two years in the White House were productive. His inaugural address and cabinet selections won wide praise. His style of leadership—examined closely in the newspapers—appeared refreshingly unassuming. The Cleveland agenda included issues like tariff reform (cutting rates on the "necessaries of life"), navy modernization, civil service, expansion, and land law reform. The president oversaw passage of the Presidential Succession Act and the Electoral Count Act, changes in currency policy, and labor controversies.

As during his terms as mayor of Buffalo and governor of New York, Cleveland icily refused to compromise his values. But when he became party leader, this steadfastness proved to be a problem. Thousands of Democratic party workers went to Washington seeking jobs in the new administration only to be disappointed. "Ah, I suppose you mean that I should appoint two horse thieves a day instead of one," Cleveland said in response to one party leader.[42] In vetoing pension bills, Cleveland called their sponsors "blood-suckers," "coffee-boilers," "pension leeches," and "bums."[43] The president appeared just as aloof to labor when a record number of strikes and disturbances swept the nation in 1886; the federal troops that Cleveland sent to the Haymarket riot in Chicago killed thirty people.

When Cleveland did bend to political realities, his timing was off. After standing firm against patronage when party enthusiasm was at its height, Cleveland disappointed reformers when he allowed lieutenants such as First Assistant Postmaster Adlai E. Stevenson to distribute favors.

The biggest controversy of the Cleveland administration involved tariffs. Concerned about federal budget surpluses that threatened to stall economic activity, Cleveland prodded the House of Representatives to pass tariff reductions. The Senate responded with a highly protective tariff measure. The unpopular tariff issue propelled the two parties into the 1888 election. The Democrats nominated Cleveland by acclamation and chose seventy-five-year-old judge Allen G. Thurman of Ohio for the vice presidency. The Democrats tried to soften their low-tariff image by promising that domestic industries would get larger markets. Lower tariffs were said to be necessary for avoiding disastrous federal budget surpluses, preventing the development of monopolies, and ensuring consumers reasonable prices for basic goods.

The 1888 Republican Recovery

A politics-weary James Blaine sent word from Florence and Paris that he would not be a candidate in 1888. The race was left open to some lesser lights, including Sen. John Sherman of Ohio, Gov. Russell Alger of Michigan, Sen. William Allison of Iowa, and Sen. Benjamin Harrison of Ohio. Sherman led the early balloting but quickly lost ground to Alger and Harrison. After extensive back-room maneuvering, including a last-minute plea to Blaine to accept the nomination, Harrison, who had the backing of state party bosses, won on the ninth ballot. Levi Morton, a banker, got the vice-presidential nomination.

Harrison, a senator from Indiana, was a former Civil War brigadier and the grandson of President William Henry Harrison with a scandal-free if colorless demeanor.

Harrison was a good speaker, but often appeared aloof. One historian wrote: "Those who talked with him were met with a frigid look from two expressionless steel grey eyes; and their remarks were sometimes answered in a few chill monosyllables devoid of the slightest note of interest."[44] Harrison pledged a modernized navy, civil service reforms, and traditional Republican protective trust and trade policies.

The election turned, as in 1884, on New York and Indiana—both states with extensive evidence of voter intimidation and manipulation of counting. Harrison won the two states narrowly—New York by only 14,373 votes—and won the White House. Except for Connecticut and New Jersey, Harrison swept the North and West. Cleveland won the South. Overall, Harrison won 5.4 million popular votes (47.8 percent) and 233 electoral votes; Cleveland won 5.5 million popular votes (48.6 percent) and 168 electoral votes.

Cleveland left the White House with an unusual amount of good will among the public because of his honest tariff campaign. His popularity increased during the next four years as the economy hit slumps and as the former president, while practicing law, delivered speeches calling for a more egalitarian brand of politics. Cleveland would be back in 1892 for vindication.

With the first one-party majority in both the executive and legislative branches in a dozen years, the Republicans went about their business briskly after the election. Postmaster General John Wanamaker dispensed patronage with zeal. President Harrison signed into law the McKinley Tariff Act and the Sherman Silver Purchase Act. The former raised duties on manufactured goods to their highest level ever but also included provisions for negotiating with other countries to bring the rates down. The silver act

After Frank Beard in *Judge*; Library of Congress

Captioned "Another Voice for Cleveland," this 1884 cartoon played on Cleveland's admission that he had fathered an illegitimate son.

loosened the money supply, which stimulated economic activity (but angered creditors and bankers since money, when it is more readily available, is worth less).

Cleveland's Comeback, 1892

The 1890 midterm elections brought huge Democratic gains. Voters all over the country—but especially in the depressed farm belt—rebelled against the inflation that high tariffs brought. The Republicans held on to the Senate, but the new House of Representatives had 235 Democrats, 88 Republicans, and 9 Farmers' Alliance members. The brief experiment in party government ended with two years of stalemate.

President Harrison evoked widespread discontent in 1892 both for his demeanor and policies, but no Republican could mount an effective challenge. Through their strong party government, Republicans had cast their lot with Harrison and had few places to turn for an alternative. Political wizard Mark Hanna, a wealthy coal magnate who became a powerful behind-the-scenes political strategist, promoted William McKinley, and Secretary of State Blaine became an alternative when he abruptly quit the administration just before the GOP convention. But Harrison received a first-ballot nomination. Former minister to France Whitelaw Reid of New York got the vice-presidential nomination.

Cleveland enjoyed widespread backing among rank-and-file voters, but party leaders were suspicious. New York governor David B. Hall got a head start when he called a "snap" state convention and won the delegation. An "anti-snapper" convention from New York sent a rival delegation to the national party convention. Democrats across the country rebelled at Hall's move and rapidly switched their support to Cleveland.

Another problem for Cleveland was the rising sentiment in agrarian states for free and unlimited coinage of silver—a way of boosting sagging farm prices by inducing inflation in the overall economy. Cleveland always had opposed this solution. The former president's consistent, principled stance on the issue not only added to his reputation for integrity but kept business- and finance-dominated states in the Northeast in the Democratic camp. Cleveland defeated Hill for the nomination on the first ballot and selected Stevenson of Illinois as his running mate.

The fall campaign was uneventful. Historian Eugene Roseboom wrote: "Honest bearded Benjamin Harrison confronting honest mustached Grover Cleveland in a tariff debate was a repeat performance that did not inspire parades with torches or the chanting of campaign ditties. . . . Democrats, out of power, could assail Republican tariff policy without clarifying their own position." [45]

Cleveland won easily. He received 5.6 million popular votes (46.1 percent) to Harrison's 5.2 million (43.0 percent) and 277 electoral votes to Harrison's 145. Populist general James B. Weaver, advocating expansion of currency and limits of interest rates, won 1.0 million popular votes (8.5 percent) and 32 electoral votes.

The Age of Reform

Throughout the period dominated by Republican conservatism—from Grant's election in 1868 until William C. McKinley's 1896 win—movements for reform of political and economic institutions gathered strength at all levels of the American political system. The so-called Populists and progressives did not overturn the system, as their rhetoric sometimes suggested, but over time they made major changes in the operation and discourse of U.S. politics.

Depending on the time and place, people who called themselves "Populists" and "progressives" promoted such contradictory ideas as strict morals and free spirits, tight money and loose money, redistribution to the masses and control of the economy by elites, federal intervention and local control of politics, the opening and closing of electoral participation, technological progress and a return to a pastoral ideal long gone, individualism and community action, ethnic celebration and immigration barriers, scientific investigation and religion, and internationalism and isolationism.

Reformism was the response to the pressures of national expansion, urban development, and growth. Both major parties had adopted probusiness, laissez-faire policies in the latter part of the nineteenth century; the parties existed to make sure the terrain was suitable for economic expansion. But the lack of any program to deal with the undesired consequences of explosive growth led to an accumulation of problems that demanded attention. The most obvious problems evolved on the opposite ends of the rural-urban continuum: on the farms and in the cities.

The farm problem developed as the United States became a major economic power throughout the world. Agriculture expanded on a vast scale to feed the booming cities and, with international trade, to bring foreign capital to the United States. By 1880, the value of U.S. wheat and flour exports nearly equaled that of cotton exports. [46] As agriculture became part of the international market, farmers became dependent not only on the vagaries of the weather but also on the fluctuations of currency in the larger economy.

In the thirty years after the Civil War, prices for farm staples fell steadily. A debt that could have been paid by producing one thousand bushels of grain immediately after the war required three thousand bushels in 1895. The more farmers produced to meet their obligations, the more prices fell to exacerbate their problems. Confronting the problem required attention to a wide array of issues, including tight money, bankers who charged 20 percent interest for loans, monopolies among farm-equipment producers, high tariffs, railroad gouging, shipping inflation, warehouse monopolies, and land speculation. Throughout the farm belt, particularly in the West, tens of thousands of farmers developed an "intense class consciousness." [47]

All of these issues received attention from a variety of third parties and independent organizations, but the two major parties were usually inattentive. The Granger Movement of the 1870s, for example, took hold in several farm states and elected new legislatures and high state officials. The Greenback party attempted to merge a labor-farmer alliance with a doctrine of silver use for public debts. Later, the Farmers' Alliance politicized the same issues. In 1892, the Populist party won 8.5 percent of the vote on a platform calling for free coinage of silver.

Another site of growing reformist strength was the city. The dominance of machines of both parties in the cities established an electoral system based on patronage but stubbornly opposed to any coherent program for addressing urban ills, such as poverty, poor housing, unsanitary conditions, transportation, education, and unfair workplace practices. Electoral fraud spurred mostly middle-class reformers to devise new electoral and city government machinery, while social problems spurred some insurgent class politics.[48] The labor movement developed strength during this period.[49]

Other parts of the progressive agenda developed with a greater understanding of the nationalization of the economic and political systems. The wider sphere of economic activities created calls for regulation of economic corporations, railroads, and banks, attention to health and environmental concerns, and product safety.

Until the ascendance of William Jennings Bryan, the Democratic presidential nominee in 1896, 1900, and 1908, the reformers were unable to capture a major party. Partly because political activism was based at the state and local level, neither national party adopted the reformers' widely variegated program as its own. The depression of 1888 caused the Populist forces to pull together more than they had during previous economic downturns, probably because of the accumulated effects of inaction. The panic of 1873 created a sectional rather than a party split, with the Democrats eventually adopting a more conservative stance on the debate over whether the currency should be expanded to spur economic activity and redistribute social burdens.[50]

The Republican presidential candidates steadfastly opposed the class-oriented proposals of the progressive movement, especially the loose-money demands.

The only Democrat to win the presidency since the Civil War was Cleveland, a stubborn advocate of hard money and other conservative economic policies, in 1884 and 1892. President Cleveland vetoed dozens of private pension bills, only grudgingly accepted railroad regulation, and did not address domestic problems in any comprehensive way. Cleveland's public statements on the currency question were especially strong. He called the use of silver "a dangerous and reckless experiment" that was "unpatriotic."[51] On the question of labor, Cleveland was just as conservative: he called out federal troops to put down the Pullman strike of 1894 and regularly preached about the evils of disorder that the labor movement seemed to foster.

Despite the complexity of the agriculture issue, the most concerted Populist action concentrated on the currency question alone. The drive to overturn the prevailing conventional economic thought by moving from a gold (tight) to a gold and silver (loose) money standard captured the imagination of the entire farm belt stretching from the Southeast to the prairie and silver-producing states of the West. The silver standard was a very simple answer to the problem of farm prices: "If money was scarce, the farmer reasoned, then the logical thing was to increase the money supply.[52]

Gold-runs on banks, manipulation of the gold crisis by J. P. Morgan and other leading financiers, procorporation Supreme Court decisions, and antilabor actions all stirred up resentment in the South and West. Silver sentiment escalated. The Democratic convention in 1896 called for the issuance of silver and rejected a resolution praising President Cleveland.[53] The movement for a silver currency found an eloquent advocate in Bryan, a member of the House of Representatives from Nebraska, who defeated Richard P. Bland of Missouri for the 1896 Democratic presidential nomination on the strength of his fiery "Cross of Gold" speech.

That speech was one of the most emotional and successful in U.S. history. Bryan attacked eastern financiers

G. Y. Coffin, 1893; Library of Congress

Grover Cleveland is welcomed back on board the "Ship of State" in this 1893 cartoon. Having served as president from 1885 to 1889, he lost the 1888 election but regained the White House in the 1892 contest. Cleveland remains the only president to serve two nonconsecutive terms.

and businessmen who exploited farmers. In an important theme to which his fall campaign would return, Bryan sought to expand the traditional Democratic conception of the independent working man to include farmers and factory workers.[54] In his speech's fortissimo, Bryan declared: "You shall not press down upon the brow of labor this crown of thorns, you shall not crucify mankind upon a cross of gold."[55]

In 1896 the Republicans nominated Ohio governor William McKinley after brilliant maneuvering by his manager, Mark Hanna. Hanna's chief strengths were fund raising and his mastery over state party organizations.

McKinley had little difficulty defeating Bryan. McKinley outspent the prairie populist by as much as ten to one, and he attracted the disaffected progold wing of the Democratic party.[56] The GOP platform called for retention of the gold standard unless international negotiations could produce a bimetallic (that is, silver and gold) currency system. The platform also called for restored tariff protections and an aggressive foreign policy in the Western Hemisphere.

Bryan's campaign was a political hurricane. He spent just $650,000, most of it donated by silver interests, compared with the millions McKinley spent. But Bryan traveled eighteen thousand miles and gave some six hundred speeches, and his campaign staffers put out an impressive quantity of literature. Several million copies of *Coin's Financial School*, a prosilver pamphlet, were distributed during the fall of 1896. Other silverites also maintained busy speaking schedules in the fall.

Bryan's appeal to industrial workers to join his coalition of independent businessmen failed, largely because they depended for their livelihoods on the very eastern interests that Bryan attacked. McKinley won not only the East but also the small cities and towns in Bryan's southern and western belt of support. Bryan was unable to win rural areas of the East. McKinley won the popular vote 7.1 million (51.0 percent) to 6.5 million (46.7 percent) and the electoral vote 271-176.

The effect of the 1896 presidential election was lasting. Political scientist James Sundquist wrote: "For 20 years the two-party system had been based on dead issues of the past. It had offered the voters no means of expressing a choice on the crucial issues of domestic policy around which the country had been polarizing. . . . Then suddenly, with the nomination of Bryan in 1896, the party system took on meaning once again." [57]

The new Republican coalition included residents of cities, where capital and labor were both reasonably content with the economic growth that the GOP tariff policy promoted; farmers in the East and Midwest, who had strong ties to the "party of Lincoln" and who came to favor high tariffs; Catholic, German Lutheran, and other liturgical Christian denominations; and some border states. Sundquist noted: "It was the persistence of the Civil War attachments that made the realignment of the North so largely a one-way movement—pro-Republican." [58]

After 1896, the competitive party balance that had prevailed for years gave way to lopsided party strength according to region—Democrats in the South, Republicans in the North. Strong opposition parties disappeared in all regions of the country, vesting political power in the hands of those already part of the system.

As political scientist E. E. Schattschneider has observed:

> The 1896 party cleavage resulted from the tremendous reaction of conservatives in both major parties to the Populist movement. . . . [S]outhern conservatives reacted so strongly that they were willing to revive the tensions and animosities of the Civil War and the Reconstruction in order to set up a one-party sectional southern political monopoly in which nearly all Negroes and many poor whites were disenfranchised. One of the most important consequences of the creation of the Solid South was that it severed permanently the connection between the western and the southern wings of the Populist movement. [59]

Conservative Republicans won the White House in all but two (1912 and 1916) of the nine elections from 1896 to 1928.

The country experienced economic prosperity that blunted the possible activism of workers and the previous activism of farmers. With good harvests and rising commodity prices, the agrarian revolt fizzled. The development of new ore extraction methods and discovery of new gold deposits made calls for silver to expand the currency supply superfluous. The war with Spain, which McKinley reluctantly entered and the burgeoning mass media publicized, created a patriotic fervor.

McKinley's reelection in 1900 was even stronger than his 1896 election. He won 7.2 million popular votes (51.7 percent) to Bryan's 6.4 million (45.5 percent), and 292 electoral votes to Bryan's 155. McKinley swept to victory with all states except the silver states of the West (Colorado, Montana, Idaho, and Nevada).

The Rise of Theodore Roosevelt

To replace Vice President Garret A. Hobart, who died in office in 1899, the Republicans selected New York's Progressive governor Theodore Roosevelt to run with McKinley. Roosevelt, an independent-minded environmentalist and trustbuster, was promoted for vice president by New York GOP boss Thomas Platt to rid the state of progressive politics. Roosevelt was reluctant to take the job—"I am a comparatively young man yet and I like to work. . . . It would not entertain me to preside in the Senate" [60]—but accepted when a convention movement and McKinley prevailed upon him.

When McKinley was assassinated in 1901 and Roosevelt became president, U.S. presidential politics came under the influence of a variant of the progressive movement. As Gabriel Kolko and other historians have demonstrated, Roosevelt's administration was friendly to many of the traditional conservative allies. But Roosevelt's rhetoric and his legacy of regulation and conservation had strong progressive or reformist elements. [61]

Roosevelt's leadership of progressives is an example of generational politics. The new president grew up in an era in which economic expansion strained the nation's fabric, causing political figures to seek idealistic but pragmatic solutions to a wide variety of problems. The previous generation had grown up in a simpler age when "politics were devoid of substance, built around appeals to tradition and old loyalties and aimed at patronage." [62]

Roosevelt steered his party toward conservation of natural resources, enforcement of antitrust laws, promotion of the concerns of labor, and railroad regulation. The government's suit to dissolve the Northern Securities Company under the Sherman Anti-Trust Act and Roosevelt's intervention in the anthracite coal miners' strike, both in 1902, established the tenor for an activist presidency. TR (the first president identified by his initials) also used his office as a "bully pulpit" to promote his increasingly sophisticated progressive ideology.

Roosevelt had no trouble winning nomination for election as president in his own right in 1904. The Republican convention, arranged in advance at the White House, unanimously voted for Roosevelt and his platform of trustbusting, tariffs, labor relations, and activist foreign policy. Sen. Charles W. Fairbanks of Indiana was the GOP vice-presidential nominee.

To oppose the rambunctious Roosevelt, the Democrats selected a sober-visaged judge. Alton Parker, the chief justice of the New York State Court of Appeals, received the backing of the Democratic party's conservative establishment when former president Cleveland turned down entreaties to make a fourth presidential run. Parker was opposed by William Randolph Hearst, a member of Congress and newspaper magnate. Bryan forced the party to adopt a liberal platform, as a balance to the conservative judge.

The Roosevelt victory was a landslide. He won 7.6 million votes (56.4 percent) to Parker's 5.1 million (37.6 percent) and won all but the southern states. Roosevelt won 336 electoral votes to Parker's 140. Both houses of Congress were overwhelmingly Republican.

President Roosevelt pledged not to seek a second term of his own because he had served most of McKinley's second term. He occupied himself with his progressive agenda and groomed his secretary of war, William Howard Taft, as his successor.

Roosevelt Picks Taft

Roosevelt appeared to be genuinely dismayed by talk in 1907 of a possible third term, so he made public shows of support for Taft. Roosevelt was able to line up state delegations for Taft, and the nomination was never in doubt. Taft, through Roosevelt, was particularly strong among Republicans in the South. Attempts to restrict southern representation and pass a more liberal party platform were defeated.

Taft had impressive government experience. Before joining Roosevelt's cabinet, he had been a Cincinnati judge, U.S. solicitor general, federal circuit judge, head of the U.S. Commission on the Philippines, and the first civil governor of the Philippines.

Roosevelt's only problem in pushing Taft at the convention was avoiding a stampede in his own favor. Despite a highly disciplined convention, the galleries demonstrated wildly for Roosevelt. But Taft—a newcomer to electoral politics—easily won the nomination on the first ballot. He had 702 votes to the runner-up's 68. Rep. James S. Sherman of New York was selected as his running mate.

The Democrats nominated Bryan for the third time. The electoral disaster that befell Judge Parker in 1904 was said to be evidence that the party needed an aggressive challenger to the Republicans rather than another conservative candidate. The Democrats were bereft of new talent, especially in close states in the East and Midwest, and turned to Bryan despite his disastrous campaign record and the warnings of former president Cleveland.

The campaign was void of serious discussion. Taft campaigned on the Roosevelt record. Bryan called for government ownership of railroads and other liberal measures—such as a lower tariff, campaign finance reform, a graduated income tax, labor reforms, and greater enforcement of antitrust and other business regulations.

With Roosevelt and Taft promoting much of the progressive agenda, Bryan's message was no longer distinctive. Taft easily won. He gathered 7.7 million popular votes (51.6 percent) to Bryan's 6.4 million (43.1 percent), and 321 electoral votes to Bryan's 162. The North, most of the West, and the border states went into the Republican column.

Wilson and the Divided Republicans

Taft was not, by temperament, an ideal executive. His lifelong ambition had been to serve on the Supreme Court, and his disciplined legal mind and collegial nature eventually would enable Taft to become one of the high court's most able chief justices. But Taft foundered in the presidency. He carried out Roosevelt's program of business regulation and conservation, yet Roosevelt responded not with gratitude but with a series of nasty statements and plans for a campaign against Taft.

The tariff issue proved to be Taft's early trouble spot. Taft was committed to reducing tariffs—he was less political than Roosevelt, who fudged the divisive issue—and quickly became embroiled in a fight with Congress—which wanted to raise tariffs. The Senate remolded House legislation to push up various duties, and Taft publicly promoted the legislation after he managed to secure new corporate taxes and tariff reductions for raw materials. Taft proved ineffective and indecisive on the tariff issue and, as a consequence, began losing the party.

Library of Congress   Harvard College Library

The Democrats selected sober-visaged judge Alton B. Parker to run against the outgoing Theodore Roosevelt in the 1904 election. Roosevelt won by a wide margin.

The Glavis-Ballinger affair further muddied the image of the administration. The scandal broke when the chief forester of the Interior Department, Gifford Pinchot, charged that Secretary Richard A. Ballinger had betrayed the cause of conservation and had even engaged in corrupt practices regarding minerals and water power. Pinchot also charged that Ballinger had wrongly fired another Interior official, Louis Glavis, for trying to expose the scandal. Pinchot took his complaints directly to Taft, but Taft sided with Ballinger and urged Pinchot to drop the matter. After an indignant Pinchot went public with the issue, Taft fired him, fueling suspicion of a coverup at Interior. The incident was a major embarrassment to Taft because of the priority that conservation had received under Roosevelt and because of the inevitable complaints that Taft was betraying his mentor on the issue.[63]

Divisions within the Republican party eventually created the movement toward rival Taft and Roosevelt factions. Tariffs, Arizona's new state constitution (which included a provision that Taft opposed for recall of the governor), treaties, and antitrust issues split the former president and the sitting president. In many ways, the dispute was over personalities. Taft carried out Roosevelt's program but lacked his evangelical fervor and decisiveness. In a still conservative age, progressives felt they needed more aggressive leadership than the judicially tempered Taft would ever give them.

Roosevelt spent more than a year of Taft's term hunting in Africa, but he was an active speaker and campaigner when he returned to the United States. He gave a detailed accounting of his philosophy of government at a 1912 speech in Columbus, Ohio, calling for voter referenda and initiatives, recall of elected officials, and curbs on judicial power. When a dump-Taft movement decided that Wisconsin's Sen. Robert La Follette had no chance to defeat the president for the GOP nomination, party discontents turned to the energetic and still young (fifty years) Roosevelt.

Roosevelt made an all-out effort for the Republican nomination, entering twelve primaries and winning all but three. Roosevelt won 278 delegates in states with primaries to Taft's 48 and La Follette's 36. In today's system, Roosevelt probably would have marched to a first-ballot nomination (because today more delegates are allocated by popular votes than by the party organizations, which then dominated the process). Three crucial Republican states—Pennsylvania, Illinois, and Ohio—went for Roosevelt. Roosevelt clearly had great popular appeal and vote-getting ability—perhaps more than ever.

But Taft won the nomination. The president controlled the party machinery, and most of the convention's delegates were sent by the state machines. Roosevelt challenged the credentials of Taft delegates at the Chicago convention, and the nomination's outcome turned on battles over almost one-fourth of the delegates. The fight went to the floor of the convention, but Taft's smooth operation defeated Roosevelt. Roosevelt appeared at the convention to buoy his forces and cry foul.

When Roosevelt, after the defeat, urged his supporters to continue their fight, some bolting progressive delegates organized a convention in August to mount a third party effort. The bolters formed the Progressive party for the effort. When Roosevelt remarked to a reporter during the GOP convention, "I'm feeling like a bull moose," his vigorous campaign had a symbol. With the Republicans divided, the Democrats saw their first opportunity to win the presidency since Cleveland.

As the 1912 Democratic convention in Baltimore neared, several national candidates and favorite sons were vying for the nomination. The front-runner was House Speaker James Beauchamp (Champ) Clark of Missouri, a party regular who had party organization support and years of experience to recommend him.

Gov. Woodrow Wilson of New Jersey—who held a doctorate in political science and moved into politics after a distinguished career as professor and president at Princeton University—was another strong candidate. Wilson's virtues were the opposite of Clark's. He did not have an extensive record for opponents to attack, and he was supported enthusiasticallly because of his dynamic presence and reformist rhetoric rather than a long political apprenticeship. The New Jersey machine had brought Wilson into politics, but he quickly asserted his independence and became something of a crusader. Wilson had guided an election bill, an anticorruption act, public utilities regulation, and worker's compensation legislation through the state legislature. Although he had dealt with the state's party bosses, he also put a distance between himself and the machine.

Other Democratic candidates were the conservative representative Oscar Underwood of Alabama, author of a historic tariff act; another conservative, Gov. Judson Harmon of Ohio; and four favorite-son governors.

Clark appeared to have won the nomination when a Tammany bloc of delegates moved to support him after he won a tenth-ballot majority. The requirement for a two-thirds majority, however, gave other candidates time to maneuver. Wilson almost dropped out of the race, but Bryan's late transfer of his support from Clark to Wilson created a bandwagon effect for Wilson. On the forty-sixth ballot, Wilson accumulated the necessary two-thirds of delegates for the nomination. Gov. Thomas Marshall of Indiana, one of the favorite-son candidates, was picked to be the vice-presidential candidate because Underwood, Wilson's choice, would not accept.

The Democratic platform was progressive. It called for tariff reduction, utility regulation, banking reforms, legislation to curb monopolies, a national income tax, direct election of senators, campaign finance reforms, and a national presidential primary.

Wilson easily won the election, receiving 435 electoral votes to Roosevelt's 88 and Taft's 8. The Republican splits obviously helped Wilson; if Roosevelt and Taft had combined their totals of 4.1 million votes (27.4 percent) and 3.5 million votes (23.2 percent), they would have topped Wilson's 6.3 million (41.8 percent). But even though Wilson was a minority president, there was a clear Democratic trend, since the Democrats had taken over the House and replaced several Republican governors in the 1910 midterm elections. It was the worst showing ever for an incumbent president—third place with only two states.

Whatever the strength of Wilson's "mandate," he acted as though he had won by a landslide. His first term was one of the most productive in U.S. history. With the Democrats in control of Congress, and with a shrewd political adviser in Col. Edward M. House, Wilson adopted a reform agenda that had been percolating at various levels of government for years. He broke precedent by delivering his first State of the Union message to Congress in person. At the center of the message was a call for reductions in tariff rates. After a bitter fight raged for a month, Wilson went public with a demand that members of Congress reveal their property holdings. The revelations showed close links between their holdings and the kinds of tariff protections on the books. Congress soon was shamed into passing tariff cuts of 15 percent. Some one hundred items were placed on a free-trade list for the first time.

Library of Congress

Woodrow Wilson traveled widely in the 1912 election campaign. His dynamic presence and reformist rhetoric appealed to the crowds who came to hear him.

Wilson also addressed other areas successfully: taxes (institution of a graduated income tax in 1913); banking regulation (the Glass-Owen Act of 1913, which created the Federal Reserve System); antitrust legislation (the Clayton Anti-Trust Act of 1914, creation of the Federal Trade Commission in 1914); labor relations (Section 6 of the Sherman Anti-Trust Act, which exempted unions from antitrust strictures); agriculture (the Smith-Lever Act of 1914, the Federal Farm Loan Act of 1916); environmentalism (creation of the National Park Service in 1916); and the judiciary (the appointment of Louis Brandeis to the Supreme Court).

Despite his strong leadership—highlighted by his stirring oratory—Wilson still faced the prospect of a tough reelection. He had won the presidency in 1912 with only 41.8 percent of the popular vote, and the growing war in Europe was beginning to disturb the American process of contented economic growth.

Public opinion on the war was volatile, largely because more than a third of the U.S. population was either foreign-born or offspring of foreign-born parents. Some eleven million Americans surveyed in the 1910 census were of direct German or Austrian descent, and another five million were from Ireland. Other immigrants were Russian, Italian, Hungarian, British, and French. Wilson sought to diffuse feelings for the immigrants' native lands when he denounced "hyphenism"—the tendency of many citizens to identify themselves with appellations that linked their ethnic origins and American status—but politicians at lower levels tailored their campaigns to specific nationality voting blocs.[64]

Wilson and Vice President Marshall won renomination without any opposition. The most significant event of the Democratic convention was the passage of the platform, which indicated the party's main campaign theme. By calling for national universal suffrage, Wilson helped himself in the eleven western states where women had already won the vote. The platform praised "the splendid diplomatic victories of our great president, who has preserved the vital interests of our government and its citizens, and kept us out of war." The latter phrase would be repeated endlessly during the fall.[65]

The Republicans nominated Supreme Court Justice Charles Evans Hughes. Hughes was silent in the months before the convention, but a number of party leaders lined up enough delegates for him to win a third-ballot nomination. Other potential candidates that year included former president Roosevelt, former senator Elihu Root of New York, former vice president Fairbanks, and senators John Weeks, Albert Cummins, and Lawrence Sherman. Fairbanks won the vice-presidential nomination.

Prosperity and reformism limited the campaign themes of the Republicans. The GOP railed against Wilson's foreign policy as "shifty expedients" and "phrasemaking" that put the United States in danger of entering the war. Hughes turned out to be a bad campaigner, but he bridged the gap between conservative and progressive Republicans that cost the party the 1912 election.

Wilson was occupied with Congress throughout the summer of 1916, but he emerged to give a series of speeches in the fall. Democratic strategists, meanwhile, conceived and executed a masterful strategy to return Wilson to the White House. The Democrats concentrated all their resources on "swing states" and ignored states they thought Wilson was sure to lose. Illinois, for example, was ignored since it was a certain Republican state. Bryan,

Wilson's secretary of state, toured the West.

Wilson won one of the closest elections in history. California, an uncertain state, ensured Wilson's victory when, because of the urban vote, it went the president's way late in the campaign. The margin of victory was 3,420 votes in that state. The president defeated Hughes by a margin of 9.1 million (49.2 percent) to 8.5 million popular votes (46.1 percent). The electoral college gave Wilson 277 votes and Hughes 254.

The "Return to Normalcy" and the Roaring Twenties

After the tumult of Woodrow Wilson's domestic reforms, the First World War, and the divisive battle over the Versailles treaty, the time was ripe for a period of conservatism and Republican government. Deep resentments developed toward Wilson and the Democratic party, and the Democrats were divided over many issues, including economic regulation, Prohibition, and race relations.

Blessed with good luck, strong financial backing, and a strong trend toward split-ticket voting, the Republicans were able to resume their dominance over national politics with three successful presidential campaigns. Warren G. Harding was elected in 1920, Calvin Coolidge in 1924, and Herbert C. Hoover in 1928.

The 1920s are usually pictured as a time of steady, unexciting politics. The conservatives dominated the federal government, and occupying the White House were men who spoke of "normalcy" and a noninterventionist brand of politics in both domestic and foreign affairs. One of the symbols of the age is President Coolidge's program of tax cuts, which reduced the rates on the wealthy. The wartime Revenue Act of 1918 had driven tax rates to the highest point in U.S. history. The total tax rate in the highest brackets was 77 percent. In 1921, 1923, and 1926, Secretary of the Treasury Andrew Mellon presented to Congress proposals to cut taxes, the most controversial being the reduction in the maximum surtax from 77 to 25 percent. Congress eventually cut the surtax to 40 percent in 1924 and 20 percent in 1926.[66]

But the three sober men who filled the presidency met challenges from progressives of both parties in Congress and in the state governments. On a wide range of issues—including relief of the poor, subsidies for the depressed farm sector, regulation of utilities, immigration, race relations, states' rights, tax cuts, and Prohibition—the conservative presidents encountered strong challenges. They frequently responded by vetoing legislation, but such an expedient would not prevent the pressures for a more activist government from developing.

Harding and "Normalcy"

Sen. Warren Harding, a product of the GOP machine of Ohio, emerged from a crowded and largely unknown pack to win the Republican nomination in 1920 at a convention dominated by economic interests such as oil, railroads, and steel.

The early candidates were Gen. Leonard Wood, an old Roosevelt ally; Gov. Frank Lowden of Illinois, who married into the Pullman family and therefore had ample financing for a campaign; and Sen. Hiram Johnson of California, whose progressive and isolationist stances put him in good stead with voters in many states. A dozen favorite sons hoped that a deadlocked convention might bring the nomination their way. All of the candidates were on hand in Chicago to maneuver for the nomination.

While Wood, Johnson, and Lowden performed reasonably well in the primaries, Harding won only his home state of Ohio and did not arouse much popular enthusiasm. Under the direction of a shrewd campaign manager, Harry Daughtery, Harding gained the support of the party's bosses and won the nomination on the tenth ballot after a brief interview in the "smoke-filled room" that was synonymous with boss control. Gov. Calvin Coolidge of Massachusetts, a favorite-son contender for president, became Harding's vice-presidential candidate.

The Democrats selected Gov. James Cox, also from Ohio, after lengthy platform battles and balloting for the nomination. Early balloting put former Treasury secretary William McAdoo and Attorney General Mitchell Palmer in the lead, but Cox gained steadily and had the nomination

by the forty-fourth roll call. Franklin D. Roosevelt of New York, the assistant secretary of the navy, was the quick selection for Cox's running mate.

The image of Woodrow Wilson hung over the convention and would hang over the fall campaign. The Democratic platform praised Wilson's conduct of the war and his domestic reform program. The results in the November election indicated deep unease over the Democratic administration, however. Harding's landslide victory was termed "election by disgust" by political analysts.

Harding amassed 16.1 million popular votes (60.3 percent) to Cox's 9.1 million (34.2 percent), and 404 electoral votes to Cox's 127. Harding carried the North and West including Oklahoma and all of the southern and border states except Tennessee and Kentucky.

The sacrifices demanded under Wilson were widely perceived as the cause of Harding's victory rather than a desire for the ideology or policy proposals that Harding offered. The *New York Post* editorialized: "We are in the

Democratic presidential candidate James M. Cox of Ohio, left, and vice-presidential candidate Franklin D. Roosevelt (one year before he was stricken with polio), campaign in the 1920 election. They lost to Republican presidential candidate Warren G. Harding and his running mate, Gov. Calvin Coolidge of Massachusetts.

backwash from the mighty spiritual and physical effort to which America girded herself when she won the war for the Allies. . . . The war has not been repudiated, though the administration that fought it has been overwhelmed. We are now in the chill that comes with the doctor's bills." [67]

The electorate's ability to shift allegiances from the Republicans to the Democrats and back again—from one period to the next, and from one level of government to the next—suggested a dissolution of partisan alignments. The addition of women to the electorate after the Nineteenth Amendment in 1920 and increasing independence among all voters added uncertainty. Apathy resulted from the national exhaustion from the war and the lack of sharp ideological differences between the candidates. The electorate's instability was suggested by the divisions within both parties on high-profile issues such as Prohibition, the League of Nations, agricultural policies, and other social and economic issues such as technical assistance and trust busting. The appearance of numerous "blocs" in both parties represented "little if anything more than a transitory alignment upon a particular vote or issue." [68]

The shifts in control of congressional and state offices also indicated electoral instability. The Democrats had comfortable control of Congress under Wilson, but in 1920 the Republicans gained a majority of 301 to 131 in the House and 59 to 37 in the Senate. Impressive liberal gains in congressional and state elections in 1922 appeared to be a slap at the Harding administration. The high turnover of votes also indicates unstable party affiliations: the 14.2 percentage point increase in the Republican vote between the 1916 and 1920 presidential elections was the largest since the Civil War, obviously a time of turmoil.[69]

President Harding died on August 2, 1923, of a heart attack, just as revelations of kickbacks and favoritism in the administration began to surface and several members of the administration quit and two committed suicide. The investigation into the so-called Teapot Dome scandal—so named after the site of naval oil reserves that were transferred to private hands in exchange for bribes—would last five years. The Democrats hoped to make the scandal a major issue in 1924, but Democratic complicity in the wrongdoing and the integrity of Harding's successor, Calvin Coolidge, defused the issue.

Coolidge Cleans Up

President Coolidge fired Attorney General Harry M. Daugherty and other members of Harding's clique and projected an image of puritan cleanliness. Coolidge—a taciturn man who had slowly climbed the political ladder in Massachusetts from city council member, city solicitor, mayor, state legislator, lieutenant governor, and governor before he became vice president—expounded a deeply individualistic Yankee philosophy that helped to separate him from the corrupt men in the Harding White House.

Except for appointing as attorney general Harlan Fiske Stone, former dean of the Columbia University School of Law, Coolidge allowed others to clean up the mess left behind by Harding. The new president was concerned about unnecessarily alienating himself from party leaders.

By the time Coolidge sought the presidency in his own right in 1924, the economy had rebounded. One of the most conservative presidents ever, Coolidge's platform called for

additional tax cuts but said nothing substantive about increasingly salient agriculture and labor issues. Coolidge also pushed an isolationist foreign policy plank. He won the nomination on the first ballot.

While the Republicans were able to "Keep Cool with Coolidge," the Democrats spent sixteen days in a seemingly endless attempt to pick a nominee in New York's sweltering Madison Square Garden. The fight developed because the party was badly split between its northeastern urban bloc and its more conservative southern and western rural bloc. New York governor Alfred Smith and former Treasury secretary William McAdoo of California were the key combatants at the convention until the delegates were freed from boss instructions on the 100th ballot.

Suspicions between the two regions were intense. A platform plank denouncing the Ku Klux Klan created the most controversy. Northerners wanted an explicit repudiation of the society that preached hatred of Catholics, Jews, and blacks; in the end, southerners would settle only for a vaguely worded rebuke. The Klan infiltrated the party in many rural areas. Another divisive issue was Prohibition, with northerners attacking the initiative and southerners supporting it. These sectional splits would cripple the Democrats in the next two elections.

After the delegates were freed from instructions, a stampede developed for John W. Davis of West Virginia, a lawyer with Wall Street connections. The ticket was balanced with the vice-presidential selection of Charles Bryan of Nebraska, the younger brother of three-time presidential candidate William Jennings Bryan.

The Progressive candidacy of Robert La Follette complicated the calculations of voters, particularly those on the liberal end of the spectrum. Since the Democrats had a nearly impenetrable hold on the South, La Follette was not given a reasonable chance of winning. But the conservatism of both Coolidge and Davis meant that La Follette was the only genuine liberal in the race. Still, many liberals voted for Davis or even Coolidge because of the fear of an inconclusive election that would have to be resolved in the House of Representatives.

Coolidge won the election easily, with the Democrats polling their smallest percentage ever. Coolidge won 54.1 percent of the vote, Davis won 28.8 percent, and La Follette won 16.6 percent. Coolidge attracted 15.7 million popular votes and 382 electoral votes; Davis, 8.4 million and 136; and La Follette, 4.8 million and 13.

On August 2, 1927, when Coolidge announced his decision not to seek reelection by passing out a brief note to reporters and then refusing further comment, the Republicans began jockeying for the nomination for the 1928 election.

The Hoover Succession

Secretary of Commerce Herbert Hoover was the obvious choice to replace Coolidge at the head of the GOP ticket. A native of Iowa who learned mining engineering at Stanford University, Hoover was immensely popular with most of the party. Hoover's administration of Belgian relief and food distribution programs during World War I had earned him the status of statesman and humanitarian.

Hoover began working for the nomination soon after Coolidge dropped out, spending $400,000 in the nomination phase of the election. He won the nomination on the

Smithsonian Institution

"Keep Cool with Coolidge" was the Republican incumbent's 1924 campaign slogan, used on posters, banners, buttons, and decorative stamps such as this one from Wisconsin.

first ballot over Lowden and Gov. Charles Curtis of Kansas. Curtis was named Hoover's running mate.

Hoover was religious in his zeal for what he called "the American system" of free enterprise and individualism. He did not see any inconsistency in having the government vigorously support businesses with tax breaks, tariffs, public provision of infrastructures, and police protection, while at the same time denying relief to people in need. Hoover appeared to be less rigid than Coolidge, however. He proposed creation of a special farm board and said he would consider legislation to protect labor unions from abuses in the use of court injunctions.

Al Smith, the Tammany-schooled governor of New York, was the Democratic nominee. Smith had the support of all the party's northern states, and he won a first-ballot nomination. Sen. Joseph Robinson of Arkansas was the vice-presidential candidate.

Smith's candidacy polarized the electorate, particularly the South. He was the first Catholic to be nominated for president by a major party, and he endured religious slurs throughout the fall. He favored repeal of Prohibition, still a divisive issue. He was an urbanite, a problem for a nation that had nurtured a rural ideal since Thomas Jefferson. He was a machine politician, a problem for anyone outside (and many people inside) the nation's great cities. He was a strong opponent of the Klan, which put him in trouble in the South. Finally, he was an unabashed liberal who proposed public works, farm relief programs, stronger protection of workers, and regulation of banking and industry.

During the fall campaign, Hoover acted like the incumbent and Smith barnstormed the country, trying in vain to pick up support in the South and West. The 1928 campaign was the first with extensive radio coverage, and Hoover generally fared better than Smith on the airwaves. Hoover, the small-town boy who made good, represented fulfillment of the American Dream; Smith, the inner-city boy who made good, also embodied that ideal, but he had too many alien traits for much of the nation to realize it.

The November election produced another Republican landslide. Hoover carried forty states with 21.4 million popular votes (58.2 percent) and 444 electoral votes, while Smith carried only eight states with 15.0 million popular votes (40.8 percent) and 87 electoral votes. As disastrous as

the election appeared to be for the Democrats, it put them in position to build a wide-ranging coalition in future years.

Smith carried only six southern states, but the defection of the others was temporary. More important to the Democrats' long-range fortunes was the movement of cities into the Democratic column, probably for the rest of the century. In all, Smith diverted 122 northern counties from the GOP to the Democratic party. Catholics, whose turnout previously was low, turned out in record numbers. Immigrants in cities also expanded their vision from local politics to the national stage for the first time. Smith also seemed to pick up some of the Progressive farm vote that La Follette had tapped before; in Wisconsin, for example, the Democratic vote jumped from 68,000 to 450,000 from 1924 to 1928. Smith's candidacy also put the Democrats solidly in the "wet" column, just as the national temper began to resent Prohibition.

President Hoover impressed political observers with his managerial skills and "coordinating mind." With passage of the Agricultural Marketing Act in June 1929, the administration appeared to address the most pressing economic problem for the business-minded president. He met some legislative setbacks, but overall the Great Engineer appeared to be in good political condition as the nation looked back over his record when Congress began its recess in the summer of 1929.

The national economic and social fiesta that began at the close of World War I came to an abrupt end on October 29, 1929. After climbing to dizzying new heights for months, the stock market crashed. First described by economists and politicians as a temporary interruption of the good times, the crash quickly led to a wave of business and bank failures, mortgage foreclosures, wage cuts, layoffs, and a crisis of political leadership. By the end of Hoover's term in 1932, more than twelve million workers had lost their jobs; the unemployment rate was approximately 25 percent. An October 1931 advertisement for 6,000 jobs in the Soviet Union brought 100,000 American applications.[70]

President Hoover, who had celebrated his inauguration with a prediction that poverty and hunger were near an end, did not know how to cope with the crisis. In a special session that Hoover called, Congress created the Federal Farm Board to coordinate marketing of agricultural products, but Hoover steadfastly opposed further moves, especially subsidies. Hoover also signed the Smoot-Hawley tariff bill to protect manufacturers, but, true to the predictions of economists and bankers, the tariff only aggravated economic conditions by hurting foreign trade.

Hoover later approved agricultural relief and public works programs and established the Reconstruction Finance Corporation. The president refused to approve direct relief to the unemployed and businesses, but he did approve some loans and aid to specific sectors of the economy.

Despite his earnest and tireless efforts, Hoover became a figure of widespread enmity. The low point of his distinguished career came when World War I veterans petitioned for early receipt of their service bonuses, which, by contract, were not to be paid until 1945. They set up camp in Washington, singing old war songs and carrying placards that bore their pleas. The "Bonus Army" numbered twenty thousand at its height. When Hoover feared a protracted protest, he ordered federal troops to take over buildings where some veterans were camping. In two skirmishes, two veterans were killed. The president then sent in Gen. Douglas MacArthur with tanks, infantry, and calvary soldiers. (MacArthur's junior officers included Dwight D. Eisenhower and George Patton.) After successfully removing the veterans, the military forces overran nearby veterans' camps in a rain of fire and tear gas. Thousands of veterans and their families fled the burning district.

The administration's tough stance against a defeated, ragtag band of former war heroes shocked and embittered the nation. The barricaded White House and administration statements about "insurrectionists" symbolized a dangerous gulf between the government and the people.

Partly because of the economic crisis he did not create, but also because of a dour and unimaginative demeanor, Hoover probably never had a chance to win reelection. The 1930 midterm elections indicated a loss of confidence in the administration. The House went Democratic, 219 to 214, and the Senate came within a seat of going Democratic as well.

Those election results did not convey the bitterness and despair that the depression would aggravate before the next presidential campaign. Hoover was mercilessly ridiculed in newspapers and in Democratic speeches. The Democratic party coordinated a comprehensive anti-Hoover campaign that made the president politically impotent.

Election of 1932

Franklin D. Roosevelt, fifth cousin to Theodore Roosevelt, was the perfect candidate to oppose Hoover. The New York governor had been an activist in state politics, first opposing the state's Tammany machine and then pioneering many relief and reconstruction programs that Hoover refused to expand to the national scale. Roosevelt had been the party's vice-presidential candidate twelve years before, and he had served in the federal government as assistant secretary of the navy.

Perhaps more important than any of his political accomplishments was FDR's image of strength and opti-

mism and his deft handling of hot issues and disparate members of the potential Democratic coalition. Although he was a polio victim, Roosevelt often smiled—a devastating contrast to Hoover. (Gutzon Borglum, the sculptor, wrote: "If you put a rose in Hoover's hand, it would wilt." [71]) Roosevelt was able to campaign for the presidency without putting forth a comprehensive program: the simple promise of a change in leadership was enough.

Some observers found the man from Hyde Park wanting. Journalist Walter Lippmann, for example, complained that Roosevelt was "a pleasant man who, without any important qualifications for the office, would like very much to be president." [72] But those detractors and a large field of Democrats were not able to keep Roosevelt from his "rendezvous with destiny." [73]

The Democratic field included the 1928 Democratic standard-bearer, Al Smith; John Nance Garner, the Speaker of the House; Gov. Albert Ritchie of Maryland; Gov. George White of Ohio; Gov. Harry Byrd of Virginia; and Sen. James Reed of Mississippi. Most considered Smith more of a "stalking horse" for the anti-FDR forces than a serious candidate in his own right. Garner had impressive backing from the newspaper magnate William Randolph Hearst amd former Democratic candidate William G. McAdoo.

The many favorite sons in the race threatened to deadlock the convention and deny the nomination to the front-runner, as they had done so often in the past. Roosevelt had difficulty with his own region of the country because of his opposition to the Tammany machine in New York. The goal of the two-thirds vote of delegates for the nomination for Roosevelt or any other candidate was difficult, but FDR eventually won on the fourth ballot when he promised the vice-presidential slot to Garner.

Franklin Roosevelt was the first candidate to appear before the convention that nominated him. In an acceptance speech to the conventioneers who had staged wild rallies in his support, Roosevelt made passing reference to

The Bettmann Archive

In 1932, World War I veterans, seeking early receipt of their service bonuses, staged a protest by setting up camps near the Capitol. On July 28, President Herbert C. Hoover ordered federal troops, headed by Gen. Douglas MacArthur, to disperse the veterans with tear gas.

Franklin D. Roosevelt campaigns in West Virginia, October 19, 1932.

a "new deal" that his administration would offer Americans. That phrase, picked up in a newspaper cartoon the following day, would symbolize the renewal that Americans yearned for as riots and radicalism seemed to threaten the nation's spirit and the legitimacy of its institutions.

Roosevelt conducted an active fall campaign, traveling twenty-three thousand miles in all but seven states to quell suspicions that his physical handicaps would deter him from performing his job. Besides barnstorming the nation, Roosevelt also took to the radio airwaves—he was the first sophisticated electronic media candidate—and conveyed a sense of warmth and confidence. He also showed an intellectual bent and an open mind when he called on academics and professionals—the famed "brains trust"—for their expert advice on the issues.

Roosevelt won 22.8 million votes (57.4 percent) to Hoover's 15.8 million (39.6 percent). Forty-two of the forty-eight states and 472 of the 531 electoral votes went for Roosevelt. The election was a landslide and a realignment of the major forces in U.S. politics.

The New Deal Coalition

The profound effect of Roosevelt's victory on U.S. politics can hardly be overstated. The New Deal coalition that Roosevelt assembled shaped the political discourse and electoral competition of the United States until the late 1960s. In many respects, that coalition is a central element of politics today.

The new Democratic coalition brought together a disparate group of interests: southerners, blacks, immigrants, farmers, capital-intensive producers, international businessmen, financiers, urbanites, trade unions, Catholics, and Jews. Rexford Tugwell called it "the most miscellaneous coalition in history." [74] These blocs were not always in perfect harmony—for example, the Democrats juggled the demands of blacks and white southerners with great diffi-

culty—but they were solid building blocks for national political dominance.

The dominance was impressive. Between 1932 and 1964, the Democrats won seven of nine presidential elections. The only successful Republican, Eisenhower, could just as easily have run as a Democrat. Party leaders in fact asked him to run as a Democrat in 1948 and 1952, and his name was entered in some Democratic primaries in 1952.

The strength of the Roosevelt rule is attributable partly to the president's personality. He could be soothing. When he gave his first "fireside chat" about the banking crisis, the nation responded with cooperation; the raids and violence at banks ended in a matter of weeks. More important than his soothing nature was his ability to experiment and shift gears. Professor James David Barber described Roosevelt's many public postures:

> Founder of the New Deal, modern American democracy's closest approximation to a common political philosophy, Roosevelt came on the scene as the least philosophical of men—"a chameleon in plaid," Hoover called him. Firm fighter of yet another Great War, Roosevelt appeared to H.L. Mencken in 1932 as "far too feeble and wishy-washy a fellow to make a really effective fight." Architect of world organization, he introduced himself as totally concerned with America's domestic drama. His name is inseparable from his generation's great social revolution; in 1932, nearly all the heavy thinkers scoffed at him as just another placebo politician—a "pill to cure an earthquake," said Professor [Harold] Laski. [75]

More important than personality was what Roosevelt had to offer the many groups in his coalition. As historian Richard Hofstadter has noted, the New Deal was "a series of improvisations, many adopted very suddenly, many contradictory." [76] The Roosevelt credo was "Save the people and the nation, and if we have to change our minds twice a day to accomplish that end, we should do it." [77]

Until the vast expenditures of World War II, there was not enough pump priming to end the depression, but Roosevelt's initiatives touched almost everyone affected by the slump.[78] For the jobless, there were unemployment insurance and public works programs like the Works Progress Administration and the Civilian Conservation Corps. For the poor, there were categorical aid programs. For westerners, there were conservation measures. For the banks, there was the famous holiday that stopped runs on holdings, and there were currency and securities reforms. For farmers, there were incentives and price supports and cooperatives. For the aged, there was Social Security. For the southeasterners, there was the Tennessee Valley Authority. For southern whites, there was a hands-off policy on race matters. For blacks, there was sympathy. For those living in rural areas, there was electrification. For families, there were home loans. For the weary worker eager for a few rounds at the local pub, there was the repeal of Prohibition. For laborers, there was acknowledgment of the right to negotiate for their share of the national wealth. For business, there were the Federal Emergency Relief Act and the National Industrial Recovery Act, as well as negotiation to reduce trade barriers.

The remarkably divergent interests in the coalition were underscored by the politics of race. Blacks moved en masse to the Democratic party from their traditional position in the "Party of Lincoln," partly because of Hoover's failure but also because of the inclusive rhetoric of the New Deal. Yet, Roosevelt was too concerned about his bloc of southern support even to accept antilynching legislation.

Scholars have argued that the New Deal coalition did not indicate a wholesale shift in existing political loyalties, but rather that new forces had joined an already stable alliance to tip the competitive balance of U.S. parties. The political discourse in the United States changed not because all or even most groups changed their behavior, but because new groups and issues became involved.[79]

The core of Roosevelt's winning coalition is easy to describe: "Southern white Protestants, Catholics, and non-Southern white Protestants of the lowest socioeconomic stratum together accounted for roughly three-fourths of all Americans of voting age in 1940 who thought of themselves as Democrats. By way of contrast, these three groups provided only about 40 percent of the smaller cadre of Republican identifiers."[80] Within this coalition, there were both new and old elements.

Although the Democratic party encompassed new constituencies and addressed new issues, it retained many of its traditional supporters. The "Jim Crow" South had consistently been in the Democratic column; in 1896, for example, the South's percentage support for Democrat William Jennings Bryan exceeded that of the rest of the nation by 15.3 points. Even in 1928, when Al Smith's Catholicism brought the Democratic support for the Democrats below 50 percent for the only time, the Deep South supported the Democrats more than the border South.[81] To the South, the Democrats were reliably the party of white supremacy and agricultural interests, while Republicans favored the industrial interests of the North.

Outside the South, the Democrats were the party of immigrants and Catholics. Since Andrew Jackson's day, the overwhelming monolithic Democratic voting patterns of Catholics contrasted with the split vote of Protestants in the United States. The Catholic-Protestant divisions "represent not so much religious as more general ethnocultural traditions."[82] The Democratic hold on the Catholic vote was reinforced by the heavy immigration into northern cities in the last half of the nineteenth century. While the

anti-Catholic Ku Klux Klan received Democratic backing in the South, it received Republican backing in the North, pushing Catholics decisively into the Democratic party.

A steady base in the Democratic party consisted of laborers and the poor. From the first party machines in the early nineteenth century to William Jennings Bryan's campaign on behalf of the depressed farm belt in 1896 to Woodrow Wilson's acceptance of labor bargaining in 1914, the Democrats had shown sympathy for the less privileged classes. Such sympathies were often constricted by prejudice, but the Democrats offered more hope of representation than the business-oriented Republicans. Roosevelt solidified the support of the poor and laboring classes.[83] Sundquist has written: "The party system undoubtedly reflected some degree of class before the realignment, but there can be little doubt that it was accentuated by the event. It was in the New Deal era that tight bonds were formed between organized labor and the Democratic Party, that ties equally close if less formal and overt were formed between business and the GOP, and that politics for the first time since 1896 sharply accented class issues."[84] Roosevelt consistently received the support of more than two-thirds of the voters of low socioeconomic status.[85]

New converts to the Democratic party included blacks and Jews. The inclusion of blacks into the New Deal coalition underscores a "multiplier effect" at work with thriving interest group politics. The Republicans received the black vote in the seventeen elections from Reconstruction to 1932. Roosevelt received 35 percent of the black vote in 1932, and his black support was as low as 23 percent in Chicago and 29 percent in Cincinnati.[86] Even though Roosevelt did little to promote black interests in the South, where most blacks lived, the black vote for him increased to 70 percent in 1936 and 1940. Migration of blacks to the North and spillover effects of Roosevelt's many domestic programs brought blacks to the Democratic party.

Jews, who had voted Republican since their numbers swelled during immigration around the turn of the century, turned to the Democrats as they became the more liberal party. Roosevelt got 85 percent of the Jewish vote in 1936 and 84 percent in 1940. New Deal assistance programs and Roosevelt's efforts to fight Nazism appealed to Jews, but perhaps more important was "the historic pattern of discrimination which forced or disposed Jews to oppose conservative parties."[87] The class division that split other social groups was absent in the Jewish population.

In many ways, the whole of the New Deal was greater than the sum of its parts. Political scientist Samuel Beer has argued that two long-competing visions of U.S. politics—the national idea and the democratic idea—at last came together during Roosevelt's administration. With the New Deal, the Democratic party was able to combine its traditional concern for local, individualistic interests with a national vision. By bringing "locked-out" groups into the system, the Democrats enhanced both nation building and individual freedoms. The parts, put together, created a stronger whole. Beer quotes the French sociologist Emile Durkheim: "The image of the one who completes us becomes inseparable from ours. . . . It thus becomes an integral and permanent part of our conscience. . . ."[88]

The political genius of "interest-group liberalism"[89] was not just that it offered something to everyone, but that it created a new age of consumerism in which everyone's interest was in growth rather than structural change. The general good was defined as growth. The potentially divisive competition over restricted and unequally distributed resources was avoided with a general acceptance of growth as the common goal. When there was growth, everyone could get a little more. That public philosophy became a permanent part of American political discourse.

The Four-term President

Roosevelt's coalition and leadership were so strong that he became the only president to win more than two elections. He won four elections and served a little more than twelve years in the White House before dying in office.

Roosevelt's four electoral triumphs caused Republicans to fume about his "imperial" presidency; all they could do in response to FDR was promote a constitutional amendment to limit presidents to two terms. More important was the way Roosevelt shaped the American political agenda. For many people of the time, it was difficult to imagine the United States under any other leadership.

Roosevelt's three successful reelection drives evoked a changing response from Republicans. Roosevelt's first re-election opponent, in 1936, was Gov. Alfred M. Landon of Kansas, who strongly criticized every aspect of the New Deal. After 1936, Republican candidates did not criticize federal intervention in economic and social affairs but rather the speed and the skill of Democratic intervention. In the third election, the Republicans argued that Roosevelt was a "warmonger" because he tilted toward Great Britain in World War II. The GOP argued in the third and fourth elections that Roosevelt threatened to become a "dictator" by breaking the traditional two-term limit.

Landon was the early favorite for the Republican nomination in 1936. Sen. Charles McNary of Oregon, Sen. Arthur Vandenberg of Michigan, and *Chicago Daily News* publisher Frank Knox provided weak opposition. Landon was attached to neither the old-guard nor the younger liberal Republicans. A Republican bolter for Theodore Roosevelt's "Bull Moose" candidacy in 1912, Landon was consistently to the left of the GOP. Historian James MacGregor Burns observed: "Landon had just the qualities of common sense, homely competence, cautious liberalism and rocklike 'soundness' that the Republicans hoped would appeal to a people tiring, it was hoped, of the antics and heroics in the White House." [90]

In 1936 the Republicans could not have stated their opposition to the popular New Deal in any stronger terms. The platform read: "America is in peril. The welfare of American men and women and the future of our youth are at stake. We dedicate ourselves to the preservation of their political liberty, their individual opportunity, and their character as free citizens, which today for the first time are threatened by government itself." [91]

The Republicans called for ending a wide range of government regulations, returning relief to state and local governments, replacing Social Security, balancing the budget, and changing tariff and currency policies. Landon's only innovation was a call for a constitutional amendment allowing the states to regulate the labor of women and children; the Supreme Court had struck down a New York minimum-wage law. After Landon won the nomination on the first ballot, he selected Knox as his running mate.

The only time the two presidential candidates met was at a meeting Roosevelt called with state governors to discuss farm relief and a recent drought. The candidates sparred inconclusively.

Landon's campaign possessed a lavish war chest of $9 million, the defections of Democratic stalwarts such as Al Smith and John Davis, well-coordinated campaign work by business lobbies, and smear campaigns that portrayed Social Security as a simple "pay reduction" measure and Roosevelt as physically and mentally ill. Landon also argued that New Deal spending was just another form of spoils politics, a charge Roosevelt addressed by folding postmasters into the civil service system.

The only important departure at the Democratic convention was the repeal of the party's requirement that a candidate receive two-thirds of the delegates to win the nomination. After some arm twisting, southern delegates backed the change, but the governor of Texas wondered aloud if the change was designed for a third Roosevelt run in 1940. Roosevelt was renominated without opposition. He asked Garner to run with him a second time.

In response to Landon's GOP nomination and agitation by leaders of the left—including Huey Long of Louisiana, Father Charles Coughlin of Detroit, Dr. Francis Townsend of California (who espoused a federal pension plan for senior citizens), and the Socialist Norman Thomas of New York—President Roosevelt in his acceptance speech launched a rhetorical war against "economic royalists" who opposed his programs. He dropped the idea of a "unity" campaign in favor of a partisan ideological attack intended to gain a mandate for a variety of stalled programs rather than a personal vote of confidence. [92]

Roosevelt at first had planned a low-key campaign of "conciliation" but decided to wage the more aggressive campaign when Landon got the GOP nomination. Landon had run an impressive nomination campaign and was thought to appeal to American pinings for governmental stability. In the early stages of the fall campaign, Roosevelt pretended not to be a partisan politician. He moved around the country to make "official" inspections of drought states and public works programs and to deliver speeches on electrical power, conservation, and social welfare programs, among other topics. Roosevelt assigned Postmaster General James Farley the task of addressing party rifts and Republican charges of spoils.

At the end of September, Roosevelt returned to his role as partisan leader. The president answered Republican charges point by point, then lashed out at the Republicans in biting, sarcastic terms. As the campaign progresssed and Roosevelt sensed a strong response from the large crowds to his attacks, the attacks became stronger. At the close of the campaign, he said:

> We have not come this far without a struggle and I assure you that we cannot go further without a struggle. For 12 years, our nation was afflicted with a hear-nothing, see-nothing, do-nothing government. The nation looked to the government but the government looked away. Nine mocking years with the golden calf and three long years of the scourge! Nine crazy years at the ticker and three long years at the breadlines! Nine mad years of mirage and three long years of despair! And, my friends, powerful influences strive today to restore that kind of government with its doctrine that that government is best which is most indifferent to mankind. . . . Never before in all of our history have these forces been so united against one candidate as they stand today. They are unanimous in their hate for me—and I welcome their hatred.[93]

Especially to sophisticated campaign technicians of the modern age, a poll that predicted a big Landon victory provides some amusement. The *Literary Digest,* which had

Library of Congress   Library of Congress   New York Historical Society

President Franklin D. Roosevelt's Republican opponents during his three reelection campaigns were, from left: Gov. Alfred M. Landon of Kansas in 1936; former Democrat and business executive Wendell L. Willkie in 1940; and Gov. Thomas E. Dewey of New York in 1944.

predicted past elections with accuracy, conducted a post-card poll that pointed toward a Landon landslide. The heavy middle- and upper-class bias of the magazine's readership meant that the views of the voters on the lower rungs of the economic ladder were left out of the sample. To this day, the poll is cited as the prime example of bad survey-group selection.

The failure of the *Literary Digest*'s survey pointed to the most salient aspect of the election results: the heavy class divisions among the voters. Polls show that class divisions widened starting around the midpoint of Roosevelt's first term. The broad support FDR had enjoyed because of a common economic disaster hardened along class lines by 1936.

Roosevelt won 27.7 million popular votes (60.8 percent) to Landon's 16.7 million (36.5 percent). Roosevelt won all but two of the forty-eight states, and he took 523 of the 531 electoral votes. In addition, the Senate's Democratic majority increased to 75 of 96 seats, and the House majority increased to 333 of 435 seats. Roosevelt ran ahead of candidates such as gubernatorial candidate Herbert Lehman of New York, who had been recruited to boost his vote totals in various states. The Democratic victory was almost too overwhelming, Roosevelt suggested, because it would encourage Democrats to fight among themselves rather than with Republicans.

The Third Term

Soon after his landslide, Roosevelt tempted fate with a proposal that would have increased the size of the Supreme Court from nine to fifteen members in order to "pack" the court with justices closer to the president's political philosophy. The high court had constantly struck down important New Deal initiatives such as the Agriculture Adjustment Act, the National Recovery Administration, and the tax on food processing.

Roosevelt shrouded his proposal in statements of concern for the capacities of some of the court's older and more conservative justices. In a fireside speech, Roosevelt said the Court's failure to keep pace with the other "horses" in the "three-horse team" of the federal government constituted a "quiet crisis." [94] The elderly chief justice Charles Evans Hughes belied that charge with the energy he brought to the tribunal. Roosevelt refused to compromise on the bill, and it became an executive-legislative dispute. The proposal was widely seen as a brazen power play, and by the summer Congress had defeated it.

President Roosevelt eventually got the judicial approval he wanted for his initiatives—what wags called "the switch in time that saved nine." The Court appeared to shift its philosophy during the court-packing affair, and, before long, enough justices had retired so that Roosevelt could put his own appointees on the Court.

Other problems awaited Roosevelt in the second term. Splits in the labor movement gave rise to violence during organizing drives, and the president responded haltingly. After his rift with business over the full range of New Deal policies, Roosevelt appeared to be drifting. Conservatives in Congress were more assertive than ever in opposing the "socialist" measures of the Roosevelt years. The only major New Deal legislation in the second term was the Fair Labor Standards Act of 1938, which abolished child labor and set a minimum wage and an official rate of time-and-a-half for overtime.

As Roosevelt looked toward a third term in 1940, the widening war in Europe posed a difficult problem. Nazi Germany had invaded the Rhineland, Poland, France, Norway, Denmark, Holland, Belgium, and Luxembourg and had made alliances with Italy and the Soviet Union, while Japan invaded China. Adolf Hitler launched the Battle of Britain in the summer of 1940 and all-night air raids of London soon afterwards.

British prime minister Winston Churchill desperately petitioned President Roosevelt to provide fifty destroyers. Britain's need for the destroyers was so great that Roosevelt balked at asking Congress for help. He reasoned that congressional action probably would take three months, and isolationists might even block action—dealing a crippling blow to Britain. After lengthy administration debate, Roosevelt agreed to send Churchill the destroyers as part of a "lend-lease" agreement. The United States would receive bases in the Caribbean as part of the deal.

A favorite parlor game as the 1940 election approached was guessing whom Roosevelt might tap as his successor. Roosevelt publicly maintained that he did not want another term, but he refused to issue a definitive statement begging off the race. Despite the historic precedent against third terms, however, Roosevelt wanted to remain president. To avoid the appearance of overzealousness, Roosevelt wanted the Democrats to draft him in 1940.

While the nation waited for Roosevelt to act, Vice President Garner announced his candidacy. Postmaster General Farley and Secretary of State Cordell Hull also wanted to be president, and Roosevelt gave both vague assurances of support. Roosevelt, whose relations with Garner had been sour for years, simply watched the vice president struggle to gain a respectable public profile. The Farley and Hull prospects withered without the help of the old master.

From a distance, Roosevelt watched state Democratic delegations declare their support. Polls showed Roosevelt's fortunes rising with the deepening European crisis. Just before the GOP convention, Roosevelt appointed Republicans Henry Stimson and Frank Knox to his cabinet. Roosevelt did not reveal his plans even to his closest aides. The president did not forbid aides such as Harry Hopkins to work on a draft, but he did not get involved because he wanted the Democrats to call on him and not the other way round.

At the Chicago convention, Sen. Alben Barkley told the convention: "The president has never had, and has not today, any desire or purpose to continue in the office of president. . . . He wishes in all earnestness and sincerity to make it clear that all the delegates of this convention are free to vote for any candidate." [95] The statement was followed by an hour-long demonstration and Roosevelt's first-ballot nomination.

The convention mood turned sour, however, when Roosevelt announced that he wanted the liberal secretary of agriculture, Henry Wallace, as his running mate. The announcement disgruntled delegates who had already lined up behind other candidates. Wallace eventually beat Alabama representative William Bankhead, his strongest opponent for the nomination.

The Republicans mounted their strongest challenge to Roosevelt in 1940, largely on their charge that Roosevelt was moving the United States toward involvement in the world war. Several moves toward military preparedness had failed at the hands of isolationists in Congress. When Roosevelt asked for increases in defense spending after Gen. Francisco Franco's victory in Spain and Hitler's invasion of Austria in 1938, critics asserted that the president was attempting to cover up domestic failures with foreign adventures. Roosevelt pressed on, however, and Congress passed the Selective Service Act and increases in military spending in 1940.

The Republican field in 1940 included several fresh faces—Sen. Robert A. Taft of Ohio, son of the former president; District Attorney Thomas E. Dewey of New York City; and Sen. Charles L. McNary of Oregon and Sen. Arthur H. Vandenberg of Michigan who had sought the Republican nomination in 1936. The freshest face of all was Wendell L. Willkie, a utility executive who had never run for political office. A large and affable man, former Democrat Willkie had barnstormed the country for seven years speaking in opposition to the New Deal. [96]

Hundreds of "Willkie clubs" sprang up in the summer of 1940, and a number of publications including Henry Luce's *Time* magazine chronicled Willkie's career and encouraged the Willkie groundswell. Despite concern about Willkie's lack of political experience that led to a "stop Willkie" movement, the Indianan won a sixth-ballot nomination by acclamation. Senator McNary, the Republicans' Senate floor leader, reluctantly accepted the vice-presidential nomination.

Traveling thirty thousand miles in thirty-four states, Willkie gave some 540 speeches. By the time his campaign ended, his already husky voice turned hoarse. The Republicans spent lavishly and organized grass-roots clubs for Willkie across the country. Charges against Roosevelt of managerial incompetence, "warmongering," and imperial ambitions punctuated the Willkie effort. A dramatic mo-

ment came when labor leader John L. Lewis called on workers to back Willkie.

After a period of strictly "presidential" behavior, Roosevelt took to the campaign trail with partisan vigor. He answered Willkie's warmongering charges with a promise never to involve the United States in "foreign wars" (which left Roosevelt free to respond to a direct attack).

The importance of alienated Democratic and independent voters was symbolized by Vice President Garner, who did not even vote. Roosevelt won, but by the slimmest margin of any race since 1912. Roosevelt received 27.3 million popular votes (54.7 percent) to Willkie's 22.3 million (44.8 percent). The electoral vote tally was 449-82.

The War and Its Legacy

Roosevelt's third term and fourth election were dominated by the Second World War. Japan attacked U.S. bases at Pearl Harbor, Hawaii, on December 7, 1941. The president, speaking before Congress, declared the surprise attack "a day that will live in infamy," and Congress shook off its isolationist inclinations to declare war.

The war did for the economy what the New Deal, by itself, could not: it brought economic prosperity. The number of unemployed workers fell from eight million to one million between 1940 and 1944. The boom brought seven million more people, half of them women, into the job market. Inflation, worker shortages, and occasional shortages in raw materials posed problems for wartime agencies. The number of U.S. families paying taxes quadrupled, and by 1945 tax revenues were twenty times their 1940 level. Budget deficits reached new heights. [97]

The war effort was grim for two years of the president's new term. Isolationist sentiment built up in Congress, with the Midwest proving the region most resistant to Roosevelt's foreign policy. Criticism of war administration was rampant. The administration won key congressional votes on the war but faced stubborn resistance on domestic measures. In the 1942 midterm elections, the Republicans gained ten seats in the Senate and forty-seven seats in the House—a major repudiation of Roosevelt.

After several setbacks, the Allied forces won impressive victories. Roosevelt and Churchill worked together closely. Allied forces led by Gen. Dwight D. Eisenhower routed the Axis powers in North Africa in 1942. The Soviet Union beat back a Nazi assault on Stalingrad in the winter of 1942-1943. The Allies took over Italy in 1943 and struggled with the Nazis in France. By September 1944, British and American troops entered Germany. In the Pacific war, American offensives secured Australia in 1942 and the Philippines in 1944.

Despite the bitterness that prevailed through much of his administration, Roosevelt had no trouble winning a fourth term in 1944. The Allies found greater success on the battlefield and on the sea, and the nation did not appear willing to risk untested leadership to prosecute the war. The Republicans turned to the smooth governor of New York, Thomas Dewey. Willkie wanted another shot at the White House, and his best-selling book *One World* put him in the public eye, but old-line conservatives blamed him for the 1944 election defeat. Governors John Bricker of Ohio and Harold Stassen of Minnesota and Gen. MacArthur were the other hopefuls.

Dewey's primary victories over Willkie in the Wisconsin, Nebraska, and Oregon primaries finished Willkie's public career. Dewey was too far in front to stop. At the convention, he won a nearly unanimous, first-ballot nomination after Bricker and Stassen dropped out. After Gov. Earl Warren of California refused the vice-presidential nomination, Bricker accepted it.

The party platform extolled the virtues of free enterprise but did not criticize the concept of the New Deal and even made bids for the votes of blacks and women. In his acceptance speech, Dewey criticized "stubborn men grown old and tired and quarrelsome in office." [98]

The 1944 election marked the early resistance of the South to the modern Democratic party. Roosevelt was a shoo-in for the nomination, but southerners wanted a replacement for Wallace as vice president, restoration of the two-thirds nominating rule, and a platform declaration of white supremacy. Unsatisfied Dixiecrats threatened to bolt the party in November, but when the party adopted only a vague civil rights plank in its platform, southern discontent dissipated. The rest of the platform called for an internationalist thrust in foreign policy and further New Deal-style reforms domestically.

Roosevelt expressed support for Wallace but said he would allow the convention to pick his running mate. Wallace gave a stirring convention speech but disturbed conservatives with his stand against the poll tax and for equal opportunity for all "regardless of race or sex." Sen. Harry S Truman of Missouri, who had won fame as a critic of defense spending, beat Wallace for the vice-presidential nomination on the second ballot.

The Democratic campaign was dominated by references to the need for wartime unity and reminders of the Republican rule under Hoover. One leaflet bore the words "Lest We Forget" and a photograph of an unemployed man selling apples in front of a "Hoover Club"; an inset photograph showed Dewey conferring with former president Hoover. The Republicans spent nearly as much money as they did in the record-setting 1936 election.

Roosevelt won with 25.6 million popular votes (53.4 percent) to Dewey's 22.0 million (45.9 percent). The electoral vote score was 432-99. President Roosevelt—who reshaped U.S. politics at all levels—did not have the opportunity to see the end of the war or to participate in the making of the postwar world. On April 12, 1945, less than two months after his fourth inauguration, Roosevelt collapsed while sitting for a portrait in Warm Springs, Georgia.

The Truman Presidency

The shock of President Roosevelt's death was perhaps greatest for the former haberdasher and machine politician who succeeded him. Truman had been a last-minute choice as FDR's running mate the previous year, and he never became a part of Roosevelt's inner circle. Truman did not have any knowledge of the most important military program of the age—the Manhattan Project, which, in a race with the Nazis, was developing a nuclear bomb in the secrecy of the brand-new town of Oak Ridge, Tennessee.

Truman also faced a problem of stature. Roosevelt had done nothing less than redefine the presidency in his twelve years in office. He not only effected the longest-lasting partisan realignment in U.S. history, but he changed the very scope of government activity. As would become clear during the Eisenhower presidency, even conservative Republicans came to accept, grudgingly, the no-

tion that the government ought to play an active role in stimulating the economy and addressing the needs of specific constituency groups. Many people could not fathom a presidency without Roosevelt. One member of the White House staff said later: "It was all so sudden, I had completely forgotten about Mr. Truman. Stunned, I realized that I simply couldn't comprehend the presidency as something separate from Roosevelt. The presidency, the White House, the war, our lives—they were all Roosevelt." [99] Other aides could not bring themselves to call Truman "Mr. President," as if so doing would dishonor the late president.

Truman's personality could not have presented a greater contrast to Roosevelt. Plain-speaking, blunt, middle-class, midwestern, not college educated, wheeling-and-dealing, and surrounded by old pals from the Pendergast machine of Missouri (the Democratic organization that dominated politics in the state), Truman offended people who had been accustomed to the charisma of Roosevelt. Truman's wife, Bess, also paled in comparison to the dynamic, more public Eleanor Roosevelt as First Lady. Truman showed absolute loyalty to the New Deal, but that would never be enough for many old Roosevelt hands and a nation entering a difficult period of postwar readjustment.

By the time the 1948 elections neared, Truman was in grave political shape. He brought former president Hoover back from exile for special projects—one of the many ways he rankled the sensibilities of former Roosevelt aides and Mrs. Roosevelt. Truman professed a desire to "keep my feet on the ground" and avoid the "crackpots and lunatic fringe" that had surrounded FDR. [100] Toward that end, Truman got rid of Commerce Secretary Henry Wallace and others. The independent journalist I. F. Stone wrote of Truman's personnel moves: "The little nameplates outside the little doors . . . began to change. In Justice, Treasury, Commerce and elsewhere, the New Dealers began to be replaced by the kind of men one was accustomed to meeting in county court-houses." [101]

The politics of postwar adjustment were difficult. The Republican Congress elected in 1946 sought to dismantle many New Deal programs, and it frustrated anti-inflation efforts. Truman duelled with Congress, vetoing 250 bills (eleven of these vetoes were overridden). Tentative civil rights initiatives disgruntled the South. Labor unrest was on the rise. Postwar mapmaking and subsequent efforts to "contain" Soviet geopolitical ambitions not only created splits among Democrats but also brought attacks from Republican isolationists. Truman also was said to have performed inadequately at Potsdam, the summer 1945 conference of World War II victors that established many geographic borders in Europe.

The situation was so bad that Roosevelt's own son promoted General Eisenhower and Supreme Court Justice William O. Douglas for a 1948 run for the Democratic nomination against Truman. Truman, in other words, was doing a good job antagonizing both the left and the right. The Democratic convention in August 1948 appeared to show a dangerously polarized nation. The convention began with a feeling of desperation when Eisenhower and Douglas refused to run. Then a "states' rights" plank offered by southern delegates was defeated, and, after strong speeches by Minneapolis mayor Hubert H. Humphrey and others, a strong northern plank passed. The party's New Deal and northern machine elements decided that southern defection would be less damaging than northern defection.

Defect is just what the southerners did. The Dixiecrats, under the leadership of South Carolina's governor J. Strom Thurmond, left the convention to conduct their own fall campaign. Thurmond's candidacy ran under the Democratic party label in four states (Alabama, Louisiana, Mississippi, and South Carolina) and under the States' Rights party elsewhere in the South. Meanwhile, the party's left wing, behind Henry Wallace, protested Truman's Marshall Plan, military buildup, and confrontational stance toward the Soviet Union; it, too, ran its own fall campaign under the banner of the Progressive Citizens of America (the Progressive party).

The seeds of Dixie defection were planted long before the convention. In 1947 the President's Committee on Civil Rights issued a report calling for the protection of the rights of all minorities. It was just the kind of spark southern segregationists needed to begin a dump-Truman drive and to organize their own campaign in 1948. The Southern Governors Conference in March 1948 recommended that southern states send delegates to the Democratic convention and electors to the electoral college who would refuse to back a pro-civil rights candidate.

As political scientist V. O. Key, Jr., has shown, the degree of resistance to civil rights in southern states depended on two basic factors: the proportion of blacks and the strength of the two-party system. Key argued that the existence of a large black population led to stronger Democratic measures against black enfranchisement and led whites to support the party in greater numbers. "To them [the whites in such districts], a single Negro vote threatened the whole caste system." [102] Alabama, Louisiana, Mississippi, and South Carolina ended up voting for the Thurmond ticket. Other southern states found broader economic and political issues more compelling than race.[103]

Many of FDR's old political allies eventually got behind the new man, but Truman's election prospects looked bleak. Some support was grudging—Mrs. Roosevelt offered a straightforward endorsement only to rebut newspaper reports that she favored the Republicans. While the Democratic party was badly fractured, the Republican party united behind Dewey.

Dewey was part of a new breed of Republican leaders—pragmatic and accepting of the New Deal and the international role that the United States would play in the postwar era. He expressed support for the basic tenets of postwar liberalism, including Social Security, civil rights, and the United Nations. In the 1948 campaign, Dewey planned to put himself above the slashing attack style of President Truman. His constant calls for national unity—spoken in a baritone voice and perfect English—expressed acceptance of the vast changes in U.S. politics over the previous twenty years.

Dewey, the 1944 GOP candidate, survived a large field in 1948 to become the nominee once again. Senator Taft of Ohio was the main threat, but his isolationism and dull public demeanor were liabilities. The most spirited opposition came from Governor Stassen of Minnesota, who appealed to the more liberal and internationalist wing of the party. An anathema to party bosses, Stassen proved his strength in a series of primary victories. Other candidates or potential convention contenders included generals Eisenhower and MacArthur, Governor Warren, and Senator Vandenberg. Polls showed all of the Republicans but Taft beating Truman.[104]

Dewey gained the preconvention momentum he needed with an impressive primary victory over Stassen in Oregon. Dewey spent three weeks in the state, while Stassen frittered away his time and resources with a hopeless challenge to Taft in the Ohio primary. Dewey was especially tough in a primary debate about Communism. Dewey also had impressive organizational strength and mastery

UPI/Bettmann Newsphotos

In 1944, pollsters and the media fed Republican candidate Thomas E. Dewey's overconfidence in his campaign to unseat President Harry S Truman. Truman had the last laugh on the press and his opponent.

over convention mechanics, and he won the nomination on the third ballot. Warren was selected the vice-presidential nominee.

From the beginning of the campaign, the media and professional politicians gave Truman little chance of retaining the White House. Early polls showed Dewey with such a strong lead that pollsters simply stopped surveying voters. But the polls failed because of a bias in the way the questions were asked and a presumption that the large undecided vote would cast their ballots in the same way as the rest of the population, when it in fact heavily favored Truman.[105]

Dewey was so certain of victory that he ran as if he were the incumbent. He made a series of bland, almost diplomatic statements rather than energetic campaign speeches. Dewey appeared confident that his advice to one audience—"Vote your own interests"—would attract an amalgam of disaffected groups. Never even mentioning the president's name, Dewey calmly canvassed the country and just smiled when people called him "President Dewey." Dewey was careful to avoid the overaggressive posture that he thought ruined his 1944 campaign against Roosevelt. He even made some initial cabinet and policy decisions.

From the beginning, Truman's strategy was simply to mobilize the New Deal coalition. The biggest danger was apathy, he and campaign aide Clark Clifford reasoned, so the best strategy was to give the voters a reason to go to the polling booths. Since the Democrats were the majority party, they had to concentrate mainly on getting their longtime supporters to the polls.

Truman ran a scrappy and blunt underdog campaign that could have been mistaken for an outsider's effort. Truman was the president, but he ran against the Washington establishment. Crisscrossing the nation on a "whistle-stop" train tour, Truman traveled some thirty-one thousand miles and spoke before six million people. He turned his record of vetoes into an asset, claiming that the "do nothing" Republican Eightieth Congress made him do it. He assailed the conservative Republican record on inflation, housing, labor, and farm issues, and foreign affairs. The president drew large crowds—sometimes many times the size of Dewey's crowds—but he was the only political professional who thought he would win.

Truman himself predicted in October that he had 229 solid electoral votes to Dewey's 109 and Thurmond's 9; he said 189 votes could go either way. The best anyone would say about the Truman campaign was that its fighting spirit improved the Democrats' chances to win the Senate. Truman answered the Republicans' claims of liberalism and reformism by criticizing the GOP for obstruction of his policies. Truman's outsider taunt was constant: "that no-account, do-nothing, Republican 80th Congress!"[106]

Despite the *Chicago Tribune*'s now famous headline— "Dewey Defeats Truman"—President Truman prevailed. Early returns put Truman in front, but it was expected that the later-reporting western states would give Dewey the win. When California and Ohio went into the Truman column midmorning Wednesday, Dewey conceded defeat. Especially considering the Democratic defections, Truman's appeal was widespread. Truman won twenty-eight states with 24.11 million votes (49.51 percent) and might have won more in the South and North with a united party. Thurmond won 22 percent of the vote in the South. Dewey won 21.97 million votes (45.12 percent), and Thurmond polled 1.17 million votes (2.40 percent). Henry Wallace won some 1.16 million votes (2.38 percent) but no electoral

This campaign button from the 1952 election expresses support for a candidate coveted by the Democratic and Republican parties.

Dwight D. Eisenhower Library

votes. Wallace's candidacy may have cost Truman New York, Michigan, and Maryland. On the other hand, Wallace may have done Truman a favor by freeing him from the taint of being the most liberal candidate in a time when the electorate was weary of liberalism. Particularly because the Republicans did not have a midwesterner on their ticket and talked about cutting back agricultural subsidies, farmers felt safer with Truman. In all, Truman won 303 electoral votes, Dewey 189, and Thurmond 39.

The Democratic defections might have helped Truman by making him the candidate of the center. The Wallace campaign freed the president from suspicions on the right, and the Thurmond defection strengthened Truman's more liberal northern constituency. In addition, the defections might have inspired Democratic voters to turn out in larger numbers than they would have had victory seemed certain.

In the end, the election merely confirmed long-held partisan allegiances. In the words of political scientist Angus Campbell and his colleagues, it was a "maintaining" election: "The electorate responded to current elements in politics very much in terms of its existing partisan loyalties. Apparently very little of the political landscape attracted strong feeling in that year. But what feeling there was seemed to be governed largely by antecedent attachments to one of the two major parties."[107]

The Eisenhower Years

Truman's political fortunes worsened during his second term to the extent that he belatedly decided against making a bid for the Democratic nomination. In 1952, for the first time in twenty-four years, neither party had an incumbent president as its nominee.

Election of 1952

The Democrats suffered from a weariness that is bound to affect any party that has been in power for twenty years. Problems and opponents' frustrated ambitions were piling up, and in Dwight Eisenhower the Republicans were able to recruit a candidate with universal appeal who was coveted by both parties. The national mood in the years before the 1952 election was sour. The nation was tiring of the Korean War, which the administration had entered in 1950 but did not appear interested in winning or leaving; price controls; and recurring scandals among members of the White House staff. The Republicans asked for a chance to "clean up the mess" in Washington and punctuated their appeals with the question "Had Enough?"

The Truman administration met with repeated frustration in dealing with the Congress that the president ran against in 1948. On civil rights, tariffs, taxes, labor reform, and the sensationalized question of Communist sympathizers in the government, Truman met a stubborn Democratic Congress—which, in turn, became more stubborn after Republican gains in the 1950 midterm elections. When Truman seized control of the steel mills because he said the steelworkers' strike threatened the nation's security, he was rebuffed by the Supreme Court.[108]

Truman's biggest problems, however, concerned cronyism and war. Republicans in congressional investigations and on the stump hammered away at conflict-of-interest scandals in Truman's administration—creating nationwide sentiment to "clean up" Washington with a new administration. Meanwhile, the United States was mired in a stalemate in Korea—a distant war that was being fought inconclusively under the aegis of the United Nations, with uncertain goals (was it to protect South Korea or replace North Korea as well?) and uncertain enemies (was the People's Republic of China an opponent as well as North Korea?). Truman evoked ire with his firing of General MacArthur, who wanted to take the war into China, and with the slow movement toward a settlement. Just as the nation tired of sacrifices in World War I under Woodrow Wilson, it tired of sacrifices under Truman.

General Eisenhower—who had just left the presidency of Columbia University to take charge of the forces of the North Atlantic Treaty Organization (NATO)—was recruited by Republicans to run when it appeared that other GOP candidates lacked the national appeal to win the White House. Senator Taft was again running, but his isolationism was considered a liability in the postwar age of internationalism. Stassen, MacArthur, and Warren were other likely Republican candidates.

Eisenhower's popular appeal was revealed when he attracted 50.4 percent of the vote in the New Hampshire primary to Taft's 38.7 percent and Stassen's 7.1 percent. Eisenhower performed well in the Northeast, and Taft generally performed well in the Midwest. A write-in campaign for Eisenhower almost upset Stassen in his home state of Minnesota.

When the GOP convention finally met in Chicago, Taft had the lead in convention delegates. In crucial delegate-seating contests, many of them played out on national

television, Eisenhower defeated Taft and won the right to seat pro-Eisenhower insurgents from the South. Taft had relied on the old strategy of mobilizing state machines, but such tactics looked unsavory on television. Eisenhower had undisputed popular appeal, and he won on the first ballot after his early lead turned into a stampede.

Eisenhower selected Sen. Richard Nixon of California as his running mate. The thirty-nine-year-old conservative had won national recognition with his activities on the controversial House Committee on Un-American Activities, which investigated the alleged Soviet ties of Alger Hiss, a former State Department official. Hiss served time for a perjury conviction.

The Democrats moved haltingly toward putting together a ticket. Truman did not announce his decision to stay out of the race until April, after two primary losses. Sen. Estes Kefauver of Tennessee, who gained fame with his televised hearings of organized crime, ran an aggressive primary campaign and entered the convention with the lead in delegates. Other candidates included Gov. Averell Harriman of New York, Vice President Alben Barkley, Sen. Robert Kerr of Oklahoma, and Sen. Richard Russell of Georgia.

The eventual nominee was Gov. Adlai Stevenson of Illinois, son of Grover Cleveland's second vice president. Stevenson had experience in the Navy and State departments before running for governor. President Truman privately recruited Stevenson for the race—at first unsuccessfully. Truman and Illinois backers set up a draft movement for Stevenson, which the governor disavowed until the last minute. Kefauver was the early leader in convention balloting, but Stevenson was always close, and he pulled into the lead on the third ballot.

Stevenson's campaign was an eloquent call to arms for liberals and reformers. Years later, Democrats would recall that the campaign had inspired the generation that would take the reins of power under John F. Kennedy. Democratic politics at all levels in subsequent years would revolve around battles of party regulars and reformers.

Stevenson did not have a chance, however, against the popular Eisenhower. Some southern states bolted the party in response to Stevenson's pro-civil rights stance. While the Republicans had them as a gift, they hammered away at the misdeeds of the Democratic administration under Truman. Issues like the Communist revolution in China of 1949 ("Who lost China?"), the protracted Korean War, administration corruption, and the alleged Communist infiltration of the government captured the nation's attention more than Stevenson's oratory.

More than anything, however, the desire for party change rather than policy change determined the election. The Republican evocation of the theme of "Corruption, Korea, and Communism" did not challenge the policies that the Democrats offered the nation as much as the way they executed those policies. Eisenhower was a proven administrator and was free of the taint of everyday U.S. politics. Stevenson was a reformer himself, but his campaign had the conspicuous backing of President Truman. Stevenson's divorce and public support of Hiss were constant if only vaguely stated issues.

The campaign's biggest controversy developed when newspaper reports alleged that Nixon used a "secret fund" provided by California millionaires to pay for travel and other expenses. To a Democratic party weary of charges of impropriety, the revelation offered an opportunity to charge that Nixon was beholden to special interests. Nixon

In 1952, Dwight D. Eisenhower selected Sen. Richard Nixon of California as his running mate. The thirty-nine-year-old conservative had won national recognition with his activities on the controversial House Committee on Un-American Activities.

admitted the existence of the fund but maintained that he used the money solely for travel and that his family did not accept personal gifts.

Nixon originally reacted to the story by asserting that it was a Communist smear. When Eisenhower would not publicly back his running mate, speculation developed that Ike would ask him to leave the ticket—and the Republican *New York Herald-Tribune* openly called for him to drop out. When Nixon decided to confront his accusers with a television speech, campaign aides told him he would be dropped if the public reaction was not favorable.

Nixon's speech was remarkable. He denied any impropriety and stated that the Stevenson campaign was hypocritical in its criticisms because it had similar funds. He denied that he accepted gifts such as a mink coat for his wife, Pat; he said that his wife wears a "Republican cloth coat." Nixon acknowledged receiving a pet dog named Checkers from a Texas admirer: "And you know, the kids love that dog, and I just want to say this right now, that regardless of what they say about it, we're going to keep it." [109] His folksy message and appeal for telegrams created a wave of sympathy, which Eisenhower rewarded with a pledge of support. The crisis was over.

In a personal victory—surveys showed that the nation still favored the programs of the New Deal and simply wanted to put the cronyism, sacrifices, and Korean War behind it—Eisenhower swept to the White House. Ike won the entire North and West, parts of the South, and some border states—a total of thirty-nine states to Stevenson's nine. His 442 electoral votes and 33.9 million popular votes (55.1 percent) overwhelmed Stevenson's 89 electoral votes and 27.3 million popular votes (44.4 percent). The election of 1956 would bring more of the same.

Election of 1956

Despite his age and a heart attack in 1955, Eisenhower was the strong favorite to be the GOP nominee for another term. Close cooperation with the congressional leadership and a "hidden-hand" leadership style seemed to comport with the electorate's wishes for normalcy. [110] The White House apparatus was ably run by the chief of staff, Sherman Adams, and foreign policy was supervised by Secretary of State John Foster Dulles. The genius of Eisenhower's management style was the use of aides as "lightning rods" for unpopular policies.

Even without lightning rods, Eisenhower probably would have fared well. The economy was booming, and Eisenhower quickly brought the Korean War to a close. His nuclear policy gave the nation a "bigger bang for the buck" in defense spending and kept the troop requirements low. Federal housing and highway programs gave impetus to suburbanization, now considered part of the middle-class American Dream. Issues that would in the future become divisive, such as civil rights, were muffled.

The only unsettled Republican issue was whether Nixon would again be the vice-presidential candidate. Eisenhower offered him a cabinet post, and Stassen mounted a campaign to replace Nixon with Massachusetts governor Christian Herter. After some hesitation, however, Eisenhower stood by his controversial running mate.

Kefauver challenged Stevenson for the right to face Eisenhower in the fall. After impressive primary victories in New Hampshire and Minnesota, the Stevenson campaign fought back with a string of primary wins in states as varied as California, Florida, and Oregon.

Former president Truman continued his stormy relationship with Stevenson when he endorsed New York governor Harriman at the opening of the Democratic convention. A variety of other favorite sons entered the race. With the help of Eleanor Roosevelt, Stevenson was able to win the nomination for a second time with careful campaigning among the convention's delegations. Stevenson won on the first ballot.

Stevenson left the vice-presidential slot open to the convention delegates. Kefauver, after battling senators John Kennedy, Albert Gore, and Hubert Humphrey and New York mayor Robert Wagner, eventually won. The open contest highlighted the future potential of Kennedy, who, according to later accounts, mainly intended not to win the second spot but to gain visibility for a 1960 presidential run.

The campaign was bereft of real issues. Eisenhower's campaigning was a tempered appeal to American values and bipartisan consensus. To Nixon was left the job of hacking away at the opposition; he called Stevenson "Adlai the Appeaser" and a "Ph.D. graduate of Dean Acheson's cowardly College of Communist Containment." [111] Overall, however, the campaign was an example of what James David Barber calls "the politics of conciliation," with little conflict or desire for change.

Whether or not the electorate was "asleep," as frustrated critics charged, Eisenhower won another strong victory. He won forty-two states, 457 electoral votes, and 35.6 million popular votes (57.4 percent), compared with Stevenson's six states, 73 electoral votes, and 26.0 million popular votes (42.0 percent). In an unprecedented development, however, both houses of Congress went to the opposition.

Kennedy and the Politics of Change

The periodic national desire for change came at the expense of the Republicans in 1960, when Sen. John F. Kennedy of Massachusetts became the youngest person elected president by defeating Vice President Richard Nixon in the tightest election in history.

The presidential election took shape in the 1958 midterm election, when the Democrats made impressive gains in Congress. An economic recession and generational politics created the first major shift toward liberalism since the administration of Franklin D. Roosevelt. The "Class of '58" decisively changed the discourse of U.S. politics. After the election the Democrats held 64 of 98 Senate seats and 283 of 435 House seats, and thirty-five states had Democratic governors. The time appeared ripe for reopening issues that had long been stifled. [112]

The 1960 Democratic field was dominated by senators—Kennedy, Lyndon B. Johnson of Texas, Hubert H. Humphrey of Minnesota, and Stuart Symington of Missouri. Each had important advantages and disadvantages. Kennedy was from a wealthy and politically minded family, but his Catholicism and undistinguished Senate record were liabilities. Johnson was a masterful majority leader, but no southerner had won the White House since James K. Polk in 1844. Humphrey was popular in the Midwest, but he lacked financial backing and was considered too loquacious and liberal. Symington had a strong Senate record and Harry S Truman's backing, but he was considered colorless, and Truman's backing carried liabilities.

Former Illinois governor Adlai E. Stevenson, the par-

In the 1960 presidential campaign, John F. Kennedy worked hard to win the West Virginia primary. His victory in this overwhelmingly Protestant state blunted the issue of his Catholicism and set him on the way to a first-ballot nomination.

---

ty's nominee in 1952 and 1956, and Sen. Estes Kefauver of Tennessee stood on the sidelines, hoping that a convention deadlock or draft movement would finally bring them a ticket to the White House. Early speculation was that the convention would be deadlocked and a compromise candidate would have to emerge. It appeared likely that the nomination would go to Symington, Johnson, Humphrey, or one of the two senior candidates, Stevenson and Kefauver; the other candidates were good bets for the vice-presidential slot.

Kennedy presented the most intriguing candidacy. He was the son of Joseph P. Kennedy, the millionaire who had been Franklin Roosevelt's ambassador to Britain before their bitter break over U.S. involvement in World War II. John Kennedy was also an Ivy League graduate (of Harvard University), a war hero (described in the book *P.T. 109*), and a Pulitzer Prize-winner (for *Profiles in Courage*). With an experienced campaign staff, he had won an overwhelming reelection to the Senate in 1958. Moreover, he had been planning a run for the White House for years.

There were Kennedy skeptics, however. No Catholic since Alfred Smith had been a major-party nominee, and Smith's bitter loss and the anti-Catholic sentiments he aroused made political professionals wary of naming another Catholic. Others focused on the influence of Joseph Kennedy, who bankrolled his sons' political careers.[113] Some considered Kennedy, at age forty-three, to be too young. Truman's comment captured the crux of Kennedy's liabilities: "It's not the Pope I'm afraid of, it's the Pop."[114]

To address the doubts, Kennedy entered political primaries that would enable him to demonstrate vote-getting ability and to confront the religion problem. The two key primaries were Wisconsin and West Virginia. In Wisconsin, Kennedy would answer the charge that he was too conservative and uncommitted to expanding the New Deal. The Kennedy strategists were divided about whether to oppose Senator Humphrey of nearby Minnesota; Wisconsin's growing independence in party politics eventually convinced them it would present a low risk for the possibility of beating Humphrey in his native region. In West Virginia, Kennedy would attempt to blunt the religion issue by attracting the votes of an overwhelmingly Protestant electorate.

Kennedy defeated Humphrey in Wisconsin, a state close to Humphrey's home state of Minnesota not only geographically but also culturally and ideologically. Kennedy's impressive campaign treasury enabled him to staff offices in eight of the ten congressional districts in the state; Humphrey had only two offices. Humphrey maintained that the defeat stemmed from crossover Republican Catholic votes and was therefore illegitimate. (Most of the state's Catholics, 31 percent of the population, belonged to the GOP.) But to Kennedy and many political observers, it was still an important victory.

Humphrey wanted to even the score in West Virginia. If Humphrey had quit the campaign and left Kennedy with no opponents, as many advised him to do, a Kennedy victory would have attracted little attention.[115] But Kennedy was able to use the Appalachian state as a way to deflect the religion issue as well as the "can't win" problem. Kennedy had a thorough organization in the state, and he worked hard. He had commissioned polls in the state as far back as 1958 in anticipation of the presidential race.

Kennedy's handling of the religion question in the primaries was shrewd and would be repeated in the fall campaign. He framed the question as one of tolerance—which put Humphrey on the defensive since he had never tried to exploit the religion issue. Kennedy had his campaign workers plant questions about how his religious beliefs would affect his loyalty to the nation, to which the candidate replied with a stock answer: "When any man stands on the steps of the Capitol and takes the oath of office as president, he is swearing to uphold the separation of church and state; he puts one hand on the Bible and raises the other hand to God as he takes the oath. And if he breaks the oath, he is not only committing a crime against the Constitution, for which the Congress can impeach him—but he is committing a sin against God."[116]

Kennedy's direct confrontation of the religion issue worked to his benefit. Kennedy had the money to get his message across: his television expenditures alone in the state totaled $34,000, while Humphrey had only $25,000 for the whole primary campaign in West Virginia.[117] Early polls gave Humphrey wide leads, and interviews elicited strong reservations about Kennedy's Catholicism. As the commercials aired and the primary neared, the lead became smaller, and voters privately said they would vote for Kennedy.

JFK, as he asked headline writers to call him instead of the youthful-sounding "Jack," easily won the primary. He was on his way to a first-ballot nomination.

The Kennedy campaign staffers managed the convention with consummate skill. Had they failed to gain a majority by the first ballot, pressure might have developed for another candidate. But the Kennedy team efficiently lobbied delegations to augment support; the vice-presidential slot was vaguely offered to several politicians. In the end, Johnson was the surprise choice for running mate. Even Kennedy supporters had doubts about Johnson, but the selection of the southerner was a classic ticket-balancing move.[118]

Central to Kennedy's winning campaign was his younger brother Robert F. Kennedy. A former counsel to Republican senator Joseph McCarthy, Robert developed into the consummate political operative. He was JFK's confidant, chief strategist, delegate counter, fund-raiser, taskmaster, and persuader. Biographer Arthur M. Schlesinger, Jr., wrote that Robert Kennedy's strength "lay in his capacity to address a specific situation, to assemble an able staff, to inspire and flog them into exceptional deeds, and to prevail through sheer force of momentum." [119]

Vice President Richard Nixon was the overwhelming choice for the Republican nomination. Nelson A. Rockefeller, elected governor of New York in 1958, was a liberal alternative, but he announced in 1959 that he would not run. There was a brief surge for Rockefeller when he criticized the party and its "leading candidate," but meetings with Nixon settled the differences. Some conservatives were disgruntled with Nixon, but their efforts for Sen. Barry Goldwater of Arizona would have to wait until 1964.

Nixon selected United Nations Ambassador Henry Cabot Lodge as his running mate, and the party platform and rhetoric stressed the need for experience in a dangerous world. Nixon promised to continue President Dwight D. Eisenhower's policies. He attempted to portray Kennedy as an inexperienced upstart, even though he was Kennedy's senior by only four years and the two had entered Congress the same year. Nixon led in the polls at the traditional Labor Day start of the fall campaign.

Kennedy's campaign was based on a promise to "get the nation moving again" after eight years of calm Republican rule. Specifically, he assured voters he would lead the nation out of a recession. The real gross national product increased at a rate of only 2.25 percent annually between 1955 and 1959. Economists puzzled over the simultaneously high unemployment and high inflation rates.[120] Kennedy repeatedly called for two related changes in national policy: pumping up the economy and increasing defense spending dramatically.

The Democrat faced up to the religion issue again with an eloquent speech before the Greater Houston Ministerial Association, and he attracted attention from civil rights leaders when he offered moral and legal support to the Rev. Martin Luther King, Jr., after King was arrested for taking part in a sit-in at an Atlanta restaurant. While Kennedy appealed to the party's more liberal and moderate wing, Johnson toured throughout the South to appeal to regional pride and to assuage fears about an activist government.

The high point of the campaign came on September 26, 1960, when the candidates debated on national television before seventy million viewers. Kennedy was well-rested and tanned and spent the week before the debate with friends and associates. Nixon was tired from two solid weeks of campaigning, and he spent the preparation period by himself. Their appearances alone greatly influenced the outcome of the debates.

Kennedy's main objective had been simply to look relaxed and "up to" the presidency. He had little to lose. Nixon was always confident of his debating skills, and he performed well in the give-and-take of the debate. But the rules of debating—the way "points" are allocated—are different in formal debating from what they are in televised encounters. Kennedy's managers prepared their candidate better for the staging of the debate. Nixon's five-o'clock shadow reinforced the cartoon image of him as darkly sinister. Polls of radio listeners found that Nixon had "won" the debate, but polls of television viewers found that Kennedy had "won" the debate. Historian Theodore H. White wrote: "It was the picture image that had done it— and in 1960 it was television that had won the nation away from sound to images, and that was that." [121]

While Kennedy called for a more activist and imaginative approach to world problems, Nixon stressed the candidates' similarities so much that their differences paled into insignificance. Kennedy called for a crusade to eliminate want and to confront tyranny. Nixon responded: "I can subscribe completely to the spirit that Sen. Kennedy has expressed tonight." [122] With ideology an unimportant part of the debate, the images of personal character the candidates were able to project gained in importance.

The candidates held three more debates and addressed issues including Fidel Castro's Cuba, the Chinese offshore islands of Quemoy and Matsu, and relations with Nikita Khrushchev's Soviet Union. None of the debates had the effect of the first, which neutralized Nixon's incumbency advantage. Nor was Nixon greatly helped by President Eisenhower, who did not campaign for his protégé until late in the campaign.

The election results were so close that Nixon did not concede his defeat until the afternoon of the day following the election. Nixon later said he considered contesting some returns more than a week after the election. After a vacation in Florida and Nassau, Nixon returned to Washington on November 19 to consider a series of charges that voter fraud had cost him the election. A shift of between eleven thousand and thirteen thousand votes in a total of five or six states could have given Nixon the electoral vote triumph. Nixon said he decided against demanding a recount because it would take "at least a year and a half" and would throw the federal government into turmoil.[123]

When the electoral college voted, Kennedy won 303 electoral votes to Nixon's 219. Democratic senator Harry F. Byrd of Virginia attracted 15 electoral votes. Kennedy won twenty-three states to Nixon's twenty-six. (A slate of eight independent electors won Mississippi; these eight, plus six from Alabama and one from Oklahoma voted for Byrd.) The overall popular vote went 34.2 million for Kennedy and 34.1 million for Nixon. The margin was about one-tenth of 1 percent, or 115,000 votes. The margins in many states were very close. Kennedy won Illinois by 8,858 votes and Texas by 46,242 votes. Despite statements that the religion question would hurt Kennedy, it probably helped him by mobilizing Catholics on his behalf. Gallup polls showed that 78 percent of Catholics voted for JFK. Although Catholics were a traditional Democratic constituent group—by margins of three or four to one—they had voted for Eisenhower by large margins.[124] In addition, Kennedy put together a predictable coalition: he won the support of voters in the Northeast, in most of the South, and in cities, plus blacks and union workers. Upper New England, the Midwest, and the West went primarily to Nixon.

In an informal way, Kennedy and Goldwater discussed the way they would conduct their campaigns for the presidency in 1964. The two expected to win their party nominations easily, and they talked about crisscrossing the nation in head-to-head debates, which would set a new standard for national campaigns.[125]

U.S. News & World Report; Library of Congress

In accepting the 1964 Republican presidential nomination, Sen. Barry Goldwater called for a moral crusade, declaring, "Extremism in defense of liberty is no vice; moderation in pursuit of justice is no virtue."

"All the Way with LBJ"

From the time of his sad but graceful ascension to the White House, Johnson was never in doubt as the Democrats' 1964 nominee. He was expected to select an eastern or midwestern liberal as his running mate, and he did so when he tapped Senator Humphrey of Minnesota at the convention, which his campaign organization stage-managed to the last detail. The only dissent from the Democratic unity was provided by Gov. George C. Wallace of Alabama, whose segregationist campaign took advantage of a backlash against the civil rights movement. Wallace entered three primaries against Johnson-allied favorite sons. He polled 43 percent of the vote in Maryland. Wallace talked about mounting a third party bid in the fall, but he backed off.

The Republicans were divided into two bitter camps led by Senator Goldwater of Arizona, the eventual nominee, and Governor Rockefeller of New York. The nomination contest was a struggle for the soul of the party. Other active and inactive candidates included Ambassador to Vietnam Henry Cabot Lodge, former vice president Nixon, and Gov. William Scranton of Pennsylvania. After a New Hampshire primary victory by Lodge, achieved through a well-organized write-in drive while he was still ambassador to Vietnam, Goldwater and Rockefeller scrapped through a series of primaries. The moderate Lodge later helped Scranton in a late effort to recruit uncommitted delegates to stop Goldwater, but by then it was too late. Goldwater lined up strong delegate support to get the nomination before the primary season even began, but he needed to use the primaries to show that he had vote-getting ability. The state organizations that backed him needed evidence that his conservative message would find popular acceptance.

In the "mixed" system then in place, candidates were able to pick and choose the primaries that best suited their strategy. Front-runners avoided risks, and long shots entered high-visibility and often risky contests as a way to attract the attention of party professionals. As expected, Goldwater won widespread support in the southern state conventions and had strong primary showings in Illinois and Indiana. Rockefeller beat Lodge in Oregon, but the decisive test came when Goldwater narrowly upset Rockefeller in California.

More important than the confusing preconvention contests was the rhetoric. Both the conservative Goldwater and the liberal Rockefeller vowed to save the party from the other's ideology. Goldwater, who rode the bestseller success of his *Conscience of a Conservative* to hero worship among conservatives, made a vigorous case against New Deal politics and for American sway in world politics: "I don't give a tinker's damn what the rest of the world thinks about the United States, as long as we keep strong militarily." [128] Rockefeller implied that Goldwater risked nuclear war and would recklessly dismantle basic social programs.

The nomination contest was a regional as well as an ideological struggle. The westerner Goldwater—backed by labor-intensive manufacturers, small business and agricultural enterprises, and domestic oil producers—opposed internationalist banking and commercial interests.[129] Goldwater made eastern media the objects of scorn. Rockefeller and his family, of course, represented the apex of the eastern establishment. Because of his strategy, Goldwater made himself an outsider to the growth-oriented consumer politics of the period.

The Kennedy-Goldwater campaign never came. On November 22, 1963, while riding in a motorcade in Dallas, Texas, President Kennedy was assassinated by a gunman named Lee Harvey Oswald.[126] Vice President Johnson assumed the presidency.[127]

In his brief administration, Kennedy had compiled a record disappointing even to many of his supporters. The Bay of Pigs fiasco in which a Central Intelligence Agency plan to overthrow the Cuban government failed miserably, the inability to obtain passage of landmark civil rights legislation, budget deficits and a drain of gold supplies from the United States, confrontations with the Soviet Union in Cuba, Hungary, and Berlin, and the nascent U.S. involvement in the Vietnam War created doubts about the young president's control of the government.

Still, Kennedy had made a start on many important issues. Arms control initiatives such as the test-ban treaty, economic growth through tax cuts, modernization of the military, the successful management of the Cuban missile crisis, civil rights and other domestic initiatives, the Peace Corps and Alliance for Progress, and growing world stature all offered hope for the second term. It would fall to Johnson, the legendary former Senate majority leader, to bring the Kennedy plans to fruition. First acting as the loyal servant of the slain president, then as his own man, Johnson was able to bring to legislative enactment many of the long-cherished initiatives of the U.S. liberal establishment—most notably the Civil Rights Act of 1964, which was considerably stronger than the Kennedy bill that had stalled in Congress.

Bitter battles over the party platform and unseemly heckling of Rockefeller displayed the party's divisions at the convention. When the conservatives won the nomination and the platform, there was no reconciliation. Goldwater selected Rep. William Miller of New York, another conservative, as his running mate and vowed to purify the party of liberal and moderate elements.

In a defiant acceptance speech, Goldwater painted a picture of the United States as inept in international affairs and morally corrupt in domestic pursuits, and he vowed an all-out crusade to change the situation: "Tonight there is violence in our streets, corruption in our highest offices, aimlessness among our youth, anxiety among our elderly, and there's a virtual despair among the many who look beyond the material successes toward the inner meaning of their lives. . . . Extremism in defense of liberty is no vice; moderation in pursuit of justice is no virtue." [130]

To a nation experiencing prosperity and unaware of the true proportions of its involvement in Vietnam, the "choice, not an echo" that Goldwater offered was a moral crusade. But the American consensus was built on material, consumer foundations, and an "outsider" appeal would have to wait until the system's foundations became unstable.

The divided GOP made for easy pickings for Johnson. The fall campaign was dominated by Goldwater's gaffes, which started long before the campaign began. He said, for example, that troops committed to the North Atlantic Treaty Organization (NATO) in Europe "probably" could be cut by "at least one-third" if NATO "commanders" had the authority to use tactical nuclear weapons in an emergency.[131] Goldwater also proposed a number of changes in the Social Security system, called for selling off the Tennessee Valley Authority, criticized the civil rights movement, and denounced the Supreme Court, the National Labor Relations Board, and the federal bureaucracy. Except for use of nuclear weapons and changes in Social Security, most of Goldwater's proposals when taken alone were not shocking. But the sum of his proposals—and his sometimes halting explanations—scared many voters.

President Johnson campaigned very actively to win a mandate for an activist new term. He traveled throughout the country making speeches to build a consensus for his domestic programs as well as his reelection. Johnson resisted Goldwater's constant calls for televised debates. The nation's prosperity was probably enough to keep the president in the White House.[132]

Johnson desperately wanted a personal mandate to pursue a variety of domestic programs that fell under the rubric "the Great Society"—a term that Johnson used in a 1964 commencement address (borrowed from a book of the same title by British socialist Graham Wallas). The desired landslide—underscored by his campaign slogan, "All the Way with LBJ"—was essential to initiatives in civil rights, health care, community action, education, welfare, housing, and jobs creation. Central to the landslide was not only economic prosperity but also peace in the world's trouble spots. Johnson therefore ran as a "peace" candidate.

But while he was trying to build a coalition that would sustain his domestic initiatives, Johnson faced an increasingly difficult dilemma about U.S. involvement in Vietnam. The United States had been involved in opposing Ho Chi Minh's revolution against French colonial rule in the 1940s and 1950s, and under presidents Eisenhower and Kennedy the United States had made a commitment to the leaders of South Vietnam (created after the failure of the 1954 Geneva accord) as a bastion against Communist expansion in Asia. But talk of war would likely imperil the domestic initiatives of the Great Society.

So while Johnson was campaigning as the peace candidate in 1964, he also was preparing for a major increase in U.S. involvement in Vietnam. As early as February 1964 the administration began elaborate covert operations in Southeast Asia and prepared a resolution to give the president a "blank check" in Vietnam.[133] By June the resolution was ready, and the Pentagon had chosen ninety-four bombing targets in North Vietnam and made provisions for bombing support systems. But on June 15, Johnson decided to delay major offensives until after the election.[134] In August Johnson sent to Congress what would be known as the Tonkin Gulf Resolution, which passed quickly and nearly unanimously. The president instructed congressional leaders to get an overwhelming majority so his policy would be bipartisan.

Johnson also seized on Rockefeller's use of the peace issue during the Republican primaries against Goldwater. He alluded to some of Goldwater's scarier statements about war, and he pledged that "we are not about to send American boys nine or ten thousand miles away from home to do what Asian boys ought to be doing for themselves." [135] A week before the election, Johnson said: "The only real issue in this campaign, the only one you ought to get concerned about, is who can best keep the peace." [136]

Johnson's landslide was the largest in U.S. history. He won 61 percent of the popular vote to Goldwater's 38 percent (or 43.1 million to 27.2 million votes). In the electoral college Johnson received 486 votes to Goldwater's 52, and he carried forty-four states—all but Goldwater's home state of Arizona and five southern states. In addition, the Democratic party amassed huge majorities in both the Senate (67-33) and the House of Representatives (295-140).

On election day Johnson created a working group to study "immediately and intensively" the U.S. options in Southeast Asia.[137] The war was increasing far beyond what most supporters of the Tonkin Gulf Resolution or "peace" supporters of the president imagined. In 1965 alone the number of U.S. troops in Vietnam increased from 15,000 to nearly 200,000.[138]

The Breakup of Consensus

A long period of uncertainty in American politics began sometime after Johnson's landslide victory over Goldwater in 1964.

By 1968, some thirty thousand Americans had been killed in action, and television was bringing the war into the living rooms of American families. Despite repeated assertions that the United States was defeating the North Vietnamese enemy, U.S. bombing efforts and ground troops did not break the resolve of the Communists in the North or their sympathizers who had infiltrated the South. The corrupt South Vietnamese government and army appeared to lack the resolve to fight the war on their own.

The opposition to the war developed as the casualties mounted, and the administration experienced a "credibility gap" because of its statements about the war. Before the United States left Vietnam in 1975, fifty-five thousand Americans had died in combat. Perhaps more important than the number of casualties—about the same as in the Korean War—was the long-term commitment that the

United States appeared to make with little evidence of progress. The "quagmire," as *New York Times* reporter David Halberstam called the war, was perhaps typified by the program of intense U.S. bombing raids that were judged by many experts to be ineffectual against the North's guerrilla warfare strategy.[139]

As opposition to the war grew among an increasingly vocal and well-organized minority, strains developed in Johnson's economic and domestic programs. Starting with the Watts riots in Los Angeles in 1965, urban areas sizzled with resentment to the mainstream liberal establishment. Detroit, Newark, and many major U.S. cities erupted in riots that burned miles of city streets and caused millions of dollars in damage. The assassination of civil rights leader Martin Luther King, Jr., in Memphis April 4, 1968, led to riots throughout the nation. Even before the riots, however, a conservative reaction against the Great Society had developed.

The activities of the Great Society were many and varied: the Civil Rights Act of 1964, the Voting Rights Act of 1965, Head Start, Model Cities, mass transit legislation, food stamps, Medicaid, the Elementary and Secondary Education Act, college loans, housing programs that included subsidies for poor, to name just the most prominent programs.

The conservative backlash was apparent before many programs had time to do their work. Efforts such as the Model Cities program and the Community Action Program, which mandated that poverty programs promote "maximum feasible participation" by the poor themselves, were often badly organized. They also were the source of additional struggles over jurisdiction in cities that already were notorious for divisive politics. Liberal efforts that predated the Great Society, such as school desegregation, created other tensions in cities.

One of the greatest sources of backlash in the late 1960s was an alarming increase in street crime. Even though blacks and the poor were the chief victims of the increase, the issue was most salient for conservative whites. Many tied the breakdown in order to the growth of the welfare state inspired by the Great Society. The crime rate seemed to many to be nothing less than ingratitude on the part of the poor. James Sundquist writes: "While increasing millions were supported by welfare, rising state and local taxes made the citizen more and more aware of who paid the bill. And while he armed himself for protection against thieves or militants, the liberals were trying to pass legislation to take away his guns."[140]

The crime problem was an important element in both national and metropolitan politics. Polls showed that half the women and a fifth of the men in the country were afraid to walk alone in their own neighborhoods at night.[141] In Alabama, Gov. George Wallace was whipping up his supporters in a frenzy of prejudice and resentment. The fear of crime also would be an important element in Richard Nixon's 1968 campaign.

The Election of 1968

With the nation divided over the war and domestic policy, the Democrats entered the 1968 campaign in an increasingly perilous state. In December 1967, Sen. Eugene McCarthy of Minnesota challenged President Johnson for the Democratic nomination, a move based almost entirely on his antiwar stance. McCarthy did unexpectedly well against Johnson's write-in candidacy in the New Hampshire primary on March 12, 1968 (drawing 42.4 percent of the vote to Johnson's 49.5 percent). Anticipating a devastating defeat in the Wisconsin primary April 2, Johnson dramatically announced his withdrawal from the campaign in a televised address March 31.

After the New Hampshire primary, New York senator Robert F. Kennedy declared his antiwar candidacy, which put in place all the elements for a Democratic fight of historic proportions. Vice President Humphrey took Johnson's place as the administration's candidate; he eschewed the primaries but eventually won the nomination on the strength of endorsements from state party organizations.

McCarthy and Kennedy fought each other in the primaries, and Kennedy appeared to have the upper hand when he closed the primary season with a victory in California on June 5. But after making his acceptance speech, he was assassinated, and the party was in greater turmoil than ever.

At the party convention in Chicago, a site Johnson had chosen for what he thought would be his own nomination, Humphrey became the Democratic party's candidate. The vice president took the nomination on the first ballot after Mayor Richard Daley of Chicago committed the Illinois delegation to his effort. Humphrey won with support from the traditional elements of the Democratic coalition—labor, blacks, urban voters—plus the backers of President Johnson. Humphrey appealed to many of the party's "moderates" on the Vietnam War.

Preliminary battles over rules and delegate seating, the representativeness of the party, and Vietnam War policies caused ugly skirmishes on the convention floor. The party's platform eventually endorsed the administration's war policy, including bombing, but strong opposition to this plank left the party divided.[142]

Outside the convention halls, demonstrations for civil rights and an end to the war met brutal rejection from the police. After three days of sometimes harsh verbal and physical battles with antiwar demonstrators in parks, the police charged a group of protesters that planned a march on the convention. Theodore H. White described the scene that played on national television:

> Like a fist jolting, like a piston exploding from its chamber, comes a hurtling column of police from off Balbo into the intersection, and all things happen too fast: first the charge as the police wedge cleaves through the mob; then screams, whistles, confusion, people running off into Grant Park, across bridges, into hotel lobbies. And as the scene clears, there are little knots in the open clearing— police clubbing youngsters, police dragging youngsters, police rushing them by their elbows, their heels dragging, to patrol wagons, prodding recalcitrants who refuse to enter quietly.[143]

Humphrey and his running mate, Sen. Edmund Muskie of Maine, faced an uphill fight.

The Republicans united behind Richard Nixon, the 1960 nominee whose political career seemed at an end after a loss in the 1962 California gubernatorial election. The GOP did not have to deal with any of the divisiveness of the 1964 Goldwater-Rockefeller battle. Nixon outspent Humphrey two-to-one, and followed a carefully devised script that avoided the exhausting schedule of his 1960 campaign. Nixon capitalized on the national discontent created by the Vietnam War, urban riots, political assassinations, and general concern about the speed of change wrought by the Great Society. Nixon traveled the high road

Popular support for Richard Nixon won him the 1968 presidential election. Promising an "open administration," his main campaign promise was change.

in his own campaign by calling for the nation to unite and heal its wounds. Promising an "open administration," Nixon's main offer was change. "I must say the man who helped us get into trouble is not the man to get us out."[144] To avoid scrutiny by the national media, Nixon gave few major addresses, preferring instead a series of interviews with local newspapers and broadcasters.

As President Johnson resisted calls for a halt in the bombing of North Vietnam, Nixon said he had a "secret plan" to end the war. He appealed to weary Democrats with his pledge of an activist administration and alternative approaches to dealing with some of the problems the Great Society addressed. Nixon promised to give blacks, in his words, "a piece of the action with a program to encourage entrepreneurial activity in cities." The "new Nixon" appeared willing to deal with the Soviet Union, which he had scorned earlier in his career. Meanwhile, his vice-presidential nominee, Gov. Spiro T. Agnew of Maryland, offered a slashing critique of the Democrats to middle-class and blue-collar Americans who resented the civil rights laws, government bureaucracy, Vietnam War protesters, and the young protest generation.

Governor Wallace of Alabama ran one of the strongest third party campaigns in U.S. history. He ran as an anti-establishment conservative, decrying desegregation, crime, taxes, opponents of the war in Vietnam, social programs, and "pointy-head" bureaucrats and "intellectual morons." His American Independent party was the strongest effort since Theodore Roosevelt's Bull Moose campaign in 1912 and Robert La Follette's Progressive run in 1924. Like earlier third party campaigns, the Wallace run caused concern about the soundness of the electoral college system. Because the race was so close, it was conceivable that no candidate would win an electoral college victory. In that

event, Wallace could have held the balance of power.[145]

Despite the early disadvantage, Humphrey made steady inroads into Nixon's support by disassociating himself from Johnson's Vietnam policies. When Johnson on November 1 ordered a halt to all bombing of North Vietnam, Humphrey appeared to be free at last from the stigma of the administration. But this change in administration policy was not enough to win the election for Humphrey.

The 1968 election was one of the closest in U.S. history. Nixon's victory was not confirmed until the day after the election when California, Ohio, and Illinois—each with very close counts—finally went into the Nixon column. Nixon attracted 31.8 million votes (43.4 percent of all votes cast); Humphrey, 31.3 million votes (42.7 percent); and Wallace, 9.9 million votes (13.5 percent). Nixon won 32 states and 301 electoral votes, compared with Humphrey's 13 states and 191 electoral votes. Nixon won six southern states (Wallace won five others), all of the West except Texas, Washington, and Hawaii, and all the midwestern states except Michigan and Minnesota. Humphrey won all of the East except New Hampshire, Vermont, New Jersey, and Delaware, plus West Virginia, Maryland, and the District of Columbia.

One long-lasting effect of 1968 was a transformation of the nomination process. In response to the bitter complaints about the 1968 Democratic convention, the party adopted rules that would make the primaries the center of the nomination process. The Chicago convention, dominated by party professionals at the expense of many important constituencies—blacks, women, youths—nominated a candidate who did not compete in any primaries. The key reform was a limit on the number of delegates that state committees could choose—after 1968, no more than 10 percent of the delegation.

Nixon's Reelection

McGovern was the miracle candidate of 1972, but his miracle did not last long enough.

Edmund Muskie, a veteran of the U.S. Senate and the vice-presidential nominee in 1968, was the early favorite to win the Democratic nomination. But because of party reforms enacted in response to the disastrous 1968 convention, the nomination process was bound to create surprises and confusion.

No fewer than fifteen contenders announced their candidacy, twelve with serious hopes of winning or influencing the final selection. Some twenty-two primaries to choose 60 percent of the party's delegates—a third more than in 1968—were to take place over four months. The marathon would be decided by accidents, media strategy, and a confusing array of voter choices that changed with each new development.

Muskie was badly damaged before the primary when he appeared to cry while lashing back at the *Manchester Union Leader*'s vicious and unrelenting attacks on his campaign and on his outspoken wife, Jane. The *Union Leader* had printed a series of attacks on Jane, then falsely reported that Muskie had laughed at a derogatory joke about French Canadians. Muskie later said of the incident: "It changed people's minds about me, of what kind of a guy I was. They were looking for a strong, steady man, and here I was weak." [146]

Muskie won the first-in-the-nation New Hampshire primary, but his 46.4 percent of the vote was considered a "disappointing" showing. McGovern of South Dakota, the antiwar candidate who won 37.1 percent of the vote, was pronounced the real winner by media and pundits. His strong showing—engineered by imaginative young political operatives, such as Gary Hart and Patrick Caddell, and a corps of youthful volunteers—was a surprise.

After New Hampshire, the Democrats battled through the summer. Wallace parlayed his antibusing rhetoric into an impressive victory in the Florida primary. Better organized than the others, McGovern swept the Wisconsin delegation by winning 29.6 percent of the state vote. McGovern then won an easy Massachusetts victory with 52.7 percent of the vote to Muskie's 21.3 percent. Humphrey edged McGovern in Ohio by 41.2 to 39.6 percent, but McGovern claimed a moral victory.

In the popular primary vote before the late summer California primary, McGovern actually stood in third place behind Wallace and Humphrey. But the delegate allocation rules gave the edge to the candidate who could squeeze out narrow victories in congressional districts, and that was McGovern. McGovern had 560 delegates to Humphrey's 311. Wallace had 324 delegates, but he was paralyzed after being shot in a Maryland shopping center and therefore no longer appeared to have a chance at the nomination.

The big McGovern-Humphrey showdown was California, which offered 271 delegates to the winner. It was a spirited campaign that included a head-to-head debate and strong Humphrey assaults on McGovern's positions on welfare and defense spending. McGovern went on to beat Humphrey by five percentage points in the winner-take-all primary. McGovern also won a majority of the delegates in New Jersey, South Dakota, and New Mexico in the last day of the primary season.[147]

After platform battles over welfare, busing, and the Vietnam War, McGovern won the nomination handily. He then selected Sen. Thomas Eagleton of Missouri as his running mate after several others declined. McGovern did not get to deliver his acceptance speech—perhaps the best speech of his career—until 2:48 a.m., when most television viewers were already in bed.

President Nixon and Vice President Agnew were renominated with barely a peep out of other Republicans. Rep. Paul N. (Pete) McCloskey of California opposed Nixon in the primaries but won only one delegate (from New Mexico).

McGovern would have been an underdog in the best of circumstances, but his chances were badly damaged by what came to be known as the "Eagleton affair." As the McGovernites celebrated their hard-won nomination, rumors circulated that Eagleton had been hospitalized for exhaustion after the 1960 campaign. Eagleton finally told McGovern operatives that he had been hospitalized three times for nervous exhaustion and fatigue, and that his treatment had included electroshock therapy. Despite McGovern's public statement that he was "1,000 percent for Tom Eagleton, and I have no intention of dropping him," Eagleton left the ticket less than two weeks after his nomination.

McGovern eventually replaced Eagleton with his sixth choice, R. Sargent Shriver, the former Peace Corps and Office of Economic Opportunity executive. But the aura of confusion that surrounded the Eagleton affair and the search for a new vice-presidential candidate hurt the campaign badly. The columnist Tom Braden likened it to a school teacher who could not control the class: "Nice people, too. One looks back with sympathy and a sense of shame. But at the time—was it that they were too nice?— their classes were a shambles. The erasers flew when they turned their backs." [148]

Nixon was in command of the fall campaign. He paraded a litany of accomplishments—the Paris peace talks over the Vietnam War, the diplomatic opening to China, the arms limitation treaty with the Soviet Union, and a number of domestic initiatives. Most of all, he was a strong figure; and if he still aroused suspicion, he was at least a known commodity.

Nixon won all but Massachusetts and the District of Columbia in the fall election. His popular vote margin was 47.2 million to McGovern's 29.2 million; the electoral college cast 521 votes for Nixon and only 17 for McGovern. Nixon's 60.7 percent share of the popular vote stood second only to Johnson's 61.1 percent in 1964.

Nixon's Downfall: The Watergate Scandals

On the surface, it appeared in 1972 that American politics were entering an age of calm consensus. At the time of the election, the economy was temporarily strong: opposition to the Vietnam War had faded as the two sides negotiated in Paris for an end to the war; the United States had signed an important nuclear arms treaty with the Soviet Union and had made important diplomatic moves with that country and the People's Republic of China. Nixon's landslide victory appeared to be a mandate and a vote of confidence.

But trouble loomed behind the apparent stability and consensus. The war in Vietnam continued, as did the antiwar protests, and generational cleavages remained. The economy experienced the first of many "shocks" in 1973 when the Organization of Petroleum Exporting Countries agreed to increases in the world prices of oil. The economic turmoil was topped off with a wage and price freeze. In addition, a warlike atmosphere between the White House and the media (as well as other perceived enemies of the administration that appeared on Nixon's "enemies list") and the mushrooming Watergate scandal combined to create a dark side to U.S. politics in the 1970s.[149]

The Watergate affair was perhaps the greatest political scandal in U.S. history. For the first time, a president was forced to leave office before his term expired. President Nixon resigned on August 9, 1974, when it became apparent that the House of Representatives would impeach him for "high crimes and misdemeanors" and the Senate would convict him. In addition, a number of Nixon aides, including his first attorney general and campaign manager, John Mitchell, would spend time in jail because of the scandal.

At its simplest level, the Watergate affair was "a third-rate burglary" and a subsequent coverup by President Nixon and his aides. In the summer of 1972, several employees of the Committee to Re-elect the President were arrested after they were discovered breaking into and bugging the Democratic National Committee's offices at the posh Watergate complex in Washington. The break-in was not a major issue in the 1972 election, but the next year congressional committees began an investigation.

During the investigation, a presidential aide revealed that Nixon had secretly taped Oval Office conversations with aides. When the Watergate special prosecutor, Archibald Cox, ordered Nixon to surrender the tapes in October 1973, Nixon ordered Cox fired. Nixon's attorney general and assistant attorney general refused to fire Cox; eventually, the solicitor general, Robert Bork, fired Cox, and a constitutional crisis dubbed the "Saturday night massacre" ensued. Nixon soon handed over the tapes Cox sought. In the summer of 1974, the Supreme Court ruled that Nixon had to surrender even more tapes, which indicated that he had played an active role in covering up the Watergate scandal. Nixon resigned the presidency when his impeachment and conviction appeared certain. The impeachment articles put forth by the House charged him with obstruction of justice, abuse of presidential powers, and contempt of Congress.

Many students of the Watergate affair maintain that the illegal campaign activities were just part of a tapestry of illegal activities in the Nixon administration—including secretly bombing Cambodia, accepting millions of dollars of illegal campaign contributions, offering government favors in return for contributions, "laundering" money through third parties, wiretapping and burglarizing a wide variety of people thought to be unsupportive of the president, offering executive clemency to convicted campaign workers, engaging in "dirty tricks" to discredit other political figures, compromising criminal investigations by giving information to the people under scrutiny, and using government funds to renovate the president's private residence.

The decade saw other political scandals as well. In 1973, Nixon's vice president, Spiro T. Agnew, resigned after pleading "no contest" to charges of bribe taking while he was governor of Maryland. Members of Congress became enmeshed in the "Koreagate" and "Abscam" influence-peddling scandals. Congressional investigations uncovered massive abuses by the Federal Bureau of Investigation and the CIA reaching back into the 1950s.

After Agnew's resignation on October 10, 1973, Nixon named House Minority Leader Gerald Ford, a longtime GOP stalwart, to become vice president under the Twenty-fifth Amendment for presidential succession.

Ford, who had never entered a national election, became president upon Nixon's resignation and quickly attracted the support of the American public with his modest, earnest disposition. Ford responded to the widespread feeling that Nixon's isolation in the Oval Office contributed to his downfall by promising to work closely with Congress and to meet with the press regularly.

Less than two months after becoming president, however, Ford ignited a firestorm of criticism with his full pardon of Nixon for crimes he may have committed while president. Ford testified before Congress that he believed Nixon had suffered enough and that the nation would have been badly torn if a former president were brought to court to face criminal charges. Critics asserted that Ford had made a "deal" in which Nixon resigned the presidency in exchange for the pardon.[150]

Ford selected former New York governor Nelson Rockefeller to be his vice president. Rockefeller received Senate and House confirmation on December 10 and 19, respectively, after long and difficult hearings that centered on his financial dealings.

Jimmy Who?

With the benefit of the Watergate scandal and Ford's pardon of Nixon, the Democrats won resounding victories in the 1974 midterm elections. The Democrats' gains of fifty-two House seats and four Senate seats not only created stronger majorities but also cut the number of members with allegiance to the old system of organizing congressional business.

The moralistic zeal of the "Watergate class" forced major changes on Congress that affected not only the legislative process but also the presidency and the nation's process of pluralistic political bargaining. The new crop of legislators was so large that it was able to undermine the seniority system that had ordered the way Congress had operated for years. The new system of committee assignments led to a proliferation of subcommittees on which most members had prominent roles. That, in turn, created a fragmented policy-making process—less susceptible to coercion by presidents and party leaders and more susceptible to interest group politics.[151]

The 1976 campaign was the first governed by campaign finance reform legislation enacted in 1971 and 1974. The Federal Election Campaign Act (FECA) of 1971 limited campaign expenditures and required disclosure of campaign receipts and expenditures. The Revenue Act of 1971 created a tax check-off in which taxpayers could designate $1.00 of their taxes to be allocated for public financing of elections. The FECA amendments of 1974 limited spending and donations for both primary and general election campaigns, established a system of partial public funding of elections, and created the Federal Election Commission to monitor campaign activities.

The Democrats and their eventual nominee, Jimmy Carter, were able to continue exploiting the nation's discontent through the 1976 election. Ronald Reagan, the former movie actor and California governor, added to the Republican party's vulnerability by waging a a stubborn primary campaign against President Ford.

The Democrats appeared headed for a long and bitter nomination struggle for the third time in a row. A few candidates—such as senators Henry Jackson of Washing-

Virtually unknown to the nation at the outset of the 1976 presidential campaign, former Georgia governor Jimmy Carter emerged from a field of candidates to win the Democratic nomination and the presidency. His casual and honest approach appealed to many voters.

ton and Birch Bayh of Indiana and Governor Wallace of Alabama—had greater stature than others, but their appeal was limited to specific factions of the Democratic coalition. Other candidates included Rep. Morris Udall of Arizona, Sen. Fred Harris of Oklahoma, Sen. Frank Church of Idaho, and Gov. Edmund G. Brown, Jr., of California. Church and Brown entered the race late, and senators Humphrey of Minnesota and Edward M. Kennedy of Massachusetts awaited a draft in the event of a deadlocked convention.

The moderate Carter, whose name recognition in polls stood in single figures as the campaign began, executed a brilliant campaign strategy to win the nomination on the first ballot. Constructing strong organizations for the Iowa caucus and the New Hampshire primary, Carter won both contests by slim margins. Although liberal candidates Udall and Bayh together polled better than Carter, it was Carter who received cover billings on national magazines and live interviews on morning television talk shows.[152] Within a matter of days, Carter changed from long shot to front-runner.

Udall performed well in the primaries but never won a single state. He and other liberals constantly split their vote; Udall's chance for a Wisconsin primary win fizzled when Harris refused to back out to create a one-on-one matchup of a liberal with Carter.[153] Carter ran into strong challenges from Church and Brown in later primaries, but he had the delegates and endorsements by the time of the Democratic convention in New York for a first-ballot nomination.

The Democratic convention was a "love-feast" with the Democrats united behind Carter and his running mate, Sen. Walter F. Mondale of Minnesota.

The GOP was divided between Ford and Reagan. Ford won the early contests, but Reagan scored big wins in the North Carolina and Texas primaries. Reagan was put on the defensive with his proposals for transferring welfare obligations to the states, but when he focused on foreign policy issues he had success. He attacked Ford for his policy of détente with the Soviet Union and his negotiation of a treaty that would forfeit U.S. control of the Panama Canal.

With Ford and Reagan locked in a close contest for delegates in the late summer, Reagan tried to gain advantage by breaking precedent and naming his vice-presidential candidate before the convention. Reagan's choice was Sen. Richard Schweicker of Pennsylvania, a moderate who widened Reagan's ideological appeal but angered many of his conservative supporters. Reagan tried to force Ford to name a vice-presidential candidate in advance, and the convention vote on the issue was a crucial test of the candidates' delegate strength. Ford won that test and the nomination. He selected the acerbic senator Robert Dole of Kansas as his running mate as a consolation prize for disappointed conservatives.

Carter emerged from the Democratic convention with a wide lead over Ford, but the race was too close to call by election day. A number of gaffes—such as Carter's interview with *Playboy* magazine, his ambiguous statements about abortion, and his confused observations on tax reform—hurt the Democratic contender.[154] Ford also gained in the polls when he began to use the patronage powers of the presidency and effectively contrasted his twenty-seven years of Washington experience to Carter's four years as governor of Georgia.

For the first time since 1960, the major candidates took part in televised debates. As the outsider, Carter helped himself by demonstrating a good grasp of national issues and by appealing to Democrats to vote the party line. Ford hurt himself with a claim that Eastern European nations did not consider themselves to be under the control of the Soviet Union.[155] The remark was intended to be testimony to the Europeans' sense of national identity, but it was interpreted as evidence of the president's naiveté.

Carter's main advantage was regional pride. The Democrats had long since lost their hold over the South, but Carter gained widespread support as the first candidate nominated from the region on his own in more than a century. The Democratic party's many factions—including big-city mayors such as Daley of Chicago and Abraham Beame of New York, civil rights activists, and organized labor—put on a rare display of unity.

Carter defeated Ford by a slim margin, winning 40.8 million votes (50.1 percent) to Ford's 39.1 million (48.0 percent). In the electoral college, 297 votes went to Carter, 240 to Ford. Carter won by pulling together the frazzled New Deal coalition of industrial and urban voters, blacks, Jews, and southerners. Ford won the West, and Carter won the South, except Virginia. Ford won all the states from the Mississippi River westward except Texas and Hawaii, plus states in his native Midwest like Iowa, Illinois, Michigan, and Indiana. Ford also won Connecticut and the three northernmost New England states—New Hampshire, Vermont, and Maine.

Carter's Uncertain Leadership

After his election, President Carter's ability to hold the coalition together was limited. The growing influence of nationalized media politics and interest group politics, poor relations with Congress, and difficult "crosscutting" issues—inflation and unemployment, oil shocks and the more general energy crisis, the Iran hostage crisis, relations with the Soviet Union, and budget austerity moves such as proposed cutbacks in water projects and social welfare—all damaged Carter's governing ability.

As the 1980 election approached, Carter appeared to have lost all but his institutional strength and the reluctance of voters to reject a president for the fourth time in a row. Carter controlled party processes, such as the primary schedule; he had access to key financial support and skilled political operatives; and he shaped much of the political agenda. But Kennedy hit him hard from the left, and Reagan and others hit him hard from the right. Carter was unable to forge a lasting consensus on important issues. Kennedy led Carter in polls by a two-to-one margin when he announced his challenge to Carter in November 1979. But Carter overcame that lead by the start of the nominating season when the seizure of American hostages in Iran rallied the nation around the president and Kennedy made a series of political mistakes. Kennedy was unable to develop campaign themes or answer questions about his personal conduct in the 1969 Chappaquiddick incident, in which a woman died after a car he was driving went off a bridge. Other "character" issues, such as Kennedy's alleged "womanizing," and more substantive issues, such as his liberal voting record, also hurt him in a year dominated by conservative themes. Kennedy's campaign also was in financial jeopardy early because of lavish spending on transportation, headquarters, and other expenses.

The campaign of Governor Brown of California was unable to find much support for his appeal for recognition of economic and environmental limits. He dropped out of the race on April 1, 1980.

The president was able to manipulate the primary and caucus schedule to bunch states favorable to him and to match pro-Kennedy states with pro-Carter states. The result was an early, strong Carter lead in delegates. Kennedy came back with some strong primary wins in New York and Pennsylvania, but his campaign by then was reduced to a vehicle for anti-Carter expressions. Many Kennedy voters hoped for a deadlocked convention at which a third candidate could win the nomination.

Carter won the nomination on the first ballot despite a variety of stop-Carter efforts and Kennedy's attempt to free delegates to vote for any candidate. When Carter won the crucial floor vote on the "open convention" question, Kennedy did not have a chance. The Carter-Mondale ticket entered the fall campaign as a wounded army with little enthusiasm from the troops.

The Republicans united early behind Reagan. By April 22, 1980, less than two months after the New Hampshire primary, six candidates had dropped out of the race, and George Bush, Reagan's only surviving competitor, was desperately behind in the delegate count. Reagan's campaign experienced an early scare when Bush beat Reagan in the Iowa caucus; but Reagan rebounded, changed campaign managers and tactics, and won a string of primaries and caucuses. By the time of the convention, Reagan was the consensus candidate, and he improved party unity by adding Bush to the fall ticket.

Reagan called for the electorate to replace politics that he said were marked by "pastels," or compromising and uncertain policies, with "bold colors." Reagan's proposed bold strokes included a 30 percent reduction in marginal tax rates based on a "supply-side" economic theory—which even some Republicans said was a dangerous kind of "voodoo economics"—and massive increases in military expenditures. Reagan criticized at the same time Carter's alleged vacillation and his commitment to liberal policies.

President Carter—vulnerable as the hostage crisis neared its first anniversary (which was November 4, election day) and high inflation and unemployment rates persisted—attempted to portray Reagan as a dangerous, heartless, and inexperienced amateur. Reagan managed to use Carter's attacks to his own advantage by assuming a posture of hurt feelings at the unfair criticism. When in a televised debate Carter attacked Reagan's previous opposition to social welfare programs, Reagan cut him off with a line, "There you go again," that suggested Carter was unfairly and relentlessly distorting Reagan's record.

Carter strategists also were concerned about the independent candidacy of Rep. John B. Anderson of Illinois, a moderate who dropped out of the Republican race when it became clear that conservatives would dominate that party. After some stronger support in the polls, Anderson stood at about 10 percent for the final two months of the campaign. Carter was concerned that Anderson would take more votes from him than from Reagan, even though analysis of Anderson support suggested otherwise.[156]

Private money almost doubled the amount that Reagan was legally entitled to spend under the federal financing system. Well-organized groups on the "new right" that opposed abortion, gun control, détente, and many social welfare programs spent lavishly on television commercials and efforts to register like-minded voters. These groups also made a "hit list" of leading liberals in Congress; these candidates were so weakened by the new right's attacks that they put a local and regional drag on an already dragging Democratic ticket.[157]

Polls before election day predicted a close race. Reagan, however, won all but six states and took the White House in an electoral landslide, 489 electoral votes to 49. Reagan won 51 percent of the vote, while Carter managed 41 percent and Anderson 7 percent. Carter ran tight races in ten additional states that could have gone his way with a shift of less than one and a half percentage points. In twenty-one states, Anderson's vote totals made up most or all of the difference between Reagan and Carter. Despite these factors and polls that regularly showed preference for Carter's policy positions, Reagan's victory was impressive. He beat Carter by better than a two-to-one margin in nine states.

Even more surprising than Reagan's electoral landslide was the Republican takeover of the Senate. The new right's targeting of several Senate liberals—such as McGovern, Bayh, Gaylord Nelson of Wisconsin, John Tunney of California, and John Culver of Iowa—created the biggest Senate turnover since 1958. The Republicans now held the Senate by a 53-to-46 margin.

President Reagan was able to parlay his claims of an electoral mandate into wide-ranging changes in tax, budget, and military policies. Reagan won passage of a three-year, 25 percent cut in tax rates that would reduce federal revenues by $196 billion annually by the time the three-stage program was in place. He also secured omnibus legislation that cut the domestic budget by $140 billion over four years and increases in defense spending of $181 billion over the same period. The media hailed Reagan as the most successful handler of Congress since Lyndon Johnson.

Reagan's 1984 Landslide

Reagan's popularity dipped to 44 percent in 1983—about the average for modern presidents—but Reagan rebounded when the economy later picked up.[158] As the 1984 election approached, Reagan faced no opposition from Republicans, but a large field of Democrats sought the right to oppose him in the fall.

The Democrats' early front-runner was former vice president Mondale, who accumulated a wide range of endorsements (AFL-CIO, National Education Association, United Mine Workers, and the National Organization for Women) and an impressive campaign treasury. The more conservative senator John Glenn of Ohio, the first American to orbit earth, was considered a strong challenger. Other candidates included senators Gary Hart of Colorado, Alan Cranston of California, and Ernest Hollings of South

UPI/Bettmann Newsphotos

Democratic presidential candidate Walter F. Mondale and his running mate, Geraldine Ferraro, the first woman to receive a major party nomination for national office, campaign in the 1984 presidential race.

Carolina, civil rights leader Jesse Jackson, former presidential candidate George McGovern, and former governor Reubin Askew of Florida.

The early results eliminated all but Mondale, Hart, and Jackson just sixteen days after the New Hampshire primary. Hart became the serious challenger to Mondale when he finished second in Iowa and first in New Hampshire, creating an explosion of media coverage. Mondale recovered, and the two fought head-to-head until the convention. Jackson, the second black to run, stayed in the race to promote his liberal party agenda.[159]

After interviewing a wide range of candidates, Mondale selected Rep. Geraldine Ferraro as his running mate—the first woman ever to receive a major-party nomination for national office. Representative Ferraro's vice-presidential candidacy probably was a drag on the ticket, not so much because she is a woman but because of the controversy created by her husband's finances and her stand on the abortion question. The controversies hindered the Democratic campaign's effort to articulate its own vision for the nation.[160]

Ferraro appeared knowledgeable and strong in her debate with Vice President Bush, and she often drew large and enthusiastic crowds. But she was stuck in controversy when details of her husband's questionable real estate, trusteeship, and tax practices became public. Opponents of abortion held prominent and often loud protests at the sites of her speeches, and she got involved in a lengthy public dispute over abortion with Catholic archbishop John O'Connor. Ferraro also did not help the ticket in regions where the Democrats were weak, such as the South and West.

Mondale ran a generally conservative campaign, concentrating on a proposed tax increase to address the unprecedented budget deficit of more than $200 billion and proposing no new social programs. Mondale criticized Reagan's record on the arms race but did not outline basic disagreements on other foreign affairs issues. He charged that Reagan, the oldest president in history, was lazy and out of touch. Only late in the campaign, when his speeches became unabashedly liberal and combative, did Mondale create any excitement.

Just once—in the period after the first presidential debate—did Mondale appear to have a chance to defeat President Reagan. Political pundits had marked Mondale as a poor television performer, but the challenger outfoxed Reagan in the debate and afterwards appeared to be gaining ground for a few days. Before the debate, Mondale aides leaked erroneous information that suggested he would make a slashing attack. But Mondale surprised Reagan. At the advice of strategist Patrick Caddell, Mondale adopted a "gold-watch approach" suitable to a family business retiring an oldtimer—"sort of embracing a grandfather, and gently pushing him aside."[161] Mondale gave the president credit for helping to restore national patriotism and beginning a national debate on education reform, but he said it was time for new leadership. Reagan appeared confused and, in the rush to demonstrate statistical knowledge of policies, he failed to outline broad themes.

Although the first debate boosted the Mondale campaign's morale, it never brought Mondale within striking range of Reagan. He never came within ten percentage points of Reagan in the polls. Reagan's campaign was a series of rallies with masses of colorful balloons and confident talk about the United States "standing tall" in domestic and world affairs. Reagan was so sure of victory that he

Although Reagan's popularity dipped to 44 percent in 1983, he rebounded when the economy later picked up. Here, Reagan campaigns with Vice President George Bush.

made a last-minute trip to Mondale's home state of Minnesota with the hope of completing a fifty-state sweep of the nation.

Reagan's triumph was resounding almost everywhere. He won 54.5 million votes (58.8 percent) to Mondale's 37.6 million (40.6 percent). In the electoral college, he received 525 votes to Mondale's 13 votes. Reagan won forty-nine states, with 2-to-1 margins in eight states. Idaho, Nebraska, and Utah each gave Reagan more than 70 percent of the vote. Mondale won only the District of Columbia and his home state of Minnesota, where he beat Reagan by only two-tenths of 1 percent.

Reagan's two landslides and the conservative discourse of his administration led many experts to wonder if they were witnessing a "realignment"—that is, a major shift in political alliances among a variety of social, economic, and ethnic groups.[162] The noteworthy aspect of U.S. politics in the last two decades appeared to be the Democratic hold on congressional and state elections and the Republican dominance of presidential elections. Some experts pointed to the electorate's ticket-splitting tendencies as evidence of "dealignment"—that is, breakdown of the old system without development of an entirely new system.[163]

Perhaps the most noteworthy development of recent years, which fits the dealignment thesis, has been the convergence of the appeal of the two parties. Michael Barone, in *The Almanac of American Politics*, wrote:

> Political preferences in the America of the 1940's correlated to a fair degree with income. Republican strength was greater than average in high income states ..., while Roosevelt and Truman carried virtually every state with incomes below the national average. But today there is virtually no correlation between income level and political preference. Utah, with one of the lowest per capita incomes, was one of the nation's most Republican states in 1980.... In the Midwest, high income Illinois is more Democratic than low income Indiana.[164]

The New Conservative Discourse

Reagan's rise ushered in a new age of conservatism in the American political discourse. The vigorous conservative campaigns for the presidency and Congress were accompanied by a host of new "think tanks" and publications with a restyled set of philosophical and policy pronouncements.

The most celebrated event of the conservative revival was the publication of George Gilder's *Wealth and Poverty,* a far-reaching attack on welfare state policies that rested on supply-side economic theory. Gilder argued that free markets and low taxes promoted not only economic efficiency and growth but also other benefits such as family strength and artistic creativity. Gilder's book was a central element of Reagan's campaign for major tax cuts.[165] But the supply-side tracts of Gilder and others were only the most prominent signs of the conservative movement. Reagan's criticism of the Supreme Court decisions on abortion and school prayer helped to bring evangelical Christians into the political process. Businesses and conservative philanthropists, meanwhile, sponsored an unprecedented level of public policy research that shaped the debate of elections and government policy.[166]

Reagan's political appeal, according to scholar Garry Wills, turned on his ability to blend contradictory elements of American culture such as capitalism, conservatism, and individualism. While Reagan decried the decline of "traditional American values," for example, he extolled the dynamic economic system that demanded constant change. Wills writes: "There are so many contradictions in this larger construct that one cannot risk entertaining serious challenge to any of its details. In Reagan, luckily, all these clashes are resolved. He is the ideal past, the successful present, the hopeful future all in one."[167]

Using the "bully pulpit" of the presidency, Reagan was able to overwhelm his opponents with his vision. When Democrats criticized specific Reagan policies, Reagan deflated them with expressions of disdain for "little men with loud voices [that] cry doom." [168] Jeane Kirkpatrick's depiction of Democrats as the "blame America first crowd" neatly expressed the way the Reagan rhetoric foreclosed debate on major policy issues such as the budget and trade deficits, military spending, the U.S. role in the third world, and U.S.-Soviet relations.

By the time the 1984 campaign took place, much of the nation had adopted Reagan's terms of debate. Mondale's strongest performance, in fact, was in the first debate when he congratulated Reagan for restoring national pride and suggested not that Reagan should be ousted but rather given a graceful retirement. Mondale's campaign was basically conservative: he did not propose a single new social program and called the federal budget deficit the nation's top problem.

The Post-Reagan Era

The election of 1988 was the first since 1968 in which an incumbent president did not run. With no major figure and no major issues, the campaign was a tumultuous affair. As fourteen candidates struggled to develop an identity with the voters, the campaign lurched from one symbolic issue to the next and never developed the overarching themes of previous campaigns.

In the absence of any major new issues, and in a time of general peace and prosperity, Republican vice president George Bush won the presidency. Bush defeated Democratic Massachusetts governor Michael S. Dukakis by a margin of 54 percent to 46 percent—47.9 million votes to 41.0 million votes. Bush's electoral vote margin was more impressive, 426-112. A negative campaign and limited voter-registration efforts resulted in the lowest voter turnout in modern times. Just more than 50 percent of all eligible citizens voted for president.

Bush won with the Nixon-Reagan presidential coalition. He won all the states of the old Confederacy, the entire West except Oregon and Washington, and several northern industrial states. Dukakis originally hoped to crack the South by selecting a favorite son, Sen. Lloyd Bentsen of Texas, as his running mate; but that failed. Dukakis lost crucial states that he fought for to the end, such as California, Pennsylvania, Illinois, Ohio, and Missouri. He won New York, Massachusetts, Wisconsin, Minnesota, Oregon, Washington, West Virginia, Iowa, Rhode Island, Hawaii, and the District of Columbia.

President Ronald Reagan's retirement after two full terms created a void as the campaign began. By most accounts, Reagan was the most popular president since Dwight D. Eisenhower. His dominance of national politics left little room for other figures to establish presidential stature.

Reagan's fiscal and social policies reduced the possibility for candidates to offer ambitious new programs. The national government's huge budget deficits—which exceeded $200 billion, compared with the previous high of about $80 billion in the last year of the Carter administration—checked any grandiose new spending plans. The Reagan debt exceeded the debt of the previous thirty-nine presidents.

President Reagan also reshaped the dialogue on foreign affairs. He maintained strong opposition to the Soviet Union and other "Marxist" nations with his policies in Nicaragua, Afghanistan, and Angola. He also projected an image of strength with military action in Libya and Grenada. At the same time, however, he co-opted critics by meeting Soviet leader Mikhail Gorbachev several times and signing a nuclear arms control agreement. Reagan even asserted that the Gorbachev regime was fundamentally different from previous Soviet regimes, which he had called the "evil empire."

The early Republican front-runners were Bush and Sen. Robert J. Dole of Kansas; former senator Gary Hart of Colorado was considered the early Democratic leader. The campaign got scrambled before it began, however. Hart left the race in 1987 when the Miami *Herald* augmented rumors of Hart's infidelity with a report that he had spent the night with a young model. Hart, considered by many to be the brightest and most issue-oriented candidate, had long faced criticism about his "character."

Sen. Joseph R. Biden, Jr., of Delaware was the next casualty of the media's 1987 concern with "character" issues.[169] Media reports that he had committed plagiarism on a law school paper and in campaign speeches led to Biden's early exit from the campaign. Biden had been considered a leading candidate because of his experience and strong speaking style.

With Hart and Biden out of the race, the Democrats were in disarray. Dubbed "dwarfs," the remaining candidates—Rev. Jesse Jackson of Illinois, Gov. Dukakis, Rep. Richard A. Gephardt of Missouri, Sen. Albert A. Gore, Jr., of Tennessee, Sen. Paul M. Simon of Illinois, and former Arizona governor Bruce Babbitt—lacked the combination of extensive government experience and strong national bases many observers thought necessary to win the presidency.

The Republicans had problems of their own. Vice President Bush was the early favorite, and he benefited from his association with President Reagan. But Bush's public fealty to Reagan created a problem: he was considered a "wimp," unable to stand on his own. Every major position Bush had held in his political career was the result of appointment: ambassador to the United Nations, chairman of the Republican National Committee, envoy to China, director of the Central Intelligence Agency, and vice president. Bush had represented Texas for two terms in the House and lost two Senate races.

Dole, too, was considered strong at the outset of the race. As Republican leader in the Senate, he had a high profile in national politics and proven fund-raising abilities. His wife, Elizabeth, was prominent as secretary of transportation. Dole also had an acerbic wit, which gave spark to his campaigning style but also irritated some voters. Other GOP candidates were Rep. Jack Kemp of New York, former secretary of state Alexander M. Haig, Jr., of Pennsylvania, former Delaware governor Pierre S. (Pete) du Pont IV and television minister Marion G. (Pat) Robertson of Virginia.

The marathon campaign for the nomination began with the Iowa caucuses, a significant event only because of intense media attention. Gephardt barely edged Simon in the Democratic contests, and Dole won the Republican race. The big story was just how badly Bush performed: he finished third behind Dole and Robertson.

The Iowa loss caused the Bush campaign to emerge from its isolation. Bush had been the most restrained and cautious candidate as he tried to benefit from the prestige of the White House. But in the New Hampshire primary, Bush beat Dole. Bush won with a series of television advertisements charging that Dole would raise taxes. Bush also was more animated on the campaign trail than he had been before. Dole failed to respond quickly to the Bush offensive, and when he snapped on national television about Bush's "lying about my record," he reinforced his image as a mean-spirited candidate.

Among the Democrats, Governor Dukakis easily won the New Hampshire primary. Capitalizing on his regional popularity, Dukakis beat Gephardt and Simon. Most of the Democratic fire in that race took place between the two runners-up. Dukakis escaped without any major criticism, and his already strong fund-raising machine went into high gear.

The decisive stage of the GOP campaign was Super Tuesday—March 8—when twenty-two states held presidential primaries or caucuses. Benefiting from a well-organized campaign, Bush won seventeen of the eighteen GOP contests. Dole staked his campaign on the ensuing Illinois primary, but he lost badly, and Bush was virtually ensured the Republican nomination.

The one issue that threatened Bush throughout 1988 was the Iran-contra scandal. Revelations that the administration had traded arms to Iran in exchange for the release of hostages, then used the proceeds illegally to fund the war in Nicaragua, raised questions about Bush's role. Administration officials admitted lying to Congress, destroying evidence, and operating outside normal government channels; one top official even attempted suicide. But the question of Bush's involvement fizzled after months of inconclusive questioning of Bush.

The Democrats sorted things out slowly on Super Tuesday. Dukakis won Texas and Florida and five northern states and confirmed his shaky front-runner status. Civil rights leader Jesse Jackson was the big surprise, however, winning five southern states. Gore won seven states.

The Democratic marathon continued into Illinois, Michigan, and New York. Dukakis took and maintained the lead in delegates with steady wins over Jackson and Gore. Gore dropped out after finishing third in a divisive New York primary, and the rest of the campaign was a one-on-one race between Dukakis and Jackson. Only once—after his victory over Dukakis in the Michigan caucuses—did Jackson appear to have a chance to win the Democratic nomination.

Jackson was a mixed blessing for the party. An energetic campaigner, he attracted support from blacks and from farmers and blue-collar workers who were disgruntled by the uneven rewards of economic growth. But Jackson was considerably to the left of the rest of the party and never had held any government office. Race also was a factor: no political professional believed that a black could be elected president.

Dukakis practically clinched the nomination with his victory over Jackson in the New York primary. The issue of race was at the center of the campaign. New York City mayor Edward I. Koch, a Gore supporter, called Jackson a "radical" and said Jews would be "crazy" to vote for him. Such remarks aggravated tensions between blacks and Jews that had festered since the 1960s. Dukakis avoided the race issue and won the primary.

As the summer conventions approached, Bush and Dukakis each had the full support of his party. The parties' internal divisions were on display as the prospective nominees considered possible vice-presidential candidates. Blacks lobbied for Jackson's selection by Dukakis, while "New Right" GOP leaders lobbied against a "moderate" running mate.

Dukakis selected conservative senator Lloyd M. Bentsen, Jr., of Texas as his running mate before the Atlanta Democratic convention. Jackson complained publicly and privately, but he eventually embraced Bentsen for the sake of party unity. Dukakis hoped Bentsen would be able to help carry Texas: no Democrat has won the presidency without winning Texas since the state became part of the nation in 1845.

The July convention was a success for the Democrats. After a week of Bush-bashing and Democratic conciliation, Dukakis gave an effective acceptance speech peppered with statements in Spanish and Greek. Dukakis left the conven-

David Valdez; The White House

On August 18, 1988, George Bush and his vice-presidential running mate, Dan Quayle, celebrate their victory at the Republican national convention.

tion with a double-digit lead over Bush in the polls.

The Republican convention in August did not start out as well. Bush announced his selection of Sen. Dan Quayle of Indiana as he arrived in New Orleans. After revelations that Quayle had avoided military service in the Vietnam War by enlisting in the Indiana National Guard, many Republicans criticized Bush's choice. Some even said Quayle might have to be dropped from the ticket. By the end of the convention, however, the Republicans had weathered the storm. Bush delivered a crisp address, which provided the self-portrait that the vice president needed, and moved into the fall campaign for a close battle with Dukakis.

Bush took the offensive immediately after the August GOP convention and hit Dukakis as a "liberal" out of touch with American "values." Bush attacked Dukakis for his membership in the American Civil Liberties Union, his veto of a bill requiring Massachusetts teachers to lead children in the Pledge of Allegiance, and a Massachusetts program allowing prisoners time off for weekends. As he pounded away at these symbolic issues, Dukakis's "negative" ratings with voters soared. Not believing the attacks would affect his standing with undecided voters—and believing they might even hurt Bush—Dukakis did not respond forcefully to the attacks until October. By then, however, Bush had effectively defined Dukakis, a newcomer to national politics. Dukakis's counteroffensive in the last two weeks of the campaign came too late.

Other major national issues—the national debt, the trade deficit, housing, education, U.S.-Soviet relations, the environment, and ethics in government—were drowned out by the emphasis on symbolic issues.

As Dukakis fell behind Bush, his campaign pinned its hopes on two nationally televised debates. Dukakis performed well in the first debate, but Bush appeared to "win" the second debate. Dukakis failed to gain on Bush.

The only major problem for Bush was Quayle. Most political professionals considered Quayle a "lightweight." The forty-one-year-old Quayle was a poor student and marginal member of Congress.[170]

Dukakis said Bush's selection of Quayle amounted to failure in his "first presidential decision." Dukakis compared Quayle with the more experienced Bentsen, who performed much better in a vice-presidential debate. Public polls revealed that most voters thought that Quayle was a bad choice.

The Bush campaign minimized the damage by limiting Quayle's public exposure and carefully scripting his statements. Quayle rarely spoke in major media markets; many of his campaign stops were accessible only by bus. While Bush delivered speeches in several states each day, Quayle often made just one speech before schoolchildren or partisan audiences.

After months of inconsistent and confusing strategy, Dukakis finally developed a strong appeal in the last two weeks of the campaign. He told voters he was "on your side" and portrayed Bush as a toady to the wealthy. Dukakis said the middle class was "squeezed" by the policies of the Reagan administration and that the Democrats would provide good jobs, affordable housing and health care, and tough enforcement of environmental protection laws.

It was not enough. Bush, who had made a fortune in the oil business before entering politics and was the son of a former U.S. senator, convinced more voters that his experience and values were what they wanted in the very personal choice of a president.

Democrats gained one seat in the Senate and three seats in the House of Representatives—a warning to Bush, since winning presidential candidates usually help their party gain seats in Congress. A period of divided government appeared in the offing, as congressional Democrats developed their own agenda for the next four years.

Notes

Original Constitutional Provisions

1. Richard M. Pious, *The American Presidency* (New York: Basic Books, 1979), 22.
2. Ibid., 25-29.
3. The term *electoral college* does not appear in the text of the Constitution. Citing Andrew C. McLaughlin, Edward Corwin wrote that the term "was used by Abraham Baldwin in 1800 and by John Randolph in 1809, and 'officially' in 1845" (Edward S. Corwin, *The President: Office and Powers*, 4th ed. [New York: New York University Press, 1957], 339 n.21).
4. The original compromise called for the Senate to make the final decision in such circumstances.
5. Richard Hofstadter, *The Idea of a Party System* (Berkeley: University of California Press, 1969), 16-39.
6. John F. Hoadley, *Origins of American Political Parties* (Lexington: University Press of Kentucky, 1986), 34.
7. A. E. Dick Howard, *Commentaries on the Constitution of Virginia*, vol. I (Charlottesville: University Press of Virginia, 1974), 318-19; ibid.
8. Howard, *Commentaries*, 320.
9. Quoted in ibid., 323.
10. Ibid., 325-26.
11. See, for example, Hoadley, *Origins*, 34-35; Robert E. Brown, *Charles Beard and the Constitution* (Princeton, N.J.: Princeton University Press, 1956), 61-72.

The Electoral College

1. Laurence H. Tribe and Thomas M. Rollins, "Deadlock: What Happens if Nobody Wins," *Atlantic Monthly,* October 1980, 49.
2. U.S. Constitution, Amendment XII, Section I.
3. U.S. Constitution, Amendment XX, Section 3.
4. Tribe and Rollins, "Deadlock," 60-61.
5. Allan P. Sindler, "Presidential Selection and Succession in Special Situations," in *Presidential Selection,* ed. Alexander Heard and Michael Nelson (Durham, N.C.: Duke University Press, 1987), 355.
6. Ibid.
7. U.S. Constitution, Amendment XX, Section 3.
8. Sindler, "Presidential Selection," 356.
9. Edward S. Corwin, *The President: Office and Powers*, 4th ed. (New York: New York University Press, 1957), 55-56.
10. Sindler, "Presidential Selection," 355; Tribe and Rollins, "Deadlock," 58-60.
11. Quoted in Tribe and Rollins, "Deadlock," 60.
12. Milton Lomask, *Aaron Burr: The Years from Princeton to Vice President (1756-1805)* (New York: Farrar, Straus, Giroux, 1979), 291-294.
13. Eugene H. Roseboom and Alfred E. Eckes, Jr., *A History of Presidential Elections,* 4th ed. (New York: Macmillan, 1979), 38.
14. Tribe and Rollins, "Deadlock,"60.
15. Edward Stanwood, *A History of the Presidency from 1788 to 1897,* rev. ed. by Charles Knowles Bolton (Boston: Houghton Mifflin, 1926), 187.
16. Tribe and Rollins, "Deadlock," 50.
17. Ibid., 56. Wallace's terms were delivered in a press conference on February 19, 1968.
18. Ibid., 50.

Chronology

1. Richard P. McCormick, *The Presidential Game: The Origins of American Presidential Politics* (New York: Oxford University Press, 1982), chap. 1.
2. Ibid., 33-34.
3. Roy F. Nichols, *The Invention of the American Political Parties* (New York: Macmillan, 1967), 192.
4. Edward Stanwood, *A History of the Presidency* (Boston: Houghton Mifflin, 1898), 63.
5. Ibid., 110.
6. Matthew A. Crenson, *The Federal Machine* (Baltimore: Johns Hopkins University Press, 1971), 11-30.
7. Jackson biographer Robert V. Remini explains the nickname "Old Hickory." In an arduous, five-hundred-mile march, Jackson gave his three horses to wounded soldiers and marched on foot with his troops to give them moral support. The soldiers serving under him agreed that their general was as tough as hickory. "Not much later," Remini writes, "they started calling him 'Hickory' as a sign of their respect and regard; then the affectionate 'Old' was added to give Jackson a nickname ... that admirably served him thereafter throughout his military and political wars" (Robert V. Remini, *Andrew Jackson* [New York: Harper and Row, 1969], 54).
8. Arthur M. Schlesinger, Jr., *The Age of Jackson* (New York: New American Library, 1945), 34.
9. *Guide to Congress*, 2d ed. (Washington, D.C.: Congressional Quarterly Inc., 1982), 613.
10. Russell L. Hanson, *The Democratic Imagination in America: Conversations with Our Past* (Princeton, N.J.: Princeton University Press, 1985), 125.
11. Eugene H. Roseboom, *A History of Presidential Elections* (New York: Macmillan, 1970), 106.
12. Schlesinger, *Jackson*, 55.
13. Estimates of vote totals vary, especially in the years before standardized methods of balloting. Discrepancies developed because of disputes about stuffing ballot boxes, the eligibility of some voters, absentee ballots, and simple counting and reporting difficulties in the pre-media age.
14. Roseboom, *Presidential Elections*, 112.
15. Hanson, *Democratic Imagination*, 54-120.
16. Ibid., 140-141.
17. Ibid., 136.
18. See Albert O. Hirschman, *Exit, Voice, and Loyalty* (Cambridge: Harvard University Press, 1970).
19. Hanson, *Democratic Imagination*, 138.
20. Richard P. McCormick, "Political Development and the Second Party System," in *The American Party Systems: Stages of Development*, ed. William Nisbet Chambers and Walter Dean Burnham (New York: Oxford University Press, 1967), 102.
21. James L. Sundquist, *Dynamics of the Party System*, rev. ed. (Washington, D.C.: Brookings, 1983), 51.
22. Roseboom, *Presidential Elections*, 143.
23. Richard Hofstadter, *The American Political Tradition* (New York: Vintage, 1948), 113.
24. Ibid.
25. Hanson, *Democratic Imagination*, 176.
26. Roseboom, *Presidential Elections*, 177-181.
27. Paul N. Angle, ed., *The Lincoln Reader* (New York: Pocket Books, 1954), 523.
28. Ibid., 531.
29. Roseboom, *Presidential Elections*, 201.
30. Eric Foner, *Reconstruction: America's Unfinished Revolution, 1863-1877* (New York: Harper and Row, 1988).
31. William S. McFeely, *Grant* (New York: Norton, 1981), 283.
32. Ibid., 288-289.
33. Ibid., 381.
34. Bernhard Bailyn, et al., *The Great Republic: A History of the American People* (Boston: Little, Brown, 1977), 802.
35. C. Vann Woodward, *Reunion and Reaction* (New York: Doubleday Anchor Books, 1951).
36. Kenneth M. Stampp, *The Era of Reconstruction, 1865-1877* (New York: Vintage, 1965), 210-211.
37. Michael Nelson, "A Short, Ironic History of American National Bureaucracy," *Journal of Politics* 44 (Winter 1982): 747-777.
38. Roseboom, *Presidential Elections*, 264.
39. Harry Thurston Peck, *Twenty Years of the Republic, 1885-1905* (New York: Dodd, Mead, 1906), 20.
40. Michael E. McGerr, *The Decline of Popular Politics: The American North, 1865-1928* (New York: Oxford University Press), 82-106.
41. Peck, *Twenty Years of the Republic*, 41.
42. Ibid., 78.
43. Ibid., 144.
44. Ibid., 169.
45. Roseboom, *Presidential Elections*, 290.
46. Bailyn et al., *Great Republic*, 786.
47. Sundquist, *Party System*, 107.
48. For a concise account of the machine-reform struggle, see Dennis R. Judd, *The Politics of American Cities* (Boston: Little, Brown, 1984), 50-110.
49. See David Montgomery, *The Fall of the House of Labor* (New York: Cambridge University Press, 1987).
50. Sundquist, *Party System*, 116-118.
51. Ibid., 143, 152.
52. Hofstadter, *American Political Tradition*, 187.
53. Sundquist, *Party System*, 149-152.
54. Hofstadter, *American Political Tradition*, 192-193.
55. See "William Jennings Bryan, Cross of Gold Speech," in *Great Issues in American History: From Reconstruction to the Present Day, 1864-1969*, ed. Richard Hofstadter (New York: Vintage, 1969), 166-173.
56. Jasper B. Shannon, *Money and Politics* (New York: Random House, 1959), 30-32.
57. Sundquist, *Party System*, 158.
58. Ibid., 169; for a general discussion of the 1896 election's resulting realignment, see pp. 160-169.
59. E. E. Schattschneider, *The Semisovereign People* (Hinsdale, Ill.: Dryden Press, 1975), 76-77.
60. Edmund Morris, *The Rise of Theodore Roosevelt* (New York: Ballantine, 1979), 718.
61. See Gabriel Kolko, *The Triumph of Conservatism* (New York: Free Press, 1963).
62. Sundquist, *Party System*, 176.
63. See Alpheus I. Mason, *Bureaucracy Convicts Itself* (New York: Viking Press, 1941); and James Penick, Jr., *Progressive Politics and Conservation* (Chicago: University of Chicago Press, 1968).
64. J. Leonard Bates, *The United States, 1898-1928* (New York: McGraw-Hill, 1976), 187.
65. Roseboom, *Presidential Elections*, 384.
66. John L. Shover, ed., *Politics of the Nineteen Twenties* (Waltham, Mass.: Ginn-Blaisdell, 1970), 148.
67. Ibid., 4.
68. Ibid., 12.
69. Ibid., 10.
70. James David Barber, *The Pulse of Politics* (New York: Norton, 1980), 239.
71. William E. Leuchtenberg, *Franklin D. Roosevelt and the New Deal* (New York: Harper and Row, 1963), 13.
72. Frank Friedel, *Franklin D. Roosevelt: The Triumph* (Boston: Little, Brown, 1956), 248-249.
73. Barber, *Pulse of Politics*, 243.
74. Ibid., 244.
75. Ibid., 238.
76. Hofstadter, *American Political Tradition*, 332.
77. Barber, *Pulse of Politics*, 244.
78. See Robert Lekachman, *The Age of Keynes* (New York: Random, 1966).
79. Schattschneider argues in *The Semisovereign People* that the key element of any conflict is the extent to which the protagonists are able to control how many people get involved. Every "scope of conflict" has a bias. The size of the

group involved in the conflict is almost always open to change. Schattschneider writes: "A look at political literature shows that there has indeed been a long-standing struggle between the conflicting tendencies toward the privatization and socialization of conflict" (p. 7). The New Deal was a stage of socialization of conflict.

80. Everett Carll Ladd, Jr., and Charles D. Hadley, *Transformations of the American Party System* (New York: Norton, 1978), 86.

81. Ibid., 43.

82. Ibid., 46.

83. Ibid., 64-74, 112; Sundquist, *Party System*, 214-224.

84. Sundquist, *Party System*, 217.

85. Ladd and Hadley, *American Party System*, 82.

86. Ibid., 58-59.

87. Ibid., 63.

88. Samuel H. Beer, "Liberalism and the National Interest," *The Public Interest*, no. 1 (Fall 1966): 81.

89. Theodore J. Lowi, *The End of Liberalism* (New York: Norton, 1969). See also Russell Hanson, *The Democratic Imagination in America* (Princeton, N.J.: Princeton University Press, 1985), 257-292.

90. James MacGregor Burns, *Roosevelt: The Lion and the Fox* (New York: Harcourt, Brace, and World, 1956), 282-283.

91. Roseboom, *Presidential Elections*, 447.

92. Burns, *Lion and the Fox*, 269-271.

93. Burns, *Roosevelt*, 282-283.

94. Ibid., 300.

95. Ibid., 427.

96. James David Barber, *The Pulse of Politics* (New York: W. W. Norton, 1980) tells the story behind the Willkie movement and the role played by Henry R. Luce, the founder of Time, Inc.

97. See Lekachman, *Age of Keynes*, esp. chaps. 5 and 6.

98. Roseboom, *Presidential Elections*, 483.

99. William E. Leuchtenberg, *In the Shadow of F.D.R.: From Harry Truman to Ronald Reagan* (Ithaca, N.Y.: Cornell University Press, 1983), 1-2.

100. Ibid., 15.

101. Ibid., 21.

102. V. O. Key, *Southern Politics in State and Nation* (Knoxville: University of Tennessee Press, 1984), 649.

103. Ibid., 330-344.

104. Barber, *Pulse of Politics*, 50.

105. Nelson W. Polsby and Aaron Wildavsky, *Presidential Elections* (New York: Scribner's, 1984), 205-206.

106. Barber, *Pulse of Politics*, 61.

107. Angus Campbell, Gerald Gurin, and Warren E. Miller, *The American Voter* (New York: Wiley, 1960), 532.

108. Richard Neustadt, *Presidential Power* (New York: Wiley, 1980), 10, 12-14, 16, 18, 19, 22-25, 43, 67-68, 178.

109. Garry Wills, *Nixon Agonistes* (New York: New American Library, 1969), 91.

110. Fred Greenstein, *The Hidden-Hand Presidency* (New York: Basic Books, 1982).

111. Barber, *Pulse of Politics*, 269.

112. Eric F. Goldman quipped, "The returns, as the gangsters said, made even Alf Landon look good" (*The Crucial Decade* [New York: Vintage, 1960], 326).

113. The elder Kennedy always planned for his sons to enter national politics. He originally pushed his eldest son, Joseph, Jr., but the son died in combat in World War II. John was next; he ran for Congress in 1946. Robert, the third Kennedy son, served as an aide to Sen. Joseph McCarthy before managing John's 1960 presidential campaign and serving as his attorney general. Edward, the youngest, worked on the 1960 campaign and won a Senate seat in 1962.

114. Merle Miller, *Plain Speaking* (New York: Berkley, 1974), 199.

115. Theodore H. White, *The Making of the President 1960* (New York: Atheneum, 1961), 114-116.

116. Ibid., 128.

117. Ibid., 130.

118. Ibid., 198-204.

119. Arthur M. Schlesinger, Jr., *Robert F. Kennedy and His Times* (Boston: Houghton Mifflin, 1978), 193.

120. Henry Fairlie, *The Kennedy Promise* (New York: Dell, 1972), 30-31.

121. White, *Making of the President 1960*, 329.

122. Ibid., 327.

123. Richard M. Nixon, *Six Crises* (Garden City, N.Y.: Doubleday, 1962), 412.

124. White, *Making of the President 1960*, 397-401.

125. Sen. Barry Goldwater, letter to the author, January 25, 1988.

126. The Warren Commission, appointed by Johnson, concluded that Oswald acted alone, but Oswald himself was killed before he had a chance to give full testimony. Many experts dispute the Warren Commission conclusion.

127. The Kennedy assassination fomented passage of the Twenty-fifth Amendment, which provides for a more orderly system of replacement. Previously, when a vice president ascended to the White House after the death or removal of a president, the vice presidency was left vacant. The amendment provides for presidential appointment of a vice president to fill the vacant spot. It also provides for at least temporary replacement of the president in the case of disability. The latter provision developed out of a concern that the country could have become leaderless had Kennedy been physically or mentally impaired but not killed.

128. Barber, *Pulse of Politics*, 167.

129. Thomas Ferguson and Joel Rogers, *Right Turn: The Decline of the Democrats and the Future of American Politics* (New York: Hill and Wang, 1986), 53.

130. Theodore H. White, *The Making of the President 1964* (New York: New American Library, 1965), 261.

131. Ibid., 353.

132. The central importance of economic conditions to electoral politics is widely documented. See, for example, Stanley Kelley, Jr., *Interpreting Elections* (Princeton, N.J.: Princeton University Press, 1983); Edward R. Tufte, *Political Control of the Economy* (Princeton, N.J.: Princeton University Press, 1978); and Angus Campbell, Gerald Gurin, and Warren E. Miller, *The American Voter* (New York: Wiley, 1960). On the link between economic conditions and the 1964 election, see Kelley, *Interpreting Elections*, 194.

133. Stanley Karnow, *Vietnam: A History* (New York: Viking, 1983), 358.

134. Ibid., 362.

135. Ibid., 395.

136. James David Barber, *The Presidential Character* (Englewood Cliffs, N.J.: Prentice-Hall, 1972), 34.

137. Karnow, *Vietnam*, 403.

138. Ibid., 479.

139. David Halberstam, *The Best and the Brightest* (New York: Random, 1969).

140. Sundquist, *Party System*, 384.

141. Ibid., 383.

142. The administration plank supported a bombing halt only when it would not endanger the lives of our troops in the field, did not call for a reduction in search-and-destroy missions or a withdrawal of troops until the end of the war, and advocated a new government in Saigon only after the war had ended. The minority plank, drafted by McCarthy and McGovern, called for an immediate halt to the bombing, reduction of offensive operations in the South Vietnamese countryside, a negotiated troop withdrawal, and encouragement of the South Vietnamese government to negotiate with Communist insurgents. After nearly three hours of debate, the minority plank was defeated, 1,567-3/4 to 1,041-1/4.

143. White, *Making of the President 1968*, 371.

144. Roseboom, *Presidential Elections*, 603.

145. See Russell Baker, *The Next President* (New York: Dell, 1968).

146. David Broder, "The Story That Still Nags at Me," *Washington Monthly*, February 1987, 29-32; see also White, *Making of the President 1972*, 82.

147. White, *Making of the President 1972,* 129.

148. Ibid., 207.

149. On the politics of the period, see Sundquist, *Party System,* 393-411; and Theodore H. White, *America in Search of Itself* (New York: Harper and Row, 1981). Good accounts of the Watergate scandal include Theodore H. White, *Breach of Faith* (New York: Atheneum, 1975); Jonathan Schell, *The Time of Illusion* (New York: Knopf, 1976); and Lewis Chester, et al., *Watergate* (New York: Ballantine, 1973).

150. Seymour Hersch, "The Pardon," *Atlantic,* August 1983, 55-78.

151. David J. Vogler, *The Politics of Congress* (Boston: Allyn and Bacon, 1977), 15-20, 25-26, 34, 147-155, 243-245.

152. For a good account of Jimmy Carter's 1976 Iowa victory, see Hugh Winebrenner, *The Iowa Precinct Caucuses* (Ames: University of Iowa Press, 1987), 67-93.

153. Jules Witcover, *Marathon* (New York: Viking, 1977), 274-288.

154. Ibid., 545-560.

155. Responding to a question during a debate, Ford said: "There is no Soviet domination of Eastern Europe, and there never will be under a Ford administration.... I don't believe ... that the Yugoslavians consider themselves dominated by the Soviet Union. I don't believe that the Rumanians consider themselves dominated by the Soviet Union. I don't believe that the Poles consider themselves dominated by the Soviet Union" (Ibid., 597, 598).

156. Richard Harwood, ed., *The Pursuit of the Presidency 1980* (New York: Berkley, 1980), 305-307.

157. Thomas Byrne Edsall, *The New Politics of Inequality* (New York: Norton, 1984), 77-78.

158. Thomas Ferguson and Joel Rogers, *Right Turn* (New York: Hall and Wang, 1986), 26.

159. Rep. Shirley Chisholm of Brooklyn, New York, was the first black to seek a major-party nomination. Her participation in the 1972 Democratic primaries won 151 delegates.

160. Geraldine Ferraro, with Linda Bird Francke, *Ferraro: My Story* (New York: Bantam, 1985), 164.

161. Paul R. Abramson, John H. Aldrich, and David W. Rohde, *Change and Continuity in the 1984 Elections,* rev. ed. (Washington, D.C.: CQ Press, 1986), 58.

162. V. O. Key, Jr., "A Theory of Critical Elections," *Journal of Politics* 17 (February 1955): 3-18.

163. Abramson, Aldrich, and Rohde, *Change and Continuity,* 286-287.

164. Michael Barone and Grant Ujifusa, *The Almanac of American Politics: 1984* (Washington, D.C.: National Journal, 1983), xiv. See also Ladd and Hadley, *American Party System,* 237-249.

165. George Gilder, *Wealth and Poverty* (New York: Basic Books, 1980). Another prominent supply-side tract is Jude Wanniski, *The Way the World Works* (New York: Basic Books, 1978). A sympathetic summary of the whole movement can be found in Robert Craig Paul, *The Supply-Side Revolution* (Cambridge, Mass.: Harvard University Press, 1984).

166. Ferguson and Rogers, *Right Turn,* 86-88, n. 245.

167. Garry Wills, *Reagan's America: Innocents at Home* (Garden City, N.Y.: Doubleday, 1987), 387.

168. Ibid., 385.

169. Also that year, two Supreme Court nominees, Robert H. Bork and Douglas H. Ginsburg, failed to win Senate confirmation. Bork lost because of his views on a wide variety of social issues, but many criticisms focused on his personality. Ginsburg withdrew from consideration after revelations that he had smoked marijuana as a student and law school professor.

170. Quayle did not meet the requirements set for political science majors and failed the first general examination at DePauw University in Indiana. He also failed to gain admission to law school under the usual application procedure. A study of Quayle's congressional career concludes that Quayle had no policy achievements in the House of Representatives but mastered some policy issues in the Senate. See Anthony Lewis, "The Intimidated Press," *New York Times,* January 19, 1989, 27, and Richard F. Fenno, Jr., *The Making of a Senator: Dan Quayle* (Washington, D.C.: CQ Press, 1988).

U.S. Presidents and Vice Presidents

President and political party	Born	Died	Age at inauguration	Native of	Elected from	Term of service	Vice president
George Washington (F)	1732	1799	57	Va.	Va.	April 30, 1789-March 4, 1793	John Adams
George Washington (F)			61			March 4, 1793-March 4, 1797	John Adams
John Adams (F)	1735	1826	61	Mass.	Mass.	March 4, 1797-March 4, 1801	Thomas Jefferson
Thomas Jefferson (DR)	1743	1826	57	Va.	Va.	March 4, 1801-March 4, 1805	Aaron Burr
Thomas Jefferson (DR)			61			March 4, 1805-March 4, 1809	George Clinton
James Madison (DR)	1751	1836	57	Va.	Va.	March 4, 1809-March 4, 1813	George Clinton
James Madison (DR)			61			March 4, 1813-March 4, 1817	Elbridge Gerry
James Monroe (DR)	1758	1831	58	Va.	Va.	March 4, 1817-March 4, 1821	Daniel D. Tompkins
James Monroe (DR)			62			March 4, 1821-March 4, 1825	Daniel D. Tompkins
John Q. Adams (DR)	1767	1848	57	Mass.	Mass.	March 4, 1825-March 4, 1829	John C. Calhoun
Andrew Jackson (D)	1767	1845	61	S.C.	Tenn.	March 4, 1829-March 4, 1833	John C. Calhoun
Andrew Jackson (D)			65			March 4, 1833-March 4, 1837	Martin Van Buren
Martin Van Buren (D)	1782	1862	54	N.Y.	N.Y.	March 4, 1837-March 4, 1841	Richard M. Johnson
W. H. Harrison (W)	1773	1841	68	Va.	Ohio	March 4, 1841-April 4, 1841	John Tyler
John Tyler (W)	1790	1862	51	Va.	Va.	April 6, 1841-March 4, 1845	
James K. Polk (D)	1795	1849	49	N.C.	Tenn.	March 4, 1845-March 4, 1849	George M. Dallas
Zachary Taylor (W)	1784	1850	64	Va.	La.	March 4, 1849-July 9, 1850	Millard Fillmore
Millard Fillmore (W)	1800	1874	50	N.Y.	N.Y.	July 10, 1850-March 4, 1853	
Franklin Pierce (D)	1804	1869	48	N.H.	N.H.	March 4, 1853-March 4, 1857	William R. King
James Buchanan (D)	1791	1868	65	Pa.	Pa.	March 4, 1857-March 4, 1861	John C. Breckinridge
Abraham Lincoln (R)	1809	1865	52	Ky.	Ill.	March 4, 1861-March 4, 1865	Hannibal Hamlin
Abraham Lincoln (R)			56			March 4, 1865-April 15, 1865	Andrew Johnson
Andrew Johnson (R)	1808	1875	56	N.C.	Tenn.	April 15, 1865-March 4, 1869	
Ulysses S. Grant (R)	1822	1885	46	Ohio	Ill.	March 4, 1869-March 4, 1873	Schuyler Colfax
Ulysses S. Grant (R)			50			March 4, 1873-March 4, 1877	Henry Wilson
Rutherford B. Hayes (R)	1822	1893	54	Ohio	Ohio	March 4, 1877-March 4, 1881	William A. Wheeler
James A. Garfield (R)	1831	1881	49	Ohio	Ohio	March 4, 1881-Sept. 19, 1881	Chester A. Arthur
Chester A. Arthur (R)	1830	1886	50	Vt.	N.Y.	Sept. 20, 1881-March 4, 1885	
Grover Cleveland (D)	1837	1908	47	N.J.	N.Y.	March 4, 1885-March 4, 1889	Thomas A. Hendricks
Benjamin Harrison (R)	1833	1901	55	Ohio	Ind.	March 4, 1889-March 4, 1893	Levi P. Morton
Grover Cleveland (D)	1837	1908	55			March 4, 1893-March 4, 1897	Adlai E. Stevenson
William McKinley (R)	1843	1901	54	Ohio	Ohio	March 4, 1897-March 4, 1901	Garret A. Hobart
William McKinley (R)			58			March 4, 1901-Sept. 14, 1901	Theodore Roosevelt
Theodore Roosevelt (R)	1858	1919	42	N.Y.	N.Y.	Sept. 14, 1901-March 4, 1905	
Theodore Roosevelt (R)			46			March 4, 1905-March 4, 1909	Charles W. Fairbanks
William H. Taft (R)	1857	1930	51	Ohio	Ohio	March 4, 1909-March 4, 1913	James S. Sherman
Woodrow Wilson (D)	1856	1924	56	Va.	N.J.	March 4, 1913-March 4, 1917	Thomas R. Marshall
Woodrow Wilson (D)			60			March 4, 1917-March 4, 1921	Thomas R. Marshall
Warren G. Harding (R)	1865	1923	55	Ohio	Ohio	March 4, 1921-Aug. 2, 1923	Calvin Coolidge
Calvin Coolidge (R)	1872	1933	51	Vt.	Mass.	Aug. 3, 1923-March 4, 1925	
Calvin Coolidge (R)			52			March 4, 1925-March 4, 1929	Charles G. Dawes
Herbert Hoover (R)	1874	1964	54	Iowa	Calif.	March 4, 1929-March 4, 1933	Charles Curtis
Franklin D. Roosevelt (D)	1882	1945	51	N.Y.	N.Y.	March 4, 1933-Jan. 20, 1937	John N. Garner
Franklin D. Roosevelt (D)			55			Jan. 20, 1937-Jan. 20, 1941	John N. Garner
Franklin D. Roosevelt (D)			59			Jan. 20, 1941-Jan. 20, 1945	Henry A. Wallace
Franklin D. Roosevelt (D)			63			Jan. 20, 1945-April 12, 1945	Harry S Truman
Harry S Truman (D)	1884	1972	60	Mo.	Mo.	April 12, 1945-Jan. 20, 1949	
Harry S Truman (D)			64			Jan. 20, 1949-Jan. 20, 1953	Alben W. Barkley
Dwight D. Eisenhower (R)	1890	1969	62	Texas	N.Y.	Jan. 20, 1953-Jan. 20, 1957	Richard Nixon
Dwight D. Eisenhower (R)			66		Pa.	Jan. 20, 1957-Jan. 20, 1961	Richard Nixon
John F. Kennedy (D)	1917	1963	43	Mass.	Mass.	Jan. 20, 1961-Nov. 22, 1963	Lyndon B. Johnson

Choosing a Running Mate: The Balancing Act

In modern times veteran political convention watchers have come to look forward to the almost-traditional night of uncertainty as the new presidential nominee tries to come up with a running mate. But this hectic process is a recent one. During the country's first years the runner-up for the presidency automatically took the second slot.

That system did not last long, however. In 1800 Thomas Jefferson and Aaron Burr found themselves in a tie for electoral votes. Neither man's supporters were willing to settle for the lesser office. The deadlock went to the House of Representatives, where Jefferson needed thirty-six ballots to clinch the presidency. It also led to the Twelfth Amendment to the U.S. Constitution, ratified in 1804, providing for electoral college balloting for presidents and vice presidents. With the emergence of political parties after 1800, candidates ran as teams. Once party conventions began in 1831, delegates, with the guidance of party bosses, began to do the choosing.

In fact, it was only in 1940 that presidential nominees began regularly handpicking their running mates. That year, after failing to persuade Secretary of State Cordell Hull to accept the vice presidency, Franklin D. Roosevelt forced Henry A. Wallace on a reluctant Democratic convention by threatening to refuse his own nomination if Wallace was rejected. The only exception to the practice Roosevelt established came in 1956, when Democrat Adlai E. Stevenson left the choice to the convention.

If the selection of a running mate often has seemed an afterthought, it could be because the position is not a particularly coveted one. John Adams, the first man to hold the job, once complained, "My country has in its wisdom contrived for me the most insignificant office that ever the intention of man contrived or his imagination conceived." More than a century later Thomas R. Marshall, Woodrow Wilson's vice president, expressed a similarly dismal view: "Once there were two brothers. One ran away to sea; the other was elected Vice President. And nothing was ever heard of either of them again."

Writing in *Atlantic* in 1974, historian Arthur Schlesinger, Jr., suggested the office be done away with. "It is a doomed office," he commented. "The Vice President has only one serious thing to do: that is, to wait around for the President to die." But there is a reasonable chance that whoever fills the position will get a chance to move up, either by succession or election. As of 1989 fourteen presidents had held the second-ranking post, seven in the twentieth century.

Also, during the 1970s and 1980s, the vice presidency evolved from the somnolent office it once had been; during this period vice presidents enjoyed responsibility their predecessors did not. Nelson A. Rockefeller, who served under Gerald R. Ford, was given considerable authority in domestic policy coordination. Both Walter F. Mondale and George Bush helped set policy for their respective presidents. As president, Bush in April 1989 named his vice president, Dan Quayle, to head the National Space Council, one of the administration's showcase projects.

Yet whoever is selected vice president is scrutinized not so much as a policy maker but as how the choice balances the ticket. One important consideration is geography, but other traditional concerns weighed by nominees are religion and ethnicity. In national politics of the 1980s, however, those considerations seemed to be losing their place to race and gender. Although a black candidate for either spot had not been seriously considered as of the 1984 election, the Democrats chose Rep. Geraldine A. Ferraro of New York to be their vice-presidential candidate, the first woman to receive a major party nomination. In 1988, when black presidential contender Jesse Jackson lost the Democratic nomination to Michael Dukakis, Jackson's supporters lobbied for him to be the vice-presidential candidate. Lloyd Bentsen of Texas was chosen, and Jackson for the sake of party unity stood behind the Democratic ticket.

President and political party	Born	Died	Age at inauguration	Native of	Elected from	Term of service	Vice president
Lyndon B. Johnson (D)	1908	1973	55	Texas	Texas	Nov. 22, 1963-Jan. 20, 1965	
Lyndon B. Johnson (D)			56			Jan. 20, 1965-Jan. 20, 1969	Hubert H. Humphrey
Richard Nixon (R)	1913		56	Calif.	N.Y.	Jan. 20, 1969-Jan. 20, 1973	Spiro T. Agnew
Richard Nixon (R)			60		Calif.	Jan. 20, 1973-Aug. 9, 1974	Spiro T. Agnew Gerald R. Ford
Gerald R. Ford (R)	1913		61	Neb.	Mich.	Aug. 9, 1974-Jan. 20, 1977	Nelson A. Rockefeller
Jimmy Carter (D)	1924		52	Ga.	Ga.	Jan. 20, 1977-Jan. 20, 1981	Walter F. Mondale
Ronald Reagan (R)	1911		69	Ill.	Calif.	Jan. 20, 1981-Jan. 20, 1985	George Bush
Ronald Reagan (R)			73			Jan. 20, 1985-Jan. 20, 1989	George Bush
George Bush (R)	1924		64	Mass.	Texas	Jan. 20, 1989—	Dan Quayle

Source: Presidential Elections Since 1789, 4th ed. (Washington, D.C.: Congressional Quarterly Inc., 1987), 4.

Note: D—Democrat; DR—Democratic-Republican; F—Federalist; R—Republican; W—Whig.

Official 1984 Presidential Election Results

(Based on reports from the secretaries of state for the fifty states and the District of Columbia)

State	Total vote	Ronald Reagan (Republican)		Walter F. Mondale (Democrat)		David Bergland (Libertarian)		Lyndon H. LaRouche Jr. (Independent)		Other *		Plurality	
		Votes	%	Votes	%	Votes	%	Votes	%	Votes	%		
Alabama	1,441,713	872,849	60.5	551,899	38.3	9,504	0.7			7,461	0.5	320,950	R
Alaska	207,605	138,377	66.7	62,007	29.9	6,378	3.1			843	0.4	76,370	R
Arizona	1,025,897	681,416	66.4	333,854	32.5	10,585	1.0			42	—	347,562	R
Arkansas	884,406	534,774	60.5	338,646	38.3	2,221	0.3	1,890	0.2	6,875	0.8	196,128	R
California	9,505,423	5,467,009	57.5	3,922,519	41.3	49,951	0.5			65,944	0.7	1,544,490	R
Colorado	1,295,380	821,817	63.4	454,975	35.1	11,257	0.9	4,662	0.4	2,669	0.2	366,842	R
Connecticut	1,466,900	890,877	60.7	569,597	38.8	204				6,222	0.4	321,280	R
Delaware	254,572	152,190	59.8	101,656	39.9	268	0.1			458	0.2	50,534	R
D.C.	211,288	29,009	13.7	180,408	85.4	279	0.1	127	0.1	1,465	0.7	151,399	D
Florida	4,180,051	2,730,350	65.3	1,448,816	34.7	754				131	—	1,281,534	R
Georgia	1,776,120	1,068,722	60.2	706,628	39.8	152		34		584	—	362,094	R
Hawaii	335,846	185,050	55.1	147,154	43.8	2,167	0.6	654	0.2	821	0.2	37,896	R
Idaho	411,144	297,523	72.4	108,510	26.4	2,823	0.7			2,288	0.6	189,013	R
Illinois	4,819,088	2,707,103	56.2	2,086,499	43.3	10,086	0.2			15,400	0.3	620,604	R
Indiana	2,233,069	1,377,230	61.7	841,481	37.7	6,741	0.3			7,617	0.3	535,749	R
Iowa	1,319,805	703,088	53.3	605,620	45.9	1,844	0.1	6,248	0.5	3,005	0.2	97,468	R
Kansas	1,021,991	677,296	66.3	333,149	32.6	3,329	0.3			8,217	0.8	344,147	R
Kentucky	1,369,345	821,702	60.0	539,539	39.4			1,776	0.1	6,328	0.5	282,163	R
Louisiana	1,706,822	1,037,299	60.8	651,586	38.2	1,876	0.1	3,552	0.2	12,509	0.7	385,713	R
Maine	553,144	336,500	60.8	214,515	38.8					2,129	0.4	121,985	R
Maryland	1,675,873	879,918	52.5	787,935	47.0	5,721	0.3			2,299	0.1	91,983	R
Massachusetts	2,559,453	1,310,936	51.2	1,239,606	48.4					8,911	0.3	71,330	R
Michigan	3,801,658	2,251,571	59.2	1,529,638	40.2	10,055	0.3	3,862	0.1	6,532	0.2	721,933	R
Minnesota	2,084,449	1,032,603	49.5	1,036,364	49.7	2,996	0.1	3,865	0.2	8,621	0.4	3,761	D
Mississippi	941,104	582,377	61.9	352,192	37.4	2,336	0.2	1,001	0.1	3,198	0.3	230,185	R
Missouri	2,122,783	1,274,188	60.0	848,583	40.0					12	—	425,605	R
Montana	384,377	232,450	60.5	146,742	38.2	5,185	1.3					85,708	R
Nebraska	652,090	460,054	70.6	187,866	28.8	2,079	0.3			2,091	0.3	272,188	R
Nevada	286,667	188,770	65.8	91,655	32.0	2,292	0.8			3,950	1.4	97,115	R
New Hampshire	389,066	267,051	68.6	120,395	30.9	735	0.2	467	0.1	418	0.1	146,656	R
New Jersey	3,217,862	1,933,630	60.1	1,261,323	39.2	6,416	0.2			16,493	0.5	672,307	R
New Mexico	514,370	307,101	59.7	201,769	39.2	4,459	0.9			1,041	0.2	105,332	R
New York	6,806,810	3,664,763	53.8	3,119,609	45.8	11,949	0.2			10,489	0.2	545,154	R
North Carolina	2,175,361	1,346,481	61.9	824,287	37.9	3,794	0.2			799	—	522,194	R
North Dakota	308,971	200,336	64.8	104,429	33.8	703	0.2	1,278	0.4	2,225	0.7	95,907	R
Ohio	4,547,619	2,678,560	58.9	1,825,440	40.1	5,886	0.1	10,693	0.2	27,040	0.6	853,120	R
Oklahoma	1,255,676	861,530	68.6	385,080	30.7	9,066	0.7					476,450	R
Oregon	1,226,527	685,700	55.9	536,479	43.7					4,348	0.4	149,221	R
Pennsylvania	4,844,903	2,584,323	53.3	2,228,131	46.0	6,982	0.1			25,467	0.5	356,192	R
Rhode Island	410,492	212,080	51.7	197,106	48.0	277	0.1			1,029	0.3	14,974	R
South Carolina	968,529	615,539	63.6	344,459	35.6	4,359	0.5			4,172	0.4	271,080	R
South Dakota	317,867	200,267	63.0	116,113	36.5					1,487	0.5	84,154	R
Tennessee	1,711,994	990,212	57.8	711,714	41.6	3,072	0.2	1,852	0.1	5,144	0.3	278,498	R
Texas	5,397,571	3,433,428	63.6	1,949,276	36.1			14,613	0.3	254	—	1,484,152	R
Utah	629,656	469,105	74.5	155,369	24.7	2,447	0.4			2,735	0.4	313,736	R
Vermont	234,561	135,865	57.9	95,730	40.8	1,002	0.4	423	0.2	1,541	0.7	40,135	R
Virginia	2,146,635	1,337,078	62.3	796,250	37.1			13,307	0.6			540,828	R
Washington	1,883,910	1,051,670	55.8	807,352	42.9	8,844	0.5	4,712	0.3	11,332	0.6	244,318	R
West Virginia	735,742	405,483	55.1	328,125	44.6					2,134	0.3	77,358	R
Wisconsin	2,211,689	1,198,584	54.2	995,740	45.0	4,883	0.2	3,791	0.2	8,691	0.4	202,844	R
Wyoming	188,968	133,241	70.5	53,370	28.2	2,357	1.2					79,871	R
	92,652,842	54,455,075	58.8	37,577,185	40.6	228,314	0.2	78,807	0.1	313,461	0.3	16,877,890	

Source: America Votes 17, ed. Richard M. Scammon and Alice V. McGillivray (Washington, D.C.: Congressional Quarterly Inc., 1987), 40-41.

* Others receiving votes: Sonia Johnson (Citizens), 72,200; Bob Richards (Populist), 66,336; Dennis L. Serrette (Alliance), 46,868; Gus Hall (Communist), 36,386; Mel Mason (Socialist Workers), 24,706: Larry Holmes (Workers World), 15,329, and Gabrielle Holmes (Workers World), 2,656; Delmar Dennis (American), 13,161; Edward Winn (Workers League), 10,801; Earl F. Dodge (Prohibition), 4,242; John B. Anderson (National Unity), 1,486; Gerald Baker (Big Deal), 892; Arthur J. Lowery (United Sovereign Citizens), 825; "None of these candidates," 3,950; Scattered write-in votes, 13,623.

Official 1988 Presidential Election Results

(Based on reports from the secretaries of state for the fifty states and the District of Columbia)

State	Total vote	George Bush (Republican) Votes	%	Michael S. Dukakis (Democrat) Votes	%	Ron Paul (Libertarian) Votes	%	Lenora B. Fulani (New Alliance) Votes	%	Other * Votes	%	Plurality	
Alabama	1,378,476	815,576	59.2	549,506	39.9	8,460	0.6	3,311	0.2	1,623	0.1	266,070	R
Alaska	200,116	119,251	59.6	72,584	36.3	5,480	2.7	1,024	0.5	1,773	0.9	46,667	R
Arizona	1,171,873	702,541	60.0	454,029	38.7	13,351	1.1	1,662	0.1	290	—	248,512	R
Arkansas	827,738	466,578	56.4	349,237	42.2	3,297	0.4	2,161	0.2	6,465	0.8	117,341	R
California	9,887,065	5,054,917	51.1	4,702,233	47.6	70,105	0.7	31,181	0.3	28,629	0.3	352,684	R
Colorado	1,372,394	728,177	53.1	621,453	45.3	15,482	1.1	2,539	0.2	4,743	0.3	106,724	R
Connecticut	1,443,394	750,241	52.0	676,584	46.9	14,071	1.0	2,491	0.1	7	—	73,657	R
Delaware	249,891	139,639	55.9	108,647	43.5	1,162	0.5	443	0.2			30,992	R
D.C.	192,877	27,590	14.3	159,407	82.6	554	0.3	2,901	1.5	2,425	1.3	131,817	D
Florida	4,302,313	2,618,825	60.9	1,656,701	38.5	19,796	0.5	6,655	0.2	276	—	962,184	R
Georgia	1,809,672	1,081,331	59.8	714,792	39.5	8,435	0.5	5,099	0.3	15	—	366,539	R
Hawaii	354,461	158,625	44.8	192,364	54.3	1,999	0.6	1,003	0.3	470	0.1	33,739	D
Idaho	408,968	253,881	62.1	147,272	36.0	5,313	1.3	2,502	0.6			106,609	R
Illinois	4,559,120	2,310,939	50.7	2,215,940	48.6	14,944	0.3	10,276	0.2	7,021	0.2	94,999	R
Indiana	2,168,621	1,297,763	59.8	860,643	39.7			10,215	0.5			437,120	R
Iowa	1,225,614	545,355	44.5	670,557	54.7	2,494	0.2	540	—	6,668	0.5	125,202	D
Kansas	993,044	554,049	55.8	422,636	42.6	12,553	1.3	3,806	0.4			131,413	R
Kentucky	1,322,517	734,281	55.5	580,368	43.9	2,118	0.2	1,256	0.1	4,494	0.3	153,913	R
Louisiana	1,628,202	883,702	54.3	717,460	44.1	4,115	0.3	2,355	0.1	20,570	1.3	166,242	R
Maine	555,035	307,131	55.3	243,569	43.9	2,700	0.5	1,405	0.3	230	—	63,562	R
Maryland	1,714,358	876,167	51.1	826,304	48.2	6,748	0.4	5,115	0.3	24	—	49,863	R
Massachusetts	2,632,805	1,194,635	45.4	1,401,415	53.2	24,251	0.9	9,561	0.4	2,943	0.1	206,780	D
Michigan	3,669,163	1,965,486	53.6	1,675,783	45.7	18,336	0.5	2,513	0.1	7,045	0.2	289,703	R
Minnesota	2,096,790	962,337	45.9	1,109,471	52.9	5,109	0.2	1,734	0.1	18,139	0.9	147,134	D
Mississippi	931,527	557,890	59.9	363,921	39.1	3,329	0.4	2,155	0.2	4,232	0.5	193,969	R
Missouri	2,093,713	1,084,953	51.8	1,001,619	47.8	434	—	6,656	0.3	51	—	83,334	R
Montana	365,674	190,412	52.1	168,936	46.2	5,047	1.4	1,279	0.3			21,476	R
Nebraska	661,465	397,956	60.2	259,235	39.2	2,534	0.4	1,743	0.3			138,721	R
Nevada	350,067	206,040	58.9	132,738	37.9	3,520	1.0	835	0.2	6,934	2.0	73,302	R
New Hampshire	451,074	281,537	62.4	163,696	36.3	4,502	1.0	790	0.2	549	0.1	117,841	R
New Jersey	3,099,553	1,743,192	56.2	1,320,352	42.6	8,421	0.3	5,138	0.2	22,449	0.7	422,840	R
New Mexico	521,287	270,341	51.9	244,497	46.9	3,268	0.6	2,237	0.4	944	0.2	25,844	R
New York	6,485,683	3,081,871	47.5	3,347,882	51.6	12,109	0.2	15,845	0.2	27,976	0.4	266,011	D
North Carolina	2,134,370	1,237,258	58.0	890,167	41.7	1,263	0.1	5,682	0.3			347,091	R
North Dakota	297,261	166,559	56.0	127,739	43.0	1,315	0.4	396	0.1	1,252	0.4	38,820	R
Ohio	4,393,699	2,416,549	55.0	1,939,629	44.1	11,989	0.3	12,017	0.3	13,515	0.3	476,920	R
Oklahoma	1,171,036	678,367	57.9	483,423	41.3	6,261	0.5	2,985	0.3			194,944	R
Oregon	1,201,694	560,126	46.6	616,206	51.3	14,811	1.2	6,487	0.5	4,064	0.3	56,080	D
Pennsylvania	4,536,251	2,300,087	50.7	2,194,944	48.4	12,051	0.3	4,379	0.1	24,790	0.5	105,143	R
Rhode Island	404,620	177,761	43.9	225,123	55.6	825	0.2	280	0.1	631	0.2	47,362	D
South Carolina	986,009	606,443	61.5	370,554	37.6	4,935	0.5	4,077	0.4			235,889	R
South Dakota	312,991	165,415	52.8	145,560	46.5	1,060	0.3	730	0.2	226	0.1	19,855	R
Tennessee	1,636,250	947,233	57.9	679,794	41.5	2,041	0.1	1,334	0.1	5,848	0.4	267,439	R
Texas	5,427,410	3,036,829	56.0	2,352,748	43.3	30,355	0.6	7,208	0.1	270	—	684,081	R
Utah	647,008	428,442	66.2	207,343	32.0	7,473	1.2	455	0.1	3,295	0.5	221,099	R
Vermont	243,328	124,331	51.1	115,775	47.6	1,000	0.4	205	0.1	2,017	0.8	8,556	R
Virginia	2,191,609	1,309,162	59.7	859,799	39.2	8,336	0.4	14,312	0.7			449,363	R
Washington	1,865,253	903,835	48.5	933,516	50.0	17,240	0.9	3,520	0.2	7,142	0.4	29,681	D
West Virginia	653,311	310,065	47.5	341,016	52.2			2,230	0.3			30,951	D
Wisconsin	2,191,608	1,047,499	47.8	1,126,794	51.4	5,157	0.2	1,953	0.1	10,205	0.5	79,295	D
Wyoming	176,551	106,867	60.5	67,113	38.0	2,026	1.1	545	0.3			39,754	R
	91,594,809	48,886,097	53.4	41,809,074	45.6	432,179	0.5	217,219	0.2	250,240	0.3	7,077,023	R

Source: America Votes 18, ed. Richard M. Scammon and Alice V. McGillivray (Washington, D.C.: Congressional Quarterly Inc., 1989), 6-7.

* Others receiving votes: David E. Duke (Populist), 47,047; Eugene Joseph McCarthy (Consumer), 30,905; James C. Griffin (American Independent), 27,818; Lyndon H. LaRouche (Independent), 25,562; William A. Marra (Right to Life), 20,504; Edward Winn (Workers League), 18,693; James Warren (Socialist Workers), 15,604; Herbert Lewin (Peace and Freedom), 10,370; Earl F. Dodge (Prohibition), 8,002; Larry Holmes (Workers World), 7,846; Willa Kenoyer (Socialist), 3,882; Delmar Dennis (American), 3,475; Jack E. Herer (Grassroots), 1,949; Louie Youngkeit (Independent), 372; John G. Martin (Third World Assembly), 236; "None of these candidates," 6,934; scattered write-in votes, 21,041.

Where They Voted ... and Where They Didn't

(1988 presidential-election turnout as percentage of voting-age population)

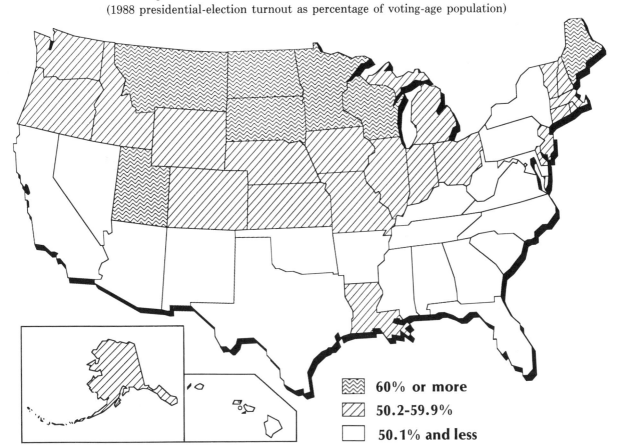

	60% or more
	50.2-59.9%
	50.1% and less

		1988 turnout rate (as percentage of voting-age pop.)	Change, 1984-1988 (in percentage points)			1988 turnout rate (as percentage of voting-age pop.)	Change, 1984-1988 (in percentage points)
		50.1%	−3.0	26.	Alaska	51.7	−7.5
1.	Minnesota	66.3	−1.9	27.	Louisiana	51.3	−3.2
2.	Montana	62.4	−2.7	28.	Delaware	51.0	−4.4
3.	Maine	62.2	−2.6	29.	Wyoming	50.3	−3.0
4.	Wisconsin	62.0	−1.5	30.	Pennsylvania	50.1	−3.9
5.	North Dakota	61.5	−1.2	31.	Mississippi	49.9	−2.3
	South Dakota	61.5	−1.0	32.	Maryland	49.1	−2.3
7.	Utah	60.0	−1.6	33.	Oklahoma	48.7	−3.4
8.	Iowa	59.3	−2.9	34.	Kentucky	48.2	−2.6
9.	Vermont	59.1	−0.7		Virginia	48.2	−2.5
10.	Oregon	58.6	−3.2	36.	New York	48.1	−3.1
11.	Idaho	58.3	−1.6	37.	California	47.4	−2.2
12.	Massachusetts	58.1	+0.5	38.	New Mexico	47.3	−4.0
13.	Connecticut	57.9	−3.2	39.	Arkansas	47.0	−4.8
14.	Nebraska	56.8	+1.2	40.	West Virginia	46.7	−5.0
15.	Colorado	55.1	0.0	41.	Alabama	45.8	−4.1
	Ohio	55.1	−2.9	42.	Arizona	45.0	−0.2
17.	Missouri	54.8	−2.5	43.	Nevada	44.9	+3.4
18.	New Hampshire	54.7	+1.7	44.	Florida	44.7	−3.5
19.	Washington	54.6	−3.8		Tennessee	44.7	−4.4
20.	Kansas	54.3	−2.5	46.	Texas	44.2	−3.0
21.	Michigan	54.0	−3.9	47.	North Carolina	43.4	−4.0
22.	Illinois	53.3	−3.8	48.	Hawaii	43.0	−1.3
	Indiana	53.3	−2.6	49.	District of Columbia	39.4	−3.8
24.	Rhode Island	53.0	−2.8	50.	South Carolina	38.9	−1.8
25.	New Jersey	52.1	−4.5	51.	Georgia	38.8	−3.2

Source: Congressional Quarterly Weekly Report, January 21, 1989, 136.

1988 Electoral Votes

		Bush (Republican)
		Dukakis (Democrat)

States	Electoral votes	Bush	Dukakis	Bentsen	States	Electoral votes	Bush	Dukakis	Bentsen
Alabama	(9)	9	-	-	Montana	(4)	4	-	-
Alaska	(3)	3	-	-	Nebraska	(5)	5	-	-
Arizona	(7)	7	-	-	Nevada	(4)	4	-	-
Arkansas	(6)	6	-	-	New Hampshire	(4)	4	-	-
California	(47)	47	-	-	New Jersey	(16)	16	-	-
Colorado	(8)	8	-	-	New Mexico	(5)	5	-	-
Connecticut	(8)	8	-	-	New York	(36)	-	36	-
Delaware	(3)	3	-	-	North Carolina	(13)	13	-	-
District of					North Dakota	(3)	3	-	-
Columbia	(3)	-	3	-	Ohio	(23)	23	-	-
Florida	(21)	21	-	-	Oklahoma	(8)	8	-	-
Georgia	(12)	12	-	-	Oregon	(7)	-	7	-
Hawaii	(4)	-	4	-	Pennsylvania	(25)	25	-	-
Idaho	(4)	4	-	-	Rhode Island	(4)	-	4	-
Illinois	(24)	24	-	-	South Carolina	(8)	8	-	-
Indiana	(12)	12	-	-	South Dakota	(3)	3	-	-
Iowa	(8)	-	8	-	Tennessee	(11)	11	-	-
Kansas	(7)	7	-	-	Texas	(29)	29	-	-
Kentucky	(9)	9	-	-	Utah	(5)	5	-	-
Louisiana	(10)	10	-	-	Vermont	(3)	3	-	-
Maine	(4)	4	-	-	Virginia	(12)	12	-	-
Maryland	(10)	10	-	-	Washington	(10)	-	10	-
Massachusetts	(13)	-	13	-	West Virginia *	(6)	-	5	1
Michigan	(20)	20	-	-	Wisconsin	(11)	-	11	-
Minnesota	(10)	-	10	-	Wyoming	(3)	3	-	-
Mississippi	(7)	7	-	-					
Missouri	(11)	11	-	-	Totals	(538)	426	111	1

Source: *Congressional Quarterly's Guide to the Presidency,* ed. Michael Nelson (Washington, D.C.: Congressional Quarterly Inc., 1989), 1427.

* Margaret Leach, a Dukakis elector, voted for Dukakis's running mate, Sen. Lloyd Bentsen of Texas.

Distribution of House Seats and Electoral Votes

(Based on Censuses of 1950, 1960, 1970, and 1980)

	U.S. House seats							Electoral votes			
	1953-1963	1960 Census changes	1963-1973	1970 Census changes	1973-1983	1980 Census changes	1983-1985	1952, 1956, 1960	1964, 1968	1972, 1976, 1980	1984, 1988
Alabama	9	−1	8	−1	7	0	7	11	10	9	9
Alaska	1	—	1	—	1	0	1	3	3	3	3
Arizona	2	+1	3	+1	4	+1	5	4	5	6	7
Arkansas	6	−2	4	—	4	0	4	8	6	6	6
California	30	+8	38	+5	43	+2	45	32	40	45	47
Colorado	4	—	4	+1	5	+1	6	6	6	7	8
Connecticut	6	—	6	—	6	0	6	8	8	8	8
Delaware	1	—	1	—	1	0	1	3	3	3	3
District of Columbia	—	—	—	—	—	—	—	—	3	3	3
Florida	8	+4	12	+3	15	+4	19	10	14	17	21
Georgia	10	—	10	—	10	0	10	12	12	12	12
Hawaii	1	+1	2	—	2	0	2	3	4	4	4
Idaho	2	—	2	—	2	0	2	4	4	4	4
Illinois	25	−1	24	—	24	−2	22	27	26	26	24
Indiana	11	—	11	—	11	−1	10	13	13	13	12
Iowa	8	−1	7	−1	6	0	6	10	9	8	8
Kansas	6	−1	5	—	5	0	5	8	7	7	7
Kentucky	8	−1	7	—	7	0	7	10	9	9	9
Louisiana	8	—	8	—	8	0	8	10	10	10	10
Maine	3	−1	2	—	2	0	2	5	4	4	4
Maryland	7	+1	8	—	8	0	8	9	10	10	10
Massachusetts	14	−2	12	—	12	−1	11	16	14	14	13
Michigan	18	+1	19	—	19	−1	18	20	21	21	20
Minnesota	9	−1	8	—	8	0	8	11	10	10	10
Mississippi	6	−1	5	—	5	0	5	8	7	7	7
Missouri	11	−1	10	—	10	−1	9	13	12	12	11
Montana	2	—	2	—	2	0	2	4	4	4	4
Nebraska	4	−1	3	—	3	0	3	6	5	5	5
Nevada	1	—	1	—	1	+1	2	3	3	3	4
New Hampshire	2	—	2	—	2	0	2	4	4	4	4
New Jersey	14	+1	15	—	15	−1	14	16	17	17	16
New Mexico	2	—	2	—	2	+1	3	4	4	4	5
New York	43	−2	41	−2	39	−5	34	45	43	41	36
North Carolina	12	−1	11	—	11	0	11	14	13	13	13
North Dakota	2	—	2	−1	1	0	1	4	4	3	3
Ohio	23	+1	24	−1	23	−2	21	25	26	25	23
Oklahoma	6	—	6	—	6	0	6	8	8	8	8
Oregon	4	—	4	—	4	+1	5	6	6	6	7
Pennsylvania	30	−3	27	−2	25	−2	23	32	29	27	25
Rhode Island	2	—	2	—	2	0	2	4	4	4	4
South Carolina	6	—	6	—	6	0	6	8	8	8	8
South Dakota	2	—	2	—	2	−1	1	4	4	4	3
Tennessee	9	—	9	−1	8	+1	9	11	11	10	11
Texas	22	+1	23	+1	24	+3	27	24	25	26	29
Utah	2	—	2	—	2	+1	3	4	4	4	5
Vermont	1	—	1	—	1	0	1	3	3	3	3
Virginia	10	—	10	—	10	0	10	12	12	12	12
Washington	7	—	7	—	7	+1	8	9	9	9	10
West Virginia	6	−1	5	−1	4	0	4	8	7	6	6
Wisconsin	10	—	10	−1	9	0	9	12	12	11	11
Wyoming	1	—	1	—	1	0	1	3	3	3	3

Electoral Votes for Vice President, 1804-1988

The following list gives the electoral votes for vice president from 1804 to 1988. Unless noted otherwise, the state-by-state breakdown of electoral votes for each vice-presidential candidate was the same as for his or her party's presidential candidate.

Before 1804, under Article II, Section 1, of the Constitution, each elector cast two votes, each vote for a different person. The electors did not distinguish between votes for president and vice president. The candidate receiving the second highest total became vice president. The Twelfth Amendment, ratified in 1804, required electors to vote separately for president and vice president.

In some cases persons received electoral votes although they had never been formally nominated. The word *candidate* is used in this section to designate persons receiving electoral votes.

Year	Candidate	Electoral votes
1804	George Clinton (Democratic-Republican)	162
	Rufus King (Federalist)	14
1808	George Clinton (Democratic-Republican)[a]	113
	John Langdon (Democratic-Republican)	9
	James Madison (Democratic-Republican)	3
	James Monroe (Democratic-Republican)	3
	Rufus King (Federalist)	47
1812	Elbridge Gerry (Democratic-Republican)[b]	131
	Jared Ingersoll (Federalist)	86
1816	Daniel D. Tompkins (Democratic-Republican)	183
	John E. Howard (Federalist)[c]	22
	James Ross (Federalist)	5
	John Marshall (Federalist)	4
	Robert G. Harper (Federalist)	3
1820	Daniel D. Tompkins (Democratic-Republican)[d]	218
	Richard Rush (Democratic-Republican)	1
	Richard Stockton (Federalist)	8
	Daniel Rodney (Federalist)	4
	Robert G. Harper (Federalist)	1
1824	John C. Calhoun (Democratic-Republican)[e]	182
	Nathan Sanford (Democratic-Republican)	30
	Nathaniel Macon (Democratic-Republican)	24
	Andrew Jackson (Democratic-Republican)	13
	Martin Van Buren (Democratic-Republican)	9
	Henry Clay (Democratic-Republican)	2
1828	John C. Calhoun (Democratic-Republican)[f]	171
	William Smith (Independent Democratic-Republican)	7
	Richard Rush (National Republican)	83
1832	Martin Van Buren (Democratic)[g]	189
	William Wilkins (Democratic)	30
	Henry Lee (Independent Democratic)	11
	John Sergeant (National Republican)	49
	Amos Ellmaker (Anti-Masonic)	7
1836	Richard M. Johnson (Democratic)[h]	147
	William Smith (Independent Democratic)	23
	Francis Granger (Whig)	77
	John Tyler (Whig)	47

Year	Candidate	Electoral votes
1840	John Tyler (Whig)	234
	Richard M. Johnson (Democratic)[i]	48
	L. W. Tazewell (Democratic)	11
	James K. Polk (Democratic)	1
1844	George M. Dallas (Democratic)	170
	Theodore Frelinghuysen (Whig)	105
1848	Millard Fillmore (Whig)	163
	William O. Butler (Democratic)	127
1852	William R. King (Democratic)	254
	William A. Graham (Whig)	42
1856	John C. Breckinridge (Democratic)	174
	William L. Dayton (Republican)	114
	Andrew J. Donelson (American)	8
1860	Hannibal Hamlin (Republican)	180
	Joseph Lane (Southern Democratic)	72
	Edward Everett (Constitutional Union)	39
	Herschel V. Johnson (Democratic)	12
1864	Andrew Johnson (Republican)	212
	George H. Pendleton (Democratic)	21
1868	Schuyler Colfax (Republican)	214
	Francis P. Blair (Democratic)	80
1872	Henry Wilson (Republican)	286
	Benjamin G. Brown (Democratic)[j]	47
	Alfred H. Colquitt (Democratic)	5
	John M. Palmer (Democratic)	3
	Thomas E. Bramlette (Democratic)	3
	William S. Groesbeck (Democratic)	1
	Willis B. Machen (Democratic)	1
	George W. Julian (Liberal Republican)	5
	Nathaniel P. Banks (Liberal Republican)	1
1876	William A. Wheeler (Republican)	185
	Thomas A. Hendricks (Democratic)	184
1880	Chester A. Arthur (Republican)	214
	William H. English (Democratic)	155
1884	Thomas A. Hendricks (Democratic)	219
	John A. Logan (Republican)	182
1888	Levi P. Morton (Republican)	233
	Allen G. Thurman (Democratic)	168
1892	Adlai E. Stevenson (Democratic)	277
	Whitelaw Reid (Republican)	145
	James G. Field (Populist)	22
1896	Garret A. Hobart (Republican)	271
	Arthur Sewall (Democratic)[k]	149
	Thomas E. Watson (Populist)	27
1900	Theodore Roosevelt (Republican)	292
	Adlai E. Stevenson (Democratic)	155
1904	Charles W. Fairbanks (Republican)	336
	Henry G. Davis (Democratic)	140
1908	James S. Sherman (Republican)	321
	John W. Kern (Democratic)	162
1912	Thomas R. Marshall (Democratic)	435

Year	Candidate	Electoral votes
	Hiram W. Johnson (Progressive)	88
	Nicholas M. Butler (Republican)	8
1916	Thomas R. Marshall (Democratic)	277
	Charles W. Fairbanks (Republican)	254
1920	Calvin Coolidge (Republican)	404
	Franklin D. Roosevelt (Democratic)	127
1924	Charles G. Dawes (Republican)	382
	Charles W. Bryan (Democratic)	136
	Burton K. Wheeler (Progressive)	13
1928	Charles Curtis (Republican)	444
	Joseph T. Robinson (Democratic)	87
1932	John N. Garner (Democratic)	472
	Charles Curtis (Republican)	59
1936	John N. Garner (Democratic)	523
	Frank Knox (Republican)	8
1940	Henry A. Wallace (Democratic)	449
	Charles L. McNary (Republican)	82
1944	Harry S Truman (Democratic)	432
	John W. Bricker (Republican)	99
1948	Alben W. Barkley (Democratic)	303
	Earl Warren (Republican)	189
	Fielding L. Wright (States' Rights Democratic)	39
1952	Richard Nixon (Republican)	442
	John J. Sparkman (Democratic)	89

Year	Candidate	Electoral votes
1956	Richard Nixon (Republican)	457
	Estes Kefauver (Democratic)	73
	Herman Talmadge (Democratic)	1
1960	Lyndon B. Johnson (Democratic)	303
	Strom Thurmond (Democratic)[l]	14
	Henry Cabot Lodge (Republican)	219
	Barry Goldwater (Republican)	1
1964	Hubert H. Humphrey (Democratic)	486
	William E. Miller (Republican)	52
1968	Spiro T. Agnew (Republican)	301
	Edmund S. Muskie (Democratic)	191
	Curtis E. LeMay (American Independent)	46
1972	Spiro T. Agnew (Republican)	520
	R. Sargent Shriver (Democratic)	17
	Theodora Nathan (Libertarian)	1
1976	Walter F. Mondale (Democratic)	297
	Robert Dole (Republican)[m]	241
1980	George Bush (Republican)	489
	Walter F. Mondale (Democratic)	49
1984	George Bush (Republican)	525
	Geraldine A. Ferraro (Democratic)	13
1988	Dan Quayle (Republican)	426
	Lloyd Bentsen (Democratic)[n]	111
	Michael S. Dukakis (Democratic)	1

Source: Congressional Quarterly's Guide to the Presidency, ed. Michael Nelson (Washington, D.C.: Congressional Quarterly Inc., 1989), 1429-1431.

a. New York cast 13 presidential electoral votes for Democratic-Republican James Madison and 6 votes for Clinton; for vice president, New York cast 13 votes for Clinton, 3 votes for Madison, and 3 votes for Monroe.

Langdon received Ohio's 3 votes and Vermont's 6 votes.

b. The state-by-state vote for Gerry was the same as for Democratic-Republican presidential candidate Madison, except for Massachusetts and New Hampshire. Massachusetts cast 2 votes for Gerry and 20 votes for Ingersoll; New Hampshire cast 1 vote for Gerry and 7 votes for Ingersoll.

c. Four Federalists received vice-presidential electoral votes: Howard—Massachusetts, 22 votes; Ross—Connecticut, 5 votes; Marshall—Connecticut, 4 votes; Harper—Delaware, 3 votes.

d. The state-by-state vote for Tompkins was the same as for Democratic-Republican presidential candidate Monroe, except for Delaware, Maryland, and Massachusetts. Delaware cast 4 votes for Rodney; Maryland cast 10 votes for Tompkins and 1 for Harper; Massachusetts cast 7 votes for Tompkins and 8 for Stockton.

New Hampshire, which cast 7 presidential electoral votes for Monroe and 1 vote for John Quincy Adams, cast 7 vice-presidential electoral votes for Tompkins and 1 vote for Rush.

e. The state-by-state vice-presidential electoral vote was as follows:

Calhoun—Alabama, 5 votes; Delaware, 1 vote; Illinois, 3 votes; Indiana, 5 votes; Kentucky, 7 votes; Louisiana, 5 votes; Maine, 9 votes; Maryland, 10 votes; Massachusetts, 15 votes; Mississippi, 3 votes; New Hampshire, 7 votes; New Jersey, 8 votes; New York, 29 votes; North Carolina, 15 votes; Pennsylvania, 28 votes; Rhode Island, 3 votes; South Carolina, 11 votes; Tennessee, 11 votes; Vermont, 7 votes.

Sanford—Kentucky, 7 votes; New York, 7 votes; Ohio, 16 votes.

Macon—Virginia, 24 votes.

Jackson—Connecticut, 8 votes; Maryland, 1 vote; Missouri, 3 votes; New Hampshire, 1 vote.

Van Buren—Georgia, 9 votes.

Clay—Delaware, 2 votes.

f. The state-by-state vote for Calhoun was the same as for Democratic-Republican presidential candidate Jackson, except for Geor-

gia, which cast 2 votes for Calhoun and 7 votes for Smith.

g. The state-by-state vote for Van Buren was the same as for Democratic-Republican presidential candidate Jackson, except for Pennsylvania, which cast 30 votes for Wilkins.

South Carolina cast 11 presidential electoral votes for Independent Democratic presidential candidate Floyd and 11 votes for Independent Democratic vice-presidential candidate Lee.

Vermont cast 7 presidential electoral votes for Anti-Masonic candidate Wirt and 7 vice-presidential electoral votes for Wirt's running mate, Ellmaker.

h. The state-by-state vote for Johnson was the same as for Democratic presidential candidate Van Buren, except for Virginia, which cast 23 votes for Smith.

Granger's state-by-state vote was the same as for Whig presidential candidate Harrison, except for Maryland and Massachusetts. Maryland cast 10 presidential electoral votes for Harrison and 10 vice-presidential votes for Tyler; Massachusetts cast 14 presidential electoral votes for Whig candidate Webster and 14 vice-presidential votes over Granger.

Tyler received 11 votes from Georgia, 10 from Maryland, 11 from South Carolina, and 15 from Tennessee.

No vice-presidential candidate received a majority of the electoral vote. As a result the Senate, for the only time in history, selected the vice president under the provisions of the Twelfth Amendment. Johnson was elected vice president by a vote of 33 to 16 over Granger.

i. The Democratic party did not nominate a vice-presidential candidate in 1840. Johnson's state-by-state vote was the same as for presidential candidate Van Buren, except for South Carolina and Virginia. South Carolina cast 11 votes for Tazewell. Virginia cast 23 presidential electoral votes for Van Buren, 22 vice-presidential votes for Johnson, and 1 vice-presidential vote for Polk.

j. Liberal Republican and Democratic presidential candidate Horace Greeley died November 29, 1872. As a result eighteen electors pledged to Greeley cast their presidential electoral votes for Brown, Greeley's running mate.

The vice-presidential vote was as follows:

Brown—Georgia, 5 votes; Kentucky, 8 votes; Maryland, 8 votes;

Missouri, 6 votes; Tennessee, 12 votes; Texas, 8 votes.

  Colquitt—Georgia, 5 votes.

  Palmer—Missouri, 3 votes.

  Bramlette—Kentucky, 3 votes.

  Groesbeck—Missouri, 1 vote.

  Machen—Kentucky, 1 vote.

  Julian—Missouri, 5 votes.

  Banks—Georgia, 1 vote.

k. The state-by-state vote for Sewell was the same as for Democratic-Populist candidate William Jennings Bryan, except for the following states, which cast electoral votes for Watson: Arkansas, 3 votes; Louisiana, 4; Missouri, 4; Montana, 1; Nebraska, 4; North Carolina, 5; South Dakota, 2; Utah, 1; Washington, 2; Wyoming, 1.

l. Democratic electors carried Alabama's 11 electoral votes. Five of the electors were pledged to the national Democratic ticket of Kennedy and Johnson. Six electors ran unpledged and voted for Harry F. Byrd for president and Strom Thurmond for vice president.

Mississippi's eight electors voted for Byrd and Thurmond.

In Oklahoma the Republican ticket of Nixon and Lodge carried the state, but one of the state's eight electors voted for Byrd for president and Goldwater for vice president.

m. One Republican elector from the state of Washington cast his presidential electoral vote for Reagan instead of the Republican nominee, Ford. But he voted for Dole, Ford's running mate, for vice president. Dole thus received one more electoral vote than Ford.

n. One Democratic elector from West Virginia cast her vice-presidential electoral vote for Dukakis, the Democratic nominee for president, and her presidential vote for his running mate, Bentsen.

Backgrounds of U.S. Presidents

President	Age at first political office	First political office	Last political office[a]	Age at becoming president	State of residence[b]	Father's occupation	Higher education[c]	Occupation
1. Washington (1789-1797)	17	County surveyor	Commander in chief	57	Va.	Farmer	None	Farmer, surveyor
2. Adams, J. (1797-1801)	39	Surveyor of highways	Vice president	61	Mass.	Farmer	Harvard	Farmer, lawyer
3. Jefferson (1801-1809)	26	State legislator	Vice president	58	Va.	Farmer	William and Mary	Farmer, lawyer
4. Madison (1809-1817)	25	State legislator	Secretary of state	58	Va.	Farmer	Princeton	Farmer
5. Monroe (1817-1825)	24	State legislator	Secretary of state	59	Va.	Farmer	William and Mary	Lawyer, farmer
6. Adams, J. Q. (1825-1829)	27	Minister to Netherlands	Secretary of state	58	Mass.	Farmer, lawyer	Harvard	Lawyer
7. Jackson (1829-1837)	21	Prosecuting attorney	U.S. Senate	62	Tenn.	Farmer	None	Lawyer
8. Van Buren (1837-1841)	30	Surrogate of county	Vice president	55	N.Y.	Tavern keeper	None	Lawyer
9. Harrison, W. H. (1841)	26	Territorial delegate to Congress	Minister to Colombia	68	Ind.	Farmer	Hampden-Sydney	Military
10. Tyler (1841-1845)	21	State legislator	Vice president	51	Va.	Planter, lawyer	William and Mary	Lawyer
11. Polk (1845-1849)	28	State legislator	Governor	50	Tenn.	Surveyor	U. of North Carolina	Lawyer
12. Taylor (1849-1850)	—	None	a	65	Ky.	Collector of internal revenue	None	Military
13. Fillmore (1850-1853)	28	State legislator	Vice president	50	N.Y.	Farmer	None	Lawyer
14. Pierce (1853-1857)	25	State legislator	U.S. district attorney	48	N.H.	General	Bowdoin	Lawyer
15. Buchanan (1857-1861)	22	Assistant county prosecutor	Minister to Great Britain	65	Pa.	Farmer	Dickinson	Lawyer
16. Lincoln (1861-1865)	25	State legislator	U.S. House of Representatives	52	Ill.	Farmer, carpenter	None	Lawyer
17. Johnson, A. (1865-1869)	20	City alderman	Vice president	57	Tenn.	Janitor-porter	None	Tailor
18. Grant (1869-1877)	—	None	a	47	Ohio	Tanner	West Point	Military
19. Hayes (1877-1881)	36	City solicitor	Governor	55	Ohio	Farmer	Kenyon	Lawyer
20. Garfield (1881)	28	State legislator	U.S. Senate	50	Ohio	Canal worker	Williams	Educator, lawyer
21. Arthur (1881-1885)	31	State engineer	Vice president	51	N.Y.	Minister	Union	Lawyer
22. Cleveland (1885-1889) 24. (1893-1897)	26	Assistant district attorney	Governor	48	N.Y.	Minister	None	Lawyer
23. Harrison, B. (1889-1893)	24	City attorney	U.S. Senate	56	Ind.	Military	Miami of Ohio	Lawyer
25. McKinley (1897-1901)	26	Prosecuting attorney	Governor	54	Ohio	Ironmonger	Allegheny	Lawyer

President	Age at first political office	First political office	Last political office[a]	Age at becoming president	State of residence[b]	Father's occupation	Higher education[c]	Occupation
26. Roosevelt, T. (1901-1909)	24	State legislator	Vice president	43	N.Y.	Businessman	Harvard	Lawyer, author
27. Taft (1909-1913)	24	Assistant prosecuting attorney	Secretary of war	52	Ohio	Lawyer	Yale	Lawyer
28. Wilson (1913-1921)	54	Governor	Governor	56	N.J.	Minister	Princeton	Educator
29. Harding (1921-1923)	35	State legislator	U.S. Senate	56	Ohio	Physician, editor	Ohio Central	Newspaper editor
30. Coolidge (1923-1929)	26	City councilman	Vice president	51	Mass.	Storekeeper	Amherst	Lawyer
31. Hoover (1929-1933)	43	Relief and food administrator	Secretary of commerce	55	Calif.	Blacksmith	Stanford	Mining engineer
32. Roosevelt, F. (1933-1945)	28	State legislator	Governor	49	N.Y.	Businessman, landowner	Harvard	Lawyer
33. Truman (1945-1953)	38	County judge (commissioner)	Vice president	61	Mo.	Farmer, livestock	None	Clerk, store owner
34. Eisenhower (1953-1961)	—	None	[a]	63	Kan.	Mechanic	West Point	Military
35. Kennedy (1961-1963)	29	U.S. House of Representatives	U.S. Senate	43	Mass.	Businessman	Harvard	Newspaper reporter
36. Johnson, L. (1963-1969)	23	Assistant to member, U.S. House of Representatives	Vice president	55	Texas	Farmer, real estate	Southwest Texas State Teacher's College	Educator
37. Nixon (1969-1974)	29	Office of Price Administration	Vice president	56	Calif.	Streetcar conductor	Whittier	Lawyer
38. Ford (1974-1977)	36	U.S. House of Representatives	Vice president	61	Mich.	Businessman	U. of Michigan	Lawyer
39. Carter (1977-1981)	38	County Board of Education	Governor	52	Ga.	Farmer, businessman	U.S. Naval Academy	Farmer, businessman
40. Reagan (1981-1989)	55	Governor	Governor	69	Calif.	Shoe salesman	Eureka	Entertainer
41. Bush (1989-)	42	U.S. House of Representatives	Vice president	64	Texas	Businessman, U.S. senator	Yale	Businessman

Source: Richard A. Watson and Norman C. Thomas, *The Politics of the Presidency,* 2d ed. (Washington, D.C.: CQ Press, 1988), 515-519.
a. This category refers to the last civilian office held before the presidency. Taylor, Grant, and Eisenhower had served as generals before becoming president.
b. The state is where the president spent his important adult years, not necessarily where he was born.
c. Refers to undergraduate education.

What They Did Before They Became President

This list gives the terms of office for each president and the public jobs each held before becoming president.

George Washington. 1759-1774, Virginia House of Burgesses; 1774-1775, delegate to Continental Congress; 1775, commander of colonial Army; 1787, delegate to Constitutional Convention; 1789-1797, president.

John Adams. 1771, Massachusetts colonial legislature; 1774-1775, Continental Congress; 1778, minister to France; 1779, delegate to Massachusetts constitutional convention; 1780, minister to the Netherlands; 1785, minister to Great Britain; 1789-1797, vice president; 1797-1801, president.

Thomas Jefferson. 1769-1774, Virginia House of Burgesses; 1775, delegate to Continental Congress; 1775, delegate to Virginia convention; 1776, delegate to Continental Congress; 1776-1779, Virginia House of Delegates; 1779-1781, governor of Virginia; 1784-1789, envoy and minister to France; 1789-1793, secretary of state; 1797-1801, vice president; 1801-1809, president.

James Madison. 1774, Colonial Committee of Safety; 1776, delegate to Virginia convention; 1776-1777, Virginia House of Delegates; 1777, Virginia State Council; 1778, Virginia Executive Council; 1779-1783, Continental Congress; 1784-1786, Virginia House of Delegates; 1786-1788, Continental Congress; 1787, delegate to Constitutional Convention; 1789-1797, U.S. House of Representatives (Va.); 1801-1809, secretary of state; 1809-1817, president.

James Monroe. 1780, Virginia House of Delegates; 1781-1783, governor's council; 1783-1786, Continental Congress; 1786, Virginia House of Delegates; 1787, delegate to Constitutional Convention; 1790-1794, U.S. Senate (Va.); 1794-1796, minister to France; 1799-1803, governor of Virginia; 1803, minister to England and France; 1804, minister to Spain; 1810, Virginia House of Delegates; 1811-1817, secretary of state; 1814-15, secretary of war; 1817-1825, president.

John Quincy Adams. 1794, minister to Netherlands; 1796, minister to Portugal; 1797, minister to Prussia; 1802, Massachusetts Senate; 1803-1808, U.S. Senate (Mass.); 1809-1814, minister to Russia; 1815-1817, minister to Great Britain; 1817-1825, secretary of state; 1825-1829, president.

Andrew Jackson. 1788, solicitor for western North Carolina; 1796, delegate to Tennessee constitutional convention; 1796-1797, U.S. House (Tenn.); 1797-1798, U.S. Senate (Tenn.); 1798-1804, Tennessee Supreme Court; 1807, Tennessee Senate; 1812, commander, U.S. militia; 1814, general U.S. Army; 1821, governor of Florida; 1823-1825, U.S. Senate (Tenn.); 1829-1837, president.

Martin Van Buren. 1813-1820, New York Senate; 1815-1819, New York attorney general; 1821-1828, U.S. Senate; 1829, governor of New York; 1829, secretary of state; 1831, minister to Great Britain; 1833-1837, vice president; 1837-1841, president.

William Henry Harrison. 1798-1799, secretary of Northwest Territory; 1799-1800, U.S. House (territorial delegate); 1801-1813, territorial governor of Indiana; 1812-1814, general, U.S. Army; 1816-1819, U.S. House (Ohio); 1819-1821, Ohio Senate; 1825-1828, minister to Colombia; 1841, president.

John Tyler. 1811-1816, Virginia House of Delegates; 1816, Virginia State Council; 1817-1821, U.S. House (Va.); 1823-1825, Virginia House of Delegates; 1825-1827, governor of Virginia; 1827-1836, U.S. Senate (Va.); 1829, Virginia House of Delegates; 1841, vice president; 1841-1845, president.

James Knox Polk. 1821-1823, chief clerk, Tennessee Senate; 1823-1825, Tennessee House; 1825-1839, U.S. House (Tenn.); 1839-1841, governor of Tennessee; 1841-1845, president.

Zachary Taylor. 1808-1849, U.S. Army; 1849-1850, president.

Millard Fillmore. 1828-1831, New York Assembly; 1833-1835, U.S. House (N.Y.); 1837-1843, U.S. House (N.Y.); 1848-1849, New York controller; 1849-1850, vice president; 1850-1853, president.

Franklin Pierce. 1829-1833, New Hampshire House; 1833-1837, U.S. House (N.H.); 1837-1842, U.S. Senate (N.H.); 1850, New Hampshire constitutional convention; 1853-1857, president.

James Buchanan. 1814-1815, Pennsylvania House; 1821-1831, U.S. House (Pa.); 1832-1833, minister to Russia; 1834-1845, U.S. Senate (Pa.); 1845-1849, secretary of state; 1853, minister to Great Britain; 1857-1861, president.

Abraham Lincoln. 1833, postmaster, New Salem, Illinois; 1835-1836, Illinois General Assembly; 1847-1849, U.S. House (Ill.); 1861-1865, president.

Andrew Johnson. 1828-1829, alderman, Greeneville, Tenn.; 1830-1833, mayor, Greeneville, Tenn.; 1835-1837, Tennessee House; 1839-1841, Tennessee House; 1841, Tennessee Senate; 1843-1853, U.S. House (Tenn.); 1853-1857, governor of Tennessee; 1857-1862, U.S. Senate (Tenn.); 1862-1865, military governor of Tennessee; 1865, vice president; 1865-1869, president.

Ulysses S. Grant. 1843-1854, U.S. Army; 1861-1865, general, U.S. Army; 1867-1868, secretary of war; 1869-1877, president.

Rutherford B. Hayes. 1857-1859, Cincinnati city

solicitor; 1865-1867, U.S. House (Ohio); 1868, governor of Ohio; 1876-1877, governor of Ohio; 1877-1881, president.

James A. Garfield. 1859, Ohio Senate; 1863-1880, U.S. House (Ohio); 1881, president.

Chester A. Arthur. 1871-1878, collector for Port of New York; 1881, vice president; 1881-1885, president.

Grover Cleveland. 1863-1865, assistant district attorney of Erie County, N.Y.; 1871-1873, sheriff of Erie County, N.Y.; 1882, mayor of Buffalo, N.Y.; 1883-1885, governor of New York; 1885-1889, president; 1893-1897, president.

Benjamin Harrison. 1864-1868, reporter of decisions, Indiana Supreme Court; 1879, member, Mississippi River Commission; 1881-1887, U.S. Senate (Ind.); 1889-1893, president.

William McKinley. 1869-1871, prosecutor, Stark County, Ohio; 1877-1883, U.S. House (Ohio); 1885-1891, U.S. House (Ohio); 1892-1896, governor of Ohio; 1897-1901, president.

Theodore Roosevelt. 1882-1884, New York State Assembly; 1889-1895, U.S. Civil Service Commission; 1895, president of New York City board of police commissioners; 1897, assistant secretary of the Navy; 1898, U.S. Army; 1899-1901, governor of New York; 1901, vice president; 1901-1909, president.

William Howard Taft. 1881-1882, assistant prosecutor, Cincinnati; 1887, assistant city solicitor, Cincinnati; 1887-1890, Cincinnati Superior Court; 1890-1892, U.S. solicitor general; 1892-1900, U.S. Circuit Court; 1900-1901, president of Philippines Commission; 1901, governor general, Philippine Islands; 1904-1908, secretary of war; 1907, provisional governor of Cuba; 1909-1913, president.

Woodrow Wilson. 1911-1913, governor of New Jersey; 1913-1921, president.

Warren G. Harding. 1895, auditor of Marion County, Ohio; 1899-1903, Ohio Senate; 1904-1905, lieutenant governor of Ohio; 1915-1921, U.S. Senate (Ohio); 1921-1923, president.

Calvin Coolidge. 1899, city council of Northampton, Mass.; 1900-1901, city solicitor of Northampton, Mass.; 1903-1904, clerk of the courts, Hampshire County, Mass.; 1907-1908, Massachusetts House; 1910-1911, mayor of Northampton, Mass.; 1912-1915, Massachusetts Senate; 1916-1918, lieutenant governor of Massachusetts; 1919-1920, governor of Massachusetts; 1921-1923, vice president; 1923-1929, president.

Herbert Hoover. 1914-1915, chairman of American Committee in London; 1915-1918, chairman, Commission for the Relief of Belgium; 1917-1919, U.S. food administrator; 1919, chairman, Supreme Economic Conference in Paris; 1920, chairman, European Relief Council; 1921-1928, secretary of commerce; 1929-1933, president.

Franklin D. Roosevelt. 1911-1913, New York Senate; 1913-1920, assistant secretary of the Navy; 1929-1933, governor of New York; 1933-1945, president.

Harry S Truman. 1926-1934, administrative judge, court of Jackson County, Missouri; 1935-1945, U.S. Senate; 1945, vice president; 1945-1953, president.

Dwight D. Eisenhower. 1915-1948, U.S. Army; 1950-1952, commander of NATO forces in Europe; 1953-1961, president.

John F. Kennedy. 1947-1953, U.S. House (Mass.); 1953-1961, U.S. Senate (Mass.); 1961-1963, president.

Lyndon B. Johnson. 1935-1937, Texas director of National Youth Administration; 1937-1948, U.S. House (Texas); 1949-1961, U.S. Senate (Texas); 1961-1963, vice president; 1963-1969, president.

Richard M. Nixon. 1947-1951, U.S. House (Calif.); 1951-1953, U.S. Senate (Calif.); 1953-1961, vice president; 1969-1974, president.

Gerald R. Ford. 1949-1973, U.S. House (Mich.); 1973-1974, vice president; 1974-1977, president.

Jimmy Carter. 1955-1962, chairman, Sumter County (Ga.) Board of Education; 1963-1967, Georgia Senate; 1971-1975, governor of Georgia; 1977-1981, president.

Ronald Reagan. 1942-1946, Army Air Corps; 1967-1975, governor of California; 1981-1989, president.

George Bush. 1942-1945, U.S. Navy; 1967-1971, U.S. House (Texas); 1971-1972, U.S. ambassador to the United Nations; 1974-1975, chief of U.S. Liaison Office, Beijing, People's Republic of China; 1976-1977, director of Central Intelligence Agency; 1981-1988, vice president; 1989—, president.

Summary of Presidential Elections, 1824-1988

Year	No. of states	Candidates		Electoral vote		Popular vote	
1824[a]	24	Dem.-Rep.	Dem.-Rep.	Dem.-Rep.	Dem.-Rep.	Dem.-Rep.	Dem.-Rep.
		Andrew Jackson	John Q. Adams	99	84	151,271	113,122
				38%	32%	41.3%	30.9%
1828	24	Dem.-Rep.	Nat.-Rep.	Dem.-Rep.	Nat.-Rep.	Dem.-Rep.	Nat.-Rep.
		Andrew Jackson	John Q. Adams	178	83	642,553	500,897
				68%	32%	56.0%	43.6%
1832[b]	24	Dem.	Nat.-Rep.	Dem.	Nat.-Rep.	Dem.	Nat.-Rep.
		Andrew Jackson	Henry Clay	219	49	701,780	484,205
				76%	17%	54.2%	37.4%
1836[c]	26	Dem.	Whig	Dem.	Whig	Dem.	Whig
		Martin Van Buren	William H. Harrison	170	73	764,176	550,816
				58%	25%	50.8%	36.6%
1840	26	Dem.	Whig	Dem.	Whig	Dem.	Whig
		Martin Van Buren	William H. Harrison	60	234	1,275,390	1,128,854
				20%	80%	52.9%	46.8%
1844	26	Dem.	Whig	Dem.	Whig	Dem.	Whig
		James Polk	Henry Clay	170	105	1,339,494	1,300,004
				62%	38%	49.5%	48.1%
1848	30	Dem.	Whig	Dem.	Whig	Dem.	Whig
		Lewis Cass	Zachary Taylor	127	163	1,361,393	1,223,460
				44%	56%	47.3%	42.5%
1852	31	Dem.	Whig	Dem.	Whig	Dem.	Whig
		Franklin Pierce	Winfield Scott	254	42	1,607,510	1,386,942
				86%	14%	50.8%	43.9%

Year	No. of states	Candidates		Electoral Vote		Popular Vote	
		Dem.	Rep.	Dem.	Rep.	Dem.	Rep.
1856[d]	31	James Buchanan	John C. Fremont	174	114	1,836,072	1,342,345
				59%	39%	45.3%	33.1%
1860[e]	33	Stephen A. Douglas	Abraham Lincoln	12	180	1,380,202	1,865,908
		Herschel V. Johnson	Hannibal Hamlin	4%	59%	29.5%	39.8%
1864[f]	36	George B. McClellan	Abraham Lincoln	21	212	1,812,807	2,218,388
		George H. Pendleton	Andrew Johnson	9%	91%	45.0%	55.0%
1868[g]	37	Horatio Seymour	Ulysses S. Grant	80	214	2,708,744	3,013,650
		Francis P. Blair, Jr.	Schuyler Colfax	27%	73%	47.3%	52.7%
1872[h]	37	Horace Greeley	Ulysses S. Grant		286	2,834,761	3,598,235
		Benjamin Gratz Brown	Henry Wilson		78%	43.8%	55.6%
1876	38	Samuel J. Tilden	Rutherford B. Hayes	184	185	4,288,546	4,034,311
		Thomas A. Hendricks	William A. Wheeler	50%	50%	51.0%	47.9%
1880	38	Winfield S. Hancock	James A. Garfield	155	214	4,444,260	4,446,158
		William H. English	Chester A. Arthur	42%	58%	48.2%	48.3%
1884	38	Grover Cleveland	James G. Blaine	219	182	4,874,621	4,848,936
		Thomas A. Hendricks	John A. Logan	55%	45%	48.5%	48.2%
1888	38	Grover Cleveland	Benjamin Harrison	168	233	5,534,488	5,443,892
		Allen G. Thurman	Levi P. Morton	42%	58%	48.6%	47.8%
1892[i]	44	Grover Cleveland	Benjamin Harrison	277	145	5,551,883	5,179,244
		Adlai E. Stevenson	Whitelaw Reid	62%	33%	46.1%	43.0%

Year	No. of states	Candidates Dem.	Candidates Rep.	Electoral Vote Dem.	Electoral Vote Rep.	Popular Vote Dem.	Popular Vote Rep.
1896	45	William J. Bryan Arthur Sewall	William McKinley Garret A. Hobart	176 39%	271 61%	6,511,495 46.7%	7,108,480 51.0%
1900	45	William J. Bryan Adlai E. Stevenson	William McKinley Theodore Roosevelt	155 35%	292 65%	6,358,345 45.5%	7,218,039 51.7%
1904	45	Alton B. Parker Henry G. Davis	Theodore Roosevelt Charles W. Fairbanks	140 29%	336 71%	5,028,898 37.6%	7,626,593 56.4%
1908	46	William J. Bryan John W. Kern	William H. Taft James S. Sherman	162 34%	321 66%	6,406,801 43.0%	7,676,258 51.6%
1912[j]	48	Woodrow Wilson Thomas R. Marshall	William H. Taft James S. Sherman	435 82%	8 2%	6,293,152 41.8%	3,486,333 23.2%
1916	48	Woodrow Wilson Thomas R. Marshall	Charles E. Hughes Charles W. Fairbanks	277 52%	254 48%	9,126,300 49.2%	8,546,789 46.1%
1920	48	James M. Cox Franklin D. Roosevelt	Warren G. Harding Calvin Coolidge	127 24%	404 76%	9,140,884 34.2%	16,133,314 60.3%
1924[k]	48	John W. Davis Charles W. Bryant	Calvin Coolidge Charles G. Dawes	136 26%	382 72%	8,386,169 28.8%	15,717,553 54.1%
1928	48	Alfred E. Smith Joseph T. Robinson	Herbert C. Hoover Charles Curtis	87 16%	444 84%	15,000,185 40.8%	21,411,991 58.2%
1932	48	Franklin D. Roosevelt John N. Garner	Herbert C. Hoover Charles Curtis	472 89%	59 11%	22,825,016 57.4%	15,758,397 39.6%
1936	48	Franklin D. Roosevelt John N. Garner	Alfred M. London Frank Knox	523 98%	8 2%	27,747,636 60.8%	16,679,543 36.5%
1940	48	Franklin D. Roosevelt Henry A. Wallace	Wendell L. Willkie Charles L. McNary	449 85%	82 15%	27,263,448 54.7%	22,336,260 44.8%
1944	48	Franklin D. Roosevelt Harry S Truman	Thomas E. Dewey John W. Bricker	432 81%	99 19%	25,611,936 53.4%	22,013,372 45.9%
1948[l]	48	Harry S Truman Alben W. Barkley	Thomas E. Dewey Earl Warren	303 57%	189 36%	24,105,587 49.5%	21,970,017 45.1%
1952	48	Adlai E. Stevenson John J. Sparkman	Dwight D. Eisenhower Richard M. Nixon	89 17%	442 83%	27,314,649 44.4%	33,936,137 55.1%
1956[m]	48	Adlai E. Stevenson Estes Kefauver	Dwight D. Eisenhower Richard M. Nixon	73 14%	457 86%	26,030,172 42.0%	35,585,245 57.4%
1960[n]	50	John F. Kennedy Lyndon B. Johnson	Richard M. Nixon Henry Cabot Lodge	303 56%	219 41%	34,221,344 49.7%	34,106,671 49.5%
1964	50*	Lyndon B. Johnson Hubert H. Humphrey	Barry Goldwater William E. Miller	486 90%	52 10%	43,126,584 61.1%	27,177,838 38.5%
1968[o]	50*	Hubert H. Humphrey Edmund S. Muskie	Richard M. Nixon Spiro T. Agnew	191 36%	301 56%	31,274,503 42.7%	31,785,148 43.4%
1972[p]	50*	George McGovern Sargent Shriver	Richard M. Nixon Spiro T. Agnew	17 3%	520 97%	29,171,791 37.5%	47,170,179 60.7%
1976[q]	50*	Jimmy Carter Walter F. Mondale	Gerald R. Ford Robert Dole	297 55%	240 45%	40,830,763 50.1%	39,147,793 48.0%
1980	50*	Jimmy Carter Walter F. Mondale	Ronald Reagan George Bush	49 9%	489 91%	35,483,883 41.0%	43,904,153 50.7%
1984	50*	Walter F. Mondale Geraldine Ferraro	Ronald Reagan George Bush	13 2%	525 98%	37,577,185 40.6%	54,455,075 58.8%

Year	No. of states	Candidates		Electoral Vote		Popular Vote	
		Dem.	Rep.	Dem.	Rep.	Dem.	Rep.
1988[r]	50*	Michael S. Dukakis	George Bush	111	426	41,809,074	48,886,097
		Lloyd Bentsen	Dan Quayle	21%	79%	45.6%	53.4%

Source: Congressional Quarterly's Guide to the Presidency, ed. Michael Nelson (Washington, D.C.: Congressional Quarterly Inc., 1989), 1439-1441.

Note: Dem.-Rep.—Democratic-Republican; Nat.-Rep.—National-Republican; Dem.—Democratic; Rep.—Republican.

a. 1824: All four candidates represented Democratic-Republican factions. William H. Crawford polled 41 electoral votes and Henry Clay polled 37 votes. Because no candidate received a majority, the election was decided (in Adams's favor) by the House of Representatives.
b. 1832: 2 electoral votes were not cast.
c. 1836: Other Whig candidates receiving electoral votes were Hugh L. White, who polled 26 votes, and Daniel Webster, who polled 14 votes.
d. 1856: Millard Fillmore, Whig-American, polled 8 electoral votes.
e. 1860: John C. Breckinridge, Southern Democrat, polled 72 electoral votes. John Bell, Constitutional Union, polled 39 electoral votes.
f. 1864: 81 electoral votes were not cast.
g. 1868: 23 electoral votes were not cast.
h. 1872: Horace Greeley, Democrat, died after the election. In the electoral college, Democratic electoral votes went to Thomas Hendricks, 42 votes; B. Gratz Brown, 18 votes; Charles J. Jenkins, 2 votes; and David Davis, 1 vote. 17 electoral votes were not cast.
i. 1892: James B. Weaver, People's party, polled 22 electoral votes.
j. 1912: Theodore Roosevelt, Progressive party, polled 86 electoral votes.
k. 1924: Robert M. La Follette, Progressive party, polled 13 electoral votes.
l. 1948: J. Strom Thurmond, States' Rights party, polled 39 electoral votes.
m. 1956: Walter B. Jones, Democrat, polled 1 electoral vote.
n. 1960: Harry Flood Byrd, Democrat, polled 15 electoral votes.
o. 1968: George C. Wallace, American Independent party, polled 46 electoral votes.
p. 1972: John Hospers, Libertarian party, polled 1 electoral vote.
q. 1976: Ronald Reagan, Republican, polled 1 electoral vote.
r. 1988: Lloyd Bentsen, the Democratic vice presidential nominee, polled 1 electoral vote for president.
* Fifty states plus District of Columbia.

Part III

Congressional and Gubernatorial Elections

Politics and Issues: 1945-1989

This chapter is a narrative chronology of the political and legislative events of the years after World War II, outlining the trends that have brought the country to its present circumstances. Following the chapter are the final, official election returns for the Senate, House, and governorships in 1986 and 1988 and a breakdown of gubernatorial and senatorial primary votes for 1986-1988.

The Postwar Years

By the end of World War II the American people had come to two fundamental decisions that would have a deep influence on the political life of the nation in the postwar years from 1945 through the mid-1960s. In domestic affairs Americans in general had concluded that the social and economic reforms of the New Deal years ought to be preserved and that government had a legitimate role in protecting the individual against economic disaster. On the international front isolationism clearly was rejected in favor of acceptance of a role of active leadership for the United States in world affairs.

These two decisions paved the way for a politics of national consensus in the postwar years. The ideological conflicts of the 1930s were softened, and it was possible for the two major political parties to argue more about means and less about basic national aims.

The main issue usually was which party could best provide for the needs of the people in a steadily expanding economy and at the same time provide firm, reliable leadership for the United States and the free world in a protracted cold war with the Communist bloc. Implicit in both parties' appeals were two basic elements: an acceptance of government's role in the social welfare field and close industry-government ties at home, coupled with a desire to avoid nuclear confrontation with the Soviet Union abroad. When, in 1964, one of the two major national parties sought to deny this postwar consensus in both its domestic and foreign aspects, it encountered the most sweeping electoral repudiation in a quarter-century.

By and large the Democratic party was more successful than the Republican in presenting itself as the party better able to carry out the national consensus in the postwar years. Three Democrats were elected to the presidency—Harry S Truman, John F. Kennedy, and Lyndon B. Johnson—while only one Republican, Dwight D. Eisenhower,

was successful, and then largely because of his status as a hero of World War II. Of the ten Congresses elected in the postwar period, eight had Democratic and only two had Republican majorities. Except for brief periods in 1947-1948 and 1951-1954 the Democrats held a majority of the state governorships. Democrats maintained regular majorities in most state legislatures. Even the eight-year incumbency of a Republican president failed to strengthen the Republican party appreciably.

The frequent Democratic victories, however, did not reflect the depth of loyalty to the Democratic party that had existed in the 1930s, when the fresh recollection of the Great Depression maintained an unwavering Democratic mandate. In fact, the political movements of the postwar period demonstrated a rapidly changing and ambiguous electoral mandate: Republicans scored major victories in 1946 and 1952, but the Democrats achieved significant and far-reaching success in 1948, 1958, and 1964.

Even in the years of party sweeps voters showed an increasing tendency to vote for the candidate rather than the party. The trend toward split tickets was especially evident in 1956, when Eisenhower was reelected by a landslide but the Democrats held Congress, and in 1964, when numerous Republican candidates eked out narrow victories despite the massive national vote for Johnson. Part of the trend toward split tickets could be attributed to an increasingly well educated electorate. But it also seemed to reflect a willingness among the voters to support superior candidates of either party—candidates who represented, in large part, the domestic and foreign policy consensus of the postwar era.

In the early 1960s a new awareness emerged on the issue of civil rights. Civil rights for black citizens had divided northern and southern Democrats in Congress for decades and had even caused a rump southern Dixiecrat party in the 1948 presidential election. But pressures for equal rights for blacks continued to increase and reached a climax with a series of nationwide demonstrations in 1963. Many white Americans, with church and union groups at the fore, joined the fight for legislative action for equal rights. The result was the comprehensive, bipartisanly sponsored Civil Rights Act of 1964.

Throughout the postwar period Congress was slower to reflect the national consensus on major issues than were the president or the judicial branch of the government. As a rule it was the executive branch that proposed major new programs in fields such as education, welfare, and domestic aid—programs that Congress accepted slowly if at all. And it was the Supreme Court that, with its 1954 decision outlawing segregation in the public schools, sparked the movement toward bringing blacks into the mainstream of American life. Other decisions of the Court on constitutional rights, ranging from legislative apportionment to the rights of witnesses and the accused, far outstripped anything Congress was willing to consider.

When Congress did assume a more central role—helping, for instance, to formulate and develop foreign aid programs from the mid-1940s on, pushing aggressively for broader domestic programs while Eisenhower was in the White House, or remolding and expanding the scope of the 1964 Civil Rights Act—its actions stood out as exceptions to the pattern of executive or judicial initiative.

Congress's conservatism and its reticence in initiating programs were based in large part on the committee seniority system and restrictive legislative rules. Committee chairmen often were southern Democrats or midwestern Republicans, representing the most rigidly held districts and states. The congressional representatives least able to build up seniority, and thus the least likely to head committees, were those from the politically volatile suburbs and city fringe areas where the major new population movements—and many major problems—of the postwar era occurred.

During this period the House, intended by the Framers of the Constitution to be the chamber closest to the people, actually was the more conservative body, blocking a substantial amount of legislation approved by the Senate. The Senate, especially after the liberal Democratic sweep of 1958, became markedly liberal in its orientation. A principal explanation for the Senate's position was that metropolitan centers, with their pressing demands, had sprung up in virtually every state, prompting senators to be responsive to their needs.

The postwar era might be remembered as one in which both American parties became truly national. Democrats extended their power and influence into midwestern and northern New England territory that had been unwaveringly Republican in the past. Republicans made significant new breakthroughs in the growing industrial South and in their best years won the votes of millions of Americans who had never voted Republican before.

The 1964 election, at the end of the era, left the Democratic party in control of most of the power centers, from the presidency to the state legislatures. But many Republicans, noting the somber outcome of an election in which their party had moved far to the right and by implication had repudiated the national stance on most matters, began to work to return the party to a central course. The 1964 election, by underlining the strength of the American consensus on vital issues of domestic economy, civil rights, and foreign policy, had demonstrated anew the broad opportunities for a party willing to offer solutions to national needs.

1945-1947:
The Seventy-ninth Congress

The death of a president who had led his country through twelve years of economic and military crisis, the end of the greatest war in history, and the inauguration of the atomic age all took place in the two-year interval between Franklin D. Roosevelt's election to a fourth term in 1944 and the 1946 midterm congressional elections.

The president died April 12, 1945, of a cerebral hemorrhage. Two weeks later, on April 25, delegates from Allied powers gathered in San Francisco to write the United Nations charter. (The U.S. Senate ratified the charter July 28, a contrast to the unwillingness of the Senate in 1919 to join the League of Nations.) On April 28 Italian partisans captured and butchered dictator Benito Mussolini. Adolf Hitler was reported to have committed suicide April 29 in his ruined Berlin chancery while Soviet troops poured into the city. Germany surrendered unconditionally on May 7.

In the Pacific, American airplanes administered the coup de grace to the tottering Japanese empire by dropping the first atomic bomb on Hiroshima August 6, 1945; another was used on Nagasaki August 9. World War II ended with the unconditional surrender of Japan on August 14.

In 1944, running on the theme that the nation shouldn't "change horses in the middle of the stream," President Roosevelt had won an unprecedented fourth term with a national vote plurality of 3,598,564 (of 47,974,819 cast) and a total of 432 (of 531) electoral votes. Reversing Democratic losses in the 1942 midterm elections, Congress went heavily Democratic. After the 1944 election 57 Democrats and 38 Republicans were in the Senate, and the House was balanced 243-190 in favor of the Democrats. Eighty-three days later Roosevelt was dead.

Roosevelt's successor, Harry S Truman, took office April 12. He faced a perplexing task as he sought to hold together the coalition of big-city machines, organized labor, conservative southern Democrats, farmers, minority groups, ethnic and religious blocs, and intellectual liberals, which FDR had brought together for his successive electoral victories.

Pent-up tensions erupted with the end of World War II. The country was hit by strikes, climaxed in June 1946 by a nationwide rail strike, which President Truman tried to break with a "labor draft," thus incurring deep resentment in the ranks of organized labor. On the right wing southern Democrats continued to bolt the administration on almost every item of domestic legislation as they had since 1938. Conservative forces in Congress pressed for a relaxation of wartime price controls far more rapidly than Truman thought advisable.

Despite its failure to reach agreement on such basic issues as labor-management relations, a national housing program, federal aid to schools, and national health insurance, the Seventy-ninth Congress produced some notable legislation, including the Atomic Energy Act of 1946, which transferred control over all aspects of atomic energy development from the War Department to a civilian Atomic Energy Commission.

The Employment Act of 1946, considerably weaker than the "Full Employment" bill first proposed—which bordered on a government guarantee of jobs for all—nevertheless broke new ground in fixing responsibility for national economic policies. The Hospital Survey and Construction Act of 1946 authorized a program of matching federal grants to state and local health bodies for hospital construction. The Legislative Reorganization Act of 1946 cut the number of standing committees in the House and the Senate, provided for preparation of an annual legislative budget to complement the president's budget, and raised the salaries of senators and representatives from $10,000 to $12,500, plus a $2,500 tax-free expense account. Included in the law, as a separate title, was the Federal Regulation of Lobbying Act, requiring lobbyists to register and report their lobbying expenses.

Congress also authorized a fifty-year loan of $3.75 billion to Great Britain, intended to assist the British in removing trade and currency exchange restrictions hampering postwar programs for economic reconstruction and trade liberalization.

The 1946 Midterm Elections

The 1946 congressional election campaign was marked by two events disadvantageous to the administration. First, President Truman on September 20, 1946, dismissed Secretary of Commerce Henry A. Wallace, former vice president (1941-1945) and only original New Dealer still remaining in the cabinet and a spokesman of labor and progressive groups. The dismissal followed a speech Wallace gave—which Wallace had read to Truman in advance—criticizing the allegedly anti-Soviet tone of foreign policy Under Secretary of State James F. Byrnes. The incident encouraged Republicans to pin the "red" label on all candidates for whom Wallace subsequently spoke during the campaign.

A second bad break for the administration came in a seven-week national meat shortage just before the election. Truman was forced to issue an order, October 14, ending all meat price controls. His action drew sharp criticism from organized labor and a charge by the Republican national chairman, Rep. B. Carroll Reece of Tennessee, that he was taking action "after the horse has gone to the butcher shop." The mood of the country was clearly in favor of an early end to all remaining wartime controls. The pent-up frustrations of wartime were directly appealed to in the Republican slogans—"Had enough?" and "It's time for a change." Reece promised that a Republican Congress would restore "orderly, capable and honest government in Washington and replace controls, confusion, corruption and communism."

Symptomatic of the tone of the times—pictured by contemporary observers as a desire to return to "normalcy"—were two election-morning newspaper headlines. One read, "Gay Crowd Hails Return of National Horse Show." A second read, "Crackers, Sugar Back in Stores."

The Democratic congressional campaign was lackadaisical. Democratic national Chairman Robert E. Hannegan did warn the country that a GOP victory would be a "surrender to the will of a few who want only large profits for themselves." But Truman failed to hit the campaign trail and offered scarcely any comment on the important races and issues.

The Democrats appeared to depend in large measure on frequent radio broadcasts of the late president Roosevelt's campaign addresses recorded in earlier years. The most publicized activity for Democratic candidates was carried out by the political action committee of the CIO (Congress of Industrial Organizations), headed by the controversial Sidney Hillman.

Results of the 1946 Elections

The 1946 campaign proved to be the most successful for the Republicans since the 1920s—and the best year they would have for many years to come. Across the nation Republicans swept Senate, House, and gubernatorial contests. The Republicans increased their Senate membership from 38 to 51 seats, while the Democrats slipped from 57 to 45 seats.

Among the new Republican senators were John W. Bricker of Ohio, Irving M. Ives of New York, William E. Jenner of Indiana, William F. Knowland of California (who had been appointed to the Senate in 1945), George W. Malone of Nevada, Arthur V. Watkins of Utah, and John J. Williams of Delaware. The Progressive candidate, Robert La Follette, Jr., of Wisconsin, lost to Republican Joseph R. McCarthy. With the exception of Ives, all represented their party's most conservative wing.

The House Republican delegation rose from 190 seats to 246 seats, while the Democratic delegation dropped from 243 to 188; this was the lowest figure since the 1928 elections. The ratio among the nation's governorships changed from 26-22 in favor of the Democrats to 25-23 in favor of the Republicans.

Important Republican gubernatorial victories included the reelection of Thomas E. Dewey of New York and Earl Warren of California and the elections of Robert F. Bradford of Massachusetts, Alfred E. Driscoll of New Jersey, James H. Duff of Pennsylvania, Thomas J. Herbert of Ohio, Kim Sigler of Michigan, and L. W. Youngdahl of Minnesota. The only Democrats to win in generally two-party states were William L. Knous of Colorado, William P. Lane, Jr., of Maryland, and Lester C. Hunt of Wyoming.

1947-1949:
The Eightieth Congress

In 1947 and 1948 the nation proceeded to shake off most of the remaining wartime economic controls and to enjoy an economic boom marred somewhat by substantial inflation and the beginnings of the first postwar recession in late 1948. Americans began to realize that the postwar period would be one of continuing international tensions rather than a return to "normalcy."

The foreign scene was darkened by increasing Soviet intransigence at the United Nations; by the civil war in Greece and Communist pressures on Turkey, which led to announcement of the Truman Doctrine in 1947; by the ouster of non-Communists from the Hungarian government in May 1947; by the Communist coup d'état in Czechoslovakia in February 1948; and by the beginning of the Soviet blockade of Berlin in April 1948. Faced with the responsibility of formulating new solutions for the new problems of the postwar era, the Republican-controlled Eightieth Congress wrote some basic laws that governed domestic and foreign policy for many years to come.

On May 15, 1947, Congress approved the Greek-Turkish aid program requested by President Truman (the Truman Doctrine). The concept of massive economic aid to European countries to assist them in their postwar recovery, suggested by Secretary of State George C. Marshall, received final congressional approval in passage of the European Recovery Program (Marshall Plan) April 2, 1948. International tensions paved the way for congressional approval of a peacetime draft law June 19, 1948.

The legislation that placed the most strain on bipartisan foreign policy was extension of the Reciprocal Trade Agreements Act. Congress in 1948 turned down presidential requests for a three-year extension, granting only a single year's extension in a limited form.

During its first session the Eightieth Congress approved legislation for unifying the armed forces under a single Department of Defense with separate Army, Navy, and Air Force departments under the secretary of defense, and for forming the Central Intelligence Agency.

In domestic affairs the Democratic president and Republican Congress generally were at loggerheads. Presidential recommendations to extend New Deal social welfare concepts were largely ignored by Congress. The most significant single piece of domestic legislation approved by the Congress was the Taft-Hartley Labor-Management Relations Act, passed over President Truman's veto June 23, 1947. The bill outlawed the closed shop, jurisdictional strikes, and secondary boycotts and was bitterly opposed by organized labor. Its chief provisions were to remain on the statute books throughout the postwar period.

The Eightieth Congress completed two significant actions concerning the office of president: it passed a bill, approved by Truman on July 18, 1947, making the Speaker and the president pro tempore of the Senate the next two in line of succession to the presidency after the vice president, ahead of the secretary of state and other cabinet members. In a slap at President Roosevelt's four terms, it sent to the states a constitutional amendment limiting the tenure of future presidents to two terms. The Twenty-second Amendment became law in February 1951.

The Communist issue monopolized national attention in the summer of 1948, as Elizabeth Bentley and Whittaker Chambers, self-confessed former Communist party members, spread before the House Un-American Activities Committee charges that numerous high administration officials during the 1930s and war years had been members of Communist spy rings. Chambers's August 3 testimony that former State Department aide Alger Hiss had been a Communist spy became the most celebrated case of all. It was highly dramatized on nationwide television on August 25, when Hiss and Chambers confronted each other at a hearing of the committee.

The 1948 Campaigns

Truman's underdog victory in the 1948 presidential election set the pattern of rapid and startling reversals in domestic political trends during the postwar years. His victory was accompanied by a Democratic congressional and gubernatorial sweep that reversed, in overwhelming measure, the Republican triumph of 1946.

The year 1947 had appeared to be a favorable one for Truman. The Marshall Plan, his "get-tough-with-Russia" policy, his advocacy of government action to curb rising prices, and his willingness to deal firmly with labor leader John L. Lewis had all increased the president's popularity in sharp contrast to its nadir at the time of the 1946 elections. In November 1947 elections the Democrats were especially successful, electing a governor in Kentucky and winning other important races.

By the late spring of 1948, however, Truman's popularity had plummeted to such depths that leaders of his own party cast about for another nominee to head the Democratic ticket. Several developments contributed to the sharp dip in presidential popularity. Reacting in part to Henry A. Wallace's December 1947 announcement that he was forming a third party, Truman included in his 1948 State of the Union address requests for new social welfare legislation plus a call for a straight $40 tax cut for each individual in the nation. Even some liberal Democrats accused the president of having made a "political harangue" in the most partisan spirit.

In February the president's advocacy of a far-sweeping civil rights program, based on recommendations of his civil rights commission, created a predictably bitter reaction in the southern wing of his party. The stage was set for the States' Rights ticket, putting four parties in the upcoming presidential campaign. Truman's reelection in the face of open revolts on the left wing (Wallaceites) and the right wing (Dixiecrats) seemed almost impossible.

Fearing defeat for the party in the November elections, an unusual coalition of Democrats began to press in late spring for General Dwight D. Eisenhower's nomination by the Democratic National Convention. The coalition included states' rights southerners, big-city bosses from the North, and party liberals. In statements on June 5 and 9, however, Eisenhower made clear his refusal to consider seeking or accepting the nomination. Neither Eisenhower's political philosophy nor his party was known; it was not until 1952 that he identified himself as a Republican.

A brief effort to draft Supreme Court Justice William O. Douglas also collapsed. No further obstacle remained to Truman's renomination when the Democrats assembled gloomily in Philadelphia July 12 for their thirtieth national convention.

Truman was nominated on the first ballot on July 15, receiving 947-1/2 votes to 263 for Sen. Richard Russell of Georgia. Senate Democratic leader Alben W. Barkley of Kentucky, who had roused the delegates with a fiery keynote speech July 12, was later nominated for vice president.

Truman's acceptance speech created a sensation. Lashing into the Republicans as "the party of special interests," he called for repeal of the Taft-Hartley Act, criticized Congress for its failure to control prices or pass a housing bill, and said that the tax reduction measure approved was a "Republican rich-man's tax bill." He then announced it was his duty to call Congress back into session on July 26 to act on anti-inflation legislation, housing, aid to education, a national health program, civil rights, an increase in the minimum wage from 40 cents to 75 cents hourly, extension of Social Security, public power and cheaper electricity projects, and a new "adequate" displaced-persons bill.

The closing day of the Democratic convention was marked by a walkout of delegations from Mississippi and Alabama, when the convention, at the instigation of Minneapolis mayor Hubert H. Humphrey and other party liberals, adopted a tough substitute civil rights plank. Following an impassioned speech by Humphrey in behalf of the stronger plank, the convention approved it by a 651-1/2 to 582-1/2 vote, substituting it for a noncontroversial plank recommended by the Resolutions (Platform) Committee.

Rebellious southerners from thirteen states convened in Birmingham, Alabama, on July 17 as the States' Rights party and nominated Gov. J. Strom Thurmond, D-S.C., for president and Gov. Fielding L. Wright, D-Miss., for vice president. They urged southern Democratic parties to substitute Thurmond and Wright for Truman and Barkley as the Democratic candidates on the ballot. The convention adopted a platform terming the national Democratic civil rights plank "this infamous and iniquitous program" that would mean a "police state in a totalitarian, centralized, bureaucratic government." The platform said, "We stand for the segregation of the races and the integrity of each race."

Another group met in Philadelphia in July. Calling itself the Progressive party, it nominated Henry A. Wallace for president and Sen. Glen H. Taylor, D-Idaho, for vice president. Party leaders denied that the party was Communist-dominated, though most observers considered it heavily influenced by the extreme left. In his acceptance speech Wallace blamed Truman for the Berlin crisis. He said there had been a "great betrayal" following President Roosevelt's death in which the administration inaugurated its "get tough" policy, thus "slamming the door" on peace talks with the Soviet Union. The Progressive platform called for a program of U.S. disarmament, a conciliatory policy toward the Soviet Union, an end to segregation, nationalization of key industries, repeal of Taft-Hartley, high farm price supports, and the Townsend plan, giving a $100 monthly pension to everyone at the age of sixty.

Scenting victory, Republicans engaged in a lively contest for their party's presidential nomination. The three chief candidates were New York governor Thomas E. Dewey, former Minnesota governor Harold E. Stassen, and Sen. Robert A. Taft of Ohio. Taft enjoyed the support of most of the more conservative party regulars.

As the primaries developed during the spring, it first appeared that Stassen might be on his way to the nomination. After losing to Dewey in New Hampshire, he won an overwhelming victory in Wisconsin over Dewey and native son Gen. Douglas MacArthur, who had been considered the strong favorite. Stassen won nineteen delegates to eight for MacArthur and none for Dewey. In the Nebraska primary Stassen again won against Dewey, Taft, and several other candidates whose names were placed on the ballot.

Observers began to predict Stassen's nomination, but he then made what later appeared to be a serious error. He entered the May 4 Ohio primary, bluntly antagonizing the Taft wing of the party. (He won only nine of the twenty-three contested delegate spots, the rest going to Taft.) In Oregon, where Stassen had been an early favorite, he lost to Dewey in the May 21 primary (117,554 votes to 107,946), after a radio debate between the two men in which Stassen endorsed and Dewey opposed outlawing the Communist party. Observers believe the debate and primary returns effectively finished Stassen's chances.

When the twenty-fourth Republican National Convention opened in Philadelphia June 21, the Dewey victory already seemed probable. Taft was handicapped because many conservatives considered his stands for federal aid to education and housing too liberal, while many party professionals feared his co-authorship of the Taft-Hartley Act might harm the party among union voters. California governor Earl Warren and Michigan senator Arthur Vandenberg both had hopes that a convention deadlock might turn the delegates toward them, but neither ambition was justified. Dewey began with the solid bloc of New York State and enjoyed substantial support in delegations from every part of the country.

In first ballot voting June 24, with 547 needed to win, Dewey received 434 votes to 224 for Taft and 157 for Stassen. Favorite-son candidates shared the rest. On the second ballot Dewey's total rose to 515 against 274 for Taft and 149 for Stassen. Following this, the other candidates quickly fell behind Dewey. His nomination on the third roll call was merely a formality.

During the following night Dewey conferred with influential party leaders and decided on Governor Warren as his running mate. The party adopted a platform backing a "bipartisan" foreign policy, foreign aid to anti-Communist countries, "full" recognition of Israel, housing, anti-inflation, and civil rights legislation, and promised a fight against Communists inside and outside government.

The Truman and Dewey campaigns became historic examples. The Truman effort showed how a determined candidate can win by going to the people, even with the odds against him; the Dewey performance was an example of how a supposedly sure candidate can lose by waging a lackluster campaign of overconfidence.

Truman undertook a thirty-one-thousand-mile "barnstorming" whistle-stop tour by train, appearing before an estimated six million persons. At each opportunity the president would appear to give one of his "give-'em-hell" attacks on the Republicans. The "do-nothing Republican Eightieth Congress" was Mr. Truman's chief target: "When I called them back into session what did they do? Nothing. Nothing. That Congress never did anything the whole time it was in session." If the Republicans win, "they'll tear you apart." The Republicans are "predatory animals who don't care if you people are thrown into a depression. . . . They like runaway prices."

Toward the end of the campaign Truman began a special appeal to minority racial and religious groups, calling for strong civil rights legislation and condemning Republican leaders for passing the Displaced Persons Act, which he said discriminated against Catholics and Jews.

Dewey's campaign was characterized by his aloofness and cool manner, his skirting of issues, and his diffuse, repetitious calls for "national unity." Dewey called the Eightieth Congress "one of the best," but he failed to come to the defense of its individual programs even when they were under direct attack from Truman. Assured by the pollsters, campaign strategists, advertising consultants, and reporters that he had the election well in hand, Dewey refrained from direct or forceful answers to any of the Truman attacks. Even more than Dewey, vice-presidential candidate Warren disdained to enter the partisan fray.

The Dewey program was particularly vague on farm legislation, which was a new field to him as a New York governor. "There are some people who would like to inject politics into the necessities of food raising in our country. I don't believe in that," Dewey said. He expressed a general support for price supports, not indicating whether they should be at parity or close to it or on a flexible or rigid scale. Meanwhile, farm prices were taking a nosedive which was concerning farmers across the Midwest. Also storage capacity in grain elevators was short, adding to rural dissatisfaction.

Both the Progressive and Dixiecrat movements, meanwhile, were faltering. Wallace became increasingly identified with the Communists and few "liberal" leaders joined his cause. His campaign crowds dwindled to a fraction of their size earlier in the year.

The Dixiecrat ticket failed to make substantial headway as most southern governors and senators—including some who had been most vociferous in denouncing Truman's civil rights proposals—chose the route of party regularity and backed the president. Only four southern Democratic parties—those in Alabama, Mississippi, South Carolina, and Louisiana—followed through on the plea of the Birmingham convention to put Thurmond and Wright on the ballot as the regular Democratic nominees. They went on the ballot as States' Rights party candidates in ten other states: Arkansas, California, Florida, Georgia, Kentucky, North Carolina, North Dakota, Tennessee, Texas, and Virginia.

With the first election eve returns from the northeastern states, Truman took a lead that he never lost despite the closeness of the election. As the night wore on state after state considered "safe Republican" moved into the Truman column. Dewey carried Pennsylvania, New Jersey,

Indiana, Maryland, Michigan, and New York (the last three evidently because of usual Democratic voters defecting to Wallace). But the president carried Massachusetts, won the border states, took all but four southern states (Alabama, Louisiana, Mississippi, and South Carolina) that were in the Dixiecrat column, carried the farm belt, and finally California fell in his column. When Ohio conclusively went for Truman at eleven o'clock Wednesday morning, November 3, Dewey conceded.

The election returns seemed to indicate that the Democratic New Deal philosophy was so generally accepted by the electorate that the president's warnings of a return to "Republican" depression days remained a telling point. On a less philosophical level many observers felt the Truman "Mr. Average" approach, compared to Dewey's "Olympian airs," drew a large sympathy vote from the average people in the street for the conceded "underdog."

Results of the 1948 Elections

With the Truman victory the Democrats took control of Congress with commanding majorities in both the Senate and the House. The Democrats picked up 9 Senate seats to make the new balance 54-42 in their favor. Among the new Democratic senators were Lyndon B. Johnson (Texas), Paul H. Douglas (Illinois), Hubert H. Humphrey (Minnesota), Estes Kefauver (Tennessee), Robert S. Kerr (Oklahoma), and Clinton P. Anderson (New Mexico). Republican Margaret Chase Smith was elected senator from Maine. And in House elections Democrats made a net gain of 75 seats; the new total was 263 Democrats and 171 Republicans.

The Democrats also ran strong in gubernatorial contests, winning 20 of the 32 seats up for election and reversing the Republican trend of the immediate past years. The new totals were 30 Democratic and 18 Republican governorships. Among the new Democratic governors were Chester Bowles (Connecticut), Adlai E. Stevenson (Illinois), and G. Mennen Williams (Michigan).

1949-1951: The Eighty-first Congress

The international situation in the years 1949 and 1950 was marked by stabilization and cooling of tensions in Europe, in sharp contrast to renewed Communist conquest and the threat of nuclear war in Asia. In April 1949 the North Atlantic Treaty was signed by the United States, Canada, and ten European nations, agreeing that "an armed attack against any one or more of them in Europe and North America shall be considered an attack against all." A direct reaction to Communist power moves, which included the 1948 takeover of Czechoslovakia, the NATO treaty laid down a policy of containment of Soviet expansionist ambitions that helped to preserve a territorial status quo on the European continent for years to come. On September 30, 1949, the Soviets lifted a blockade of Berlin, which had been in effect since April 1, 1948.

In Asia, however, the Western position was disintegrating rapidly. On January 22, 1949, the Chinese Communists took Beijing. On April 23 they crossed the Yangtze and captured Nanjing. On August 6 Secretary of State Dean Acheson blamed Generalissimo Chiang Kai-shek's "reactionary" clique for the Communist victory and gave notice that no further aid would be given Chiang's govern-

---

Actions of the "Do-Nothing" Eightieth Congress

The Eightieth Congress (1947-1948), characterized by a hard-campaigning President Truman as the "do-nothing Republican Eightieth Congress," actually produced a great deal of legislation, some of which Truman wanted, some over his serious objections. A partial list of Eightieth Congress actions:

~ Truman doctrine of aid to Greece and Turkey.
~ Marshall Plan for aid to Europe.
~ Peace treaties ratified with Italy, Hungary, Bulgaria, and Rumania.
~ Inter-American Treaty of Mutual Assistance ratified.
~ Vandenberg Resolution favoring collective and regional mutual assistance pacts.
~ Unification of armed forces under Department of Defense; creation of Central Intelligence Agency.
~ $65 million building loan for UN headquarters.
~ Peacetime draft law.
~ Passage of Taft-Hartley Act, over veto.
~ Presidential succession change.
~ Constitutional amendment to limit presidential tenure to two terms.
~ Hope-Aiken flexible price support bill.
~ Newsboys excluded from Social Security system, over veto.
~ A tax-reduction bill, over veto.
~ Liberalized housing credit terms.
~ Extended rent control.

---

ment. On December 7, 1949, the Nationalist Chinese government fled to Formosa.

The takeover of mainland China by a hostile Communist power did not shake the Western world, however, as did the surprise attack of Communist North Korean troops on South Korea June 25, 1950. The UN Security Council immediately ordered a cease-fire. Two days later President Truman ordered U.S. forces under Gen. Douglas MacArthur to repel the North Koreans. This became a UN "peace action" but was largely an American venture. U.S. involvement in Korea led to a near-wartime mobilization of the U.S. economy. It also led to President Truman's dispute with General MacArthur over the proposed bombing of Manchuria, which in turn led to MacArthur's dismissal in April 1951. As the war dragged on for two years with heavy U.S. casualties, it became a source of great frustration for the American people.

In other important developments the Soviet Union in September 1949 exploded its first atomic bomb, ending the U.S. atomic monopoly; India was proclaimed independent in January 1950; Alger Hiss was found guilty of perjury on January 21, 1950; and Truman, in January 1950, authorized the Atomic Energy Commission to produce the hydrogen bomb.

In his inaugural address January 20, 1949, President Truman included a "Point IV" proposal of American foreign policy for "a bold new program for making the benefits of our scientific advances and industrial progress available for the improvement and growth of underdeveloped areas." Over the succeeding years, foreign aid assistance for capital investment to build up the economies of fledgling nations of Africa, Asia, and Latin America became a cornerstone of U.S. foreign policy.

When the heavily Democratic Eighty-first Congress assembled in Washington January 3, 1949, liberals had high hopes that it would enact a new body of social welfare legislation such as that proposed by Truman in the 1948 campaign. The first signs for the Truman program seemed bright as the House on January 3 adopted a new rule to break the power of its Rules Committee to bottle up legislation indefinitely. The "twenty-one-day rule" provided that if the Rules Committee failed to clear a bill after twenty-one legislative days the chairman of the legislative committee that originally approved it could ask the House to vote on whether to consider the measure or not, with a majority vote required to bring the bill to the floor. The rule lasted only through the Eighty-first Congress and was rejected by the House when the Eighty-second Congress organized in 1951.

On January 5 Truman appeared before Congress to urge a sweeping new Fair Deal program of social reform. But Congress in general proved to be a disappointment to the liberal camp on domestic issues. Approval was given to a long-range housing bill providing for expanded federal programs in slum clearance, public housing, and farm improvement programs, which Truman signed into law July 15, 1949, "with deep satisfaction." The administration also scored an important victory in passage of the Social Security Expansion Act of 1950 and a limited victory in a 1949 minimum wage increase. But otherwise the Fair Deal program hit formidable obstacles.

Legislation to continue the Marshall Plan, military assistance to friendly foreign nations, and a two-year extension of the Trade Agreements Act cleared Congress with some bipartisan support. The Senate on July 21, 1949, ratified the North Atlantic Treaty by a 2-1 margin. In domestic affairs important steps toward streamlining the executive branch of the government were made in the Government Reorganization Act of 1949.

An explosive new issue, meanwhile, had developed on the domestic scene. In a February 11, 1950, speech in Wheeling, West Virginia, Sen. Joseph R. McCarthy, R-Wis., charged that there were fifty-seven Communists working in the State Department, a charge promptly denied by the department. Until his formal censure by the Senate in 1954, McCarthy and his freewheeling accusations of Communist sympathies among high- and low-placed government officials absorbed much of the public attention. The phenomenon of McCarthyism had a major effect on the psychological climate of the early 1950s.

The 1950 Midterm Elections

The liberal Democratic trend apparent in Truman's surprise 1948 victory was sharply reversed in the 1950 elections as Republicans exploited the issues of inflation, Korea, Communism, and corruption, to make strong comebacks in congressional and gubernatorial elections.

Truman, delivering his only major speech of the campaign November 4, 1950, sought to bolster the Democratic effort with charges similar to those he leveled against the Republicans in 1948: that they were captives of "special interests," that they would undo the country's progress toward peace and prosperity if they gained control of the national government. Truman said the Republicans were "isolationists" and that "any farmer who votes for the Republican party ought to have his head examined."

The Republican campaign assumed a far more aggressive tone than it had had in 1948. Sen. Robert A. Taft, R-Ohio, said the administration was responsible for high prices, high taxes, the loss of China to the Communists, and the Korean conflict. (Republicans pointed frequently to a January 12, 1950, speech by Secretary of State Dean Acheson before the National Press Club in which Acheson described the U.S. defensive line in the Far East in such a way as to exclude Korea.)

Typical of other Republican attacks was a November 4 reply to Truman by Harold Stassen, charging that the "blinded, blundering, bewildering" Far East policy of the "spy-riddled" Truman administration was directly to blame for American casualties in Korea.

McCarthy's charges of Communism in high places in the government played an important part in the campaign. Whether or not the voters believed in all of McCarthy's charges, many seemed to accept the thesis that there was something drastically wrong with U.S. foreign policy and that Acheson was a likely villain.

In Maryland the prominent veteran Democratic senator Millard E. Tydings was defeated by John Marshall Butler, an obscure Republican, after a campaign in which Tydings was accused of having "whitewashed" the State Department as head of a Senate committee investigating McCarthy's charges of Communism in the department. Butler was later accused of countenancing distribution of a campaign leaflet with a doctored photograph showing Tydings with U.S. Communist leader Earl Browder.

In California Republican representative Richard M. Nixon ran for the Senate against Rep. Helen Gahagan Douglas, a prominent liberal Democrat. Nixon's charges that Douglas voted frequently with New York representative Vito Marcantonio, a member of the American Labor party, whose voting record was often depicted as pro-Communist, established the image of Nixon as a ruthless campaigner, an image that would harm him in future races.

Another Senate contest with Communism as the chief issue was in North Carolina, where Willis Smith defeated incumbent Frank P. Graham in a June 24 Democratic primary runoff. Smith charged that Graham was badly tainted with socialism because of his alleged "associations with Communism."

Among major issues stressed by the Republicans was Truman's program for compulsory health insurance for all, termed "socialized medicine" by doctors who fought it both in the primaries and in the general elections. The issue was thought to have contributed to the defeat of several Democratic senators, including Claude Pepper of Florida and Graham of North Carolina in primaries and Elbert D. Thomas of Utah and Glen H. Taylor of Idaho in the general election. But in each one of these cases and in the California Senate race the "soft-on-Communism" issue, at its peak in 1950, played a more important role.

Results of the 1950 Elections

The two most closely watched Senate battles were in Ohio, where Republican senator Robert Taft was the target of an all-out attempt by organized labor to defeat him because of his co-authorship of the Taft-Hartley Act, and in Illinois, where Senate majority leader Scott W. Lucas was challenged by former Republican representative Everett McKinley Dirksen, who campaigned as a conservative near-isolationist. The election returns showed Taft the winner in Ohio by a gigantic 431,184 vote margin (57.5 percent), while Dirksen upset Lucas with 294,354 votes to spare (53.9 percent). Both men later became their party's Senate leader.

Assessment of the election returns showed that, while the Democrats retained nominal control of Congress (the Senate by 2 votes, the House by 35), the Truman-Fair Deal influence on Congress had been virtually nullified. Outside the conservative southern states, the Democrats elected only 126 House members to 196 for the Republicans.

On the Senate side the Republicans won 18 and the Democrats 9 of the nonsouthern contests. Among the new senators were Richard M. Nixon, R-Calif., George A. Smathers, D-Fla., Everett McKinley Dirksen, R-Ill., A. S. Mike Monroney, D-Okla., and James H. Duff, R-Pa., who was one of the prime movers for the nomination of Eisenhower in 1952.

1951-1953:
The Eighty-second Congress

The Korean conflict continued to dominate American life in 1951 and 1952 and led directly to the defeat of the Democrats in the 1952 elections. On April 11, 1951, President Truman removed General of the Army Douglas MacArthur from his command of UN and U.S. forces in the Far East. MacArthur had wanted to pursue the Chinese Communists across the Yalu River to their sanctuary in Manchuria in order to destroy the air depots and lines of supply being used to sustain their war effort in Korea. On March 25 MacArthur had threatened Communist China with air and naval attack. These steps, running contrary to the Truman administration policy under Secretary of State Dean Acheson, led to MacArthur's removal. Negotiations for a truce along the thirty-eighth parallel began July 10, 1951, but the fighting continued for another two years.

In other international developments the Japanese peace treaty was signed in San Francisco on September 8, 1951. War between Germany and the United States was formally ended October 19. On May 26, 1952, a peace contract between Germany and the Western allies was signed. In November 1952 the first hydrogen bomb was exploded by the United States.

A major domestic controversy developed in 1952 when Truman on April 8 ordered seizure of the nation's steel mills to avert a strike by six-hundred-thousand CIO steel workers. On June 2, however, the Supreme Court ruled the seizure illegal. The workers struck from June 3 to July 25.

The eighty-second Congress accomplished very little outside the realm of foreign and military affairs. None of the Fair Deal proposals expounded by the president and the Democratic leadership in 1948 and 1950—national health insurance, aid to education, and increased public health benefits—was enacted into law.

In 1951 the nation's interest was captured by the televised crime hearings of a Senate subcommittee chaired by Sen. Estes Kefauver, D-Tenn. The hearings exposed nationwide criminal organizations that reaped huge illegal profits, influencing local politicians and buying protection.

The 1952 Campaigns

President Truman ended any speculation about his third-term ambitions by announcing March 29 that he would not be a candidate for reelection. The field of possible Democratic nominees included Senator Kefauver; Gov. Adlai E. Stevenson, D-Ill.; W. Averell Harriman of New York; Vice President Alben W. Barkley of Kentucky; Sen. Robert S. Kerr, D-Okla.; and Sen. Richard B. Russell, D-Ga. Stevenson was Truman's personal choice for the nomination and was offered presidential support as early as January. Truman was willing to back Barkley after Stevenson's repeated disavowals of interest in the nomination; however, influential labor leaders vetoed Barkley's nomination, forcing him to withdraw on the eve of the convention.

Stevenson consistently professed his disinterest in the nomination and only submitted to a draft movement in his behalf while the 1952 Democratic convention, which convened in Chicago July 21, was in progress. The support for Stevenson, already strong, began to snowball with the July 24 announcement of Thomas J. Gavin, President Truman's alternate as a delegate from Missouri, that he would vote for Stevenson on Truman's instructions. Stevenson ran second to Kefauver in both the first and second ballots in polling.

Only on the third ballot, not completed until 12:25 a.m. on July 26, did Stevenson move close to nomination as Harriman withdrew in his favor. A unanimous nomination by acclamation was then moved and carried. Following a conference with President Truman, Stevenson chose Sen. John J. Sparkman, D-Ala., a backer of the national Democratic party on most issues except civil rights, as his running mate. The convention then confirmed his choice by acclamation.

The contest for the Republican presidential nomination, despite other entries in the field, was fought out between the supporters of two relatively clearly defined groups within the party: Sen. Robert A. Taft of Ohio represented the conservative midwestern and southern wing of the party, and Gen. Dwight D. Eisenhower became the candidate of the "internationalist" wing of the party centered on the east and west coasts. Other announcements of candidacy were made by California governor Earl Warren and by Harold E. Stassen.

Eisenhower in early 1952 was on duty in Paris as commanding general of the new North Atlantic Treaty Organization. The major political question as 1952 began was whether he would permit his name to be put forth for the Republican nomination. Previously he had always rejected talk of his running for president, and he had declined to make his political affiliations known. The mystery ended on January 7 when Sen. Henry Cabot Lodge, R-Mass., announced that he was entering Eisenhower's name in the March 11 New Hampshire primary after having received assurances from the general that he was a Republican. In a January 8 statement from Paris, Eisenhower confirmed his Republican loyalties and said he would run for president if he received a "clear-cut call to political duty." Eisenhower said, however, that he would not actively seek the nomination. Despite his refusal to campaign, Eisenhower ran strongly in most of the primaries where his name was entered.

When the twenty-fifth Republican National Convention opened in Chicago on July 7, the delegate issue was the hottest—and one of the first—items of business. In a preliminary test the convention voted 658-548 against allowing delegates with disputed seats to vote on other delegate contests until their own credentials were accepted. This resolution, which had been endorsed by twenty-five of the nation's Republican governors, prevented disputed Taft delegates from the South from voting for each other's seating. The victory of the Eisenhower forces on this issue foreshadowed the general's eventual nomination.

Korea, foreign affairs, corruption in government, internal Communism, and the domestic economy were the major issues of the 1952 campaign. Of these, only the domestic economy—booming through the stimulation of the Korean War—proved to be in any way a plus for the Democrats. The other issues aided the Republican campaign.

The most dramatic episode of the campaign opened September 18 with an article in the *New York Post,* charging that Nixon had been the beneficiary of an allegedly secret fund financed by California businesses. For a week controversy raged with many demands that Nixon resign from the ticket so that the corruption issue against the Democrats would not be diluted.

Eisenhower declined to take a firm stand on Nixon's continuance on the ticket. Finally, Nixon on September 23 went on nationwide television for a melodramatic defense of the moral rectitude of the fund and to make a complete accounting of his own relatively limited personal assets. In this speech Nixon referred to his wife's "respectable Republican cloth coat" and the gift dog, Checkers—"regardless of what they say about it, we're going to keep it."

Response to Nixon's speech overwhelmingly favored keeping him on the ticket. Eisenhower immediately issued a statement lauding Nixon for his bravery in a "tough situation." At a September 24 meeting between the two men in Wheeling, West Virginia, Eisenhower announced that Nixon had completely "vindicated himself."

Results of the 1952 Elections

In contrast to 1948, when the pollsters and commentators had all foreseen a sweeping Dewey victory, there was a marked reluctance to make a firm prediction on the outcome of the 1952 campaign. But when the returns started to roll in election eve, it was clear that Eisenhower had won by a landslide and that his victory had probably never been in doubt.

Only nine of the forty-eight states went for Stevenson, and they were in the South or border areas (West Virginia, Kentucky, Alabama, Arkansas, Georgia, Louisiana, Mississippi, and North and South Carolina). Every state across the East, Midwest, and Far West went for Eisenhower. And the tide rolled on into many parts of the South, with the Eisenhower-Nixon ticket carrying Texas, Oklahoma, Florida, Virginia, and Tennessee.

The electoral vote count was 442 for Eisenhower, 89 for Stevenson. In popular votes Eisenhower won a 6,621,485-vote plurality. He polled 33,936,137 votes, the highest number of votes ever received by a presidential candidate. But in defeat Stevenson won 27,314,649 votes, the highest number ever received by a losing candidate.

Seeking explanations for the Eisenhower landslide, observers found a multitude of reasons. The doubts, fears, and frustrations stemming from the stalemated Korean War, the Hiss case, and the Communist spy trials, revelations of corruption in the federal government, rising prices and high taxes—all contributed to a strong desire for a change in executive leadership. Stevenson's divorce and wit were thought to be unpopular with many voters. Sparkman's identification with the white supremacy views of the

Alabama Democratic party harmed the ticket among black voters.

The lack of enthusiasm for the Republican congressional leadership, the memory of the depression, and fear of reversal of social-economic gains of the Democratic years might have nullified these Republican advantages, however, if the Republicans had not found in Eisenhower an ideal candidate to allay such fears. A national hero, a man whose leadership had already been proven in World War II and in laying the groundwork for the North Atlantic Alliance, Eisenhower also had the invaluable asset of a magic personality that charmed voters and the image of being "above politics." Few could seriously believe that "Ike" would scuttle the New Deal reforms.

The uniquely personal aspect of Eisenhower's victory was underlined by the narrow margins with which Republicans moved into control of Congress, despite the presidential landslide. Republicans made a net gain of 22 House seats to a new total of 221, only 3 more than the 218 needed to give them control. The Democratic House total slipped from 235 to 213. In Senate elections the Republicans made a net gain of only one seat, just enough to give them a one-seat edge in the new Senate. The new Senate totals were 48 Republicans, 47 Democrats, and 1 Independent (Wayne Morse of Oregon, formerly a Republican).

In what proved to be a significant Senate race thirty-five-year-old Democratic representative John F. Kennedy defeated Republican Henry Cabot Lodge, Jr., a top leader in the Eisenhower drive for the GOP presidential nomination, by a 70,737-vote margin in Massachusetts. Other newly elected senators included Barry Goldwater, R-Ariz., Stuart Symington, D-Mo., Mike Mansfield, D-Mont., Henry M. Jackson, D-Wash., and Albert Gore, D-Tenn.

On the gubernatorial level Republicans solidified the national lead they had achieved in 1950 by winning 5 new seats. The winners were Christian A. Herter, R-Mass., William G. Stratton, R-Ill., J. Caleb Boggs, R-Del., George N. Craig, R-Ind., and Hugo Aronson, R-Mont. The new governorship totals were 30 Republicans and 18 Democrats.

1953-1955:
The Eighty-third Congress

Many Americans had hoped that Eisenhower's election to the presidency would usher in an era of domestic tranquillity and international stability. In some respects these wishes were fulfilled. There was a more harmonious relationship between the president and Congress than at any time since World War II. A Korean armistice was finally signed July 27, 1953, with prisoner repatriation following shortly thereafter.

Republicans claimed that President Eisenhower's action in instructing the U.S. Seventh Fleet to stop shielding Communist China from any possible Nationalist Chinese attacks, combined with information relayed to the Chinese that the United States would resort to full-scale war in Korea if the Communists refused to come to peace terms, were decisive factors in persuading the Communists to come to terms. Democrats replied that the terms of the armistice were no better than those the Truman administration had previously rejected.

Even with a return to relative stability in Korea, however, the international situation remained in flux on other fronts. Soviet Premier Joseph Stalin died March 5, setting off a contest for succession in the USSR. On July 7, 1953, an uprising that broke out in Communist-held East Germany was quelled when the Communists called in Soviet troops and tanks, which mowed down civilians revolting in the streets of East Berlin. The United States did not intervene, drawing into question the wisdom of the "liberation" policy spelled out by Republican campaigners in 1952.

On August 20, 1953, the Soviet Union announced the successful testing of its first hydrogen bomb. President Eisenhower went before the United Nations on December 8 to urge the major powers to cooperate in developing the peaceful uses of atomic energy. The United States on January 21, 1954, launched the *Nautilus*, the first atomic-powered submarine.

The curtain began to go down on France's colonial empire as she admitted defeat in the seven-and-a-half-year war against Communist infiltration in Indo-China and submitted to a partition of Vietnam at the spring 1953 Geneva conference on Far Eastern affairs; France subsequently withdrew forces from Vietnam, Cambodia, and Laos. Threatened Communist inroads in South America were reversed, however, by U.S.-supported anti-Communist forces, which invaded Guatemala and overthrew the Communist-oriented government of President Jacobo Arbenz Guzman in June 1954.

The Eighty-third Congress produced few innovations in domestic or foreign policy, but neither did it reverse New Deal social reforms. During the first session (1953), foreign aid and military appropriations were pared, the controversial Reconstruction Finance Corp. was abolished, legislation was passed giving the states title to the oil-rich coastal lands previously claimed by the federal government, and Congress permitted the president to carry out a governmental reorganization creating a new Department of Health, Education, and Welfare, which it had denied President Truman in 1949 and 1950.

Sen. Joseph R. McCarthy and his unrestrained accusations of Communist influence throughout the government remained a domestic issue. Taking over chairmanship of the Senate Government Operations Committee in 1953, McCarthy conducted hearings and investigated the State Department, Voice of America, Department of the Army, and other agencies. An opinion-stifling "climate of fear" in many government agencies was said to be one of the results of his probes. The Army-McCarthy hearings, televised in the spring of 1954, were the climax of McCarthy's career and led finally to his censure by the Senate on December 2, 1954. McCarthy's influence waned steadily thereafter. He died May 2, 1957.

The Supreme Court on May 17, 1954, handed down a unanimous decision declaring racial segregation in the public schools to be unconstitutional. The opinion, written by Chief Justice Earl Warren (whom Eisenhower had appointed on the death of Chief Justice Fred M. Vinson in 1953), began a major movement toward racial desegregation across the nation. It inspired bitter hostility in the southern states.

A potential Democratic comeback with the nation's voters was presaged by special elections held during 1953. The traditional Republican hold on New Jersey was broken by the election of Democrat Robert B. Meyner to the governorship. Special elections in the New Jersey Sixth and Wisconsin Ninth Districts resulted in the election of two Democrats, Harrison A. Williams, Jr., in New Jersey and Lester Johnson in Wisconsin. They were the first members of their party ever to win in either of these districts.

The 1954 Midterm Elections

The Republican success under Eisenhower in winning both houses of Congress in 1952 was not repeated in 1954. Democrats made significant comebacks, recapturing control of both House and Senate and reversing the Republican gubernatorial trend of recent years. But the swing back to the Democrats, while it indicated that the Republican party was probably much weaker than its popular president, was by no means strong enough to spell a major change in the nation's mood. Although it was in the majority, much of the Democratic party strength was concentrated in the conservative South.

President Eisenhower appealed to the voters to return a Republican Congress and he campaigned harder and longer than any other president had ever done in a midterm election. He claimed that Congress had enacted 54 of 64 legislative proposals he had submitted and that this "batting average of .830" was "pretty good in any league." (Congressional Quarterly figures showed Congress had approved 150 of 232 specific Eisenhower requests for a batting average of .647.)

In an October 8 televised address he warned that a Democratic congressional victory would start "a cold war of partisan politics between the Congress and the Executive Branch," which would block "the great work" his administration had "begun so well." Congressional Democratic leaders Sam Rayburn and Lyndon B. Johnson, both of Texas, replied in a joint telegram to the president that "there will be no cold war conducted against you by the Democrats" and complained that the president had made an "unjust attack on the many Democrats who have done so much to cooperate with your Administration and to defend your program against attacks by members of your own party."

In a last-minute effort to bolster the Republican vote in critical states, Eisenhower made an unprecedented one-day, 1,521-mile flying trip on October 29, 1954, to address crowds in Cleveland, Detroit, Louisville, and Wilmington, Delaware. In these speeches he implied that Democratic administrations had been able to boast of full employment and prosperity only during war. Following the campaign some observers speculated that Eisenhower may have kept many women's votes by reminding them that the Republicans had put an end to the "futile casualties" in Korea. There was general agreement that his campaign activities averted a still stronger Democratic trend, especially in congressional elections.

Vice President Nixon played a controversial role in the campaign, charging that the Democrats were unfit to govern because of their record on the Communist issue.

On the issue of mounting unemployment in several areas of the country, Democrats charged Republicans with a "callous" attitude toward the problem, while Republicans replied that they had provided jobs without war. Public power was also an issue, with Democrats accusing Republicans of "give-aways" to private interests, while Republicans replied that Democratic public power policy had tended toward socialism and government monopoly.

Results of the 1954 Elections

Democrats moved into control of the Senate by a 48-47-1 margin as compared with the 49-46-1 Republican edge before the election. Among the new senators were Richard L. Neuberger, D-Ore., former vice president Alben W. Barkley, D-Ky., and Clifford P. Case, R-N.J.

In the House the new lineup was 232 Democrats and 203 Republicans, a net Democratic gain of 19 seats over the previous Congress, which had had 221 Republicans and 213 Democrats.

The Democratic congressional majorities grew throughout the remainder of the Eisenhower years. Sam Rayburn, D-Texas, again became Speaker of the House, and Lyndon B. Johnson, D-Texas, Senate majority leader—posts they held through the rest of the decade.

Republicans fared even worse in the governorship races. Including the Democratic victory of Edmund S. Muskie in the September 13 Maine election, the Democrats ousted Republicans from eight state governments, and the Republicans failed to take a single Democratic seat. The gubernatorial balance shifted from 29-19 in favor of the Republicans to 27-21 in favor of the Democrats. In the New York governorship election to succeed retiring three-term governor Thomas E. Dewey, a Republican, Democrat Averell Harriman won a narrow 11,125-vote plurality over Republican senator Irving M. Ives. Other Democratic gubernatorial winners included Abraham Ribicoff in Connecticut, Orville Freeman in Minnesota, and George M. Leader in Pennsylvania.

1955-1957:
The Eighty-fourth Congress

Cooperation between a middle-of-the-road president and a middle-of-the-road Congress, tension in the Formosa Strait, growing pressures in Africa and Asia for independence from colonial rule, the Geneva "summit" conference, presidential illnesses, "de-Stalinization" in the Soviet empire, revolt in Poland and Hungary, war over the Suez Canal, these events were highlights of the last half of President Eisenhower's first term in office.

Divided responsibility for government brought unexpectedly harmonious sessions of Congress, with nothing resembling the "cold war of partisan politics" predicted in 1954 by Eisenhower if the Democrats were to take control of Congress. Administration measures fared almost as well as they had during the Republican Eighty-third Congress, again with substantial aid from Democrats.

Especially in foreign affairs the Democratic leadership cooperated substantially with the president. Early in 1955 Congress approved the resolution Eisenhower had requested to give him authority to employ U.S. armed forces to defend Formosa. Prompted by Communist Chinese bombardment of the off-shore islands of Quemoy and Matsu, the resolution also gave the president authority to defend, in addition to Formosa, "related positions and territories now in friendly hands," an evident reference to Quemoy and Matsu. Senate moves to delete this authority were overwhelmingly rejected.

The Senate ratified, by almost unanimous votes, the Southeast Asia Collective Defense Treaty (which created the Southeast Asia Defense Organization—SEATO), plus protocols ending the occupation of Germany, restoring sovereignty to West Germany, and permitting West German rearmament and NATO membership. The peace treaty with Austria, creating an independent, neutral state, was signed in Vienna on May 15 and was ratified by the Senate June 7, 1955. The controversial constitutional amendment offered by Sen. John W. Bricker, R-Ohio, to trim the president's treaty-making powers was reported out of the Senate Foreign Relations Committee in 1956, but it was not brought up for Senate debate because of the president's firm opposition. In 1955 the Reciprocal Trade Agreements Act was extended for three years, the longest single extension since 1945. Foreign aid appropriations came fairly close to matching presidential requests.

Domestic enactments by the politically divided government were less impressive. The two most important measures approved by Congress appeared to be the multibillion dollar federal highway program, providing for a forty-one-thousand-mile interstate superhighway program as part of the most extensive public works project in the nation's history, and the Agricultural Act of 1956, which included the soil bank program that supporters hoped would limit farm surpluses and raise farmers' incomes. Congress also voted an increase in the minimum wage to $1 an hour (as opposed to the 90-cent figure recommended by the administration).

On the international scene the first conference of Asian-African countries met April 18-27, 1955, in Bandung, Indonesia. Delegates endorsed an end to colonialism, called for national independence, and demanded UN membership for all states qualified in terms of the UN charter (including Communist China). In the following month the Warsaw Treaty, counterpart to NATO for the Communist satellites of Eastern Europe, was ratified.

At the twentieth Congress of the Soviet Communist Party in Moscow, February 14-25, 1956, Nikita Khrushchev proclaimed a new party line, which included destruction of Joseph Stalin as a national idol. The rush to "de-Stalinize" however, loosed forces in the Communist world that the Soviet Union was able to control only by bloody repressions of the June 28, 1956, workers revolt in Poznan, Poland, and the revolt of Hungarians in October and November of 1956.

Reacting adversely to Egyptian president Gamal Abdel Nasser's acceptance of Soviet-bloc arms and economic agreements with the Communist world, the United States on July 19, 1956, informed Egypt that it was withdrawing its offer to aid in construction of the Aswan Dam on the Nile River. Britain on July 20 announced it was also withdrawing from the project. On July 26 Egypt seized the British-held Suez Canal and denounced the Western powers. Prolonged negotiations during the summer and fall failed to persuade Egypt to modify its decision on nationalizing the canal, and on October 29 Israel launched an invasion of Egypt. The move was coordinated with the British and French governments, which attacked Egypt on October 31. The Suez Canal was blocked by sunken and scuttled ships. The Soviet Union stepped into the controversy, threatening atomic war if Britain and France refused to retreat. The United Nations, led by the United States, condemned the French, British, and Israeli moves. A UN cease-fire ended the fighting November 7, and a UN international peace force moved in to enforce the peace, the terms of which allowed Egypt to regain control of the canal and forced Israeli withdrawal.

The question of President Eisenhower's health hung over the nation for a year before the November 1956 election. On September 24, 1955, the sixty-four-year-old president was stricken by a heart attack, which totally incapacitated him for a period of days and necessitated his hospitalization for almost two months. Republican leaders, who had confidently expected Eisenhower to seek (and easily win) reelection in 1956, suddenly faced the possibility that he might not be available. As the president gradually improved, party leaders, particularly GOP national chairman Leonard W. Hall, repeatedly urged him to run again despite his illness. After thorough physical examinations Eisenhower on February 29, 1956, announced that he was convinced that his health would permit him to carry the "burdens of the Presidency" under a reduced work schedule and that he would seek reelection.

On June 8 the president was again hospitalized, this time with ileitis. He underwent successful surgery on June 9 and was once more hospitalized for several weeks. Again the possibility arose that he might not seek reelection. But on July 10 Eisenhower made it clear he would go ahead with his campaign for reelection.

Without the question of presidential illness, there would probably have been little doubt, at any time, that Ike could achieve reelection. The presidential illness, however, added an element of uncertainty to the entire campaign and made the Democratic nomination appear far more "worth having" than might otherwise have been the case.

The 1956 Campaigns

A familiar cast stepped forward to seek the Democratic presidential nomination: Adlai E. Stevenson, the 1952 nominee; Tennessee senator Estes Kefauver, the popular primary choice of 1952; and New York governor Averell Harriman. Senate majority leader Lyndon B. Johnson of Texas was supported for the nomination by several southern leaders, but he had little backing outside the South.

Early in the spring it appeared that Kefauver might again sweep the primaries. After winning the New Hampshire Democratic primary without opposition on March 13, he went on to pick up 56 percent of the vote in the March 20 Minnesota primary against Stevenson. The decisive contest came on June 5 in California, where both men had waged vigorous campaigns. The results: Stevenson, 1,139,964; Kefauver, 680,722. The Kefauver campaign limped along for a few more weeks. On July 26 Kefauver announced his withdrawal in favor of Stevenson.

When the Democratic National Convention met in Chicago on August 13, Stevenson and Harriman were the only two serious candidates for the nomination. The Harriman candidacy, discounted by most observers, received a boost when former president Truman on August 11 endorsed him. But in the vital contest for actual delegate votes, Stevenson, with Kefauver's support, was too far ahead to be stopped. On the first ballot on August 16 Stevenson was nominated with 905-1/2 votes to 210 for Harriman, 80 for Johnson, and the remainder scattered.

Historically, the most significant event at the 1956 convention was the cliff-hanging decision about the Democratic vice-presidential nominee. Following his nomination Stevenson made a brief appearance before the convention to tell the delegates he had decided "to depart from the precedents of the past." He said "the selection of the Vice Presidential nominee should be made through the free processes of this convention."

After a stiff two-ballot contest, Kefauver, on August 17, narrowly won the vice-presidential nomination over Massachusetts senator John F. Kennedy. With 686-1/2 votes required for nomination, Kennedy's total moved as high as 648 at one point during the second ballot. But a series of vote switches gave the nomination to Kefauver, who had 755-1/2 votes against 589 for Kennedy and 27-1/2 scattered. Other unsuccessful aspirants for the vice-presidential nomination, all of whom received substantial first-ballot votes, were Sen. Hubert H. Humphrey of Minnesota,

Sen. Albert Gore of Tennessee, and New York mayor Robert F. Wagner.

The vice-presidential fight marked Kennedy's entry into presidential politics. The good showing that Kennedy had made, particularly in southern delegations, convinced his backers that despite his Roman Catholic faith Kennedy could be elected president.

The convention on August 16 adopted a platform including a compromise civil rights plank. It termed Supreme Court rulings "the law of the land" but made no specific pledge to apply the Court's decisions and denounced the use of force to implement them. A move by a northern liberal group led by Gov. G. Mennen Williams of Michigan, Sen. Paul H. Douglas of Illinois, and Sen. Herbert H. Lehman of New York to insert a pledge to "carry out" the Court's decisions, was defeated by voice vote on the convention floor.

On the Republican side from February 29, when Eisenhower announced he would seek a second term, there was no visible opposition to his renomination. Senate minority leader William F. Knowland, R-Calif., had previously announced his "provisional" candidacy, if Eisenhower were not to run, but he quickly withdrew it. The president swept all the primaries where his name was entered.

With the GOP presidential nomination a foregone conclusion, interest centered on the Republican vice-presidential nomination. Eisenhower declined to make an early clear-cut endorsement of Richard M. Nixon for renomination as vice president and was reported to have suggested to Nixon that he consider a cabinet assignment or another government post, if Nixon planned to seek the GOP presidential nomination at a later date.

Presidential disarmament adviser Harold E. Stassen on July 25 attempted to spark a "stop Nixon" movement, claiming that Nixon's presence on the ticket might cost Eisenhower as much as 6 percent of the vote in the fall and endanger Republican congressional campaigns. No major Republican leaders came forward to support Stassen and the stop-Nixon move quickly faded. At Eisenhower's request Stassen actually ended by making a seconding speech for Nixon at the convention, which met in San Francisco August 20-23.

The convention adopted without dissent a platform pledging a "continuation of peace, prosperity and progress." Threatened opposition to the civil rights plank evaporated after the Resolutions Committee modified an earlier and "stronger" version and proposed a plank acceptable to both northern and southern delegates.

The attack on Egypt and uprisings in Hungary and Poland dominated the news during the last weeks of the 1956 campaign, eclipsing domestic issues and changing the emphasis in international policy debates.

Early in the campaign Eisenhower boasted that his administration had offered, "in all levels of government," an "honest" regime of "good judgment," "tolerance" and "conciliation." The voters were asked to reelect him in order to keep the country "going down the straight road of prosperity and peace." Vice President Nixon, answering Democratic criticisms of Eisenhower administration foreign policy, said the families of "157,000 Americans who were killed, wounded or missing in Korea" could testify "whether we have peace today." Nixon said "the great majority of the American people have enjoyed the best four years of their lives under the Eisenhower Administration."

Stevenson's first approach was to challenge the effectiveness of Eisenhower's executive leadership, putting forth his own gospel of "the New America" under a Democratic party that "can build as we have to build." He criticized the administration for failing to pass school aid legislation and other vitally needed domestic programs. He said the administration had "pilloried innocent men and women under the pretense of conducting loyalty and security investigations."

The tone of the campaign began to change as debate mounted over Stevenson's proposals to end the draft and stop U.S. testing of hydrogen bombs. The Stevenson proposal to end the draft drew the reply from Eisenhower that he saw "no chance of ending the draft and carrying out the responsibilities for the security of the country."

The debate was disturbed, however, by the beginning of the Hungarian uprising on October 23 and the Israeli attack on Egypt on October 29. Whatever the merits of the Stevenson proposals, they appeared to be badly timed in view of the international situation. Eisenhower again stressed that "we need our military draft for the safety of our nation" and that the country must have the "most advanced military weapons." With war threatening both in the Mideast and in Eastern Europe, the general public reaction seemed to be that it was a bad time to change leaders, especially considering the president's military background.

Results of the 1956 Elections

President Eisenhower was reelected with the largest popular vote in history and a plurality second only to that of Franklin D. Roosevelt in 1936. Eisenhower came out with 35,585,245 votes (457 electoral votes) and Stevenson, 26,030,172 (73 electoral votes). Eisenhower's plurality was 9,555,073 votes.

In the North the president carried or ran unusually well in many urban areas formerly considered safe Democratic areas. More blacks voted Republican than in any election since pre-New Deal days. The only states where Eisenhower pluralities dropped from 1952 were several farm states where Secretary of Agriculture Ezra Taft Benson and administration agricultural policies were highly unpopular.

The presidential election did not have the necessary coattail effect to give Republicans control of Congress. Although the returns indicated Ike's tremendous popularity with voters, the outcome for other offices made it clear that most citizens still identified their interests with those of the Democratic party. For the first time since 1848 the winning presidential candidate was unable to carry at least one house of Congress for his party.

The Democrats amazingly maintained their 49-47 lead in the Senate, taking Republican seats in Colorado, Idaho, Ohio, and Pennsylvania to make up for their losses in New York, West Virginia, and Kentucky. Democratic senator Wayne Morse, the man whom the Republicans had wanted most to defeat, won over former secretary of the interior Douglas McKay. Newly elected senators included Thruston B. Morton, R-Ky., Joseph S. Clark, D-Pa., Jacob K. Javits, R-N.Y., Frank Church, D-Idaho, and Frank J. Lausche, D-Ohio.

In the House the Democrats added to the 29-seat margin they had achieved in 1954. The new House totals were Democrats 234 and Republicans 201.

The Democrats made a net gain of one new governorship for a new 28-20 balance in their favor. Important Democratic gubernatorial victories included two in nor-

mally Republican farm states: Herschel C. Loveless in Iowa and George Docking in Kansas. Other Democrats winning previously held Republican governorships were Foster Furcolo in Massachusetts and Robert D. Holmes in Oregon. Republicans winning Democratic gubernatorial seats were C. William O'Neill in Ohio, Cecil Underwood in West Virginia, and Edwin L. Mechem in New Mexico.

1957-1959:
The Eighty-fifth Congress

The first two years of Eisenhower's second term in office were marked by two major events, one domestic and one foreign, in the fall of 1957.

On September 4 a controversy over admission of black students to the previously all-white Central High School in Little Rock, Arkansas, reached a showdown as the National Guard, ordered out by Gov. Orval Faubus, prevented the black students from entering the school. A federal court on September 21 ordered removal of the National Guard. But when the black students reentered the school two days later, they were ordered to leave by local authorities because of fear of mob violence. Eisenhower then ordered federal troops sent into Little Rock to enforce the court's order, and the school began operation on an integrated basis.

The spectacle of angry, racist-minded crowds in the face of fixed bayonets rioting to prevent black children from entering the school shocked the world. The scene was offset in part by the use of federal troops to enforce the constitutional rights of U.S. citizens. Throughout the South, however, the reaction was one of bitterness toward Eisenhower for using troops to enforce a deeply resented Supreme Court decision.

The second major event in the fall of 1957 was the Soviet Union's successful launching, on October 4, of the first manufactured satellite, Sputnik I, into an orbit around the world. Congress and the nation responded with anger, frustration, and alarm, directed chiefly at the Eisenhower administration because it had not pressed the U.S. effort to beat the Soviets into outer space and showed, at least initially, little concern about the Soviet achievement. More profound concern developed about the quality of U.S. education, especially in scientific fields. The first successful U.S. satellite, Explorer I, was launched by the Army from Cape Canaveral, Florida, on January 31, 1958.

Other major international events in 1957 and 1958 were the following:

~ On March 25, 1957, the Common Market (European Economic Community) and Euratom (European Atomic Energy Community) treaties among six Western European powers were signed in Rome. (The countries were France, Belgium, Netherlands, Luxembourg, Italy, and West Germany.) These treaties were significant steps toward the U.S.-supported goal of a united Europe.

~ Vice President and Mrs. Nixon narrowly escaped injury from Communist-inspired riots while on a good-will tour in Caracas, Venezuela, on May 13, 1957.

~ Great Britain exploded its first hydrogen bomb, May 15, 1957.

~ Former premier Georgii M. Malenkov, former foreign minister V. M. Molotov, and L. M. Kaganovich were purged by the Soviet Presidium under Nikita Khrushchev's leadership, July 3-4, 1957, for alleged pro-Stalinist activities. On March 27, 1958, Chairman Khrushchev completed solidification of power by succeeding Nikolai A. Bulganin as premier.

~ Charles de Gaulle became head of the French government on June 1, 1958, averting threatened civil war.

~ At the request of the Lebanese government, U.S. Marines were dispatched to Lebanon on July 15, 1958, to forestall a threatened effort by Egyptian president Gamal Abdel Nasser's United Arab Republic and the Soviet Union to overthrow Lebanon's pro-Western regime. U.S. troops withdrew in August after calm was restored.

~ In the fall of 1958 the United States and the Soviet Union began a three-and-one-half-year unpoliced moratorium on nuclear weapons tests.

Major domestic events included the development of the most serious postwar recession, in mid-1957 lasting through 1958; a stroke suffered by President Eisenhower November 25, 1957, from which he was pronounced "completely recovered" on March 1, 1958; and the resignation of Sherman Adams, assistant to the president. Adams's resignation in September 1958 followed revelations before a House subcommittee that he had interceded with various federal agencies in behalf of his friend, Boston industrialist Bernard Goldfine, and that he had received gifts from Goldfine. The Goldfine-Adams episode hurt the Eisenhower administration on the corruption-in-government issue and was one of several elements contributing to the Democratic sweep in the 1958 congressional and gubernatorial elections.

The Eighty-fifth Congress established a record of moderate productivity, all its chief enactments bearing the "middle-of-the-road" stamp that was the natural result of compromise between a "mildly conservative" president and the "mildly liberal" congressional leadership of House Speaker Sam Rayburn and Senate majority leader Lyndon B. Johnson, both of Texas.

The mounting recession pushed the federal budget increasingly into the red, with a $2.8 billion deficit in fiscal 1958 and a $12.4 billion deficit for the fiscal 1959 budget, approved in mid-1958.

In foreign policy the Senate in 1957 approved the International Atomic Energy treaty (stemming from President Eisenhower's Atoms for Peace program). During its first session Congress approved the Mideast Resolution (Eisenhower Doctrine), in response to the president's request for advance authority to use U.S. troops to protect free Middle East nations from "overt armed aggression" by "power hungry Communists." During the second session Congress acceded readily to the president's request for authority to extend financial aid and technical assistance to the newly formed European Atomic Energy Community.

A military reorganization bill was approved by Congress in 1958. This bill eliminated the "separately administered" provision for Army, Navy, and Air Force written into the 1947 National Security Act and made it clear that the three military departments were to operate under the direction and control of the secretary of defense. Legislation passed in July 1958 established a civilian-controlled National Aeronautics and Space Administration. Both houses organized permanent standing committees on space matters.

The major domestic bill passed in 1957 was the Civil Rights Act. The bill created the executive Commission on Civil Rights and empowered the attorney general to seek injunctions when individuals are denied the right to vote. With strengthening amendments in succeeding years, this legislation gave more and more black citizens the power of the ballot, viewed by the bill's advocates as the foundation of most other civil liberties.

The most notable accomplishment of Congress's 1958 session was passage and signature by the president of the Alaska statehood bill, culminating decades of pressure to admit the territory to the Union.

Other important actions of the second session included emergency housing and highway construction legislation to help stem the recession; passage of the National Defense Education Act of 1958, including $295 million for loans to needy college students; the Transportation Act of 1958, designed to revive the failing railroads; and passage of a low-support farm bill with few controls generally in line with administration proposals.

Under the leadership of Democratic national chairman Paul M. Butler, a policy-making Democratic Advisory Committee was organized in November 1956 and became the chief voice for the militantly liberal Democratic point of view. It made sharp partisan attacks on the Eisenhower administration. Democratic congressional leaders Rayburn and Johnson had been asked to join but instead actively opposed it, expressing a preference for policy formulation through regular Democratic congressional leadership channels. Many of the committee's statements reflected severe criticism of the Democratic congressional leadership for alleged lack of sufficiently aggressive opposition to the Eisenhower administration. (The committee was eventually abolished in March 1961 after the Democratic takeover of the executive office. The new Democratic National Chairman, John M. Bailey, said the committee had "served a function" only when the party was out of power.)

The 1958 Midterm Elections

The swing of the political pendulum against the Republicans and in favor of the Democrats was apparent as early as mid-1957. It ended November 25, 1958, with a clean Democratic sweep in Alaska's first election as a state. The over-all national result was the most thorough Democratic victory since the Roosevelt landslide year of 1936.

In August 1957 Democrat William Proxmire easily won the Wisconsin Senate seat of the late Republican senator Joseph R. McCarthy, who had died May 2 of the same year. In the November 1957 off-year elections the Democrats reelected New Jersey Democratic governor Robert B. Meyner by a plurality of nearly two hundred thousand votes, also scoring important victories in Virginia and New York. In the September 8, 1958, Maine elections the Democrats swept that normally Republican state, electing a Democratic governor, a Democratic senator, and two Democratic representatives.

The Republicans began the 1958 campaign with a number of handicaps. The Adams-Goldfine incident had been a source of profound embarrassment for the Eisenhower administration, only partly relieved by Adams's resignation in September. Although recovery from the 1957-1958 recession was already under way, the recession had served to weaken seriously voter confidence in the Eisenhower prosperity formula. Another crisis in the Formosa Strait, with renewed Communist shelling of Quemoy and Matsu, reminded voters that the administration had yet to find a solution for the China problem. Sputnik had weakened voter confidence in the Eisenhower administration's defense and space programs.

In many states the Republicans backed ballot initiative proposals for right-to-work laws that were bitterly opposed by organized labor. This inspired labor to work particularly hard to get its members out to vote: against right-to-work and for Democrats. A major portion of the blame for Republican debacles in states such as Ohio and California was attributed to GOP right-to-work stands. Still another incident harming the Republicans was deep southern resentment against Eisenhower's ordering of paratroops into Little Rock in 1957. This effectively curtailed Republican efforts for new inroads in the South.

In the campaign the Democrats charged that the Republicans had callously allowed the country to slip into a serious recession, showing little regard for the interests of the unemployed. Adlai Stevenson on October 18 said that the crises over Quemoy, desegregation, education, and recession "could have been avoided if we had an administration which thought in advance instead of waiting placidly on the fairways until the mortal danger is upon us and then angrily calling out the Marines." "The tragedy of the Eisenhower Administration," Stevenson said, "is that its only weapons seem to be platitudes or paratroops."

Alarmed by the apparent Democratic inroads, the Republicans held an October 6 White House strategy session that produced a manifesto declaring that if a new Democratic Congress were elected, "we are certain to go down the left lane which leads inseparably to socialism." In Baltimore, on October 31, Eisenhower used such terms as "political free spenders," "gloomdoggler," and "extremist" to describe his Democratic opponents.

House Speaker Rayburn on November 1 predicted that a new Democratic-controlled Congress would not fight the president despite "desperation" oratory in which Rayburn said Eisenhower went "pretty far in accusing us of being radicals and left-wingers." Rayburn said that "in the past about 85 percent of the time Eisenhower's programs were just an extension of Democratic principles. . . . We're not going to hate Eisenhower bad enough for us to change our principles."

Much of the hard campaigning for Republican candidates throughout the country was done by Vice President Nixon. On October 21 Nixon said that the Democratic party was split between "essentially moderate" Democratic leaders in Congress and the group "which presently controls the Democratic National Committee, which is radical in its approach to economic problems (and) bitterly partisan in its criticism of the Eisenhower foreign policy."

As the campaign progressed, the Republicans came under increasingly heavy Democratic fire for being antilabor. Eisenhower and Nixon refused to endorse the right-to-work laws, but the president called for legislation to let workers "free themselves of their corrupt labor bosses who have betrayed their trust."

In reply to the potent Democratic "missile gap" issue of allegedly slow U.S. progress in rockets and missiles, Eisenhower repeatedly declared that no more than $1 million had been spent on development of long-range missiles in any year before he became president, but that "the so-called missile gap is being rapidly filled."

Results of the 1958 Elections

As election returns poured in during the evening of November 4, it was clear that the Democratic tide had engulfed Republicans in virtually every area of the nation. Including the November 25 Alaska election, the results showed a new Senate of 64 Democrats and 34 Republicans, a Democratic gain of 15 seats and a Republican loss of 13

from the 49-47 Democratic edge in 1956. Democrats gained seats in California (where Republicans were embroiled in internecine fights and the right-to-work issue), Connecticut, Indiana, Maine, Michigan, Minnesota, Nevada, New Jersey, Ohio, Utah, West Virginia (2 seats), Wyoming, and the 2 new seats from Alaska.

The new Democratic senators included Eugene J. McCarthy of Minnesota, Thomas J. Dodd of Connecticut, Clair Engle of California, and Harrison A. Williams, Jr., of New Jersey. New Republicans elected to the Senate were Kenneth B. Keating of New York and Hugh Scott of Pennsylvania.

In the House there were 282 Democrats, 48 more than the previous Congress's total and the highest figure since the 1936 elections. Republicans slipped from 201 to 154 seats. Republican House losses were heaviest in the Midwest, where 23 seats were lost (many in the traditional Republican heartland), and in the East, where 20 were lost. Only two incumbent Democratic House members were defeated: Rep. Coya Knutson of Minnesota, evidently as a result of her marital difficulties, and Rep. Brooks Hays of Arkansas, a moderate on racial issues defeated on a write-in vote by Dale Alford, a Democratic archsegregationist in Arkansas's Fifth (Little Rock) District.

In gubernatorial races there was a net switch of 5 governorships, plus the new Alaska governorship, to the Democrats for a new total of 35 Democratic and 14 Republican governors. Important Democratic gubernatorial victories included Edmund G. Brown in California (over Senate minority leader William F. Knowland); Michael V. DiSalle, Ohio; Ralph G. Brooks, Nebraska; Ralph Herseth, South Dakota; Gaylord A. Nelson, Wisconsin; and J. Millard Tawes, Maryland. Democrats also reelected Gov. Abraham A. Ribicoff in Connecticut by a record majority and reelected Democratic governor George Docking in traditionally Republican Kansas.

The brightest spot in the entire picture for the Republicans was the New York governorship victory by Nelson A. Rockefeller over incumbent governor Averell Harriman by a 573,034-vote margin. Republicans also won the Oregon governorship with Mark Hatfield and the Rhode Island governorship with Christopher Del Sesto.

1959-1961:
The Eighty-sixth Congress

Relations between the United States and the Soviet Union dominated the international news, running the gamut from cordial to extremely bitter during 1959-1960.

In November 1958 Soviet premier Nikita S. Khrushchev had demanded an end to the four-power occupation of Berlin and threatened to turn control of Allied supply lines to West Berlin over to East Germany, asking that Berlin be made into a demilitarized "free city." The Soviet Union set May 27, 1959, as the deadline for the end of the occupation of Berlin. An international crisis, threatening atomic war, appeared to develop over the ensuing months. But when the Big Four foreign ministers sat down for consultations in Paris the following May, the Soviet deadline had been lifted and no changes in the Berlin status quo evolved.

Meanwhile, President Eisenhower had lost his key foreign policy adviser when Secretary of State John Foster Dulles was stricken by cancer early in 1959. Dulles resigned by April 15 and died on May 24. Under Secretary Christian

A. Herter, former Massachusetts congressman and governor, succeeded Dulles.

A period of moderation in U.S.-Soviet relations followed. Vice President Richard Nixon on July 22 left for a thirteen-day tour of the Soviet Union. Nixon received a friendly reception by Russian crowds. In September, at Eisenhower's invitation, Khrushchev visited the United States for consultations with the president and a transcontinental tour. But the 1959 "spirit of Camp David" failed to result in a lasting thaw in the cold war.

In May 1960, just before a scheduled Big Four summit conference in Paris, the Soviet Union announced that an American plane had been shot down over its territory. The United States at first said no violation of Soviet air space had been intended. After Khrushchev revealed that the pilot of the U-2 reconnaissance plane had confessed being on an intelligence-gathering flight for the U.S. Central Intelligence Agency, Secretary of State Herter admitted that the United States had engaged in "extensive aerial surveillance of the USSR." President Eisenhower took full responsibility for the flights, terming them a "distasteful but vital necessity."

When the Big Four met May 16, Khrushchev denounced the "spy flight" and demanded a U.S. apology and punishment of responsible officials before the summit conference could continue. He withdrew an already-accepted invitation to Eisenhower to visit the Soviet Union in June 1960. Eisenhower said the flights had been discontinued and would not begin again, but he refused to accept Khrushchev's ultimatum. The conference collapsed, and leaders withdrew to their capitals amid mutual recriminations.

The incident weakened the confidence of many voters in the Republicans' skill in handling foreign affairs. Some observers later speculated that if there had been no U-2 incident, and if the summit conference and the Eisenhower trip to the Soviet Union had proceeded as planned, the country might have been in no mood to replace the Republican hold on the White House in the November elections.

Other important international developments in 1959 and 1960 included the following:

~ Fidel Castro assumed power in Cuba after collapse of the Batista dictatorship on January 1, 1959. Communist influence and control over the Castro revolution became increasingly evident in the succeeding years.

~ A revolt by the Tibetan people against Chinese Communist rule was crushed in March 1959.

~ Eisenhower made good-will missions to Europe, Asia, and Africa in December 1959, to Latin America in February-March 1960, and to the Far East in early summer 1960. Leftist riots in Japan protesting the new U.S.-Japanese treaty of mutual security and cooperation forced Eisenhower to cancel plans to include that country in his Far Eastern tour.

~ The French tested their first nuclear device in the Sahara, February 13, 1960.

~ The Belgian Congo gained independence, becoming the Republic of the Congo on June 30, 1960; soon thereafter the country was plunged into civil war, resulting in UN intervention in July 1960.

On the domestic front heavy Democratic majorities in the Eighty-sixth Congress failed to produce the kind of prolabor, liberal legislation for which many observers had seen a mandate in the 1958 election returns. The two major accomplishments of Congress—Hawaiian statehood and a labor reform law—were in fact just as much administration as Democratic bills.

Statehood for Hawaii, signed into law March 18, 1959, after fifty-nine years of territorial status for the one-time island kingdom, added a fiftieth state to the Union. The new state elected the nation's first two representatives of Chinese and Japanese ancestry: Sen. Hiram L. Fong, a Republican, and Rep. Daniel K. Inouye, a Democrat.

In the waning days of the 1959 session Congress passed a "strong" labor regulation law (the Landrum-Griffin bill), which contained major Taft-Hartley Act amendments favored by business and opposed by organized labor. The continuing exposure of union corruption and labor-management collusion by the Senate Select Committee on Improper Activities in the Labor or Management Field had produced a deluge of letters, telegrams, and editorials calling for action.

The relatively mild Kennedy bill for labor regulation was passed by the Senate April 25. The House, on August 13, by a 229-201 roll call, approved an even tougher measure, the Landrum-Griffin bill, which incorporated important Taft-Hartley reforms sought by President Eisenhower. The vote was a major victory for Eisenhower and the House Republican leadership under the newly chosen minority leader, Charles A. Halleck, R-Ind. It was a defeat for House Speaker Sam Rayburn, who preferred a milder measure. Most of Landrum-Griffin was incorporated in the conference committee compromise.

Determined to prevent adoption of expensive domestic programs suggested by liberal Democrats, Eisenhower sought to dramatize the issue of "spending" in his press conferences and other public utterances. Grass-roots response was so positive that he was able to galvanize the Republican minority and invigorate the Republican-southern Democratic coalition, preventing passage of most liberal measures and rallying sufficient strength to sustain his vetoes of all but a handful of those that did pass. Thus Democratic proposals for a wide program of aid for school construction and teachers' salaries, for a massive area redevelopment program, for an increased minimum wage, and for medical care for the aged under Social Security all came to naught.

During 1960, however, the liberals found a new issue on which to base their call for increased social welfare legislation: the need for a rapid rate of growth in the national economy. The issue of economic growth developed too late to assist in passage of liberal measures in the Eighty-sixth Congress, but it provided campaign fodder for Democratic nominee John F. Kennedy in the 1960 presidential campaign.

The failure of many important domestic bills to clear Congress was largely attributed to the continuing party division between the executive and legislative branches and the approaching presidential elections. In 1959, for instance, the Senate took time out for a long and bitter debate that ended in rejection of the president's nomination of Lewis L. Strauss to be secretary of commerce. In 1960 a $750 million pay raise for federal employees was passed over the president's veto. Scenting victory in the upcoming elections, Democrats refused to pass a bill creating thirty-five badly needed new federal judgeships.

After long debate over the "missile gap" and the general adequacy of the nation's defense effort, Congress passed the president's defense budget with few overall changes in 1959 but in 1960 added $600 million more than Eisenhower had requested. The missile gap became a major issue in the 1960 presidential campaign, only to recede as an apparent mirage early in 1961.

During the postconventions session of Congress that began August 8, 1960, Democratic presidential candidate John F. Kennedy, a Massachusetts senator, and his running mate, Senate majority leader Lyndon B. Johnson, failed in their efforts to complete action on major Democratic legislation planks. The Senate approved the Kennedy minimum wage bill, but the measure died when House conferees refused to budge from their own truncated version. Medical care for the aged under the Social Security system—a second "must" bill—was rejected by the Senate, and a school construction bill expired when the House Rules Committee refused to send it to conference. As Congress adjourned September 1 and the campaign began in earnest, Republicans made the most of their opponents' plight.

The 1960 Campaigns

The Twenty-second Amendment to the Constitution, placing a two-term limitation on the presidency, meant that Eisenhower was ineligible to seek reelection in 1960. Adlai E. Stevenson's record of two defeats for the presidency appeared to preclude him from choice as the Democrats' candidate, barring a convention deadlock. Thus both parties were faced with the prospect of coming up with new nominees in 1960. For the Republicans the choice appeared relatively easy since Vice President Richard Nixon had been in the public eye for eight full years. Nixon had been an extremely active vice president, he was a tireless campaigner for GOP candidates, and he had strong support in Republican organizations throughout the country. For the Democrats the choice was more difficult because no members of the party had clearly established themselves as leaders of presidential stature.

In a departure from the American tendency to select governors for presidential nominees, all four chief contenders for the Democratic nomination were senators. In order of their announcements they were Hubert H. Humphrey of Minnesota, John F. Kennedy of Massachusetts, Stuart Symington of Missouri, and Majority Leader Lyndon B. Johnson of Texas. Of these four only Kennedy and Humphrey chose to campaign in the primaries. In the end the primaries were the decisive factor in Kennedy's victory.

Symington dismissed primary contests as useless and Johnson maintained that he could not carry out his Senate duties properly and simultaneously run in numerous individual primaries. (CQ 1960 Senate Voting Participation scores showed an average of 80 percent for all Democrats. Kennedy scored 35 percent, Humphrey 49 percent; both campaigned extensively during the session. Symington scored 58 percent, and Johnson, 95 percent.)

The issue of Kennedy's religion dominated much of the preconvention and general-election debate and speculation about his chances. Not since 1928, when the Democrats nominated Alfred E. Smith of New York for the presidency, had a Roman Catholic headed a national ticket. Smith had been resoundingly defeated, with many normally Democratic but heavily Protestant states going against him, although other considerations than religion, perhaps equally important, ran against Smith. In the intervening years Roman Catholics had become a far larger segment of the population than before (16 percent in 1928; 22.8 percent by 1960, with especially large concentrations in the urban areas in the biggest states). The consensus was that the nation had become far more tolerant in its religious outlook.

The spring primaries produced a string of unbroken victories for Kennedy. Unopposed, he piled up an impressive 43,372 vote total in the early-bird New Hampshire primary March 8. In May Humphrey withdrew after the West Virginia primary, leaving Symington and Johnson as opponents for Kennedy. Just before the convention it appeared that Stevenson might reenter the race.

At the Democratic National Convention, which opened in Los Angeles on July 11, Kennedy won on the first ballot. After conferring with Democratic leaders, he announced that Lyndon B. Johnson would be his running mate. Most observers were surprised that Johnson, powerful Senate majority leader and almost ten years Kennedy's senior, would accept the nomination. Most party liberals expressed consternation at Kennedy's selection. Later it became evident that Johnson's presence on the ticket was probably an essential element in holding most of the South behind Kennedy and effecting Democratic victory in one of the closest presidential elections in U.S. history.

Without any significant opposition, Nixon breezed through the primaries and at the Republican National Convention was nominated July 27, receiving 1,321 votes to 10 for Barry Goldwater. He selected UN ambassador and former Massachusetts senator Henry Cabot Lodge as his running mate.

By election day, November 8, Kennedy had covered seventy-five thousand miles and visited forty-six states, while Nixon had traveled more than sixty thousand miles and appeared in all fifty states. Speaking as often as a dozen times a day, both candidates were seen and heard by millions of voters, in person as well as on radio and television, in what may have been the most talkative as well as the most expensive campaign on record.

The central issue, Kennedy asserted time and again, was the need for strong presidential leadership to reverse the nation's declining prestige abroad and lagging economy at home. Arguing that the position of the United States relative to that of the Soviets had deteriorated under the Eisenhower administration, he called for a stepped-up defense effort and an enlarged federal role in a wide variety of fields at home and abroad "to get America moving again."

In an unprecedented series of face-to-face encounters, candidates Kennedy and Nixon appeared on four nationally televised, hour-long programs during which they were questioned by panels of journalists and permitted to rebut each other's answers. The time was provided free of charge by the networks when Congress suspended the equal time provision of the Communications Act for the duration of the 1960 campaign. The audiences for the four debates were estimated by the Arbitron rating service at seventy to seventy-five million, sixty-one million, sixty-five million, and sixty-four million, respectively.

Republicans generally were dismayed by Nixon's appearance on the first debate, blaming it on poor lighting and their candidate's unaggressive stance, but they found little fault with the remaining three programs. Democrats regarded all the debates as highly successful on grounds that they served to demolish the GOP theme of Kennedy's "immaturity" and to project his personality to millions of undecided voters, many of whom were disturbed by his Catholic faith.

Results of the 1960 Elections

On election day 68,828,960 Americans—the largest number in history—cast ballots for president. Kennedy emerged the victor with a solid majority in the electoral college. But his popular-vote plurality over Nixon was only 114,673 votes, the smallest vote margin of the twentieth century. In eleven states—eight won by Kennedy, three by Nixon—a shift of less than 1 percent of the vote would have switched the state's electoral votes.

The Kennedy-Johnson ticket carried twenty-three states with 303 electoral votes. They put together a coalition of eastern states (including New York, Pennsylvania, and New Jersey), central industrial states (Illinois, Michigan, and Minnesota), and several of the traditionally Democratic southern states (including Johnson's own Texas) that was sufficient to win, despite loss of almost the entire West and farm belt and several southern states.

Democrats maintained their heavy majorities in Congress and among the nation's governors in 1960, but Republicans were able to make some important gains, especially in the House of Representatives. Republican gains, taking place in the face of a victory for Democratic candidate Kennedy, appeared due in part to the return of normally Republican seats to the GOP to offset the serious losses suffered by Republicans in the 1958 Democratic sweep.

The continued heavy Democratic congressional majority, especially in the Senate, made it appear unlikely that Republicans would be able to regain control of Congress at any time during President-elect Kennedy's first term in the White House.

The Republicans made a gain of 2 Senate seats, replacing Democrats in Delaware and Wyoming. Despite advance predictions of possible trouble for Republican Senate incumbents in Massachusetts and New Jersey, both were able to withstand the Kennedy tide in those states. Democrats held their seats in Minnesota, Missouri, Michigan, and Montana, where Republican challengers ran energetic campaigns. The new Senate balance was 64 Democrats and 36 Republicans.

The Republican Senate gain was reduced when Senator-elect Keith Thomson, R-Wyo., died on December 9 and was replaced by Democrat J. J. Hickey. But the Senate balance returned to 64-36 in May 1961, when Republican John Tower won the Texas Senate seat vacated by Lyndon B. Johnson, the new vice president.

In House elections Republicans made a net gain of 20 seats. The new House had 263 Democrats and 174 Republicans, as compared to a 283-154 balance in the previous Congress.

In contrast to most presidential elections, the victory of the national Democratic ticket did not appear to play an important part in most congressional contests. If Kennedy coattails existed at all, they were probably evident in New York State, which he carried by a wide margin and where 3 incumbent GOP congressmen were defeated; in Connecticut, where Democrats held 2 close seats; and in New Jersey, where 1 Republican seat went Democratic. All other Democratic House gains appeared to be the result of special local conditions.

The most important Republican congressional gains came in the Midwest, where Nixon ran a strong race. Widespread and deep-seated anti-Catholic sentiment, combined with a marked cooling off of the farm issue, which hurt midwestern Republicans so badly in 1958, appeared to form the basis of much of the increased Republican midwestern strength in both presidential and local races.

Many Republican gains, through midwestern farm states but also in Connecticut, Maine, Ohio, Vermont, Oregon, and Pennsylvania, seemed to mark the return to the GOP fold of traditionally Republican congressional districts, which had gone Democratic in 1958 in a temporary protest against Republican policies.

In gubernatorial races the Democrats captured 7 seats from the Republicans, and the Republicans captured 6 from the Democrats. The new lineup was 34 Democrats to 16 Republicans, a net gain of 1 for the Democrats. Among the governors elected were Democrats Otto Kerner of Illinois, Matthew E. Welsh of Indiana, John B. Swainson of Michigan, and Frank B. Morrison of Nebraska. Republican governors elected included John A. Volpe of Massachusetts, Elmer L. Andersen of Minnesota, Norman A. Erbe of Iowa, and John Anderson, Jr., of Kansas.

1961-1963:
The Eighty-seventh Congress

Hopes were high, both in America and abroad, when John F. Kennedy, took office as president January 20, 1961. In his inaugural address Kennedy called on Americans and all free people "to bear the burden of a long twilight struggle ... against the common enemies of man: tyranny, poverty, disease and war itself." Kennedy urged Americans: "Ask not what your country can do for you—ask what you can do for your country."

Some of this idealism was translated into specific programs and action during the next two years. A Peace Corps was established, sending young Americans to underdeveloped nations, to provide trained personnel for development projects. Fulfilling another campaign promise, Kennedy got congressional approval of a U.S. Arms Control and Disarmament Agency. On March 14, 1961, the president announced an Alliance for Progress with the countries of Latin America, under which the United States would step up aid to the other Americas but expect to see political and social reforms to guarantee true democracy and promote stability and progress in those countries.

In the domestic field several items of "liberal" legislation that had failed passage because of a stalemate between President Eisenhower and a Democratic Congress were enacted into law. Chief among these were a hike in the minimum wage to $1.25, a subsidy program for economically distressed areas in the United States, widening of Social Security benefits, a $4.88 billion omnibus housing bill, stepped-up federal aid to localities to battle water pollution, and a vastly increased public works program.

The first two years of Kennedy's term, however, contained disappointments, both foreign and domestic. In January 1961 the administration had high hopes of a period of relaxed tensions with the Soviet world. Congratulating Kennedy on his election, Soviet premier Nikita S. Khrushchev had expressed the "hope that while you are at this post the relations between our countries will again follow the line along which they were developing in Franklin Roosevelt's time." Khrushchev made specific mention of chances for early conclusion of a nuclear test ban treaty and a German peace treaty. During the first week of Kennedy's presidency the Soviet government freed two U.S. Air Force RB-47 pilots who had been held in the USSR since their plane was downed off Soviet shores in July 1960. But the optimism of January 1961 seemed more like overconfidence by late 1961 as the tide of events continued to run almost consistently against the nation's foreign policy objectives.

On April 17, 1961, twelve hundred Cuban refugees—recruited, trained, and supplied by the U.S. Central Intelligence Agency—landed ninety miles south of Havana; their announced goal was to overthrow the Communist-oriented regime of Fidel Castro. Within three days the invasion had been crushed, inflicting a disastrous blow to American prestige and to that of the new president.

Kennedy met with Khrushchev June 3-4, 1961, in Vienna. At this summit conference Khrushchev made clear his determination to sign a peace treaty with the East German Communist regime, a move long interpreted in the West as part of the effort to force the Western powers out of West Berlin. The Vienna confrontation convinced Kennedy that it was time to muster public support in behalf of a "firm stand" in Berlin. In a July 25 televised report to the nation, he called for an immediate buildup of U.S. and NATO forces along with an extra $3.5 billion in U.S. defense funds. Congress promptly granted his requests.

Khrushchev's reply was to threaten Soviet mobilization and to boast that the Soviets could build a hundred-megaton nuclear warhead. Much more damaging to the West, however, was the Communists' unexpected action on August 13 in sealing off the border between East and West Berlin. The wall virtually stopped the large flow of refugees from East to West that had bled the Communist regime of much of its most valuable personnel during the postwar years.

Adding immeasurably to the tension over Berlin was the Soviet announcement on August 30, 1961, that it would break the three-year voluntary moratorium on testing of nuclear weapons because of the "ever increasing aggressiveness of the policy of the NATO military bloc." The Soviet test series began September 1 and concluded in November 1961. Their tests completed, the Soviets returned to the test ban negotiations in Geneva on November 28. The United States, however, refused to reimpose an uncontrolled moratorium on itself and, between April 25 and November 4, 1962, carried out a series of tests underground and in the atmosphere.

Two Southeast Asian nations, Laos and Vietnam, were thorny problems for the new administration. Fearful that a Communist takeover of Laos would make the Western position in Vietnam untenable, the administration supported establishment of a "neutral" government in Laos, in the hope that the tiny kingdom could serve as a buffer. In Vietnam increased Communist guerrilla activity forced increased commitment of U.S. military "advisers," who soon found themselves in the thick of military engagements.

Cuba, however, remained the chief foreign policy problem of the administration. The Castro regime became increasingly identified as a Soviet satellite and was expelled from the Organization of American States. During the summer of 1962 Soviet arms began to pour into Cuba. On October 22 President Kennedy told the American people in a radio-television address that U.S. aerial surveillance of the Soviet military buildup in Cuba had produced "unmistakable evidence" that "a series of offensive missile sites is now in preparation on that imprisoned island. The purpose of these bases can be none other than to provide a nuclear strike capacity against the Western Hemisphere."

As countermeasures the president announced "a strict quarantine on all offensive military equipment under shipment to Cuba" and said that U.S. ships would begin checking incoming shipments to the island. He called on the Soviet leader to withdraw his offensive weapons from Cuba.

For several days the Soviets continued preparation of their missile sites, and the world wondered whether it might be plunged into war. On October 27 Khrushchev, apparently unwilling to take the ultimate risk, sent a note to Kennedy in which he agreed to remove the offensive weapons systems from Cuba under UN observation and supervision in return for removal of the U.S. quarantine and agreement not to launch an invasion of the islands.

In succeeding weeks the removal of the bases took place at a relatively rapid rate. Castro, however, blocked UN inspection, and the United States never formalized its agreement not to invade Cuba. Thousands of Soviet troops and technical personnel remained on the island, along with a heavy array of "defensive" weapons.

Kennedy's chief domestic problem during his first two years in office was the lagging condition of the U.S. economy. The new administration made clear its commitment to a general monetary and fiscal policy aimed at the inducement of economic growth, even at the price of heavy federal budget deficits. Federal expenditures rose from $81.5 billion in fiscal 1961 to $87.8 billion in fiscal 1962 and $94.3 billion in estimated figures for fiscal 1963. The federal deficit rose from $3.8 billion in 1961 to $6.4 billion in 1962, and dropped slightly to $6.2 billion for fiscal 1963.

Aided in part by the sharply increased federal expenditures under Kennedy, the 1960 recession tapered off by mid-1961. But the basic underlying problems remained.

Although President Kennedy had himself served in the House for six years and in the Senate for eight, relations between his administration and Congress were far from ideal. The change in Democratic leadership in both houses, some congressional apprehension about use of political power by the new administration, and a continuing "conservative coalition" between Republicans and southern Democrats all tended to slow down if not wreck parts of the Kennedy program.

Most apparent and serious was the shift in leadership. The elevation of Lyndon B. Johnson to the vice presidency removed one of the strongest majority leaders in the history of the Senate. He was succeeded by Sen. Mike Mansfield, D-Mont., a mild-mannered man who lacked Johnson's drive.

On November 16, 1961, House Speaker Sam Rayburn, D-Texas, died of cancer. Rayburn had been a member of the House for almost forty-nine years and had served as Speaker for seventeen years (twice interrupted by brief periods of Republican majorities). Any successor would have faced difficulties in filling the shoes of "Mr. Sam," a man who understood the House and, until his later years, could draw together the disparate elements of his party with remarkable success. John W. McCormack of Massachusetts, elevated from the majority leadership to be Speaker, faced the unenviable task of succeeding Rayburn. His first year in office was considered a qualified success.

The Eighty-seventh Congress ended on an acrimonious note. A year-long feud between the House and Senate on procedural issues regarding appropriation bills was symptomatic of a broader rift between the two chambers that had been growing for several years. The dispute held up several fund bills for months (well beyond July 1, the start of the new fiscal year) and helped prolong the 1962 session to October 13. Not since the Korean War year of 1951 had a session lasted until so late in the autumn.

During the ensuing months increasing discussion was heard of the need to modernize and streamline congressional procedures.

The 1962 Midterm Elections

The Kennedy administration entered the 1962 campaign determined to reinforce the narrow margin by which the president had been elected in 1960 and to prevent serious losses in Democratic congressional strength. The off-year elections of 1961 had produced mixed results. In a May 1961 special election in Texas the Democrats had lost the Senate seat vacated by Vice President Johnson to Republican John Tower. Not since Reconstruction days had Texas sent a Republican to the Senate.

But in the November 1961 elections, Democrat Richard J. Hughes, aided by a personal appearance on his behalf by President Kennedy, won the New Jersey governorship against no less an opponent than Republican James P. Mitchell, secretary of labor in the Eisenhower administration.

Mayor Robert F. Wagner, a political ally of the president, easily won reelection in New York City. The administration felt confident that with sufficient presidential campaigning, the party could fare well in the 1962 elections.

Kennedy set the tone for the 1962 battle in a July 23 press conference. Declaring that the congressional Republicans were almost wholly negative on domestic social legislation, he said that he would go all-out to defeat them in the fall campaign. Kennedy said a Democratic gain of one or two Senate seats and five or ten House seats would make it possible to enact controversial administration bills in such fields as Medicare, public works, mass transit, and urban affairs. He said the 1962 elections would give the American people a "clear" choice: to "anchor down" by voting Republican or to "sail" by voting Democratic.

In midsummer the president began to make flying campaign trips to various states every weekend and some weekdays. Until halted by the Cuban crisis October 20, the president's campaigning promised to be the most vigorous of any U.S. president in a midterm election. In every appearance he went down the line for all Democratic candidates. The president was accorded a warm personal reception in most cities, confirming the high degree of personal popularity with the people that had been recorded in Gallup polls. Whether his plea to elect "more Democrats" was making a serious impression remained in doubt, however.

By October public uneasiness over the Communist arms buildup in Cuba was growing. Republicans made a central campaign issue of Cuba, and most observers thought the GOP would make some gains. But the president's October 22 announcement of a naval quarantine of Cuba and his ultimatum to Khrushchev blunted the Republican arguments and rallied the country behind him.

The Republicans began the 1962 campaign in hopes they could win important congressional and gubernatorial gains and thereby increase their effectiveness as an opposition party in Washington and prepare for a possible presidential comeback. They counted on the traditional pattern of midterm gains for the party out of power to help them in the congressional elections.

The party, however, was suffering from image problems. The congressional wing of the GOP, headed by Senate minority leader Everett Dirksen, R-Ill., and House minority leader Charles Halleck, R-Ind., had dominated the news of Republican activity in Washington since Eisenhower's retirement. Deprived of the expertise of the executive branch, Hill Republicans came up with few legislative initiatives and had few counterproposals to the stream of legislative requests that flowed from the White House.

The only serious competition to Dirksen and Halleck for the Republican spotlight was Sen. Barry Goldwater of Arizona, whose outspoken conservatism made him the favorite of the right wing throughout the country. Moderate and liberal Republicans received scant attention. Eisenhower had retired; Nixon was embroiled in California politics; New York governor Nelson A. Rockefeller was busy preparing for his own reelection campaign in New York and wrestling with possible adverse effects of his divorce announced late in 1961.

The Republicans waged the 1962 campaign with familiar issues: the need for fiscal responsibility in government, calls for a balanced budget, and warnings of the dangers of encroaching federal (especially executive) power. But the GOP lacked any single strong issue, such as the demand for an end to wartime controls in 1946 or alleged Democratic responsibility for the Korean War in 1950, with which to rout the Democrats. For a while they hoped Cuba would be that issue, but the president's firm action in late October effectively deprived them of it. In the end improved Republican organizations, especially in the big cities, helped the party to some victories. But the only region of the country in which they made any significant congressional gains was the South, where they jumped from nine to fourteen seats.

Results of the 1962 Elections

The Democratic party confirmed its heavy majorities in both houses of Congress and among the states' governors. Democrats avoided "normal" midterm losses of the party in power by gaining 4 Senate seats and suffering only a nominal loss in the House. Not since 1934 had the presidential party fared so well in a midterm election. Democrats said that, in contrast to the familiar patterns of major midterm loses by the presidential party, the 1962 results constituted a real vote of confidence in the administration.

Republicans replied that they saw "no endorsement of the New Frontier and its policies." They pointed out that President Kennedy had not carried Democrats into office with him in 1960, actually losing 20 House seats that year, so that there were fewer vulnerable seats for the GOP to pick off in 1962. The Republicans argued that the national House vote for the GOP had actually risen to 47.7 percent, 4.0 points higher than 1958 and 2.7 points higher than 1960. Privately, however, Republicans expressed deep disappointment that they had not been able to register important gains, especially in the House.

Congressional reapportionment after the 1960 census had caused major shifts in the distribution of seats in the House. The eastern states lost a net of 7 seats; the South, 1; and the Midwest, 4. The western states were the beneficiaries, picking up 10 new seats; 8 of them went to California.

Democrats controlled the California legislature, which redistricted in 1961. As a result they gained 8 seats from California in the 1962 elections. A similar Republican gerrymander in New York State misfired, and Republican gains in other areas barely balanced the Democratic bonus from California.

Republicans were especially disappointed by their net loss of 4 Senate seats. The new Senate was so heavily Democratic that the Republicans had no real hope of regaining control until 1968 or later.

Despite a heavy turnover in the governorship elections (Democrats took 7 from the Republicans and lost a like number), the gubernatorial party balance remained 34-16 in favor of the Democrats. The Republicans, however, did seize control of several important state governorships including those of Pennsylvania, Ohio, and Michigan.

The most devastating defeat of the year was suffered by former vice president Richard M. Nixon, who was soundly defeated for governor of California only two years after barely missing election to the presidency. Other political veterans retired by the voters included longtime senators Homer E. Capehart, R-Ind., and Alexander Wiley, R-Wis.; Rep. Walter H. Judd, R-Minn.; and Gov. Michael V. DiSalle, D-Ohio.

The potential national leaders elected in 1962 included Republican representative William W. Scranton, elected governor of Pennsylvania by a 486,651 majority; former auto maker George W. Romney, a Republican who ended fourteen years of Democratic control of the Michigan governorship; youthful Democratic state representative Birch Bayh, who toppled Homer Earl Capehart in the Indiana Senate race; Edward M. "Ted" Kennedy, youngest brother of the president, who was elected U.S. senator from Massachusetts; and Robert Taft, Jr., a Republican who was elected congressman at large from Ohio.

Among the new senators elected in 1962 was Democrat Abraham A. Ribicoff, former governor of Connecticut and first secretary of Health, Education, and Welfare in the Kennedy administration. Hawaiian voters sent Rep. Daniel K. Inouye, a Democrat, to the Senate. He was the first U.S. senator of Japanese ancestry. The new governorship roster included James A. Rhodes, R-Ohio, John A. Love, R-Colo., Karl Rolvaag, D-Minn., John B. Connally, D-Texas, and John A. Burns, D-Hawaii.

Among the "miracle men" of 1962 were Philip H. Hoff, who became the first Democratic governor of Vermont in more than a century, and Henry Bellmon, who became Oklahoma's first Republican governor since the state joined the Union.

Incumbents who won impressive victories included Sen. Jacob K. Javits, R-N.Y., reelected by a plurality of almost one million; Republican Senate whip Thomas H. Kuchel, R-Calif., reelected by a quarter-million vote margin despite the 296,758-vote triumph of Democratic governor Edmund G. "Pat" Brown over Nixon in the same state's balloting; Sen. Thruston B. Morton, former national chairman of the Republican party, reelected against powerful Democratic opposition in Kentucky; and New York governor Nelson A. Rockefeller, whose plurality was down slightly from its 1958 level but still big enough to make him appear the top contender for the 1964 Republican presidential nomination.

Across the nation, voters showed a continuing tendency to disregard traditional party lines in choosing people for high office. The success of Democrats in rock-ribbed Republican states of northern New England and breakthroughs for the Republicans in the South—including a near miss in the Alabama Senate race—attested to the possible development of significant new voting patterns.

1963-1965:
The Eighty-eighth Congress

The years 1963-1964 were good years for most Americans as the nation enjoyed continued economic prosperity and international affairs remained relatively tranquil. These same years, however, witnessed the assassination of a president, the launching of the most profound equal rights drive since the Civil War, and seizure of control of one of the major American political parties by a right-wing faction.

John F. Kennedy was shot on November 22, 1963, as his motorcade moved through cheering crowds in downtown Dallas. Approximately one-half hour later the president was pronounced dead. A special presidential commission, headed by Chief Justice Earl Warren, reported September 27, 1964, that Lee Harvey Oswald, "acting alone and without advice or assistance," had shot the president. The report said Jack Ruby was on his own in killing Oswald and that neither was part of "any conspiracy, domestic or foreign," to kill President Kennedy. The report called for an overhauling and modernization of the Secret Service, the group entrusted with physical protection of the president, and of FBI procedures.

At 1:39 p.m., November 22, Vice President Lyndon Baines Johnson took the oath of office as the thirty-sixth president aboard the presidential jet plane just before its departure from Dallas to Washington. The next few days witnessed President Kennedy's funeral; the confluence in Washington of heads of state, dignitaries, and emissaries from governments of all the world to pay their respects to the dead president; and the resolute grasp of the reins of power by Lyndon Johnson.

The new president's political roots reached into the liberalism of the New Deal on the one hand and into the conservatism of political life in his native Texas on the other. His wealth of experience in American political life, especially in Congress, served him well as he moved into the presidency. He quickly embraced the salient features of President Kennedy's program, especially the tax cut bill and civil rights legislation; moved to win the confidence of the liberal community by a well-publicized "war on poverty" in America; and won the confidence of the business community and many conservatives by ordering strict economies in federal spending. Johnson's foes accused him of political sleight-of-hand in being both liberal and conservative at the same time, but opinion polls—and the 1964 elections—indicated the American people approved wholeheartedly.

The issue of civil rights produced a profound domestic crisis for the United States in 1963 and 1964. Discontented with the pace of their advances in all spheres of life, black Americans pressed for full rights in every field from voting to employment, from education to housing.

President Kennedy, in February 1963, had sent his first civil rights legislative program to Congress—one characterized by liberals of both parties as "thin." On April 3 mass demonstrations for equal rights began in Birmingham, Alabama. Dramatized by the use of children in the demonstrations and the use of dogs and hoses by the police against the blacks, events in Birmingham sparked a determined nationwide series of protests. By the end of 1963 demonstrations had taken place in more than eight hundred cities and towns, climaxed by a gigantic but orderly "March on Washington for Jobs and Freedom" in which more than two hundred thousand persons participated on August 28.

The demonstrations began primarily with black protestors, but millions of white Americans—most noticeably church groups and college students—took interest in the lot of black Americans. At the same time, however, many northern whites showed their hostility to the civil rights drive because it appeared to threaten de facto segregation in housing, employment, and education. Capitalizing on white northern fears, Alabama's segregationist governor,

George C. Wallace, entered spring 1964 Democratic presidential primaries in Wisconsin, Indiana, and Maryland and won 33.8, 29.8, and 42.8 percent of the vote in the respective races. But when the new Republican national leadership sought to cultivate the "white backlash" vote in the 1964 presidential campaign, the effort proved singularly unsuccessful outside a few Deep South states.

In early June 1963 congressional Republicans and liberal Democrats began to press for strong civil rights legislation, and on June 11 President Kennedy told the nation: "We cannot say to 10 percent of the population that . . . the only way they are going to get their rights is to go into the streets and demonstrate." A week later he submitted a new and broadened civil rights program to combat discrimination in public accommodations, schools, jobs, and voting, which he urged Congress to enact.

For a while it appeared the bill might go aground, but in November the House Judiciary Committee reported a bipartisan civil rights measure, the fruit of conferences between administration leaders and Republican congressional civil rights advocates. Working under cloture the Senate passed the bill June 19, 1964, by a 73-27 vote. The House passed the amended bill July 2, and President Johnson signed it into law a few hours later. Among other things the bill expanded federal power to protect voting rights; guaranteed access to all public accommodations and public facilities for all races, with federal power to back up the pledge; gave the federal government power to sue for school desegregation; outlawed denial of equal job opportunities in businesses or unions with twenty-five or more workers; and authorized the federal government to intervene in any court suit alleging denial of equal protection of the laws. It was the most sweeping civil rights measure in American history.

Determined to prevent economic stagnation and give the country's economy a major boost forward, President Kennedy in January 1963 proposed a $10.3 billion personal and corporate income tax cut to take effect July 1, 1963. After protracted hearings in the House and Senate, the final version, reducing taxes $11.5 billion annually, was signed into law by President Johnson February 26, 1964.

In the meantime the economy, which the tax bill had been designed to help, was doing surprisingly well on its own. The 1963 gross national product reached $585 billion, and the Council of Economic Advisers predicted a $623 billion level in 1964. With the exception of unemployment, which remained above 5 percent of the work force, most economic indicators continued a gradual upward rise during 1963 and 1964. In October 1964, 71.2 million Americans were employed. Despite the rise in the economy, only a few economists saw any serious threat of inflation.

In his State of the Union message January 8, 1964, Johnson called for an "unconditional" declaration of "war on poverty in America." The poverty program constituted the chief innovation in the president's legislative proposals. Submitting his specific program to Congress March 16, he called for a fiscal 1965 outlay of $962.5 million to fight poverty. When Congress finished action on his request in August, it had authorized $947.5 million, only $15 million less than the draft proposal, with approval of almost all the president's requests. As enacted, the bill authorized ten separate programs under the supervision of the Office of Economic Opportunity, created by the bill. Major sections authorized a Job Corps to provide youths with work experience and training in conservation camps and in residential training centers, a work-training program to employ youths locally, a community action program under which the government would assist a variety of local efforts to combat poverty, an adult education program, and a "domestic peace corps" program.

The years 1963 and 1964 witnessed a steady relaxation in the tensions of the cold war, perhaps the closest approximation to an East-West detente since 1945. At the beginning of 1963 U.S.-Soviet relations were at a standoff, produced by Russian withdrawal of missiles from Cuba in October 1962. By mid-1963 a Soviet-Chinese rift had deepened, and a lessening of U.S.-Soviet tensions was evident.

In a speech on June 10, 1963, Kennedy announced that the United States, the Soviet Union, and Great Britain would begin talks on a partial test ban, apart from the seventeen-nation Geneva talks that had dragged on intermittently without much hope since 1958. Then, before many realized that progress was at last to be made, a limited treaty was initialed in Moscow July 25. The Senate consented to ratification September 24.

A moderately optimistic tone pervaded U.S.-Soviet relations in 1964. On April 20 both the United States and the Soviet Union announced they were going to cut back their production of nuclear materials for weapons use. The growing tensions between China and the Soviet Union caused the Soviets to turn their attention more and more inward. On October 16 the Western world was shocked to hear that Nikita S. Khrushchev had been ousted from his duties as premier and also as first secretary of the Soviet Communist party. He was replaced as premier by Aleksei N. Kosygin and as party secretary by Leonid Brezhnev, possibly presaging a prolonged struggle for power within the Soviet hierarchy. The new Soviet leaders quickly made it clear they would follow Khrushchev's policy of "peaceful coexistence" with the West.

The Kennedy-Johnson administration's Alliance for Progress suffered as democratically elected regimes were deposed in Ecuador, Guatemala, Honduras, the Dominican Republic, and Bolivia. The Johnson administration faced its first major foreign policy crisis in January 1964 when large-scale violence broke out in Central America as Panamanians protested the 1903 treaty under which the United States administered the Panama Canal and Americans enjoyed special privileges in the Canal Zone. The United States was encouraged, however, when President Joao Goulart of Brazil, accused of conducting a leftist and chaotic administration, was deposed in a bloodless coup on April 1, 1964.

Apparently upset by Vietnam government moves against Buddhists, suicidal burnings by Buddhist monks, corruption within the government, and inadequate military success against the Communist Viet Cong, the State Department in 1963 gradually curtailed aid to the Vietnamese regime of Catholic president Ngo Dinh Diem. On November 1 a military coup ended the Diem regime. The State Department denied participation in the coup, but unofficially it admitted that it might have encouraged the "proper climate" for such a revolt. The new ruling junta in Vietnam was itself overturned by a coup in January 1964, starting a series of bewildering governmental shifts that lasted through 1964 as the military situation continued to deteriorate.

The off-year elections of November 1963 provided no definite clue to possible trends for 1964. Democrats maintained control of the Kentucky and Mississippi governorships and the Philadelphia mayoralty in the top three races, but the GOP vote was up sharply in all three areas.

Top Republican takeovers of the year were scored in New Jersey, where the Assembly reverted to GOP hands to give the Republicans majorities in both houses, and in Indiana, where the GOP elected twenty-five new mayors. The Republicans also scored gains in Virginia and Mississippi legislative elections. Democratic Representative John F. Shelley won election as mayor of San Francisco, ending fifty-five years of GOP control in technically nonpartisan elections. Suburban New York also showed some Democratic gains.

The 1964 Campaigns

From the beginning of 1964 it was apparent that President Johnson was the strong favorite to win a full four-year White House term in his own right. As the Democrats gathered in Atlantic City for their convention on August 24, Johnson kept silence about his final decision for a running mate. In a move unprecedented in American politics, he appeared before the Democratic National Convention just before his own nomination the same evening to announce to the delegates that Sen. Hubert H. Humphrey of Minnesota was his choice for the vice-presidential slot.

The most fascinating story of the 1964 presidential campaign, however, lay in the opposition party. Throughout the postwar years, the Republican party, despite its conservative inclinations, had generally embraced the wide consensus of U.S. politics: agreement on basic social welfare responsibilities of the government together with a firm but not bellicose policy toward the Communist world. But in 1964 the Republican party turned abruptly from the moderate course. For president it nominated a militantly conservative two-term Arizona senator, Barry Goldwater, known for his hostile views toward the power of the federal government and his apparent willingness to risk nuclear confrontation with the Soviets to advance the Western cause. The course set by Goldwater brought the Republican party its most devastating defeat in more than a quarter-century. Republican ranks in Congress and the state legislatures were greatly reduced. Even worse, national confidence in the party was so badly shaken that it might take years to recoup.

Early in 1964, however, only one Republican of national stature was willing to speak out on the possible dangers of Goldwater and his philosophy for the Republican party. That man was New York governor Nelson A. Rockefeller, who had entered the race for the GOP nomination November 7, 1963. Rockefeller symbolized the eastern progressive wing of the Republican party that had dominated Republican National Conventions since 1940. The other leaders of the Republican party's moderate wing—governors William W. Scranton of Pennsylvania and George W. Romney of Michigan, Ambassador Henry Cabot Lodge, and former vice president Richard M. Nixon—all were thought to harbor some presidential ambitions, but none was willing to take the plunge in the presidential primaries or to risk an open challenge to the Goldwater wing of the party.

The "National Draft Goldwater Committee," which organized formally in the spring of 1963, aimed both at nominating Goldwater and at remaking the entire Republican party into a vehicle for militant conservatism. Their aim appeared to be the reforming of two U.S. political parties along straight liberal versus conservative lines. By the autumn of 1963 the years of Goldwater stewardship

within the ranks of the Republican party had begun to bear fruit. Goldwater supporters held important positions in the Republican party apparatus. Rep. William E. Miller, R-N.Y., who would later become Goldwater's vice-presidential running mate, was the Republican national chairman.

The Republican National Convention, meeting in San Francisco July 13-16, turned sharply to the right, rejecting the party's moderate tone of the postwar years and substituting instead an unabashed conservatism in domestic affairs and all-out nationalism in foreign policy.

Goldwater's controversial stands and his failure to advance meaningful alternative solutions to national problems relieved Johnson of having to spell out in any substantial detail what his plans for the "great society" were. For the most part Johnson confined himself to calls for national unity and remarks aimed at broadening the breach between Goldwater and the bulk of moderate and liberal Republicans. Johnson was so successful in preempting the vital "middle ground" of American politics that a Democratic victory was assured long before election day.

Results of the 1964 Elections

In the November 3 elections President Johnson led the Democratic party to its greatest national victory since 1936. Not only did Johnson win a four-year White House term in his own right, amassing the largest vote of any presidential candidate in history, but his broad coattails helped the Democrats score major gains in the House of Representatives and increase their already heavy majority in the Senate.

The Johnson-Humphrey ticket ran 15,948,746 votes ahead of the Goldwater-Miller ticket, easily exceeding the previous national popular vote plurality of 11,068,093 by which Franklin D. Roosevelt defeated Alfred M. Landon in 1936. The final, official vote for Johnson-Humphrey was 43,126,584; for Goldwater-Miller, 27,177,838.

Johnson won forty-four states and the District of Columbia (which voted for the first time for president, under the terms of the Twenty-third Amendment to the Constitution). His electoral vote total was 486. Goldwater won six states with a total of 52 electoral votes. The Democratic presidential victory began in New England and the East, where Johnson carried every state and chalked up a better than 2-1 majority.

The Democratic sweep continued through the Republican midwestern heartland, where every state also cast its electoral vote for Johnson. The president was the winner in every mountain and Pacific state except Arizona, Goldwater's home state. California, which had boosted Goldwater to the Republican nomination in the June primary, went for Johnson by over a million votes.

Only an unusual degree of ticket splitting saved the Republican party from almost total annihilation in races for congressional and state posts. As it was, the Republicans were reduced to their lowest congressional levels since depression days. In elections to the House the Republicans suffered a net loss of 38 seats. The new House balance was 295 Democrats and 140 Republicans, the lowest GOP membership figure since the 1936 elections. Among the more serious Republican House losses were 7 seats in New York, 5 in Iowa, and 4 each in New Jersey, Michigan, Ohio, and Washington. Many of the northern Republican representatives defeated were among their party's most conservative, representing formerly "safe Republican" seats. For example, 54 Republican House members had backed Goldwater's nomination drive in June by signing a statement saying his nomination would "result in substantial increases in Republican membership in both houses of Congress." Of these, 17 were defeated, another 3 retired but saw their districts go Democratic, and all but 6 saw their winning percentages dwindle. Of the 21 northern Republicans who had voted with Goldwater against the 1964 Civil Rights Act, 11 were defeated. Republicans who disassociated themselves from Goldwater and his policies were generally more successful. The most spectacular Republican House victory of the year was scored by Rep. John V. Lindsay of New York, who refused to endorse Goldwater but won a 71.5 percent victory in his district, while Johnson was carrying it by more than 2-1.

The only area of significant Republican House gains was in the deep South, where Goldwater coattails helped the party elect 5 new representatives in Alabama and 1 each in Georgia and Mississippi. They were the first Republican House members from these states since Reconstruction. But at the same time 3 conservative GOP southern House members—2 in Texas, 1 in Kentucky—were going down to defeat.

One result of the election was to erode the power base of the "conservative coalition" between Republicans and southern Democrats. Not only would there be less conservative representation in the House, but the relative strength of northern liberals in the Democratic House Caucus would be increased substantially.

The Senate elections resulted in a net Democratic gain of 2 seats, making the new balance 68 Democrats and 32 Republicans. Not since the elections of 1940 had the Democrats held such a heavy majority. But the major story was not the new Democratic Senate gains of 1964 but the fact that the members of the liberal Democratic class of 1958 were all reelected to office. The Democrats' gain of 13 formerly Republican seats in 1958 had effected a basic realignment of power within the Senate, giving it a much more liberal orientation than the House. The Republicans had long looked forward to 1964 as the year when they would win back many of the class of 1958 seats.

The Democrats actually won 3 GOP Senate seats in 1964: Kenneth Keating's seat in New York, taken by Robert F. Kennedy (thus making Kennedy a potential future contender for the Democratic presidential nomination); J. Glenn Beall's seat in Maryland, won by Democrat Joseph D. Tydings; and the New Mexico seat of interim senator Edwin L. Mechem, won by Rep. Joseph M. Montoya. The sole GOP gain was in California, where George Murphy scored an upset victory over interim senator Pierre Salinger, former presidential press secretary.

A major blow to the GOP was the defeat in Ohio of Robert Taft, Jr., who was challenging Democratic senator Stephen M. Young. Before the election Taft had been looked to as a major future leader of his party. But the Goldwater "drag"—Johnson won Ohio by 1,027,466 votes—was too much for Taft to overcome.

In gubernatorial elections the Republicans scored gains in Washington, Wisconsin, and Massachusetts and lost seats they had held in Arizona and Utah. The result was a net gain of 1 for the GOP. But the already heavy Democratic majority was not weakened significantly. The new lineup was 33 Democrats and 17 Republicans.

Without Goldwater at the head of the ticket the Republicans might have scored much better. Their most disappointing defeat came in Illinois, where Charles H. Percy,

who had been regarded as a possible future presidential candidate, went down to defeat in the Democratic landslide.

The most spectacular GOP governorship win was scored by Michigan governor George R. Romney, seeking reelection. He withstood a Johnson landslide of more than 2-1 to win reelection. The outcome established Romney, who had refused to endorse Goldwater's candidacy, as a powerful future leader of his party.

Among the new governors elected were Samuel P. Goddard, D-Ariz., Roger D. Branigin, D-Ind., Daniel J. Evans, R-Wash., and Warren P. Knowles, R-Wis.

Democratic governors who won substantial reelection victories despite the Republican complexion of their states included Frank B. Morrison of Nebraska, Harold E. Hughes of Iowa, John W. King of New Hampshire, and Philip H. Hoff of Vermont. But in normally Democratic Rhode Island, Republican governor John H. Chafee won reelection with 61.3 percent of the vote, while Goldwater received only 19.1 percent of the state's vote.

The Vietnam War Years

The years of the 1960s and 1970s were some of the most turbulent in the nation's history. The seeds of the great upheavals ahead were already sprouting even before President Kennedy's death in November 1963. The country's role in the Vietnam War was inching upward. Black Americans were becoming ever more insistent in demanding an end to all forms of racial discrimination. A huge generation of teen-agers, born in the post-World War II baby boom, were reaching college age and were preparing to challenge authority on a scale unprecedented in American history. And there were growing indications of conservative political strength, especially within the Republican party.

In the late 1960s the nation experienced a series of cataclysmic changes that, while they did not appear to endanger the basic economic health of the nation, did jeopardize the postwar politics of consensus and promise as yet unpredictable changes in the social and political climate of American life. Only when the nation found itself entangled in a seemingly endless and unwinnable war in Vietnam in the mid-1960s did the first major cracks appear in the general national consensus behind U.S. foreign policy. For the first time serious doubts were raised about the role of the nation as a global policeman, and there were indications that a period of limited isolationism might come in the wake of any Vietnam settlement.

Through the 1964 election the United States had enjoyed remarkably stable two-party politics in the postwar years. No major ideological gulfs existed between the parties, and although the Democrats were more frequently victorious at the polls than the Republicans (an apparent legacy of Franklin Roosevelt's New Deal), few Americans were deeply concerned when the party in power changed in Washington or the state capitals. Indeed, two-party politics infused virtually every region of the country for the first time in its history. And as the parties became more competitive, personal allegiances shifted more frequently and ticket splitting became an American electoral pastime.

When Barry Goldwater was repudiated at the polls in 1964, the post-New Deal consensus seemed to have been reaffirmed. Indeed, the year 1965 saw the last major burst of legislative accomplishments and national optimism that the country was to witness for some time. With the large Democratic majorities created by the Johnson landslide, Congress enacted federal aid to education, a national health insurance program, and a voting rights act.

But the Johnson administration's fortunes soon changed. The decision to commit massive American ground forces to Vietnam resulted in increased opposition at home to American participation in the war. The war further stimulated student unrest on the campuses resulting in siege conditions at some universities. Blacks burst forth in anger and destroyed large sections of American cities. And the Rev. Martin Luther King, Jr., and Sen. Robert F. Kennedy were assassinated in 1968.

The Democratic party coalition broke open under these strains in 1968, with the challenge to President Johnson's renomination and the Independent candidacy of Alabama governor George C. Wallace. The result was that Republican Richard Nixon was elected to the presidency.

At the end of the 1960s both parties were clearly in transition. The Democrats, in order to hold their solid base among the low-income voters and the minorities, would be obliged to remain strong advocates of wide-ranging social reform. But that very course could possibly seal their eventual downfall in the South, even if an increased black vote in that region compensated for some of that loss. And while organized labor had turned out a strong Democratic vote in 1968, its leaders were having increasing difficulty in convincing workers that they should remain unswervingly loyal to the Democratic party.

The Republicans, even in winning the presidential election of 1968, received only 43 percent of the national vote and had to recognize that in their major base of support—the predominantly white, middle-class rural areas and small cities—they faced a diminishing asset in overall population terms. It was clear that the Republicans' growing strength in the burgeoning white suburban areas of America would hold solidly only as long as the party maintained domestic prosperity and found a way to calm inner-city tensions.

During his first term President Nixon too had to deal with antiwar demonstrations. But his policy of gradual withdrawal of American troops, climaxing with the peace settlement of January 1973, finally removed the war from the top of the American political agenda.

At the same time, with the passage of the baby-boom generation out of college and into the labor market, the nation's campuses became more peaceful. And the movement of many blacks onto the voter rolls, into public office, and into more jobs and better housing seemed to relieve some of the racial tension.

But at the very moment when things began looking better, the nation was hit by a fresh series of calamities. Throughout 1973 and 1974 the Watergate scandal implicated several top public officials, including the president himself, in illegal activities. The immediate result was the first presidential resignation in U.S. history, but the deeper ramification could be found in the damage it did to the confidence of the people in their government and leaders.

While the revelations were continuing, the United States was hit with an energy crisis when the Arab states cut off the flow of oil during the October 1973 war in the Middle East. Even when the flow was resumed, the price had been jacked up more than 300 percent, and this increase, combined with other trends in the economy, produced some of the worst inflation in the nation's history.

Buffeted by these forces, seemingly beyond their control, many Americans wondered about the future of their country and the stability of their economic and political system.

President Gerald Ford, with his low-key personality and image of personal integrity, helped calm the country after these misfortunes. But he was not seen by many as a strong leader and was almost defeated for the presidential nomination of his own party in the 1976 primaries.

1965-1967:
The Eighty-ninth Congress

Buoyed by the largest party majorities enjoyed by any president in three decades, Lyndon Johnson led the Eighty-ninth Congress in an amazingly productive 1965 session. The scope of the legislation was even more impressive than the number of major new laws. In the course of the year Congress approved programs that had long been on the agenda of the Democratic party—in the case of medical care for the aged under Social Security, for as long as twenty years. Other longstanding objectives were met by enactment of aid to primary and secondary schools, college scholarships, and immigration reform.

The pace of the 1965 session was so breathless as to cause a major revision of the image, widely prevalent in preceding years, of Congress as structurally incapable of swift decision. The change was because of three primary elements not always present in past years: the decisive Democratic majorities elected in 1965, the personal leadership of President Johnson, and the shaping of legislation to obtain maximum political support in Congress.

The expanded Democratic pluralities were most significant in the House, where the Democrats had not only scored a thirty-eight-seat net gain over the Republicans in the 1964 elections but had also traded a number of conservative Democratic votes in the South for liberal Democratic votes in the North. The new liberal strength in the House showed itself most dramatically in passage of the aid to education and medical care (Medicare) bills. The Senate had passed similar measures in previous years only to see them blocked by the hitherto powerful coalition of Republicans and conservative southern Democrats in the House. But the "conservative coalition," where it did appear in House roll call votes, was victorious only 25 percent of the time in 1965, compared with 67 percent in 1962 and 1964 and 74 percent in 1961, the first year of President Kennedy's term.

The president gained maximum political effect from his efforts to build a broad consensus of support. An excise tax cut, designed to keep the economy growing steadily, appealed to business and consumer interests alike. Lack of strong opposition from business circles made it easier for Democrats to mount the Great Society program of greatly increased civil benefits and tended to smother Republican protests that Congress was merely rubber stamping ill-conceived administration proposals.

The Voting Rights Act of 1965, the most comprehensive legislation to ensure the right to vote in ninety years, was prompted by the brutal suppression of demonstrations in Selma, Alabama, and other parts of the South. The bill went beyond the milder courtroom remedies of earlier civil rights acts. In the wake of this legislation an additional 500,000 southern blacks were registered by the time of the 1966 elections.

Other legislation was a housing bill authorizing $7.8

billion to fund new and existing housing programs through 1969 and a bill establishing a cabinet-level Department of Housing and Urban Development.

The year 1965 was punctuated by major crises in Vietnam. Faced with the threat of success by the Viet Cong Communist insurgents in South Vietnam, President Johnson initiated large-scale bombing raids in North Vietnam, which was giving major aid to the Viet Cong. When this tactic failed to turn the unfavorable course of the war, he ordered a vast increase—from about 20,000 to eventually more than 140,000—in American troop strength in the South and an aggressive prosecution of the land war. Both steps required new outlays for personnel and materiel. Despite highly vocal criticism of his Vietnam policy by a small band of senators, Congress overwhelmingly approved Johnson's special request for funds.

The Vietnam budget pressures soon had serious effect on the domestic economy. As 1966 began the U.S. economy was already strained to its noninflationary limit. After fifty-nine months of stable economic growth, it was near full employment. Plant capacity was in full use. Any sizable increase in demand under these conditions would be bound to result in inflation. This is precisely what occurred as the defense budget shot upward, without any significant offsetting measures to cut back on other purchasing power. The cost-of-living index jumped from 111.0 percent in January to 113.8 percent in August. The president early in the year asked and received congressional approval of a $5.9 billion bill to accelerate certain types of tax payments and reimpose 1965 excise tax levies, but the measure was hardly adequate to counter the Vietnam spending boom. Almost every leading economist in the nation called for a general tax increase, but President Johnson refused.

With the public increasingly concerned with inflation and the Vietnam War, congressional Republicans found new Democratic allies in the effort to curb the Great Society—not only its spending programs but almost any measure providing social reform. Despite strong persuasive efforts by the president, the administration was rebuffed on many major bills.

An important reason for the defeat of the administration's new civil rights proposals was a wave of summertime riots in black "ghetto" areas of the large cities. In August 1965 a six-day disturbance had erupted in Los Angeles's 95 percent black Watts area, with six to seven thousand youths participating in rioting, looting, and arson. The National Guard finally restored order, but only after thirty-four deaths. In summer 1966 other riots followed in the black areas of several other American cities. The 1966 riots were attributed not only to decades of frustration among urban blacks in education, housing, and employment fields but to the growth of a new philosophy of "black power," expounded by extremist civil rights groups such as the Congress of Racial Equality (CORE) and the Student Nonviolent Coordinating Committee (SNCC).

In the House, Rep. John William McCormack of Massachusetts continued as Speaker, and Sen. Mike Mansfield of Montana remained as Senate majority leader, with Sen. Everett Dirksen of Illinois his Republican counterpart. House minority leader Charles Halleck of Indiana was defeated for reelection to his leadership post by Rep. Gerald R. Ford of Michigan, just before formal opening of the Eighty-ninth Congress. Ford's election as minority leader was a continuation of the revolt of younger House Republicans that had begun with Ford's election as House GOP Conference chairman two years before. As in 1963 the

leadership struggle seemed to be based less on ideological differences than on the question of which representative could give the most forceful leadership to the depleted Republican House ranks.

The 1964 elections had left the Republicans at such a low point that some resurgence seemed inevitable. In 1965 it began in a spectacular way as Republican-Liberal John V. Lindsay won election as mayor in heavily Democratic New York City. Lindsay's victory, combined with the victories of liberally inclined Republican candidates for district attorney in Philadelphia and mayor in Louisville, Kentucky, signaled a potential Republican resurgence on the left in the very areas where Goldwater had been weakest—in the major cities and especially among blacks and other minority groups.

In New Jersey, however, the Republican gubernatorial candidate took a conservative tack similar to that of the 1964 Goldwater campaign and found himself defeated by Democratic governor Richard J. Hughes by a record 363,572-vote margin. Democrats also held the Virginia governorship and legislature and easily maintained control of the mayors' offices in major cities such as New Haven, St. Louis, Pittsburgh, and Detroit. In Cleveland a black state legislator running as an Independent came within 2,143 votes of upsetting the incumbent Democratic mayor. In the smaller cities some of the most interesting contests took place on June 8 in Hattiesburg and Columbus, Mississippi, where the first Republicans of the twentieth century—all staunch conservatives—were elected mayors.

The 1966 Midterm Elections

From the beginning of the 1966 campaign the Democrats realized that they faced formidable odds if they hoped to maintain their overwhelming margins of control in Congress and in the state governorships and legislatures. Yet at the end of 1965 it looked as if the minority Republicans might be held to minimal gains. The first session of the Eighty-ninth Congress had passed laws with benefits for almost every segment of the population. President Johnson still enjoyed the wide "consensus" support he had enjoyed in 1964, from every group from organized labor to big business and the minorities. And the economy was booming on virtually every front.

By the beginning of the 1966 campaign, however, it was apparent that the odds had shifted significantly to the benefit of the Republicans. Behind the change was the escalation of the Vietnam War, with its heavy toll both in American lives and dollars. The conflict in Vietnam, because of its limited nature, increased frustrations across the country and began to undermine public support of the administration in power.

The war effort generated inflationary pressures that were being felt throughout the country by mid-1966. The Republicans were able to argue with some effectiveness that the Johnson administration should be cutting down, rather than increasing, national expenditures for a wide variety of Great Society programs. Moreover, those very social welfare programs that had looked so politically attractive at the end of 1965 were beginning to encounter serious administrative difficulties, with wide gaps between the administration's promises to improve educational standards, end conditions of poverty, and ensure racial peace and its ability to deliver those promises.

President Johnson's own popularity plummeted during the year; wide splits appeared in the Democratic party in many important states; and at the same time several attractive Republican candidates appeared to lead the GOP in critical states—in sharp contrast to the unpopularity of Goldwater, the party's 1964 standard bearer.

Early in 1965 the Democrats had launched an ambitious Operation Support from within the Democratic National Committee, designed to reelect a large portion of the seventy-one freshman Democratic representatives who came into office in the 1964 Democratic sweep—thirty-eight of them from formerly Republican districts. But while Operation Support functioned smoothly in 1965, it tended to fall off in 1966 as the national committee obeyed presidential orders to cut back on its activities in order to pay off a heavy debt left from the 1964 campaign.

The Republican congressional effort, on the other hand, was bolstered by a massive fund-raising campaign that made it possible to funnel thousands of dollars into every doubtful congressional district in the country. Reports just before the elections showed national-level gifts of $1.6 million to GOP congressional candidates from their party headquarters, compared with only $250,000 from national-level Democratic committees.

The primary season indicated some significant shifts in the political landscape. In California, long a bastion of liberal Republicanism, actor Ronald Reagan, an outspoken conservative, won a sweeping primary victory over more liberal opposition. In the Virginia primary two aging representatives of traditional conservative southern Democracy were defeated by younger men of more moderate persuasion. In Florida the mayor of Miami, Robert King High, won the Democratic gubernatorial primary with liberal support over the more conservative incumbent governor. Staunch segregationist candidates, on the other hand, won Democratic gubernatorial primaries in the Deep South: Jim Johnson in Arkansas, Lester Maddox in Georgia, and Lurleen Wallace, wife of outgoing governor George C. Wallace (who was ineligible to succeed himself), in Alabama.

As the campaign gathered steam in the fall, the Republicans concentrated their fire increasingly on the issues of inflation, Vietnam, crime, and the alleged credibility gap between what President Johnson and his administration said they were doing and their actual performance.

Results of the 1966 Elections

The Republican party reasserted itself as a major force in American politics by capturing 8 new governorships, 3 new seats in the Senate, and 47 additional House seats in the November 8 elections. In a striking comeback from its devastating defeat of 1964, the GOP elected enough new governors to give it control of twenty-five of the fifty states with a substantial majority of the nation's population. The Senate and House gains left the party still short of a majority but in a position of new power and relevance on the national scene.

A new vigor shown by Republican candidates across the country marked a return to more competitive two-party politics and the possibility that the 1968 presidential election could be closely contested. The vast majority of successful Republican candidates, both for congressional and state offices, appeared to have rejected the ultraconservative ideology symbolized by former senator Barry Goldwater. But the winning Republicans did represent a somewhat more conservative philosophy than that of the president and his administration, reflecting a national movement to the right, which many observers felt was reflected in the

slowdown on major domestic reforms in the closing session of the Eighty-ninth Congress. The 1966 elections appeared to lay the groundwork for a strong moderate Republican challenge to Johnson in 1968.

The party control among the state governorships shifted form 33-17 in favor of the Democrats to 25-25, the greatest Republican strength since the early 1950s. The Republicans gained California and held New York, Pennsylvania, Ohio, and Michigan to give them control of five of the nation's seven largest states. In addition to California, the Republicans added Alaska, Arizona, Arkansas, Florida, Maryland, Minnesota, Nebraska, Nevada, and New Mexico to the list of governorships under their control. Among the new Republican governors were Winthrop Rockefeller of Arkansas; Claude R. Kirk, Jr. (in traditionally Democratic Florida); and Spiro T. Agnew of Maryland, a political moderate who defeated George P. Mahoney, the narrow victor in a three-way Democratic primary who had pitched his campaign to the "white backlash" vote. (In general, "backlash" candidates were unsuccessful in the elections.) Republican gubernatorial candidate Howard Callaway won a plurality of the votes in the one-time impregnable Democratic stronghold of Georgia. But Callaway failed to poll an absolute majority, and under the Georgia constitution, the election was thrown into the state legislature, which chose the Democratic runner-up, Lester Maddox.

The Republicans' most spectacular gain was in the House, where they picked up 52 seats and lost only 5 to the Democrats. The new party lineup in the House would be 248 Democrats and 187 Republicans. The Republican total in the thirteen southern states rose to 28 seats, compared with only 14 in 1962. In Senate elections Republicans gained seats in Illinois, Oregon, and Tennessee, giving them 36 seats to the Democrats' 64. Democrats failed to take any Senate seats from the Republicans.

In the state legislatures the Republicans scored net gains of 156 senate seats and 401 seats in the lower houses, reflecting not only the strong party trend running in the Republicans' favor but the fact that reapportionment, by adding seats in suburban areas, was helping them as much as it helped the Democrats, if not more.

1967-1969:
The Ninetieth Congress

The United States in 1967-1968 underwent two of the most trying years in its history as a rising wave of rioting and looting swept over its largely black central cities, the Vietnam War continued to build in human and dollar costs, inflationary pressures mounted, and two major national leaders were assassinated. President Johnson, recognizing the inability of his administration to command continued strong popular support, announced in March 1968 that he would not seek reelection to a second full term in the White House.

The Vietnam War became increasingly troublesome. It often overshadowed civil rights and city problems, distorted the U.S. economy, and loomed over U.S. foreign policy. Its cost soared to more than $2 billion a month. Reflecting the expense of the war, the federal budget by fiscal 1969 was at a record $186 billion, with $80 billion of that for defense.

Hopes for a political settlement in Vietnam were buoyed on October 31, when President Johnson announced he was ordering a complete halt to all American bombing of the North. Though not officially confirmed, it was believed that the bombing halt was undertaken with tacit agreement that it would last only so long as the North Vietnamese did not use it to their military advantage. A new and complicated round of negotiations then began in Paris on the means and protocol for substantive peace negotiations.

The patterns of violence in American life reasserted themselves when two prominent Americans became victims of assassins' bullets. The first was the Rev. Martin Luther King, Jr., who was shot and killed April 4, 1968, in Memphis, Tennessee. Following his death, rioting, looting, and burning broke out in black districts in more than one hundred cities. On June 5 another apostle of social progress and reconciliation between the races was struck down. Leaving the Los Angeles hotel ballroom in which he had made his California presidential primary victory statement, Sen. Robert F. Kennedy was shot in the head and died twenty-five hours later.

The 1968 Campaigns

Few presidential election years in the history of the nation brought as many surprising developments as 1968. Just a year before the election, it appeared likely that the two candidates might be President Johnson for the Democrats and Michigan's governor George W. Romney for the Republicans. But by late winter 1968 both Johnson and Romney were out of the picture, and each of the major parties was plunged into spirited fights for their presidential nominations. During 1968 continued racial tensions in the nation led to fears that Alabama's former governor George C. Wallace, running as the candidate of his own American Independent Party, might win a major share of the national vote or at least cause deadlock in the electoral college.

For the Democrats the year of surprises began November 30, 1967, when Minnesota's Eugene McCarthy announced that he would enter four 1968 presidential primaries to demonstrate opposition to the Johnson policies. McCarthy's candidacy struck an immediate chord of response, especially among younger Americans who shared his fervent distaste for the war in Vietnam. Most political observers discounted the seriousness of McCarthy's candidacy, but in the March 12 presidential primary in New Hampshire, McCarthy scored an amazing "moral" victory by gathering 42 percent of the vote against the president's 49 percent.

The McCarthy vote in New Hampshire then triggered another major surprise: the entry of Robert Kennedy into the Democratic presidential race, announced March 16. And on March 31 President Johnson stunned the nation by announcing, at the end of a lengthy radio and television address on Vietnam policy, that he would not seek reelection in 1968.

After Johnson withdrew, the race for the Democratic nomination turned into a three-way affair: McCarthy, Kennedy, and Vice President Hubert Humphrey, who entered the fray in April. On June 4, in the conclusive California primary, Kennedy emerged the narrow victor over McCarthy, only to be assassinated as he left the hotel ballroom where he had claimed victory.

The death of Kennedy, who had shared McCarthy's Vietnam views while taking a far more aggressive stance on urban and minorities' problems, was followed by an eerie moratorium in Democratic politics as the shaken party factions sought to decide on their next move. But within weeks Humphrey emerged as the odds-on favorite for the nomination.

While violence flared in the city streets and thousands of police and guards imposed security precautions unprecedented in the annals of American presidential conventions, the thirty-fifth Democratic National Convention met August 26-29 in Chicago to nominate Hubert H. Humphrey of Minnesota for the presidency and to endorse the controversial Vietnam policies of the Johnson-Humphrey administration. Humphrey's selection as running mate was Maine's Sen. Edmund S. Muskie. In the campaign that followed Muskie's calm-voiced appeals for understanding between the groups in American society would prove an asset for the Democratic ticket.

In a minority were the antiwar factions that rallied around the candidacies of McCarthy and McGovern. The McCarthy forces mounted a series of challenges to the Humphrey faction, on credentials, rules, the platform, and the nomination itself. An unprecedented number of credentials were challenged. McCarthy, McGovern, and other liberal factions won their greatest breakthrough on convention rules, obtaining abolition of a mandatory unit rule for the 1968 convention and at every level of party activity leading up to and including the 1972 convention. Many Humphrey-pledged delegates also backed the move. For the first time in recent party history, the functioning of party machinery at every level had been questioned. Humphrey won his party's nomination, but he would lead a bitterly divided party into the autumn campaign.

In the Republican party George Romney had established himself as the early leader in the race for the nomination, but his liberalism was distasteful to many orthodox Republicans. He was followed into the GOP race by Richard Nixon, who made his long-anticipated candidacy formal on February 1. The two front-runners entered the New Hampshire presidential primary, but it soon became apparent to Romney that he faced a likely loss, and on February 28 he surprised the nation by withdrawing from the contest. Nixon won an overwhelming victory in the March 12 New Hampshire GOP primary. Moderate and liberal Republicans hoped that New York's Gov. Nelson A. Rockefeller would step into the void created by Romney's withdrawal, but Rockefeller declared on March 21 that he would not run because "the majority of (Republican) leaders want the candidacy of Richard Nixon."

Without significant opposition Nixon swept the Wisconsin, Indiana, Nebraska, Oregon, and South Dakota primaries, shedding most of the "loser" image he had acquired from his 1960 defeat for president and 1962 defeat for governor of California. Rockefeller reversed his ground once again by entering the race on April 30, but even in the primaries where write-ins were permitted, the vote for him was generally low.

The Republican National Convention, meeting in Miami Beach August 5-8, wrote a moderately progressive party platform and then chose candidates for president and vice president who, at the moment of their selection, seemed to be taking increasingly restrictive attitudes on the sensitive national issues of law, order, and civil rights.

Nixon won nomination for the presidency on the first ballot, bearing out the predictions of his campaign organization. For vice president, at Nixon's suggestion, the Republicans selected Spiro T. Agnew, governor of Maryland since his election in 1966. The selection of Agnew, one of the major surprises of the year, was announced by Nixon the morning after his own nomination, and in the wake of almost-solid all-night conferences with Republican leaders, chiefly those of a conservative bent. Liberal Republicans were outraged at Agnew's designation.

Nixon seemed to represent the middle ground of the Republican party of 1968, substantially to the right of Governor Rockefeller and well to the center of the road compared to the conservative Ronald Reagan. The Republican platform of 1968, adopted by the Convention August 6 without a floor fight or any amendments, was generally moderate in tone and contained a preamble calling for major national effort to rebuild urban and rural slums and attack the root causes of poverty, including racism.

To conduct his second campaign for the presidency, Nixon assembled a massive—and doubtless the best financed—campaign organization in U.S. history. Nixon was intent on avoiding the mistakes of his 1960 campaign, when a frenetic campaign pace resulted in exhaustion and snap decisions.

A central theme of Nixon's campaign was an appeal to a group he called the "forgotten Americans," whom Nixon defined as "the nonshouters," those who "work in America's factories, run America's business, serve in Government, provide most of the soldiers who died to keep us free." By suggesting that his administration would look chiefly to the interest of this group, Nixon was able to make a strong bid for the support of white suburban and small-town America, traditional heartland of GOP strength in the nation.

Humphrey's bid for the presidency got off to a depressing start in September 1968 with sparse crowds, disordered schedules, and vicious heckling by left-wing, antiwar elements virtually everywhere he sought to speak. Humphrey's first task was to establish some measure of independence from the vastly unpopular Johnson administration. A significant step to win some of the antiwar Democrats to his side came in a September 30 televised address from Salt Lake City, when he said he would stop the bombing of North Vietnam "as an acceptable risk for peace." When President Johnson actually took that step on October 31, Humphrey could hardly restrain his glee. The combination of his own softened stand and the presidential position won him, at least at the last moment, the support of many of the Democrats who had been most disaffected at Chicago.

Humphrey endorsed virtually all the social advances of the Kennedy-Johnson years but called for a substantial broadening of domestic efforts to meet minorities and other problems. He charged that Nixon's economic policies would bring America "back to McKinley," with recession and unemployment like the country experienced during Eisenhower years.

George Wallace had announced on February 8, that he would run for president as a third party candidate under the banner of the American Independent party. campaign had a narrower goal: to win the balance of in electoral college voting, thus depriving either party of the clear electoral majority required for e Wallace made it clear that he would then expect on major party candidates to make concessions in re sufficient support from the Wallace supporters to tion. Wallace indicated he expected the electic resolved in the electoral college and not go to the Representatives for resolution. At the end of the it was revealed that he had obtained affidavits fr electors in which they promised to vote for W whomsoever he may direct" in the electoral co

Results of the 1968 Elections

In one of the closest elections of the century Richard Nixon on November 5 was elected president. In percentage terms Nixon had 43.4 percent of the popular vote, the lowest winning percentage for a winning presidential candidate since 1912, when Woodrow Wilson won by 41.9 percent. Humphrey's percentage was 42.7; Wallace's was 13.5.

For the Republican party Nixon's victory had special significance. He was the first successful GOP presidential contender since the 1920s who was closely identified with the party organization. The victories of Dwight D. Eisenhower in the 1950s, followed by Nixon's defeat in 1960, had raised the possibility that the Republicans might lack the broad appeal ever to win a presidential victory unless their candidate possessed special nonparty appeal.

The Democrats had feared that the election would bring a final dissolution of the grand Democratic coalition that had controlled the federal government in most elections since the 1930s. The election returns did show the South deserting the Democratic party in presidential voting, the Deep South to Wallace, the border South to Nixon. But the other elements of the Democratic coalition held together remarkably well, helping the party to win the electoral votes of several major states and to return a high proportion of its congressional incumbents.

Preelection surveys of Wallace voters had indicated that if they had been obliged to choose between Nixon and Humphrey, about twice as many would have preferred Nixon as Humphrey. If Wallace had not been on the ballot, Nixon would very possibly have carried some of the five Deep South states that went for Wallace, possibly building up a stronger national vote lead in the process. But it was difficult to tell from the election returns whether Wallace had hurt Nixon or Humphrey the more in the nonsouthern

spot for the Republicans was on the GOP added 5 seats for a new ol of both

seats, for a since 1956. GOP. It was ns also won ate was 58 th Congress, ns. Republi- Democrats, ld by Repub- 5. No incum- was defeated, for additional

ected to result he right. While the Ninetieth rs dropped and orrespondingly. ate seats previ- oldwater, former epublican presi- ose previous ser- epublican fresh- dent pro tempore

also won Senate

seats previously held by Democrats. They were Edward J. Gurney of Florida, Charles McC. Mathias, Jr., of Maryland, and Richard S. Schweiker of Pennsylvania. Other Republicans winning seats previously held by Democrats were Henry Bellmon of Oklahoma and William B. Saxbe of Ohio. The other two freshman Republicans were Marlow W. Cook of Kentucky and Rep. Robert Dole of Kansas. The two Democrats who won seats previously held by Republicans were Alan Cranston of California and Iowa governor Harold E. Hughes.

In the House the party breakdown when the Ninety-first Congress convened was 243 Democrats and 192 Republicans. In all Republicans took 9 seats from the Democrats and lost 5 of their own for a 4-seat net gain. Republicans had scored a net gain of 47 seats in the 1966 elections and had won a special election to fill a Democratic vacancy earlier in 1968. The Republicans had lost 38 seats in the 1964 elections.

Of the 435 representatives elected in November 396 were incumbents (223 Democrats and 173 Republicans), and only 39 (20 Democrats and 19 Republicans) were newcomers. The new winners included two former representatives, one a Democrat and the other a Republican.

The new Congress would have the smallest crop of freshman members in years. Between 1940 and 1948 an average of 96 newcomers were elected to each new House. The average dropped to 68 between 1950 and 1958 but rose to 72 between 1960 and 1966. In 1964 there were 91 newcomers elected and in 1966, 73.

In gubernatorial races the Republican party, winning 13 of the year's 21 races and capturing 7 seats held by Democrats, increased its control of the nation's statehouses from 26 to 31. Even after the selection of a Democrat to succeed Vice President-elect Agnew, the GOP would boast 30 governors, equaling its holdings after the Eisenhower sweep of 1952, when there were two fewer states.

In light of the extremely close presidential race and the continuing, though narrowed, control of Congress by the Democrats, the Republican margin of 10 governorships gave the party its most broad-based mandate for leadership. The GOP scored a net gain of 3 seats each in the East and the Midwest and lost 1 in the West. There were no party changes in the South.

Nixon's coattails had a less decisive effect than did Eisenhower's four national elections earlier. Nixon did carry 6 of the 7 states in which Republicans took governorships formerly held by Democrats (including 2 incumbents). But it was far from clear who helped whom in several of those races. In Montana an easy Nixon win failed to save Gov. Tim M. Babcock, an early Nixon backer. In Rhode Island, the only other race in which a Republican incumbent was beaten, Gov. John H. Chafee's advocacy of a state income tax appeared to be the major factor in his defeat.

Battling for seats vacated by Democratic incumbents, Republicans won in Indiana, Iowa, West Virginia, New Hampshire, and Vermont. State matters, primarily fiscal, were the main issues in all five states. The Democrats suffered particularly through the voluntary retirement of their popular governors in normally Republican Iowa, New Hampshire, and Vermont. Except for Montana and Rhode Island the Democrats picked up no seats formerly held by Republicans.

Republicans scored minimal gains in the contests for state legislature seats around the country. As a result of the elections, they would control 20 legislatures, the same number controlled by the Democrats. (The other 10 were split in control or nonpartisan.) The GOP rose in strength from 41.8 to 43.4 percent of the seats in all senate chambers around the country but held static at just over 42 percent of all seats in lower houses.

1969-1971:
The Ninety-first Congress

The Ninety-first Congress, which adjourned on January 2, 1971, compiled a substantial record of domestic accomplishments despite drawn-out disputes with President Nixon over foreign policy and spending.

The Senate made the first substantial attempt since World War II to challenge the president's authority on foreign policy and military involvement. Although the House generally agreed to uphold President Nixon's requests to finance new weapons systems and to send money and troops into Southeast Asia, the Senate engaged in numerous long debates on those issues.

It was in domestic legislation, however, that Congress compiled its most substantial record of accomplishment. This legislation included major air and water pollution control measures, a $25-billion education authorization, and a bill extending the 1965 Voting Rights Act and allowing eighteen-year-olds to vote in national elections. In the final days of the 1970 session Congress completed action on a bill extending the food stamp program that, for the first time, provided free food stamps for the poorest families.

Congress and the administration worked to establish new federal agencies. Foremost among these was the government-owned postal corporation to replace the Post Office Department. Congress also agreed to the president's reorganization plans to set up an independent Environmental Protection Agency and a National Atmospheric and Oceanic Administration in the Commerce Department.

Problems concerning the economy dominated Nixon's first two years in office, and Congress attempted periodically to deal with these problems. In 1969 it enacted a major overhaul of the tax code. It sliced funds from military, foreign aid, and space requests and added money to numerous domestic programs, notably education, health, training, and pollution control. For the third year in a row Congress enacted a federal spending ceiling for fiscal 1971.

Congress engaged in debates over the Vietnam War in attempts to limit deployment of troops and reduce spending. The Senate voted twice to repeal the 1964 Tonkin Gulf resolution, and the House eventually agreed to repeal the resolution.

The 1970 Midterm Elections

Despite the unprecedented off-year campaign efforts of President Nixon and Vice President Agnew, most observers felt the Republicans suffered a net loss in the elections of November 3, 1970. In their drive to improve the Republican position in Congress and in state capitals, the president campaigned for candidates in twenty-three states during the weeks preceding the election, and the vice president visited twenty-nine states.

Although the effect of a presidential appearance for a candidate was unclear, Nixon and Agnew could point to victories in several states where they campaigned: Senate victories in Maryland, Connecticut, Ohio, and Tennessee, for example, and gubernatorial victories in Connecticut, Tennessee, California, Arizona, Iowa, Vermont, and Wyoming. Administration efforts failed to pay off in other states on the Republican target list. Democratic candidates were elected to the Senate in Utah, New Mexico, Wyoming, Nevada, North Dakota, and Indiana, despite the high-level administration campaigning. And Nixon or Agnew visits failed to persuade voters to elect Republican Senators in California, Texas, Illinois, or Florida.

The most spectacular third party victory of the year was that of James L. Buckley of New York, a Conservative who was elected to the Senate with a minority of the votes. Buckley's election was made possible by a division of the votes for the Republican-Liberal incumbent, Charles E. Goodell, and the Democratic candidate, Rep. Richard L. Ottinger.

Another third party success belonged to Sen. Harry F. Byrd, Jr, of Virginia. In March 1970 the veteran Democrat announced that he would not run as a Democrat because of a party "loyalty oath" that he claimed would force him to commit himself to the Democratic presidential candidate in 1972. Byrd ran as an Independent, easily defeating the Democratic and Republican candidates.

A second incumbent Democratic senator who ran as an Independent was Thomas J. Dodd of Connecticut. Dodd had been censured by the Senate in 1967 for diverting testimonial funds to his personal use. He was regarded as unlikely to win the Senate nomination in a Democratic primary. His Independent candidacy divided the Democratic vote and helped elect a Republican, Rep. Lowell P. Weicker, Jr., to his seat.

Results of the 1970 Elections

Republicans registered a net gain of 2 Senate seats in the November 3 elections, leaving Democrats with a majority of 55 to 45 in the Ninety-second Congress. Of the 35 Senate seats being contested, 11 were won by Republicans, 22 by Democrats, 1 by a Conservative party candidate, and 1 by an Independent. Democrats had held 25 of the seats and Republicans, 10. Republicans who captured Democratic seats were Rep. Weicker, Rep. J. Glenn Beall, Jr., of Maryland, Rep. Robert Taft, Jr., of Ohio, and Rep. W. E. Brock III of Tennessee.

In Minnesota Hubert H. Humphrey won back a seat in the Senate, where he had served from 1949 to 1965, when he became vice president. He defeated Republican representative Clark MacGregor for the seat of retiring Democrat Eugene J. McCarthy. In Texas former Democratic representative Lloyd M. Bentsen, Jr., defeated Rep. George Bush for the seat held by Ralph W. Yarborough, a Democrat defeated in the May 2 primary.

The Democratic party showed renewed strength in the Great Plains and the Far West in the 1970 elections as it gained 9 House seats to open up a 255-180 margin for the Ninety-second Congress. Republicans claimed success in limiting Democratic gains to less than the 38-seat average pickup recorded by the nonpresidential party in off-year elections during this century. Democrats said their gains were significant because President Nixon's 1968 victory carried in few of the marginal candidates, who are normally easy prey to the party out of power in off-year contests.

Registering the most impressive net gain in statehouses by any party since 1938, Democrats in 1970 took 13 governorships from Republican control, while losing only 2, in Tennessee and Connecticut. The balance of state power shifted dramatically from 18 Democratic and 32 Republican governors before the election to 29 Democratic and 21 Republican governors.

State-level gains were doubly significant in 1970. Democratic control of a majority of the states furnished vital power bases for the 1972 presidential elections. Democrats won Ohio and Pennsylvania and held Texas, thus controlling three of the most populous states. Democrats also wrested from Republican control Alaska, Florida, Arkansas, and Oklahoma and the western and midwestern states of Idaho, Minnesota, Nebraska, Nevada, New Mexico, South Dakota, and Wisconsin. Republicans continued to hold New York, California, Michigan, and Illinois.

Republicans went into the 1970 elections holding 51 of the 99 state legislative bodies (Nebraska has a unicameral legislature). This figure included the two nominally nonpartisan legislatures of Minnesota and Nebraska, which were controlled by conservative, Republican-oriented majorities. Democrats held the other 48 chambers. Following the 1970 elections Democrats gained control of 8 new legislative bodies, giving them control of 56.

1971-1973:
The Ninety-second Congress

The years 1971-1973 saw some of the boldest and most dramatic presidential initiatives in years. In the summer of 1971 President Nixon imposed wage and price controls on the economy, announced that he would visit Communist China, and planned a summit meeting with Soviet leaders. His visits to China and the Soviet Union in 1972 gave Nixon a strong boost in his campaign for reelection.

Dissent over the Vietnam War, which seemed on the rise in the spring of 1971, had waned by midyear following further troop withdrawal announcements by Nixon. At year's end 45,000 additional troops were scheduled for withdrawal, practically bringing to an end the offensive combat involvement of U.S. ground forces. By late 1972 it appeared that a settlement of the Vietnam War, or at least a cease-fire and return of U.S. prisoners, was imminent. Presidential aide Henry Kissinger and North Vietnamese officials had hammered out a nine-point agreement, but the Saigon government balked, and the elusive peace had to await a final agreement in January 1973.

In October 1972 Congress gave President Nixon a major legislative victory: passage of a general revenue-sharing measure. The bill was the only one of the president's "six great goals" to pass during the Ninety-second Congress. In 1972 Congress also approved the Equal Rights Amendment, forty-nine years after it was introduced. The amendment was sent to the states for ratification March 22 after the Senate passed it 84-8.

On June 17, 1972, five men were arrested in the Democratic national headquarters at the Watergate building in Washington, D.C. This incident was the beginning of a process that was to continue over the next two years and destroy a presidency. The break-in was immediately tagged the "Watergate caper" by the press. But by the time the election arrived it had become the "Watergate affair," and it was being examined seriously. In the months following the celebrated break-in, allegations of a widespread network of political espionage and sabotage engineered by the Republicans were carried in the news media. Charges of involvement were leveled by the Democrats and the press against persons in high positions in the White House and the Committee for the Reelection of the President.

Seven men were indicted on criminal charges, three civil suits were filed, and one man was found guilty in a Florida court on a minor charge related to Watergate. Two congressional committees initiated staff investigations of the allegations. And Watergate repeatedly surfaced in the presidential campaign, with Democratic nominee George McGovern and his campaign pursuing the charges and President Nixon and his staff denouncing them. Investigators and reporters began to backtrack: meetings, phone calls, financial transactions, and other related events were traced back months before the incident.

The 1972 Campaigns

President Nixon was in a strong position to seek another term as the 1972 presidential election year opened. His wage and price control system had curbed the inflationary spiral, while increased federal spending cut into the unemployment rate. His scheduled trips to Beijing and Moscow promised widespread publicity and a focus on the "peace" half of a peace and prosperity theme. And although he had alienated small groups of Republicans on the left and right wings of his party, Nixon could count on being renominated without much trouble.

The Democrats, meanwhile, headed toward a bruising battle for the nomination that would result in ripping their party apart. Although Maine senator Edmund S. Muskie looked like a strong possibility for the nomination in late 1971, his centrist liberal political stance was not enough to hold the party together. His candidacy soon collapsed in the rush of primary voters toward the left or right wings of the party. Still angry over the Vietnam War, left-wing party activists gathered behind Sen. George McGovern of South Dakota. On the right Alabama governor George C. Wallace gathered voters angry with busing and the rapid pace of social change in general.

Other well-known candidates who entered the fray for the Democratic presidential nomination were Sen. Henry M. Jackson of Washington and Sen. Hubert H. Humphrey of Minnesota. Several other hopefuls failed to gain any significant momentum; among them were former senator Eugene J. McCarthy of Minnesota and Rep. Shirley Chisholm of New York. Chisholm was the first black to run in a series of presidential primaries.

McGovern began his upward climb to the nomination by a stronger than expected showing in the New Hampshire primary. Although Muskie won the popular vote there, he was labeled a loser because he received far fewer votes than expected. From there it was downhill for Muskie, and after he ran fourth in the Pennsylvania primary on April 25, he ceased active campaigning. McGovern, meanwhile, ran first in Wisconsin on April 4, then won Massachusetts, Nebraska, Oregon, and beat Humphrey in a June 6 showdown in California. From there on he was practically assured of the nomination, although there was a last-minute effort at the convention to stop him.

McGovern's highly vocal and longstanding opposition to the Vietnam War caused many political analysts to look on him as a one-issue candidate. But his major problem was one of recognition. Public opinion polls indicated that he had only 2 percent support from the voters in the field of prospective Democratic nominees. By mid-March, after two months of extensive campaigning, McGovern had gained only 3 percentage points in the polls.

Beyond any doubt the reform commission that McGovern had headed after the disastrous Democratic convention of 1968 had changed the face of the Democratic party. And beyond any doubt the changes favored McGovern's candidacy by expanding the party's base and bringing more women, minorities, and youths into the process.

At the convention, McGovern's winning of the nomination was never really in doubt, even before the balloting began, and he moved steadily toward his goal. The Democrats chose Sen. Thomas F. Eagleton of Missouri as their nominee for vice president. But on July 25 Eagleton disclosed that he had voluntarily hospitalized himself three times between 1960 and 1966 for "nervous exhaustion and fatigue." Since 1966, said the candidate, he had "experienced good, solid, sound health." But Eagleton's statement, culminating an investigation by reporters of his past difficulties under stress, started a sequence of developments that included increasing pressure for Eagleton to withdraw from the ticket. After a meeting with McGovern on July 31, Eagleton withdrew from the ticket.

His presidential campaign sidetracked, McGovern announced August 5 that his choice to replace Eagleton was R. Sargent Shriver, former director of the Peace Corps and the Office of Economic Opportunity and U.S. ambassador to France. In a display of unity and anti-Nixon oratory, the newly enlarged Democratic National Committee at an August 8 meeting in Washington nominated Shriver with 2,936 of the 3,013 votes cast.

In the Republican camp the renomination of President Nixon did not go completely unchallenged. He had opposition from both the left and the right. Assailing the president from the left was California representative Paul N. McCloskey, Jr., who based his campaign on opposition to administration policies and its deception of the news media. McCloskey withdrew six days after the New Hampshire primary because of insufficient funds, but his name remained on the ballot in twelve other states as a symbolic protest. Nixon's opponent on the right was Ohio representative John M. Ashbrook, who attacked the president for what he called his failure to live up to 1968 promises in fiscal matters, foreign affairs, and defense posture. Ashbrook's name was on the ballot in eleven state presidential primaries.

The Republican National Convention was a gigantic television spectacular from start to finish. The main business of the convention, the nomination of President Nixon and Vice President Agnew to a second term, was a preordained ritual.

Nixon did little campaigning for his second term. Because of his strong lead in the polls and lack of speech making, the president also was in the enviable position of making few, if any, concrete campaign pledges to the electorate. He enunciated the major themes of the campaign in his acceptance speech before the Republican convention, emphasizing the divisions in the Democratic party and urging dissatisfied Democrats to downplay traditional party loyalty.

From almost every standpoint the Democratic campaign contrasted sharply with that of the Republicans. McGovern and his running mate were on the road incessantly from Labor Day until election day. McGovern tried in vain to draw Nixon into debate. His initial tax and welfare reform proposals attracted widespread criticism and helped alienate several traditional sources of Democratic strength, such as ethnic groups and blue-collar workers. When he substituted Shriver for Eagleton, he was attacked for poor judgment and vacillation. His chief issue, administration conduct of the Vietnam War, lost whatever remaining effect it might have had when an administration-negotiated peace appeared to be in sight during the last days of the campaign.

Rather than moving into the offensive against the administration, McGovern was kept on the defensive throughout the campaign, constantly forced to explain earlier positions and rebut Republican charges. The break-in at Democratic headquarters at Watergate in June and ensuing disclosures of the alleged involvement of administration officials in espionage and sabotage directed against the Democrats was potentially damaging, but the charge failed to excite the voters enough to head off the Nixon sweep.

Results of the 1972 Elections

Nixon swept back into the White House on November 7 with a devastating landslide victory over McGovern. He carried a record of forty-nine states for a total of 520 electoral votes. Only Massachusetts and the District of Columbia, with a meager 17 electoral votes between them, went for McGovern.

The Nixon landslide was the first Republican sweep since Reconstruction of the once solid Democratic South. By runaway margins Nixon took all eleven states of the old Confederacy, plus all the border states.

Americans engaged in massive ticket splitting in the 1972 election. Nixon's landslide victory was not reflected in significant Republican gains in Congress or in governorships. Despite the avalanche of votes for Nixon, the Democrats scored a net gain of 2 seats in the Senate, thereby increasing their majority to 57-43 in the Ninety-third Congress. Of the 33 seats contested, the Democrats won 16 and the Republicans won 17. Nineteen of those seats had been controlled by the Republicans in the Ninety-second Congress, 14 by the Democrats.

The most significant, and surprising, element of the Democratic gain was the upset of four seemingly well entrenched Republican incumbents: Gordon Allott of Colorado, J. Caleb Boggs of Delaware, Jack Miller of Iowa, and Margaret Chase Smith of Maine. If it had not been for Republican gains in three Southern states (North Carolina, Oklahoma, and Virginia), the Democratic majority in the Senate would have been much larger.

Half of the eight new Democrats were considered significantly more liberal than the incumbent Republicans they upset. In this category were Floyd K. Haskell, who beat Allott in Colorado; Joseph R. Biden, Jr., who defeated Boggs in Delaware; Dick Clark, who retired Miller in Iowa; and Rep. William D. Hathaway, who upset Smith in Maine. A fifth Democrat, Rep. James Abourezk, defeated Republican Robert W. Hirsch in South Dakota to take the seat of retiring Republican incumbent Karl E. Mundt. Abourezk was considered far more liberal than the conservative Mundt.

Two more Democrats were conservatives who replaced conservatives. Sam Nunn of Georgia and J. Bennett Johnston, Jr., of Louisiana defeated Republican opponents to fill the seats of Democratic incumbents David H. Gambrell of Georgia and the late Allen J. Ellender of Louisiana. The remaining Democrat, Walter "Dee" Huddleston, defied the southern election trend by winning his race against Republican Louie B. Nunn in Kentucky for the seat of retiring Republican John Sherman Cooper. Both the incumbent

and his successor were moderates.

Final returns showed that Republicans gained 13 House seats in the 1972 elections, far short of the number they needed to win control of the House. The 13-seat pickup was slightly more than the 4 House seats gained when President Nixon first was elected in 1968, but it was far less than the winning party usually has gained in a presidential landslide. A close look at the House figures showed that the president not only lacked coattails, but appeared to have little if any perceptible effect on House races.

The only semblance of coattail effects in the election was in the South, where the Republicans took 7 House seats out of Democratic hands. For several states the election of Republican representatives meant drastic breaks with tradition.

The 1972 election was the first to take place after the reapportionment and redistricting that followed the 1970 census. More than a dozen entirely new districts were created, and others had major changes in their boundary lines. Most of these changes tended to favor the Republicans, because many new districts were placed in fast-growing Republican suburbs and because legislatures in several key states drew the lines to partisan Republican advantage.

Redistricting also played a significant part in the defeat of House incumbents. Thirteen incumbents, 8 Democrats and 5 Republicans, were defeated. For 9 of these incumbents, 7 of them Democrats, redistricting was the dominant factor in their defeat. Three lost because redistricting forced them to run against other incumbents.

The House of Representatives in the Ninety-third Congress looked quite a bit different from its predecessor, but the reasons were mainly because of redistricting and retirement, not election defeats. The new count was 243 Democrats and 192 Republicans.

Chalking up a net gain of 1, the Democrats in 1972 retained the wide margin of statehouse control they won in 1970, holding 31 governorships to the Republicans' 19. (Democrats gained the Kentucky governorship in the 1971 off-year elections.) Of the 18 seats up for election in 1972, Democrats won 11 and Republicans won 7. Despite upsets in several states, the net result was only a minimal change in party power.

Republicans lost governorships in Delaware, Illinois, and Vermont, while ousting Democrats in Missouri and North Carolina. Close races in New Hampshire, North Carolina, Washington, and West Virginia were won by Republicans, who also upset a favored Democratic candidate in Indiana. As expected, Republicans won gubernatorial contests in Iowa and Missouri.

Incumbent or favored Republicans were upset by Democrats in Illinois, North Dakota, Rhode Island, and Vermont, while Democratic incumbents were reelected in Arkansas, Kansas, South Dakota, and Utah. In Montana and Texas, Democrats were elected to succeed retiring Democratic governors. As expected, the Democratic challenger unseated Delaware's Republican incumbent by capitalizing on the issue of taxes.

In West Virginia's gubernatorial race, which drew national attention, Republican governor Arch A. Moore put together his general popularity and campaigning ability with Nixon's strong showing in the state—and the obvious incongruity of a millionaire populist candidate running in one of the nation's poorest states—to defeat Democratic challenger John D. "Jay" Rockefeller IV, the secretary of state.

1973-1975:
The Ninety-third Congress

The legislative activities of the Ninety-third Congress were overshadowed by one of the nation's greatest political crises: Watergate. Watergate dominated the news from the beginning of the second Nixon administration in January 1973 until the president's resignation on August 9, 1974. The year 1973 opened with the trial of the seven Watergate burglars beginning January 8. Five of the seven defendants pleaded guilty a few days after the trial opened, while the remaining two stood trial and were found guilty by the end of the month. Sentencing was March 23.

From mid-May until early August 1973 American television screens were filled with politicians and former government officials testifying before the Senate Select Committee on Presidential Campaign Activities—the Watergate committee. Most important of all information produced by the hearings was the revelation that tape recordings had been made of many presidential conversations in the White House during the period in which the break-in occurred and the cover-up began. The tapes contained evidence that ultimately led to Nixon's resignation.

Immediately after the existence of the tapes was made public on July 16, a struggle for the recordings began. The legal battle would last almost a year, from July 23, 1973, to July 24, 1974, when the Supreme Court ruled that Nixon had to turn over the tapes to U.S. District Judge John J. Sirica for use as evidence in the Watergate cover-up trial.

In the midst of the tapes battle, Spiro Agnew, on October 10, 1973, became the second vice president in American history to resign. Under investigation for multiple charges of alleged conspiracy, extortion and bribery, Agnew agreed to resign and avoided imprisonment by pleading nolo contendere to charges of income tax evasion.

Two days after Agnew's resignation President Nixon nominated House Minority Leader Gerald R. Ford of Michigan as his successor. Ford became the fortieth vice president of the United States on December 6, 1973.

While Americans were reeling from these events, they were overtaken by an energy crisis, as a result of the Arab oil embargo, and some of the worst inflation to hit the economy in peacetime history.

But even as public attention focused on the presidency and the economic problems of the country, Congress was passing landmark legislation representing an attempt to change the balance of power between the presidency and Congress. Among measures enacted were limits on a president's right to impound money, the establishment of a more thorough method for Congress to consider the federal budget, and restrictions on the president's war-making powers.

Investigation of Watergate continued. After two months of closed congressional hearings beginning May 9, 1974, and a series of televised debates beginning July 24, the House Judiciary Committee voted to recommend three articles of impeachment.

On August 5 Nixon released three previously undisclosed transcripts. The conversations showed clearly Nixon's participation in the cover-up. In a written statement the president acknowledged that he had withheld the contents of the tapes despite the fact that they contradicted his previous declarations that he had not known of or participated in the cover-up. These admissions destroyed almost all of Nixon's remaining support in Congress. On

August 8 Nixon announced his resignation, to be effective at noon the next day, and Vice President Ford became the nation's thirty-eighth president.

A month after assuming office, Ford pardoned Nixon "for all offenses against the United States which he, Richard Nixon, has committed or may have committed" during his years as president.

Ford was succeeded in the vice presidency by Nelson A. Rockefeller, who became vice president December 19, 1974, after the House confirmed his nomination by President Ford, 287-128. The Senate had given its approval December 10, 90-7. Thus the nation for the first time had both a president and a vice president chosen under the Twenty-fifth Amendment to the Constitution rather than by a national election.

Reacting to presidential campaign abuses, Congress in 1974 enacted a landmark campaign reform bill that radically overhauled the existing system of financing election campaigns. The new measure cleared Congress October 10, 1974, and was signed into law five days later by President Ford. It established the first spending limits ever for candidates in presidential primary and general elections and in primary campaigns for the House and Senate.

Although the Arab nations had lifted their oil embargo, they and other oil producing states refused to lower the posted price for oil. The energy situation became intertwined with the grave economic problems President Ford inherited on taking office. Within months, he and Congress were trying to get together on an economic-energy package that reflected the inseparability of the two crises. The continuing high oil prices played havoc with the international monetary system and contributed heavily to the deepening worldwide recession.

The 1974 Midterm Elections

Republicans paid the bill in November 1974 for two years of scandal and economic decline, losing heavily in congressional and gubernatorial elections throughout the country and slipping deeper into a minority status. Democrats gained 43 seats in the House, 3 seats in the Senate, and 4 new governorships.

As soon as the November 5 election returns were in, Republicans began looking for comfort in the fact that parties holding the White House normally lose heavily in midterm elections. But it was a small comfort. Democrats went into the 1974 election with nearly 60 percent of the seats in the Senate and House. For the most part the Democratic gains in the House were not marginal seats won by Republicans in a previous presidential sweep but solid Republican districts.

If there was one region that disappointed Republicans the most, it was the South. Shortly before the election the South was thought to be the one Republican bright spot. Losses were expected to be lightest in that area, and there was a good chance for the party to gain half a dozen House seats. As it turned out Republicans lost 10 House seats in the South and won only 2 Democratic ones.

The Midwest proved even more disastrous for Republicans. Before the election the Midwest had been the only region of the country in which Republicans held a majority of the House seats. But with a net Democratic gain of 14 seats there, that was no longer true.

A look at the demographics of the election yielded another interesting conclusion: Republicans suffered badly in the suburbs, where much of the so-called emerging Republican majority was supposed to lie. The striking fact about these suburban districts was that they were not marginal. In many cases the suburban districts that went Democratic contained thousands of former Democrats who left their party behind as they became prosperous enough to move outside the city limits. The new suburban middle class had been hard hit by recession and inflation, and Republicans may have paid the price.

Perhaps more important, however, was the prevalence in the suburbs of independent and ticket-splitting voters. Surveys had consistently shown a clear majority of independent voters favoring Democratic congressional candidates in 1974, and the switch in the independent vote probably was concentrated in the suburbs.

The heavy turnover decreed by the election—11 new senators, 92 new representatives, 40 incumbent representatives defeated—broke one of the most consistent political patterns of previous years. The tendency since World War II had been for incumbents to seek reelection as long as they were physically able to serve and for nearly all of them to win.

In 1974 that changed. Thanks to the combination of retirement and defeat, there were more first termers elected to the Ninety-fourth House than in any other since 1949. More than one-third of the new House was elected either in 1972 or 1974.

Results of the 1974 Elections

The Democrats scored a net gain of 3 Senate seats in the November 5 elections. A fourth gain came later in New Hampshire, where the state ballot law commission had at first declared Republican Louis C. Wyman the winner by two votes. But the Senate refused to seat Wyman, eventually declaring a vacancy which Democrat John Durkin won in a special election in September 1975. In addition, the Democrats had gained a seat in Ohio by appointment early in 1974, which they held in the November balloting.

Two incumbents, both Republicans, were defeated in the election. Marlow W. Cook of Kentucky lost by a substantial margin to Democratic governor Wendell H. Ford. In Colorado, Republican Peter H. Dominick was swamped by Democrat Gary W. Hart.

Democrats also captured 2 seats from which incumbent Republicans were retiring. In a major upset in Vermont Patrick J. Leahy beat Rep. Richard W. Mallary in a close race and became the first Democratic senator in the state's history. Leahy replaced retiring George D. Aiken, the Senate's senior Republican.

The Republicans' only Senate gain was in Nevada, where former governor Paul Laxalt was the winner by 624 votes.

In other races for vacant seats there were no shifts in party lineup. Democratic representative John C. Culver won the seat of retiring Harold E. Hughes in Iowa. In North Carolina former state attorney general Robert B. Morgan easily held the seat of Sam J. Ervin, Jr. Two Democrats who defeated incumbents in primaries, former astronaut John H. Glenn, Jr., of Ohio and Gov. Dale Bumpers of Arkansas, won landslide victories over weak Republican opposition.

Republicans, while losing Aiken's seat, held onto the Utah Senate seat of Wallace F. Bennett, who retired. Salt Lake City mayor Jake Garn won easily over Democratic representative Wayne Owens.

The Democratic gain was kept modest because the Republicans managed to hold their vulnerable Utah seat and to reelect three incumbents who had been in serious trouble: Senators Robert Dole of Kansas, Henry Bellmon of Oklahoma, and Milton R. Young of North Dakota.

Three Democratic incumbents in difficult races won reelection. They were Birch Bayh of Indiana, George McGovern of South Dakota, and Mike Gravel of Alaska. Other incumbents in both parties won easily.

In the House Democrats gained 43 seats, pushing their number just above the two-thirds mark. They had already made a net gain of 5 seats in special elections and a party switch, raising their total in the last days of the Ninety-third Congress to 248. Thus, after the elections, they had won 291 seats.

The Democratic trend was as broad as it was deep. It took away 4 Republican seats in New Jersey and 4 in California. It took 5 in Indiana, 5 in New York, 3 in Illinois, and 2 in Michigan. In nearly all cases the change to a new member of the House appeared to mean at least a slight shift to the left. There were a few new conservative Democratic representatives in the new House, such as John Birch Society member Lawrence P. McDonald of Georgia, but they were exceptions. For the most part liberal Democrats who retired were replaced by persons of similar persuasion, and conservative Republicans were replaced by Democrats who ran against them from the left.

The Republican group in the House was also expected to shift slightly toward liberalism even as it shrank by 43 members. Nearly every House Republican beaten November 5 was counted among the conservatives; the liberal and moderate Republicans generally had little trouble winning reelection. The only serious casualty among the Republican moderates was John Dellenback of Oregon. Moderates such as John B. Anderson of Illinois and Paul N. McCloskey, Jr., of California won without serious contest.

It was not a pleasant night for Republicans who remained loyal to President Nixon in the days just before his resignation. Four Republicans who supported Nixon during the House Judiciary Committee's impeachment inquiry were beaten decisively. They were David W. Dennis of Indiana, Wiley Mayne of Iowa, and Joseph J. Maraziti and Charles W. Sandman, Jr., of New Jersey. Harold V. Froehlich of Wisconsin, who supported two articles of impeachment against Nixon but opposed the third, also was defeated. All the Republicans on the Judiciary Committee who consistently voted to impeach Nixon were reelected, as were several Nixon defenders.

Democrats increased their firm hold on the nation's governorships from 32 to 36. Of the 35 seats up for election Democrats won 27, Republicans won 7, and an Independent was elected in Maine. The new lineup of governorships was 36 Democrats, 13 Republicans, and 1 Independent. Not since the 1930s had the Democrats—or any party—held as many as 36 of the nation's governorships.

Republicans lost governorships in three of the nation's ten largest states—New York, California, and Massachusetts. They suffered three losses in the mountain states—Wyoming, Colorado, and Arizona. Besides these states Republicans also lost control of governorships in Oregon, Connecticut, and Tennessee, for a total loss of 9.

The Democrats also suffered some gubernatorial reverses, despite their overall net gain. In Alaska, Ohio, Kansas, and South Carolina, Republicans picked up state capitols held by Democrats, leaving the Republicans with a net loss of 5. Democrats also lost Maine to an Independent.

Perhaps the two greatest upsets in the gubernatorial

races occurred in Maine and Ohio. In Maine voters rejected both major political parties, choosing instead James B. Longley, who ran as an Independent. Longley was the first Independent to be elected governor of any state since 1930. In Ohio, Democratic governor John J. Gilligan lost to former Republican governor James A. Rhodes.

Minority groups fared well in gubernatorial contests. Both Arizona and New Mexico elected Spanish-surnamed governors, Arizona for the first time in history and New Mexico for the first time in fity-six years. In Hawaii Democrat George R. Ariyoshi became the first Japanese-American to hold the governorship of any state.

There were 15 other newcomers, for a total of 19 new governors. Among them were Edmund G. Brown, Jr., D-Calif., Ella T. Grasso, D-Conn., Michael S. Dukakis, D-Mass., David L. Boren, D-Okla., James B. Edwards, R-S.C., and Jay Hammond, R-Alaska.

Years of Uneasy Peace

By the time Jimmy Carter took the oath as president in January 1977, America's confidence had been shaken by almost a decade and a half of violence and scandal. The country had in effect lost its first war; had gone through a series of political assassinations and its first case of presidential resignation; had been besieged by urban, campus, and racial violence; and had experienced the strains of an energy crisis and rampant inflation. In large part Carter's victory stemmed from the weariness of the voters with the normal political leadership of the country and their search for a new start.

But however great the hopes, President Carter soon became embroiled in national problems and Washington politics. Critics charged him with inflexibility and lack of leadership. His energy bill was stalled and dismantled in Congress. And inflation resumed its seemingly inexorable rise. By mid-1979 few were optimistic that the nation's energy shortages and economic ills would be resolved any time soon. The debate over solutions continued to preoccupy the nation and its leaders.

The Democrats saw a reversal of fortunes in the 1980 election when conservative Ronald Reagan swept Carter from office. Reagan was the first GOP president since Dwight D. Eisenhower to have his party in a majority position in either chamber. The election gave conservatives a chance to control or influence national policy in the executive and legislative branches of government.

In line with his conservative ideology, President Reagan instigated huge tax cuts, which were largely credited with moving the country from recession to prosperity. The president came into office speaking in a traditional Republican manner, calling for a balanced budget. But he presided over the biggest deficits in American history, transforming the United States from the world's biggest creditor nation to the world's biggest debtor nation. During his tenure the national debt increased nearly threefold, from $931 billion to $2.69 trillion.

The Reagan foreign policy took many turns, gradually toning down an early ideological bent and a tendency to exert military muscle—such as in the 1983 invasion of Grenada and the 1986 bombing of Libya. But the focus always was on the Soviet Union. Over the years the United States had grown accustomed to dealing with a Soviet

Union that was predictable. Kremlin leaders came and went, but the fundamental Soviet policies remained the same, and Washington did not have to be particularly creative in responding to them. Gorbachev, who came to power in March 1985, during the early stage of Reagan's second term, upset many of the underlying assumptions about Soviet behavior.

At the outset President Reagan vested much of his energy in strengthening the armed forces. He left the presidency as an apostle of superpower disarmament, welcoming U.S.-Soviet summitry that he had once disdained and discarding his earlier belief that the Soviet Union was an "evil empire." Reagan had vowed never to deal with terrorists, but he suffered the humiliation of a White House scandal that involved the secret sale of arms to Iran in an attempt to release American hostages in Lebanon—and which illegally siphoned the sale proceeds to Central American contra guerrillas.

President Reagan's final year in office was one of warming relations between Washington and Moscow. He took his unique brand of politicking to Moscow May 29-June 2, 1988, for an upbeat summit meeting at which he and Gorbachev exchanged documents ratifying an arms control treaty they had signed the previous December in Washington. It was the first arms treaty ratified by the two countries since 1972 and the first to ban an entire class of nuclear weapons—ground-launched intermediate-range nuclear-force missiles.

Perhaps Reagan's ultimate accolade from the nation's voters was their elevation of his vice president and preferred successor, George Bush, to the Oval Office. In winning the party's nomination and then the presidency in 1988, Bush portrayed himself as the rightful heir to the Reagan legacy.

1975-1977:
The Ninety-fourth Congress

The years 1975-1976 gave America a significant respite from the high political temperature of the previous several years. With Richard Nixon gone and the Vietnam War over, the two great issues that had convulsed the country for so long were gone. But even as the country was cooling off, it found itself stalemated on the prime issues facing it. Congress and the president failed to agree on a workable energy program. A strategic arms limitation treaty with the Soviet Union was put off. And while inflation lessened, unemployment jumped to alarming heights.

As the Ninety-fourth Congress opened, there were clear differences over what steps to take to cure the continuing economic ills of inflation and recession. The Democrats were calling for a massive tax cut, emergency jobs for the unemployed, housing construction subsidies, an end to certain tax shelters, and other proposals aimed at closing tax loopholes.

Ford, who in late 1974 had called for a tax increase to combat inflation, in March 1975 reluctantly agreed to a tax cut package drafted by the Democrats that was retroactive to January 1. He and his advisers insisted that it was just as important to fight inflation as to reduce taxes. For this reason, he vetoed as too inflationary the Democrats' bill to create more than one million jobs; the veto was sustained by Congress even though the national unemployment rate was climbing to its high of 9.2 percent in May. Ford subsequently made an about-face and agreed to a compromise version that had a lower price tag but contained many of the same jobs programs.

No subject consumed more time during the first session of the Ninety-fourth Congress than energy legislation. But despite the amount of time expended in debate and hearings on energy issues, the legislation enacted fell far short of setting a national energy policy. Congress and the White House were deadlocked on fundamental energy questions, with Ford unable to sell his programs and the Democratic majority unable to draft viable alternatives. After a temporary compromise allowed extension of energy controls until mid-December, a more lasting resolution was attained under which controls would continue until early 1979.

In 1976 Congress generally agreed with the administration's request for increased defense spending. Impressed by evidence of a Soviet military buildup, Congress gave the Defense Department virtually all Ford had requested and accepted the principle that defense spending must continue to grow beyond the amount needed to cover inflation.

The 1976 Campaigns

Both parties witnessed an intense struggle for the presidential nominations in 1976, with President Ford barely surviving an effort by former California governor Ronald Reagan to deny him the Republican nomination and the Democrats selecting an obscure former governor of Georgia, Jimmy Carter.

Because of the scandals of the Nixon regime and the perceived weakness of the Ford administration, Carter was heavily favored to take the presidency at the beginning of the fall campaign. But the race gradually narrowed, until on election day Carter won by only 2.1 percentage points.

Carter's nomination represented a repudiation of the political establishment by Democratic primary voters. Such well-known names as Sen. Henry M. Jackson of Washington, Gov. George C. Wallace of Alabama, 1972 vice-presidential nominee Sargent Shriver, and Rep. Morris K. Udall of Arizona, all fell before the little-known Georgian who espoused an anti-Washington rhetoric combined with an appeal to the old virtues. Tired of political corruption and what they perceived as too much government interference in their lives, voters responded positively to Carter's appeal, despite his lack of experience in the federal government.

On December 2, 1974, Carter announced his candidacy for the 1976 presidential nomination. His speech before the national press club included most of the themes of his campaign: restoration of public trust in government; reforms to make government more open and more efficient; comprehensive energy policy; thorough tax reform; "a simplified, fair, and compassionate welfare program"; and a comprehensive national health program.

Carter won the New Hampshire primary February 24 with 28.4 percent in a field of nine candidates, including write-ins. In Massachusetts on March 2, Carter ran behind Jackson, Udall, and Wallace but picked up 16 delegates. The same day he won Vermont's advisory primary with more than 42 percent against three other candidates. His next major test came March 9 in Florida, where he had vowed to defeat Wallace. When all the votes were counted, Carter had beaten Wallace 34.5 to 30.5 percent. Jackson was third with 23.9. Most observers felt that if Jackson had stayed out of the race Carter's victory over Wallace would have been much stronger.

Carter ended the longest primary season ever with 38.8 percent of all votes cast. In the twenty-seven presidential preference primaries Carter finished first in seventeen and second in eight. On the way to the nomination, he eliminated a dozen candidates who entered the campaign and showed enough strength to block his greatest potential rival, Sen. Hubert H. Humphrey.

Jimmy Carter brought the Democratic party's diverse elements together in July at its national convention. The four-day convention in New York City was the party's most harmonious in twelve years and a stark contrast to the bitter and divisive conventions of 1968 and 1972.

Balloting for president was merely a formality. Besides Carter, three other names were placed in nomination: Udall, Brown, and antiabortion crusader Ellen McCormack. The proceedings, however, turned into a love-feast as Udall before the balloting and Brown afterwards appeared at the convention to declare their support for Carter. On the presidential roll call Carter received 2,238-½ of the convention's 3,008 votes, topping the needed majority little more than halfway through the balloting with the vote from Ohio. The following morning Carter announced that his choice for vice president was Minnesota senator Walter F. Mondale.

Gerald Ford ran his primary campaign on his two-year performance record as president. The plan was to cultivate the image of an America healed of its divisive internal wounds, involved in a promising economic recovery, and at peace both at home and abroad. In doing this Ford had many of the incumbent's powers of policy making, media access, and patronage. All of these were to be used against Ronald Reagan, who announced his candidacy November 20, 1975.

Ford began early to capitalize on his position, spending considerable time in the fall of 1975 traveling across the country. Knowing that Reagan would have to make bold stands on key issues, Ford hoped to remain presidential in his own low-key manner.

And at first the plan seemed to work. Ford won New Hampshire by about 1,500 votes. In Florida, where he was once thought far behind, the president was helped by older voters' fears that Reagan would alter the Social Security system. Ford scored a convincing victory. Following a big win in Illinois March 16, Ford strategists hoped to build a party consensus that would force Reagan to withdraw and support the president's nomination before the campaign moved into Reagan's Sun Belt strongholds. As they had done privately before the campaign had begun, Ford's supporters began publicly urging Reagan to pull out of the race in the name of party unity. It was at that point that the plan, as scheduled, began to bog down.

Reagan scored a series of important victories in the South and Southwest. By mid-May the Ford candidacy had fallen behind in the convention delegate count. Ford survived with a large victory in his home state on May 18, breaking Reagan's momentum. Added to that victory were stepped-up efforts to cash in on Ford's incumbency with a flurry of patronage in key primary states and more effective usage of Ford's access to the press. The two candidates split the six May 25 primaries evenly, with Ford taking Kentucky, Tennessee, and Oregon. The border state wins were interpreted as a success for Ford, showing he could compete with Reagan for conservative votes.

The president finally regained the edge in the delegate count in late May by persuading his technically uncommitted supporters in New York and Pennsylvania to declare for him. Ford ended the primary season with an easy win in New Jersey and a hefty margin in Ohio. Reagan kept close with a landslide victory in California, ensuring that the nomination would turn on the status of the uncommitted delegates to the convention.

The Republican delegates arrived in Kansas City for their convention in August more evenly split than they had been since 1952. Both President Ford, breaking with tradition, and Ronald Reagan arrived in town three days before the balloting to continue their pursuit of delegates.

On the presidential roll call, Reagan, bolstered by the votes in California and some Deep South states, took a healthy lead. But Ford's strength in the big northeastern states—New York, New Jersey, Pennsylvania, Connecticut, Ohio—and others such as Minnesota and Illinois pushed Ford ahead. There was a pause as the Virginia delegation was individually polled. And then West Virginia put the president over the top.

The final vote was 1,187 for Ford, 1,070 for Reagan, 1 vote from the New York delegation for Commerce Secretary Elliot L. Richardson, and 1 abstention. On a voice vote the convention made the nomination unanimous.

Ford the next day selected Sen. Robert Dole of Kansas as his running mate after Reagan ruled out his acceptance of the second spot. Dole was seen as an effective gut fighter against the Carter forces who would allow Ford to keep his campaign style presidential.

Ford's basic campaign strategy was to portray himself as an experienced leader, a calm and reasonable man who had restored openness and respect to the presidency. Carter's strategy was to attack Ford as an inept leader who lacked the imagination and instincts to move the country forward.

Also campaigning was Eugene J. McCarthy, who ran as an Independent, unaffiliated with any party. The McCarthy campaign was aimed at people who had been frequent nonvoters in the past, a group making up nearly half the potential electorate. The Democrats, however, saw the McCarthy voter as a liberal Democrat who would choose Carter over Ford in a two-way race.

Results of the 1976 Elections

On November 2 Jimmy Carter swept the South, took a majority in the East, and did well enough in the Midwest to struggle home with a victory. But it was not easy. Carter's win in Ohio by 11,000 votes still left him with the smallest electoral college margin since Woodrow Wilson won reelection in 1916. Without Ohio's 25 electoral votes, Carter's total would have dropped to 272, giving him the smallest edge in a hundred years.

In several states McCarthy's Independent candidacy appeared to have tipped the balance to Ford, although in the national popular vote count McCarthy made little impact, receiving less than 1 percent of the total.

Carter won by welding together varying proportions of Roosevelt's New Deal coalition: the South, the industrial Northeast, organized labor, minorities, and the liberal community. Carter won majorities in each of these regions and voting groups and made a better than usual showing for a Democratic candidate in the rural Midwest.

Ford made his best showing in the West, winning 53 percent of the popular vote and carrying all but one state, Hawaii. Neither Ford nor Carter ran well in the region during the primaries, but the president benefited from traditional Republican strength and the absence of an intensive Carter effort in the region to score a series of one-sided victories.

In the Senate an unusual number of new people were elected in 1976, but it changed little in ideology and none at all in party lineup. Voters turned 9 incumbent senators out of office, more than in any year since 1958. But they took care to treat both parties about the same way, and when the Ninety-fifth Congress convened in January, there were 62 Senate Democrats and 38 Republicans, just as there were in the Senate that had left in October.

It was an extraordinarily large freshman class—18, including the replacement for Vice President-elect Mondale. Ten of the first-termers were Democrats; 8 were Republicans. The large-scale rejection of incumbents had not been expected. The 9 who lost represented more than one-third of all the incumbents seeking reelection. By some stroke of challengers' luck virtually every senator who found himself in a difficult race lost.

Three Democratic senators in the "class of 1958"—Vance Hartke of Indiana, Gale W. McGee of Wyoming, and Frank E. Moss of Utah—lost decisively. The other four were easy winners. They were Robert C. Byrd of West Virginia, Harrison A. Williams, Jr., of New Jersey, Howard W. Cannon of Nevada, and Edmund S. Muskie of Maine.

But the group of senators that did even worse in 1976 was the Republican "class of 1970," many of whom won their first terms six years earlier with Nixon administration help. All six senators ran for second terms in 1976, and four were beaten: J. Glenn Beall, Jr., of Maryland, Bill Brock of Tennessee, James L. Buckley of New York (elected as a Conservative), and Robert Taft, Jr., of Ohio.

The classes of 1958 and 1970 thus accounted for seven of the nine incumbent defeats on November 2. The other two beaten incumbents were Democrats John V. Tunney of California and Joseph M. Montoya of New Mexico.

The ten new Democrats were Dennis DeConcini of Arizona, Spark M. Matsunaga of Hawaii, John Melcher of Montana, Howard M. Metzenbaum of Ohio, Daniel Patrick Moynihan of New York, Donald W. Riegle, Jr., of Michigan, Paul S. Sarbanes of Maryland, Jim Sasser of Tennessee, Edward Zorinsky of Nebraska, and Wendell R. Anderson, appointed from Minnesota.

The eight new Republicans were John H. Chafee of Rhode Island, John C. Danforth of Missouri, Orrin G. Hatch of Utah, S. I. "Sam" Hayakawa of California, John Heinz of Pennsylvania, Richard G. Lugar of Indiana, Harrison "Jack" Schmitt of New Mexico, and Malcolm Wallop of Wyoming.

In the House the Democratic freshmen taught the Republicans a lesson in the power of incumbency, winning reelection almost unanimously to ensure a Democratic majority by the same 2-1 margin the party held in the Ninety-fourth Congress. Democrats won 292 House seats, and the Republicans, 143.

The Democratic freshmen used the perquisites of office with consummate skill to build political strength and resist close identification with the rest of Congress and the federal bureaucracy. The nationwide Republican effort to brand them as big-spending radicals flopped and left the House GOP in the same minority status as before the elections.

Only 13 House incumbents—8 Democrats and 5 Republicans—lost their seats. This was far below the number retired by the voters in 1974, when 36 Republicans and 4 Democrats were defeated in the Watergate landslide that raised the Democrats to overwhelming dominance in the chamber.

The majority of the Democratic seats were safe, while most of the Republican ones were up for grabs, and many were won by the Democrats. The GOP held onto only 9 of its 17 seats while winning 3 held by Democrats, for a net loss of 5 in this open category.

In gubernatorial races the Democrats gained one more governorship, defeating Republican candidates in 9 states out of the 14. The new lineup was 37 Democrats, 12 Republicans, and 1 Independent, James B. Longley of Maine. Most of the races for governor ended as expected. Voters reelected five incumbents, defeated two others, and elected nine new governors.

The one real upset was in Missouri, where Democrat Joseph P. Teasdale defeated Republican governor Christopher S. "Kit" Bond by 13,000 votes. Bond, Missouri's first GOP governor since World War II, was expected to win a second term.

Four states—Montana, North Dakota, Utah, and Washington—chose Ford over Carter but elected Democratic governors. Delaware voted for Carter but elected a Republican as governor.

1977-1979:
The Ninety-fifth Congress

With a new and unknown president taking office in January 1977, Congress and the nation waited expectantly to see how Carter would tackle the intractable problems of energy and the economy. In addition, the new president would have to work out a constructive relationship with a Congress that had asserted its power after a long period of presidential dominance. It was also a Congress that had selected new Democratic leadership on both sides of the Capitol, caused by the retirement of Senate Majority Leader Mike Mansfield, D-Mont., and House Speaker Carl Albert, D-Okla.

In foreign affairs the country was at peace, but the administration had to plunge into the labyrinths of relations with the Soviet Union and China and wrestle with attempts to achieve peace in the Middle East.

Carter did not hesitate to get to work on these difficult problems, early proposing an economic stimulus package and an energy program. It soon became clear, however, that major roadblocks stood in the way of enacting significant legislation, especially in the energy area.

The lack of consensus on crucial issues, both in Congress and among the public, was one problem. Another was the continued rivalry between the legislative and executive branches, with congressional leaders accusing the new administration of ineptness and lack of leadership and the executive pointing to Congress' inherent inability to lead.

The partial deadlock reflected the malaise of a country that seemed to be ending its era of predominance in the world and continued economic expansion at home. How the country would cope with the new era remained unclear at the close of 1978.

The House installed Thomas P. O'Neill, Jr., D-Mass., as Speaker. In a sharp contest for House majority leader, moderate representative Jim Wright of Texas won out. In the Senate, Democratic whip Robert C. Byrd of West Virginia was chosen unanimously as the new majority leader. Republicans also had a leadership contest for Senate mi-

nority leader, with Sen. Howard H. Baker, Jr., R-Tenn., the victor.

In January 1978 President Carter presented Congress with his major tax cut and reform program. After working on taxes most of the year, Congress gave final approval October 15 to an $18.7 billion tax cut for 1979 that included a substantial reduction in the tax on capital gains. The bill provided individual income tax reductions that were designed to offset Social Security and inflation-induced tax increases for 1979. In addition, it provided about 4.3 million taxpayers—mostly in the middle- and upper-income ranges—with generous capital gains tax reductions. For businesses, the bill included a reduction in corporate income tax rates and expanded investment tax credits.

In April 1977 Carter introduced his energy policy. For most of 1978 the measure was bogged down in the conference committee trying to resolve differences over the natural gas pricing section. Finally, on October 15, 1978, Congress cleared the bill and sent it to the president.

In the summer of 1977 a political scandal hit the Carter administration that damaged the president's popularity. Questions were raised in the press about the propriety of a number of transactions that Bert Lance, Carter's director of the Office of Management and Budget, had engaged in during his banking career. The Lance matter preoccupied the White House until Lance's resignation in September 1977.

The Carter administration in 1977 laid the groundwork for two treaties with Panama, which were ratified by the Senate in April 1978. One would turn over the Panama Canal to Panama by the year 2000; the second guaranteed the United States' right to defend the canal after that date.

Carter's greatest foreign policy triumph came in September 1978 when he met at Camp David with Egyptian president Anwar Sadat and Israeli prime minister Menachem Begin to hammer out the outlines of a Middle East peace. The success of that effort gave Carter a major boost in prestige and in the polls. And it laid the groundwork for a possible solution to the thirty-year-old Middle East conflict.

President Carter had one more big foreign policy surprise for 1978. In a joint communiqué issued December 15, the United States and the People's Republic of China announced that they would formally recognize each other January 1, 1979, and would exchange ambassadors and establish embassies March 1. This announcement ended another thirty-year-old dispute: the refusal of the United States to recognize the Communists as the rulers of China.

The 1978 Midterm Elections

Republicans in the 1978 midterm campaign were curiously unable to capitalize on their own carefully developed issues in what ought to have been their kind of year. Without a Republican president to have to defend, GOP congressional candidates were free to run against every branch of the federal government, a traffic that brought them enormous gains the last time they tried it, in 1966. Besides, the rise of tax resentment gave them a drum to beat, and they pounded on it in virtually every contested congressional district in the country.

Humiliated by their failure to gain any House or Senate seats at all in 1976, Republicans redesigned their strategy for the 1978 campaign. In the House they abandoned their attempts to defeat many of the Democrats first elected in 1974, switching to place their emphasis on older incumbents weak in constituent service and name identification. In both the House and Senate they involved themselves in primaries to see that promising candidates won.

But Republican leaders made one other decision that did not work as well as they had hoped: they chose to base congressional campaigns throughout the country on a plan, proposed by Rep. Jack F. Kemp of New York and Sen. William V. Roth, Jr., of Delaware, to cut federal income taxes by one-third. It was difficult to find a Republican nominee in any contested state or district who did not talk about Kemp-Roth.

The Republican approach allowed Democratic opponents to seize the popular side of the issue by charging that a Kemp-Roth tax cut was inflationary. Democrats insisted that spending cuts were the proper course, co-opting normal Republican rhetoric.

Results of the 1978 Elections

The 1978 elections produced a Republican gain of 3 seats in the Senate, along with the second largest freshman Senate class in the history of popular elections. The new Senate lineup for the Ninety-sixth Congress was 59 Democrats and 41 Republicans. The Democratic total included Harry F. Byrd, Jr., of Virginia, elected as an Independent. While the GOP increase was not overwhelming, it was slightly greater than what GOP officials themselves expected a year before.

The GOP newcomers included Nancy Landon Kassebaum of Kansas, the first woman elected to the Senate without being preceded in Congress by her husband, and Thad Cochran, the first Republican senator elected in Mississippi since 1875. The only black in the Senate during the Ninety-fifth Congress, Edward W. Brooke of Massachusetts, was defeated.

The large freshman classes of 1976 and 1978 differed markedly from their counterparts of the previous generation. The new freshman classes represented no distinct national trends. The 1976 class of 18 was composed of 8 Republicans and 10 Democrats, and the 1978 newcomers included 11 Republicans and 9 Democrats. The large Senate turnover in the 1970s meant that nearly half the members—48—were in their first terms as of January 1979.

The most notable conservative gains in the Senate occurred in Iowa, where Republican Roger Jepsen unseated incumbent Dick Clark, and in New Hampshire, where incumbent Democrat Thomas J. McIntyre lost to Gordon Humphrey.

The Democratic class of 1972 turned out to be somewhat more vulnerable than the Republican group. Democrats lost Clark, William D. Hathaway of Maine, and Floyd K. Haskell of Colorado. In addition to their defeats, the seat of retiring Democratic senator James Abourezk of South Dakota was upturned by the Republicans.

Other freshmen Democrats included Howell Heflin and Donald Stewart (both of Alabama), David Pryor (Arkansas), Paul E. Tsongas (Massachusetts), Carl Levin (Michigan), Max Baucus (Montana), J. James Exon (Nebraska), Bill Bradley (New Jersey), and David L. Boren (Oklahoma). Republican newcomers were William L. Armstrong (Colorado), William S. Cohen (Maine), Rudy Boschwitz and David Durenberger (Minnesota), Larry Pressler (South Dakota), John Warner (Virginia), and Alan K. Simpson (Wyoming).

In the House, Republicans made modest inroads on the lopsided Democratic majority, making a net gain of 11 seats. But Democrats remained in firm control, winning 277 seats to 158 for the GOP. With a record 58 open seats in the House, Republicans hoped to make their biggest gains in the 39 open districts held by Democrats. But that strategy brought only a net gain of 2, as Republicans captured 8 Democratic-held open seats but lost 6 of their 19 vacant seats to the Democrats.

Campaigning against incumbents, usually a harder task, proved surprisingly successful for the GOP, as 14 Democratic House members were defeated, compared to 5 Republicans. It was the largest number of Democratic defeats since 1966, when 39 House Democrats, many of them brought in during the 1964 presidential landslide, lost their jobs.

In gubernatorial politics Republicans moved a step closer to respectability, increasing the number of statehouses under their control from 12 to 18. William Clements's upset election in Texas, Richard L. Thornburgh's come-from-behind triumph in Pennsylvania, and James A. Rhodes's narrow survival in Ohio guaranteed that the GOP would enter the 1980 election year with governors in five of the ten "megastates." That news diluted the Republican disappointment at failing to oust Democratic governor Hugh L. Carey in New York or even to come close against incumbent Democrat Edmund G. Brown in California.

1979-1981:
The Ninety-sixth Congress

The first session of the Ninety-sixth Congress passed into history as a contradiction. Members came to Washington in 1979 spurred by a nationwide antigovernment mood. Legislators, even some of the more liberal ones, talked bravely of the need to limit federal spending. Contrary to the rhetoric, which continued throughout the year, that session of Congress voted for massive new spending efforts and laid the groundwork for significant new federal involvement in the lives of American businesses and citizens.

The most massive expansion of the federal role was in the package of energy legislation, which was the focus of congressional debate most of the year. It called for spending billions of dollars on synthetic fuels development and imposing a major federal presence in the energy industry. It also was a year when advocates of more defense spending finally recouped from the travails of the Vietnam era and won a pledge of extra billions for the military from a president who initially opposed such increases.

Support for the energy package was grounded in troubled U.S. relations with oil-exporting nations and a continuing upward spiral in the cost of imported oil. Those trends were exacerbated by the crumbling of relations between the United States and Iran after militant Iranians seized the U.S. Embassy in Tehran and held fifty-three Americans hostage for the return of that nation's deposed shah, Mohammed Reza Pahlavi.

Advocates of higher defense spending, using the Iranian hostage situation as an example, argued more vigorously than ever before that America's strength and influence in the world were declining and that U.S. military strength was falling far behind that of the Soviet Union.

But if Congress acted with determination on energy and some other issues, it acted virtually not at all on the economic troubles of the nation. Faced with double-digit inflation and the threatened onset of a recession, Congress—much like the president—did not seem to know what to do. It appeared both were marking time until 1980 to decide whether federal action would help or worsen America's economic problems.

Congress showed little interest in social, consumer, and environmental legislation. The realization was growing that the federal budget was not open-ended and that government spending decisions required some distasteful choices. Nevertheless, members approved Carter's request to create a separate Department of Education.

In 1980, facing an aggressive and unified Republican party and worried by its own reputation for big spending, the Democratic-controlled Congress began the election year concentrating on trimming programs in order to balance the federal budget. A recession combined with spiraling inflation soon dashed the Democrats' balanced-budget hopes. But these new economic woes also did nothing to encourage the Democrats to resume pushing for some of their favorite programs. In addition, because of escalating campaign pressures, Democratic leaders delayed until after the election consideration of the budget and a number of other key bills.

By year's end, however, the Democrats found their scheme had backfired. Instead of rewarding them for their restraint, the elections had deprived them of their control of the White House and Senate and put them in a substantially weaker position in the House in 1981.

The 1980 Campaigns

President Carter won enough delegates at his party's primaries and caucuses to win the Democratic presidential nomination. But he faced significant opposition at the convention from Sen. Edward M. Kennedy of Massachusetts. Carter led Kennedy throughout the primary season, but as the convention neared, the momentum seemed to be with Kennedy. Although Carter continued to win more caucus delegates, Kennedy won five of the last eight primaries, which kept him in contention.

At the same time, the president's position in the popularity polls dropped, and Carter found himself in the midst of an embarrassing controversy over his brother Billy's connection with the Libyan government.

Alarmed by Carter's apparently diminishing reelection prospects, several party leaders grew concerned that a Carter defeat in November would drag down dozens of state and local candidates across the country. They called for an "open convention" that could nominate a compromise candidate. And they teamed up with Senator Kennedy to urge defeat of a proposed convention rule that would bind all delegates to vote on the first ballot for the candidate under whose banner they were elected.

When the convention opened, Carter could count 1,981.1 delegates pledged to him—315 more than he needed for the nomination. Kennedy had 1,225.8 delegates, and the only chance he had to gain the nomination was to defeat the rule. There were 122.1 uncommitted delegates and 2 for other candidates.

In the days before the convention opening Kennedy strategists claimed that there were continuing defections from the Carter camp. On Sunday they said they were within 50 to 100 votes of the majority needed to overturn the rule binding the delegates. But the Kennedy predictions and hopes proved to be exaggerated. The final tally on the rule showed 1,936.418 delegates favoring the binding

rule and 1,390.580 opposing it. Passage of the rule ensured Carter's renomination. Shortly after the vote, Kennedy ended his nine-month challenge to the president by announcing that his name would not be placed in nomination on August 13.

But Kennedy did not withdraw from the platform debate. The bitterly contested party platform pitted Carter against Kennedy and a coalition of special interest groups. The final document was filled with so many concessions to the Kennedy forces that it won only a halfhearted endorsement from the president.

Kennedy capped his platform victories with an August 12 appearance before the delegates in which he presented a stunning speech to a tumultuous ovation. His speech created a sense of enormous energy within the hall and left the feeling that a significant political event had occurred.

By the following day Carter began to reassert control over the convention. In a statement issued just hours after the platform debate ended, the president refused to accept—as diplomatically as possible—many of the platform revisions. In his carefully worded statement, Carter did not flatly reject any of Kennedy's amendments, but he did not embrace them either. Carter concluded his statement with the unity refrain that had become the hallmark of every White House comment on the platform since the drafting process began: "The differences within our party on this platform are small in comparison with the differences between the Republican and Democratic party platforms."

Carter won his party's presidential nomination on the first ballot, and his vice president, Walter F. Mondale, easily won renomination. Kennedy pledged his support and even made a brief appearance on the platform with Carter and Mondale as the convention drew to a close. But it was uncertain whether the appeals for unity had succeeded.

On the Republican side Ronald Reagan had carefully cultivated an image as the presumed GOP front-runner for 1980 from the day Gerald Ford was defeated by Carter in 1976. During the primaries Reagan lost only four of the state preference primaries he entered. In states that chose their delegates in caucuses, Reagan was even more impressive, winning just under 400 of the 478 delegates picked by caucuses. But it was in the early primaries that Reagan was able to pare the field from a half-dozen major candidates to just two.

In South Carolina on March 8 Reagan knocked former Texas governor John B. Connally out of the race. Ten days later he deflated John B. Anderson's surging campaign with a victory in the representative's home state of Illinois. A similar result two weeks later in Wisconsin forced Anderson out of the GOP contest and into an unsuccessful Independent bid for the White House.

After four quick defeats Senate minority leader Howard H. Baker, Jr., of Tennessee dropped out. Neither Rep. Philip M. Crane of Illinois nor Sen. Robert Dole of Kansas had ever caught the voters' attention. And on March 15 former president Gerald Ford put to rest growing speculation that he might jump into the race in an effort to stop Reagan. By April the GOP contest was reduced to former Texas representative George Bush's frantic efforts to catch Reagan in a few major states. It was too little, too late.

Having outdistanced all the competition, Reagan easily won his party's 1980 nomination at the Republican National Convention in Detroit. Reagan won on the first ballot, receiving 1,939 of the 1,994 delegate votes. His nomination was then made unanimous.

The unusual flap over the selection of the vice-presidential nominee provided the only suspense at the convention. Rumors circulated that Ford was being tapped for the second spot. Ford himself had encouraged that speculation, although he declined to spell out his conditions. It became clear he wanted responsibilities that would have made him, in effect, co-president with Reagan. Late on July 16 the Reagan-Ford arrangement fell apart, and the two men agreed that it would be better for Ford to campaign for the GOP ticket rather than be a member of it. The speculation prompted Reagan to make an unusual visit to the convention hall at 12:15 a.m. on July 17 to to announce his choice of George Bush as his running mate.

The American hostage crisis was injected into the campaign in the eleventh hour when Iranian leaders miscalculated that Carter would accept their demands in return for release of the hostages before election day. Although Carter tried to keep the negotiations—which reached a peak during the weekend before November 4—out of the campaign, the publicity given them so close to the election worked against the president.

But what hurt Carter the most, in the opinion of many analysts, was his inability to improve the state of the economy. Throughout the fall campaign Reagan blamed Carter for almost tripling the inflation rate he had inherited from the Ford administration. During 1980 the rate averaged about 13 percent.

No one publicly forecast the rout that developed election night. Reagan's sweep was nationwide. In most of the states that were expected to be close or to go for Carter, Reagan won, frequently by comfortable margins. In states Reagan was expected to carry, he won overwhelmingly.

Reagan easily carried every region of the country, including the keystones of Carter's triumph four years before—the industrial Northeast and the president's native South.

Results of the 1980 Elections

The Republican victory did not stop with the presidency. The GOP rode the crest of a breathtaking sweep to take control of the Senate for the first time in a quarter-century. Although the Democrats retained their majority in the House, the national shift to the political right combined with a variety of scandals, complacency by some incumbents, and unusually strong Reagan coattails cost the Democrats a net loss of 33 seats in the House. That made the Republicans 26 seats shy of controlling the House, although conservative Democrats were expected to give the GOP an ideological edge on many issues.

The 12 Senate seats won by Republicans represented the largest net gain in the Senate for any party since 1958, when the Democrats took over 15 seats. The new lineup was 53 Republicans and 47 Democrats. The 1980 GOP Senate victory was the first since 1952 and ended the longest one-party dominance of the Senate in American history.

In addition to their increases the Republicans held on to the 10 seats that were up in 1980. That included holding 3 open seats in Pennsylvania, Oklahoma, and North Dakota and the New York seat of Republican senator Jacob K. Javits, who was defeated for renomination in the primary but ran for reelection on the Liberal party ticket.

Democrats had 24 seats before the election and lost half of them. Not only would the Senate be more Republican, it would be noticeably more conservative. Several pillars of Democratic liberalism went down to defeat, in-

cluding George McGovern of South Dakota, Warren G. Magnuson of Washington, and John C. Culver of Iowa.

To replace the Democrats, Republicans elected a freshman Senate class made up largely of dedicated conservatives. Representatives Charles E. Grassley of Iowa, Steven D. Symms of Idaho, James Abdnor of South Dakota, and Robert W. Kasten, Jr., of Wisconsin had compiled distinctively conservative records in the House. John P. East of North Carolina, an expert in conservative political thought, was expected to carry out his beliefs in the Senate.

But there was a contingent of Republican moderates that could leaven some of the conservative impulses. Warren Rudman of New Hampshire, Arlen Specter of Pennsylvania, and Slade Gorton of Washington all were from the moderate wing of their party.

Among the losing Democrats were four of the six prime targets of the National Conservative Political Action Committee, which prepared hard-hitting ads attacking the records of liberal senators. The targeted senators were Birch Bayh of Indiana, Culver of Iowa, McGovern of South Dakota, Thomas F. Eagleton of Missouri, Frank Church of Idaho, and Alan Cranston of California. Bayh, Culver, McGovern, and Church went down to defeat.

In the House the lineup going into the November election was 273 Democrats to 159 Republicans. There also were three vacancies that had been held by Democrats. When the ballots had been counted, the new lineup was 243 Democrats to 192 Republicans. The Democratic total included one Independent.

The Republican net gain of 33 seats was the largest increase for the GOP since 1966. Most of the GOP gains came at the expense of incumbents. In all, 31 of the 392 incumbents running for reelection were turned out. Of those, 27 were Democrats who lost to Republicans. Only 3 incumbent Republicans were defeated.

There were 74 new faces in the new House, 3 fewer than in 1978. Republican freshmen had the edge with 52 seats, compared to 22 for the Democrats. Four new women—all Republicans—were elected, bringing the total number of women in the House to 19. There were four black freshmen, for a total of 17 black voting members. All were Democrats.

Republicans increased their hold on governorships by 4 states, bringing their nationwide total to 23. Democrats still maintained a lead, with 27 governors' chairs. The Republican additions came in states west of the Mississippi River: Arkansas, Missouri, North Dakota, and Washington.

The Republican gain continued the party's gradual comeback on the gubernatorial level. After 1968, when the party won 31 governorships compared with the Democrats 19, GOP gubernatorial fortunes slid to a low of 12 in 1977. The party began to make gains again in 1978, boosting its total by 6. In 1979 the GOP added another governor in Louisiana.

Despite the party's success in gubernatorial races, Republicans advanced only negligibly in state legislatures, which were to redraw political boundaries in post-1980 census redistricting.

1981-1983:
The Ninety-seventh Congress

Dominated by Republicans for the first time in two and a half decades and guided by a forceful and popular president, Congress took bold steps in 1981 toward reducing the federal government's scope. Following the wishes of President Reagan, the Ninety-seventh Congress slashed government spending, cut taxes for individuals and business, and slimmed down federal regulatory activities.

The 1980 elections not only swept a conservative Republican into the White House but also floated the GOP into its first Senate majority since January 1955. The change in control meant that committee leadership shifted to the Republicans and that the Democrats were relegated to minority leadership. The new Senate majority leader was Howard H. Baker, Jr., of Tennessee.

In the House the Democrats, under the leadership of Thomas P. O'Neill, Jr., of Massachusetts, were still in the majority, though by a slimmer margin (243-192) than they enjoyed in the previous Congress. And the conservative leanings of many of their numbers made the Democratic leadership's grasp on House proceedings tentative at times.

When Reagan entered office in January 1981, he laid out what appeared to some to be contradictory goals for his presidency. To revitalize the economy and strengthen the nation, he would cut federal spending yet increase spending for defense, reduce taxes yet balance the budget. Many traditional Republicans in Congress were uneasy with this "supply-side" economic approach. But the GOP leaders in both houses proved to be effective and loyal lieutenants for their president.

Congress enacted $35.2 billion in fiscal 1982 program reductions, cut nearly $4 billion more from appropriations, approved a cut in individual and business taxes totaling $749 billion over a five-year period, and added about $18 billion to the fiscal 1982 defense budget drafted by President Carter the year before. But the federal deficit for the year appeared to be heading over the $100 billion mark, and the economy was in recession. In the process of getting his program enacted, Reagan exhausted his winning coalition, stretched congressional procedures out of shape, and bruised sensitive legislative egos.

Almost all the sweeping budget cuts Congress approved were made in one package, the budget "reconciliation" bill. The use of the reconciliation method in such a massive way was criticized by some members as an abuse of the budget process. The budget bill touched on virtually every federal activity except defense. Included in it were a multitude of changes in existing law, including provisions to tighten eligibility for public assistance, cut funds for subsidized housing programs, reduce school lunch subsidies, and cut Medicaid payments to the states.

In September, when Reagan proposed a second package of $13 billion in further spending cuts and $3 billion in unspecified revenue increases for 1982, the president's coalition began to crumble. Even members who had worked hard for Reagan's first round of cuts had no stomach for a second in a single year. Moderate House Republicans threatened to desert him unless he shielded their pet programs. Conservative Democrats threatened to bail out over the growing deficit, and the Reagan team was split over the question of tax increases.

The president maintained symbolic pressure on Congress to make additional spending cuts, even bringing the government to a halt for a day in late November by vetoing a temporary funding resolution. But Congress was unwilling to make the cuts he demanded. The appropriations process ground to a halt, and the government limped through the end of the year on a series of temporary funding resolutions.

On defense, Congress granted Reagan's request for significant spending increases. The $200 billion fiscal 1982 defense appropriation was the largest peacetime appropriations bill ever approved.

Congress grew increasingly independent of the White House in 1982. The legislators adhered to President Reagan's general course of restraining domestic programs while increasing military spending, but they rejected many of the president's specific proposals. They substantially rewrote Reagan's fiscal 1983 budget and persuaded the president to support a large tax increase only a year after passing his three-year tax cut plan.

While modifying or rejecting many of Reagan's requests, Congress did not originate much of its own legislation in 1982. Faced with soaring federal deficits, members spent a lot of their time defending existing programs from budget cuts rather than trying to create new ones.

The 1982 Midterm Elections

The 1982 midterm elections produced major change in the House but left the Senate comparatively untouched. A combination of redistricting and recession produced a huge crop of 81 House freshmen, 57 of them Democrats. In the previous thirty years only three other elections had brought in that many new Democrats.

Redistricting played a major role in 1982. This was the election in which reapportionment, the rise of the Sun Belt, and the decline of the Frost Belt were supposed to catch up with the Democrats, setting in motion a decade of conservative and Republican advance of power in the House. But it did not work out that way.

The Sun Belt proved the Republicans' greatest disappointment. The nationwide shift in population away from the industrial North gave southern and western states 17 new districts, and the GOP at one time hoped to take at least a dozen of them. But Democratic legislative cartography and unfriendly federal court action got in the way, and in the end Democrats won 10 of the 17.

Results of the 1982 Elections

The only thing remarkable about the 1982 Senate results was the sheer absence of change. Not only did the party ratio remain the same—54 Republicans and 46 Democrats—but 95 of the 100 senators returned to Washington. The class of 5 newcomers was the smallest such group in the sixty-eight-year history of popular Senate elections.

That stability was itself a dramatic reversal of recent election trends. During the previous decade a Senate seat had been one of the most difficult offices in U.S. politics to hold. While reelection rates for House incumbents regularly had run above 85 percent, senators struggled against well-financed challengers and effective special interest groups.

The Senate outcome was neither the "ratifying" election that Republicans had hoped for after their sweep of 1980 nor the "correcting" election that Democrats had wanted. But there were favorable results for both parties. Republicans kept their beachhead on Capitol Hill, ensuring that Ronald Reagan would be the first Republican president since Herbert Hoover to have a GOP Senate majority throughout his four-year term.

Democrats broke even in an election that could have relegated them to minority status in the Senate for a long time. Of the 33 seats that were contested in 1982, the

Democrats were defending 19. They ended up winning 60.6 percent of the races.

In the House, Democrats scored a 26-seat gain, as voters expressed antipathy toward President Reagan's economic program but stopped short of repudiating it altogether. The outcome revealed an unusual degree of voter frustration with a party only two years into national power.

Democrats won 269 seats to 166 seats for the GOP, giving the Democrats a 103-seat advantage. Going into the election, Democrats held 241 seats and Republicans 192, with vacancies in two districts formerly occupied by Democrats. Twenty-six Republican incumbents and 3 sitting Democrats were beaten, nearly a mirror image of the 1980 election, in which the GOP lost 3 incumbents and unseated 28 Democratic members.

Hurt by losses in the economically distressed Midwest, Republicans saw their hold on the nation's governorships dwindle to 16 in the November 2 elections. The Democrats controlled statehouses in 34 states. The GOP's net loss of 7 statehouses—the party dropped 9 and picked up 2—ended a comeback in the party's gubernatorial fortunes. Republicans had been posting gains since 1977, when they hit a low point of 12 governors' chairs.

Of the Republican governors' seats that switched to the Democrats, 5 were in the Midwest, where the recession had been most acute, hitting both manufacturing and farming. Michigan, Minnesota, Nebraska, Ohio, and Wisconsin opted for Democrats. Republican incumbents were retiring in all these states except Nebraska, where Gov. Charles Thone was turned out.

Republicans also encountered a setback in their progress in the South. They held 4 of the region's 13 governorships in 1982; in 1983 they had just 2. Only Tennessee's Lamar Alexander won reelection.

In addition, Democrats took over GOP statehouses in Alaska and Nevada. Republicans assumed power in California, where George Deukmejian edged out Democrat Tom Bradley, and in New Hampshire, where GOP challenger John H. Sununu unseated Democratic incumbent Hugh Gallen. Each party had 6 open seats at stake. Democrats held all theirs except for California. Republicans managed to retain only Iowa.

Democrats also turned the tables on the GOP in state legislative elections, regaining most of the chambers taken by the Republicans in the previous two elections and ending a six-year decline in the number of legislatures under Democratic control.

1983-1985:
The Ninety-eighth Congress

Congress and President Reagan generally kept to their own turf in 1983, each going about business with little involvement from the other side. Unlike the first two years of the Reagan administration, when the president essentially wrote the economic script, Congress conducted its 1983 debate on deficits without Reagan's overt participation. And while Congress tried to assert itself on foreign policy, Reagan consistently called the global shots.

There were important bipartisan agreements in 1983 on Social Security, jobs legislation, the War Powers Resolution, and fiscal 1984 appropriations bills. But these were rare commodities in a year in which political motivations ranked above policy considerations.

The prime example of this dilemma was the way Congress and Reagan reacted to massive federal deficits. No matter how many experts said soaring deficits hurt the economy, few people were willing to take the politically risky steps needed to cure the problem. Reagan made a calculated decision to stay out of the deficit debate, thereby ducking any responsibility for tax increases his advisers viewed as a 1984 election liability. Antideficit rhetoric was a constant refrain among legislators, but Congress took little decisive action on the issue.

Standing behind Reagan, House Speaker Thomas P. O'Neill, Jr., D-Mass., in September helped push through a measure allowing the president to keep U.S. troops in Lebanon for up to eighteen months. In backing Reagan on Lebanon, Congress for the first time invoked major parts of the 1973 War Powers Resolution. On October 23, 241 U.S. Marines, sailors, and soldiers and 58 French paratroopers were killed by a terrorist truck bomb in Beirut. Subsequent efforts to revise or revoke the measure keeping troops in Lebanon failed in both houses. Under congressional pressure, Reagan announced in February 1984 that he had ordered the troop withdrawal.

Congress reluctantly continued to back Reagan's policy in Nicaragua. The House twice voted to force Reagan to stop backing rightist forces that were fighting to overthrow that country's leftist government. When the Senate refused to go along, a compromise was reached limiting aid to the rebels and requiring Reagan to seek explicit approval from Congress for additional aid.

Reagan won widespread approval in both chambers for the October 25 invasion of the Caribbean island of Grenada. The president said the invasion was necessary to protect some thousand Americans, mostly medical students, from civil strife that erupted following the murder of Marxist prime minister Maurice Bishop.

Reagan was victorious in most of his defense fights with Congress. He won the go-ahead for production of the MX missile, although the House came within a handful of votes of killing funding for the project.

On domestic issues Reagan met many disappointments on Capitol Hill in 1984. The president could not persuade Congress to approve his social agenda, which featured constitutional amendments to ban abortion and allow school prayer. Nor did Congress adopt his plan to give tuition tax credits to parents who sent their children to private schools, or his enterprise zone system to provide tax relief to businesses that created jobs in depressed areas.

One of the biggest problems remained the massive federal deficit. Although Congress took actions designed to reduce the deficit by $149 billion over three years, the tax increases and spending cuts were viewed as a mere "down payment" on a larger remedy. While legislators spent much of 1984 talking about the evils of the swelling federal deficit, they took only a first step toward a cure. Instead, many members figured they would deal with the problem in 1985, after the November elections.

The 1984 Campaigns

The focus in the early months of the presidential election was not on Reagan but on the Democratic candidates seeking their party's nomination. Sen. Alan Cranston of California was the first to toss his hat in the ring formally, announcing his candidacy February 2, 1983. But Walter Mondale had informally started his campaign shortly after he and President Jimmy Carter lost to Reagan and George Bush in 1980.

Mondale was never particularly popular with the voters. His public personality and speaking style were bland, his traditional "New Deal" Democratic message seemed stale and, to many, ineffective, and his identification as a candidate of the special interests led voters to look closely and often approvingly at Mondale's competitors.

Before the primaries began, Mondale's main opponent seemed to be John Glenn, senator from Ohio and former astronaut. But the first delegate selection event of the season, the Iowa precinct caucuses of February 20, was disastrous for Glenn as well as two other conservative Democrats in the race, South Carolina senator Ernest F. Hollings and former Florida governor Reubin Askew. Together these three drew less than 10 percent of the vote. In New Hampshire a week later the results for Glenn, Hollings, and Askew were just as discouraging, and all three withdrew from the race.

Other challenges came from Colorado senator Gary Hart and from George McGovern, the former South Dakota senator whose losing 1972 presidential campaign Hart had managed. Glenn and McGovern withdrew from the race after Super Tuesday, leaving in contention Mondale, Hart, and the Rev. Jesse Jackson, the first black to pursue seriously the presidential nomination of any major political party.

Hart's momentum was blunted almost as quickly as it began. In the week after Super Tuesday, he ran behind Mondale in six of seven delegate selection events. Then Mondale got a much-needed boost by winning the New York and Pennsylvania primaries. His chance to eliminate Hart evaporated when Hart won Ohio and Indiana. Mondale continued to lead in the number of delegates committed to him, and with his win in New Jersey June 5 he had enough delegates to win the nomination. But his campaign ended on the same lackluster note that had characterized most of the last four months; the same day Mondale claimed the nomination, Hart won three other primaries including California's.

Despite the difficult, sometimes bitter, primary season campaign, Democrats mustered a display of party unity at their convention and made a historic vice-presidential choice. The Democratic National Convention picked Mondale to be the party standard bearer against President Reagan. As in much of his drive for the nomination, Mondale was almost overshadowed again, this time by the attention generated by his selection of New York representative Geraldine A. Ferraro to be his running mate. Ferraro was the first woman ever chosen for the national ticket by a major party.

President Reagan enjoyed the smoothest road to renomination that any presidential candidate could have. Brimming with confidence that President Reagan and Vice President Bush would be "the winning team" in November, a jubilant Republican party held its convention in Dallas August 20-23. With the ticket's renomination certain beforehand, the convention was more a celebration for GOP activists than a business meeting. Criticisms from the party's shrinking band of moderates, worried by the strongly conservative tone of the platform, did little to dispel the optimistic mood of delegates, who looked forward with confidence to Reagan's easy reelection victory.

Highlights of the fall campaign were the two presidential debates. The first, held October 7, was focused on domestic issues. Mondale made a strong showing, which lessened his negative image. Equally important was the perception that Reagan turned in a poor performance; the

seventy-three-year-old president seemed tired and disorganized, leading journalists and Democrats to suggest that age was catching up with Reagan.

The second debate, on October 21, focusing on foreign affairs, was a draw in the opinion of most analysts. The debate was not a significant boost to Mondale's campaign, and it allowed Reagan to ease concerns about his age and competence raised by his performance during the first debate. The vice-presidential candidates also held a nationally televised debate, on October 11. Most analysts viewed it as a draw or gave a slight edge to Bush.

Almost every thrust Mondale made was effectively parried by his Republican opponents. Mondale's efforts to draw attention to the massive budget deficits run up during Reagan's first term by promising a tax increase did not stand a chance against Reagan's promise not to raise taxes. Similarly Mondale's attempts to paint Reagan as a man who favored the rich over the poor, the majority over the minority, did not overcome charges that Mondale was a tool of the special interests.

In the end perhaps no Democrat could have defeated Ronald Reagan in 1984. For one thing most voters thought they were better off than they had been four years earlier when Reagan first asked that question during his 1980 run against Carter and Mondale. Perhaps more important, voters seemed to respond to Reagan's upbeat attitude and his promise of continued peace and prosperity.

Results of the 1984 Elections

There was never much doubt that Ronald Reagan, one of the most popular presidents in American history, would win reelection in 1984. And it would be hard to imagine a vote more decisive than the balloting that gave him his victory. Winning all but one state, he drew 59 percent of the popular vote, and he won a record 525 electoral votes.

Despite the size of Reagan's victory, its meaning remained unclear. The vote clearly exposed the Democrats' limited appeal in presidential elections. On the other hand, Democrats held their own in other elections. In the Senate, rather than gaining as most presidents do, Reagan lost two seats, reducing the Republican majority to 53-47. In the House of Representatives the president's party gained 14 seats, far short of the historical average for landslides. The GOP gained one governor for a lineup of 16 Republicans and 34 Democrats. Only in the state legislatures did the Republican party make gains that could be considered significant.

Neither the Republicans nor the Democrats came away with quite what they wanted from the 1984 struggle for control of the Senate. Democrats had hoped to regain the majority they lost in 1980, when Republicans won a Senate majority for the first time since the 1954 elections. Republicans hoped that President Reagan's march to reelection would bring about a modest reprise of 1980, making the GOP hold on the Senate more secure.

But in this election Reagan was no trailblazer: Democrats retained 13 of the 14 seats they were defending, and a trio of Democratic House members captured Republican seats: Illinois representative Paul Simon edged out Sen. Charles H. Percy; Iowa representative Tom Harkin defeated Sen. Roger W. Jepsen; and Tennessee representative Albert Gore, Jr., took the seat being vacated by Senate majority leader Howard H. Baker, Jr. Countering the good news for the Democrats was an unexpected outcome in

Kentucky: the defeat of Sen. Walter "Dee" Huddleston at the hands of Mitch McConnell.

Thus Democrats won a net gain of 2 Senate seats, shifting the party ratio to 53 Republicans and 47 Democrats. That standing was an improvement over the preelection ratio of 55-45 but a comedown from the Democrats' 1983 prediction that the party could recapture Senate control by picking up a number of Republican seats Democrats regarded as shaky.

As it turned out Democrats failed to win most of the GOP seats in the "at risk" category. The biggest Democratic disappointment came in North Carolina, where GOP incumbent Jesse Helms narrowly won his bitter battle with Democratic governor James B. Hunt, Jr. It was the most expensive Senate contest ever, with the campaigns spending a total of about $22 million.

In four other key states where Democrats had hoped to pull upsets, Republicans prevailed easily: Mississippi senator Thad Cochran won against former governor William Winter; Sen. Gordon J. Humphrey won a second term in New Hampshire; Texas representative Phil Gramm, who switched parties in 1983, replaced retiring GOP senator John Tower; and Sen. Rudy Boschwitz took 58 percent in Minnesota, encountering no problems with Mondale's coattails because the Democratic presidential nominee barely carried his home state.

For the second time in a little over a decade, Republicans watched with disappointment as their presidential standard bearer swept triumphantly across the nation followed by a threadbare retinue of new U.S. House members. The November 6 elections revealed considerable hesitation nationwide over an all-out endorsement of Republican policies, as voters in district after district stopped short of backing GOP challengers who campaigned on their loyalty to Ronald Reagan. After several closely contested battles were decided, Republicans had gained 14 seats, falling well short of making up the 26 seats they lost in the 1982 midterm elections. One seat, still undecided at year's end, eventually remained Democratic.

Not counting the undecided seat, Democrats retained control of the House with 252 members to the GOP's 182. Going into the election, Democrats held 266 seats and Republicans 167, with vacancies in a New Jersey district previously held by a Republican and in a Kentucky district held by a Democrat. Those seats stayed in their respective parties' hands and were filled for the remainder of the term in special elections. As a result of the election there were 43 House freshmen in 1985, a small class, due mostly to the relatively low number of open seats in 1984.

The gubernatorial elections did little to dent the 2-1 advantage the Democratic party had in governorships it controlled. Republicans notched victories in North Carolina, Rhode Island, Utah, and West Virginia, where the statehouses were left vacant by departing Democratic incumbents. But the Democrats captured 3 seats, toppling Republican incumbents in North Dakota and Washington and picking up the seat left open by retiring GOP governor Richard A. Snelling in Vermont.

Republicans thus scored a net gain of 1 seat, boosting the total governorships under their control from 15 to 16 and reducing the number of states in the Democratic column from 35 to 34. The GOP's showing represented an improvement over 1982, when the party suffered a net loss of 7 seats. Republicans still remained a long way, however, from capturing a majority of governorships, a feat they last accomplished in 1969.

1985-1987:
The Ninety-ninth Congress

The Ninety-ninth Congress compiled an extraordinary record. It revised the tax code more dramatically than in any time since World War II, rewrote immigration law, approved the most far-reaching environmental bills since the 1970s, boosted student aid, reversed President Reagan's policy toward South Africa, and joined him in openly seeking to overthrow Nicaragua's leftist government.

Congress seized the legislative initiative from the White House in 1985 and dominated the Capitol Hill agenda to a degree unmatched since President Reagan took office in 1981. Although Reagan was able to rescue his top domestic priority—tax-overhaul legislation—with a last-minute personal lobbying campaign, the close call was a testament to the altered relationship between the White House and Capitol Hill.

On other issues ranging from deficit reduction to federal farm spending, from South Africa sanctions to Middle East arms sales, Congress called the shots, in stark contrast to the opening year of Reagan's first term.

Lawmakers made a historic year-end decision: passage of the Gramm-Rudman-Hollings legislation, which mandated paring of the federal deficit over the next five years until the budget was balanced in fiscal 1991. Although Congress embraced the budget reduction plan—offered by Republican senators Phil Gramm of Texas and Warren B. Rudman of New Hampshire and Democratic senator Ernest F. Hollings of South Carolina—as the best hope for future deficit control, many who shaped the measure were skeptical about its chances for working.

Deficit reduction had been the top priority of Senate majority leader, Bob Dole, R-Kan., when the Ninety-ninth Congress opened, but the expected deficit bequeathed to the next Congress remained about $180 billion.

In the two most important elections of 1985, moderation seemed to be the winning theme. Democrats retained the governorship in Virginia with Gerald L. Baliles, who mimicked the moderate philosophy of outgoing Democratic governor Charles S. Robb. Similarly, New Jersey Republican governor Thomas H. Kean thrived at the polls by positioning himself as more moderate than his party's national image. Because neither of the gubernatorial elections produced a partisan shift, the nationwide party lineup of governors remained at 34 Democrats and 16 Republicans—unchanged from 1984.

The 1986 Midterm Elections

The 1986 Senate campaigns deserve special notice for what they said about the state of electioneering in the latter half of the 1980s. Most spectacularly they laid to rest a theory that took hold in 1980—that the GOP's superior financial resources give it an infallible ability to win close contests. The notion gained widespread currency in 1982, when the GOP's high-tech campaign techniques and last-minute infusions of money saved several endangered Republican candidates. That year the GOP won five of the six contests in which the winner took 52 percent or less of the vote.

But in 1986 nine of the eleven races won by 52 percent or less went to Democrats. That achievement came in spite of daunting obstacles: the National Republican Senatorial Committee's nearly 8-1 funding advantage over its Democratic counterpart, a $10 million nationwide GOP get-out-the-vote effort, and an army of consultants, pollsters, media advisers, and GOP field staff at the disposal of Republican candidates.

The difference lay in what each side did with the resources at its disposal. In many contests Democrats latched onto issues—of substance and of personality—that by election day were helping them frame the terms of the debate. Even more important, while the GOP was spending much of its money on TV advertising and on a technology-driven voter mobilization effort, Democrats built on their strength at the grass roots. They developed extensive local organizations and, especially in the South, reawakened old party apparatuses and alliances.

In a year when there were so many close contests, the Republicans' lack of organizational depth hurt them, particularly in states where Democrats latched onto local issues that seemed more compelling to voters than national Republican pleas to keep the Senate in GOP hands.

The most striking examples of the Democrats' ability to outcampaign their opponents came in the South. All Democrats there used a variation on a single theme: that they were home-grown state patriots, while their opponents were national Republicans with little interest in local affairs. And all used their state's traditional Democratic base to surmount better-financed Republican efforts.

Results of the 1986 Elections

Democrats on November 4, 1986, regained control of the Senate they had lost to the GOP in 1980. Six Republicans who won their seats that year were defeated in their bids for reelection, as Democrats captured 9 GOP seats and lost only 1 of their own to take a 55-45 Senate majority. The results also gave Democrats the largest class of freshman senators since 1958. Of the 13 new senators, 11 were Democrats.

The party's most significant set of victories came in the South, where Democrats won 6 of 7 Senate contests. Their gains elsewhere were scattered across the map. Farm unrest in the Midwest cost two GOP members of the class of 1980 their seats. In Washington State controversy over the possible situating of a high-level nuclear waste site in Hanford helped Brock Adams unseat Republican Slade Gorton.

The Democrats' other gains came in Maryland, where Rep. Barbara A. Mikulski easily won the seat of retiring GOP Sen. Charles McC. Mathias, Jr., and in Nevada, where Rep. Harry Reid defeated former representative Jim Santini for the right to succeed retiring GOP senator Paul Laxalt.

The sole Republican pickup was in Missouri. There, former governor Christopher S. "Kit" Bond won the seat held by retiring Democratic veteran Thomas F. Eagleton.

Not every potentially close election broke the Democrats' way. In Oklahoma and Pennsylvania, Democratic representatives James R. Jones and Bob Edgar tried to turn local economic troubles to their advantage. Neither, however, could arouse the core Democratic constituency in the western half of their states. Oklahoma representative Don Nickles and Pennsylvania Republican Arlen Specter both won handily. And in Idaho, Democratic governor John V. Evans lost to conservative Republican Steven D. Symms.

In North Carolina, Democrat Terry Sanford stressed his longstanding ties to the state. At the same time, he painted incumbent James T. Broyhill as a captive of the Washington establishment. In Alabama, Rep. Richard C. Shelby attacked Republican senator Jeremiah Denton for being more interested in his personal agenda of "family" and social issues than in helping Alabama's economy.

Democratic representative John B. Breaux overcame an early lead by GOP representative W. Henson Moore to hold on to the Louisiana seat of retiring Democratic senator Russell B. Long. Breaux hammered away at Moore as a representative of GOP policies that were hurting Louisiana's farmers and its oil and gas industry.

In Georgia, Rep. Wyche Fowler, Jr., ran an almost picture-perfect campaign against Republican incumbent Mack Mattingly. Fowler carried just under two-thirds of the state's 159 counties.

Florida's Democratic governor Bob Graham, a popular moderate, put Paula Hawkins on the defensive by portraying the first-term senator as a lightweight with a narrow focus. Hawkins won only 45 percent of the vote, the worst showing of any Senate incumbent.

Superior organization proved to be the key element in Democratic representative Timothy E. Wirth's victory over GOP representative Ken Kramer for the Senate seat left vacant by retiring Colorado Democrat Gary Hart. In California, where media ads played a crucial role, Democratic Sen. Alan Cranston ran a masterful campaign that kept Rep. Ed Zschau's legislative record in the spotlight for much of the campaign and prevented the Republicans from focusing on Cranston's performance.

House Republicans lost only 5 seats in 1986, giving the Democrats a 258-177 edge for the 100th Congress. It was an extraordinarily good election for incumbents of both parties. Only 5 Republican incumbents went down to defeat: Mike Strang of Colorado; Webb Franklin of Mississippi; Fred J. Eckert of New York; and Bill Cobey and Bill Hendon, both of North Carolina. The Democrats suffered only 1 incumbent casualty: Robert A. Young of Missouri. The number of incumbents defeated was the lowest in postwar history.

The freshman House class of 1986 included 23 Republicans and 27 Democrats. That was larger than the 43-member freshman class of 1984 but much smaller than the 74-member GOP-dominated class of 1980 and the Democrat-heavy, 80-member contingent elected in 1982.

The Republican party made a strong showing in gubernatorial contests in 1986, winning a net gain of 8 governorships. The Democrats, who entered the election holding 34 of the 50 governorships, saw their advantage drop to 26-24. The GOP count was the largest since 1970, when the party last held a majority of the governorships.

Republicans unseated Democratic incumbents in Texas and Wisconsin and won 9 open seats that had been held by Democrats, including upset wins in Alabama and Arizona and a solid victory in Florida. Those victories were offset by the loss of 3 open Republican seats: in Oregon, Pennsylvania, and Tennessee.

The base of the Republican success was a small core of popular incumbents: California's George Deukmejian, Rhode Island's Edward DiPrete, and New Hampshire's John H. Sununu. The farm crisis that helped oust at least 2 Republican senators did not hurt most of the party's gubernatorial nominees. Iowa incumbent Terry E. Branstad won, as did 3 GOP candidates for open seats: Mike Hayden in Kansas, Kay A. Orr in Nebraska, and George S. Michelson in South Dakota. Republicans also picked up the governorship in Maine.

Democratic ineptness aided the Republicans in several states, particularly in Alabama, where Guy Hunt became the state's first Republican governor since Reconstruction. In Illinois, incumbent GOP governor James R. Thompson was considered vulnerable to a challenge from Adlai E. Stevenson III, until two associates of Lyndon H. LaRouche, Jr., won Democratic primaries for state office, causing Stevenson to renounce his own nomination and run as an Independent. A three-way race in Arizona helped elect conservative Republican Evan Mecham to succeed Democratic governor Bruce Babbitt in Arizona.

Despite the GOP's poor showing in Senate elections in the South, the party made its greatest gubernatorial gains in that region. In addition to picking up Texas and Alabama, the GOP elected Tampa mayor Bob Martinez in Florida, former governor and senator Henry Bellmon in Oklahoma, and Carroll A. Campbell, Jr., in South Carolina.

Democrats claimed 3 of the 4 seats being given up by Republican incumbents. Their largest catch was Pennsylvania, where Bob Casey defeated Lt. Gov. William W. Scranton III.

Republicans, however, were disappointed in their efforts to capture state legislatures. Nationwide, Democrats improved their lead in the number of legislative seats they controlled by 179 and won control of the legislatures in 28 states, 2 more than they dominated before the election. Republicans controlled both chambers in 10 legislatures, down from 11 before the election. Legislative control was split between the two parties in 11 states. (Nebraska has a nonpartisan, unicameral legislature.)

1987-1989: The 100th Congress

The 100th Congress, by its number, had a historic resonance. It convened in the year that the United States was celebrating the bicentennial of its Constitution and the government of checks and balances created by that Constitution.

Fittingly enough, members commemorated the separation of powers that lay at the heart of the Constitution by challenging the president over the Iran-contra affair and by checking his attempt to reshape the judiciary through the appointment of a controversial justice to a pivotal Supreme Court vacancy. The budget deficit engendered partisan wrangling within Congress and between Congress and the president for much of 1987. After the October 19, 1987, stock market crash, however, Congress and Reagan reached accord on a two-year deficit-reduction package.

For the first time since 1981 Democrats were in control of both chambers. Senate Democrats returned to power with a 55-45 margin; Robert C. Byrd of West Virginia was restored to his former position as majority leader. House Democrats, who increased their already formidable edge to 258-177, named Majority Leader Jim Wright of Texas to succeed Speaker Thomas P. O'Neill, Jr., of Massachusetts, who had retired in 1986. Wright was unopposed.

Two issues consumed as much if not more congressional attention than the perennial budget battles. The Iran-contra affair rarely left the front pages from February 1987, when a White House commission said the president had all but lost control of his national security apparatus, to November, when the Senate and House select committees investigating the scandal published their report. Continual revelations about the White House plan to sell arms to Iran in exchange for U.S. hostages in the Middle East and the subsequent diversion of profits from the arms sale to the contra guerrillas in Nicaragua severely damaged Reagan's public standing.

Almost as soon as the Iran-contra hearings concluded, Reagan's nomination to fill a Supreme Court vacancy created an equally clamorous controversy. Reagan nominated Robert H. Bork, a federal appeals court judge who had gained notoriety when, as solicitor general in 1973, he fired Watergate special prosecutor Archibald Cox. After a bitter fight, Bork was rejected. Reagan's second nominee, Douglas H. Ginsburg, was forced to withdraw his nomination after he admitted that he had smoked marijuana when he was a law student and law professor. Reagan's third nominee, Anthony M. Kennedy, was confirmed unanimously in February 1988.

Despite these divisive battles and other flare-ups between the Republican White House and the Democratic Congress, the two sides managed to reconcile their differences on a number of major issues, including measures to bail out the Farm Credit System and the Federal Savings and Loan Insurance Corporation. For all its productivity, however, the 100th Congress left for its successor a pile of unfinished business, with the deficit-ridden federal budget teetering at the top.

The 1988 Campaigns

Vice President George Bush's nomination for the presidency was never in any real jeopardy. His candidacy, though, generated little enthusiasm, which encouraged several Republicans to enter the race. Two contenders, former Delaware governor Pierre S. du Pont IV and former secretary of state Alexander M. Haig, Jr., left the race early.

The Iowa caucuses gave the Bush forces a momentary scare when their candidate came in third behind Sen. Bob Dole of Kansas and television evangelist Pat Robertson. A week later Bush trounced Dole in New Hampshire and then went on to sweep sixteen states on Super Tuesday, shutting Dole out of the March 8 events altogether. New York representative Jack F. Kemp, who had hoped to win the backing of the party's conservative wing, did not fare well in the early primaries and decided to leave the race after Super Tuesday.

Bush confirmed his standing with Republican voters on March 15, decisively winning Illinois. Dole left the race two weeks later. On April 26 Bush won enough Pennsylvania delegates to clinch the Republican nomination.

On the Democratic side eight candidates entered the contest: former Arizona governor Bruce Babbitt; Delaware senator Joseph R. Biden, Jr.; Gov. Michael Dukakis of Massachusetts; Rep. Richard A. Gephardt of Missouri; Sen. Albert Gore, Jr., of Tennessee; former senator Gary Hart of Colorado; Jesse Jackson; and Sen. Paul Simon of Illinois. Dukakis did not emerge as the clear front-runner until well into the primary schedule.

By mid-March Jackson had accumulated more primary votes than any other Democrat and only four fewer delegates than Dukakis. Then came Wisconsin, where Dukakis beat Jackson by more than 200,000 votes. Dukakis followed his Wisconsin victory with a decisive win in New York. Dukakis went on to win all the remaining primaries except in the District of Columbia, which Jackson took. Even then, Dukakis was not assured of enough delegates until the last round of voting on June 7.

After years of internal warfare the Democrats staged a remarkable show of unity at their convention in Atlanta. The prospects for party peace were not at all guaranteed as the party gathered for its July 18-21 conclave. In the weeks before the convention Dukakis had two main tasks: to select a running mate and to find a way to involve Jackson in the fall campaign.

On July 12 Dukakis announced that he had chosen Texas senator Lloyd Bentsen to be his running mate. The decision angered Jackson supporters, who noted that Bentsen was both southern and conservative and who believed that Jackson and his message had been slighted. Jackson then seemed to have scaled back his implicit demands that the vice-presidential nomination be offered to him. At the same time Dukakis seemed to find ways to demonstrate his respect for Jackson without pandering to him. Both men seemed close to accommodation on platforms and rules issues.

Jackson's willingness to compromise on the platform contributed greatly to the bonhomie of Atlanta, signaling a victory of pragmatism over idealism. As a result the rest of the convention was tension-free, providing the backdrop for a Hollywood-style finale. Jackson himself kicked off the unity collaboration in an electrifying speech that unfurled his famous call for social justice and offered strong words of praise for Dukakis.

With the conclusion of Jackson's speech, his virtual domination of the convention gave way to the business at hand. On July 20 Democratic delegates nominated Dukakis, who won 2,876.25 votes to Jackson's 1,218.5. Jackson conceded by telephone, and the convention then ratified Dukakis's nomination by acclamation.

Running behind Michael Dukakis in the public opinion polls, George Bush came to the Republican National Convention in New Orleans in August with one main task: to convince delegates and the viewing public that he was not the "wimp" pictured by political cartoonists. His choice of Sen. Dan Quayle of Indiana as his running mate, however, heightened many of the doubts he had sought to dispel.

To maintain some suspense, Bush had not been expected to name his choice for vice president until the last day of the convention. But at a welcoming ceremony on August 16, he announced his selection. Concern about Quayle's youth and government inexperience quickly surfaced. A major controversy erupted when reporters questioned Quayle about whether he had used family influence to get into the Indiana National Guard in 1969 to avoid service in the Vietnam War.

While controversy swirled around Quayle's selection, the convention business proceeded as if nothing unusual were happening. With no fights over the platform or party rules (both were approved without debate), the Republicans could concentrate on positioning themselves for the fall campaign.

Although Democrats began the fall campaign with high hopes for November, the campaign turned out to be a downhill slide for Dukakis. Dukakis left the Democratic convention as much as seventeen points ahead of Bush in some polls. That lead evaporated under a withering Republican attack that began at the GOP convention. Despite continuing reservations among voters about the Quayle nomination, Bush surged ahead in the polls at the end of August. He maintained that advantage throughout the fall, emphasizing at every opportunity that Dukakis was a lib-

Table 1 Growing Franchise in the United States, 1932-1988

Presidential election year	Estimated population of voting age	Vote cast for presidential electors	
		Number	Percent
1932	75,768,000	37,732,000	52.4
1936	80,174,000	45,643,000	56.9
1940	84,728,000	49,900,000	58.9
1944	85,654,000	47,977,000	56.0
1948	95,573,000	48,794,000	51.1
1952	99,929,000	61,551,000	61.6
1956	104,515,000	62,027,000	59.3
1960	109,672,000	68,838,000	63.1
1964	114,090,000	70,645,000	61.8
1968	120,285,000	73,212,000	60.7
1972	140,068,000	77,625,000	55.4
1976	150,127,000	81,603,000	54.4
1980	162,761,000	86,515,221	53.2
1984	173,936,000	92,652,793	53.3
1988	182,628,000	91,609,673	50.2

Source: Congressional Quarterly's Guide to the Presidency, ed. Michael Nelson (Washington, D.C.: Congressional Quarterly Inc., 1989), 170.

eral out of step with the mainstream. Many scored Bush for his tactics, but few argued with their effectiveness.

Bush's ability to keep Dukakis on the defensive was reflected in the public opinion polls. A week before the election, they gave Bush as much as a twelve-point lead.

Results of the 1988 Elections

George Bush was elected the nation's forty-first president on November 8, winning 54 percent of the popular vote. He was the first sitting vice president to win the White House since Martin Van Buren in 1836. Bush's victory confirmed that, absent economic crisis or White House scandal, the burden of proof was on the Democrats to convince voters that their party could be trusted with the executive branch of the federal government.

Bush was the first candidate since John F. Kennedy to win the White House while his party lost seats in the House. And unlike Kennedy's, Bush's victory margin was substantial in a number of states. His inability to carry others into office may have been partly due to his message, which was essentially a call to "stay the course."

In reviewing the results of the 1988 Senate elections, both parties had cause for rue and relief. But it was the Republicans who felt the keener disappointment. Democrats won 19 of the 33 races and restored the 55-45 majority they had seized in the 1986 elections. In 1988 Democrats successfully defended 15 of their 18 seats and took over Republican seats in Connecticut, Virginia, Nebraska, and Nevada.

GOP Senate leader Bob Dole conceded on election night that reclaiming the Senate had not been realistic in 1988. And the party could be pleased at capturing 3 historically Democratic seats as well as holding 11 of its own 15. Of the 4 the GOP lost, the only surprise came in Connecticut, where incumbent Lowell P. Weicker, Jr., was edged out by Joseph I. Lieberman.

The GOP had all but conceded the other 3 seats to the Democrats a year before the election. In Virginia former governor Charles S. Robb succeeded Republican Paul S. Trible, Jr., who retired after a single term. David K. Karnes of Nebraska lost to former Democratic governor Robert Kerry, and Chic Hecht of Nevada lost to sitting Democratic governor Richard H. Bryan.

The only Democratic incumbent the Republicans defeated was John Melcher of Montana. Conrad Burns became the state's first Republican senator elected in forty-two years. The other 2 new Republican seats in the Senate were won by House minority whip Trent Lott of Mississippi and Rep. Connie Mack of Florida. The latest emblems of the GOP's new day in the Old South, they replaced retiring Democrats John C. Stennis and Lawton Chiles.

An important measure of a party's performance in any election year is its score in contests where no incumbent is running. In this category the GOP won four of six. The party held on to retiring Robert T. Stafford's seat in Vermont, where at-large representative James M. Jeffords had no trouble moving in. And former GOP senator Slade Gorton, whom the voters turned out two years before, was elected to succeed retiring Republican senator Daniel J. Evans. Mack and Lott picked up the other two open seats.

The two Democrats winning open seats were Robb and Herbert Kohl. Kohl succeeded Democrat William Proxmire, who retired.

In the House of Representatives election day was cause for celebration for more than 98 percent of the members seeking reelection. Only 6 of 408 incumbents on the ballot lost, 4 Republicans and 2 Democrats. The Democrats picked up a net of 2 seats, putting the partisan lineup in the House at 260 Democrats and 175 Republicans.

The most prominent member to fall was Fernand J. St Germain of Rhode Island, who was soundly rejected after being dogged by questions about his ethical conduct. And in Georgia the Democrats had little trouble knocking off Republican representative Pat Swindall, who was under indictment for allegedly lying to a grand jury about a money-laundering scheme.

Democratic representative Bill Chappell, Jr., lost his Florida district after being battered by public questions about his links to a defense-procurement scandal. Democratic representative Roy Dyson of Maryland, also plagued by unfavorable stories about his links to the procurement

scandal and his conduct in office, narrowly eked out a victory over a challenger he was expected to trounce.

Many victories in 1988 depended on more than political skills, personality, and partisan appeal. The powers of incumbency—free mailing, press attention and fund-raising advantages—played a significant role in the election.

If the advantage of incumbency helped to explain why Republicans were having trouble reducing the Democratic advantages in the House, it did little to explain why they made no headway in the battle for open seats. In all, only 3 of the 27 open seats changed partisan hands, with the Democrats winning 2 formerly GOP seats and the Republicans winning 1 seat held by the Democrats.

The 1988 results were unlikely to encourage challengers mulling the 1990 election. The 98 percent reelection rate from 1986 may well have played a role in discouraging competition in 1988, one of the quietest election years in recent memory.

There were 12 gubernatorial races on November 8. Of the 9 governors seeking reelection, 8 won, all by stressing their managerial skill. The only incumbent to fail, West Virginia Republican Arch A. Moore, Jr., was ousted because voters had lost confidence in his ability to steer the state's struggling economy toward better times. Democrat Gaston Caperton defeated Moore.

Two other GOP governors were as embattled as Moore—Edward DiPrete in Rhode Island and Norman H. Bangerter in Utah—but both eked out victories over stiff Democratic competition.

Those narrow GOP victories deflated the Democrats' high expectations of gubernatorial gains in 1988. Democrats were defending only 4 seats, compared with the GOP's 8. In addition, the 3 Democratic incumbents seeking reelection seemed solid, while Republicans looked to be struggling in at least four states. But on November 8 the Democrats scored a net gain of just 1 governorship, bringing to 28 their number of chief executives. The GOP held 22 governorships.

While Democrats may have been disappointed in the results of the gubernatorial elections, Republican hopes for taking eventual control of Congress suffered a little-noticed but substantial setback when voters across the nation cast ballots for state legislative seats. In those seats will sit, by the early 1990s, the men and women who will redefine the fifty states' congressional districts. Most of them, it would appear, will be Democrats.

1986 Elections:
Governor, Senate, and House

This list gives the final, official 1986 vote returns for the Senate, House, and governorships compiled by Congressional Quarterly from figures supplied by each state's election agency. The box shows party designation symbols.

Because of rounding and because scattered write-in votes are not listed, percentages do not always add to 100. An asterisk (*) indicates incumbents. An X denotes candidates without major-party opposition; no votes were cast.

		Vote total	Per-cent
ALABAMA			
Governor			
	Guy Hunt (R)	696,203	56.4
	Bill Baxley (D)	537,163	43.5
Senate			
	Richard C. Shelby (D)	609,360	50.3
	Jeremiah Denton (R)*	602,537	49.7
House			
1	Sonny Callahan (R)*	96,469	100.0
	(No Democratic candidate)		
2	William L. Dickinson (R)*	115,302	66.7
	Mercer Stone (D)	57,568	33.3
3	Bill Nichols (D)*	115,127	80.6
	Whit Guerin (R)	27,769	19.4
4	Tom Bevill (D)*	132,881	77.5
	Al DeShazo (R)	38,588	22.5
5	Ronnie G. Flippo (D)*	125,406	78.9
	Herb McCarley (R)	33,528	21.1
6	Ben Erdreich (D)*	139,608	72.7
	L. Morgan Williams (R)	51,924	27.1
	Martin J. Boyers	444	0.2
7	Claude Harris (D)	108,126	59.8
	Bill McFarland (R)	72,777	40.2
ALASKA			
Governor			
	Steve Cowper (D)	84,943	47.3
	Arliss Sturgulewski (R)	76,515	42.6
	Joe Vogler (AMI)	10,013	5.6
	Walter J. Hickel (write-in)	4,958	2.8
	Mary O'Brannon (LIBERT)	1,050	0.6
Senate			
	Frank H. Murkowski (R)*	97,674	54.0
	Glenn Olds (D)	79,727	44.1
	Chuck House (LIBERT)	3,161	1.7
House			
AL	Don Young (R)*	101,799	56.5
	Pegge Begich (D)	74,053	41.1
	Betty "Belle Blue" Breck (LIBERT)	4,182	2.3
ARIZONA			
Governor			
	Evan Mecham (R) [a]	343,913	39.7

		Vote total	Per-cent
	Carolyn Warner (D)	298,986	34.5
	Bill Schulz (I)	224,085	25.8
Senate			
	John McCain (R)	521,850	60.5
	Richard Kimball (D)	340,965	39.5
House			
1	John J. Rhodes III (R)	127,370	71.3
	Harry Braun III (D)	51,163	28.7
2	Morris K. Udall (D)*	77,239	73.3
	Sheldon Clark (R)	24,522	23.3
	Lorrenzo Torrez (I)	3,646	3.4
3	Bob Stump (R)*	146,462	100.0
	(No Democratic candidate)		
4	Jon Kyl (R)	121,939	43.6
	Philip R. Davis (D)	66,894	35.4
5	Jim Kolbe (R)*	119,647	64.9
	Joel Ireland (D)	64,848	35.1
ARKANSAS			
Governor			
	Bill Clinton (D)*	439,851	63.9
	Frank White (R)	248,415	36.1
Senate			
	Dale Bumpers (D)*	433,092	62.3
	Asa Hutchinson (R)	262,300	37.7

ABBREVIATIONS FOR PARTY DESIGNATIONS

AM	American		L	Liberal
AMI	American Independent		LAB F	Labor-Farm
			LIBERT	Libertarian
C	Conservative		NA	New Alliance
CIT	Citizens		PFP	Peace and Freedom
CON	Consumer			
D	Democratic		POP	Populist
DFL	Democratic Farmer-Labor		PRG SC	Progressive Social
			PROH	Prohibition
I	Independent		R	Republican
IL SOL	Illinois Solidarity		RTL	Right to Life
			SOC WORK	Socialist Workers
I-R	Independent-Republican		WL	Workers League

		Vote total	Per- cent				Vote total	Per- cent
					Bill White (LIBERT)	6,227	3.3
				13	Norman Y. Mineta (D)*	107,696	69.7

ARKANSAS
House

1	Bill Alexander (D)*	105,773	64.2
	Rick H. Albin (R)	58,937	35.8
2	Tommy F. Robinson (D)*	128,814	75.7
	Keith Hamaker (R)	41,244	24.2
3	John Hammerschmidt (R)*	145,113	79.8
	Su Sargent (D)	36,726	20.2
4	Beryl Anthony Jr. (D)*	115,335	77.5
	Lamar Keels (R)	22,980	15.4
	Stephen A. Bitely (I)	10,604	7.1

CALIFORNIA
Governor

	George Deukmejian (R)*	4,506,601	60.5
	Tom Bradley (D)	2,781,714	37.4
	Joseph Fuhrig (LIBERT)	52,628	0.7
	Maria E. Munoz (PFP)	51,995	0.7
	Gary V. Miller (AMI)	50,547	0.7

Senate

	Alan Cranston (D)*	3,646,672	49.3
	Ed Zschau (R)	3,541,804	47.9
	Edward B. Vallen (AMI)	109,856	1.5
	Breck McKinley (LIBERT)	66,261	0.9
	Paul Kangas (PFP)	33,869	0.4

House

1	Douglas H. Bosco (D)*	138,174	67.5
	Floyd G. Sampson (R)	54,436	26.6
	Elden McFarland (PFP)	12,149	5.9
2	Wally Herger (R)	109,758	58.3
	Stephen C. Swendiman (D)	74,602	39.6
	Harry Hugh Pendery (LIBERT)	4,054	2.1
3	Robert T. Matsui (D)*	158,709	75.9
	Lowell Landowski (R)	50,265	24.1
4	Vic Fazio (D)*	128,364	70.2
	Jack D. Hite (R)	54,596	29.8
5	Sala Burton (D)* b	122,688	75.1
	Mike Garza (R)	36,039	22.1
	Samuel K. Grove (LIBERT)	2,409	1.5
	Theodore Zuur (PFP)	2,078	1.3
6	Barbara Boxer (D)*	142,946	73.9
	Franklin H. Ernst III (R)	50,606	26.1
7	George Miller (D)*	124,174	66.6
	Rosemary Thakar (R)	62,379	33.4
8	Ronald V. Dellums (D)*	121,790	60.0
	Steven Eigenberg (R)	76,850	37.9
	Lawrence R. Manuel (PFP)	4,295	2.1
9	Fortney H. Stark (D)*	113,490	69.7
	David M. Williams (R)	49,300	30.3
10	Don Edwards (D)*	84,240	70.5
	Michael R. La Crone (R)	31,826	26.6
	Perr Cardestam (LIBERT)	1,797	1.5
	Bradley L. Mayer (PFP)	1,701	1.4
11	Tom Lantos (D)*	112,380	74.1
	G. M. "Bill" Quraishi (R)	39,315	25.9
12	Ernest L. Konnyu (R)	111,252	59.5
	Lance T. Weil (D)	69,564	37.2

	Bill White (LIBERT)	6,227	3.3
13	Norman Y. Mineta (D)*	107,696	69.7
	Bob Nash (R)	46,754	30.3
14	Norman D. Shumway (R)*	146,906	71.6
	Bill Steele (D)	53,597	26.1
	Bruce A. Daniel (LIBERT)	4,658	2.3
15	Tony Coelho (D)*	93,600	71.0
	Carol Harner (R)	35,793	27.2
	Richard M. Harris (LIBERT)	2,382	1.8
16	Leon E. Panetta (D)*	128,151	78.4
	Louis Darrigo (R)	31,386	19.2
	Ron Wright (PFP)	2,017	1.2
	Bill Anderson (LIBERT)	1,944	1.2
17	Charles Pashayan Jr. (R)*	88,787	60.2
	John Hartnett (D)	58,682	39.8
18	Richard H. Lehman (D)*	101,480	71.3
	David C. Crevelt (R)	40,907	28.7
19	Robert J. Lagomarsino (R)*	122,578	71.9
	Wayne B. Norris (D)	45,619	26.7
	George Hasara (LIBERT)	2,341	1.4
20	William M. Thomas (R)*	129,989	72.6
	Jules H. Moquin (D)	49,027	27.4
21	Elton Gallegly (R)	132,090	68.4
	Gilbert R. Saldana (D)	54,497	28.2
	Daniel Wiener (LIBERT)	6,504	3.4
22	Carlos J. Moorhead (R)*	141,096	73.8
	John G. Simmons (D)	44,036	23.1
	Jona Joy Bergland (LIBERT)	3,114	1.6
	Joel Lorimer (PFP)	2,930	1.5
23	Anthony C. Beilenson (D)*	121,468	65.7
	George Woolverton (R)	58,746	31.8
	Tom Hopke (PFP)	2,521	1.4
	Taylor Rhodes (LIBERT)	2,019	1.1
24	Henry A. Waxman (D)*	103,914	87.9
	(No Republican candidate)		
	George Abrahams (LIBERT)	8,871	7.5
	James Green (PFP)	5,388	4.6
25	Edward R. Roybal (D)*	62,692	76.1
	Gregory L. Hardy (R)	17,558	21.3
	Ted Brown (LIBERT)	2,163	2.6
26	Howard L. Berman (D)*	98,091	65.1
	Robert M. Kerns (R)	52,662	34.9
27	Mel Levine (D)*	110,403	63.7
	Rob Scribner (R)	59,410	34.3
	Thomas L. O'Connor Jr. (PFP)	2,078	1.2
	Larry Leathers (LIBERT)	1,429	0.8
28	Julian C. Dixon (D)*	92,635	76.4
	George Adams (R)	25,858	21.3
	Howard Johnson (LIBERT)	2,837	2.3
29	Augustus F. Hawkins (D)*	78,132	84.6
	John Van de Brooke (R)	13,432	14.5
	Waheed Boctor (LIBERT)	851	0.9
30	Matthew G. Martinez (D)*	59,369	62.5
	John W. Almquist (R)	33,705	35.5
	Kim J. Goldsworthy (LIBERT)	1,911	2.0

		Vote total	Per- cent

CALIFORNIA

31	Mervyn M. Dymally (D)*	77,126	70.3
	Jack McMurray (R)	30,322	27.6
	B. Kwaku Duren (PFP)	2,333	2.1
32	Glenn M. Anderson (D)*	90,739	68.5
	Joyce M. Robertson (R)	39,003	29.4
	John S. Donohue (PFP)	2,799	2.1
33	David Dreier (R)*	118,541	71.7
	Monty Hempel (D)	44,312	26.8
	Mike Noonan (PFP)	2,500	1.5
34	Esteban Edward Torres (D)*	66,404	60.3
	Charles M. House (R)	43,659	39.7
35	Jerry Lewis (R)*	127,235	76.9
	R. "Sarge" Hall (D)	38,322	23.1
36	George E. Brown Jr. (D)*	78,118	57.1
	Bob Henley (R)	58,660	42.9
37	Al McCandless (R)*	122,416	63.7
	David E. Skinner (D)	69,808	36.3
38	Bob Dornan (R)*	66,032	55.3
	Richard Robinson (D)	50,625	42.4
	Lee Connelly (LIBERT)	2,807	2.3
39	William E. Dannemeyer (R)*	137,603	74.5
	David D. Vest (D)	42,377	24.0
	Frank Boeheim (PFP)	2,752	1.5
40	Robert E. Badham (R)*	119,829	59.8
	Bruce W. Sumner (D)	75,664	37.7
	Steve Sears (PFP)	5,025	2.5
41	Bill Lowery (R)*	133,566	67.8
	Dan Kripke (D)	59,816	30.4
	Dick Rider (LIBERT)	3,541	1.8
42	Dan Lungren (R)*	140,364	72.8
	Michael P. Blackburn (D)	47,586	24.7
	Kate McClatchy (PFP)	4,761	2.5
43	Ron Packard (R)*	137,341	73.1
	Joseph Chirra (D)	45,078	24.0
	Phyllis Avery (LIBERT)	5,370	2.9
44	Jim Bates (D)*	70,557	64.3
	Bill Mitchell (R)	36,359	33.1
	Shirley Isaacson (PFP)	1,676	1.5
	Dennis Thompson (LIBERT)	1,244	1.1
45	Duncan Hunter (R)*	118,900	76.9
	Hewitt Fitts Ryan (D)	32,800	21.2
	Lee Schwartz (LIBERT)	2,975	1.9

COLORADO

Governor

Roy Romer (D)	616,325	58.2
Ted Strickland (R)	434,420	41.0
Earl F. Dodge (PROH)	8,183	0.8

Senate

Timothy E. Wirth (D)	529,449	49.9
Ken Kramer (R)	512,994	48.4
Michael Martin Bush (I)	11,127	1.0
Michael R. Chamberlain (SOC WORK)	3,756	0.4
Henry John Olshaw (I)	1,868	0.2
Calvin G. Dodge (PROH)	1,571	0.1

House

1	Patricia Schroeder (D)*	106,113	68.4
	Joy Wood (R)	49,095	31.6
2	David Skaggs (D)	91,223	51.5
	Michael J. Norton (R)	86,032	48.5
3	Ben Nighthorse Campbell (D)	95,353	51.9
	Mike Strang (R)*	88,508	48.1
4	Hank Brown (R)*	117,089	69.8
	David Sprague (D)	50,672	30.2
5	Joel Hefley (R)	121,153	69.8
	Bill Story (D)	52,488	30.2
6	Dan Schaefer (R)*	104,359	65.0
	Chuck Norris (D)	53,834	33.5
	John Heckman (I)	2,338	1.5

CONNECTICUT

Governor

William A. O'Neill (D)*	575,638	57.9
Julie D. Belaga (R)	408,489	41.1
Frank Longo (I)	9,565	1.0

Senate

Christopher J. Dodd (D)*	632,695	64.8
Roger W. Eddy (R)	340,438	34.8
Edward J. McCallum Jr. (I)	3,800	0.4

House

1	Barbara B. Kennelly (D)*	128,930	74.2
	Herschel A. Klein (R)	44,122	25.4
	Sally F. Cadmus (I)	735	0.4
2	Sam Gejdenson (D)*	109,229	67.4
	Francis M. "Bud" Mullen (R)	52,869	32.6
3	Bruce A. Morrison (D)*	114,276	69.6
	Ernest J. Diette Jr. (R)	49,806	30.4
4	Stewart B. McKinney (R)* c	77,212	53.5
	Christine M. Niedermeier (D)	66,999	46.5
5	John G. Rowland (R)*	98,664	60.9
	Jim Cohen (D)	63,371	39.1
6	Nancy L. Johnson (R)*	111,304	64.2
	Paul S. Amenta (D)	62,133	35.8

DELAWARE

House

AL	Thomas R. Carper (D)*	106,351	66.2
	Thomas Stephen Neuberger (R)	53,767	33.4
	Patrick F. Harrison (AM)	639	0.4

FLORIDA

Governor

Bob Martinez (R)	1,847,525	54.6
Steve Pajcic (D)	1,538,620	45.4

Senate

Bob Graham (D)	1,877,231	54.7
Paula Hawkins (R)*	1,551,888	45.3

		Vote total	Per- cent				Vote total	Per- cent

FLORIDA
House

1	Earl Hutto (D)*	97,465	63.8
	Greg Neubeck (R)	55,415	36.2
2	Bill Grant (D)	110,120	99.4
	(No Republican candidate)		
	Kim O'Connor (write-in)	625	0.6
3	Charles E. Bennett (D)*	x	x
	(No Republican candidate)		
4	Bill Chappell Jr. (D)*	x	x
	(No Republican candidate)		
5	Bill McCollum (R)*	x	x
	(No Democratic candidate)		
6	Buddy MacKay (D)*	143,583	70.2
	Larry Gallagher (R)	61,053	29.8
7	Sam Gibbons (D)*	x	x
	(No Republican candidate)		
8	C. W. Bill Young (R)*	x	x
	(No Democratic candidate)		
9	Michael Bilirakis (R)*	166,504	70.8
	Gabe Cazares (D)	68,574	29.2
10	Andy Ireland (R)*	122,368	71.2
	David B. Higginbottom (D)	49,559	28.8
11	Bill Nelson (D)*	149,036	72.7
	Scott Ellis (R)	55,904	27.3
12	Tom Lewis (R)*	150,222	99.4
	(No Democratic candidate)		
	Phil Jackson (write-in)	440	0.3
	Daniel S. Ray (write-in)	258	0.2
	George R. Spanton (write-in)	238	0.1
13	Connie Mack (R)*	187,794	75.0
	Addison S. Gilbert III (D)	62,694	25.0
14	Daniel A. Mica (D)*	171,961	73.8
	Rick Martin (R)	61,185	26.2
15	E. Clay Shaw Jr. (R)*	x	x
	(No Democratic candidate)		
16	Lawrence J. Smith (D)*	121,213	69.7
	Mary Collins (R)	52,807	30.3
17	William Lehman (D)*	x	x
	(No Republican candidate)		
18	Claude Pepper (D)*	80,047	73.5
	Tom Brodie (R)	28,803	26.5
19	Dante B. Fascell (D)*	99,203	69.1
	Bill Flanagan (R)	44,455	30.9

GEORGIA

Governor

	Joe Frank Harris (D)*	828,465	70.5
	Guy Hunt (R)	346,512	29.5

Senate

	Wyche Fowler Jr. (D)	623,707	50.9
	Mack Mattingly (R)*	601,241	49.1

House

1	Robert Lindsay Thomas (D)*	69,440	100.0
	(No Republican candidate)		

2	Charles Hatcher (D)*	72,482	100.0
	(No Republican candidate)		
3	Richard Ray (D)*	75,850	99.7
	(No Republican candidate)		
4	Pat Swindall (R)*	86,366	53.2
	Ben Jones (D)	75,892	46.8
5	John Lewis (D)	93,229	75.3
	Portia A. Scott (R)	30,562	24.7
6	Newt Gingrich (R)*	75,583	59.5
	Crandle Bray (D)	51,352	40.5
7	George "Buddy" Darden (D)*	88,636	66.4
	Joe Morecraft (R)	44,891	33.6
8	J. Roy Rowland (D)*	82,254	86.4
	Eddie McDowell (R)	12,952	13.6
9	Ed Jenkins (D)*	84,303	100.0
	(No Republican candidate)		
10	Doug Barnard Jr. (D)*	79,548	67.3
	Jim Hill (R)	38,714	32.7

HAWAII
Governor

	John Waihee (D)	173,655	52.0
	D. G. "Andy" Anderson (R)	160,460	48.0

Senate

	Daniel K. Inouye (D)*	241,887	73.6
	Frank Hutchinson (R)	86,910	26.4

House

1	Patricia Saiki (R)	99,683	59.2
	Mufi Hannemann (D)	63,061	37.5
	Blase Harris (LIBERT)	5,633	3.3
2	Daniel K. Akaka (D)*	123,830	76.1
	Maria M. Hustace (R)	35,371	21.7
	Ken Schoolland (LIBERT)	3,618	2.2

IDAHO
Governor

	Cecil D. Andrus (D)	193,429	49.9
	David H. Leroy (R)	189,794	49.0
	James A. Miller (I)	4,203	1.1

Senate

	Steve Symms (R)*	196,958	51.6
	John V. Evans (D)	185,066	48.4

House

1	Larry E. Craig (R)*	120,553	65.1
	Bill Currie (D)	59,723	32.3
	David W. Shepherd (I)	4,848	2.6
2	Richard H. Stallings (D)*	103,035	54.4
	Mel Richardson (R)	86,528	45.6

ILLINOIS
Governor

	James R. Thompson (R)*	1,655,945	52.7
	Adlai E. Stevenson (IL SOL)	1,256,725	40.0
	Democratic ticket — no candidate for governor	208,841	6.6
	Gary L. Shilts (LIBERT)	15,647	0.5
	Diane Roling (SOC WORK)	6,843	0.2

		Vote total	Per- cent

ILLINOIS

Senate

		Vote total	Per- cent
	Alan J. Dixon (D)*	2,033,926	65.1
	Judy Koehler (R)	1,053,793	33.7
	Einar V. Dyhrkopp (IL SOL)	15,805	0.5
	Donald M. Parrish Jr. (LIBERT)	13,892	0.5
	Omari Musa (SOC WORK)	5,671	0.2

House

1	Charles A. Hayes (D)*	122,376	96.4
	Joseph C. Faulkner (R)	4,572	3.6
2	Gus Savage (D)*	99,268	83.8
	Ron Taylor (R)	19,149	16.2
3	Marty Russo (D)*	102,949	66.2
	James J. Tierney (R)	52,618	33.8
4	Jack Davis (R)	61,633	51.6
	Shawn Collins (D)	57,925	48.4
5	William O. Lipinski (D)*	82,466	70.4
	Daniel John Sobieski (R)	34,738	29.6
6	Henry J. Hyde (R)*	98,196	75.4
	Robert H. Renshaw (D)	32,064	24.6
7	Cardiss Collins (D)*	90,761	80.2
	Caroline K. Kallas (R)	21,055	18.6
	Jerald Wilson (I)	1,348	1.2
8	Dan Rostenkowski (D)*	82,873	78.7
	Thomas J. DeFazio (R)	22,383	21.3
9	Sidney R. Yates (D)*	92,738	71.6
	Herbert Sohn (R)	36,715	28.4
10	John Edward Porter (R)*	87,530	75.1
	Robert A. Cleland (D)	28,990	24.9
11	Frank Annunzio (D)*	106,970	70.7
	George S. Gottlieb (R)	44,341	29.3
12	Philip M. Crane (R)*	89,044	77.7
	John A. Leonardi (D)	25,536	22.3
13	Harris W. Fawell (R)*	107,227	73.4
	Dominick J. Jeffrey (D)	38,874	26.6
14	J. Dennis Hastert (R)	77,288	52.4
	Mary Lou Kearns (D)	70,293	47.6
15	Edward R. Madigan (R)*	115,284	100.0
	(No Democratic candidate)		
16	Lynn Martin (R)*	92,982	66.9
	Kenneth F. Bohnsack (D)	46,087	33.1
17	Lane Evans (D)*	85,442	55.6
	Sam McHard (R)	68,101	44.4
18	Robert H. Michel (R)*	94,308	62.6
	Jim Dawson (D)	56,331	37.4
19	Terry L. Bruce (D)*	111,105	66.4
	Al Salvi (R)	56,186	33.6
20	Richard J. Durbin (D)*	126,556	68.1
	Kevin B. McCarthy (R)	59,291	31.9
21	Melvin Price (D)* d	65,722	50.4
	Robert H. Gaffner (R)	64,779	49.6
22	Kenneth J. Gray (D)*	97,585	53.2
	Randy Patchett (R)	85,733	46.8

INDIANA

Senate

		Vote total	Per- cent
	Dan Quayle (R)* e	936,143	60.6

		Vote total	Per- cent
	Jill Lynette Long (D)	595,192	38.5
	Bradford L. Warren (LIBERT)	8,314	0.5
	Rockland R. Snyder (AM)	5,914	0.4

House

1	Peter J. Visclosky (D)*	86,983	73.4
	William Costas (R)	30,395	25.7
	James E. Willis (LIBERT)	660	0.6
	Tracy E. Kyle (WL)	403	0.3
2	Philip R. Sharp (D)*	102,456	61.9
	Donald J. Lynch (R)	62,013	37.4
	Richard Smith (LIBERT)	1,156	0.7
3	John Hiler (R)*	75,979	49.8
	Thomas W. Ward (D)	75,932	49.8
	Kenneth K. Donnelly (LIBERT)	596	0.4
4	Dan Coats (R)*	99,865	69.6
	Gregory Alan Scher (D)	43,105	30.0
	Stephen L. Dasbach (LIBERT)	602	0.4
5	Jim Jontz (D)	80,772	51.4
	James R. Butcher (R)	75,507	48.1
	Brent Waibel (LIBERT)	727	0.5
6	Dan Burton (R)*	118,363	68.3
	Thomas F. McKenna (D)	53,431	30.9
	Pamela Webe (LIBERT)	1,371	0.8
7	John T. Myers (R)*	104,965	66.8
	L. Eugene Smith (D)	49,675	31.6
	Barbara J. Bourland (LIBERT)	2,523	1.6
8	Frank McCloskey (D)*	106,662	53.0
	Richard D. McIntyre (R)	93,586	46.5
	Marilyn Stone (LIBERT)	909	0.5
9	Lee H. Hamilton (D)*	120,586	71.9
	Robert Walter Kilroy (R)	46,398	27.7
	Douglas Boggs (LIBERT)	719	0.4
10	Andrew Jacobs Jr. (D)*	68,817	57.7
	Jim Eynon (R)	49,064	41.2
	Frederick Peterson (LIBERT)	1,285	1.1

IOWA

Governor

		Vote total	Per- cent
	Terry E. Branstad (R)*	472,712	51.9
	Lowell L. Junkins (D)	436,987	48.0

Senate

		Vote total	Per- cent
	Charles E. Grassley (R)*	588,880	66.0
	John P. Roehrick (D)	299,406	33.6
	John Masters (I)	3,370	0.4

House

1	Jim Leach (R)*	86,834	66.4
	John R. Whitaker (D)	43,985	33.6
2	Tom Tauke (R)*	88,708	61.3
	Eric Tabor (D)	55,903	38.7
3	David R. Nagle (D)	83,504	54.6
	John McIntee (R)	69,386	45.4

		Vote total	Per- cent

IOWA

		Vote total	Per- cent
4	Neal Smith (D)*	107,271	68.4
	Bob Lockard (R)	49,641	31.6
5	Jim Lightfoot (R)*	85,025	59.2
	Scott Hughes (D)	58,552	40.8
6	Fred Grandy (R)	81,861	50.9
	Clayton Hodgson (D)	78,807	49.0

KANSAS

Governor

	Mike Hayden (R)	436,267	51.9
	Tom Docking (D)	404,338	48.1

Senate

	Robert Dole (R)*	576,902	70.0
	Guy MacDonald (D)	246,664	30.0

House

1	Pat Roberts (R)*	141,297	76.5
	Dale Lyon (D)	43,359	23.5
2	Jim Slattery (D)*	110,737	70.6
	Phill Kline (R)	46,029	29.4
3	Jan Meyers (R)*	109,266	100.0
	(No Democratic candidate)		
4	Dan Glickman (D)*	111,164	64.5
	Bob Knight (R)	61,178	35.5
5	Bob Whittaker (R)*	116,800	71.1
	Kym E. Myers (D)	47,540	28.9

KENTUCKY

Senate

	Wendell H. Ford (D)*	503,775	74.4
	Jackson M. Andrews (R)	173,330	25.6

House

1	Carroll Hubbard Jr. (D)*	64,315	100.0
	(No Republican candidate)		
2	William H. Natcher (D)*	57,644	100.0
	(No Republican candidate)		
3	Romano L. Mazzoli (D)*	81,943	73.0
	Lee Holmes (R)	29,348	26.2
	Estelle DeBates (SOC WORK)	899	0.8
4	Jim Bunning (R)	67,626	55.1
	Terry L. Mann (D)	53,906	43.9
	Walter T. Marksberry (I)	735	0.6
	W. Ed Parker (AM)	485	0.4
5	Harold Rogers (R)*	56,760	100.0
	(No Democratic candidate)		
6	Larry J. Hopkins (R)*	75,906	74.3
	Jerry W. Hammond (D)	26,315	25.7
7	Carl C. Perkins (D)*	90,619	79.6
	James T. Polley (R)	23,209	20.4

LOUISIANA

Senate

	John B. Breaux (D)	723,586	52.8
	W. Henson Moore (R)	646,311	47.2

House

1	Bob Livingston (R)*	x	x

		Vote total	Per- cent
2	Lindy (Mrs. Hale) Boggs (D)*	x	x
3	W. J. "Billy" Tauzin (D)*	x	x
4	Buddy Roemer (D)* f	x	x
5	Jerry Huckaby (D)*	x	x
6	Richard Baker (R)	x	x
7	Jimmy Hayes (D)	109,205	57.0
	Margaret Lowenthal (D)	82,293	43.0
8	Clyde C. Holloway (R)	102,276	51.4
	Faye Williams (D)	96,864	48.6

MAINE

Governor

	John R. McKernan Jr. (R)	170,312	39.9
	James Tierney (D)	128,744	30.1
	Sherry E. Huber (I)	64,317	15.1
	John E. Menario (I)	63,474	14.9

House

1	Joseph E. Brennan (D)	121,848	53.2
	H. Rollin Ives (R)	100,260	43.7
	Plato Truman (I)	7,109	3.1
2	Olympia J. Snowe (R)*	148,770	77.3
	Richard R. Charette (D)	43,614	22.7

MARYLAND

Governor

	William Donald Schaefer (D)	907,301	82.4
	Thomas J. Mooney (R)	194,187	17.6

Senate

	Barbara A. Mikulski (D)	675,229	60.7
	Linda Chavez (R)	437,419	39.3

House

1	Roy Dyson (D)*	88,113	66.8
	Harlan C. Williams (R)	43,764	33.2
2	Helen Delich Bentley (R)*	96,745	58.7
	Kathleen Kennedy Townsend (D)	68,200	41.3
3	Benjamin L. Cardin (D)	100,161	79.1
	Ross Z. Pierpont (R)	26,452	20.9
4	Tom McMillen (D)	65,075	50.2
	Robert R. Neall (R)	64,651	49.8
5	Steny H. Hoyer (D)*	82,098	81.9
	John Eugene Sellner (R)	18,102	18.1
6	Beverly B. Byron (D)*	102,975	72.2
	John Vandenberge (R)	39,600	27.8
7	Kweisi Mfume (D)	79,226	86.7
	Saint George I. B. Crosse III (R)	12,170	13.3
8	Constance A. Morella (R)	92,917	52.9
	Stewart Bainum Jr. (D)	82,825	47.1

MASSACHUSETTS

Governor

	Michael S. Dukakis (D)*	1,157,786	68.7
	George Kariotis (R)	525,364	31.2

		Vote total	Per-cent			Vote total	Per-cent

MASSACHUSETTS
House

		Vote total	Per-cent
1	Silvio O. Conte (R)*	113,653	77.8
	Robert S. Weiner (D)	32,396	22.2
2	Edward P. Boland (D)*	91,033	65.9
	Brian P. Lees (R)	47,022	34.1
3	Joseph D. Early (D)*	120,222	100.0
	(No Republican candidate)		
4	Barney Frank (D)*	134,387	88.8
	(No Republican candidate)		
	Thomas D. DeVisscher (AM)	16,857	11.2
5	Chester G. Atkins (D)*	113,690	99.9
	(No Republican candidate)		
6	Nicholas Mavroules (D)*	131,051	99.9
	(No Republican candidate)		
7	Edward J. Markey (D)*	124,183	100.0
	(No Republican candidate)		
8	Joseph P. Kennedy II (D)	104,651	72.0
	Clark C. Abt (R)	40,259	27.7
9	Joe Moakley (D)*	110,026	83.8
	(No Republican candidate)		
	Robert W. Horan (I)	21,292	16.2
10	Gerry E. Studds (D)*	121,578	65.1
	Ricardo M. Barros (R)	49,451	26.5
	Alexander Byron (I)	15,687	8.4
11	Brian J. Donnelly (D)*	114,926	100.0
	(No Republican candidate)		

MICHIGAN
Governor

		Vote total	Per-cent
	James J. Blanchard (D)*	1,632,138	68.1
	William Lucas (R)	753,647	31.4
	Martin McLaughlin (WL)	9,477	0.4

House

		Vote total	Per-cent
1	John Conyers Jr. (D)*	94,307	89.2
	Bill Ashe (R)	10,407	9.8
	Peter Banta Bowen (I)	539	0.5
	Andrew Pulley (I)	529	0.5
2	Carl D. Pursell (R)*	79,567	59.0
	Dean Baker (D)	55,204	41.0
3	Howard Wolpe (D)*	78,720	60.4
	Jackie McGregor (R)	51,678	39.6
4	Fred Upton (R)	70,331	61.9
	Dan Roche (D)	41,624	36.6
	Richard H. Gillmor (I)	1,649	1.5
5	Paul B. Henry (R)*	100,577	71.2
	Teresa S. Decker (D)	40,608	28.8
6	Bob Carr (D)*	74,927	56.7
	Jim Dunn (R)	57,283	43.3
7	Dale E. Kildee (D)*	101,225	79.6
	Trudie Callihan (R)	24,848	19.5
	Gene Schenk (I)	1,099	0.9
8	Bob Traxler (D)*	97,406	72.6
	John A. Levi (R)	36,695	27.4
9	Guy Vander Jagt (R)*	89,991	64.4
	Richard J. Anderson (D)	49,702	35.6
10	Bill Schuette (R)*	78,475	51.2
	Donald J. Albosta (D)	74,941	48.8

		Vote total	Per-cent
11	Robert W. Davis (R)*	91,575	63.0
	Robert C. Anderson (D)	53,180	36.6
	Phil Bellfy (I)	648	0.4
12	David E. Bonior (D)*	87,643	66.4
	Candice S. Miller (R)	44,442	33.6
13	George W. Crockett Jr. (D)*	76,435	85.2
	Mary Griffin (R)	12,395	13.8
	Barbara L. Putnam (I)	597	0.7
	Lucy Bell Randolph (I)	318	0.3
14	Dennis M. Hertel (D)*	92,328	72.9
	Stanley T. Grot (R)	33,831	26.7
	William Osipoff (I)	506	0.4
15	William D. Ford (D)*	77,950	75.2
	Glen Kassel (R)	25,078	24.2
	James H. Stamps (I)	584	0.6
16	John D. Dingell (D)*	101,659	77.8
	Frank W. Grzywacki (R)	28,971	22.2
17	Sander M. Levin (D)*	105,031	76.4
	Calvin Williams (R)	30,879	22.5
	Charles E. Martell (I)	1,477	1.1
18	William S. Broomfield (R)*	110,099	73.8
	Gary L. Kohut (D)	39,144	26.2

MINNESOTA
Governor

		Vote total	Per-cent
	Rudy Perpich (DFL)*	790,138	55.8
	Cal R. Ludeman (I-R)	606,755	42.9
	W. Z. "Bill" Brust (WL)	4,208	0.3
	Joseph A. Rohner III (LIBERT)	3,852	0.3
	Tom Jaax (SOC WORK)	3,151	0.2

House

		Vote total	Per-cent
1	Timothy J. Penny (DFL)*	125,115	72.4
	Paul H. Grawe (I-R)	47,750	27.6
2	Vin Weber (I-R)*	100,249	51.6
	Dave Johnson (DFL)	94,048	48.4
3	Bill Frenzel (I-R)*	127,434	70.1
	Ray Stock (DFL)	54,261	29.9
4	Bruce F. Vento (DFL)*	112,662	72.9
	Harold Stassen (I-R)	41,926	27.1
5	Martin Olav Sabo (DFL)*	105,410	72.7
	Rick Serra (I-R)	37,583	25.9
	Clifford Mark Greene (I)	2,004	1.4
6	Gerry Sikorski (DFL)*	110,598	65.8
	Barbara Zwach Sykora (I-R)	57,460	34.2
7	Arlan Stangeland (I-R)*	94,024	49.7
	Collin C. Peterson (DFL)	93,903	49.6
	Jon Hall (CIT)	1,326	0.7
8	James L. Oberstar (DFL)*	135,718	72.6
	Dave Rued (I-R)	51,315	27.4

MISSISSIPPI
House

		Vote total	Per-cent
1	Jamie L. Whitten (D)*	59,870	66.4
	Larry Cobb (R)	30,267	33.6
2	Mike Espy (D)	73,119	51.7
	Webb Franklin (R)*	68,292	48.3

		Vote total	Per- cent

MISSISSIPPI

		Vote total	Percent
3	G. V. "Sonny" Montgomery (D)* (No Republican candidate)	80,575	100.0
4	Wayne Dowdy (D)*	85,819	71.5
	Gail Healy (R)	34,190	28.5
5	Trent Lott (R)*	75,288	82.3
	Larry L. Albritton (D)	16,143	17.7

MISSOURI

Senate

	Christopher S. "Kit" Bond (R)	777,612	52.6
	Harriett Woods (D)	699,624	47.4

House

1	William L. Clay (D)*	91,044	66.1
	Robert J. Wittmann (R)	46,599	33.9
2	Jack Buechner (R)	101,010	51.9
	Robert A. Young (D)*	93,538	48.1
3	Richard A. Gephardt (D)*	116,403	69.0
4	Ike Skelton (D)*	129,471	100.0
	(No Republican candidate)		
5	Alan Wheat (D)*	101,030	70.9
	Greg Fisher (R)	39,340	27.6
	Jay Manifold (LIBERT)	2,204	1.5
6	E. Thomas Coleman (R)*	95,865	56.7
	Doug R. Hughes (D)	73,155	43.3
7	Gene Taylor (R)*	114,210	67.0
	Ken Young (D)	56,291	33.0
8	Bill Emerson (R)*	79,142	52.5
	Wayne Cryts (D)	71,532	47.5
9	Harold L. Volkmer (D)*	95,939	57.5
	Ralph Uthlaut Jr. (R)	70,972	42.5

MONTANA

House

1	Pat Williams (D)*	98,501	61.7
	Don Allen (R)	61,230	38.3
2	Ron Marlenee (R)*	84,548	53.5
	Richard "Buck" O'Brien (D)	73,583	46.5

NEBRASKA

Governor

	Kay A. Orr (R)	298,325	52.9
	Helen Boosalis (D)	265,156	47.0

House

1	Doug Bereuter (R)*	121,772	64.4
	Steve Burns (D)	67,137	35.5
2	Hal Daub (R)*	99,569	58.5
	Walter M. Calinger (D)	70,372	41.3
3	Virginia Smith (R)*	136,985	69.8
	Scott E. Sidwell (D)	59,182	30.2

NEVADA

Governor

	Richard H. Bryan (D)* ᵍ	187,268	71.9

		Vote total	Percent
	Patty Cafferata (R)	65,081	25.0
	"None of these candidates"	5,471	2.1
	Louis R. Tomburello (LIBERT)	2,555	1.0

Senate

	Harry Reid (D)	130,955	50.0
	Jim Santini (R)	116,606	44.5
	"None of these candidates"	9,472	3.6
	Kent Cromwell (LIBERT)	4,899	1.9

House

1	James H. Bilbray (D)	61,830	54.1
	Bob Ryan (R)	50,342	44.0
	Gordon Michael Morris (LIBERT)	2,145	1.9
2	Barbara F. Vucanovich (R)*	83,479	58.4
	Pete Sferrazza (D)	59,433	41.6

NEW HAMPSHIRE

Governor

	John H. Sununu (R)*	134,824	53.7
	Paul McEachern (D)	116,142	46.3

Senate

	Warren B. Rudman (R)*	154,090	62.9
	Endicott Peabody (D)	79,222	32.4
	Bruce Valley (I)	11,423	4.7

House

1	Robert C. Smith (R)*	70,739	56.4
	James M. Demers (D)	54,787	43.6
2	Judd Gregg (R)*	85,479	74.2
	Laurence Craig-Green (D)	29,688	25.8

NEW JERSEY

House

1	James J. Florio (D)*	93,497	75.6
	Fred A. Busch (R)	29,175	23.6
	Jerry Zeldin (LIBERT)	931	0.8
2	William J. Hughes (D)*	83,821	68.3
	Alfred J. Bennington Jr. (R)	35,167	28.6
	Len Smith (I)	3,812	3.1
3	James J. Howard (D) * ʰ	73,743	58.7
	Brian T. Kennedy (R)	51,882	41.3
4	Christopher H. Smith (R)*	78,699	61.1
	Jeffrey Laurenti (D)	49,290	38.3
	Earl G. Dickey (I)	789	0.6
5	Marge Roukema (R)*	94,253	74.6
	H. Vernon Jolley (D)	32,145	25.4
6	Bernard J. Dwyer (D)*	67,460	69.0
	John D. Scalamonti (R)	28,286	28.9
	Rose (Zeidwerg) Monyek (I)	2,023	2.1
7	Matthew J. Rinaldo (R)*	92,254	79.0
	June S. Fischer (D)	24,462	21.0
8	Robert A. Roe (D)*	57,820	62.8
	Thomas P. Zampino (R)	34,268	37.2
9	Robert G. Torricelli (D)*	89,634	69.0
	Arthur F. Jones (R)	40,226	31.0
10	Peter W. Rodino Jr. (D)*	46,666	95.9
	(No Republican candidate)		
	Chris Brandlon (SOC WORK)	1,977	4.1

		Vote total	Per-cent
	NEW JERSEY		
11	Dean A. Gallo (R)*	75,037	68.0
	Frank Askin (D)	35,280	32.0
12	Jim Courter (R)*	72,966	63.5
	David B. Crabiel (D)	41,967	36.5
13	H. James Saxton (R)*	82,866	65.4
	John Wydra (D)	43,920	34.6
14	Frank J. Guarini (D)*	63,057	70.7
	Albio Sires (R)	23,822	26.7
	Herbert H. Shaw (I)	1,825	2.0
	William Link (I)	525	0.6

NEW MEXICO

Governor

		Vote total	Per-cent
	Garrey E. Carruthers (R)	209,455	53.0
	Ray B. Powell (D)	185,378	47.0

House

1	Manuel Lujan Jr. (R)*	90,476	70.9
	Manny Garcia (D)	37,138	29.1
2	Joe Skeen (R)*	77,787	62.9
	Mike Runnels (D)	45,924	37.1
3	Bill Richardson (D)*	95,760	71.3
	David F. Cargo (R)	38,552	28.7

NEW YORK

Governor

		Vote total	Per-cent
	Mario M. Cuomo (D, L)*	2,775,229	64.6
	Andrew P. O'Rourke (R, C)	1,363,810	31.8
	Denis E. Dillon (RTL)	130,802	3.0
	Lenora B. Fulani (NA)	24,130	0.6

Senate

		Vote total	Per-cent
	Alfonse M. D'Amato (R, C, RTL)*	2,378,197	56.9
	Mark Green (D)	1,723,216	41.2
	John Dyson (L)	60,099	1.4
	Frederick D. Newman (NA)	10,559	0.3
	Michael Shur (SOC WORK)	7,376	0.2

House

1	George J. Hochbrueckner (D)	67,139	51.2
	Gregory J. Blass (R)	55,413	42.3
	Dominic J. Santoro (C)	4,345	3.3
	William J. Doyle (RTL)	4,134	3.2
2	Thomas J. Downey (D)*	69,771	64.3
	Jeffrey A. Butzke (R, C)	35,132	32.4
	Veronica Windishman (RTL)	3,651	3.3
3	Robert J. Mrazek (D)*	83,985	56.4
	Joseph A. Guarino (R, C)	60,367	40.6
	Charles W. Welch (RTL)	4,440	3.0
4	Norman F. Lent (R, C)*	92,214	64.8
	Patricia Sullivan (D, L)	43,581	30.6
	George E. Patterson (RTL)	6,493	4.6
5	Raymond J. McGrath (R, C)*	93,473	65.3

		Vote total	Per-cent
	Michael T. Sullivan (D, L, RTL)	49,728	34.7
6	Floyd H. Flake (D)	58,317	67.7
	Richard Dietl (R, C)	27,773	32.3
7	Gary L. Ackerman (D)*	62,836	77.4
	Edward Nelson Rodriguez (R, C)	18,384	22.6
8	James H. Scheuer (D, L)*	70,605	90.2
	(No Republican candidate)		
	Gustave Reifenkugel (C)	7,679	9.8
9	Thomas J. Manton (D)*	50,738	69.4
	Salvatore J. Calise (R)	18,040	24.7
	Thomas V. Ognibene (C)	4,348	5.9
10	Charles E. Schumer (D, L)*	76,318	93.3
	(No Republican candidate)		
	Alice Gaffney (C)	5,472	6.7
11	Edolphus Towns (D, L)*	41,689	89.4
	Nathaniel Hendricks (R)	4,053	8.7
	Alfred J. Hamel (C)	874	1.9
12	Major R. Owens (D, L)*	42,138	91.5
	Owen Augustin (R)	2,752	6.0
	Joseph N. O. Caesar (C, RTL)	1,168	2.5
13	Stephen J. Solarz (D, L)*	61,089	82.4
	Leon Nadrowski (R)	10,941	14.8
	Samuel Roth (C)	2,106	2.8
14	Guy V. Molinari (R, C)*	64,647	68.8
	Barbara Walla (D)	27,950	29.7
	Joseph F. Sulley (L)	1,375	1.5
15	Bill Green (R)*	58,214	58.0
	George A. Hirsch (D, L)	42,147	42.0
16	Charles B. Rangel (D, R, L)*	61,262	96.4
	Michael R. Berns (C)	1,288	2.0
	William Seraile (NA)	995	1.6
17	Ted Weiss (D, L)*	95,094	85.5
	Thomas A. Chorba (R, C)	15,587	14.0
	James Mangia (NA)	581	0.5
18	Robert Garcia (D, L)*	43,343	93.5
	Melanie Chase (R)	2,479	5.4
	Lorraine Verhoff (C)	531	1.1
19	Mario Biaggi (D, R, L)*	87,774	90.2
	Alice Farrell (C)	6,906	7.1
	John J. Barry (RTL)	2,669	2.7
20	Joseph J. DioGuardi (R, C)*	80,220	53.9
	Bella S. Abzug (D)	66,359	44.5
	Florence T. O'Grady (RTL)	2,341	1.6
21	Hamilton Fish Jr. (R, C)*	102,070	76.5
	Lawrence W. Grunberger (D)	28,339	21.3
	Karen A. Gormley-Vitale (RTL)	2,988	2.2
22	Benjamin A. Gilman (R)*	94,244	69.5
	Eleanor F. Burlingham (D)	36,852	27.2
	Richard Bruno (RTL)	4,560	3.3
23	Samuel S. Stratton (D)*	140,759	96.4
	(No Republican candidate)		
	James Joseph Callahan (SOC WORK)	5,279	3.6
24	Gerald B. H. Solomon (R, C, RTL)*	117,285	70.4

		Vote total	Percent

NEW YORK

		Vote total	Percent
	Ed Bloch (D)	49,225	29.6
25	Sherwood Boehlert (R)*	104,216	69.0
	Kevin J. Conway (D)	33,864	22.4
	Robert S. Barstow (C, RTL)	12,999	8.6
26	David O'B. Martin (R, C)*	94,840	100.0
	(No Democratic candidate)		
27	George C. Wortley (R, C)*	83,430	49.7
	Rosemary S. Pooler (D)	82,491	49.1
	Dennis R. Burns (RTL)	2,105	1.2
28	Matthew F. McHugh (D)*	103,908	68.3
	Mark R. Masterson (R, C, RTL)	48,213	31.7
29	Frank Horton (R)*	99,704	70.7
	James R. Vogel (D)	34,194	24.2
	Robert C. Byrnes Jr. (C)	4,762	3.4
	Donald M. Peters (RTL)	2,348	1.7
30	Louise M. Slaughter (D)	86,777	51.0
	Fred J. Eckert (R, C)*	83,402	49.0
31	Jack F. Kemp (R, C, RTL)*	92,508	57.4
	James P. Keane (D)	67,574	42.0
	Gerald R. Morgan (L)	913	0.6
32	John J. LaFalce (D, L)*	99,745	91.0
	(No Republican candidate)		
	Dean L. Walker (C)	6,234	5.7
	Anthony J. Murty (RTL)	3,678	3.3
33	Henry J. Nowak (D, L)*	109,256	85.1
	Charles A. Walker (R, C)	19,147	14.9
34	Amo Houghton (R, C)	85,856	60.1
	Larry M. Himelein (D)	56,898	39.9

NORTH CAROLINA

Senate [i]

		Vote total	Percent
	Terry Sanford (D)	823,662	51.8
	James T. Broyhill (R)*	767,668	48.2

House

		Vote total	Percent
1	Walter B. Jones (D)*	91,122	69.5
	Howard Moye (R)	39,912	30.5
2	Tim Valentine (D)*	95,320	74.6
	Bud McElhaney (R)	32,515	25.4
3	Martin Lancaster (D)	71,460	64.5
	Gerald B. Hurst (R)	39,408	35.5
4	David E. Price (D)	92,216	55.7
	Bill Cobey (R)*	73,469	44.3
5	Stephen L. Neal (D)*	86,410	54.1
	Stuart Epperson (R)	73,261	45.9
6	Howard Coble (R)*	72,329	50.0
	Robin Britt (D)	72,250	50.0
7	Charlie Rose (D)*	70,471	64.2
	Thomas J. Harrelson (R)	39,289	35.8
8	W. G. "Bill" Hefner (D)*	80,959	57.9
	William G. Hamby Jr. (R)	58,941	42.1
9	J. Alex McMillan (R)*	80,352	51.3
	D. G. Martin (D)	76,240	48.7
10	Cass Ballenger (R)	83,902	57.5
	Lester D. Roark (D)	62,035	42.5
11	James McClure Clarke (D)	91,575	50.7
	Bill Hendon (R)*	89,069	49.3

NORTH DAKOTA

Senate

		Vote total	Percent
	Kent Conrad (D)	143,932	49.8
	Mark Andrews (R)*	141,797	49.1
	Anna Belle Bourgois (I)	3,269	1.1

House

		Vote total	Percent
AL	Byron L. Dorgan (D)*	216,258	75.5
	Syver Vinje (R)	66,989	23.4
	Gerald W. Kopp (I)	3,114	1.1

OHIO

Governor

		Vote total	Percent
	Richard F. Celeste (D)*	1,858,372	60.6
	James A. Rhodes (R)	1,207,264	39.4

Senate

		Vote total	Percent
	John Glenn (D)*	1,949,208	62.5
	Thomas N. Kindness (R)	1,171,893	37.5

House

		Vote total	Percent
1	Thomas A. Luken (D)*	90,477	61.7
	Fred E. Morr (R)	56,100	38.3
2	Bill Gradison (R)*	105,061	70.7
	William F. Stineman (D)	43,448	29.3
3	Tony P. Hall (D)*	98,311	73.7
	Ron Crutcher (R)	35,167	26.3
4	Michael G. Oxley (R)*	115,751	75.1
	Clem T. Cratty (D)	26,320	17.1
	Raven L. Workman (I)	11,997	7.8
5	Delbert L. Latta (R)*	102,016	65.0
	Tom Murray (D)	54,864	35.0
6	Bob McEwen (R)*	106,354	70.3
	Gordon Roberts (D)	42,155	27.8
	Amos Seeley (I)	2,829	1.9
7	Michael DeWine (R)*	119,238	100.0
	(No Democratic candidate)		
8	Donald E. Lukens (R)	98,475	68.1
	John W. Griffin (D)	46,195	31.9
9	Marcy Kaptur (D)*	105,646	77.5
	Mike Shufeldt (R)	30,643	22.5
10	Clarence E. Miller (R)*	106,870	70.4
	John M. Buchanan (D)	44,847	29.6
11	Dennis E. Eckart (D)*	104,740	72.4
	Margaret R. Mueller (R)	35,944	24.9
	Werner J. Lange (I)	3,884	2.7
12	John R. Kasich (R)*	117,905	73.4
	Timothy C. Jochim (D)	42,727	26.6
13	Don J. Pease (D)*	88,612	62.8
	William D. Nielsen Jr. (R)	52,452	37.2
14	Thomas C. Sawyer (D)	83,257	53.7
	Lynn Slaby (R)	71,713	46.3
15	Chalmers P. Wylie (R)*	97,745	63.7
	David L. Jackson (D)	55,750	36.3
16	Ralph Regula (R)*	118,206	76.3
	William J. Kennick (D)	36,639	23.7
17	James A. Traficant Jr. (D)*	112,855	72.3
	James H. Fulks (R)	43,334	27.7
18	Douglas Applegate (D)*	126,526	100.0
	(No Republican candidate)		
19	Edward F. Feighan (D)*	97,814	54.8

		Vote total	Percent

OHIO

		Vote total	Percent
	Gary C. Suhadolnik (R)	80,743	45.2
20	Mary Rose Oakar (D)*	110,976	84.9
	Bill Smith (R)	19,794	15.1
21	Louis Stokes (D)*	99,878	81.6
	Franklin H. Roski (R)	22,594	18.4

OKLAHOMA

Governor

		Vote total	Percent
	Henry Bellmon (R)	431,762	47.5
	David Walters (D)	405,295	44.5
	Jerry Brown (I)	60,115	6.6
	Nelson Freckles Little (I)	12,753	1.4

Senate

		Vote total	Percent
	Don Nickles (R)*	493,436	55.2
	James R. Jones (D)	400,230	44.8

House

		Vote total	Percent
1	James M. Inhofe (R)	78,919	54.8
	Gary D. Allison (D)	61,663	42.8
	Carl E. McCullough Jr. (I)	3,455	2.4
2	Mike Synar (D)*	114,543	73.3
	Gary K. Rice (R)	41,795	26.7
3	Wes Watkins (D)*	114,008	78.1
	Patrick K. Miller (R)	31,913	21.9
4	Dave McCurdy (D)*	94,984	76.2
	Larry Humphreys (R)	29,697	23.8
5	Mickey Edwards (R)*	108,774	70.6
	Donna Compton (D)	45,256	29.4
6	Glenn English (D)*	x	x
	(No Republican candidate)		

OREGON

Governor

		Vote total	Percent
	Neil Goldschmidt (D)	549,456	51.9
	Norma Paulus (R)	506,986	47.8

Senate

		Vote total	Percent
	Bob Packwood (R)*	656,317	63.0
	Rick Bauman (D)	375,735	36.0

House

		Vote total	Percent
1	Les AuCoin (D)*	141,585	61.7
	Anthony "Tony" Meeker (R)	87,874	38.3
2	Robert F. Smith (R)*	113,566	60.2
	Larry Tuttle (D)	75,124	39.8
3	Ron Wyden (D)*	180,067	85.9
	Thomas H. Phelan (R)	29,321	14.0
4	Peter A. DeFazio (D)	105,697	54.1
	Bruce Long (R)	89,795	45.9
5	Denny Smith (R)*	125,906	60.5
	Barbara Ross (D)	82,290	39.5

PENNSYLVANIA

Governor

		Vote total	Percent
	Bob Casey (D)	1,717,484	50.7
	William W. Scranton (R)	1,638,268	48.3
	Heidi J. Hoover (CON)	32,523	1.0

Senate

		Vote total	Percent
	Arlen Specter (R)*	1,906,537	56.4
	Bob Edgar (D)	1,448,219	42.9
	Lance S. Haver (CON)	23,470	0.7

House

		Vote total	Percent
1	Thomas M. Foglietta (D)*	88,224	74.7
	Anthony J. Mucciolo (R)	29,811	25.3
2	William H. Gray III (D)*	128,399	98.4
	(No Republican candidate)		
	Linda R. Ragin (NA)	2,096	1.6
3	Robert A. Borski (D)*	107,804	61.8
	Robert A. Rovner (R)	66,693	38.2
4	Joe Kolter (D)*	86,133	60.4
	Al Lindsay (R)	55,165	38.7
	Emily C. Fair (POP)	1,296	0.9
5	Richard T. Schulze (R)*	87,593	65.7
	Tim Ringgold (D)	45,648	34.3
6	Gus Yatron (D)*	98,142	69.1
	Norm Bertasavage (R)	43,858	30.9
7	Curt Weldon (R)	110,118	61.3
	Bill Spingler (D)	69,557	38.7
8	Peter H. Kostmayer (D)*	85,731	55.0
	David A. Christian (R)	70,047	45.0
9	Bud Shuster (R)*	120,890	100.0
	(No Democratic candidate)		
10	Joseph M. McDade (R)*	118,603	74.7
	Robert C. Bolus (D)	40,248	25.3
11	Paul E. Kanjorski (D)*	112,405	70.6
	Marc Holtzman (R)	46,785	29.4
12	John P. Murtha (D)*	97,135	67.4
	Kathy Holtzman (R)	46,937	32.6
13	Lawrence Coughlin (R)*	100,701	58.5
	Joseph M. Hoeffel (D)	71,381	41.5
14	William J. Coyne (D)*	104,726	89.6
	(No Republican candidate)		
	Richard Edward Caligiuri (LIBERT)	6,058	5.2
	Mark Weddleton (SOC WORK)	3,120	2.7
	Thomas R. McIntyre (POP)	1,487	1.3
	Phyllis Gray (WL)	1,468	1.2
15	Don Ritter (R)*	74,829	56.8
	Joe Simonetta (D)	56,972	43.2
16	Robert S. Walker (R)*	100,784	74.6
	James D. Hagelgans (D)	34,399	25.4
17	George W. Gekas (R)*	101,027	73.6
	Michael S. Ogden (D)	36,157	26.4
18	Doug Walgren (D)*	104,164	63.0
	Ernie Buckman (R)	61,164	37.0
19	Bill Goodling (R)*	100,055	72.9
	Richard F. Thornton (D)	37,223	27.1
20	Joseph M. Gaydos (D)*	136,638	98.5
	(No Republican candidate)		
	Alden W. Vedder (WL)	2,114	1.5
21	Tom Ridge (R)*	111,148	80.9
	Joylyn Blackwell (D)	26,324	19.1
22	Austin J. Murphy (D)*	131,650	100.0
	(No Republican candidate)		
23	William F. Clinger Jr. (R)*	79,595	55.5
	Bill Wachob (D)	63,875	44.5

	Vote total	Percent

RHODE ISLAND

Governor

	Vote total	Percent
Edward DiPrete (R)*	208,822	64.7
Bruce G. Sundlun (D)	104,508	32.4
Robert J. Healey Jr. (I)	5,913	1.8
Anthony D. Affigne (CIT)	3,481	1.1

House

		Vote total	Percent
1	Fernand J. St Germain (D)*	85,077	57.7
	John A. Holmes Jr. (R)	62,397	42.3
2	Claudine Schneider (R)*	113,603	71.8
	Donald J. Ferry (D)	44,586	28.2

SOUTH CAROLINA

Governor

	Vote total	Percent
Carroll A. Campbell Jr. (R)	384,565	51.0
Mike Daniel (D)	361,325	47.9
William Griffin (LIBERT)	4,211	0.6
Millard Smith (AM)	3,309	0.4

Senate

	Vote total	Percent
Ernest F. Hollings (D)*	465,500	63.1
Henry D. McMaster (R)	262,886	35.6
Steve Vandervelde (LIBERT)	4,789	0.7
Ray Hillyard (AM)	4,588	0.6

House

		Vote total	Percent
1	Arthur Ravenel Jr. (R)	59,969	52.0
	Jimmy Stuckey (D)	55,262	48.0
2	Floyd Spence (R)*	73,455	53.6
	Fred Zeigler (D)	63,592	46.4
3	Butler Derrick (D)*	79,109	68.4
	Richard Dickison (R)	36,495	31.5
4	Liz J. Patterson (D)	67,012	51.4
	Bill Workman (R)	61,648	47.3
	Bob Wilson (AM)	1,644	1.3
5	John M. Spratt Jr. (D)*	95,859	99.7
	(No Republican candidate)		
6	Robin Tallon (D)*	92,398	75.5
	Robbie Cunningham (R)	29,922	24.5

SOUTH DAKOTA

Governor

	Vote total	Percent
George S. Mickelson (R)	152,543	51.8
R. Lars Herseth (D)	141,898	48.2

Senate

	Vote total	Percent
Thomas A. Daschle (D)	152,657	51.6
James Abdnor (R)*	143,173	48.4

House

		Vote total	Percent
AL	Tim Johnson (D)	171,462	59.2
	Dale Bell (R)	118,261	40.8

TENNESSEE

Governor

	Vote total	Percent
Ned McWherter (D)	656,602	54.3
Winfield Dunn (R)	553,449	45.7

House

		Vote total	Percent
1	James H. Quillen (R)*	80,289	68.9
	John B. Russell (D)	36,278	31.1
2	John J. Duncan (R)*	96,396	76.2
	John F. Bowen (D)	30,088	23.8
3	Marilyn Lloyd (D)*	75,034	53.9
	Jim Golden (R)	64,084	46.1
4	Jim Cooper (D)*	86,997	100.0
	(No Republican candidate)		
5	Bill Boner (D)* j	85,126	57.9
	Terry Holcomb (R)	58,701	39.9
	Charlie Daniels (I)	2,033	1.4
	Russell Hancock (I)	658	0.4
	Kenneth Wayne Bloodworth (I)	609	0.4
6	Bart Gordon (D)*	102,180	76.8
	Fred Vail (R)	30,823	23.2
7	Don Sundquist (R)*	93,902	72.3
	M. Lloyd Hiler (D)	35,966	27.7
8	Ed Jones (D)*	101,699	80.4
	Dan H. Campbell (R)	24,792	19.6
9	Harold E. Ford (D)*	83,006	83.4
	(No Republican candidate)		
	Isaac Richmond (I)	16,221	16.3

TEXAS

Governor

	Vote total	Percent
William P. Clements Jr. (R)	1,813,779	52.7
Mark White (D)*	1,584,515	46.1
Theresa Doyle (LIBERT)	42,496	1.2

House

		Vote total	Percent
1	Jim Chapman (D)*	84,445	100.0
	(No Republican candidate)		
2	Charles Wilson (D)*	78,529	56.7
	Julian Gordon (R)	55,986	40.5
	Sam I. Paradice (I)	3,838	2.8
3	Steve Bartlett (R)*	143,381	94.1
	(No Democratic candidate)		
	Brent Barnes (I)	6,268	4.1
	Don Gough (LIBERT)	2,736	1.8
4	Ralph M. Hall (D)*	97,540	71.7
	Thomas Blow (R)	38,578	28.3
5	John Bryant (D)*	57,410	58.5
	Tom Carter (R)	39,945	40.7
	Bob Brewer (LIBERT)	749	0.8
6	Joe L. Barton (R)*	86,190	55.8
	Pete Geren (D)	68,270	44.2
7	Bill Archer (R)*	129,673	87.4
	Harry Kniffen (D)	17,635	11.9
	Roger Plail (LIBERT)	1,087	0.7
8	Jack Fields (R)*	66,280	68.4
	Blaine Mann (D)	30,617	31.6
9	Jack Brooks (D)*	73,285	61.5
	Lisa D. Duperier (R)	45,834	38.5
10	J. J. Pickle (D)*	135,863	72.3
	Carole Keeton Rylander (R)	52,000	27.7
11	Marvin Leath (D)*	84,201	100.0
	(No Republican candidate)		

		Vote total	Per- cent
TEXAS			
12	Jim Wright (D)*	84,831	68.7
	Don McNeil (R)	38,620	31.3
13	Beau Boulter (R)*	84,980	64.9
	Doug Seal (D)	45,907	35.1
14	Mac Sweeney (R)*	74,471	52.3
	Greg Laughlin (D)	67,852	47.7
15	E. "Kika" de la Garza (D)*	70,777	100.0
	(No Republican candidate)		
16	Ronald D. Coleman (D)*	50,590	65.7
	Roy Gillia (R)	26,421	34.3
17	Charles W. Stenholm (D)*	97,791	100.0
	(No Republican candidate)		
18	Mickey Leland (D)*	63,335	90.2
	(No Republican candidate)		
	Joanne Kuniansky (I)	6,884	9.8
19	Larry Combest (R)*	68,695	62.0
	Gerald McCathern (D)	42,129	38.0
20	Henry B. Gonzalez (D)*	55,363	100.0
	(No Republican candidate)		
21	Lamar Smith (R)	100,346	60.6
	Pete Snelson (D)	63,779	38.5
	Jim Robinson (LIBERT)	1,432	0.9
22	Thomas D. DeLay (R)*	76,459	71.8
	Susan Director (D)	30,079	28.2
23	Albert G. Bustamante (D)*	68,131	90.7
	(No Republican candidate)		
	Ken Hendrix (LIBERT)	7,001	9.3
24	Martin Frost (D)*	69,368	67.2
	Bob Burk (R)	33,819	32.8
25	Michael A. Andrews (D)*	67,435	100.0
	(No Republican candidate)		
26	Dick Armey (R)*	101,735	68.1
	George Richardson (D)	47,651	31.9
27	Solomon P. Ortiz (D)*	64,165	100.0
	(No Republican candidate)		
UTAH			
Senate			
	Jake Garn (R)*	314,608	72.3
	Craig Oliver (D)	115,523	26.6
	Hugh A. Butler (LIBERT)	3,023	0.7
	Mary C. Zins (I)	1,863	0.4
House			
1	James V. Hansen (R)*	82,151	51.6
	Gunn McKay (D)	77,180	48.4
2	Wayne Owens (D)	76,921	55.2
	Tom Shimizu (R)	60,967	43.7
	Stephen Carmichael Carr (LIBERT)	1,302	0.9
	Scott Alan Breen (I)	200	0.2
3	Howard C. Nielson (R)*	86,599	66.6
	Dale F. Gardiner (D)	42,582	32.7
	David P. Hurst (I)	893	0.7
VERMONT			
Governor [k]			
	Madeleine M. Kunin (D)*	92,379	47.0

		Vote total	Per- cent
	Peter Smith (R)	75,162	38.2
	Bernard Sanders (I)	28,430	14.5
	Richard F. Gottlieb (LIBERT)	662	0.3
Senate			
	Patrick J. Leahy (D)*	124,123	63.2
	Richard A. Snelling (R)	67,798	34.5
	Anthony N. Doria (C)	2,963	1.5
	Jerry Levy (LIBERT)	1,583	0.8
House			
AL	James M. Jeffords (R)*	168,403	89.1
	(No Democratic candidate)		
	Peter Diamondstone (LIBERT)	7,060	3.7
	John T. McNulty (I)	7,404	3.9
	Morris Earle (I)	5,850	3.1
VIRGINIA			
House			
1	Herbert H. Bateman (R)*	80,713	56.0
	Robert C. Scott (D)	63,364	44.0
2	Owen B. Pickett (D)	54,491	49.5
	A. J. "Joe" Canada Jr. (R)	46,137	41.9
	Stephen P. Shao (I)	9,492	8.6
3	Thomas J. Bliley Jr. (R)*	74,525	67.0
	Kenneth E. Powell (D)	32,961	29.7
	J. Stephen Hodges (I)	3,675	3.3
4	Norman Sisisky (D)*	64,699	99.8
	(No Republican candidate)		
5	Dan Daniel (D)* [l]	73,085	81.5
	(No Republican candidate)		
	J. F. "Frank" Cole (I)	16,551	18.5
6	Jim Olin (D)*	88,230	69.9
	Flo Neher Traywick (R)	38,051	30.1
7	D. French Slaughter Jr. (R)*	58,927	98.3
	(No Democratic candidate)		
8	Stan Parris (R)*	72,670	61.8
	James H. Boren (D)	44,965	38.2
9	Rick Boucher (D)*	59,864	99.0
	(No Republican candidate)		
10	Frank R. Wolf (R)*	95,724	60.2
	John G. Milliken (D)	63,292	39.8
WASHINGTON			
Senate			
	Brock Adams (D)	677,471	50.6
	Slade Gorton (R)*	650,931	48.7
	Jill Fein (SOC WORK)	8,965	0.7
House			
1	John R. Miller (R)*	97,969	51.4
	Reese Lindquist (D)	92,697	48.6
2	Al Swift (D)*	124,840	72.2
	Thomas S. Talman (R)	48,077	27.8
3	Don Bonker (D)*	114,775	73.6
	Joe Illing (R)	41,275	26.4
4	Sid Morrison (R)*	107,593	72.1

		Vote total	Per-cent			Vote total	Per-cent

WASHINGTON

		Vote total	Percent
	Robert Goedecke (D)	41,709	27.9
5	Thomas S. Foley (D)*	121,732	74.7
	Floyd L. Wakefield (R)	41,179	25.3
6	Norman D. Dicks (D)*	90,063	71.2
	Kenneth W. Braaten (R)	36,410	28.8
7	Mike Lowry (D)*	124,317	72.6
	Don McDonald (R)	46,831	27.4
8	Rod Chandler (R)*	107,824	65.2
	David E. Giles (D)	57,545	34.8

WEST VIRGINIA

House

		Vote total	Percent
1	Alan B. Mollohan (D)*	90,715	100.0
	(No Republican candidate)		
2	Harley O. Staggers Jr. (D)*	76,355	69.5
	Michele Golden (R)	33,554	30.5
3	Bob Wise (D)*	73,669	64.9
	Tim Sharp (R)	39,820	35.1
4	Nick J. Rahall II (D)*	58,217	71.3
	Martin Miller (R)	23,490	28.7

WISCONSIN

Governor

		Vote total	Percent
	Tommy G. Thompson (R)	805,090	52.7
	Anthony S. Earl (D)*	705,578	46.2
	Kathryn A. Christensen (LAB F)	10,323	0.7
	Darold E. Wall (I)	3,913	0.3
	Sanford Knapp (I)	1,668	0.1

Senate

		Vote total	Percent
	Bob Kasten (R)*	754,573	50.9
	Ed Garvey (D)	702,963	47.4
	Peter Y. Taylor Sr. (I)	19,266	1.3

		Vote total	Percent
	Margo Storsteen (SOC WORK)	2,926	0.2
	Eugene A. Hem (I)	2,234	0.2

House

		Vote total	Percent
1	Les Aspin (D)*	106,288	74.3
	Iris Peterson (R)	34,495	24.1
	John Graf (LAB F)	2,354	1.6
2	Robert W. Kastenmeier (D)*	106,919	55.6
	Ann J. Haney (R)	85,156	44.2
	Syed Ameen (I)	443	0.2
3	Steve Gunderson (R)*	104,393	64.1
	Leland E. Mulder (D)	58,445	35.9
4	Gerald D. Kleczka (D)*	120,354	99.6
	(No Republican candidate)		
5	Jim Moody (D)*	109,506	99.0
	(No Republican candidate)		
6	Thomas E. Petri (R)*	124,328	96.7
	(No Democratic candidate)		
	John Richard Daggett (I)	4,268	3.3
7	David R. Obey (D)*	106,700	62.2
	Kevin J. Hermening (R)	63,408	36.9
	Joseph D. Damrell (LAB F)	1,599	0.9
8	Toby Roth (R)*	118,162	67.4
	Paul F. Willems (D)	57,265	32.6
9	F. James Sensen-brenner Jr. (R)*	138,766	78.2
	Thomas G. Popp (D)	38,636	21.8

WYOMING

Governor

		Vote total	Percent
	Mike Sullivan (D)	88,879	54.0
	Pete Simpson (R)	75,841	46.0

House

		Vote total	Percent
AL	Dick Cheney (R)*	111,007	69.5
	Rick Gilmore (D)	48,780	30.5

a. Mecham was impeached and removed from office in April 1988. Rose Mofford as secretary of state succeeded him.

b. Burton died February 1, 1987. Democrat Nancy Pelosi was elected to fill her seat June 2, 1987.

c. McKinney died May 7, 1987. GOP state representative Christopher Shays won a special election August 18, 1987, to succeed him.

d. Price died April 22, 1988. Democrat Jerry F. Costello won a special election August 9, 1988, to succeed him.

e. Quayle was elected vice president in 1988. Republican Daniel R. Coats was appointed January 3, 1989, to replace him in the Senate. A special election was to be held in 1990 to fill the remaining two years of Quayle's term.

f. Roemer resigned March 14, 1988, to become governor of Louisiana. He was elected November 21, 1987. His successor, Republican Jim McCrery, was chosen in a special runoff election April 16, 1988.

g. Bryan was elected to the Senate November 8, 1988, and Bob Miller as lieutenant governor became acting governor. A gubernatorial election was to be held in 1990.

h. Howard died March 25, 1988.

i. On July 3, 1986, Rep. James T. Broyhill was appointed to replace Republican senator John P. East, who died June 29, 1986. His appointment ran through November 4, 1986. On November 4 Democrat Terry Sanford was elected both to serve a full term and to fill the vacancy. Although he was not officially sworn in until December 10, 1986, he became a member of the Senate on November 5, 1986.

j. Boner resigned October 5, 1987, to become mayor of Nashville. He was elected September 22, 1987. His successor, Democrat Bob Clement, was chosen in a special election January 19, 1988.

k. Since no candidate won a clear majority of the total vote cast for governor, the election passed to the state legislature. Sitting in joint assembly in January 1987, the legislature elected Kunin with 139 votes to 39 for Smith and 1 for Sanders.

l. Daniel died January 23, 1988. Democrat L. F. Payne was chosen in a special election June, 14, 1988, to fill the remaining term for the 100th Congress.

1988 Elections:
Governor, Senate, and House

This list gives the final, official 1988 vote returns for the Senate, House, and governorships compiled by Congressional Quarterly from figures supplied by each state's election agency. The box shows party designation symbols.

Because of rounding and because scattered write-in votes are not listed, percentages do not always add to 100. An asterisk (*) indicates incumbents. An X denotes candidates without major-party opposition; no votes were cast.

		Vote total	Percent

ALABAMA
House

		Vote total	Percent
1	Sonny Callahan (R) *	115,173	59.2
	John M. Tyson Jr. (D)	77,670	40.0
	Ken Ament (LIBERT)	1,483	0.8
2	Bill Dickinson (R) *	120,408	94.2
	(No Democratic candidate)		
	Joel Brooke King (LIBERT)	7,352	5.8
3	Bill Nichols (D) * a	117,514	96.1
	(No Republican candidate)		
	Jerome Shockley (LIBERT)	4,793	3.9
4	Tom Bevill (D) *	131,880	96.2
	(No Republican candidate)		
	John Sebastian (LIBERT)	5,264	3.8
5	Ronnie G. Flippo (D) *	120,142	64.4
	Stan McDonald (R)	64,491	34.5
	John Palmer (LIBERT)	1,989	1.1
6	Ben Erdreich (D) *	138,920	66.5
	Charles Caddis (R)	68,788	32.9
	William Wingo (LIBERT)	1,092	0.5
7	Claude Harris (D) *	136,074	67.7
	James E. "Jim" Bacon (R)	63,372	31.5
	Alan Barksdale (LIBERT)	1,421	0.7

ALASKA
House

		Vote total	Percent
AL	Don Young (R) *	120,595	62.5
	Peter Gruenstein (D)	71,881	37.3

ARIZONA
Senate

		Vote total	Percent
	Dennis DeConcini (D)	660,403	56.7
	Keith DeGreen (R)	478,060	41.1
	Rick Tompkins (LIBERT)	20,849	1.8
	Ed Finkelstein (I)	5,195	0.4

House

		Vote total	Percent
1	John J. Rhodes III (R) *	184,639	72.1
	John M. Fillmore (D)	71,388	27.9
2	Morris K. Udall (D) *	99,895	73.3
	Joseph D. Sweeney (R)	36,309	26.7
3	Bob Stump (R) *	174,453	68.9
	Dave Moss (D)	72,417	28.6
	John Parsons (I)	6,460	2.5
4	Jon Kyl (R) *	206,248	87.1
	(No Democratic candidate)		

		Vote total	Percent
	Gary Sprunk (LIBERT)	30,430	12.9
5	Jim Kolbe (R) *	164,462	67.8
	Judith E. Belcher (D)	78,115	32.2

ARKANSAS
House

		Vote total	Percent
1	Bill Alexander (D) *	x	x
	(No Republican candidate)		
2	Tommy F. Robinson (D) * b	168,889	83.5
	Warren D. Carpenter (R)	33,475	16.5
3	John Paul Hammerschmidt (R) *	161,623	74.7
	David Stewart (D)	54,767	25.3
4	Beryl Anthony Jr. (D) *	129,508	69.2
	Roger N. Bell (R)	57,658	30.8

CALIFORNIA
Senate

		Vote total	Percent
	Pete Wilson (R) *	5,143,409	52.8
	Leo T. McCarthy (D)	4,287,253	44.0
	M. Elizabeth Munoz (PFP)	166,600	1.7
	Jack Dean (LIBERT)	79,997	0.8
	Merton D. Short (AMI)	66,288	0.7

House

		Vote total	Percent
1	Douglas H. Bosco (D) *	159,815	62.9
	Samuel "Mark" Vanderbilt (R)	72,189	28.4

ABBREVIATIONS FOR PARTY DESIGNATIONS

AM	American	I-R	Independent-Republican
AMI	American Independent	L	Liberal
C	Conservative	LIBERT	Libertarian
COM	Communist	LU	Liberty Union
CON	Consumer	NA	New Alliance
D	Democratic	PFP	Peace and Freedom
DFL	Democratic Farmer-Labor	POP	Populist
I	Independent	R	Republican
IL SOL	Illinois Solidarity	RTL	Right to Life
		SOC WORK	Socialist Workers

		Vote total	Percent			Vote total	Percent
					John G. Simmons (D)	61,555	26.0
CALIFORNIA					Shirley Rachel Isaacson (PFP)	6,298	2.7
	Eric Fried (PFP)	22,150	8.7		Ted Brown (LIBERT)	4,259	1.8
2	Wally Herger (R) *	139,010	58.8	23	Anthony C. Beilenson (D) *	147,858	63.5
	Wayne Meyer (D)	91,088	38.5		Jim Salomon (R)	77,184	33.1
	Harry H. Pendery (LIBERT)	6,253	2.6		John Richard Vernon (LIBERT)	4,503	1.9
3	Robert T. Matsui (D) *	183,470	71.2		John Honigsfeld (PFP)	3,316	1.4
	Lowell Patrick Landowski (R)	74,296	28.8	24	Henry A. Waxman (D) *	112,038	72.3
4	Vic Fazio (D) *	181,184	99.3		John N. Cowles (R)	36,835	23.7
	(No Republican candidate)				James Green (PFP)	3,571	2.3
5	Nancy Pelosi (D) *	133,530	76.4		George Abrahams (LIBERT)	2,627	1.7
	Bruce Michael O'Neill (R)	33,692	19.3	25	Edward R. Roybal (D) *	85,378	85.5
	Theodore "Ted" Zuur (PFP)	3,975	2.3		(No Republican candidate)		
	Sam Grove (LIBERT)	3,561	2.0		Raul Reyes (PFP)	8,746	8.8
6	Barbara Boxer (D) *	176,645	73.4		John C. Thie (LIBERT)	5,752	5.8
	William Steinmetz (R)	64,174	26.6	26	Howard L. Berman (D) *	126,930	70.3
7	George Miller (D) *	170,006	68.4		G. C. "Brodie" Broderson (R)	53,518	29.7
	Jean Last (R)	78,478	31.6	27	Mel Levine (D) *	148,814	67.5
8	Ronald V. Dellums (D) *	163,221	66.6		Dennis Galbraith (R)	65,307	29.6
	John J. Cuddihy Jr. (R)	76,531	31.2		William J. Fulco (LIBERT)	6,214	2.8
	Tom Condit (PFP)	5,444	2.2	28	Julian C. Dixon (D) *	109,801	76.1
9	Pete Stark (D) *	152,866	73.0		George Zaldivar Adams (R)	28,645	19.8
	Howard Hertz (R)	56,656	27.0		Howard Johnson (LIBERT)	3,080	2.1
10	Don Edwards (D) *	142,500	86.2		Salomea Honigsfeld (PFP)	2,811	2.0
	(No Republican candidate)			29	Augustus F. Hawkins (D) *	88,169	82.8
	Kennita Watson (LIBERT)	22,801	13.8		Reuben D. Franco (R)	14,543	13.7
11	Tom Lantos (D) *	145,484	71.0		Gregory P. Gilmore (LIBERT)	3,724	3.5
	G. M. "Bill" Quraishi (R)	50,050	24.4	30	Matthew G. Martinez (D) *	72,253	59.9
	Bill Wade (LIBERT)	4,683	2.3		Ralph R. Ramirez (R)	43,833	36.3
	Victor Martinez (PFP)	2,906	1.4		Houston Myers (AMI)	2,694	2.2
	Nicholas W. Kudrovzeff (AMI)	1,893	0.9		Kim J. Goldsworthy (LIBERT)	1,864	1.6
12	Tom Campbell (R)	136,384	51.7	31	Mervyn M. Dymally (D) *	100,919	71.6
	Anna G. Eshoo (D)	121,523	46.0		Arnold C. May (R)	36,017	25.5
	Tom Grey (LIBERT)	6,023	2.3		B. Kwaku Duren (PFP)	4,091	2.9
13	Norman Y. Mineta (D) *	143,980	67.1	32	Glenn M. Anderson (D) *	114,666	66.9
	Luke Sommer (R)	63,959	29.8		Sanford W. Kahn (R)	50,710	29.6
	John H. Webster (LIBERT)	6,583	3.1		Marc F. Denny (LIBERT)	1,941	1.1
14	Norman D. Shumway (R) *	173,876	62.6		Vikki Murdock (PFP)	4,032	2.4
	Patricia Malberg (D)	103,899	37.4	33	David Dreier (R) *	151,704	69.2
15	Tony Coelho (D) * c	118,710	69.7		Nelson Gentry (D)	57,586	26.2
	Carol Harner (R)	47,957	28.2		Gail Lightfoot (LIBERT)	6,601	3.0
	Richard M. Harris (LIBERT)	3,526	2.1		Mike Noonan (PFP)	3,492	1.6
16	Leon E. Panetta (D) *	177,452	78.6	34	Esteban E. Torres (D) *	92,087	63.2
	Stanley Monteith (R)	48,375	21.4		Charles M. House (R)	50,954	35.0
17	Charles "Chip" Pashayan Jr. (R) *	129,568	71.5		Carl "Marty" Swinney (LIBERT)	2,686	1.8
	Vincent Lavery (D)	51,730	28.5	35	Jerry Lewis (R) *	181,203	70.4
18	Richard H. Lehman (D) *	125,715	69.9		Paul Sweeney (D)	71,186	27.7
	David A. Linn (R)	54,034	30.1		Jeff Shuman (LIBERT)	4,879	1.9
19	Robert J. Lagomarsino (R) *	116,026	50.2	36	George E. Brown Jr. (D) *	103,493	54.0
	Gary K. Hart (D)	112,033	48.5		John Paul Stark (R)	81,413	42.5
	Robert Donaldson (LIBERT)	2,865	1.2		Kenneth E. Valentine (LIBERT)	3,382	1.8
20	Bill Thomas (R) *	162,779	71.1		Fred L. Anderson (AMI)	3,360	1.7
	Lita Reid (D)	62,037	27.1	37	Al McCandless (R) *	174,284	64.3
	David Bersohn (LIBERT)	4,190	1.8		Johnny Pearson (D)	89,666	33.1
21	Elton Gallegly (R) *	181,413	69.1		Bonnie Flickinger (LIBERT)	7,169	2.6
	Donald E. Stevens (D)	75,739	28.8	38	Robert K. Dornan (R) *	87,690	59.5
	Robert Jay (LIBERT)	5,519	2.1		Jerry Yudelson (D)	52,399	35.6
22	Carlos J. Moorhead (R) *	164,699	69.5				

		Vote total	Percent			Vote total	Percent

CALIFORNIA

		Vote total	Percent
	Bruce McKay (LIBERT)	3,733	2.5
	Frank German (PFP)	3,547	2.4
39	William E. Dannemeyer (R) *	169,360	73.8
	Don E. Marquis (D)	52,162	22.7
	Lee Connelly (LIBERT)	7,470	3.3
40	C. Christopher Cox (R)	181,269	67.0
	Lida Lenney (D)	80,782	29.9
	Roger Bloxham (LIBERT)	4,539	1.7
	Gretchen J. Farsai (PFP)	3,699	1.4
41	Bill Lowery (R) *	187,380	65.6
	Dan Kripke (D)	88,192	30.8
	Dick Rider (LIBERT)	5,336	1.9
	C. T. Weber (PFP)	4,853	1.7
42	Dana Rohrabacher (R)	153,280	64.2
	Guy C. Kimbrough (D)	78,778	33.0
	Richard D. Rose (PFP)	6,563	2.8
43	Ron Packard (R) *	202,478	71.7
	Howard Greenebaum (D)	72,499	25.6
	Daniel L. Muhe (LIBERT)	7,552	2.7
44	Jim Bates (D) *	90,796	59.7
	Rob Butterfield (R)	55,511	36.5
	Dennis Thompson (LIBERT)	5,782	3.8
45	Duncan Hunter (R) *	166,451	74.0
	Pete Lepiscopo (D)	54,012	24.0
	Perry Willis (LIBERT)	4,440	2.0

COLORADO

House

		Vote total	Percent
1	Patricia Schroeder (D) *	133,922	69.9
	Joy Wood (R)	57,587	30.1
2	David E. Skaggs (D) *	147,437	62.7
	David Bath (R)	87,578	37.3
3	Ben Nighthorse Campbell (D) *	169,284	78.0
	Jim Zartman (R)	47,625	22.0
4	Hank Brown (R) *	156,202	73.1
	Charles S. Vigil (D)	57,552	26.9
5	Joel Hefley (R) *	181,612	75.1
	John J. Mitchell (D)	60,116	24.9
6	Dan Schaefer (R) *	136,487	63.0
	Martha M. Ezzard (D)	77,158	35.6
	John Heckman (I)	2,911	1.3

CONNECTICUT

Senate

		Vote total	Percent
	Joseph I. Lieberman (D)	688,499	49.8
	Lowell P. Weicker Jr. (R) *	678,454	49.0
	Howard A. Grayson Jr. (LIBERT)	12,409	0.9
	Melissa M. Fisher (NA)	4,154	0.3

House

		Vote total	Percent
1	Barbara B. Kennelly (D) *	176,463	77.2
	Mario Robles Jr. (R)	51,985	22.8
2	Sam Gejdenson (D) *	143,326	63.6
	Glenn Carberry (R)	81,965	36.4
3	Bruce A. Morrison (D) *	147,394	66.5
	Gerard B. Patton (R)	74,275	33.5
4	Christopher Shays (R) *	147,843	71.8
	Roger Pearson (D)	55,751	27.1

		Vote total	Percent
	Nicholas J. Tarzia (I)	2,379	1.1
5	John G. Rowland (R) *	163,729	73.6
	Joseph Marinan Jr. (D)	58,612	26.4
6	Nancy L. Johnson (R) *	157,020	66.3
	James L. Griffin (D)	78,814	33.3
	Louis J. Marietta (I)	1,054	0.4

DELAWARE

Governor

		Vote total	Percent
	Michael N. Castle (R) *	169,733	70.7
	Jacob Kreshtool (D)	70,236	29.3

Senate

		Vote total	Percent
	William V. Roth Jr. (R) *	151,115	62.1
	S. B. Woo (D)	92,378	37.9

House

		Vote total	Percent
AL	Thomas R. Carper (D) *	158,338	67.5
	James P. Krapf Sr. (R)	76,179	32.5

FLORIDA

Senate

		Vote total	Percent
	Connie Mack (R)	2,051,071	50.4
	Buddy MacKay (D)	2,016,553	49.6

House

		Vote total	Percent
1	Earl Hutto (D) *	142,449	66.9
	E. D. Armbruster (R)	70,534	33.1
2	Bill Grant (D) * d	134,269	99.7
	(No Republican candidate)		
3	Charles E. Bennett (D) *	x	x
	(No Republican candidate)		
4	Craig T. James (R)	125,608	50.2
	Bill Chappell Jr. (D) *	124,817	49.8
5	Bill McCollum (R) *	x	x
	(No Democratic candidate)		
6	Cliff Stearns (R)	136,415	53.5
	Jon Mills (D)	118,756	46.5
7	Sam M. Gibbons (D) *	x	x
	(No Republican candidate)		
8	C. W. Bill Young (R) *	169,165	73.0
	C. Bette Wimbish (D)	62,539	27.0
9	Michael Bilirakis (R) *	223,925	99.9
	(No Democratic candidate)		
10	Andy Ireland (R) *	156,563	73.5
	David B. Higginbottom (D)	56,536	26.5
11	Bill Nelson (D) *	168,390	60.8
	Bill Tolley (R)	108,373	39.2
12	Tom Lewis (R) *	x	x
	(No Democratic candidate)		
13	Porter Goss (R)	231,170	71.2
	Jack Conway (D)	93,700	28.8
14	Harry A. Johnston (D)	173,292	54.9
	Ken Adams (R)	142,635	45.1
15	E. Clay Shaw Jr. (R) *	132,090	66.1
	Michael A. "Mike" Kuhle (D)	67,746	33.9
16	Lawrence J. Smith (D) *	153,032	69.4
	Joseph Smith (R)	67,461	30.6
17	William Lehman (D) *	x	x
	(No Republican candidate)		
18	Claude Pepper (D) * e	x	x

		Vote total	Per- cent

FLORIDA

	(No Republican candidate)		
19	Dante B. Fascell (D) *	135,355	72.4
	Ralph Carlos Rocheteau (R)	51,628	27.6

GEORGIA

House

1	Lindsay Thomas (D) *	94,531	67.0
	John Christian Meredith (R)	46,552	33.0
2	Charles Hatcher (D) *	85,029	61.7
	Ralph T. Hudgens (R)	52,807	38.3
3	Richard Ray (D) *	97,663	100.0
	(No Republican candidate)		
4	Ben Jones (D)	148,394	60.3
	Pat Swindall (R) *	97,745	39.7
5	John Lewis (D) *	135,194	78.2
	J. W. Tibbs Jr. (R)	37,693	21.8
6	Newt Gingrich (R) *	110,169	58.9
	Dave Worley (D)	76,824	41.1
7	George "Buddy" Darden (D) *	135,056	64.8
	Robert Lamutt (R)	73,425	35.2
8	J. Roy Rowland (D) *	102,696	100.0
	(No Republican candidate)		
9	Ed Jenkins (D) *	121,800	62.9
	Joe Hoffman (R)	71,905	37.1
10	Doug Barnard Jr. (D) *	118,156	64.0
	Mark Myers (R)	66,521	36.0

HAWAII

Senate

	Spark M. Matsunaga (D) *	247,941	76.5
	Maria M. Hustace (R)	66,987	20.7
	Ken Schoolland (LIBERT)	8,948	2.8

House

1	Patricia Saiki (R) *	96,848	54.7
	Mary Bitterman (D)	76,394	43.2
	Blase Harris (LIBERT)	3,778	2.1
2	Daniel K. Akaka (D) *	144,802	88.9
	(No Republican candidate)		
	Lloyd Jeffrey Mallan (LIBERT)	18,006	11.1

IDAHO

House

1	Larry E. Craig (R) *	135,221	65.8
	Jeanne Givens (D)	70,328	34.2
2	Richard Stallings (D) *	127,956	63.4
	Dane Watkins (R)	68,226	33.8
	Donovan Bramwell (LIBERT)	5,703	2.8

ILLINOIS

House

1	Charles A. Hayes (D) *	164,125	96.0
	Stephen J. Evans (R)	6,753	4.0
2	Gus Savage (D) *	138,256	82.7
	William T. Hespel (R)	28,831	17.3
3	Marty Russo (D) *	132,111	62.2

		Vote total	Per- cent
	Joseph J. McCarthy (R)	80,181	37.8
4	George E. Sangmeister (D)	91,282	50.3
	Jack Davis (R) *	90,243	49.7
5	William O. Lipinski (D) *	93,567	61.3
	John J. Holowinski (R)	59,128	38.7
6	Henry J. Hyde (R) *	153,425	73.7
	William J. Andrle (D)	54,804	26.3
7	Cardiss Collins (D) *	135,331	100.0
	(No Republican candidate)		
8	Dan Rostenkowski (D) *	107,728	74.6
	V. Stephen Vetter (R)	34,659	24.0
	Mark J. Almberg (COM)	1,937	1.3
9	Sidney R. Yates (D) *	135,583	66.1
	Herbert Sohn (R)	67,604	32.9
	Jessie Fields (IL SOL)	2,000	1.0
10	John Porter (R) *	158,519	72.5
	Eugene F. Friedman (D)	60,187	27.5
11	Frank Annunzio (D) *	131,753	64.5
	George S. Gottlieb (R)	72,489	35.5
12	Philip M. Crane (R) *	165,913	75.2
	John A. Leonardi (D)	54,769	24.8
13	Harris W. Fawell (R) *	174,992	70.2
	Evelyn E. Craig (D)	74,424	29.8
14	Dennis Hastert (R) *	161,146	73.7
	Stephen Youhanaie (D)	57,482	26.3
15	Edward Madigan (R) *	140,171	71.7
	Thomas J. "Tom" Curl (D)	55,260	28.3
16	Lynn Martin (R) *	128,365	63.9
	Steven E. Mahan (D)	72,431	36.1
17	Lane Evans (D) *	132,130	64.9
	William E. Stewart (R)	71,560	35.1
18	Robert H. Michel (R) *	114,458	54.7
	G. Douglas Stephens (D)	94,763	45.3
19	Terry L. Bruce (D) *	132,889	64.2
	Robert F. Kerans (R)	73,981	35.8
20	Richard J. Durbin (D) *	153,341	68.9
	Paul E. Jurgens (R)	69,303	31.1
21	Jerry F. Costello (D) *	105,836	52.6
	Robert H. "Bob" Gaffner (R)	95,385	47.4
22	Glenn Poshard (D)	139,392	64.9
	Patrick J. Kelley (R)	75,462	35.1

INDIANA

Governor

	Evan Bayh (D)	1,138,574	53.2
	John M. Mutz (R)	1,002,207	46.8

Senate

	Richard G. Lugar (R) *	1,430,525	68.1
	Jack Wickes (D)	668,778	31.9

House

1	Peter J. Visclosky (D) *	138,251	77.1
	Owen W. Crumpacker (R)	41,076	22.9
2	Philip R. Sharp (D) *	116,915	53.2
	Mike Pence (R)	102,846	46.8
3	John Hiler (R) *	116,309	54.3
	Thomas W. Ward (D)	97,934	45.7
4	Daniel R. Coats (R) * f	132,843	62.1
	Jill Long (D) g	80,915	37.9
5	Jim Jontz (D) *	116,240	56.3

		Vote total	Per-cent

INDIANA

	Patricia L. Williams (R)	90,163	43.7
6	Dan Burton (R) *	192,064	72.9
	George Thomas Holland (D)	71,447	27.1
7	John T. Myers (R) *	130,578	61.8
	Mark Richard Waterfill (D)	80,738	38.2
8	Frank McCloskey (D) *	141,355	61.8
	John L. Myers (R)	87,321	38.2
9	Lee H. Hamilton (D) *	147,193	70.7
	Floyd Eugene Coates (R)	60,946	29.3
10	Andrew Jacobs Jr. (D) *	105,846	60.5
	James C. Cummings (R)	68,978	39.5

IOWA
House

1	Jim Leach (R) *	112,746	60.7
	Bill Gluba (D)	71,280	38.4
	Judy Stav-River (I)	1,670	0.9
2	Tom Tauke (R) *	113,543	56.8
	Eric Tabor (D)	86,438	43.2
3	Dave Nagle (D) *	129,204	63.4
	Donald B. Redfern (R)	74,682	36.6
4	Neal Smith (D) *	157,065	71.6
	Paul Lunde (R)	62,056	28.3
5	Jim Ross Lightfoot (R) *	117,761	63.9
	Gene Freund (D)	66,599	36.1
6	Fred Grandy (R) *	125,859	64.4
	Dave O'Brien (D)	69,614	35.6

KANSAS
House

1	Pat Roberts (R) *	168,700	100.0
	(No Democratic candidate)		
2	Jim Slattery (D) *	135,694	73.3
	Phil Meinhardt (R)	49,498	26.7
3	Jan Meyers (R) *	150,223	73.6
	Lionel Kunst (D)	53,959	26.4
4	Dan Glickman (D) *	122,777	64.0
	Lee Thompson (R)	69,165	36.0
5	Bob Whittaker (R) *	127,722	70.2
	John A. Barnes (D)	54,327	29.8

KENTUCKY
House

1	Carroll Hubbard Jr. (D) *	117,288	95.0
	(No Republican candidate)		
	Charles K. Hatchett (I)	6,106	4.9
2	William H. Natcher (D) *	92,184	60.6
	Martin A. Tori (R)	59,907	39.4
3	Romano L. Mazzoli (D) *	131,981	69.7
	Philip Dunnagan (R)	57,387	30.3
4	Jim Bunning (R) *	145,609	74.2
	Richard V. Beliles (D)	50,575	25.8
5	Harold Rogers (R) *	104,467	100.0
	(No Democratic candidate)		
6	Larry J. Hopkins (R) *	128,898	74.0
	Milton Patton (D)	45,339	26.0

		Vote total	Per-cent
7	Carl C. Perkins (D) *	96,946	58.7
	William T. "Will" Scott (R)	68,165	41.3

LOUISIANA
House

1	Bob Livingston (R) *	x	x
2	Lindy (Mrs. Hale) Boggs (D) *	x	x
3	W. J. "Billy" Tauzin (D) *	x	x
4	Jim McCrery (R) *	x	x
5	Jerry Huckaby (D) *	x	x
6	Richard H. Baker (R) *	x	x
7	Jimmy Hayes (D) *	x	x
8	Clyde C. Holloway (R) *	116,241	56.8
	Faye Williams (D)	88,564	43.2

MAINE
Senate

	George J. Mitchell (D) *	452,590	81.2
	Jasper S. Wyman (R)	104,758	18.8

House

1	Joseph E. Brennan (D) *	190,989	63.2
	Edward S. O'Meara Jr. (R)	111,125	36.8
2	Olympia J. Snowe (R) *	167,229	66.2
	Kenneth P. Hayes (D)	85,346	33.8

MARYLAND
Senate

	Paul S. Sarbanes (D) *	999,166	61.8
	Alan L. Keyes (R)	617,537	38.2

House

1	Roy Dyson (D) *	96,128	50.4
	Wayne T. Gilchrest (R)	94,588	49.6
2	Helen Delich Bentley (R) *	157,956	71.5
	Joseph Bartenfelder (D)	63,114	28.5
3	Benjamin L. Cardin (D) *	133,779	72.9
	Ross Z. Pierpont (R)	49,733	27.1
4	Tom McMillen (D) *	128,624	68.3
	Bradlyn McClanahan (R)	59,688	31.7
5	Steny H. Hoyer (D) *	128,437	78.6
	John Eugene Sellner (R)	34,909	21.4
6	Beverly B. Byron (D) *	166,753	75.4
	Kenneth W. Halsey (R)	54,528	24.6
7	Kweisi Mfume (D) *	117,650	100.0
	(No Republican candidate)		
8	Constance A. Morella (R) *	172,619	62.7
	Peter Franchot (D)	102,478	37.3

MASSACHUSETTS
Senate

	Edward M. Kennedy (D) *	1,693,344	65.0
	Joseph D. Malone (R)	884,267	33.9
	Mary Fridley (NA)	15,208	0.6
	Freda Lee Nason (LIBERT)	13,199	0.5

House

1	Silvio O. Conte (R) *	186,356	82.7
	John R. Arden (D)	38,907	17.3

		Vote total	Per- cent

MASSACHUSETTS

		Vote total	Percent
2	Richard E. Neal (D)	156,262	80.2
	(No Republican candidate)		
	Louis R. Godena (I)	38,446	19.7
3	Joseph D. Early (D) *	191,005	99.8
	(No Republican candidate)		
4	Barney Frank (D) *	169,729	70.3
	Debra R. Tucker (R)	71,661	29.7
5	Chester G. Atkins (D) *	181,860	84.1
	(No Republican candidate)		
	T. David Hudson (LIBERT)	34,339	15.9
6	Nicholas Mavroules (D) *	177,643	69.6
	Paul McCarthy (R)	77,186	30.3
7	Edward J. Markey (D) *	188,647	100.0
	(No Republican candidate)		
8	Joseph P. Kennedy II (D) *	165,745	80.4
	Glenn W. Fiscus (R)	40,316	19.6
9	Joe Moakley (D) *	160,799	99.8
	(No Republican candidate)		
10	Gerry E. Studds (D) *	187,178	66.7
	Jon L. Bryan (R)	93,564	33.3
11	Brian Donnelly (D) *	169,692	80.8
	Michael C. Gilleran (R)	40,277	19.2

MICHIGAN
Senate

		Vote total	Percent
	Donald W. Riegle Jr. (D) *	2,116,865	60.4
	Jim Dunn (R)	1,348,219	38.5
	Dick M. Jacobs (LIBERT)	27,116	0.8
	Sally Bier (I)	8,908	0.2
	Mark L. Friedman (I)	4,821	0.1

House

		Vote total	Percent
1	John Conyers Jr. (D) *	127,800	91.2
	Bill Ashe (R)	10,979	7.8
	Jonathan Paul Flint (LIBERT)	744	0.5
	Sam Johnson (I)	615	0.4
2	Carl D. Pursell (R) *	120,070	54.7
	Lana Pollack (D)	98,290	44.7
	David H. Raaflaub (LIBERT)	1,324	0.6
3	Howard Wolpe (D) *	112,605	57.3
	Cal Allgaier (R)	83,769	42.7
4	Fred Upton (R) *	132,270	70.8
	Norman J. Rivers (D)	54,428	29.2
5	Paul B. Henry (R) *	166,569	72.6
	James M. Catchick (D)	62,868	27.4
6	Bob Carr (D) *	120,581	58.9
	Scott Schultz (R)	81,079	39.6
	Tony Wright (LIBERT)	1,897	0.9
	Judith R. Christensen (I)	1,063	0.5
7	Dale E. Kildee (D) *	150,832	75.8
	Jeff Coad (R)	47,071	23.6
	Gary Walkowicz (I)	1,174	0.6
8	Bob Traxler (D) *	139,904	72.1
	Lloyd F. Buhl (R)	54,195	27.9
9	Guy Vander Jagt (R) *	149,748	69.8
	David John Gawron (D)	64,843	30.2
10	Bill Schuette (R) *	152,646	72.7
	Mathias G. Forbes (D)	55,398	26.4
	Gary R. Bradley (LIBERT)	1,812	0.9

		Vote total	Percent
11	Robert W. Davis (R) *	129,085	59.6
	Mitch Irwin (D)	86,526	40.0
	Denise Kline (LIBERT)	803	0.4
12	David E. Bonior (D) *	108,158	53.6
	Douglas Carl (R)	91,780	45.5
	Keith P. Edwards (LIBERT)	1,311	0.6
	Vincent Mario Contrera (I)	548	0.3
13	George W. Crockett Jr. (D) *	99,751	87.0
	John Wright Savage II (R)	13,196	11.5
	Alan H. Harris (LIBERT)	878	0.8
	Martinez Alfred Gomez (I)	874	0.7
14	Dennis M. Hertel (D) *	111,612	62.6
	Kenneth C. McNealy (R)	64,750	36.3
	Robert W. Roddis (LIBERT)	1,336	0.7
	James L. Breeland (I)	710	0.4
15	William D. Ford (D) *	104,596	63.8
	Burl C. Adkins (R)	56,963	34.8
	Eric Blankenburg (LIBERT)	1,613	1.0
	Ronda M. Reed Bell (I)	670	0.4
16	John D. Dingell (D) *	132,775	97.4
	(No Republican candidate)		
	Russell W. Leone (I)	3,561	2.6
17	Sander M. Levin (D) *	135,493	70.2
	Dennis M. Flessland (R)	55,197	28.6
	Charles Hahn (LIBERT)	2,333	1.2
18	William S. Broomfield (R) *	195,579	76.0
	Gary L. Kohut (D)	57,643	22.4
	Timothy J. O'Brien (LIBERT)	4,003	1.6

MINNESOTA
Senate

		Vote total	Percent
	Dave Durenberger (I-R) *	1,176,210	56.2
	Hubert H. "Skip" Humphrey III (DFL)	856,694	40.9
	Polly Mann (I)	44,474	2.1
	Derrick P. Grimmer (I)	9,016	0.4
	Arlen Overvig (LIBERT)	4,039	0.2
	Wendy Lyons (SOC WORK)	3,105	0.1

House

		Vote total	Percent
1	Timothy J. Penny (DFL) *	161,118	70.1
	Curt Schrimpf (I-R)	67,709	29.5
	Craig Honts (SOC WORK)	957	0.4
2	Vin Weber (I-R) *	131,639	57.8
	Doug Peterson (DFL)	96,016	42.2
3	Bill Frenzel (I-R) *	215,322	68.2
	Dave Carlson (DFL)	99,770	31.6
4	Bruce F. Vento (DFL) *	181,227	72.4
	Ian Maitland (I-R)	67,073	26.8
	Natasha Terlexis (SOC WORK)	1,861	0.7
5	Martin Olav Sabo (DFL) *	174,416	72.1
	Raymond C. Gilbertson (I-R)	60,646	25.1
	T. Christopher Wright (I)	6,468	2.7
6	Gerry Sikorski (DFL) *	169,486	65.4
	Ray Ploetz (I-R)	89,209	34.4
7	Arlan Stangeland (I-R) *	121,396	54.6
	Marv Hanson (DFL)	101,011	45.4
8	James L. Oberstar (DFL) *	165,656	74.5
	Jerry Shuster (I-R)	56,630	25.5

	Vote total	Percent

MISSISSIPPI

Senate

		Vote total	Percent
	Trent Lott (R)	510,380	53.9
	Wayne Dowdy (D)	436,339	46.1

House

1	Jamie L. Whitten (D) *	137,445	78.2
	Jim Bush (R)	38,381	21.8
2	Mike Espy (D) *	112,401	64.7
	Jack Coleman (R)	59,827	34.5
	Dorothy Benford (I)	1,403	0.8
3	G. V. "Sonny" Montgomery (D) *	164,651	88.8
	Jimmie Ray Bourland (R)	20,729	11.2
4	Mike Parker (D)	110,184	54.8
	Thomas Collins (R)	88,433	44.0
	Liz Gilchrist (I)	2,446	1.2
5	Larkin Smith (R) ʰ	100,185	55.0
	Gene Taylor (D)	82,034	45.0

MISSOURI

Governor

	John Ashcroft (R) *	1,339,531	64.2
	Betty Hearnes (D)	724,919	34.8
	Mike Roberts (LIBERT)	21,467	1.0

Senate

	John C. Danforth (R) *	1,407,416	67.7
	Jay Nixon (D)	660,045	31.8
	John Guze (LIBERT)	11,410	0.5

House

1	William L. Clay (D) *	140,751	71.6
	Joseph A. Schwan (R)	53,109	27.0
	Terry Inman (LIBERT)	2,798	1.4
2	Jack Buechner (R) *	186,450	66.3
	Bob Feigenbaum (D)	91,645	32.6
	Deania Lohmann (LIBERT)	3,014	1.1
3	Richard A. Gephardt (D) *	150,205	62.8
	Mark F. "Thor" Hearne (R)	86,763	36.3
	Lloyd Sloan (LIBERT)	2,128	0.9
4	Ike Skelton (D) *	166,480	71.8
	David Eyerly (R)	65,393	28.2
5	Alan Wheat (D) *	149,166	70.3
	Mary Ellen Lobb (R)	60,453	28.5
	Mike Hurley (LIBERT)	2,520	1.2
6	E. Thomas Coleman (R) *	135,883	59.3
	Doug R. Hughes (D)	93,128	40.7
7	Melton D. "Mel" Hancock (R)	127,939	53.1
	Max E. Bacon (D)	111,244	46.2
	Rob Lurvey (LIBERT)	1,728	0.7
8	Bill Emerson (R) *	117,601	58.1
	Wayne Cryts (D)	84,801	41.9
9	Harold L. Volkmer (D) *	160,872	67.9
	Ken Dudley (R)	76,008	32.1

MONTANA

Governor

	Stan Stephens (R)	190,604	51.9
	Thomas L. Judge (D)	169,313	46.1

	Vote total	Percent
William D. Morris (LIBERT)	7,104	1.9

Senate

	Conrad Burns (R)	189,445	51.9
	John Melcher (D) *	175,809	48.1

House

1	Pat Williams (D) *	115,278	60.8
	Jim Fenlason (R)	74,405	39.2
2	Ron Marlenee (R) *	97,465	55.5
	Richard "Buck" O'Brien (D)	78,069	44.5

NEBRASKA

Senate

	Bob Kerrey (D)	378,717	56.7
	David K. Karnes (R) *	278,250	41.7
	Ernie Chambers (NA)	10,372	1.6

House

1	Doug Bereuter (R) *	146,231	66.9
	Corky Jones (D)	72,167	33.0
2	Peter Hoagland (D)	112,174	50.5
	Jerry Schenken (R)	109,193	49.1
3	Virginia Smith (R) *	170,302	79.0
	John D. Racek (D)	45,183	21.0

NEVADA

Senate

	Richard H. Bryan (D)	175,548	50.2
	Chic Hecht (R) *	161,336	46.1
	"None of these candidates"	7,242	2.1
	James Frye (LIBERT)	5,523	1.6

House

1	James Bilbray (D) *	101,764	64.0
	Lucille Lusk (R)	53,588	33.7
	Patrick O'Neill (LIBERT)	3,724	2.3
2	Barbara F. Vucanovich (R) *	105,981	57.3
	James Spoo (D)	75,163	40.6
	Kent Cromwell (LIBERT)	3,953	2.1

NEW HAMPSHIRE

Governor

	Judd Gregg (R)	267,064	60.4
	Paul McEachern (D)	172,543	39.1
	Howard Wilson Jr. (LIBERT)	2,216	0.5

House

1	Robert C. Smith (R) *	131,824	60.3
	Joseph F. Keefe (D)	86,623	39.6
2	Chuck Douglas (R)	119,742	56.8
	James W. Donchess (D)	89,677	42.5
	Roy Kendel (AM)	1,454	0.7

NEW JERSEY

Senate

	Frank R. Lautenberg (D) *	1,599,905	53.5
	Pete Dawkins (R)	1,349,937	45.2
	Joseph F. Job (I)	20,091	0.7
	Jerry Zeldin (LIBERT)	12,354	0.4
	Thomas A. Fiske (SOC WORK)	5,347	0.2

		Vote total	Percent

NEW JERSEY
House

1	James J. Florio (D) *	141,988	69.9
	Frank A. Cristaudo (R)	60,037	29.5
	Richard Bartucci (LIBERT)	1,128	0.6
2	William J. Hughes (D) *	134,505	65.7
	Kirk W. Conover (R)	67,759	33.1
	Richard A. Schindenwolf Jr. (I)	2,372	1.2
3	Frank Pallone Jr. (D)	117,024	51.6
	Joseph Azzolina (R)	107,479	47.4
	Laura Stewart (LIBERT)	2,107	0.9
4	Christopher H. Smith (R) *	155,283	65.7
	Betty Holland (D)	79,006	33.4
	Judson M. Carter (I)	1,114	0.5
	Daniel A. Maiullo Jr. (LIBERT)	791	0.3
5	Marge Roukema (R) *	175,562	75.7
	Lee Monaco (D)	54,828	23.6
	Daniel M. Karlan (LIBERT)	1,546	0.7
6	Bernard J. Dwyer (D) *	120,125	61.1
	Peter J. Sica (R)	74,824	38.1
	Joan Paltrineri (SOC WORK)	1,034	0.5
	Howard F. Schoen (LIBERT)	615	0.3
7	Matthew J. Rinaldo (R) *	153,350	74.6
	James Hely (D)	52,189	25.4
8	Robert A. Roe (D) *	96,036	100.0
	(No Republican candidate)		
9	Robert G. Torricelli (D) *	142,012	67.1
	Roger J. Lane (R)	68,363	32.3
	Richard J. Kemly (I)	1,119	0.5
10	Donald M. Payne (D)	84,681	77.4
	Michael Webb (R)	13,848	12.6
	Anthony Imperiale (I)	5,422	5.0
	Mindy Brudno (SOC WORK)	4,539	4.1
	Alvin Curtis (I)	551	0.5
	Alan Bowser (I)	432	0.4
11	Dean A. Gallo (R) *	154,654	70.5
	John C. Shaw (D)	64,773	29.5
12	Jim Courter (R) *	165,918	69.3
	Norman J. Weinstein (D)	71,596	29.9
	Stephen Friedlander (LIBERT)	2,023	0.8
13	H. James Saxton (R) *	167,470	69.5
	James B. Smith (D)	73,561	30.5
14	Frank J. Guarini (D) *	104,001	67.3
	Fred J. Theemling Jr. (R)	47,293	30.6
	John A. Jones (I)	1,346	0.9
	Christopher White (LIBERT)	1,005	0.7
	John Rummel (COM)	442	0.3
	Peter Galbo (I)	353	0.2

NEW MEXICO
Senate

	Jeff Bingaman (D) *	321,983	63.3
	Bill Valentine (R)	186,579	36.7

House

1	Steven H. Schiff (R)	89,985	50.6
	Tom Udall (D)	84,138	47.3
	Allen M. Parkman (LIBERT)	3,839	2.1

2	Joe Skeen (R) *	100,324	100.0
	(No Democratic candidate)		
3	Bill Richardson (D) *	124,938	73.1
	Cecilia M. Salazar (R)	45,954	26.9

NEW YORK
Senate

	Daniel Patrick Moynihan (D, L) *	4,048,649	67.0
	Robert R. McMillan (R, C)	1,875,784	31.1
	Adelle R. Nathanson (RTL)	64,845	1.1
	Charlene Mitchell (I)	14,770	0.2
	Lydia Bayoneta (I)	13,573	0.2
	William P. McMillen (LIBERT)	12,064	0.2
	James Harris Jr. (SOC WORK)	11,239	0.2

House

1	George J. Hochbrueckner (D) *	105,624	50.8
	Edward P. Romaine (R, C, RTL)	102,327	49.2
2	Thomas J. Downey (D) *	107,646	61.6
	Joseph Cardino Jr. (R, C, RTL)	66,972	38.4
3	Robert J. Mrazek (D) *	128,336	57.2
	Robert Previdi (R, C)	91,122	40.6
	Robert J. Considine (RTL)	3,625	1.6
	Anthony Signorelli (L)	1,223	0.5
4	Norman F. Lent (R, C) *	151,038	70.1
	Francis T. Goban (D, L)	59,479	27.6
	Margaret T. McGeary (RTL)	4,869	2.3
5	Raymond J. McGrath (R, C) *	134,881	65.1
	William G. Kelly (D)	68,930	33.2
	James A. Matier (RTL)	3,502	1.7
6	Floyd H. Flake (D, L) *	94,506	85.9
	(No Republican candidate)		
	Robert L. Brandofino (C)	15,547	14.1
7	Gary L. Ackerman (D, L) *	93,120	100.0
	(No Republican candidate)		
8	James H. Scheuer (D, L) *	100,240	100.0
	(No Republican candidate)		
9	Thomas J. Manton (D) *	72,851	100.0
	(No Republican candidate)		
10	Charles E. Schumer (D, L) *	107,056	78.4
	George S. Popielarski (R)	24,313	17.8
	Alice E. Gaffney (C)	5,119	3.8
11	Ed Towns (D, L) *	73,755	88.7
	Riaz B. Hussain (R)	7,418	8.9
	Alfred J. Hamel (C)	1,271	1.5
	Lorraine Stevens (NA)	714	0.9
12	Major R. Owens (D, L) *	74,304	93.0
	Owen Augustin (R, C)	5,582	7.0
13	Stephen J. Solarz (D, L) *	81,305	74.7
	Anthony M. Curci (R, C)	27,536	25.3
14	Guy V. Molinari (R, C, RTL) *	99,179	63.3
	Jerome X. O'Donovan (D)	57,503	36.7
15	Bill Green (R) *	107,599	61.3
	Peter G. Doukas (D)	64,425	36.7
	John B. Levitt (L)	3,459	2.0
16	Charles B. Rangel (D, R, L) *	107,620	97.1

	Vote total	Per-cent

NEW YORK

		Vote total	Per-cent
	Michael Liccione (C)	1,779	1.6
	Barbara R. Taylor (NA)	1,451	1.3
17	Ted Weiss (D, L) *	157,339	84.4
	Myrna C. Albert (R, C)	29,156	15.6
18	Robert Garcia (D, L) *	75,459	91.1
	Fred Brown (R)	5,764	6.9
	Rafael Mendez (NA)	904	1.1
	Daniel Verhoff (C)	739	0.9
19	Eliot L. Engel (D, L)	77,158	56.0
	Mario Biaggi (R) [i]	37,454	27.2
	Martin J. O'Grady (RTL)	11,271	8.2
	Robert Blumetti (C)	11,182	8.1
	Michael Zagarell (I)	678	0.5
20	Nita M. Lowey (D)	102,235	50.3
	Joseph J. DioGuardi (R, C) *	96,465	47.5
	Florence T. O'Grady (RTL)	2,932	1.4
	Henry M. Levine (L)	1,631	0.8
21	Hamilton Fish Jr. (R, C) *	150,443	74.6
	Lawrence W. Grunberger (D)	47,294	23.5
	Richard S. Curtin II (RTL)	3,870	1.9
22	Benjamin A. Gilman (R) *	144,227	70.8
	Eleanor F. Burlingham (D)	54,312	26.7
	Barbara E. Braun (RTL)	5,096	2.5
23	Michael R. McNulty (D)	145,040	61.7
	Peter M. Bakal (R, C)	89,858	38.3
24	Gerald B. H. Solomon (R, C, RTL) *	162,962	72.4
	Fred Baye (D)	62,177	27.6
25	Sherwood Boehlert (R) *	130,122	100.0
	(No Democratic candidate)		
26	David O'B. Martin (R, C) *	131,043	75.0
	Donald R. Ravenscroft (D)	43,585	25.0
27	James T. Walsh (R)	124,928	57.5
	Rosemary S. Pooler (D)	90,854	41.8
	Stephen K. Hoff (RTL)	1,644	0.7
28	Matthew F. McHugh (D) *	141,976	93.2
	(No Republican candidate)		
	Mary C. Dixon (RTL)	10,395	6.8
29	Frank Horton (R) *	132,608	68.8
	James R. Vogel (D)	51,243	26.6
	Richard G. Baxter (C)	5,688	3.0
	Donald M. Peters (RTL)	3,122	1.6
30	Louise M. Slaughter (D) *	128,364	56.9
	John D. Bouchard (R)	89,126	39.5
	Thomas D. Cook (C)	6,252	2.7
	Michael P. Flanagan (RTL)	1,970	0.9
31	Bill Paxon (R, C, RTL)	117,710	53.4
	David J. Swarts (D, L)	102,777	46.6
32	John J. LaFalce (D, L) *	133,917	72.7
	Emil K. Everett (R, C, RTL)	50,229	27.3
33	Henry J. Nowak (D, L) *	139,604	100.0
	(No Republican candidate)		
34	Amo Houghton (R, C) *	131,078	96.5
	(No Democratic candidate)		
	Ian Kelley Woodward (L)	4,797	3.5

NORTH CAROLINA

Governor

	Vote total	Per-cent
James G. Martin (R) *	1,222,338	56.1

		Vote total	Per-cent
	Robert B. Jordan III (D)	957,687	43.9

House

		Vote total	Per-cent
1	Walter B. Jones (D) *	118,027	65.2
	Howard D. Moye (R)	63,013	34.8
2	Tim Valentine (D) *	128,832	100.0
	(No Republican candidate)		
3	H. Martin Lancaster (D) *	95,323	100.0
	(No Republican candidate)		
4	David E. Price (D) *	131,896	58.0
	Tom Fetzer (R)	95,482	42.0
5	Stephen L. Neal (D) *	110,516	52.6
	Lyons Gray (R)	99,540	47.4
6	Howard Coble (R) *	116,534	62.5
	Tom Gilmore (D)	70,008	37.5
7	Charlie Rose (D) *	102,392	67.3
	George "Jerry" Thompson (R)	49,855	32.7
8	W. G. "Bill" Hefner (D) *	99,214	51.5
	Ted Blanton (R)	93,463	48.5
9	Alex McMillan (R) *	139,014	65.9
	Mark Sholander (D)	71,802	34.1
10	Cass Ballenger (R) *	112,554	61.0
	Jack L. Rhyne (D)	71,865	39.0
11	James McClure Clarke (D) *	108,436	50.4
	Charles H. Taylor (R)	106,907	49.6

NORTH DAKOTA

Governor

	Vote total	Per-cent
George Sinner (D) *	179,094	59.9
Leon Mallberg (R)	119,986	40.1

Senate

	Vote total	Per-cent
Quentin N. Burdick (D) *	171,899	59.4
Earl Strinden (R)	112,937	39.1
Kenneth C. Gardner (LIBERT)	4,334	1.5

House

		Vote total	Per-cent
AL	Byron L. Dorgan (D) *	212,583	70.9
	Steve Sydness (R)	84,475	28.1
	Kris Brekke (LIBERT)	2,924	1.0

OHIO

Senate

	Vote total	Per-cent
Howard M. Metzenbaum (D) *	2,480,038	57.0
George Voinovich (R)	1,872,716	43.0

House

		Vote total	Per-cent
1	Thomas A. Luken (D) *	117,682	56.5
	Steve Chabot (R)	90,738	43.5
2	Bill Gradison (R) *	153,162	72.3
	Chuck R. Stidham (D)	58,637	27.7
3	Tony P. Hall (D) *	141,953	76.9
	Ron Crutcher (R)	42,664	23.1
4	Michael G. Oxley (R) *	160,099	99.7
	(No Democratic candidate)		
5	Paul E. Gillmor (R)	123,838	60.7
	Tom Murray (D)	80,292	39.3
6	Bob McEwen (R) *	152,235	74.3
	Gordon R. Roberts (D)	52,635	25.7
7	Mike DeWine (R) *	142,597	73.9
	Jack Schira (D)	50,423	26.1

		Vote total	Per- cent

OHIO

8	Donald E. "Buz" Lukens (R) *	154,164	75.9
	John Griffin (D)	49,084	24.1
9	Marcy Kaptur (D) *	157,557	81.3
	Al Hawkins (R)	36,183	18.7
10	Clarence E. Miller (R) *	143,673	71.6
	John M. Buchanan (D)	56,893	28.4
11	Dennis E. Eckart (D) *	124,600	61.5
	Margaret Mueller (R)	78,028	38.5
12	John R. Kasich (R) *	154,727	79.0
	Mark P. Brown (D)	41,178	21.0
13	Don J. Pease (D) *	137,074	69.8
	Dwight Brown (R)	59,287	30.2
14	Thomas C. Sawyer (D) *	148,951	74.7
	Loretta A. Lang (R)	50,356	25.3
15	Chalmers P. Wylie (R) *	146,854	74.8
	Mark S. Froehlich (D)	49,441	25.2
16	Ralph Regula (R) *	158,824	78.6
	Melvin J. Gravely (D)	43,356	21.4
17	James A. Traficant Jr. (D) *	162,526	77.2
	Frederick W. Lenz (R)	47,929	22.8
18	Douglas Applegate (D) *	151,306	76.6
	William C. Abraham (R)	46,130	23.4
19	Edward F. Feighan (D) *	168,065	70.5
	Noel F. Roberts (R)	70,359	29.5
20	Mary Rose Oakar (D) *	146,715	82.6
	Michael Sajna (R)	30,944	17.4
21	Louis Stokes (D) *	148,388	85.7
	Franklin H. Roski (R)	24,804	14.3

OKLAHOMA

House

1	James M. Inhofe (R) *	103,458	52.6
	Kurt Glassco (D)	93,101	47.4
2	Mike Synar (D) *	136,009	64.9
	Ira Phillips (R)	73,659	35.1
3	Wes Watkins (D) *	x	x
	(No Republican candidate)		
4	Dave McCurdy (D) *	x	x
	(No Republican candidate)		
5	Mickey Edwards (R) *	139,182	72.2
	Terry J. Montgomery (D)	53,668	27.8
6	Glenn English (D) *	122,887	73.1
	Mike Brown (R)	45,239	26.9

OREGON

House

1	Les AuCoin (D) *	179,915	69.6
	Earl Molander (R)	78,626	30.4
2	Bob Smith (R) *	125,366	62.7
	Larry Tuttle (D)	74,700	37.3
3	Ron Wyden (D) *	190,684	99.4
	(No Republican candidate)		
4	Peter A. DeFazio (D) *	108,483	72.0
	Jim Howard (R)	42,220	28.0
5	Denny Smith (R) *	111,489	50.2
	Mike Kopetski (D)	110,782	49.8

		Vote total	Per- cent

PENNSYLVANIA

Senate

	John Heinz (R) *	2,901,715	66.5
	Joseph C. Vignola (D)	1,416,764	32.4
	Darcy Richardson (CON)	25,273	0.6
	Henry Haller III (LIBERT)	11,822	0.3
	Samuel Cross Jr. (POP)	6,455	0.1
	Sam Blancato (NA)	4,569	0.1

House

1	Thomas M. Foglietta (D) *	128,076	76.3
	William J. O'Brien (R)	39,749	23.7
2	William H. Gray III (D) *	184,322	93.7
	Richard L. Harsch (R)	12,365	6.3
3	Robert A. Borski (D) *	135,590	63.2
	Mark Matthews (R)	78,909	36.8
4	Joe Kolter (D) *	124,041	69.8
	Gordon R. Johnston (R)	52,402	29.5
	Erich L. Kaltenhauser (POP)	1,256	0.7
5	Richard T. Schulze (R) *	153,453	78.2
	Donald A. Hadley (D)	42,758	21.8
6	Gus Yatron (D) *	114,119	63.1
	James R. Erwin (R)	65,278	36.1
	Louis R. Perugini Jr. (I)	1,348	0.7
7	Curt Weldon (R) *	155,387	67.8
	David Landau (D)	73,745	32.2
8	Peter H. Kostmayer (D) *	128,153	56.8
	Ed Howard (R)	93,648	41.5
	Donald C. Ernsberger (LIBERT)	3,765	1.7
9	Bud Shuster (R, D) *	158,702	100.0
10	Joseph M. McDade (R) *	140,096	73.2
	Robert C. Cordaro (D)	51,179	26.8
11	Paul E. Kanjorski (D) *	120,706	100.0
	(No Republican candidate)		
12	John P. Murtha (D) *	133,081	100.0
	(No Republican candidate)		
13	Lawrence Coughlin (R) *	152,191	66.6
	Bernard Tomkin (D)	76,424	33.4
14	William J. Coyne (D) *	135,181	78.6
	Richard Edward Caligiuri (R)	36,719	21.4
15	Don Ritter (R) *	106,951	57.5
	Ed Reibman (D)	79,127	42.5
16	Robert S. Walker (R) *	136,944	74.0
	Ernest Eric Guyll (D)	48,169	26.0
17	George W. Gekas (R, D) *	166,289	100.0
18	Doug Walgren (D) *	136,924	62.7
	John A. Newman (R)	80,975	37.0
	James J. Bailey (POP)	589	0.3
19	Bill Goodling (R) *	145,381	77.2
	Paul E. Ritchey (D)	42,819	22.8
20	Joseph M. Gaydos (D) *	137,472	98.5
	(No Republican candidate)		
	Richard W. Wilson (POP)	2,144	1.5
21	Tom Ridge (R) *	141,832	78.7
	George R. H. Elder (D)	38,288	21.3
22	Austin J. Murphy (D) *	123,428	72.4
	William Hodgkiss (R)	47,039	27.6
23	William F. Clinger Jr. (R) *	105,575	62.0
	Howard Shakespeare (D)	63,476	37.3
	William Smolik (POP)	1,109	0.7

		Vote total	Per-cent

RHODE ISLAND
Governor

	Vote total	Per-cent
Edward D. DiPrete (R) *	203,550	50.8
Bruce Sundlun (D)	196,936	49.2

Senate

	Vote total	Per-cent
John H. Chafee (R) *	217,273	54.6
Richard A. Licht (D)	180,717	45.4

House

		Vote total	Per-cent
1	Ronald K. Machtley (R)	105,506	55.6
	Fernand J. St Germain (D) *	84,141	44.4
2	Claudine Schneider (R) *	145,218	72.1
	Ruth S. Morgenthau (D)	56,129	27.9

SOUTH CAROLINA
House

		Vote total	Per-cent
1	Arthur Ravenel Jr. (R) *	101,572	63.8
	Wheeler Tillman (D)	57,691	36.2
2	Floyd D. Spence (R) *	94,960	52.8
	Jim Leventis (D)	83,978	46.6
	Geb Sommer (LIBERT)	1,061	0.6
3	Butler Derrick (D) *	89,071	53.7
	Henry S. Jordan (R)	75,571	45.6
	John B. Heaton (LIBERT)	1,183	0.7
4	Liz J. Patterson (D) *	90,234	52.2
	Knox White (R)	82,793	47.8
5	John M. Spratt Jr. (D) *	107,959	69.8
	Robert K. "Bob" Carley (R)	46,622	30.2
6	Robin Tallon (D) *	120,719	76.1
	Robert Cunningham Sr. (R)	37,958	23.9

SOUTH DAKOTA
House

		Vote total	Per-cent
AL	Tim Johnson (D) *	223,759	71.7
	David Volk (R)	88,157	28.3

TENNESSEE
Senate

	Vote total	Per-cent
Jim Sasser (D) *	1,020,061	65.1
Bill Andersen (R)	541,033	34.5
Khalil-Ullah Al-Muhaymin (I)	6,042	0.4

House

		Vote total	Per-cent
1	James H. Quillen (R) *	119,526	80.2
	Sidney S. Smith (D)	29,469	19.8
2	John J. "Jimmy" Duncan Jr. (R)	99,631	56.2
	Dudley W. Taylor (D)	77,540	43.8
3	Marilyn Lloyd (D) *	108,264	57.4
	Harold L. Coker (R)	80,372	42.6
4	Jim Cooper (D) *	94,129	100.0
	(No Republican candidate)		
5	Bob Clement (D) *	155,068	100.0
	(No Republican candidate)		
6	Bart Gordon (D) *	123,652	76.5
	Wallace Embry (R)	38,033	23.5
7	Don Sundquist (R) *	142,025	80.1
	Ken Bloodworth (D)	35,237	19.9

		Vote total	Per-cent
8	John Tanner (D)	94,571	62.4
	Ed Bryant (R)	56,893	37.6
9	Harold E. Ford (D) *	126,280	81.6
	(No Republican candidate)		
	Isaac Richmond (I)	28,522	18.4

TEXAS
Senate

	Vote total	Per-cent
Lloyd Bentsen (D) *	3,149,806	59.2
Beau Boulter (R)	2,129,228	40.0
Jeff Daiell (LIBERT)	43,989	0.8

House

		Vote total	Per-cent
1	Jim Chapman (D) *	122,566	62.2
	Horace McQueen (R)	74,357	37.8
2	Charles Wilson (D) *	145,614	87.7
	(No Republican candidate)		
	Gary W. Nelson (LIBERT)	20,475	12.3
3	Steve Bartlett (R) *	227,882	81.8
	Blake Cowden (D)	50,627	18.2
4	Ralph M. Hall (D) *	139,379	66.4
	Randy Sutton (R)	67,337	32.1
	Melanie A. Dunn (LIBERT)	3,152	1.5
5	John Bryant (D) *	95,376	60.7
	Lon Williams (R)	59,877	38.1
	Ken Ashby (LIBERT)	1,786	1.1
6	Joe L. Barton (R) *	164,692	67.6
	N. P. "Pat" Kendrick (D)	78,786	32.4
7	Bill Archer (R) *	185,203	79.1
	Diane Richards (D)	48,824	20.9
8	Jack Fields (R) *	90,503	100.0
	(No Democratic candidate)		
9	Jack Brooks (D) *	137,270	100.0
	(No Republican candidate)		
10	J. J. "Jake" Pickle (D) *	232,213	93.4
	(No Republican candidate)		
	Vincent J. May (LIBERT)	16,281	6.6
11	Marvin Leath (D) *	134,207	95.4
	(No Republican candidate)		
	Frederick M. King (LIBERT)	6,533	4.6
12	Jim Wright (D) * j	135,459	99.3
	(No Republican candidate)		
13	Bill Sarpalius (D)	98,345	52.5
	Larry S. Milner (R)	89,105	47.5
14	Greg H. Laughlin (D)	111,395	53.2
	Mac Sweeney (R) *	96,042	45.9
	Don Kelley (LIBERT)	1,779	0.9
15	E. "Kika" de la Garza (D) *	93,672	93.9
	(No Republican candidate)		
	Gloria Joyce Hendrix (LIBERT)	6,133	6.1
16	Ronald D. Coleman (D) *	104,514	100.0
	(No Republican candidate)		
17	Charles W. Stenholm (D) *	149,064	100.0
	(No Republican candidate)		
18	Mickey Leland (D) * k	94,408	92.9
	(No Republican candidate)		

		Vote total	Per-cent

TEXAS

		Vote total	Per-cent
	J. Alejandro Snead (LIBERT)	7,235	7.1
19	Larry Combest (R) *	113,068	67.7
	Gerald McCathern (D)	53,932	32.3
20	Henry B. Gonzalez (D) *	94,527	70.7
	Lee Trevino (R)	36,801	27.5
	Theresa S. Doyle (LIBERT)	2,368	1.8
21	Lamar Smith (R) *	203,989	93.2
	(No Democratic candidate)		
	James A. Robinson (LIBERT)	14,801	6.8
22	Tom DeLay (R) *	125,733	67.4
	Wayne Walker (D)	58,471	31.4
	George Harper (LIBERT)	2,276	1.2
23	Albert G. Bustamante (D) *	116,423	64.5
	Jerry Gonzales (R)	60,559	33.6
	Tony R. Garza (LIBERT)	3,448	1.9
24	Martin Frost (D) *	135,794	92.6
	(No Republican candidate)		
	Leo Sadovy (LIBERT)	10,841	7.4
25	Michael A. Andrews (D) *	113,499	71.4
	George H. Loefflor Jr. (R)	44,043	27.7
	Kevin Southwick (LIBERT)	1,494	0.9
26	Dick Armey (R) *	194,944	69.3
	Jo Ann Reyes (D)	86,490	30.7
27	Solomon P. Ortiz (D) *	105,085	100.0
	(No Republican candidate)		

UTAH

Governor

		Vote total	Per-cent
	Norman H. Bangerter (R) *	260,462	40.1
	Ted Wilson (D)	249,321	38.4
	Merrill Cook (I)	136,651	21.0
	Kitty K. Burton (LIBERT)	1,661	0.3
	Arly H. Pedersen (AM)	1,019	0.2

Senate

		Vote total	Per-cent
	Orrin G. Hatch (R) *	430,089	67.1
	Brian H. Moss (D)	203,364	31.7
	Robert J. Smith (AM)	6,016	0.9
	William M. Arth (SOC WORK)	1,233	0.2

House

		Vote total	Per-cent
1	James V. Hansen (R) *	130,893	59.8
	Gunn McKay (D)	87,976	40.2
2	Wayne Owens (D) *	112,129	57.4
	Richard Snelgrove (R)	80,212	41.1
	Michael Lee (LIBERT)	2,997	1.5
3	Howard C. Nielson (R) *	129,951	66.8
	Robert W. Stringham (D)	60,018	30.9
	E. Dean Christensen (AM)	3,285	1.7
	Judy Stranahan (SOC WORK)	1,207	0.6

VERMONT

Governor

		Vote total	Per-cent
	Madeleine M. Kunin (D) *	134,438	55.4
	Michael Bernhardt (R)	105,191	43.3
	Richard F. Gottlieb (LU)	2,919	1.2

Senate

		Vote total	Per-cent
	James M. Jeffords (R)	163,183	67.9

		Vote total	Per-cent
	William Gray (D)	71,460	29.8
	Jerry Levy (I)	2,533	1.0
	King Milne (I)	2,424	1.0

House

		Vote total	Per-cent
AL	Peter Smith (R)	98,937	41.2
	Bernard Sanders (I)	90,026	37.5
	Paul N. Poirier (D)	45,330	18.9
	Jim Hedbor (LIBERT)	3,110	1.3
	Peter Diamondstone (LU)	1,455	0.6
	Morris Earle (I)	1,070	0.4

VIRGINIA

Senate

		Vote total	Per-cent
	Charles S. Robb (D)	1,474,086	71.2
	Maurice A. Dawkins (R)	593,652	28.7

House

		Vote total	Per-cent
1	Herbert H. Bateman (R) *	135,937	73.3
	James S. Ellenson (D)	49,614	26.7
2	Owen B. Pickett (D) *	106,666	60.5
	Jerry R. Curry (R)	62,564	35.5
	Stephen P. Shao (I)	4,255	2.4
	Robert A. Smith (I)	2,691	1.5
3	Thomas J. Bliley Jr. (R) *	187,354	99.7
	(No Democratic candidate)		
4	Norman Sisisky (D) *	134,786	99.9
	(No Republican candidate)		
5	Lewis F. Payne Jr. (D) *	97,242	54.2
	Charles Hawkins (R)	78,396	43.7
	J. F. "Frank" Cole (I)	3,792	2.1
6	Jim Olin (D) *	118,369	63.9
	Charles E. Judd (R)	66,935	36.1
7	D. French Slaughter Jr. (R) *	136,988	99.6
	(No Democratic candidate)		
8	Stan Parris (R) *	154,761	62.3
	David G. Brickley (D)	93,561	37.7
9	Rick Boucher (D) *	113,309	63.4
	John C. Brown (R)	65,410	36.6
10	Frank R. Wolf (R) *	188,550	68.1
	Robert L. Weinberg (D)	88,284	31.9

WASHINGTON

Governor

		Vote total	Per-cent
	Booth Gardner (D) *	1,166,448	62.2
	Bob Williams (R)	708,481	37.8

Senate

		Vote total	Per-cent
	Slade Gorton (R)	944,359	51.1
	Mike Lowry (D)	904,183	48.9

House

		Vote total	Per-cent
1	John Miller (R) *	152,265	55.4
	Reese Lindquist (D)	122,646	44.6
2	Al Swift (D) *	175,191	100.0
	(No Republican candidate)		
3	Jolene Unsoeld (D)	109,412	50.1
	Bill Wight (R)	108,794	49.9
4	Sid Morrison (R) *	142,938	74.5
	J. Richard Golob (D)	48,850	25.5
5	Thomas S. Foley (D) *	160,654	76.4

		Vote total	Per-cent				Vote total	Per-cent

WASHINGTON

		Vote total	Per-cent
	Marlyn A. Derby (R)	49,657	23.6
6	Norm Dicks (D) *	125,904	67.6
	Kevin P. Cook (R)	60,346	32.4
7	Jim McDermott (D)	173,809	76.3
	Robert Edwards (R)	53,902	23.7
8	Rod Chandler (R) *	174,942	70.9
	Jim Kean (D)	71,920	29.1

WEST VIRGINIA

Governor

	Vote total	Per-cent
Gaston Caperton (D)	382,421	58.9
Arch A. Moore Jr. (R) *	267,172	41.1

Senate

	Vote total	Per-cent
Robert C. Byrd (D) *	410,983	64.8
M. Jay Wolfe (R)	223,564	35.2

House

		Vote total	Per-cent
1	Alan B. Mollohan (D) *	119,256	74.5
	Howard Tuck (R)	40,732	25.5
2	Harley O. Staggers Jr. (D) *	118,356	100.0
	(No Republican candidate)		
3	Bob Wise (D) *	120,192	74.3
	Paul W. Hart (R)	41,478	25.7
4	Nick J. Rahall II (D) *	78,812	61.3
	Marianne R. Brewster (R)	49,753	38.7

WISCONSIN

Senate

	Vote total	Per-cent
Herb Kohl (D)	1,128,625	52.1
Susan Engeleiter (R)	1,030,440	47.5
George W. Zaehringer (I)	3,965	0.2

		Vote total	Per-cent
	Patricia Grogan (I)	3,029	0.1
	Arlyn F. Wollenburg (R)	1,198	0.1

House

		Vote total	Per-cent
1	Les Aspin (D) *	158,552	76.2
	Bernie Weaver (R)	49,620	23.8
2	Robert W. Kastenmeier (D) *	151,501	58.5
	Ann Haney (R)	107,457	41.5
3	Steve Gunderson (R) *	157,513	68.3
	Karl E. Krueger (D)	72,935	31.6
4	Gerald D. Kleczka (D) *	177,283	99.7
	(No Republican candidate)		
5	Jim Moody (D) *	140,518	64.1
	Helen Barnhill (R)	78,307	35.7
6	Thomas E. Petri (R) *	165,923	74.2
	Joe Garrett (D)	57,552	25.8
7	David R. Obey (D) *	142,197	61.8
	Kevin Hermening (R)	86,077	37.4
	John Thomas Alan Duelge (I)	1,893	0.8
8	Toby Roth (R) *	167,275	69.7
	Robert Baron (D)	72,708	30.3
9	F. James Sensenbrenner Jr. (R) *	185,093	74.9
	Tom Hickey (D)	62,003	25.1

WYOMING

Senate

	Vote total	Per-cent
Malcolm Wallop (R) *	91,143	50.4
John Vinich (D)	89,821	49.6

House

		Vote total	Per-cent
AL	Dick Cheney (R) * l	118,350	66.6
	Bryan Sharratt (D)	56,527	31.8
	Craig Alan McCune (LIBERT)	1,906	1.1
	Al Hamburg (NA)	868	0.5

a. Nichols died December 13, 1988. Democrat Glenn Browder won a special election April 4, 1989, to fill his seat.

b. Robinson switched from the Democratic to the Republican party in July 1989.

c. Coelho resigned June 15, 1989. Democrat Gary Condit won a special election September 12, 1989, to fill his seat.

d. Grant switched from the Democratic to the Republican party in February 1989.

e. Pepper died May 30, 1989. Republican Ileana Ros-Lehtinen won a special election August 29, 1989, to replace him.

f. Coats was appointed January 3, 1989, to fill the Senate seat vacated by Dan Quayle, who was elected vice president in 1988. A special election was to be held in 1990 to fill the remaining two years of Quayle's term.

g. Long won a special election March 28, 1989, to win the House seat vacated by Coats.

h. Smith died August 13, 1989. When no candidate received a

majority of the vote in a nonpartisan special election held October 3, 1989, the two top finishers, Gene Taylor (D) and Tom Anderson, Jr. (R), were forced into a runoff October 17. Taylor won the seat.

i. Biaggi announced his resignation August 5, 1988, too late to remove himself from the Republican ballot. He did not campaign.

j. Wright resigned June 30, 1989. Preston M. "Pete" Geren won a runoff election September 12, 1989, to replace him. The runoff was forced when none of the eight candidates won a majority in a special election August 12.

k. Leland died August 7, 1989. A special election was to be held November 7, 1989, to fill his seat. Under Texas law, candidates of all parties were to run on a single ballot, with the top two finishers competing in a runoff if no one obtained a majority.

l. Cheney resigned March 17, 1989, to become secretary of defense. Republican Craig Thomas won a special election April 26, 1989, to succeed him.

Off-year and Special Elections, 1985-1989

This list gives the official vote returns for off-year gubernatorial elections and House special elections from 1985, after *Congressional Quarterly's Guide to U.S. Elections,* 2d edition, was published, through October 1989.

These data were gathered from figures supplied by each state's election agency and from *America Votes* 17

(1987) and 18 (1989), compiled by Richard M. Scammon and Alice V. McGillivray and published by Congressional Quarterly Inc. Other sources were the Federal Election Commission and Congressional Quarterly. The box shows party designation symbols. Because of rounding and because scattered write-in votes are not listed, percentages do not always add to 100.

		Vote total	Percent
NEW JERSEY			
1985 Governor			
	Thomas H. Kean (R)	1,372,631	70.3
	Peter Shapiro (D)	578,402	29.7
VIRGINIA			
1985 Governor			
	Gerald Baliles (D)	741,438	55.2
	Wyatt B. Durrette (R)	601,652	44.8
HAWAII			
1986 House Special			
1 [a]	Neil Abercrombie (D)	42,031	29.9
	Patricia Saiki (R)	41,067	29.2
	Mufi Hannemann (D)	39,800	28.3
	Steve Cobb (D)	16,721	11.9
	Louis Agard (D)	566	0.4
	Blase Harris (NONPART)	460	0.3
NEW YORK			
1986 House Special			
6 [b]	Alton R. Waldon Jr. (D)	12,654	31.0
	Floyd H. Flake (U)	12,376	30.3
	Richard Dietl (R, C) [c]	8,700	21.3
	Kevin McCabe (GOOD GOV)	3,738	9.2
	Andrew Jenkins (L)	3,323	8.1
NORTH CAROLINA			
1986 House Special			
10 [d]	Cass Ballenger (R)	82,973	57.5
	Lester D. Roark (D)	61,205	42.5
CALIFORNIA			
1987 House Special			
5 [e]	Nancy Pelosi (D)	46,428	63.3
	Harriet Ross (R)	22,478	30.7
	Karen Edwards (I)	1,602	2.2
	Theodore A. Zuur (PFP)	1,105	1.5
	Sam Grove (LIBERT)	1,007	1.3

		Vote total	Percent
	Cathy Sedwick (I)	659	0.9
CONNECTICUT			
1987 House Special			
4 [f]	Christopher Shays (R)	50,518	57.2
	Christine M. Niedermeier (D)	37,293	42.2
	Nicholas J. Tarzia (AIDS)	524	0.5
KENTUCKY			
1987 Governor			
	Wallace Wilkinson (D)	504,367	64.9
	John Harper (R)	273,035	35.1
LOUISIANA			
1987 Governor [g]			
	Buddy Roemer (D)	516,078	33.1
	Edwin W. Edwards (D)	437,801	28.1
	Bob Livingston (R)	287,780	18.5
	W. J. "Billy" Tauzin (D)	154,079	9.9
	Jim Brown (D)	138,223	8.9
	Speedy O. Long (D)	18,738	1.2
	Earl J. Amedee (D)	3,767	0.2
	Ken Lewis (D)	2,264	0.1
MISSISSIPPI			
1987 Governor			
	Ray Mabus (D)	387,346	53.8
	Jack Reed (R)	332,985	46.3

ABBREVIATIONS FOR PARTY DESIGNATIONS

AIDS	War Against AIDS	*LIBERT*	Libertarian
C	Conservative	*NONPART*	Nonpartisan
D	Democratic	*PFP*	Peace and Freedom
GOOD GOV	Good Government		
I	Independent	*·R*	Republican
		U	Unity

		Vote total	Per-cent			Vote total	Per-cent

ILLINOIS

1988 House Special

21 [h]	Jerry F. Costello (D)	33,144	51.5
	Robert H. Gaffner (R)	31,257	48.5

LOUISIANA

1988 House Special

4 [i]	Jim McCrery (R)	63,590	50.5
	Foster Campbell (D)	62,214	49.5

NEW JERSEY

1988 House Special

3 [j]	Frank Pallone (D)	116,988	52.0
	Joseph Azzolina (R)	106,489	47.3
	Laura Stewart (LIB)	1,713	0.8

TENNESSEE

1988 House Special

2 [k]	John J. Duncan Jr. (R)	92,929	56.1
	Dudley W. Taylor (D)	70,576	42.6
	Charles West (I)	2,114	1.2

1988 House Special

5 [l]	Bob Clement (D)	56,323	62.2
	Terry Holcomb (R)	32,847	36.3
	Suzanne Stewart (I)	685	0.8
	Joe Driscoll (I)	601	0.7

VIRGINIA

1988 House Special

5 [m]	L. F. Payne (D)	55,469	59.3
	Linda Arey (R)	38,063	40.7

ALABAMA

1989 House Special

3 [n]	Glen Browder (D)	47,229	65.4
	John Rice (R)	25,008	34.6

CALIFORNIA

1989 House Special

15 [o,p]	Gary Condit (D)	49,948	57.1
	Clare Berryhill (R)	30,635	35.0
	Robert Weimer (R)	2,879	3.3
	Cliff Burris (R)	2,331	2.7
	Roy Shrimp (LIBERT)	768	0.9
	Dave Williams (R)	365	0.4

FLORIDA

1989 House Special

18 [q]	Ileana Ros-Lehtinen (R)	49,298	53.3
	Gerald F. Richman (D)	43,274	46.7

INDIANA

1989 House Special

4 [r]	Jill Long (D)	65,272	50.7
	Dan Heath (R)	63,494	49.3

MISSISSIPPI

1989 House Special

5 [s]	Gene Taylor (D)	83,093	65.2
	Tom Anderson Jr. (R)	44,430	34.8

TEXAS

1989 House Special

12 [t]	Preston M. "Pete" Geren (D)	40,210	51.0
	Bob Lanier (R)	38,590	49.0

WYOMING

1989 House Special

AL [u]	Craig Thomas (R)	74,258	52.5
	John P. Vinch (D)	60,821	43.0
	Craig Alan McCune (LIBERT)	5,921	4.2
	Daniel Johnson (I)	500	0.3

a. Abercrombie was elected to fill the unexpired term of Cecil Heftel (D), who resigned July 11, 1986, to run for governor.

b. Waldon was elected to fill the the unexpired term of Joseph P. Addabbo (D), who died April 10, 1986.

c. Dietl received 6,502 votes as the Republican candidate and 2,198 as the Conservative candidate.

d. Ballenger was elected to fill the unexpired term of James T. Broyhill (R), who resigned in July 1986, when he was appointed to fill the Senate vacancy caused by the death of Sen. John P. East. Broyhill was defeated in a special Senate election in November 1986. See 1986 Senate election returns (p. 240).

e. Pelosi was elected to fill the unexpired term of Sala Burton (D), who died February 1, 1987.

f. Shays was elected to fill the unexpired term of Stewart B. McKinney (R), who died May 7, 1987.

g. Louisiana holds an open primary election with candidates from all parties running on the same ballot. Any candidate who receives a majority is elected. If no candidate receives 50 percent of the vote, a runoff election between the two top finishers, without regard to party affiliation, is held in November. In 1987 incumbent governor Edwards withdrew after the primary, and no runoff

election was held in November.

h. Costello was elected to fill the unexpired term of Melvin Price (D), who died April 22, 1988.

i. McCrery was elected to fill the unexpired term of Buddy Roemer (D), who resigned March 14, 1988, to become governor.

j. Pallone was elected to fill the unexpired term of James J. Howard (D), who died March 25, 1988.

k. Duncan was elected to fill the unexpired term of his father, John J. Duncan (R), who died June 21, 1988.

l. Clement was elected to fill the unexpired term of Bill Boner (D), who resigned October 5, 1987, after being elected mayor of Nashville.

m. Payne was elected to fill the unexpired term of W. C. Daniel (D), who died January 23, 1988.

n. Browder was elected to fill the unexpired term of Bill Nichols (D), who died December 13, 1988.

o. Condit was elected to fill the unexpired term of Tony Coelho (D), who resigned June 15, 1989.

p. Chris Patterakis (R) and Jack McCoy (R) had withdrawn from the race, but their names remained on the ballot. They took a total of 558 votes (0.7 percent).

q. Ros-Lehtinen was elected to fill the unexpired term of Claude Pepper (D), who died May 30, 1989.

r. Long was elected to fill the unexpired term of Daniel R. Coats (R), who resigned in January 1989 when he was appointed to the Senate to fill Dan Quayle's seat.

s. Taylor was elected to fill the unexpired term of Larkin Smith (R), who died August 13, 1989.

t. Geren was elected to fill the unexpired term of Jim Wright (D), who resigned June 30, 1989.

u. Thomas was elected to fill the unexpired term of Dick Cheney (R), who resigned March 17, 1989, to become defense secretary.

Senate Primary Returns, 1986-1988

Following are 1986, 1987, and 1988 Senate primary returns. The major source for this section was the *America Votes* series, compiled biennially by Richard M. Scammon and Alice V. McGillivray and published since 1966 by Congressional Quarterly Inc. Other sources were the returns obtained by Congressional Quarterly after each Senate election. In cases of discrepancies the *America Votes* figures were used. Candidates are listed only if they received 5 percent or more of the vote. Percentages may not equal 100 because of rounding. Where no primary is indicated for a year in which a state elected a senator, it generally means that party conventions chose the nominees.

Year	Candidates	Votes	Percent

ALABAMA
CLASS 3
1986
Republican Primary

	Votes	Percent
Jeremiah Denton (R)	29,805	88.5
Richard W. Vickers (R)	3,854	11.5

Democratic Primary

	Votes	Percent
Richard C. Shelby (D)	420,155	51.3
James B. Allen, Jr. (D)	284,206	34.7
Ted McLaughlin (D)	70,784	8.6
Others	43,445	5.1

ALASKA[a]
CLASS 3
1986
Republican Primary

	Votes	Percent
Frank H. Murkowski (R)	Unopposed	100.0

Democratic Primary

	Votes	Percent
Glenn Olds (D)	36,995	75.0
Bill Barnes (D)	4,871	9.9
Dave Carlson (D)	4,211	8.5
Others	3,263	6.6

Libertarian Primary

	Votes	Percent
Chuck House (LIBERT)	Unopposed	100.0

ARIZONA
CLASS 3
1986
Republican Primary

	Votes	Percent
John McCain (R)	Unopposed	100.0

Democratic Primary

	Votes	Percent
Richard Kimball (D)	Unopposed	100.0

CLASS 1
1988
Republican Primary

	Votes	Percent
Keith DeGreen (R)	Unopposed	100.0

Democratic Primary

	Votes	Percent
Dennis DeConcini (D)	Unopposed	100.0

Libertarian Primary [b]

	Votes	Percent
Rick Tompkins (LIBERT)	Unopposed	100.0

New Alliance Primary [c]

	Votes	Percent
Ed Finkelstein (NA)	Unopposed	100.0

ARKANSAS
CLASS 3
1986
Republican Primary

	Votes	Percent
Asa Hutchinson (R)	Unopposed	100.0

Democratic Primary

	Votes	Percent
Dale Bumpers (D)	Unopposed	100.0

CALIFORNIA
CLASS 3
1986
Republican Primary

	Votes	Percent
Ed Zschau (R)	737,384	37.1
Bruce Herschenson (R)	587,852	29.6
Michael D. Antonovich (R)	180,010	9.1
Bobbi Fiedler (R)	143,032	7.2
Ed Davis (R)	130,309	6.6
Others	207,787	10.5

Democratic Primary

	Votes	Percent
Alan Cranston (D)	1,807,242	80.7
Charles Greene (D)	165,594	7.4
John H. Abbott (D)	124,218	5.5
Others	125,293	5.6

American Independent Primary

	Votes	Percent
Edward B. Vallen (AMI)	Unopposed	100.0

Peace and Freedom Primary

	Votes	Percent
Paul Kangas (PFP)	2,495	51.6
Lenni Brenner (PFP)	2,344	48.4

Libertarian Primary

	Votes	Percent
Breck McKinley (LIBERT)	Unopposed	100.0

Year	Candidates	Votes	Per-cent

CALIFORNIA
CLASS 1
1988

Republican Primary

Pete Wilson (R)	Unopposed	100.0

Democratic Primary

Leo T. McCarthy (D)	2,367,067	81.7
John H. Abbott (D)	220,331	7.6
Robert J. Banuelos (D)	163,882	5.7
Charles Greene (D)	146,307	5.0

American Independent Primary

Merton D. Short (AMI)	Unopposed	100.0

Libertarian Primary

Jack Dean (LIBERT)	Unopposed	100.0

Peace and Freedom Primary

M. Elizabeth Munoz (PFP)	3,701	58.5
Gloria Garcia (PFP)	2,623	41.5

COLORADO
CLASS 3
1986

Republican Primary

Ken Kramer (R)	Unopposed	100.0

Democratic Primary

Timothy E. Wirth (D)	Unopposed	100.0

DELAWARE
CLASS 1
1988

Republican Primary

William V. Roth (R)	Unopposed	100.0

Democratic Primary [d]

S. B. Woo (D)	20,225	50.0
Samuel S. Beard (D)	20,154	50.0

FLORIDA
CLASS 3
1986

Republican Primary

Paula Hawkins (R)	491,953	88.7
Jon L. Shudlick (R)	62,474	11.3

Democratic Primary

Robert Graham (D)	851,586	85.0
Robert P. Kunst (D)	149,797	15.0

CLASS 1
1988

Republican Primary

Connie Mack (R)	405,296	61.8
Robert W. Merkle (R)	250,730	38.2

Democratic Primary

Bill Gunter (D)	383,721	38.0
Buddy McKay (D)	263,946	26.1
Dan Mica (D)	179,524	17.8
Patricia Prank (D)	119,277	11.8
Claude R. Kirk (D)	51,387	5.0

Democratic Runoff

Buddy McKay (D)	369,266	52.0
Bill Gunter (D)	340,918	48.0

GEORGIA
CLASS 3
1986

Republican Primary

Mack Mattingly (R)	74,743	95.0
Others	3,911	5.0

Democratic Primary

Wyche Fowler (D)	314,787	50.2
Hamilton Jordan (D)	196,307	31.3
John D. Russell (D)	100,881	16.1

HAWAII
CLASS 3
1986

Republican Primary

Frank Hutchinson (R)	20,375	67.7
Marvin Franklin (R)	9,714	32.3

Democratic Primary

Daniel K. Inouye (D)	Unopposed	100.0

Nonpartisan Primary

Elizabeth A. P. Stone (NONPART) [e]	Unopposed	100.0

CLASS 1
1988

Republican Primary

Maria M. Hustace (R)	18,124	48.7
Leonard Mednick (R)	13,590	36.4
Susanne Sydney (R)	5,526	14.8

Democratic Primary

Spark M. Matsunaga (D)	180,853	86.9
Robert Zimmerman (D)	27,360	13.1

Libertarian Primary

Ken Schoolland (LIBERT)	Unopposed	100.0

IDAHO
CLASS 3
1986

Republican Primary

Steven D. Symms (R)	Unopposed	100.0

Democratic Primary

John V. Evans (D)	Unopposed	100.0

ILLINOIS
CLASS 3
1986

Republican Primary

Judy Koehler (R)	266,214	55.0

Year	Candidates	Votes	Percent		Year	Candidates	Votes	Percent

ILLINOIS

George A. Ranney (R)   217,720   45.0

Democratic Primary

Alan J. Dixon (D)   720,571   84.8
Sheila Jones (D)   129,474   15.2

INDIANA

CLASS 3
1986

Republican Primary

Dan Quayle (R)   Unopposed   100.0

Democratic Primary

Jill L. Long (D)   258,085   73.5
Georgia D. Irey (D)   93,079   26.5

CLASS 1
1988

Republican Primary

Richard G. Lugar (R)   Unopposed   100.0

Democratic Primary

Jack Wickes (D)   Unopposed   100.0

IOWA

CLASS 3
1986

Republican Primary

Charles E. Grassley (R)   Unopposed   100.0

Democratic Primary

John P. Roehrick (D)   88,347   83.8
Juan Cortez (D)   16,987   16.1

KANSAS

CLASS 3
1986

Republican Primary

Robert Dole (R)   228,301   84.4
Shirley J. A. Landis (R)   42,237   15.6

Democratic Primary

Guy MacDonald (D)   31,942   27.7
Darrell T. Ringer (D)   30,483   26.4
W. H. Addington (D)   21,082   18.3
Lionel Kunst (D)   18,795   16.3
Jim Oyler (D)   13,201   11.4

KENTUCKY

CLASS 3
1986

Republican Primary

Jackson M. Andrews (R)   16,211   39.0
Carl W. Brown (R)   9,724   23.3
Tommy Klein (R)   8,595   20.6
Thurman J. Hamlin (R)   7,062   17.0

Senate's Three Classes

The Senate is divided into three classes, or groups, of members. A member's class depends on the year in which he or she is elected. Article I, Section 3, Paragraph 2, of the Constitution, relating to the classification of senators in the first and succeeding Congresses, provides that "Immediately after they shall be assembled in consequence of the first election, they shall be divided as equally as may be into three classes. The seats of the Senators of the first class shall be vacated at the expiration of the second year, of the second class at the expiration of the fourth year and of the third class at the expiration of the sixth year, so that one-third may be chosen every second year. . . ."

Thus senators belonging to class 1 began their regular terms in the years 1789, 1791, 1797, 1803, and so forth, continuing through the present day to 1971, 1977, 1983, and 1989, and coming up for reelection in 1994. Senators belonging to class 2 began their regular terms in 1789, 1793, 1799, 1805, and so forth, continuing through the present day to 1973, 1979, and 1985, and will be up for election in 1990. And senators belonging to class 3 began their regular terms in 1789, 1795, 1801, 1807, and so forth, continuing through the present day to 1975, 1981, 1987, and coming up for reelection in 1992.

Democratic Primary

Wendell H. Ford (D)   Unopposed   100.0

LOUISIANA[f]

CLASS 3
1986

Open Primary

W. Henson Moore (R)   529,433   44.2
John B. Breaux (D)   447,328   37.3
Samuel B. Nunez (D)   73,505   6.1
Others   146,975   12.3

MAINE

CLASS 1
1988

Republican Primary

Jaspar S. Wyman (R)   Unopposed   100.0

Democratic Primary

George J. Mitchell (D)   Unopposed   100.0

MARYLAND

CLASS 3
1986

Republican Primary

Linda Chavez (R)   100,888   73.1

Year	Candidates	Votes	Percent	Year	Candidates	Votes	Percent

MARYLAND

| | Michael Schaefer (R) | 16,902 | 12.2 |
| | Others | 20,284 | 14.7 |

Democratic Primary

	Barbara A. Mikulski (D)	307,876	49.5
	Michael D. Barnes (D)	195,086	31.4
	Harry Hughes (D)	88,908	14.3
	Others	30,054	5.0

CLASS 1
1988

Republican Primary [g]

	Thomas L. Blair (R)	68,268	45.6
	James G. Bennett (R)	19,720	13.2
	Patrick L. McDonough (R)	16,305	10.9
	E. Robert Zarwell (R)	10,725	7.2
	Albert Ceccone (R)	9,601	6.4
	John C. Webb (R)	8,405	5.6
	Horace S. Rich (R)	8,031	5.4
	Others	8,876	5.9

Democratic Primary

	Paul S. Sarbanes (D)	309,919	85.8
	B. Emerson Sweatt (D)	25,932	7.2
	A. Robert Kaufman (D)	25,450	7.0

MASSACHUSETTS

CLASS 1
1988

Republican Primary

| | Joseph Malone (R) | Unopposed | 100.0 |

Democratic Primary

| | Edward M. Kennedy (D) | Unopposed | 100.0 |

MICHIGAN

CLASS 1
1988

Republican Primary

| | Jim Dunn (R) | 245,275 | 61.1 |
| | Robert J. Huber (R) | 155,984 | 38.9 |

Democratic Primary

| | Donald W. Riegle (D) | Unopposed | 100.0 |

MINNESOTA

CLASS 1
1988

Republican Primary

| | Dave Durenberger (R) | 112,413 | 93.5 |
| | Others | 7,843 | 6.5 |

Democratic Primary

| | Hubert H. Humphrey III (D) | 153,808 | 90.6 |
| | Kent S. Herschbach (D) | 15,994 | 9.4 |

MISSISSIPPI

CLASS 1
1988

Republican Primary

| | Trent Lott (R) | Unopposed | 100.0 |

Democratic Primary

| | Wayne Dowdy (D) | 189,954 | 53.4 |
| | Dick Molpus (D) | 152,126 | 42.8 |

MISSOURI

CLASS 3
1986

Republican Primary

| | Christopher Bond (R) | 239,961 | 88.9 |
| | Others | 29,900 | 11.1 |

Democratic Primary

	Harriet Woods (D)	362,287	75.6
	James J. Askew (D)	44,292	9.2
	Oren L. Staley (D)	34,009	7.1
	Others	38,374	8.0

CLASS 1
1988

Republican Primary

| | John C. Danforth (R) | Unopposed | 100.0 |

Democratic Primary

| | Jeremiah W. Nixon (D) | Unopposed | 100.0 |

MONTANA

CLASS 1
1988

Republican Primary

| | Conrad Burns (R) | 63,330 | 84.7 |
| | Tom Faranda (R) | 11,427 | 15.3 |

Democratic Primary

| | John Melcher (D) | 88,457 | 74.5 |
| | Robert C. Kelleher (D) | 30,212 | 25.5 |

NEBRASKA

CLASS 1
1988

Republican Primary

| | David Karnes (R) | 117,439 | 54.8 |
| | Harold J. Daub (R) | 96,436 | 45.0 |

Democratic Primary

| | Bob Kerrey (D) | 156,498 | 91.4 |
| | Ken L. Michaelis (D) | 14,248 | 8.3 |

New Alliance [h]

| | Ernest Chambers (NA) | Unopposed | 100.0 |

NEVADA

CLASS 3
1986

Republican Primary

| | James Santini (R) | 55,947 | 80.3 |

Year	Candidates	Votes	Percent	Year	Candidates	Votes	Percent
					Corky Morris (R)	16,539	20.1
					Joseph J. Carraro (R)	6,928	8.4
	NEVADA				**Democratic Primary**		
	Richard Gilster (R)	3,544	5.1		Jeff Bingaman (D)	Unopposed	100.0
	"None of these candidates"	8,214	11.8				
					NEW YORK		
	Democratic Primary				**CLASS 3**		
	Harry Reid (D)	74,275	82.7	1986			
	Manny Beals (D)	7,039	7.8		**Republican Primary**		
	"None of these candidates"	8,486	9.4		Alfonse M. D'Amato (R)	Unopposed	100.0
					Democratic Primary		
	CLASS 1				John S. Dyson (D)	Unopposed	100.0
1988					**Right to Life Primary**		
	Republican Primary				Alfonse M. D'Amato (RTL)	Unopposed	100.0
	Chic Hecht (R)	55,473	82.1				
	Larry Scheffler (R)	5,618	8.3		**CLASS 1**		
	"None of these candidates"	6,460	9.6	1988			
					Republican Primary		
	Democratic Primary				Robert McMillan (R)	Unopposed	100.0
	Richard H. Bryan (D)	62,278	79.5		**Democratic Primary**		
	Patrick M. Fitzpatrick (D)	4,721	6.0		Daniel Patrick Moynihan (D)	Unopposed	100.0
	"None of these candidates"	7,035	9.0		**Conservative Primary**		
	Others	4,311	5.5		Robert McMillan (R)	Unopposed	100.0
					Liberal Primary		
	NEW HAMPSHIRE				Daniel Patrick Moynihan (L)	Unopposed	100.0
	CLASS 3				**Right to Life Primary**		
1986					Adelle R. Nathanson (RTL)	Unopposed	100.0
	Republican Primary						
	Warren Rudman (R)	Unopposed	100.0		**NORTH CAROLINA**		
	Democratic Primary				**CLASS 3**		
	Endicott Peabody (D)	20,568	61.2	1986			
	Robert L. Dupay (D)	6,108	18.2		**Republican Primary**		
	Robert A. Patton (D)	3,721	11.1		James T. Broyhill (R)	139,570	66.5
	Andrew D. Tempelman (D)	2,601	7.8		David B. Funderburk (R)	63,593	30.3
					Democratic Primary		
	NEW JERSEY				Terry Sanford (D)	409,394	60.2
	CLASS 1				John Ingram (D)	111,557	16.4
1988					Fountain Odom (D)	49,689	7.3
	Republican Primary				William I. Belk (D)	33,821	5.0
	Peter M. Dawkins (R)	Unopposed	100.0		Others	75,026	11.0
	Democratic Primary						
	Frank R. Lautenberg (D)	362,072	79.5		**NORTH DAKOTA**		
	Elnardo J. Webster (D)	51,938	11.4		**CLASS 3**		
	Harold J. Young (D)	41,303	9.1	1986			
					Republican Primary		
	NEW MEXICO				Mark Andrews (R)	Unopposed	100.0
	CLASS 1				**Democratic Primary**		
1988					Kent Conrad (R)	Unopposed	100.0
	Republican Primary						
	William Valentine (R)	35,809	43.4				
	Rick Montoya (R)	23,162	28.1				

Year	Candidates	Votes	Percent	Year	Candidates	Votes	Percent

NORTH DAKOTA
CLASS 1
1988

Republican Primary

Earl Strinden (R) — Unopposed — 100.0

Democratic Primary

Quentin N. Burdick (D) — Unopposed — 100.0

Libertarian Primary

Kenneth C. Gardner (LIBERT) — Unopposed — 100.0

OHIO
CLASS 3
1986

Republican Primary

Thomas N. Kindness (R) — Unopposed — 100.0

Democratic Primary

John H. Glenn (D) — 678,171 — 87.6
Don Scott (D) — 96,309 — 12.4

CLASS 1
1988

Republican Primary

George Voinovich (R) — Unopposed — 100.0

Democratic Primary

Howard Metzenbaum (D) — 1,070,934 — 83.6
Ralph A. Applegate (D) — 210,508 — 16.4

OKLAHOMA
CLASS 3
1986

Republican Primary

Don Nickles (R) — Unopposed — 100.0

Democratic Primary

James R. Jones (R) — 324,907 — 67.4
George Gentry (R) — 157,141 — 32.6

OREGON
CLASS 3
1986

Republican Primary

Robert W. Packwood (R) — 171,985 — 57.6
Joe P. Lutz (R) — 126,315 — 42.3

Democratic Primary [i]

James Weaver (D) — 183,334 — 61.6
Rod Monroe (D) — 44,553 — 15.0
Rick Bauman (D) — 41,939 — 14.1
Steve Anderson (D) — 26,130 — 8.8

PENNSYLVANIA
CLASS 3
1986

Republican Primary

Arlen Specter (R) — 434,623 — 76.2

Richard A. Stokes (R) — 135,673 — 23.8

Democratic Primary

Robert W. Edgar (D) — 432,940 — 47.3
Don Bailey (D) — 408,460 — 44.7
George R. H. Elder (D) — 46,663 — 5.1

CLASS 1
1988

Republican Primary

H. John Heinz (R) — Unopposed — 100.0

Democratic Primary

Joseph C. Vignola (D) — 492,153 — 45.4
Susan S. Kefover (D) — 371,443 — 34.2
Steve Douglas (D) — 145,614 — 13.4
John J. Logue (D) — 76,020 — 7.0

RHODE ISLAND
CLASS 1
1988

Republican Primary

John H. Chafee (R) — Unopposed — 100.0

Democratic Primary

Richard A. Licht (D) — Unopposed — 100.0

SOUTH CAROLINA
CLASS 3
1986

Republican Primary

Henry D. McMaster (R) — 27,695 — 53.4
Henry S. Jordan (R) — 24,164 — 46.6

Democratic Primary

Ernest F. Hollings (D) — Unopposed — 100.0

SOUTH DAKOTA
CLASS 3
1986

Republican Primary

James Abdnor (R) — 63,414 — 54.5
William J. Janklow (R) — 52,924 — 45.5

Democratic Primary

Thomas A. Daschle (D) — Unopposed — 100.0

TENNESSEE
CLASS 1
1988

Republican Primary

Bill Anderson (R) — 115,341 — 72.9
Alice W. Algood (R) — 34,413 — 21.8
Hubert D. Patty (R) — 8,358 — 5.3

Democratic Primary

James R. Sasser (D) — Unopposed — 100.0

Year	Candidates	Votes	Per-cent

TEXAS
CLASS 1
1988
Republican Primary

	Votes	Percent
Wes Gilbreath (R)	275,080	36.7
Beau Boulter (R)	228,676	30.5
Milton E. Fox (R)	138,031	18.4
Ned Snead (R)	107,560	14.4

Democratic Primary

Lloyd Bentsen (D)	1,365,736	84.8
Joe Sullivan (D)	244,805	15.2

Republican Runoff

Beau Boulter (R)	111,134	60.2
Wes Gilbreath (R)	73,573	40.0

UTAH
CLASS 3
1986
Democratic Primary [d]

Craig Oliver (D)	14,654	50.5
Terry Williams (D)	14,379	49.5

VERMONT
CLASS 3
1986
Republican Primary

Richard A. Snelling (R)	21,477	75.1
Anthony N. Doria (R)	6,493	22.7

Democratic Primary

Patrick J. Leahy (D)	Unopposed	100.0

Liberty Union Primary

Jerry Levy (LU)	Unopposed	100.0

CLASS 1
1988
Republican Primary

James M. Jeffords (R)	30,555	60.8
Mike Griffes (R)	19,593	39.0

Democratic Primary

William Gray (D)	Unopposed	100.0

Liberty Union Primary

Jerry Levy (LU)	Unopposed	100.0

WASHINGTON
CLASS 3
1986
Republican Primary

Slade Gorton (R)	291,735	93.0
Others	22,080	7.0

Democratic Primary

Brock Adams (D)	287,258	91.7
Others	26,027	8.3

Socialist Workers Primary

Jill Fein (SOC WORK)	Unopposed	100.0

CLASS 1
1988
Republican Primary

	Votes	Percent
Slade Gordon (R)	335,846	85.3
Doug Smith (R)	31,512	8.0
William C. Goodloe (R)	26,224	6.7

Democratic Primary

Mike Lowry (D)	297,399	55.2
Don Bonker (D)	241,170	44.8

Socialist Workers Primary

Daniel B. Fein (SOC WORK) [j]	3,312	100.0

WEST VIRGINIA
CLASS 1
1988
Republican Primary

M. Jay Wolfe (R)	81,286	70.3
Bernie Lumbert (R)	34,273	29.7

Democratic Primary

Robert C. Byrd (D)	252,767	80.8
Bobbie E. Myers (D)	60,186	19.2

WISCONSIN
CLASS 3
1986
Republican Primary

Robert W. Kasten (R)	Unopposed	100.0

Democratic Primary

Edward R. Garvey (D)	126,408	47.6
Matthew J. Flynn (D)	101,777	38.3
Gary R. George (D)	29,485	11.1

CLASS 1
1988
Republican Primary

Susan Engeleiter (R)	209,025	57.0
Stephen B. King (R)	148,601	40.5

Democratic Primary

Herbert Kohl (D)	249,226	46.8
Anthony S. Earl (D)	203,479	38.2
Edward R. Garvey (D)	55,225	10.4
Others	3,600	5.3

WYOMING
CLASS 1
1988
Republican Primary

Malcolm Wallop (R)	55,752	83.2
Nora M. Lewis (R)	3,933	5.9
I. W. Kinney (R)	3,716	5.5
Others	3,600	5.4

Democratic Primary

John P. Vinich (D)	23,214	47.2
Pete Maxfield (D)	14,613	29.7
Lynn Simons (D)	11,350	23.1

a. Alaska's primaries are open, with all candidates for an office on the ballot together. Thus a voter can vote for a Republican for senator, a Democrat for governor, and so on. Nominations go to the highest Republican and the highest Democrat in this so-called jungle primary.

b. No candidates appeared on the ballot; there were 180 write-in votes for Tompkins.

c. No candidates appeared on the ballot; there were 6 write-in votes for Finkelstein.

d. Data for the Democratic primary are given for the recount vote.

e. Stone withdrew from the Nonpartisan primary, and no substitution was made.

f. Louisiana holds an open primary, with candidates from all parties running on the same ballot. Any candidate who receives a majority is elected. If no candidate receives 50 percent of the vote, there is a runoff election, without regard to party affiliation, between the top two finishers.

g. Blair withdrew after the Republican primary. Alan L. Keyes was substituted by the party state central committee.

h. No New Alliance candidate names appeared on the ballot. Chambers received the nomination by write-in votes.

i. Weaver withdrew after the Democratic primary. Bauman was substituted by the party state central committee.

j. Fein did not qualify for a place on the general-election ballot because he received less than 1 percent of the total votes cast for the office.

Gubernatorial Primary Returns,
1986-1988

Following are 1986, 1987, and 1988 gubernatorial primary returns. The major source for this section was the *America Votes* series, compiled biennially by Richard M. Scammon and Alice V. McGillivray and published since 1966 by Congressional Quarterly Inc. Other sources were the returns obtained by Congressional Quarterly after each gubernatorial election. In cases of discrepancies the *America Votes* figures were used. Candidates are listed only if they received 5 percent or more of the vote. Percentages may not equal 100 because of rounding. Where no primary is indicated for a year in which a state elected a governor, it generally means that party conventions chose the nominees.

Year	Candidates	Votes	Percent

ALABAMA

1986

Republican Primary

Guy Hunt (R)	20,823	71.3
Doug Carter (R)	8,371	28.7

Democratic Primary

Bill Baxley (D)	345,985	36.8
Charles Graddick (D)	275,714	29.3
Forrest H. James (D)	195,844	20.8
George McMillan (D)	117,258	12.5

Democratic Runoff [a]

Charles Graddick (D)	470,051	50.5
Bill Baxley (D)	461,295	49.5

ALASKA [b]

1986

Republican Primary

Arliss Sturgulewski (R)	25,740	30.6
Walter J. Hickel (R)	23,733	28.3
Richard Randolph (R)	18,164	21.6
Joe L. Hayes (R)	7,989	9.5
Bob Richards (R)	4,973	5.9

Democratic Primary

Steve Cowper (D)	36,233	54.5
Bill Sheffield (D)	29,935	45.0

Alaskan Independence Primary

Joe Vogler	Unopposed	100.0

Libertarian Primary

Mary O'Brannon (LIBERT)	205	53.5
Ed Hoch (LIBERT)	178	46.5

ARIZONA

1986

Republican Primary

Evan Mecham (R)	121,614	53.7
Burton S. Barr (R)	104,682	46.3

Democratic Primary

Carolyn Warner (D)	106,687	50.6
Tony Mason (D)	92,413	43.9
Dave Moss (D)	11,588	5.5

ARKANSAS

1986

Republican Primary

Frank D. White (R)	13,831	61.9
Wayne Lanier (R)	4,576	20.5
Maurice Britt (R)	3,116	13.9

Democratic Primary

Bill Clinton (D)	315,397	60.6
Orval E. Faubus (D)	174,402	33.5
Dean Goldsby (D)	30,829	5.9

CALIFORNIA

1986

Republican Primary

George Deukmejian (R)	1,927,288	93.6
William H. R. Clark (R)	132,125	6.4

Democratic Primary

Tom Bradley (D)	1,768,042	81.5
Hugh G. Bagley (D)	141,217	6.5
Charles Pineda (D)	109,001	5.0
Others	150,365	6.9

American Independent Primary

Gary V. Miller (AMI)	Unopposed	100.0

Peace and Freedom Primary

Maria E. Munoz (PFP)	3,508	69.8
Cheryl Zuur (PFP)	1,519	30.2

Libertarian Primary

Joseph Fuhrig (LIBERT)	Unopposed	100.0

COLORADO

1986

Republican Primary

Ted Strickland (R)	66,796	35.6
Steve Schuck (R)	64,245	34.2
Bob Kirscht (R)	56,779	30.2

Democratic Primary

Roy Romer (D)	Unopposed	100.0

Year	Candidates	Votes	Percent	Year	Candidates	Votes	Percent

CONNECTICUT

1986

Republican Primary

Julie D. Belaga (R)	39,074	41.3
Richard C. Bozzuto (R)	33,852	35.8
Gerald Labriola (R)	21,610	22.9

DELAWARE

1988

Republican Primary

Michael N. Castle (R)	Unopposed	100.0

Democratic Primary

Jacob Kreshtool (D)	Unopposed	100.0

FLORIDA

1986

Republican Primary

Bob Martinez (R)	244,499	44.1
Louis Frey (R)	138,017	24.9
Tom Gallagher (R)	127,709	23.0
Chester Clem (R)	44,438	8.0

Republican Runoff

Bob Martinez (R)	259,333	66.3
Louis Frey (R)	131,652	33.7

Democratic Primary

Steve Pajcic (D)	361,359	35.9
Jim Smith (D)	310,479	30.8
Harry Johnston (D)	258,038	25.6
Mark K. Goldstein (D)	54,077	5.4

Democratic Runoff

Steve Pajcic (D)	429,427	50.6
Jim Smith (D)	418,614	49.4

GEORGIA

1986

Republican Primary

Guy Davis (R)	Unopposed	100.0

Democratic Primary

Joe Frank Harris (D)	521,704	85.3
Kenneth B. Quarterman (D)	89,759	14.7

HAWAII

1986

Republican Primary

D. G. Anderson (R)	38,790	94.6
Others	2,211	5.4

Democratic Primary

John Waihee (D)	105,579	45.6
Cecil Heftel (D)	83,939	36.2
Patsy T. Mink (D)	37,998	16.4

IDAHO

1986

Republican Primary

David H. Leroy (R)	Unopposed	100.0

Democratic Primary

Cecil D. Andrus (D)	Unopposed	100.0

ILLINOIS

1986

Republican Primary

James R. Thompson (R)	452,685	90.9
Peter Bowen (R)	45,236	9.1

Democratic Primary

Adlai E. Stevenson III (D) [c]	735,249	92.9
Larry Burgess (D)	55,930	7.1

INDIANA

1988

Republican Primary

John M. Mutz (R)	Unopposed	100.0

Democratic Primary

Evan Bayh (D)	493,198	83.1
Stephen J. Daily (D)	66,242	11.2
Frank L. O'Bannon (D)	34,360	5.8

IOWA

1986

Republican Primary

Terry E. Branstad (R)	Unopposed	100.0

Democratic Primary

Lowell L. Junkins (D)	70,605	52.6
Bob Anderson (D)	44,550	33.2
George R. Kinley (D)	15,473	11.5

KANSAS

1986

Republican Primary

Mike Hayden (R)	99,669	36.1
Larry Jones (R)	85,989	31.1
Jack H. Brier (R)	37,410	13.6
Gene Bicknell (R)	25,733	9.3
Richard J. Peckham (R)	18,876	6.8

Democratic Primary

Thomas R. Docking (D)	Unopposed	100.0

KENTUCKY

1987

Republican Primary

John Harper (R)	37,432	41.4
Joseph E. Johnson (R)	22,396	24.8
Leonard W. Beasley (R)	21,067	23.3
Thurman J. Hamlin (R)	9,475	10.5

Democratic Primary

Wallace G. Wilkinson (D)	221,138	34.9

Year	Candidates	Votes	Per-cent

KENTUCKY

	John Y. Brown, Jr. (D)	163,204	25.8
	Steven L. Beshear (D)	114,439	18.1
	Grady Stumbo (D)	84,613	13.4
	Julian M. Carroll (D)	42,137	6.6

LOUISIANA

1987

Open Primary [d]

	Charles Roemer (D)	516,078	33.1
	Edwin W. Edwards (D) [e]	437,801	28.0
	Bob Livingston (R)	287,780	18.5
	W. J. Tauzin (D)	154,079	9.9
	James H. Brown (D)	138,223	8.8

MAINE

1986

Republican Primary

	John R. McKernan (R)	79,393	68.4
	Porter D. Leighton (R)	36,705	31.6

Democratic Primary

	James Tierney (D)	44,087	37.2
	Severin M. Beliveau (D)	27,991	23.6
	G. William Diamond (D)	24,693	20.8
	David E. Redmond (D)	17,598	14.9

MARYLAND

1986

Republican Primary

	Thomas J. Mooney (R)	Unopposed	100.0

Democratic Primary

	William D. Schaefer (D)	395,170	61.7
	Stephen H. Sachs (D)	224,755	35.1

MASSACHUSETTS

1986

Republican Primary [f]

	Gregory S. Hyatt (R)	31,021	48.2
	Royall H. Switzler (R)	20,802	32.3
	George Kariotis (R)	11,787	18.3

Democratic Primary

	Michael S. Dukakis (D)	Unopposed	100.0

MICHIGAN

1986

Republican Primary

	William Lucas (R)	259,153	44.5
	Dick Chrysler (R)	198,174	34.0
	Colleen Engler (R)	63,927	11.0
	Dan Murphy (R)	61,073	10.5

Democratic Primary

	James J. Blanchard (D)	428,125	93.7
	Henry Wilson (D)	28,940	6.3

MINNESOTA

1986

Republican Primary

	Cal R. Ludeman (R)	147,674	76.9
	James H. Lindau (R)	30,768	16.0
	Others	13,711	7.1

Democratic Primary

	Rudy Perpich (D)	293,426	57.5
	George Latimer (D)	207,198	40.6

MISSISSIPPI

1987

Republican Primary

	Jack Reed (R)	14,798	78.5
	Doug Lemon (R)	4,057	21.5

Democratic Primary

	Ray Mabus (D)	304,559	35.7
	Mike P. Sturdivant (D)	131,180	16.2
	William L. Waller (D)	105,056	13.0
	John A. Eaves (D)	98,517	12.2
	Maurice Dantin (D)	83,603	10.3
	Ed Pittman (D)	73,667	9.1

Democratic Runoff

	Ray Mabus (D)	428,883	64.3
	Mike P. Sturdivant (D)	238,039	35.7

MISSOURI

1988

Republican Primary

	John Ashcroft (R)	Unopposed	100.0

Democratic Primary

	Betty C. Hearnes (D)	375,564	81.5
	Lavoy Reed (D)	85,409	18.5

MONTANA

1988

Republican Primary

	Stan Stephens (R)	44,022	50.1
	Cal Winslow (R)	37,875	43.1
	Jim Waltermire (R) [g]	6,024	6.9

Democratic Primary

	Thomas L. Judge (D)	46,412	39.3
	Frank Morrison (D)	32,124	27.2
	Mike Greely (D)	26,827	22.7
	Ted Neuman (D)	7,297	6.2
	Others	5,398	5.0

NEBRASKA

1986

Republican Primary

	Kay Orr (R)	75,914	39.4
	Kermit Brashear (R)	60,308	31.3
	Nancy Hoch (R)	42,649	22.1
	Others	13,980	7.2

Democratic Primary

	Helen Boosalis (D)	63,833	44.0

Year	Candidates	Votes	Percent	Year	Candidates	Votes	Percent

NEBRASKA

	David A. Domina (D)	37,975	26.2
	Chris Beutler (D)	31,605	21.8
	Others	11,644	8.0

NEVADA

1986

Republican Primary

	Patty Cafferata (R)	31,430	46.1
	Jim Stone (R)	12,296	18.0
	Marcia J. Wines (R)	5,599	8.2
	"None of these candidates"	15,116	22.2
	Others	3,795	5.6

Democratic Primary

| | Richard H. Bryan (D) | 71,920 | 79.9 |
| | Herb Tobman (D) | 13,776 | 15.3 |

NEW HAMPSHIRE

1986

Republican Primary

| | John H. Sununu (R) | 44,906 | 77.3 |
| | Roger L. Easton (R) | 12,702 | 21.9 |

Democratic Primary

	Paul McEachern (D)	19,731	54.6
	Paul M. Gagnon (D)	9,790	27.1
	Bruce Anderson (D)	5,816	16.1

1988

Republican Primary

| | Judd Gregg (R) | 65,777 | 79.0 |
| | Robert F. Shaw (R) | 15,133 | 18.2 |

Democratic Primary

| | Paul McEachern (D) | Unopposed | 100.0 |

NEW JERSEY

1985

Republican Primary

| | Thomas H. Kean (R) | Unopposed | 100.0 |

Democratic Primary

	Peter Shapiro (D)	101,243	31.0
	John F. Russo (D)	86,827	26.6
	Kenneth A. Gibson (D)	85,293	26.1
	Stephen B. Wiley (D)	27,914	8.6
	Robert J. Del Tufo (D)	19,742	6.0

NEW MEXICO

1986

Republican Primary

	Garrey E. Carruthers (R)	27,671	31.1
	Joseph H. Mercer (R)	23,560	26.4
	Colin R. McMillan (R)	19,807	22.2
	Frank M. Bond (R)	10,619	11.9
	Paul F. Becht (R)	6,566	26.4

Democratic Primary

| | Ray B. Pohwell (D) | Unopposed | 100.0 |

NEW YORK ʰ

1986

Republican Primary

| | Andrew P. O'Rouke (R) | Unopposed | 100.0 |

Democratic Primary

| | Mario M. Cuomo (D) | Unopposed | 100.0 |

Conservative Primary

| | Andrew P. O'Rouke (C) | Unopposed | 100.0 |

Liberal Primary

| | Mario M. Cuomo (L) | Unopposed | 100.0 |

Right to Life Primary

| | Denis E. Dillon (RTL) | Unopposed | 100.0 |

NORTH CAROLINA

1988

Republican Primary

| | James G. Martin (R) | Unopposed | 100.0 |

Democratic Primary

	Robert B. Jordan (D)	403,145	79.7
	Billy Martin (D)	60,770	12.0
	Others	42,158	8.3

NORTH DAKOTA

1988

Republican Primary

| | Leon L. Mallberg (R) | Unopposed | 100.0 |

Democratic Primary

| | George Sinner (D) | Unopposed | 100.0 |

OHIO

1986

Republican Primary

	James A. Rhodes (R)	352,261	48.2
	Paul E. Gillmor (R)	281,737	38.5
	Paul E. Pfeifer (R)	96,948	13.3

Democratic Primary

| | Richard F. Celeste (D) | Unopposed | 100.0 |

OKLAHOMA

1986

Republican Primary

	Henry Bellmon (R)	111,665	70.3
	Mike Fair (R)	33,266	20.9
	Others	13,968	8.8

Democratic Primary

	David Walters (D)	238,165	46.0
	Mike Turpen (D)	207,357	40.0
	Leslie Fisher (D)	33,639	6.5
	Others	38,149	7.4

Year	Candidates	Votes	Percent	Year	Candidates	Votes	Percent

OKLAHOMA

Democratic Runoff

David Walters (D)	235,373	50.4
Mike Turpen (D)	231,390	49.6

OREGON

1986

Republican Primary

Norma Paulus (R)	219,505	77.0
Betty Freauf (R)	36,384	12.8
Others	29,048	10.2

Democratic Primary

Neil Goldschmidt (D)	214,148	67.4
Edward N. Fadeley (D)	81,300	25.6
Others	22,069	7.0

PENNSYLVANIA

1986

Republican Primary

William W. Scranton III (R)	Unopposed	100.0

Democratic Primary

Robert Casey (D)	549,376	56.4
Edward G. Rendell (D)	385,539	39.6

RHODE ISLAND

1986

Republican Primary

Edward DiPrete (R)	Unopposed	100.0

Democratic Primary

Bruce G. Sundlun (D)	43,120	75.3
Steve White (D)	14,124	24.7

1988

Republican Primary

Edward DiPrete (R)	Unopposed	100.0

Democratic Primary

Bruce G. Sundlun (D)	68,065	90.3
Peter Van Daam (D)	7,328	9.7

SOUTH CAROLINA

1986

Republican Primary

Carroll Campbell (R)	Unopposed	100.0

Democratic Primary [i]

Mike Daniel (D)	156,077	47.4
Phil Lader (D)	86,136	26.1
Frank Eppes (D)	59,125	17.9
Hugh Leatherman (D)	28,158	8.5

SOUTH DAKOTA

1986

Republican Primary

George S. Mickelson (R)	40,979	35.3
Clint Roberts (R)	37,250	32.1

Lowell Hansen (R)	21,884	18.8
Alice Kundert (R)	15,985	13.8

Democratic Primary

R. Lars Herseth (D)	30,801	42.8
Richard F. Kneip (D)	27,811	38.7
Kenneth D. Stofferahn (D)	13,332	18.5

TENNESSEE

1986

Republican Primary

Winfield Dunn (R)	222,458	94.2
Others	13,683	5.8

Democratic Primary

Ned McWherter (D)	314,449	42.5
Jane Eskind (D)	225,551	30.5
Richard Fulton (D)	190,016	25.7

TEXAS

1986

Republican Primary

William P. Clements (R)	318,808	58.5
Tom Loeffler (R)	117,673	21.6
Kent Hance (R)	108,238	19.8

Democratic Primary

Mark White (D)	589,536	53.8
Andrew C. Briscoe (D)	248,850	22.7
A. Don Crowder (D)	120,999	11.0
Bobby Locke (D)	58,936	5.4
Others (D)	78,231	7.1

VERMONT

1986

Republican Primary

Peter Smith (R)	Unopposed	100.0

Democratic Primary

Madeleine M. Kunin (D)	Unopposed	100.0

Liberty Union Primary

Richard F. Gottlieb (LU)	Unopposed	100.0

1988

Republican Primary

Michael Bernhardt (R)	Unopposed	100.0

Democratic Primary

Madeleine M. Kunin (D)	Unopposed	100.0

Liberty Union Primary

Richard F. Gottlieb (LU)	Unopposed	100.0

WASHINGTON

1988

Republican Primary

Bob Williams (R)	187,797	56.4
Norm Maleng (R)	139,274	41.4

Democratic Primary

Booth Gardner (D)	539,243	90.6

Year	Candidates	Votes	Per-cent	Year	Candidates	Votes	Per-cent

WASHINGTON

Jeanne Dixon (D) — 31,917 — 5.4

Independent Primary

Baba J. Mangaoang (I) [j] — 5,818 — 100.0

WEST VIRGINIA

1988

Republican Primary

Arch A. Moore (R)	78,495	53.2
John R. Raese (R)	68,973	46.8

Democratic Primary

Gaston Caperton (D)	132,435	38.0
Clyde M. See (D)	94,364	27.0
Mario J. Palumbo (D)	51,722	14.8
Gus R. Douglass (D)	48,748	14.0
Others	21,617	6.2

WISCONSIN

1986

Republican Primary

Tommy G. Thompson (R)	156,875	52.1
Jonathan B. Barry (R)	67,114	22.3

George Watts (R)	58,424	19.4
Albert L. Wiley (R)	15,233	5.1

Democratic Primary

Anthony S. Earl (D)	215,183	80.2
Edmond Hou-Seye (D)	52,784	19.7

Labor-Farm Primary

Kathryn A. Christensen (LAB F) — Unopposed — 100.0

WYOMING

1986

Republican Primary

Peter Simpson (R)	25,948	27.6
Bill Budd (R)	25,495	27.1
Fred Schroeder (R)	15,013	16.0
Russ Donley (R)	12,979	13.8
David R. Nicholas (R)	11,092	11.8

Democratic Primary

Mike Sullivan (D)	29,266	70.9
Pat McGuire (D)	5,406	13.1
Keith B. Goodenough (D)	4,039	9.8
Al Hamburg (D)	2,554	6.2

a. After the Democratic runoff primary a subcommittee of Alabama's Democratic party declared Baxley the nominee, deciding that voters who voted in the Republican primary had crossed over and voted in the Democratic runoff primary for Graddick, against party rules. This decision was contested through the courts, but the Democratic party decision was upheld.

b. Alaska's primaries are open, with all candidates for an office on the ballot together. Thus a voter can vote for a Republican for governor, a Democrat for senator, and so on. Nominations go to the highest Republican and the highest Democrat in this so-called jungle primary.

c. Stevenson withdrew after the primary on the ground that the nominated candidate for lieutenant governor was a supporter of Lyndon LaRouche, whose views were so different from Stevenson's as to make a joint candidacy impossible. No replacement candidate was named by the Democratic party. A new party, Illinois Solidarity, was formed with Stevenson as its gubernatorial candidate.

d. Louisiana holds an open primary, with candidates from all parties running on the same ballot. Any candidate who receives a majority is elected. If no candidate receives 50 percent of the vote, a runoff election is held between the top two finishers, without regard to party affiliation, in November.

e. Edwards withdrew and no runoff election was held in November.

f. Hyatt withdrew after the primary, and Kariotis was substituted by the Republican state central committee.

g. Waltermire died two months before the primary.

h. The Republican candidate was also the Conservative nominee, and 152,287 of his votes were received as the Conservative candidate. The Democratic candidate was also the Liberal nominee, and 120,303 of his votes were received as the Liberal candidate.

i. Neither Lader nor the other two candidates requested a runoff primary, and Daniel was declared the nominee.

j. Mangaoang did not qualify for a place on the general-election ballot because he received less than 1 percent of the total votes cast for the office.

1985-1989 House Makeup, Party Gains and Losses

	Seats	99th Congress Dem.	Rep.	100th Congress Dem.	Rep.	101st Congress Dem.	Rep.	Gain/Loss 99th-100th	Gain/Loss 100th-101st
Ala.	7	5	2	5	2	5	2		
Alaska	1	0	1	0	1	0	1		
Ariz.	5	1	4	1	4	1	4		
Ark.	4	3	1	3	1	3	1		
Calif.	45	27	18	27	18	27	18		
Colo.	6	2	4	3	3	3	3	+1D/−1R	
Conn.	6	3	3	3	3	3	3		
Del.	1	1	0	1	0	1	0		
Fla.	19	12	7	12	7	10	9		−2D/+2R
Ga.	10	8	2	8	2	9	1		+1D/−1R
Hawaii	2	2	0	1	1	1	1	−1D/+1R	
Idaho	2	1	1	1	1	1	1		
Ill.	22	13	9	13	9	14	8		+1D/−1R
Ind.	10	5	5	6	4	6	4	+1D/−1R	
Iowa	6	2	4	2	4	2	4		
Kan.	5	2	3	2	3	2	3		
Ky.	7	4	3	4	3	4	3		
La.	8	6	2	5	3	4	4	−1D/+1R	−1D/+1R
Maine	2	0	2	1	1	1	1	+1D/−1R	
Md.	8	6	2	6	2	6	2		
Mass.	11	10	1	10	1	10	1		
Mich.	18	11	7	11	7	11	7		
Minn.	8	5	3	5	3	5	3		
Miss.	5	3	2	4	1	4	1	+1D/−1R	
Mo.	9	6	3	5	4	5	4	−1D/+1R	
Mont.	2	1	1	1	1	1	1		
Neb.	3	0	3	0	3	1	2		+1D/−1R
Nev.	2	1	1	1	1	1	1		
N.H.	2	0	2	0	2	0	2		
N.J.	14	8	6	8	6	8	6		
N.M.	3	1	2	1	2	1	2		
N.Y.	34	19	15	20	14	21	13	+1D/−1R	+1D/−1R
N.C.	11	6	5	8	3	8	3	+2D/−2R	
N.D.	1	1	0	1	0	1	0		
Ohio	21	11	10	11	10	11	10		
Okla.	6	5	1	4	2	4	2	−1D/+1R	
Ore.	5	3	2	3	2	3	2		
Pa.	23	13	10	12	11	12	11	−1D/+1R	
R.I.	2	1	1	1	1	0	2		−1D/+1R
S.C.	6	3	3	4	2	4	2	+1D/−1R	
S.D.	1	1	0	1	0	1	0		
Tenn.	9	6	3	6	3	6	3		
Texas	27	17	10	17	10	19	8		+2D/−2R
Utah	3	0	3	1	2	1	2	+1D/−1R	
Vt.	1	0	1	0	1	0	1		
Va.	10	4	6	5	5	5	5	+1D/−1R	
Wash.	8	5	3	5	3	5	3		
W.Va.	4	4	0	4	0	4	0		
Wis.	9	5	4	5	4	5	4		
Wyo.	1	0	1	0	1	0	1		
Totals	435	253	182	258	177	260	175	+5D/−5R	+2D/−2R

Sources: Elections '88 (Washington, D.C.: Congressional Quarterly Inc., 1988), 106; *Congressional Quarterly Weekly Report,* November 12, 1989, 3269.

Election Results, Congress and Presidency, 1936-1988

The following chart tracks the results of House and Senate elections from the 75th through the 101st Congress and the performance of the Democratic and Republican parties in those years. The House election figures on gains and losses measure each party's net change since the previous election in each district, including special elections.

The Senate figures reflect the partisan makeup of the Senate following each election day; the parties' gains and losses are net changes, measured from how the Senate stood on the day before election day to how it was changed by the elections.

Members are listed with the party with which they align themselves in Congress.

Election year	Congress elected	House Members elected			House Gains/losses		Senate Party lineup			Senate Gains/losses		Presidency Elected	Popular vote plurality
		Dem.	Rep.	Misc.	Dem.	Rep.	Dem.	Rep.	Misc.	Dem.	Rep.		
1936	75th	333	89	13	+11	−14	75	17	4	− 6	+ 6	Roosevelt (D)	11,073,102
1938	76th	262	169	4	−71	+80	69	23	4	− 8	+ 8		
1940	77th	268	162	5	+ 7	− 8	66	28	2	− 3	+ 4	Roosevelt (D)	4,964,561
1942	78th	222	209	4	−45	+46	57	38	1	− 8	+ 9		
1944	79th	242	101	2	+21	−19	57	38	1	− 1	+ 1	Roosevelt (D)	3,594,993
1946	80th	188	246	1	−53	+55	45	51		−11	+11	Truman	
1948	81st	263	171	1	+76	−76	54	42		+ 9	− 9	Truman (D)	2,188,054
1950	82nd	235	199	1	−27	+27	49	47		− 5	+ 5		
1952	83rd	213	221	1	−24	+24	47	48	1	− 2	+ 2	Eisenhower (R)	6,621,242
1954	84th	232	203		+19	−18	48	47	1	+ 2	− 2		
1956	85th	234	201		+ 2	− 2	49	47		0	0	Eisenhower (R)	9,567,720
1958	86th	283	153		+49	−48	64	34		+15	−13		
1960	87th	263	174		−20	+21	64	36		− 2	+ 2	Kennedy (D)	118,574[a]
1962	88th	258	176	1[b]	− 4	0	68	32		+ 4	− 4		
1964	89th	295	140		+38	−37	68	32		+ 2	− 2	Johnson (D)	15,951,296
1966	90th	248	187		−48	+48	64	36		− 3	+ 3		
1968	91st	243	192		− 7	+ 7	58	42		− 5	+ 5	Nixon (R)	510,314
1970	92nd	255	180		+12	−12	55	45		− 2	+ 2		
1972	93rd	244	191		−13	+13	57	43		+ 2	− 2	Nixon (R)	17,999,528
1974	94th	291	144		+48	−48	61	38		+ 3[c]	− 4		
1976	95th	292	143		+ 2	− 2	62	38		0	0	Carter (D)	1,682,970
1978	96th	277	158		−12	+12	59	41		− 3	+ 3		
1980	97th	243	192		−33	+33	47	53		−12	+12	Reagan (R)	8,420,270
1982	98th	269	166		−26	−26	46	54		0	0		
1984	99th	253	182		−15	+15	47	53		− 2	− 2	Reagan (R)	16,877,890
1986	100th	258	177		+ 5	− 5	55	45		+ 8	− 8		
1988	101st	260	175		+ 2	− 2	55	45		+ 0	0	Bush (R)	7,077,023

Sources: Congressional Quarterly Weekly Report, October 29, 1988, 3104; America Votes 18, ed. Richard M. Scammon and Alice V. McGillivray (Washington, D.C.: Congressional Quarterly Inc., 1989), 7.

a. Includes divided Alabama elector slate votes.
b. Vacancy—Rep. Clem Miller, D-Calif. (1959-62), died October 6, 1962, but his name remained on the ballot and he received a plurality. A special election was later held, and his Republican opponent won.

c. The race between Democrat John A. Durkin and Republican Louis C. Wyman for the open seat previously held by a Republican was too close to determine a winner; the Senate refused to seat either candidate. Durkin won a special election in September 1975.

Corrections to *Congressional Quarterly's Guide to U.S. Elections,* 2d ed. (1985)

Page ix, third head from bottom should read: "American Political Parties Since 1789 (Chart)" (changing year from 1879 to 1789).

Page xv, box, paragraph 6, third to last line should read: "and Adlai E. Stevenson II," (adding II, deleting Jr.).

Page 16, col. 6: For the year 1920 the number of presidential ballots was 44 (not 43).

Page 85, col. 1, paragraph 4 under Democrats, line 8: Change West Virginia to New York. (John W. Davis moved to New York after serving in the U.S. House from West Virginia.)

Page 186: In the 1904 Republican total votes, move footnote *a* from Ohio to Oklahoma.

Page 242, Election of 1924, Democratic Party: Change John W. Davis's state from West Virginia to New York.

Page 243, Election of 1936, Socialist Labor Party, line 1, should read: "President: John W. Aiken," (not Aikin).

Page 245, Election of 1968, Freedom and Peace Party, add: "Vice President: Mark Lane, New York."

Page 252, col. 8: The name of Vice President Nelson A. Rockefeller was misspelled.

Page 252, last line: The abbreviation (D-R) stands for Democratic-Republican (not Democrat-Republican).

Page 252, col. 2: Add 1913 as the year of birth for Gerald R. Ford.

Page 252, col. 2: Add 1924 as the year of birth for Jimmy Carter.

Page 252, col. 2: Add 1911 as the year of birth for Ronald Reagan.

Page 255, box, paragraph 1, line 12, should read: "Neil R. Peirce and Lawrence D. Longley," (adding Lawrence D. Longley).

Page 265, col. 2: The entry for Peirce, Neil, should read: "Peirce, Neil, and Lawrence D. Longley. *The People's President: The Electoral College in American History and the Direct Vote Alternative.*"

Page 268, paragraph 1, line 3, should read: "pp. 779-812" (not 779-8l2).

Page 323, col. 1, paragraph 2, sentence beginning "Only twice" should read: "Only once (in 1896) between 1868 and 1948 was there no New Yorker on the national ticket of at least one of the major parties—for president or vice president."

Page 324, col. 2, paragraph 2, line 3: The word "require" was misspelled.

Page 363, line 2, should read: "Nixon's plurality" (not Reagan's plurality).

Page 363, the figures for Alabama should read: col. 2: "728,701"; col. 3: "72.4"; col. 4: "256,923"; col. 5: "25.5"; col. 6: "11,928"; col. 7: "1.1"; col. 10: "8,559"; col. 11: ".9."

Page 363: New Mexico, col. 4, should be in roman type (141,084).

Page 366, 1984 Presidential Election table: Several states revised their final election returns after this table was published in 1985. The revised version may be found on page 163 of this book.

Page 436, Alabama, col. 1, should read: March 13 (adding March).

Page 441, col. 1, line 2: Delete the category "Unpledged Delegates" (deleting entire line 2 in col. 1).

Page 443, col. 3, John William Davis: Add N.Y. after W.Va.

Page 446, add: ROCKEFELLER, Nelson A. - N.Y. (Republican) July 8, 1908 - Jan. 26, 1979; governor, 1959-1973; U.S. vice president, 1974-1977 (nominated under the provisions of the Twenty-fifth Amendment). Candidacies: P, 1964, 1968, and 1972.

Page 454: In the box on length of governor terms, the year of change to longer term for Arizona should be 1986 (not 1984).

Page 456: In the box on party lineup of governors, one governorship was held by an Independent in 1976 (not zero).

Page 461, col. 1, line 31: The first name of William D. Jelks was misspelled.

Page 484, col. 2, Virginia, second to last line: The footnote number for Francis H. Peirpoint should be 12 (not 13).

Page 485, col. 1, Washington, line 11: Dates of service for Clarence D. Martin began Jan. 9, 1933 (not 1833).

Page 503, Louisiana: Add as footnote 3 the same footnote that appears on page 618 (footnote 2 under Louisiana).

Page 533, col. 1, 1976: Line should read: "Dixy Lee Ray (D)" [not (R)].

Page 581, Connecticut: Henry Edwards served from Oct. 8, 1823 (not Dec. 1, 1823).

Page 589, Maine: Hannibal Hamlin served from June 8, 1848 (not May 26, 1848).

Page 589, Maryland: Samuel Smith served from Dec. 17, 1822 (not Dec. 16, 1822).

Page 595, New Jersey: Nicholas F. Brady served from April 12, 1982, to Dec. 20, 1982 (not April 20, 1982, to Dec. 27, 1982).

Page 621, col. 2, class 2: For the year 1918 add opponent candidate beneath Pat Harrison: "Sumner W. Rose (S), 1,569 votes, 5.0%."

Page 798, Illinois, 16th District, second line should read: "P. E. Hosmer (R)" (not Heasmer).

Page 854, Mississippi, 6th District, second line should read: "C. W. Baylis (SOC)" (not C. W. Banks).

Page 888, Mississippi, add these statistics: 2nd District: Hubert D. Stephens (D), 10,192 votes, 97.6%; 5th District: William A. Venable (D), 11,966 votes, 94.5%; Charles Evans (SOC), 692 votes, 5.5%; 6th District: Pat Harrison (D), 12,492 votes, 94.6%, F. T. Maxwell (SOC), 716 votes, 5.4%: 8th District: James W. Collier (D) 6,147 votes, 97.6%.

Page 1053, Louisiana: Add the same footnote that appears on page 618 (footnote 2 under Louisiana).

Page 1060, Oregon, 5th District: Add the winner: Denny Smith (R), 130,424 votes, 54.5%.

Page 1082, col. 1: For the year 1975 line 1 should read: "Edwin W. Edwards (D)" etc. [not (R)].

Page 1095, Louisiana: For 1978 and subsequent elections, add the same footnote that appears on page 618 (footnote 2 under Louisiana).

Page 1105, 1st Congress, col. 6: After John Langdon, insert footnote 4.

Page 1107, 40th Congress, col. 7: After Theodore M. Pomeroy, insert footnote 11.

Page 1108, 44th Congress, col. 7: After Samuel S. Cox, change footnote 12 to 13.

Page 1108, 44th Congress, col. 7: After Milton Sayler, insert footnote 14.

Page 1110, 86th Congress, col. 3: After Jan. 7, 1959, change footnote 47 to 48.

Page 1119, footnote 8: The last sentence should read: "The 5-5 figure," etc. (not 6-5).

Page 1124, election year 1928: Change Democratic figure from 163 to 167 and Democratic loss figure from −32 to −28.

Page 1124, election year 1930: Change Democratic figure from 216 to 220 and Republican figure from 218 to 214. Change Republican loss figure from −49 to −53. An updated version of this table for election years 1936 through 1988 appears on page 276 of this book.

Page 1125: The wrong table was printed on this page, and an adhesive insert was provided. The correct table contained an additional column showing each state's electoral votes for 1984 and 1988. This version may be found on page 167 of this book.

Page 1128, col. 1, paragraph 8, line 8, should read: "may by law provide" etc. (adding by, deleting be).

Index